I0831073

CASTLES & ROYAL PALACES

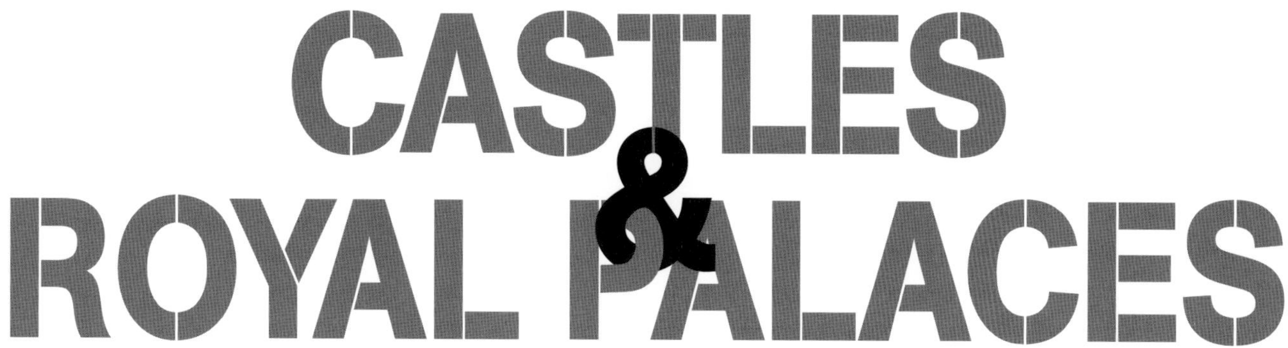

ITINERARIES TO DISCOVER

Text by Paola Hazon

whitestar

Contents

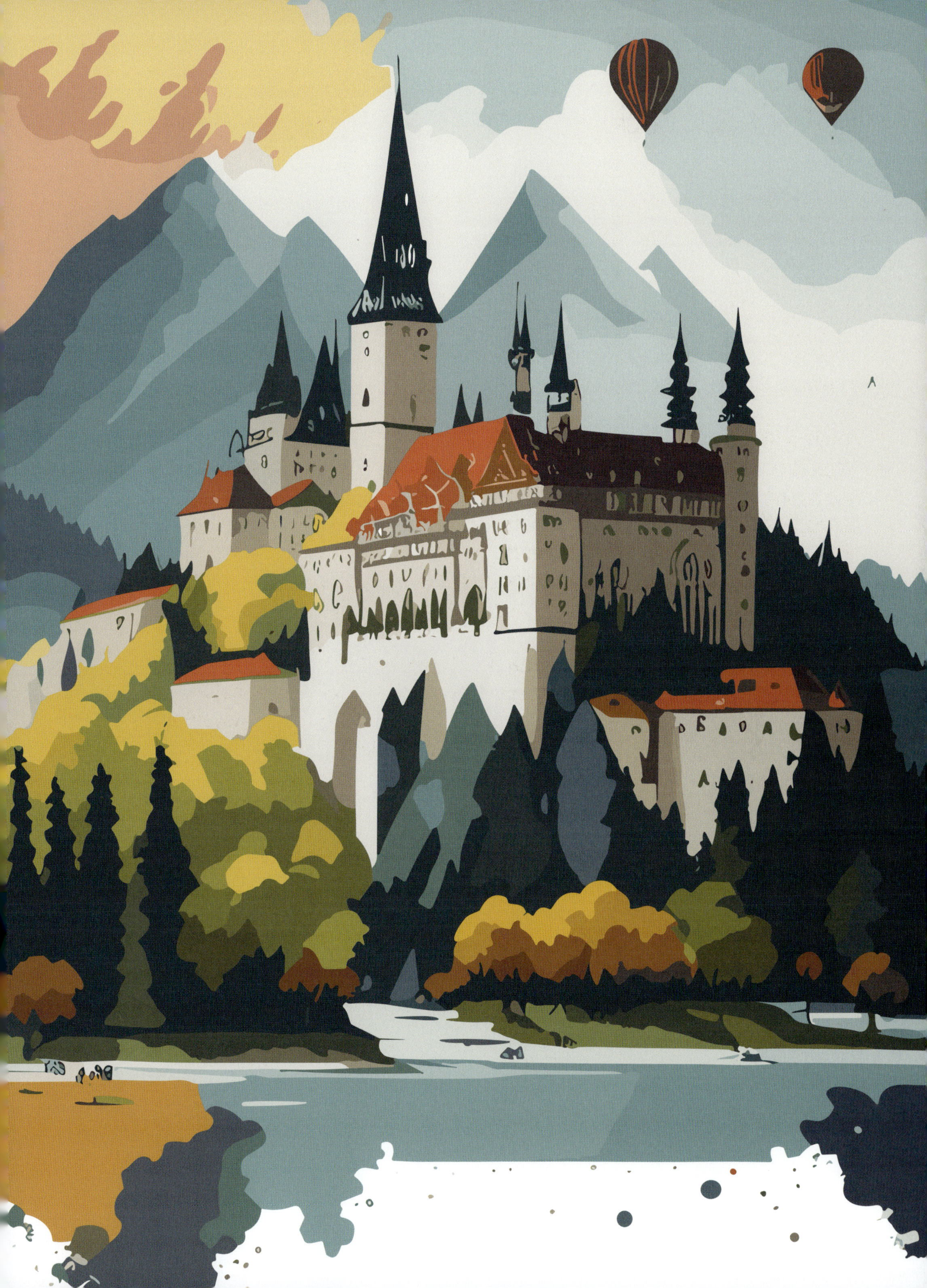

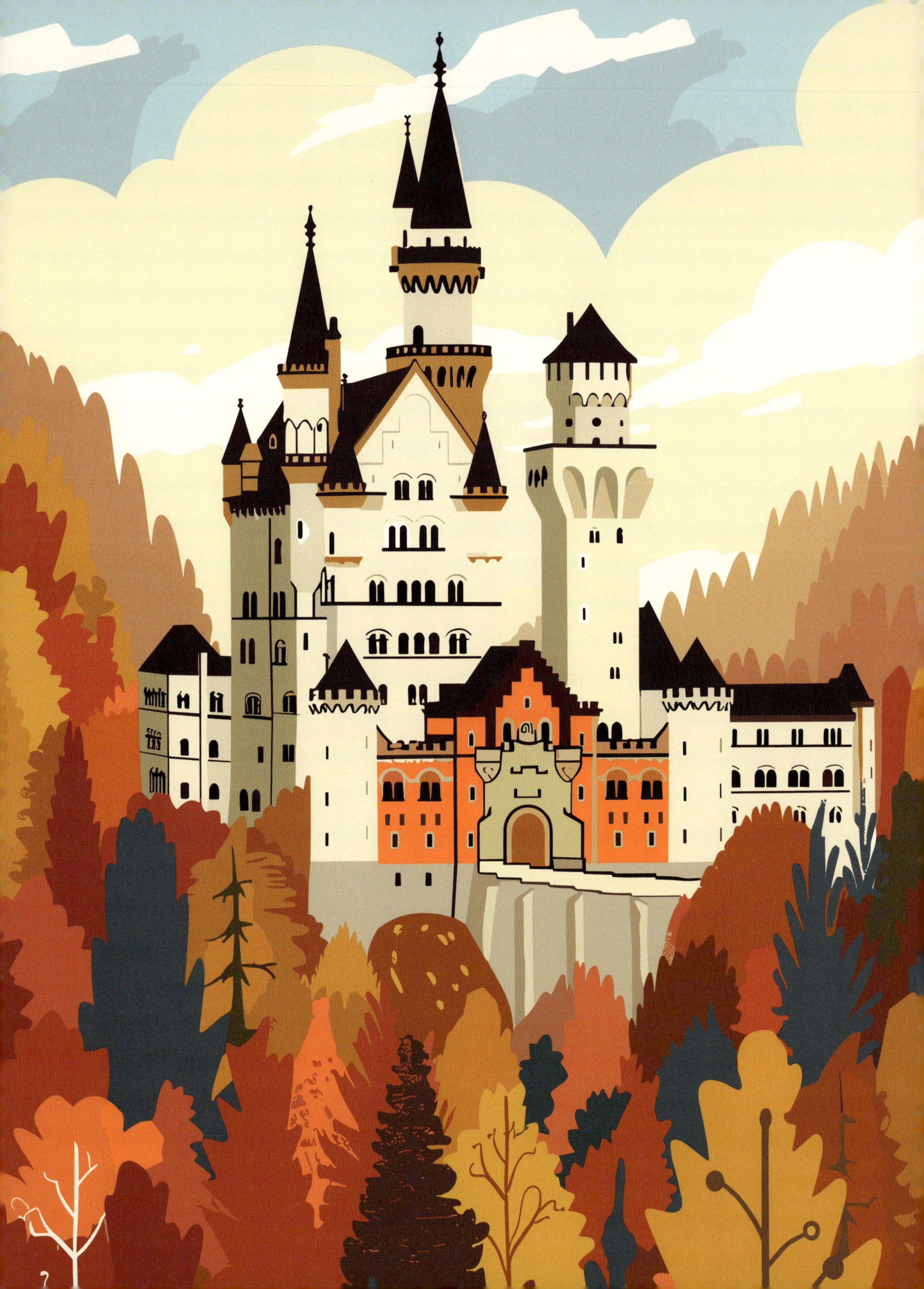

Introduction

In the collective imagination, castles are enchanted, fairytale places, settings for adventures starring dames and knights, kings and queens. Within their walls, along corridors or in dimly lit stairways, often hovers the legend of the ghost of one of the owners, as if modern visitors were unwelcome. In reality, however, castles, royal residences, fortresses, and palaces around the world, from Europe to Asia, have far more fascinating reasons to be visited. First and foremost, entering a castle means immersing oneself in the historical time in which it was built, spanning the long period from the Middle Ages to the 19th century when, with a few isolated exceptions, castles lost their function as royal and noble residences and were mostly transformed into museums. In any era, the magnificence of a residence served primarily as a representation of the political and economic power of the owner. The most striking example is the Palace of Versailles, an extention of the Sun King Louis XIV. As an absolute ruler, he made the gilded walls of the palace on the outskirts of Paris the symbol of his authoritarian rule. In the palace, he had the astute idea of "enclosing" the aristocracy and the court to keep them away from the political issues debated in the capital. The story of the Palace of Versailles transcended the borders of France, and, in the 18th century, other monarchs did everything they could to have a residence worthy of that of the Sun King and his successors (who went on making it even more sumptuous). On a visit to Versailles in the early 18th century, Tsar Peter I could not resist the temptation to own and display a similar residence upon his return to Saint Petersburg. In Poland, not far from Warsaw, Augustus III embellished the Baroque Wilanów Palace to such an extent that it was compared to a miniature Versailles.

Another aspect to consider in understanding the heritage represented by castles is linked to the architects who designed them, the artists who decorated them, and the collections housed inside. In addition to the furniture, much of which has been preserved or skillfully restored, and the precious objects, such as clocks and fine porcelain, timeless masterpieces hang on the walls of most royal palaces. At Buckingham Palace in London, for example, in the King's Gallery, founded in 1962 by Queen Elizabeth II, you can admire the masterpieces of the Royal Collection, one of the most significant art collections in the world, assembled by British kings and queens over the centuries. The same happens at the Winter Palace, one of the branches of the Hermitage in Saint Petersburg, or at the Château de Fontainebleau, where King Francis I of France summoned the greatest artists of the Italian Renaissance in the 16th century.

A third reason why learning about the history of castles is irresistible is the opportunity to "meet" their former owners and rediscover their inclinations, ambitions, and deepest weaknesses by exploring room after room or while strolling through the gardens. The dreamlike passions of King Ludwig I of Bavaria are translated into the pinnacles, turrets, and furnishings of the slender Neuschwanstein Castle. A shiver of terror is triggered by the sight of the perched Bran Castle in Romania, linked to the legend of Count Dracula. In Beijing, entering what was once the inaccessible Forbidden City of the Chinese emperors is a unique experience in itself, precisely because it was forbidden for centuries to anyone who did not have a specific role at court. The gushing fountains in the courtyards of Topkapi Palace in Istanbul or the Alhambra complex in Granada, meanwhile, evoke an atmosphere straight out of One Thousand and One Nights. So the circle closes and royal residences, castles, fortresses, and palaces once again become the protagonists of unforgettable fairy tales and legends.

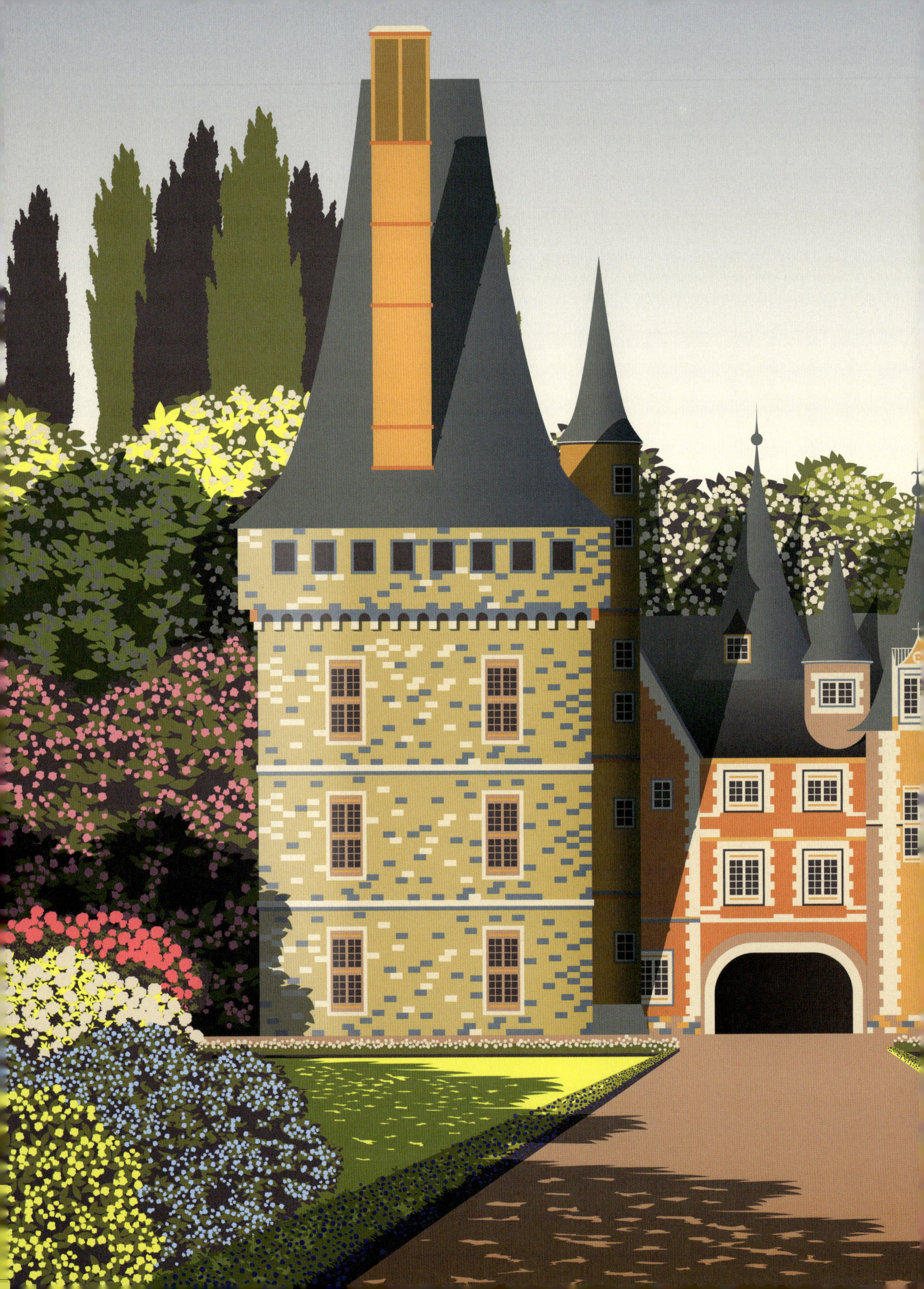

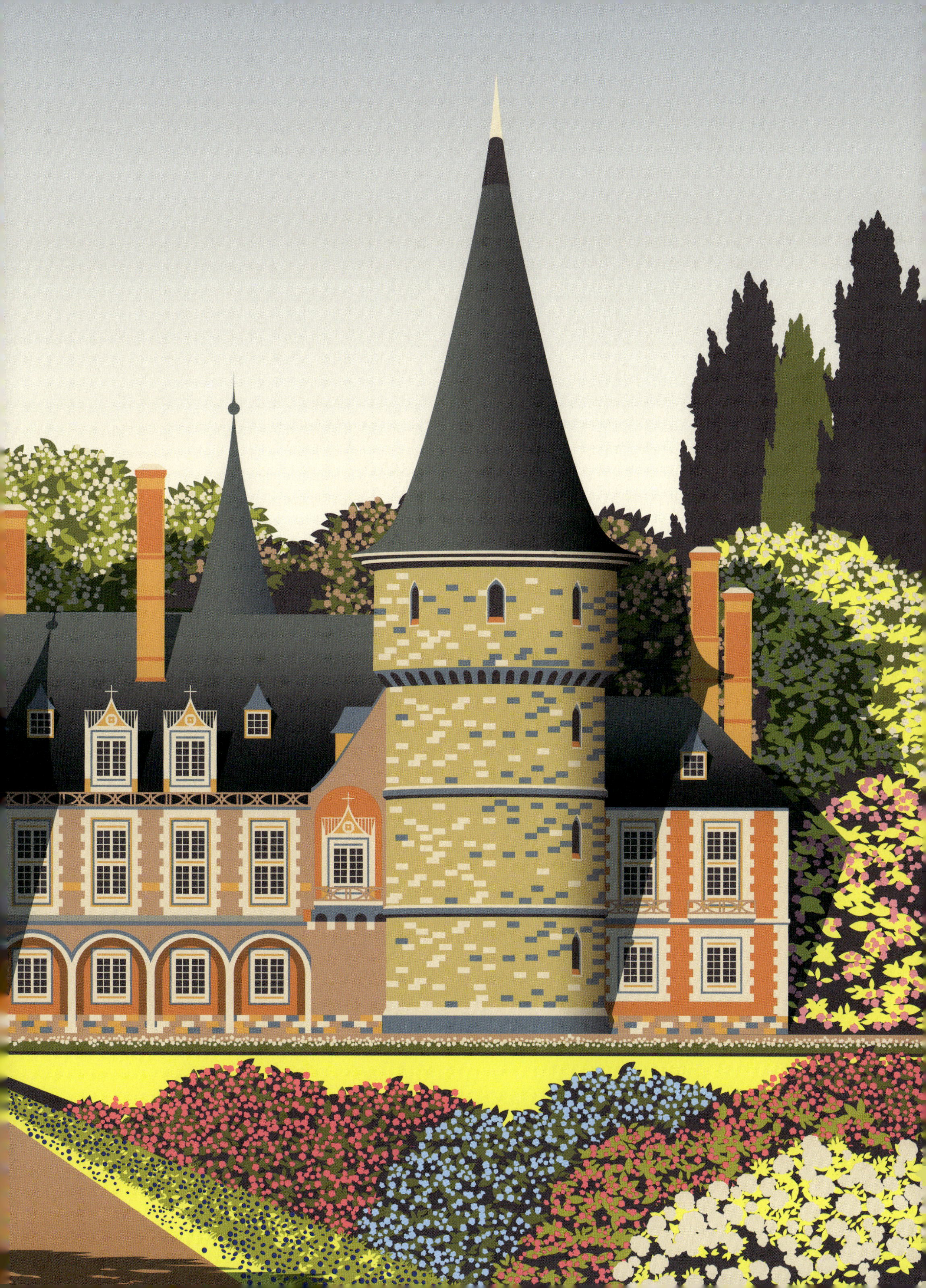

KILKENNY CASTLE

1172
Richard de Clare, Anglo-Norman conqueror better known as "Strongbow," built a wooden tower on the current site of Kilkenny Castle.

1192-1220
The Normans began construction of Kilkenny Castle on the site of their original fortification. Work continued until 1220.

1391
After passing from hand to hand, the castle was purchased by the noble and powerful Butler family, who owned it until 1935.

1650
The castle suffered extensive damage during Cromwell's conquest of Ireland. One of the four towers and the south- eastern curtain wall collapsed.

1661
With the return of the Stuarts to the throne, with Charles II as King of England, Scotland, and Ireland, the old manor was restored and modernized by James Butler.

1826
Another renovation of the castle began, restoring it to its "medieval" appearance by rebuilding the north wing and extending the south wall.

1935
The Butler family organized a large auction and sold all the furnishings of the castle.

1967
Arthur Butler sold the castle to the city of Kilkenny for the symbolic sum of £50.

With its imposing appearance, opulent interiors, and Italian gardens, Kilkenny Castle, just over 62 miles south of Dublin, is one of Ireland's most visited attractions. Built on the banks of the River Nore in a strategic position for the Earl of Pembroke at the end of the 12th century as a symbol of Norman control over the newly conquered island, for over 600 years it was the seat of power of the influential Butler clan, which boasted links with the English royal family (Lady Margaret Butler was the paternal grandmother of Anne Boleyn, the ill-fated wife of Henry VIII of England). The magnificent Long Gallery, the most admired room in the house, displays portraits of the Butler family, the oldest of which dates back to the 17th century. As for the exterior, compared to the original building from 1192, the manor, perfectly integrated into the medieval context of the town of Kilkenny, characterized by narrow alleys and cobbled streets, was repeatedly destroyed and rebuilt. Of the oldest part, the imposing structure with three cylindrical towers remains (originally there were four) while the rest dates back to 19th-century renovations in Victorian style. The building is surrounded by extensive grounds

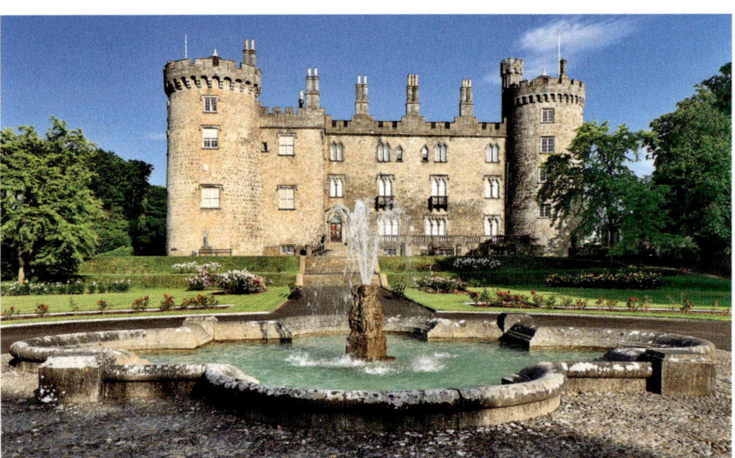

and a formal garden, on the west side of the castle, with symmetrical paths radiating from a central fountain: rearranged in the 20th century, it retains the appearance it probably had 300 years ago. Although the Butlers were forced by economic difficulties in the 20th century to auction off most of the collections of paintings and precious objects they had collected over the years, the rooms of

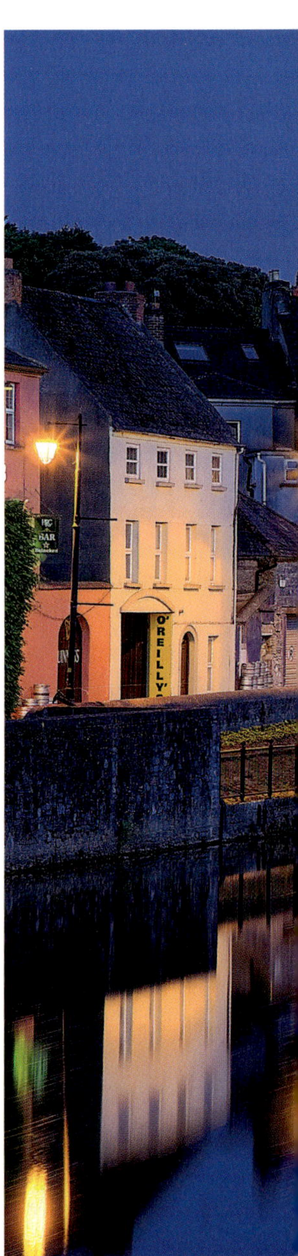

• 10 left: The first Norman tower of the complex was built in 1172, about twenty years before the construction of the castle, which, despite the centuries, retains its medieval appearance. Several excavations have uncovered parts of the original structure.

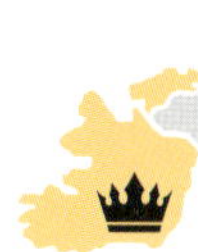

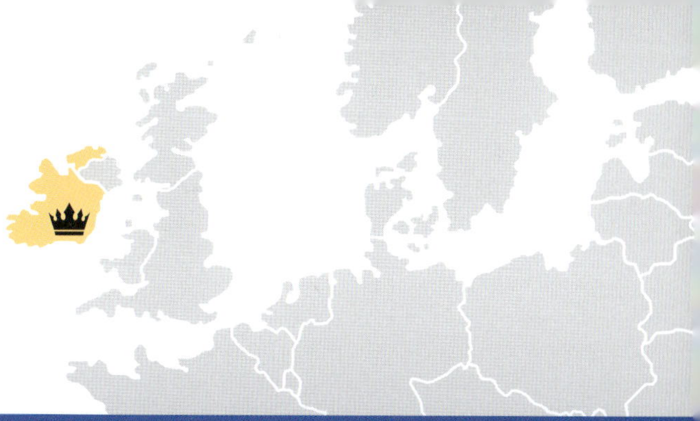

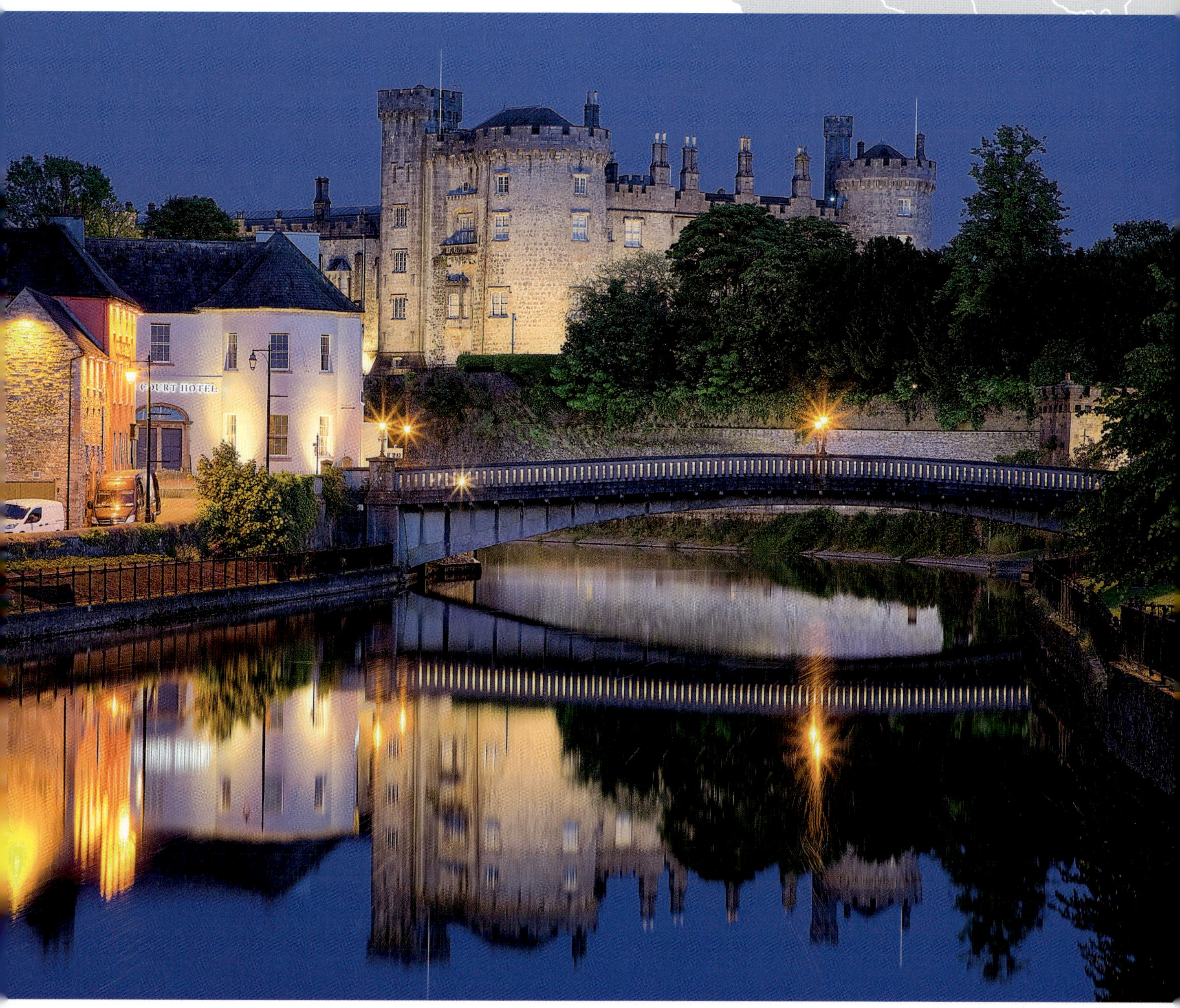

the castle are still a perfect example of a stately home, as can be seen from the 17th-century tapestries depicting the stories of Decius Mus hanging on the walls, the tapestry in the Withdrawing Room, the Victorian nursery with its antique rocking horses, and the realistic animals carved in stone decorating the exotic Moorish staircase.

• 10–11: View of the mighty Kilkenny Castle of the Butler family, who arrived in Ireland in the Middle Ages with the Norman invasion. The Irish town is nicknamed the "marble city" because of its gray limestone houses, rich in fossils.

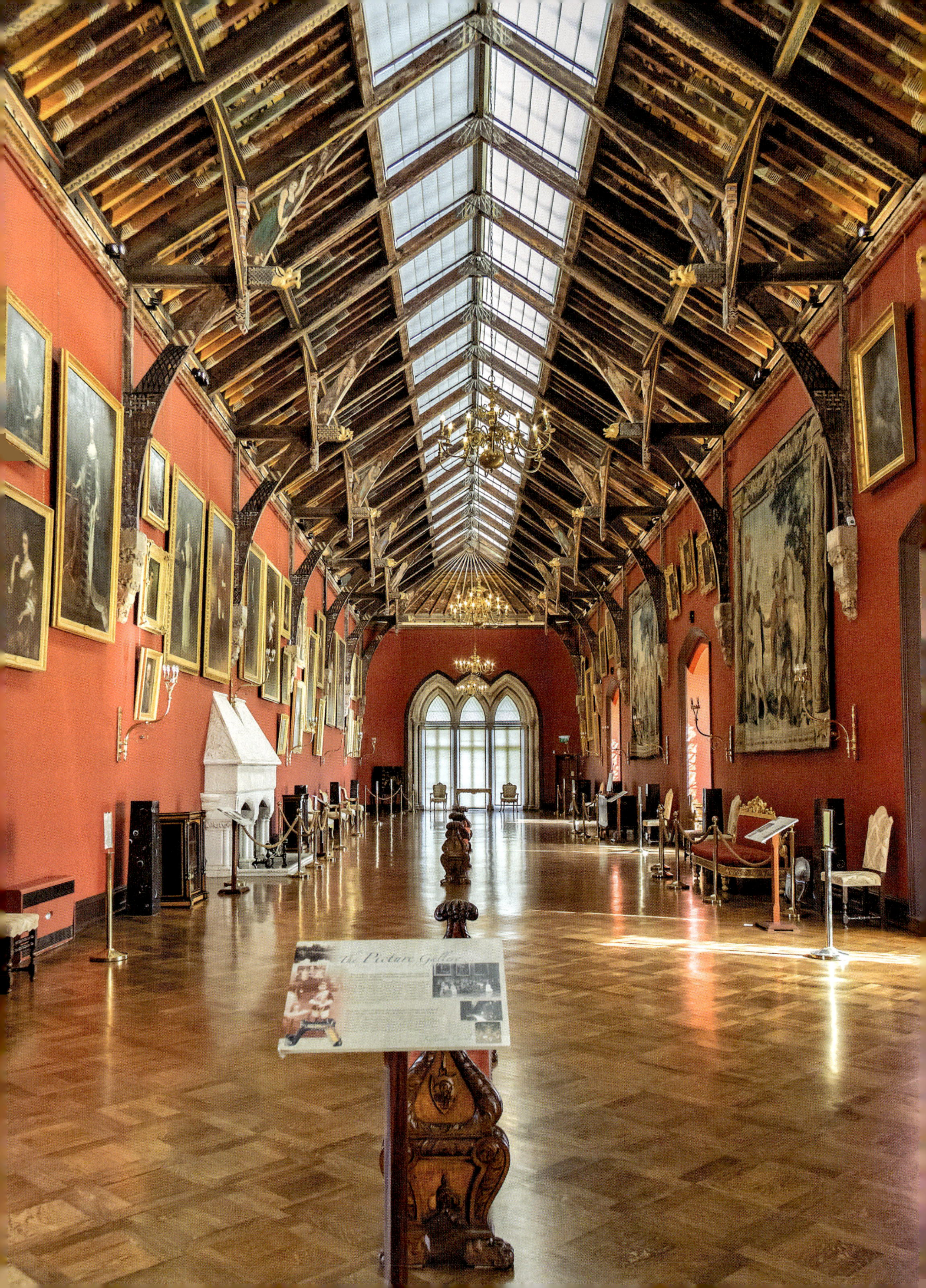
The Picture

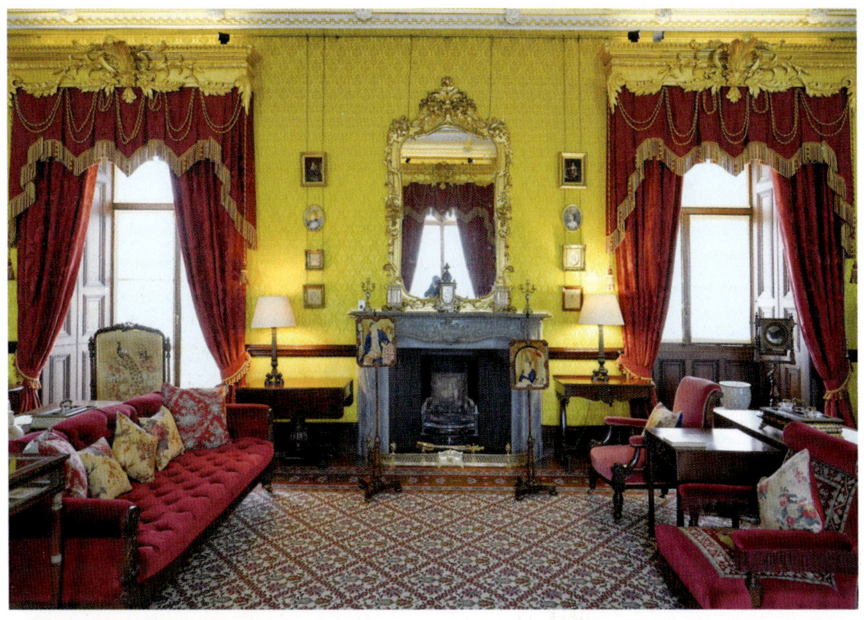

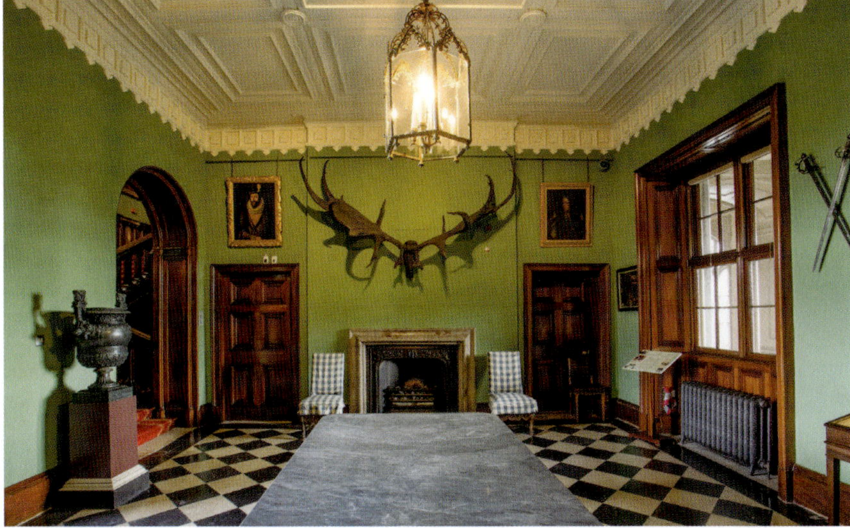

· 12: The magnificent Long Gallery, whose bright trussed ceiling features colorful Celtic motifs inspired by the Book of Kells, the work of John Hungerford Pollen. This English architect also designed the refined fireplace in pure Carrara marble, decorated with scenes from the history of the family. The walls are adorned with portraits of members of the Butler clan.

· 13 top: The Withdrawing Room or Drawing Room of the castle is a typical feature of English aristocratic residences. It was a sort of formal living room where the owners, or more often their wives and daughters, could withdraw to welcome and entertain visiting guests. This necessitated the creation of more informal but extremely elegant rooms where the owners could display their wealth through luxurious furnishings and works of art.

· 13 bottom: A majestic Italian black marble table dominates the hall: it is said to be the only piece of furniture that the Butlers were unable to sell at auction due to its weight. The room, known as the "Diamond Hall," was already being used as an entrance hall in the 17th century.

The Book of Kells

The Great Gospel Book of Saint Columba, known as the "Book of Kells," an absolute masterpiece of early medieval miniature art since 1661, is located at Trinity College in Dublin under the reference number MS 58. The date of this parchment work remains a matter of debate: tradition would have it dating back directly to Saint Columba of Iona, one of the patron saints of Ireland who lived in the 6th century—a period not justified, however, by the calligraphy, which is typical of at least two centuries later. In any case, the presence of the Gospel Book at Kells Abbey, founded by monks from Iona in the Hebrides, northwest of Dublin, is documented from the early 11th–12th centuries. The precious book contains the text of the four Gospels in Latin, accompanied by rich miniatures by magnificent colors that reveal the use of purple, lilac, red, pink, green, and yellow pigments, probably imported from Mediterranean countries, and even from Afghanistan in the case of the blue lapis lazuli. In 1953, its 680 pages were bound into four volumes, and today three are displayed in rotation, one miniated and two containing text.

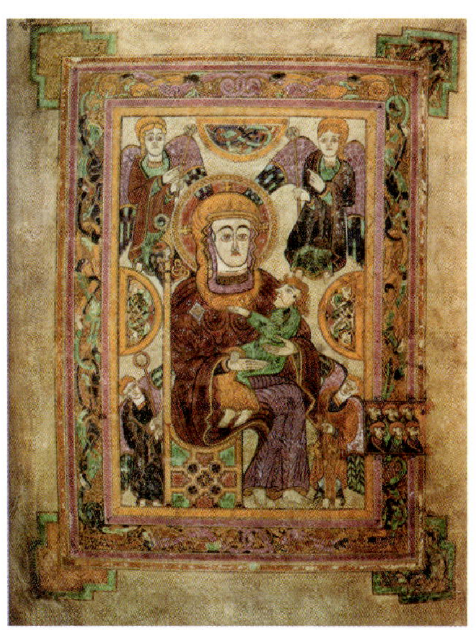

Holyrood Palace

1128
King David I of Scotland founded Holyrood Abbey as an Augustinian monastery at the eastern end of the Royal Mile in Edinburgh.

1501–1505
James IV had a new palace built next to the abbey, which became his favorite residence.

1528–1536
James V expanded the palace, adding the Tower of James V, which still stands today.

1561–1567
Mary Stuart, Queen of Scotland, resided at Holyroodhouse.

1642–1649
During the English Revolution, the palace suffered serious damage, followed by years of neglect.

1671–1678
Sir William Bruce rebuilt the palace in Baroque style for Charles II, restoring it as a royal residence.

1745
Charles Edward Stuart, known as "Bonnie Prince Charlie," briefly used the palace during the Jacobite uprising.

1822
George IV was the first British monarch to visit Holyroodhouse since the 17th century.

19th century
Queen Victoria restored the palace's royal role, making it a key venue for ceremonial visits.

21st century
Holyroodhouse is the official Scottish residence of the monarch. In 2022, the coffin of Queen Elizabeth II was laid in state there.

The Royal Mile runs down the ridge on which Edinburgh, in Scotland, has developed over the centuries. At the highest end of the street stands the Castle, which dominates the city. At the other end, at the bottom of the slope, located on the edge of a landscape that seems more rural than urban due to the presence of the large Holyrood Park, stands Holyrood Palace, also known as "Holyroodhouse," near the evocative ruins of the medieval Augustinian abbey of the same name—the site of the coronation of several Scottish kings and of royal weddings—of which the palace was originally the guest quarters. The complex

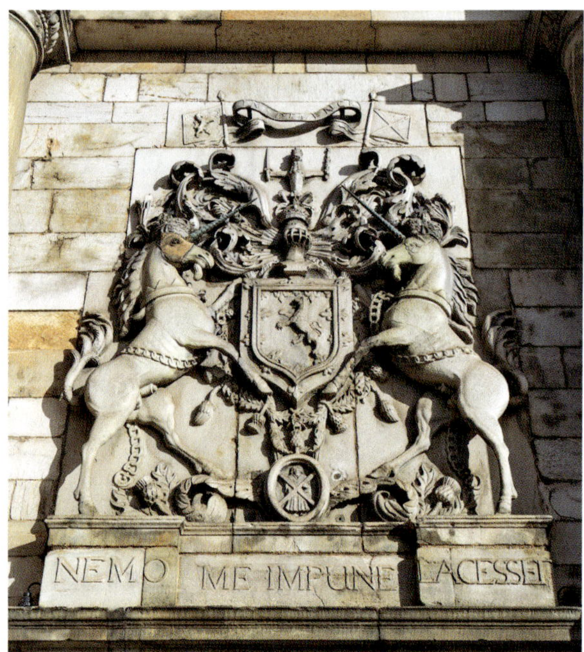

was built at the end of the 15th century by James IV as the new residence for his family, the Stuarts, and it was the home of the Scottish monarchs until 1603, when James VI became King of England and moved the court to London. Its history is therefore closely linked to that of the Stuarts and, above all, to the unfortunate story of Mary, Queen of Scots, who lived here between 1561 and 1567, so much so

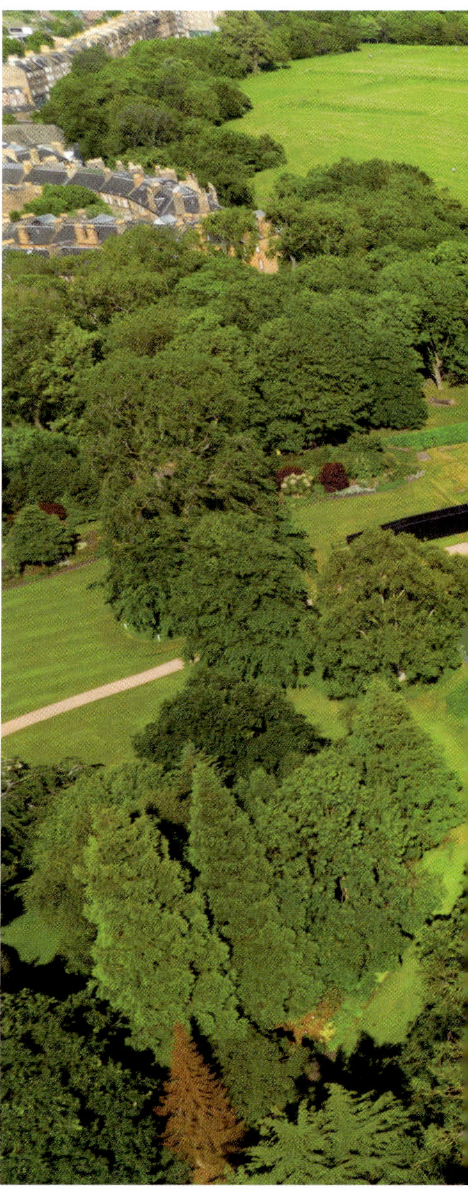

• 14 left: The unicorn is the emblem of Scotland, a symbol of pride and freedom, difficult to capture and even more difficult to kill. It was used on the royal coat of arms for the first time in the 12th century.

• 14-15: Aerial view of Holyrood Palace. The palace's inner courtyard, in Renaissance style and not very large, has a square layout and is surrounded on all sides by a portico reminiscent of a cloister. In the center of the lawn is a small fountain. The name Holyrood means "Holy Cross," referring to a relic that belonged to Queen Margaret, wife of Malcolm III and mother of David I, who died in 1093 in Edinburgh Castle. On the left side of the image, you can see the remains of the medieval Augustinian abbey.

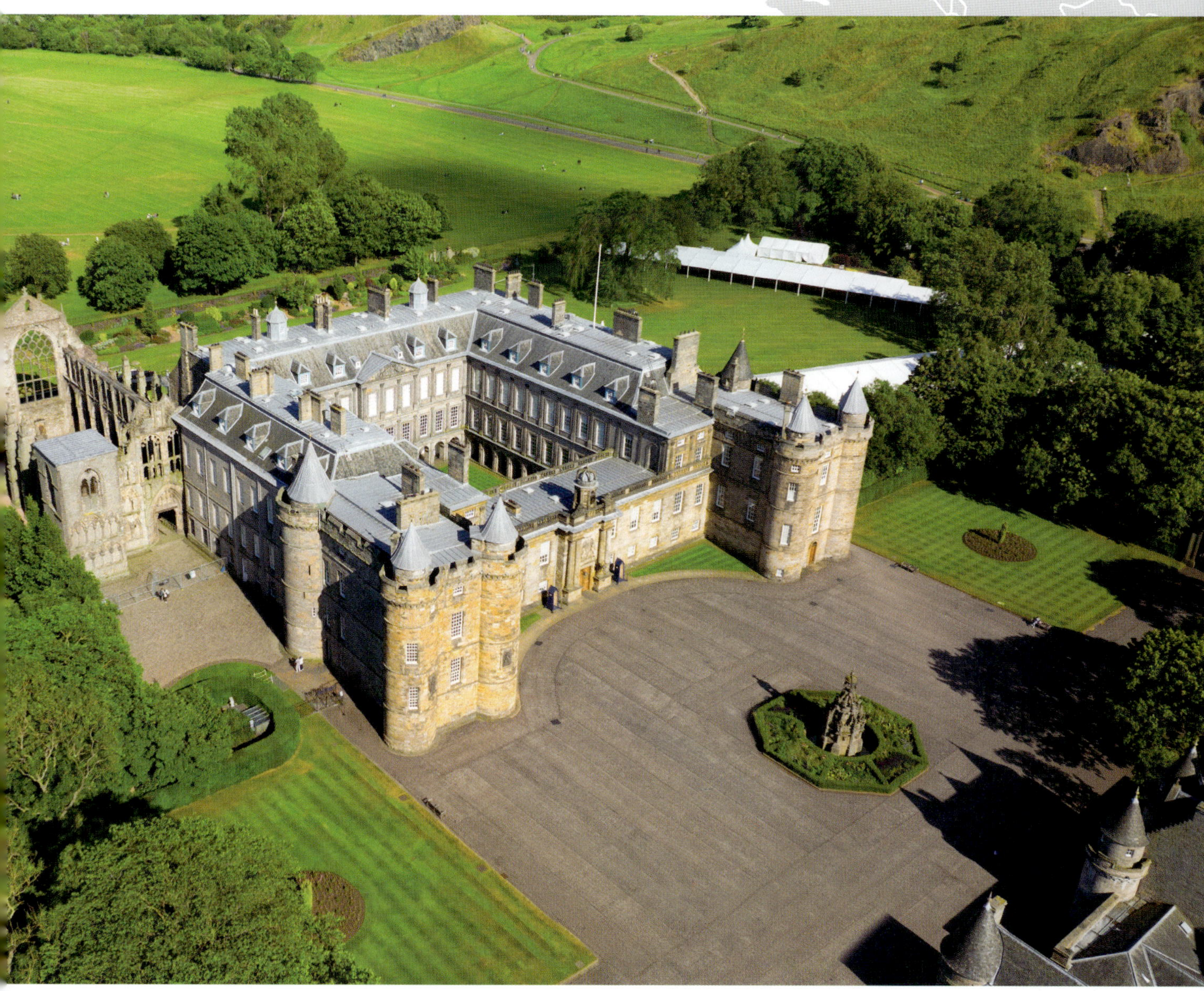

that the castle is often referred to as "the house of Mary Stuart." It was at Holyrood that Mary married her cousin Lord Darnley, and it was here that she witnessed the murder of her loyal Italian secretary Davide Rizzio, who was killed in the queen's private apartments in 1566. A century later, during the English Revolution, the palace was almost destroyed by fire and had to be rebuilt. After James VI became King of England in 1603 and moved to London, the palace was no longer the permanent seat of the royal court, although the Stuarts continued to visit it during their trips to Scotland, and in 1745 Bonnie Prince Charlie, the pretender to the throne who led the Jacobite uprising that year with the aim of restoring his family's power, established his court there for several months. Today, Holyrood Palace is the official residence of the British royal family when they are in Scotland.

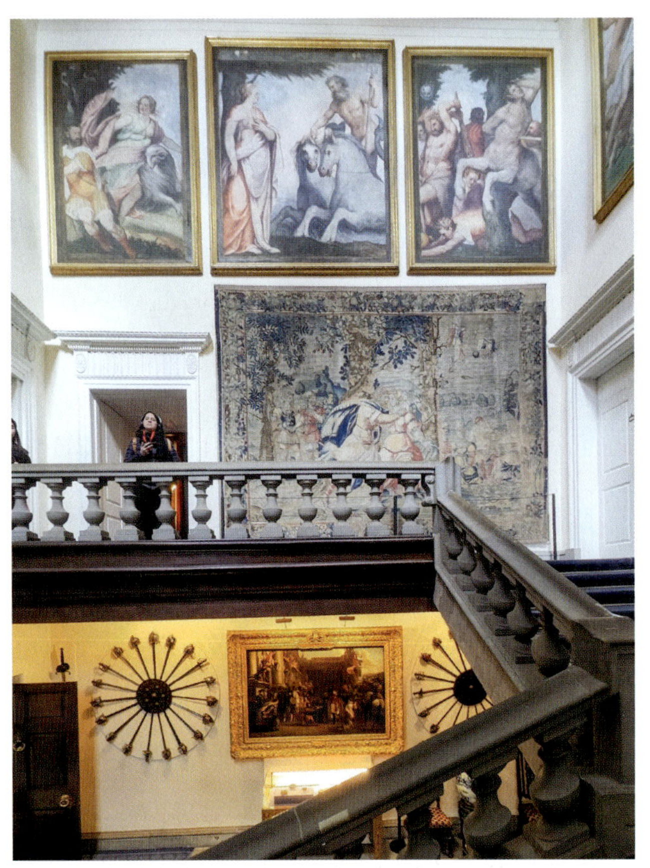

The queen in the movies

The life story of Mary Stuart, so full of twists and turns and so tragic, has never ceased to inspire artists and writers, from Vittorio Alfieri (1749–1803) to Friedrich Schiller (1759–1805), to countless screenwriters and theater, film, and television directors, who still today continue to grapple with the fascinating personality of this historical figure. Mary Stuart is striking also because she was the first female monarch to be executed in England, and the first of the Stuart dynasty to be crowned in Scotland. Mary Stuart is striking not only for her passion, but also because she was a tenacious woman who fought for power with another strong woman, Elizabeth I, in a world dominated by men and at a time torn apart by political divisions between Catholics and Protestants. The story of the Scottish queen has been told several times on the big screen, starting with silent films, but among the most memorable films are John Ford's *Mary of Scotland* (1936) with Katharine Hepburn; *Mary, Queen of Scots* (1971) by Charles Jarrott with Vanessa Redgrave (and Glenda Jackson in the role of Elizabeth I), and *Elizabeth: The Golden Age* (2007) by Shekhar Kapur with Cate Blanchett and Samantha Morton in the roles of Elizabeth and Mary, respectively.

• 16 bottom: American actress Katharine Hepburn portrayed on the set of the 1936 film **Mary of Scotland,** directed by John Ford.

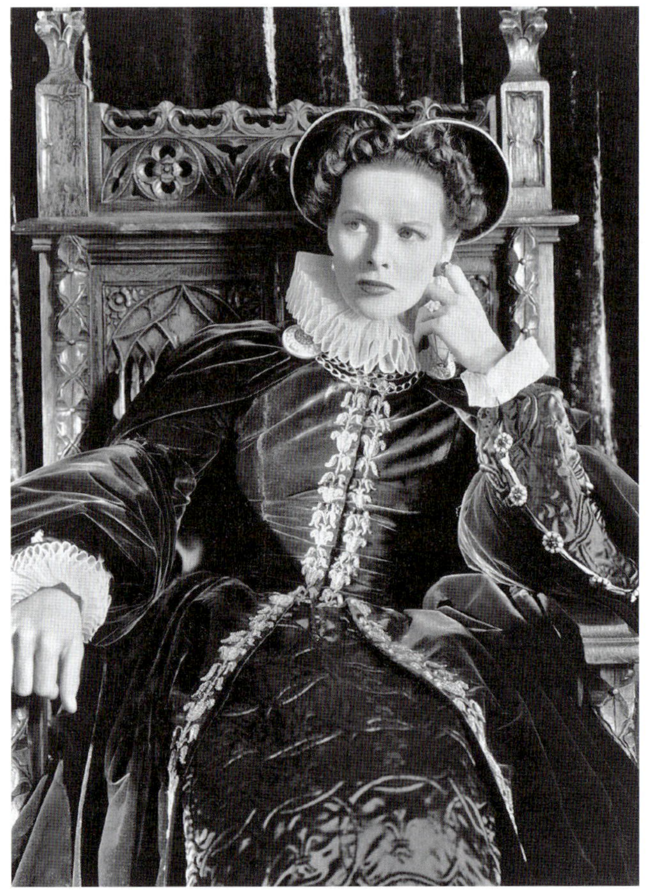

• 16 left top: The Great Staircase at Holyrood Palace is decorated with fragments of Italian Renaissance frescoes depicting mythological subjects. They were purchased by Prince Albert, husband of Queen Victoria, who had them installed on these walls in 1881.

• 16 left bottom: The dining room at Holyrood is kept with the table elegantly set as if members of the British royal family and their guests were about to arrive for dinner at any moment.

• 17: Holyrood Palace was the venue for Mary's second and third marriages. She married Lord Darnley in 1565 in the chapel and Lord Bothwell, who was Protestant, in 1567 in the Great Hall. Mary Stuart's apartments consist of two audience rooms and a bedroom, as well as two small rooms located in the corner towers of the building.

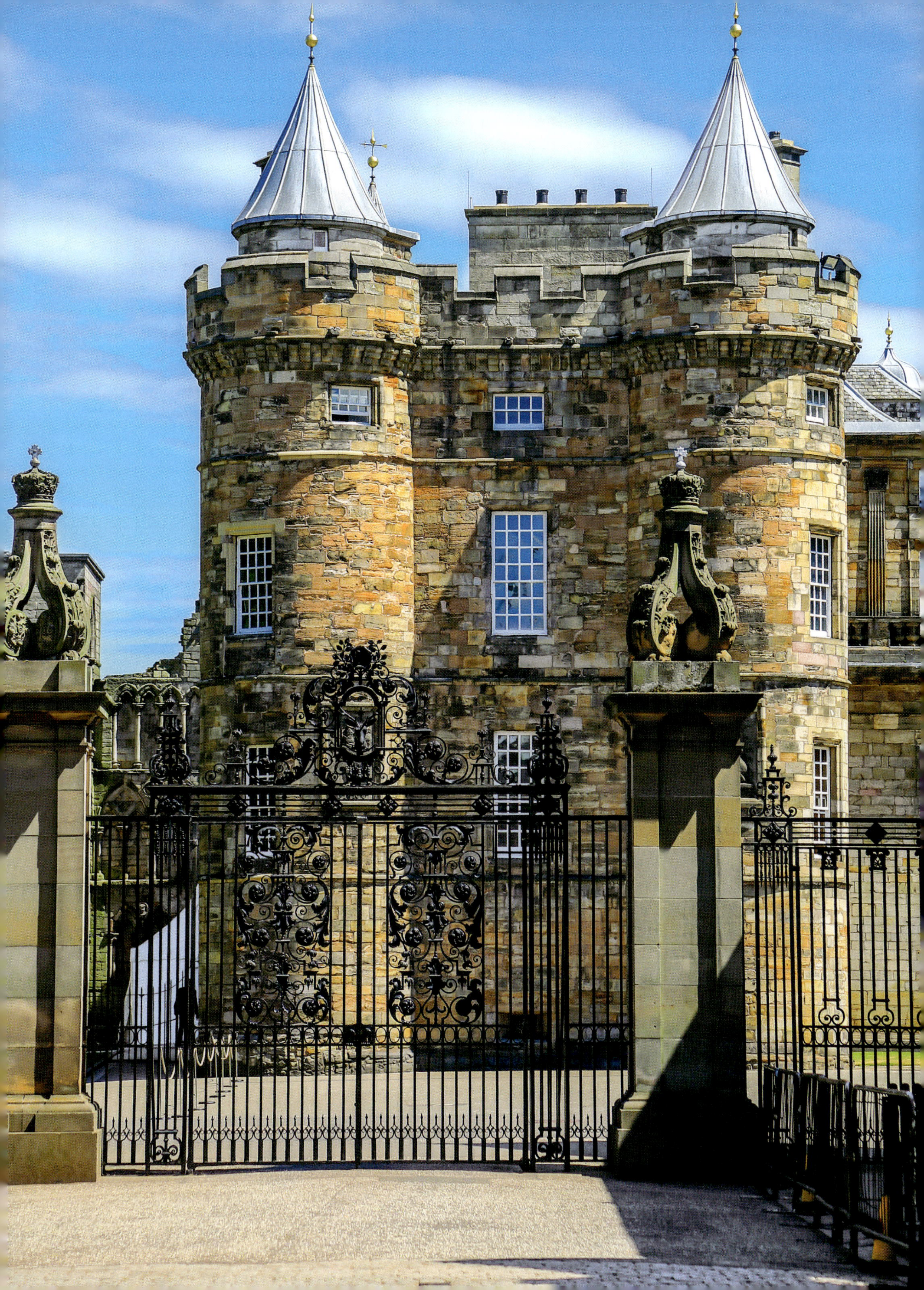

BUCKINGHAM PALACE

1703
The future Buckingham Palace was built by the Duke of Buckingham, John Sheffield, on the site of an older palace.

1761
George III purchased Buckingham House for £21,000. Starting the following year, the palace was modernized.

1826
George IV commissioned architect John Nash to transform Buckingham House into Buckingham Palace, despite initially planning to keep the old mansion as his pied-à-terre.

1837
Upon the death of William IV, his granddaughter Victoria was crowned Queen of Great Britain and Ireland on June 20. The queen moved to Buckingham Palace, which from that moment became the official residence of the monarchy of the United Kingdom.

1840–1860
Queen Victoria married Albert of Saxe-Coburg and Gotha, who was responsible for making Buckingham Palace more comfortable and for initiating work to enlarge it.

1901–1910
During the reign of Edward VII and his wife Alexandra of Denmark, Buckingham Palace once again became the center of the monarchy and was embellished and decorated in the Belle Époque style.

1948
Prince Charles, the future King Charles III, was born at Buckingham Palace. He was the first-born child of Princess Elizabeth and Prince Philip of Greece and Denmark.

1952
On February 6, 1952, Princess Elizabeth ascended to the throne of the United Kingdom. Along with her prince consort, she officially moved to Buckingham Palace.

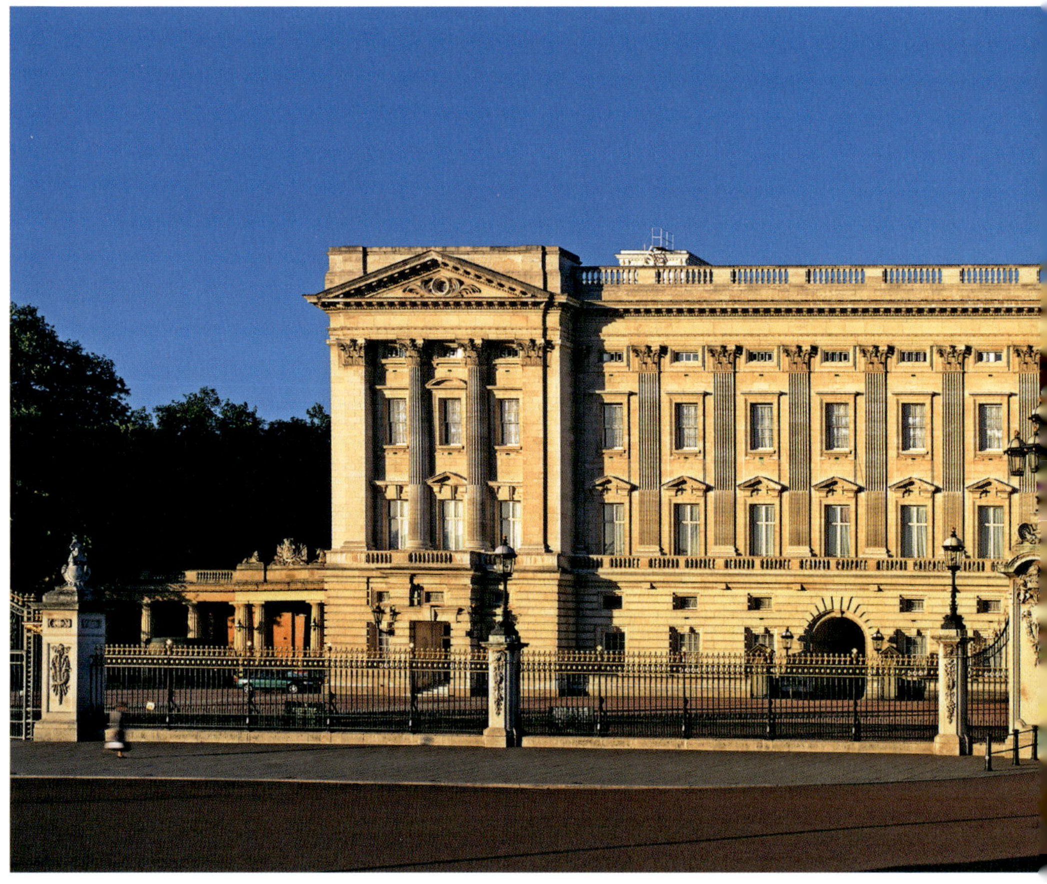

Located in the heart of London, Buckingham Palace is the headquarters of the Windsor monarchy and the residence where the Royal Family lives their private lives: when the Royal Standard, with the golden lions of England and the rampant lion of Scotland, flies at the top of the palace means that the sovereign of the United Kingdom and its Overseas Territories is inside. Conversely, the Union Flag, known as the "Union Jack," is flown over the London royal palace when the king is elsewhere. The history of the residence of the Firm, the British "company" that includes the Royal Family, but also all the institutions associated with it, the staff, courtiers, and offices responsible for managing its affairs and properties, dates back to the 18th century, but it was not until the 19th century that the palace became a royal residence. Before that, English sovereigns lived in other prestigious palaces in the English capital: Whitehall Palace (of which only the Banqueting House remains) was the residence of Henry VIII (1491–1547) and his successors

• 18–19: Buckingham Palace as it appears today is the result of a series of renovations. The façade with the balcony from which the royals appear was redesigned by Sir Aston Webb for George V in 1913.

• 19 bottom: The iconic gates of Buckingham Palace with the royal coats of arms of the British monarchy. Announcements of important events concerning the Royal Family, from the births of princes to the death of Queen Elizabeth II, are posted here.

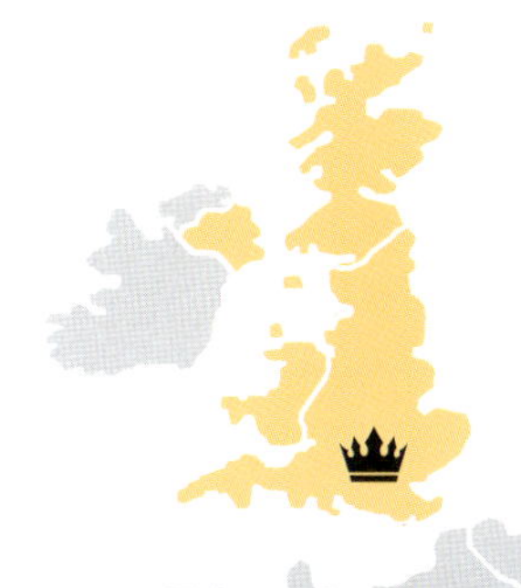

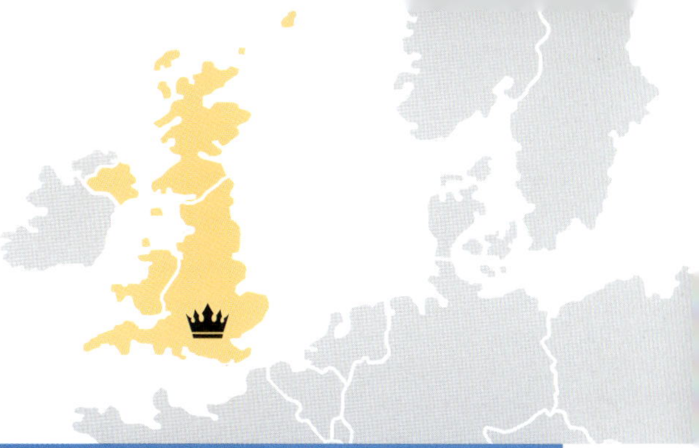

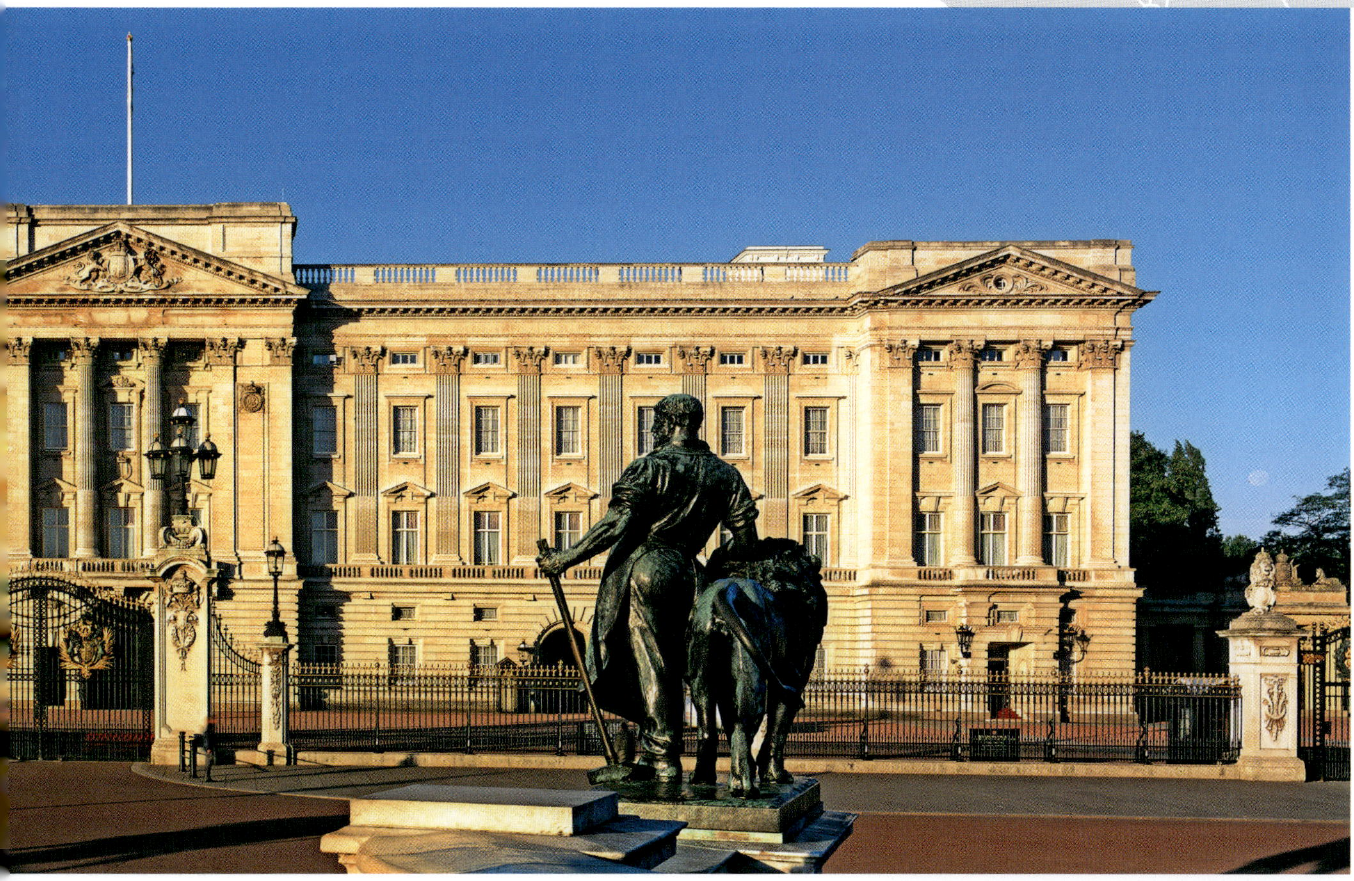

until the end of the 17th century, when it was destroyed by fire and the court moved to St James's Palace. Although the palace was not particularly opulent compared to the 18th-century palaces of European courts, George I (1660–1727) and George II (1683–1760) of the Hanover dynasty maintained their court there, while George III, after purchasing it, spent a lot of time at Buckingham House, the complex that preceded Buckingham Palace, which became the property of John Sheffield, Duke of Buckingham, in 1703, from whom it derives its name. Inspired by the sumptuous European residences, particularly Versailles, the nobleman had an aristocratic residence built overlooking the Thames, inspired by the Italian villas of Andrea Palladio, with rooms decorated with stucco, marble, and frescoes. Its grandeur attracted the attention of George III, who, taking advantage of a technicality regarding the ownership of part of the land on which the palace stood, claimed possession, forcing the duke to sell it in 1761.

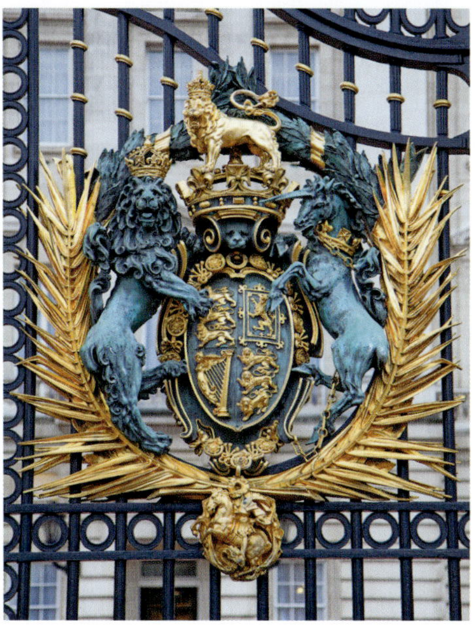

The changing of the guard

At the main entrance to Buckingham Palace, every morning at 11 a.m. in June and July, and every other day during the rest of the year (except in case of rain), one of the most symbolic ceremonies associated with the British monarchy has been taking place for centuries.

The military personnel of the Royal Guard, dressed in traditional red coats and bearskin hats, change guard at the palace where the reigning monarch resides. Until 1698, the ceremony was held at Whitehall Palace in London, the official residence of the British sovereign.

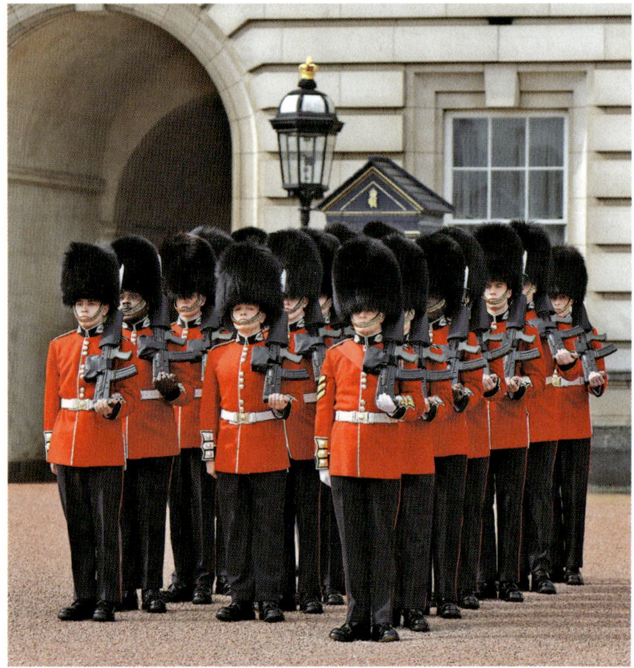

Later, when the court moved to St James's Palace, the Foot Guards—i.e., the royal infantry—continued to protect the new residence. With the current arrangement at Buckingham Palace, the Guard remains stationed at the nearby St James's Palace but maintains a garrison at Buckingham Palace, which is relieved every 24 hours. The soldiers on duty, the Old Guard, are replaced by the New Guard. The most important part is when the captains of the two Guards hand over the keys to the Palace. The garrisons are traditionally accompanied by a full military band, which plays a selection of music, which today ranges from traditional marches to popular songs.

The new residence was intended as a private residence for the king's wife, Queen Charlotte of Mecklenburg-Strelitz, and her apartments in particular were furnished with great splendor. George IV soon decided to leave Carlton House (the palace was demolished in 1826) where he lived and, spending a fortune without the consent of Parliament, hired the architect John Nash to begin a neoclassical renovation, complete with a marble triumphal arch in the style of ancient Rome (which was moved to Hyde Park in the 19th century, where it still stands today). The palace was U-shaped around a large square courtyard of honor. Compared to today's palace, there was no façade facing the Mall, which closes the quadrangle. George IV's successor was not as eager to embellish the building, and it was Queen Victoria, the first monarch to make Buckingham Palace the official residence of the monarchy and the British Empire, who decided on new changes and renovations. Overcoming a certain melancholy at leaving Kensington Palace where she had grown up, on July 13, 1837, the future queen arrived by carriage at her new home. After the death of her husband, Prince Albert, in 1861, the queen wore perpetual mourning clothes, withdrew almost completely from public life, and abandoned Buckingham Palace, preferring Windsor Castle or Balmoral Castle. In 1901, her son Edward VII brought the London palace back to life, giving the rooms a Belle Époque look, which was later revised. However, the most important work of the 20th century was the construction, designed by Aston Webb and commissioned by George V, of the new Portland stone façade with the balcony from which the Royal Family still greets its subjects on special occasions.

• 21 right top: Behind the white façade of Buckingham Palace lies the King's vast private garden, where important events are held, including garden parties attended by up to 24,000 guests from all walks of life. The park is home to a variety of plant species and features a small lake in the center.

• 21 right bottom: The Mall is the wide avenue, about 0.6 mile long, that connects Buckingham Palace and Admiral Arch from west to east. At the end of the Mall, in front of the gates of the royal palace, stands the Victoria Memorial, dedicated to Queen Victoria.

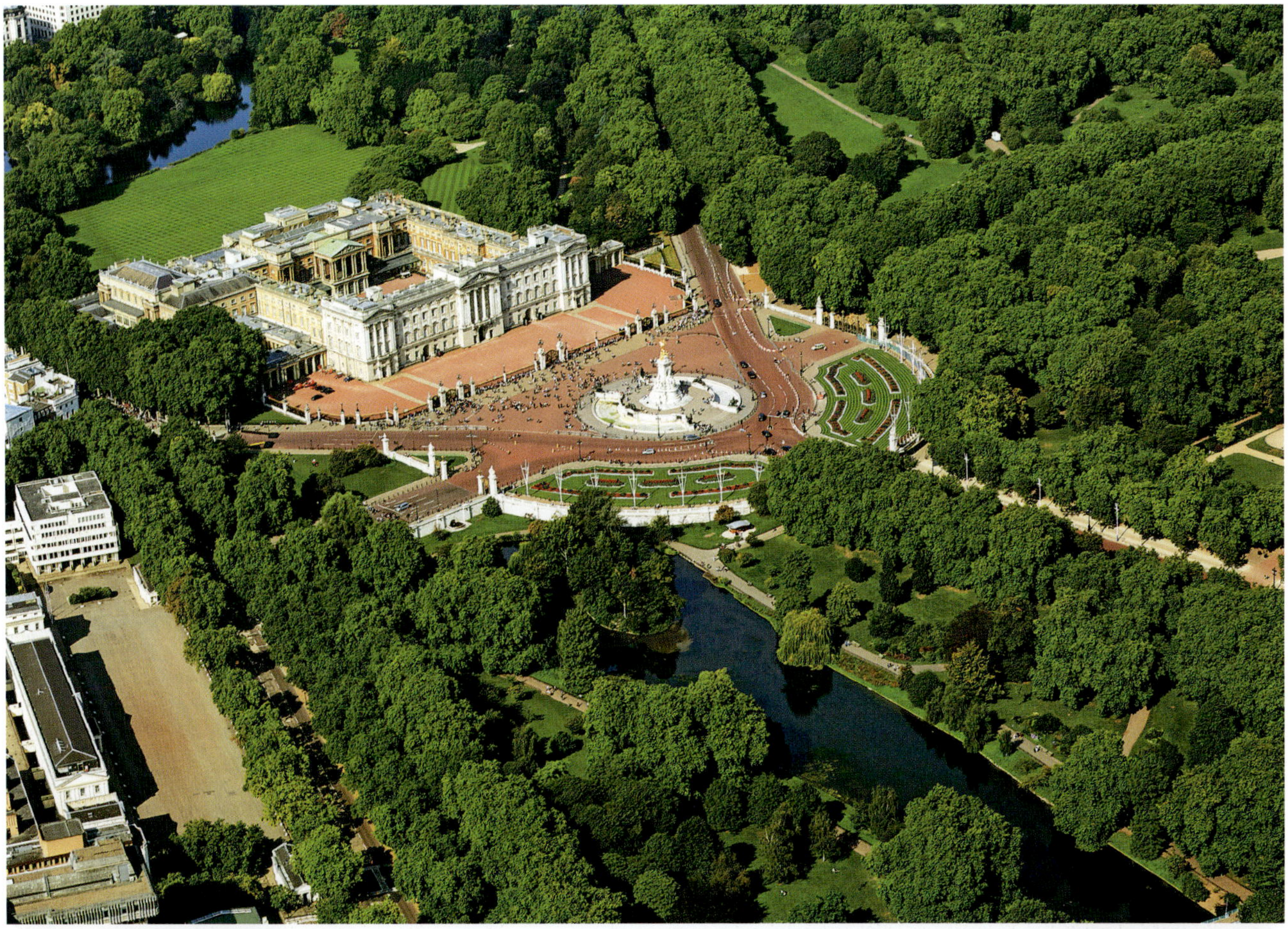

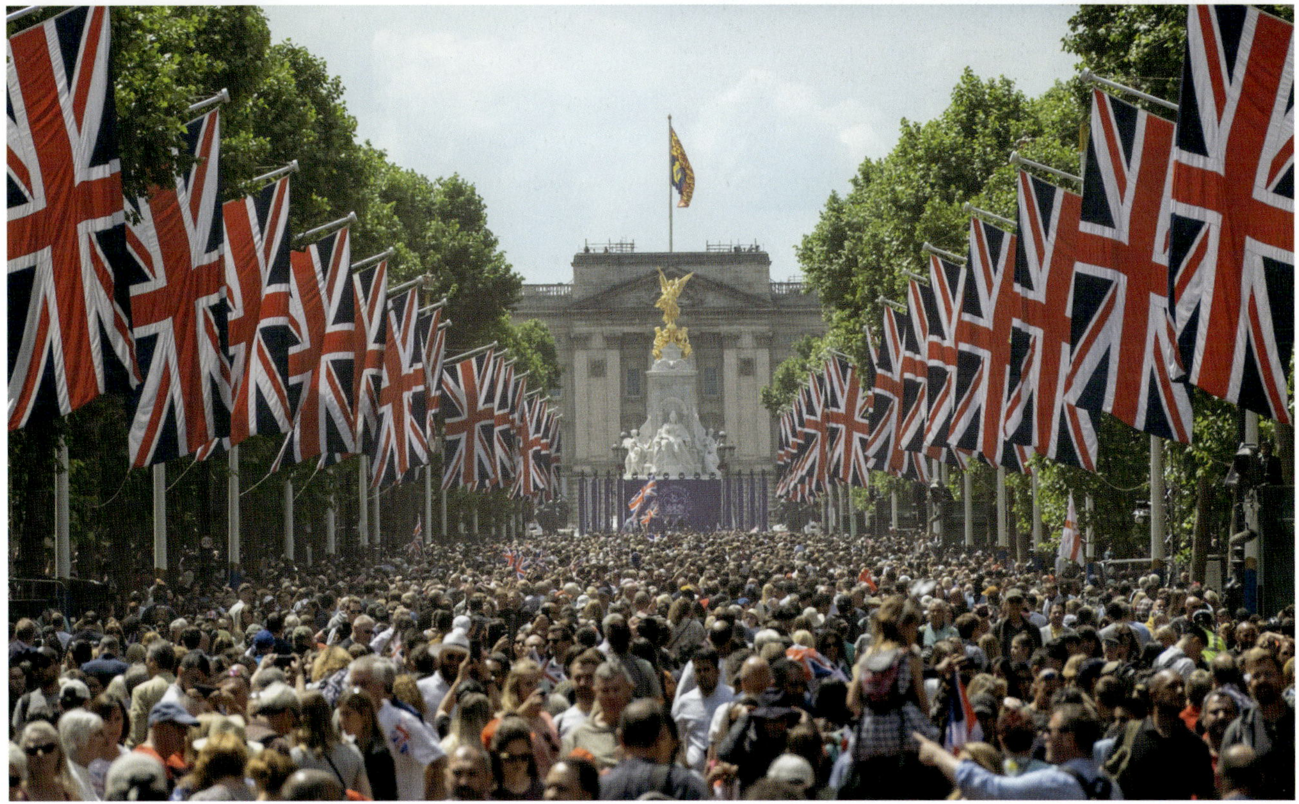

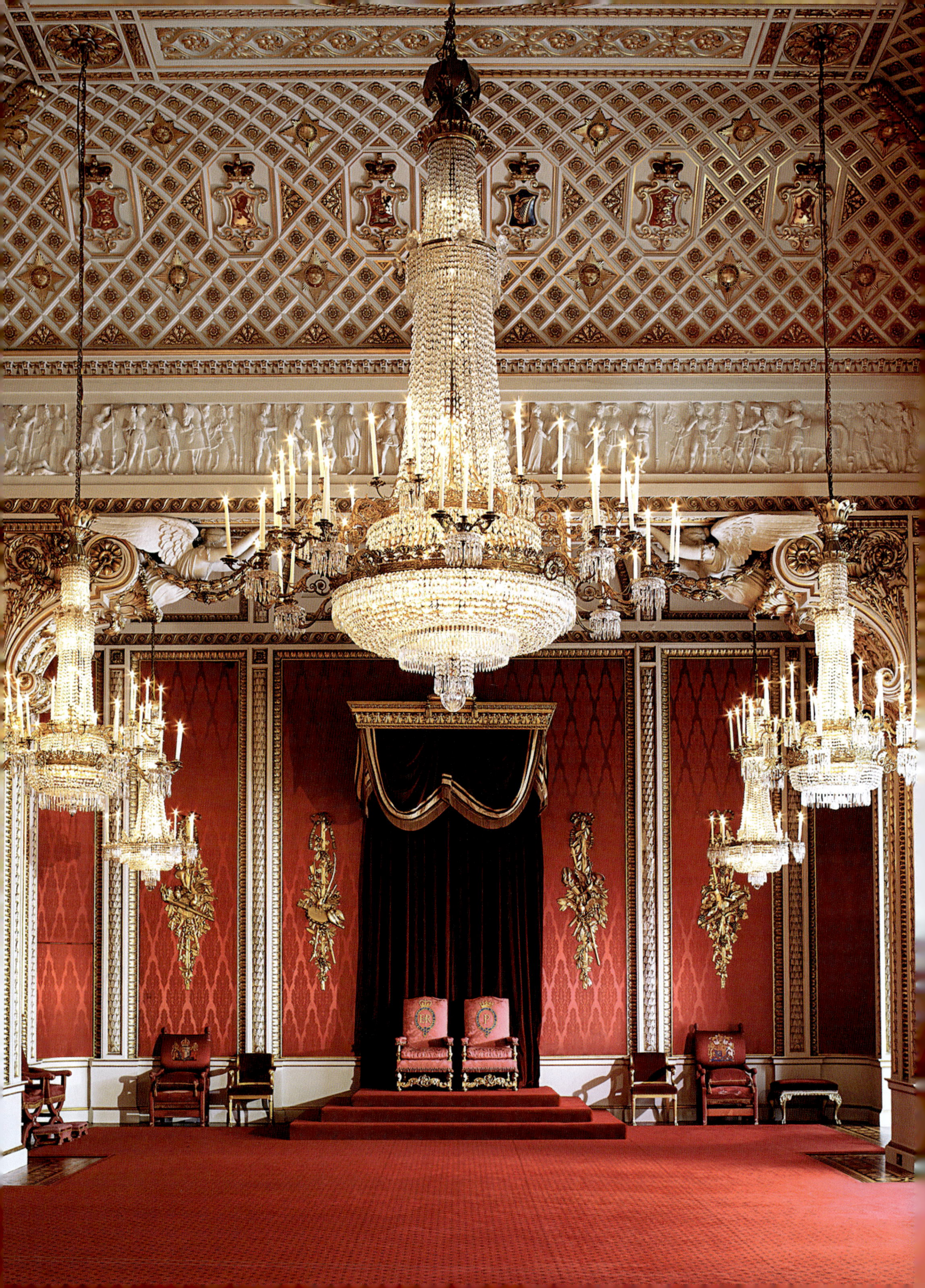

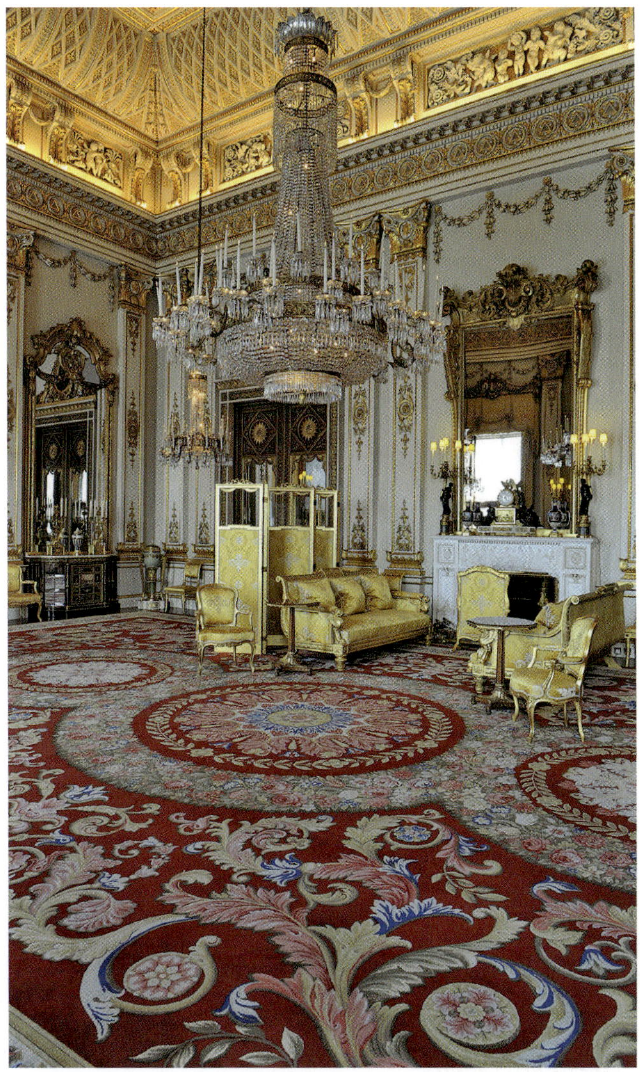

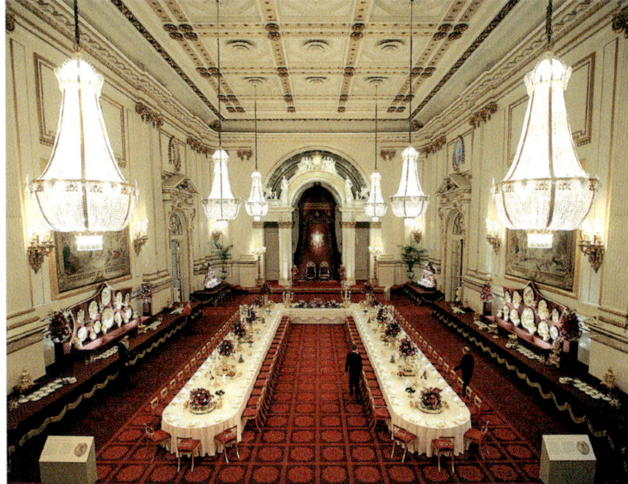

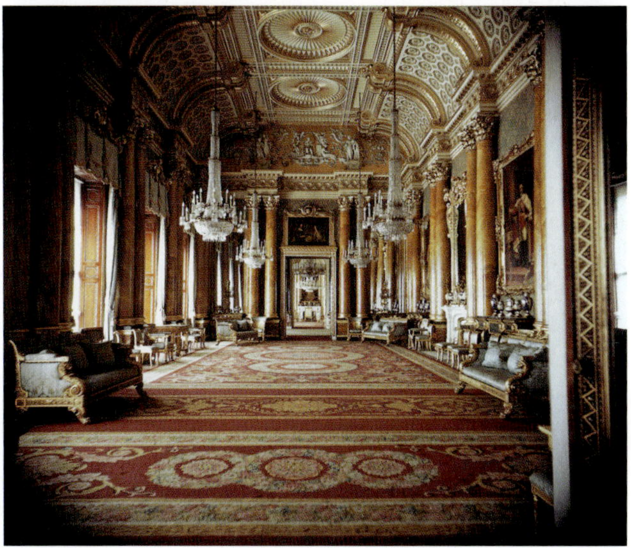

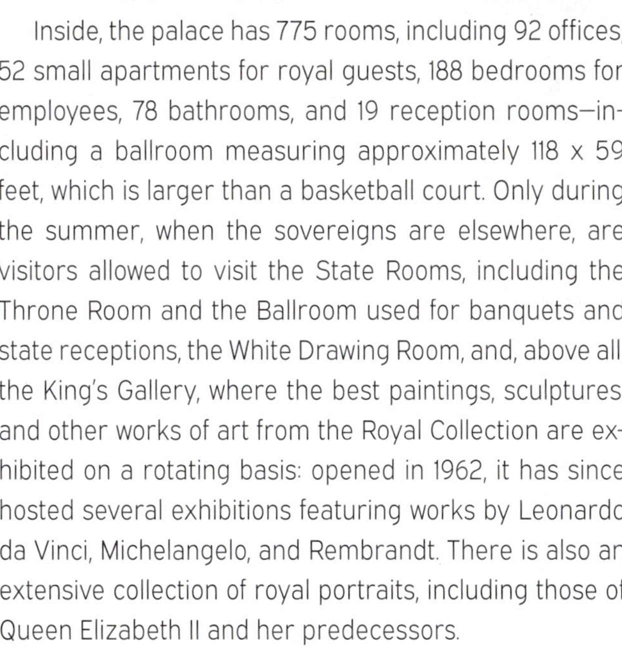

Inside, the palace has 775 rooms, including 92 offices, 52 small apartments for royal guests, 188 bedrooms for employees, 78 bathrooms, and 19 reception rooms—including a ballroom measuring approximately 118 x 59 feet, which is larger than a basketball court. Only during the summer, when the sovereigns are elsewhere, are visitors allowed to visit the State Rooms, including the Throne Room and the Ballroom used for banquets and state receptions, the White Drawing Room, and, above all, the King's Gallery, where the best paintings, sculptures, and other works of art from the Royal Collection are exhibited on a rotating basis: opened in 1962, it has since hosted several exhibitions featuring works by Leonardo da Vinci, Michelangelo, and Rembrandt. There is also an extensive collection of royal portraits, including those of Queen Elizabeth II and her predecessors.

• 22: The Throne Room houses the magnificent throne on which the sovereigns of the United Kingdom sit. Golden decorations further enrich the room, which is used mainly for ceremonies of particular importance, such as the opening of Parliament.

• 23 left: The White Drawing Room, one of the most elegant rooms in Buckingham Palace, owes its name to its color scheme, white and gold. The spectacular chandelier, which dominates the center of the room, is made of precious crystal and adds further charm to the room.

• 23 right top: In the sparkling Ballroom, completed in 1853, a dance party was held on June 17, 1856, to celebrate the end of the Crimean War. At the time, the predominant colors were not white and crimson, but the walls were painted with Renaissance-style motifs. The Gobelins tapestries were added by Victoria's son, Edward VII, who liked the Louis XVI style.

• 23 right bottom: The ceiling of the Blue Drawing Room, designed by John Nash. The room is decorated with pairs of scagliola columns, painted to resemble onyx in 1860. Sparkling cut-glass chandeliers hang from the ceiling.

WINDSOR CASTLE

1070
After conquering England in 1066, William the Conqueror began building a wooden fort in Windsor, a strategic location for controlling the region.

1165–1179
Henry II had a first stone castle built in place of the wooden fort.

1240–1263
Henry III made the walls more secure and embellished the interiors.

1344–1377
Edward III began major expansion work on the castle, transforming it into a large royal residence. The state apartments were added.

1475
Edward IV commissioned the construction of St. George's Chapel.

1668
With the Restoration following the English Revolution, Charles II decided to restore the castle to its former glory, taking inspiration from the Palace of Versailles.

1760
George III purchased valuable art collections for Windsor Castle.

1901
Edward VII had the castle modernized. All the rooms were renovated.

1910
During the reign of George V, renovation work continued. Queen Mary of Teck tracked down the furniture belonging to the residence and had them returned to their original locations.

1992
A fire severely damaged the castle, which was completely restored in the following years.

Windsor is the name of the royal dynasty of the United Kingdom of Great Britain since 1917. In reality, the name of the family is Saxe-Coburg and Gotha, but in 1917 King George V decided to replace it with Windsor, after the name of the castle in the county of Berkshire,

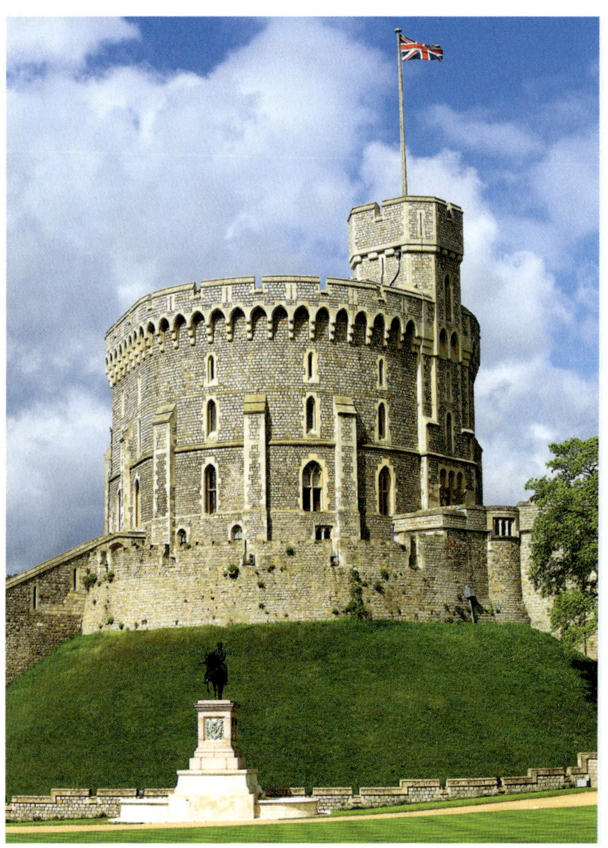

about 31 miles from London, owned by the English monarchs from the 11th century onwards. This choice was dictated by the importance of the castle in English history. Its origins date back to the period when William the Conqueror ascended to the throne of England after his victory in the Battle of Hastings (1066) at the head of his Norman army. On the site where the castle now stands, overlooking the Thames—fundamental for the transport of goods inland—and in a strategic position both for defense and for reaching

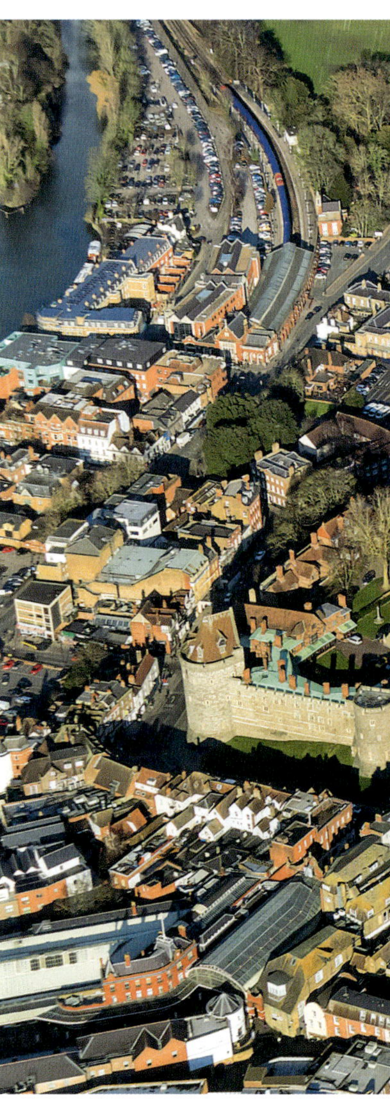

• 24 left: The Round Tower, the result of a series of renovations over the centuries, stands on the site of a previous wooden fortification built by William the Conqueror in the 11th century. The interior was renovated in the early 1990s to house the Royal Archives. The Tower is located between the two courtyards of Windsor Castle: the Lower Court, occupied by St. George's Chapel, and the Upper Court, with the private Royal Apartments and state rooms.

• 24-25: Aerial view of Windsor Castle, one of the Royal Family's favorite places. Elizabeth II used to spend her weekends here. During World War II, the future queen lived here with her sister Margaret to escape the danger of bombing.

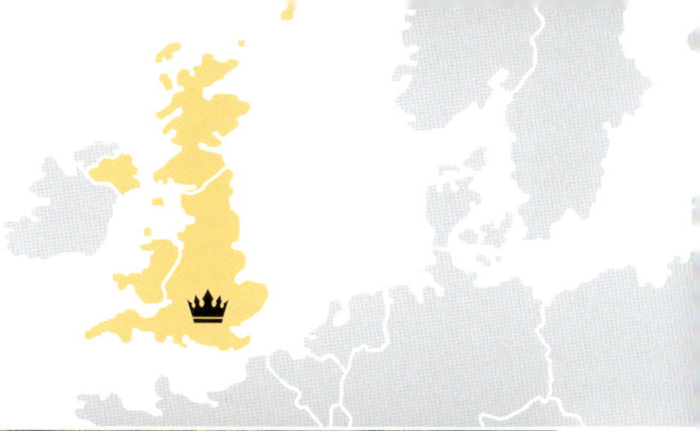

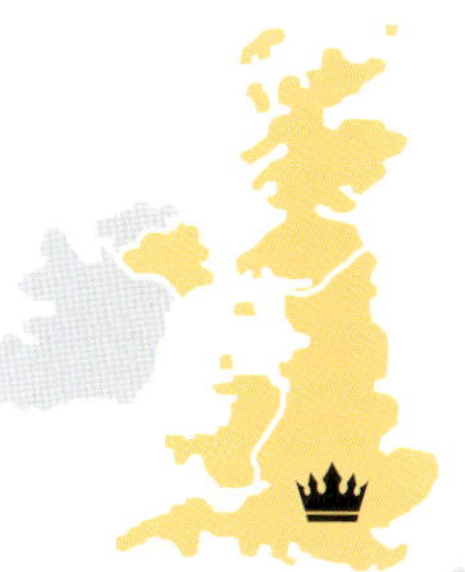

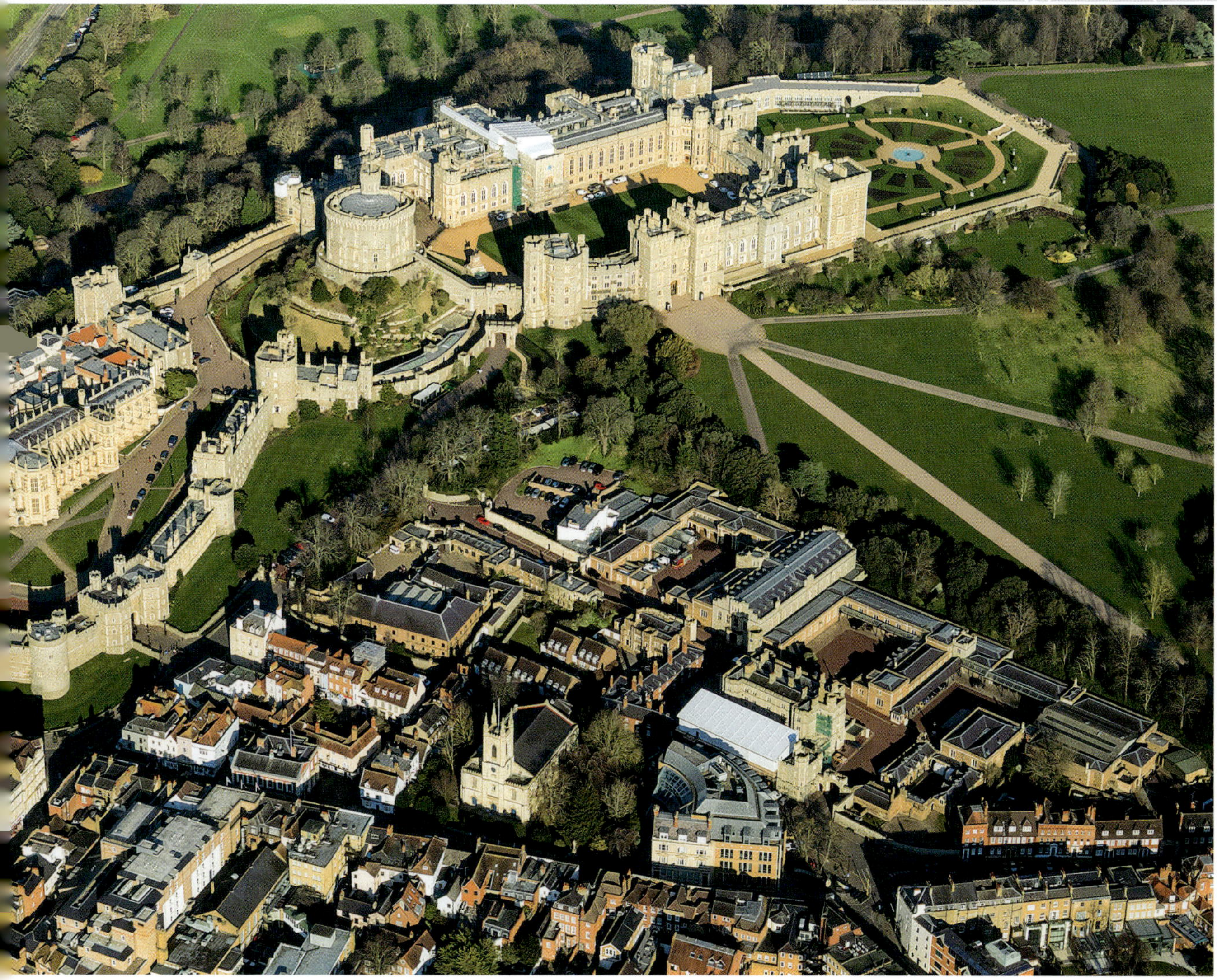

London, the Norman king had built a motte-and-bailey where he could hunt deer in the woods: this was an artificial hill (motte) made of limestone, surrounded by palisades and topped by a wooden tower that dominated the surrounding countryside. William's successors made changes to the fortification: around 1170, Henry II replaced the wooden tower on top of the motte with a stone one, which, after further alterations, became the Circular Tower that still stands today. In addition, private royal apartments overlooking the upper courtyard and reception rooms were built. The defensive walls were built in stone by Henry II and his successor Henry III, who added three semicircular towers to the lower courtyard, as well as tunnels and secret passages to allow escape in case of siege, including the Curfew Tower. When the castle was attacked twice in the 13th century, it did not surrender because its mighty walls withstood the blows of the attacking catapults.

• 26 left: The aerial image clearly shows a portion of the walled Central Courtyard, which surrounds a 49-foot-high artificial hill made of limestone in the center. The keep, called the "Circular Tower," rises above it.

• 26-27: The spectacular avenue that crosses the park laid out by Charles II between 1683 and 1685. Flanked by elm trees, it is 2.5 miles long and is where subjects gather to pay homage to the monarch as they pass by. In the center, between the two towers, is the Norman Gate, built under Edward III to protect access to the Upper Courtyard, where the royal private apartments were located.

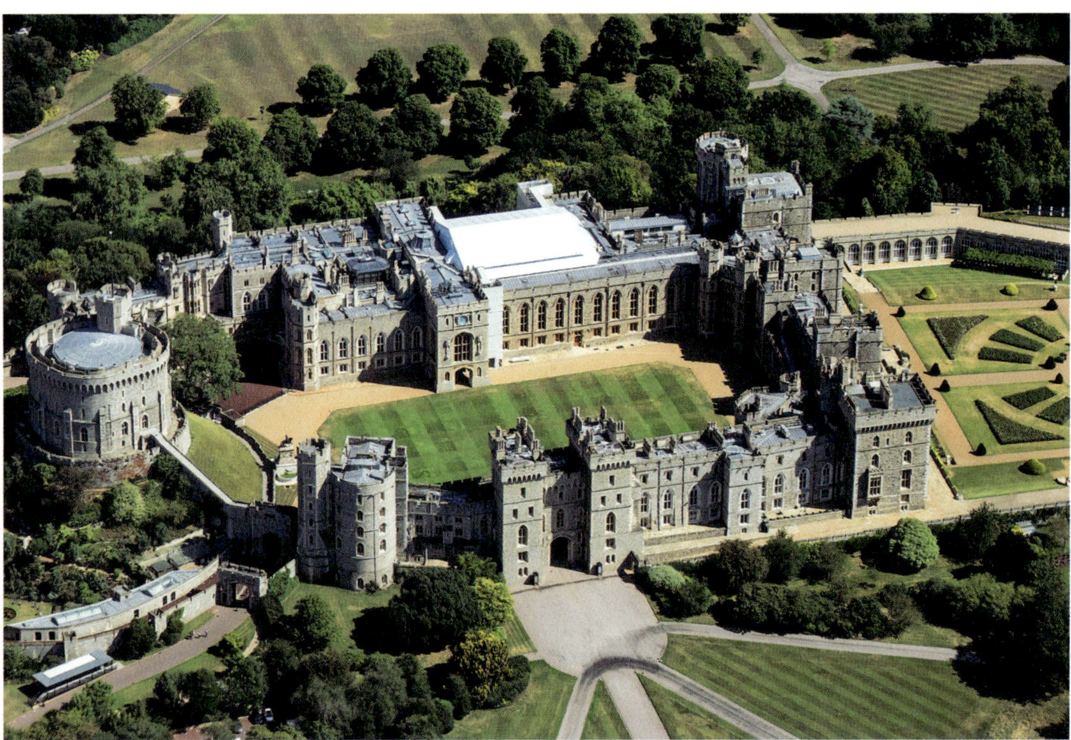

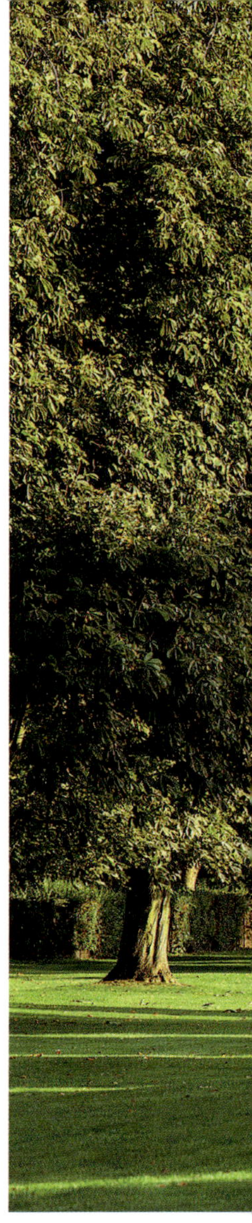

However, in the Middle Ages, it was Edward III who invested a fortune in Windsor Castle, where he was born, to transform it from a fortress into a royal residence in the second half of the 14th century. The sovereign spent £50,000 (equivalent to over 8 million dollars today): the Round Tower was rebuilt and the large entrance gate to the Upper Courtyard (renovated in Gothic style), the Norman Gate, was added. Under the Tudors, few changes were made except for the gate added by Henry VIII and a long gallery, now part of the Royal Library, requested by Elizabeth I so that she could walk there even on bad weather days. In 1348, Edward III founded two new religious colleges charged with celebrating worship in the two main royal palaces: Westminster in London and Windsor Castle. The first was dedicated to St. Stephen, the second to St. George. The king was very devoted to the patron saint of England, the Christian martyr who lived in the 5th century and is linked to the legendary slaying of a dragon, symbolizing the victory of good over evil. Initially, the Windsor college was attached to the existing Chapel of St. Edward the Confessor. The actual St. George's Chapel, a Gothic extension of the previous sacred place, was founded by Henry IV in 1475 and completed by Henry VIII fifty years later. Much later, Queen Victoria also had alterations made to the building: the eastern part at the end of the choir was dedicated to her husband, Prince Albert. The result is the splendid "cathedral" overlooking the Lower Ward, which opens its doors to funerals, weddings, and, once a year in June, to welcome members of the Order of the Garter.

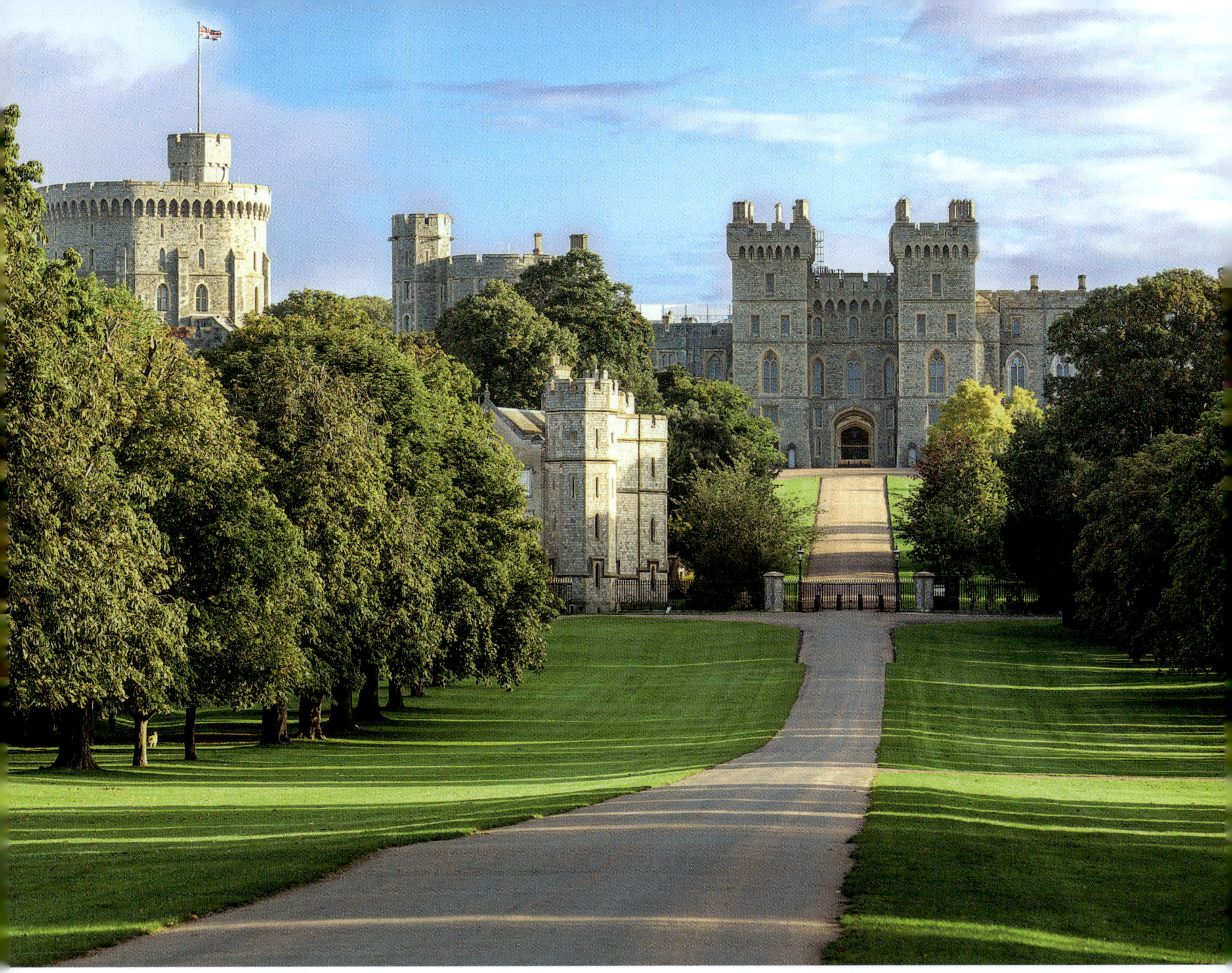

The birth of the Windsors

The House of Windsor was born on a specific day, July 17, 1917. The British and German empires were engaged in the First World War. British civilians were exasperated by the conflict, and the sovereign and emperor, whose German surname was Saxe-Coburg-Gotha, was a source of concern: George V's worst enemy was Kaiser Wilhelm II (1859–1941) of the Hohenzollern dynasty. Wilhelm was his cousin, with Prince Albert of Saxe-Coburg being their grandfather and husband of Queen Victoria, who, not coincidentally, was considered the "grandmother" of all the royals of Europe.

In short, at the outbreak of war, that surname had become a burden and a threat to the English Crown. It was therefore necessary to find a new dynastic name and implement a radical change. Someone in the king's entourage suggested a return to the past, with names such as Lancaster, York, and even Plantagenet and a sort of curious Tudor–Stuart union. There were also those who proposed Fitzroy, "son of the king," a title that usually referred to the illegitimate descendants of sovereigns.

In the end, the choice fell on the simplest and most British name, Windsor, the imposing and unmistakably English castle. In the photo, the rose, symbol of the Tudors, was placed above the Henry VIII Gate.

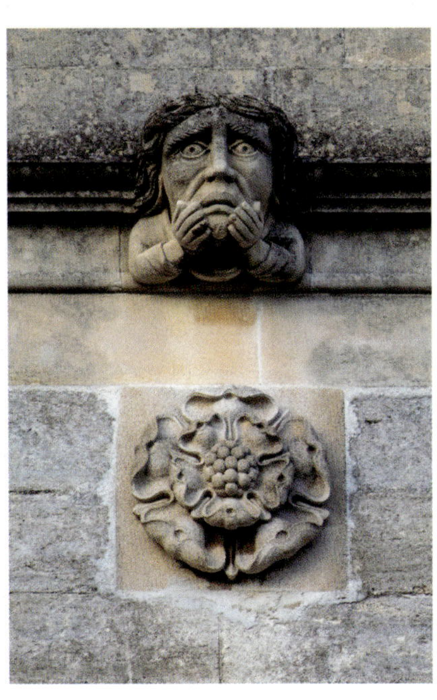

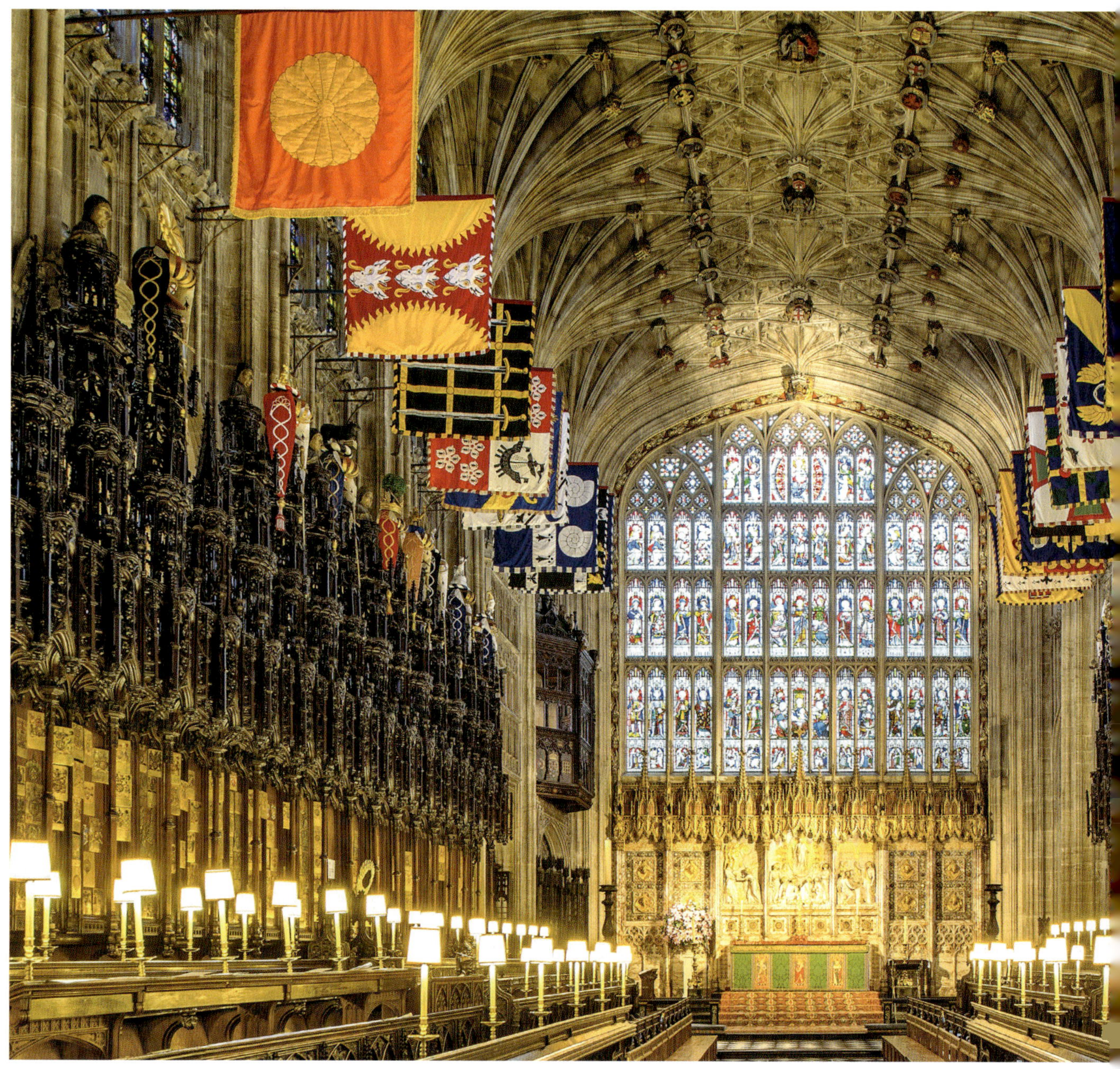

The interior of St. George's Chapel is considered a masterpiece of the Perpendicular Gothic style, typical of the late Middle Ages and characterized by the vertical accentuation of the decorative elements, the disappearance of the division into bays, and the fan vault, in this case added by Henry VIII. Looking up, above each seat in the choir hangs a flag. These are the banners bearing the coats of arms of the families to which the members of the Order of the Garter belong, the prestigious order of knights founded in 1348 by Edward III, inspired by the tales of King Arthur and the Knights of the Round Table. It consists of 24 knights—each of whom has a seat in the Chapel with their name written on it—plus the reigning sovereign and the Prince of Wales, as well as other members of the Royal Family and sovereigns of other states as honorary members. Since the 14th century, ladies and princesses known as Lady Companions have also been admitted. The emblem of the Order is a garter surmounted by the motto "Honi soit qui mal y pense," in Old French, "Shame on him who thinks evil." Legend has it that Edward III uttered these words when handing his favorite lady the garter that had fallen from her stocking.

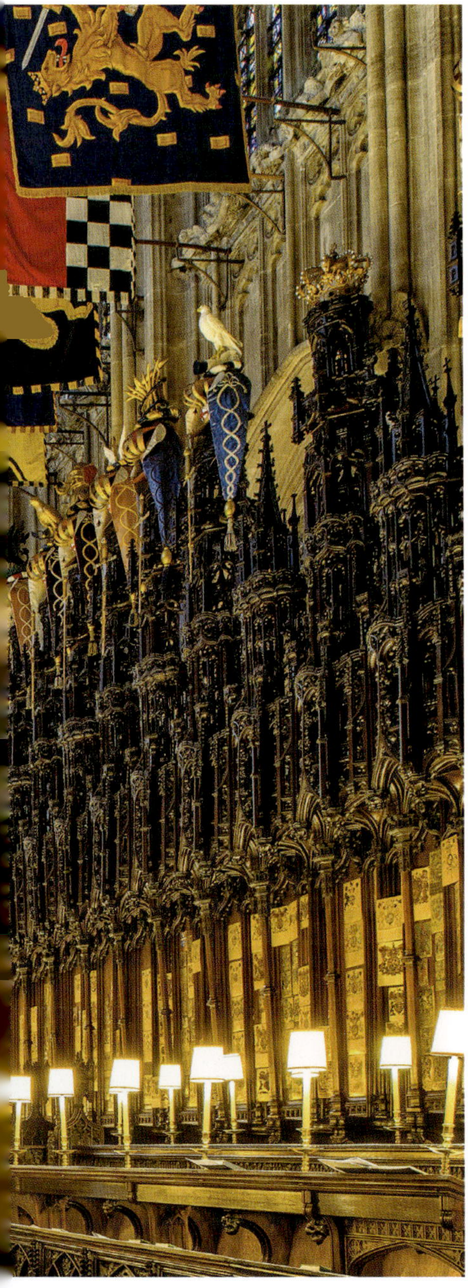

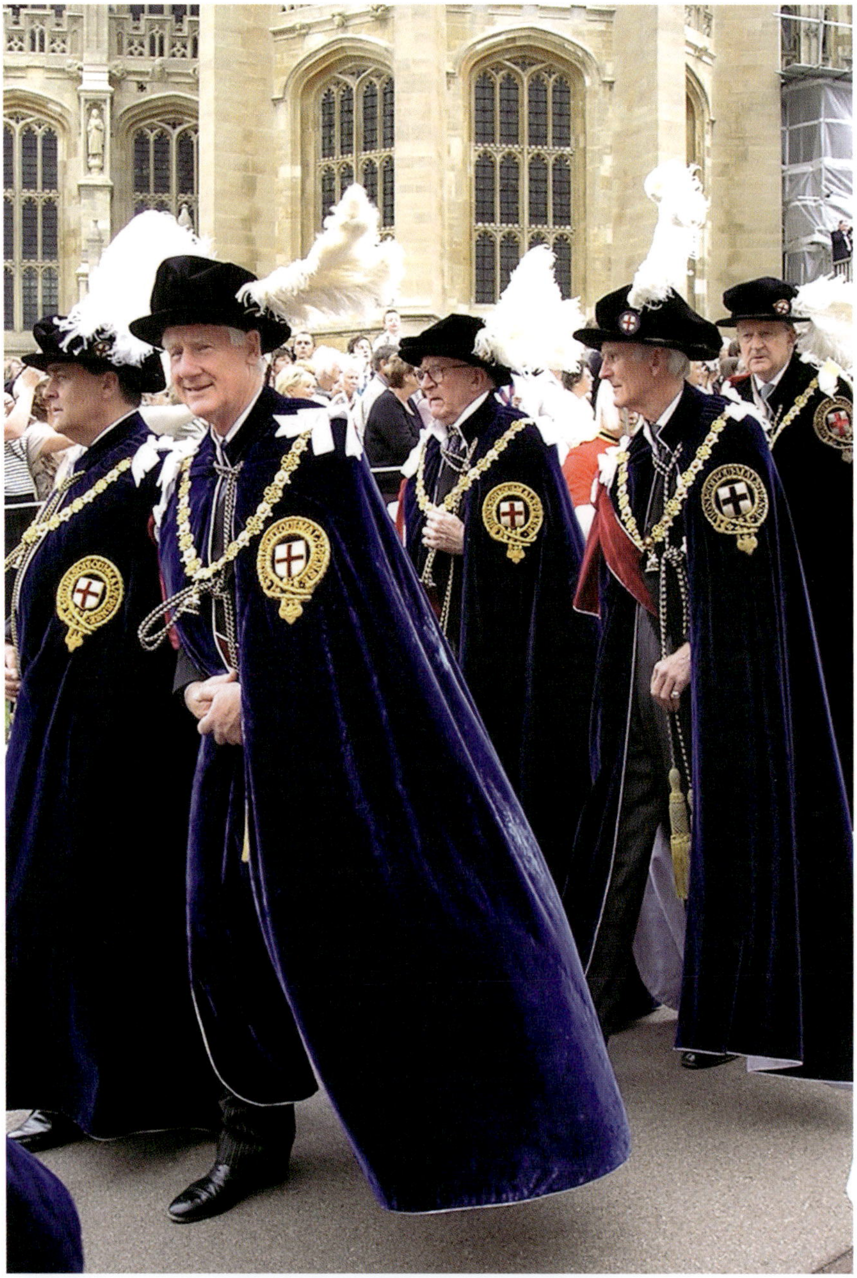

• 28-29: The Chapel of St. George at Windsor Castle is considered one of the most significant examples of Perpendicular Gothic architecture in the United Kingdom. The Chapel, which has undergone various alterations and renovations over the years, is characterized by a spectacular soaring ceiling, fan vaults, and beautiful stained-glass windows dating back to the 15th century.

• 29 right top: The prestigious Order of the Garter, founded by Edward III in 1348, consists of 24 knights.

• 29 right bottom: The Gothic exterior of St. George's Chapel overlooking the Lower Ward of Windsor Castle.

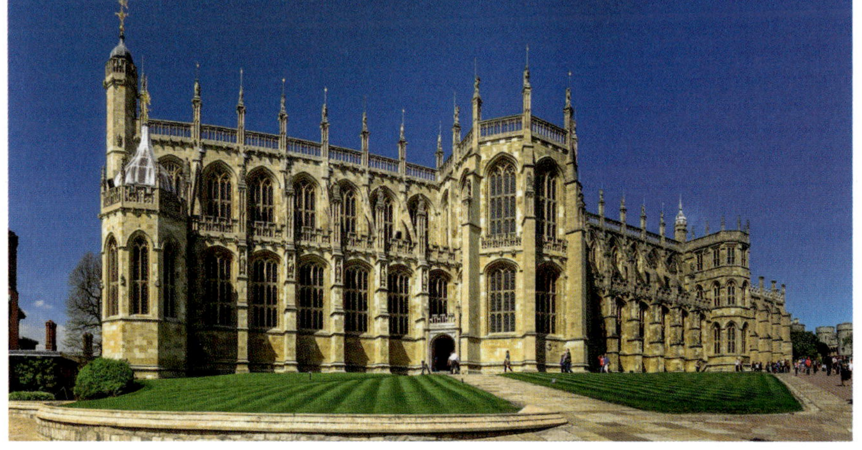

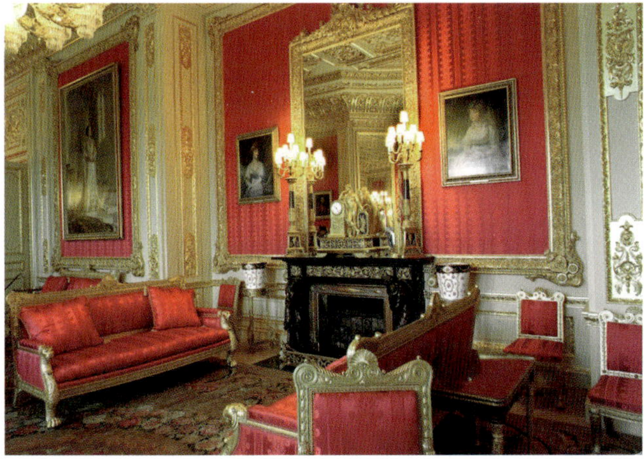

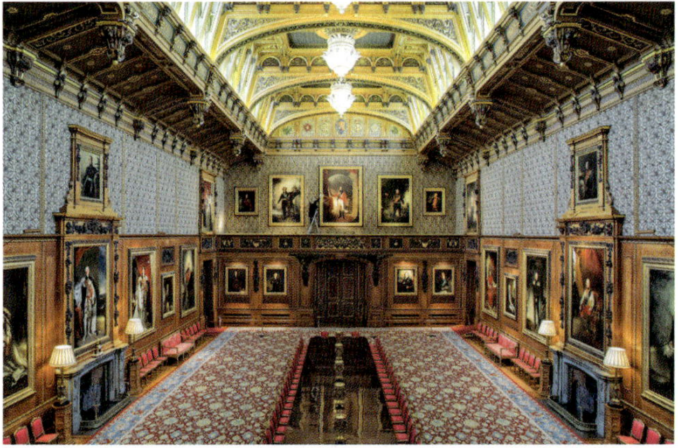

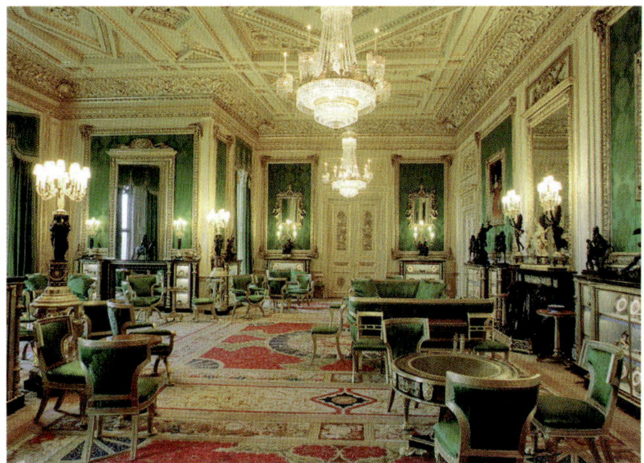

• 30 top: The Crimson Drawing Room is part of the private apartments created by George IV. The king, who loved luxury and comfort, took a personal interest in the decoration and in the rooms' furnishings, hiring the best architects and artists. The work was very expensive and time-consuming, but the sovereign settled in his palace nonetheless, despite the fact that several hundred workers were still employed there. The renovation of the castle continued under his brother and successor, William IV, but was only completed during the reign of his granddaughter, Queen Victoria.

• 30 center: The Waterloo Chamber, built between 1830 and 1831, is a large hall, designed by architect Jeffry Wyatville and dedicated to Napoleon Bonaparte's famous defeat.

The royal rooms and apartments of Windsor Castle reflect the changes in taste and style brought about by the kings and queens who lived in these luxurious surroundings, filling them with masterpieces: just think of Charles I's art collection, which includes the famous triple portrait of the king by Antoon van Dyck. After the English Revolution, with the sacking and transformation of the Norman Tower into a prison for royalists and Charles I himself (1600–1649), the restored Charles II ensured that the Castle was brought back to its former glory with Baroque furnishings and decorations: the State Apartments rivaled those of Versailles and are still furnished with some of the finest works of art in the Royal Collection. The magnificent state rooms, such as St. George's Hall and the colossal Waterloo Chamber, built to commemorate the defeat of Napoleon Bonaparte, date from the 19th century, as do the apartments of George IV. Queen Victoria, who spent many years of her life at Windsor, made the palace the center of the monarchy and the British Empire, hosting monarchs, ambassadors, and ministers from all over the world. Unfortunately, a fire broke out in 1992 in Queen Victoria's private chapel, destroying the ceilings of St. George's Hall and other rooms. However, at a cost of £37 million and after five years of work, the castle was restored to its former glory by Elizabeth II.

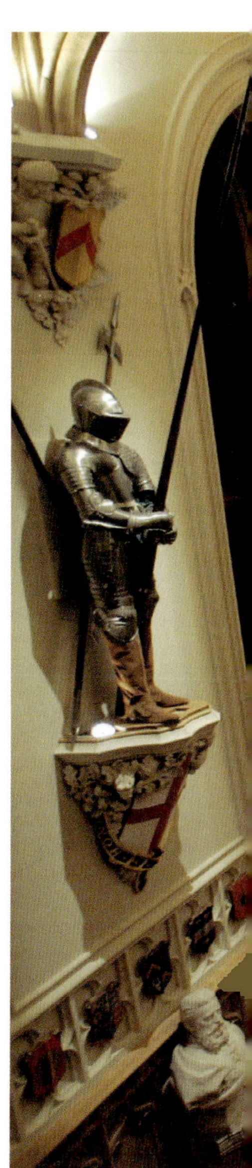

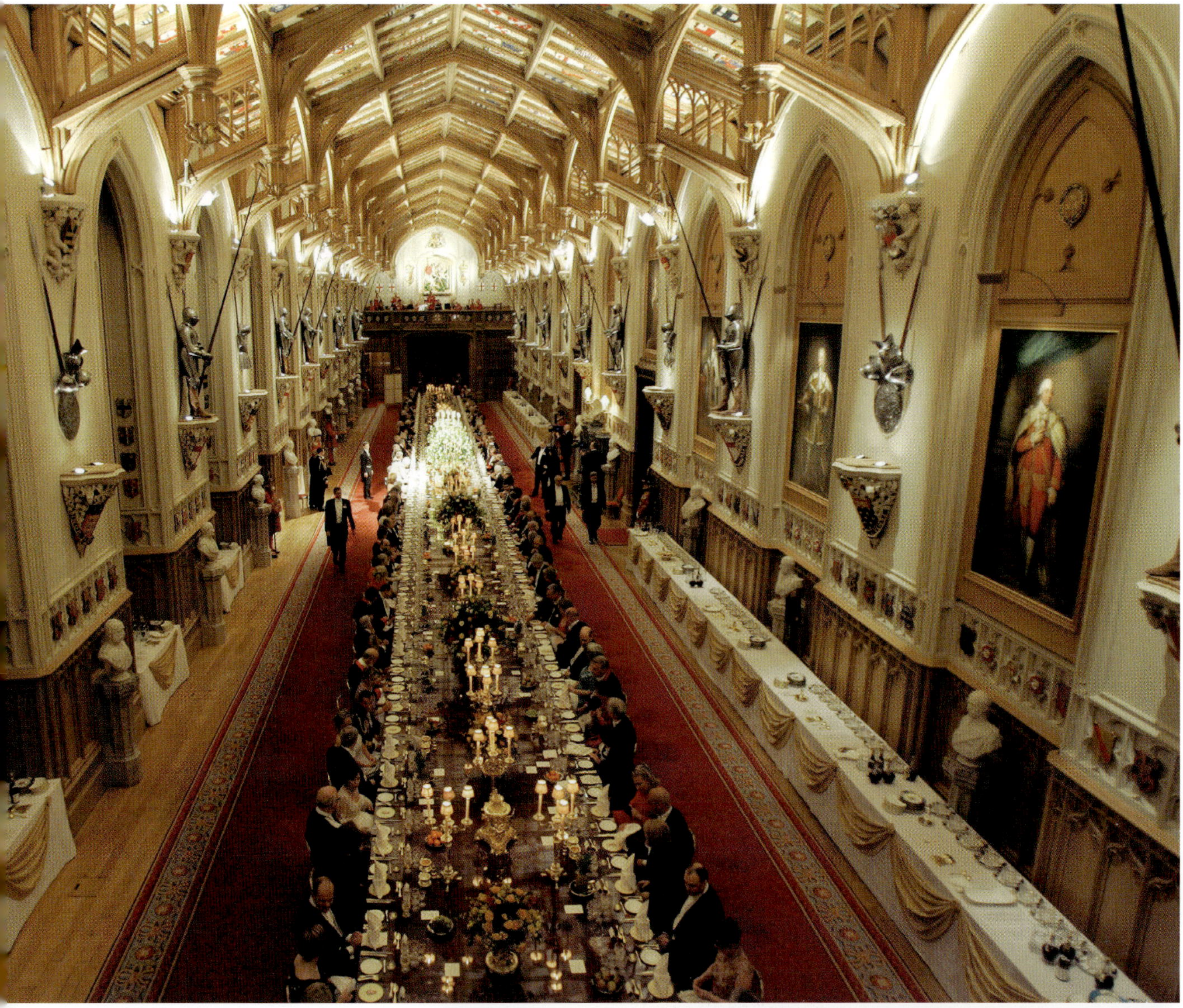

• 30 bottom: The Green Drawing Room is one of the main rooms in the State Apartments of Windsor Castle. It is adjacent to the Queen's Closet to the east and the Queen's State Bedchamber to the west.

• 30–31: St. George's Hall is 180 feet long. In the picture, it is set up for a state banquet. On the ceiling, restored after the fire of 1992, are painted the coats of arms of every single Knight of the Garter since the order was founded.

• 31 bottom: The Queen's State Bedchamber, a clear example of the grandeur of the royal apartments, is characterized by sumptuous decoration: the walls are covered with red silk, and the ceiling, frescoed by Verrio, depicts the myth of Diana and Endymion.

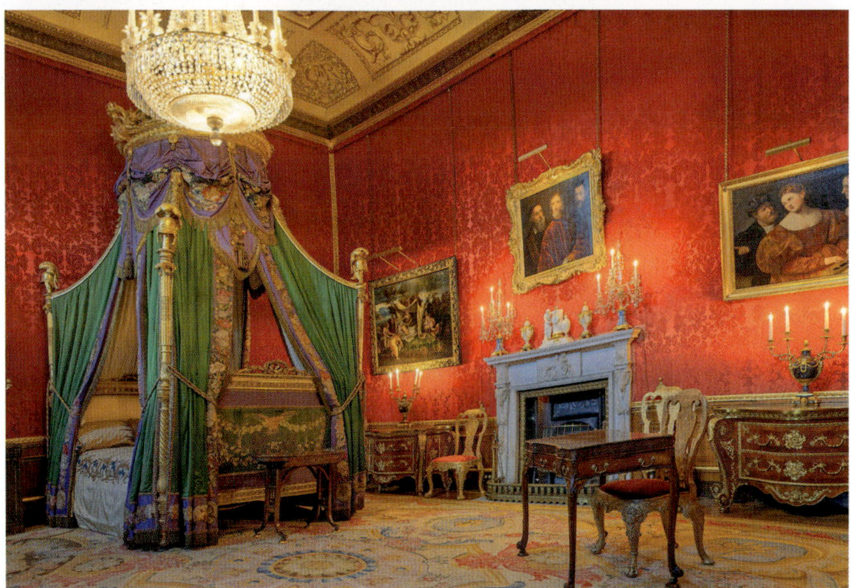

• 32–33: View of Hampton Court Palace. Despite various inevitable renovations, the castle is a powerful testament to the Tudor style and is considered by many to be the most beautiful of the English royal residences, which were home to the British monarchy until the second half of the 18th century. Queen Victoria (1819–1901) opened the complex to the public in 1838 and is said to have preferred it greatly to Windsor Castle. The vast palace complex is built around several large courtyards: the Base Court and the Clock Court, dominated by Henry VIII's astronomical clock. Among the surviving Tudor features are the magnificent Chapel Royal and, on the ground floor, the vast royal kitchens.

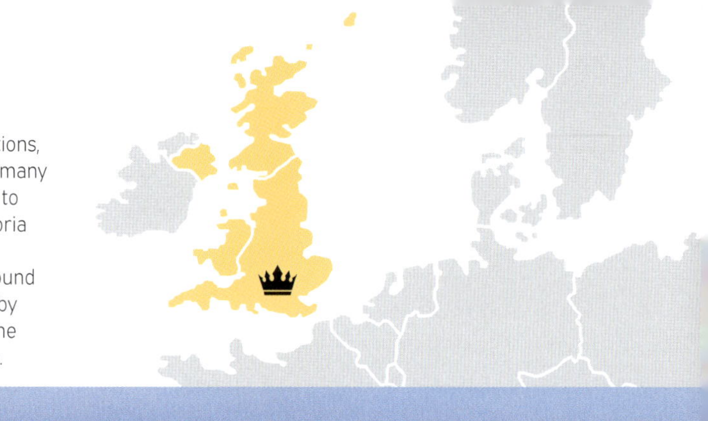

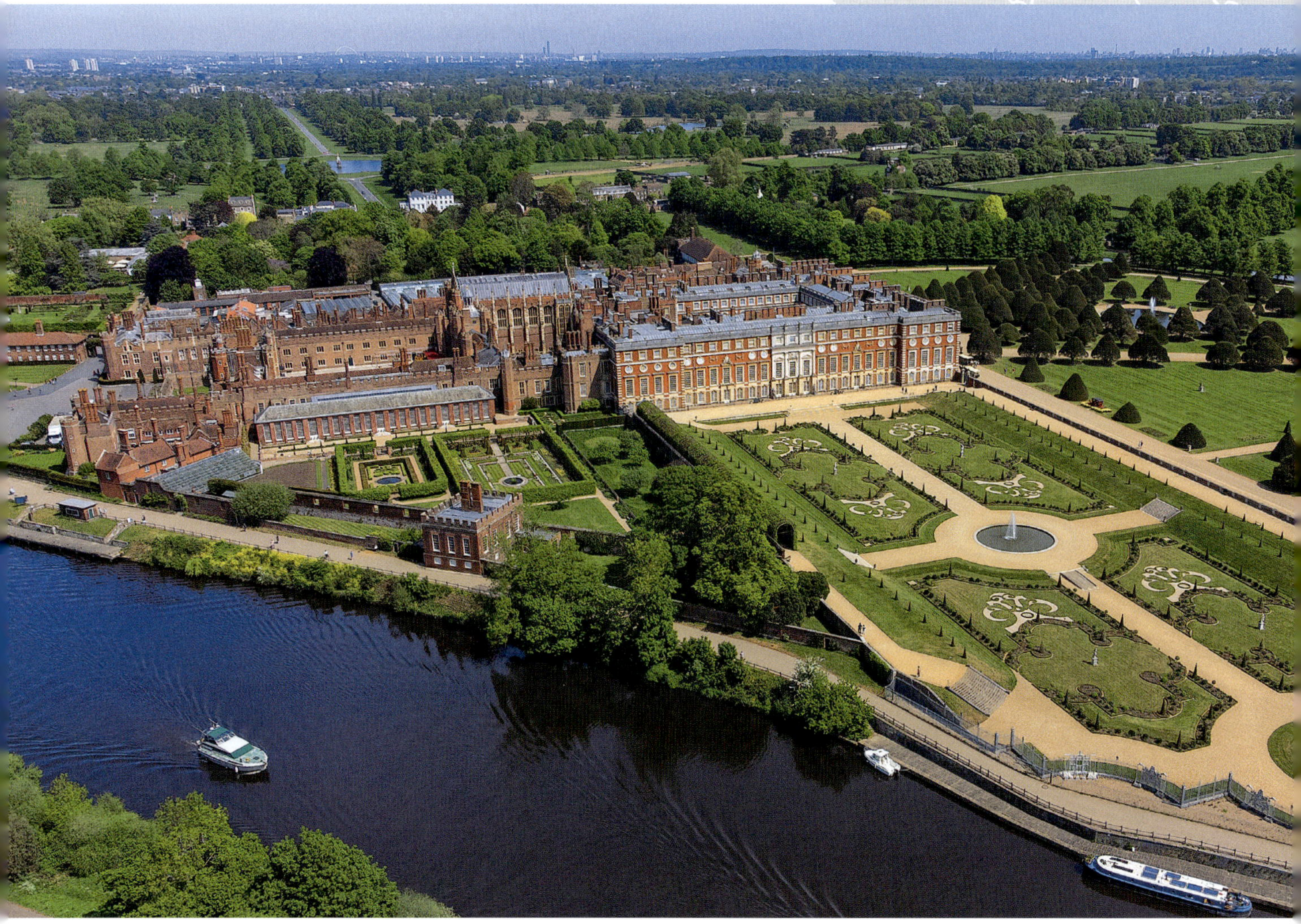

The majestic Hampton Court Palace, nestled on the banks of the River Thames, is located in the London borough of Richmond upon Thames, approximately 12 miles from the center of the UK capital. The castle's heyday coincided with the period when the Tudor dynasty ruled England, from 1485, the year King Henry VII ascended the throne and founded the dynasty, to 1603, the date of Elizabeth I's death: a period of extraordinary change (the break with Rome, the establishment of the Anglican Church, and the defeat of the Spanish Armada), which saw personalities such as Henry VIII, William Shakespeare, and Thomas More emerged. The first person to make the modest country house of Hampton Court worthy of hosting kings and dignitaries was Cardinal and Archbishop Thomas Wolsey, Henry VIII's powerful adviser and statesman. After taking possession of it, he did not hesitate to spend considerable sums—thought to be 200,000 gold crowns—to make it one of the most magnificent palaces in the country, strategically located along the River Thames. Despite his undoubted political acumen, however, Wolsey was unable to obtain from Pope Clement VII the

HAMPTON COURT

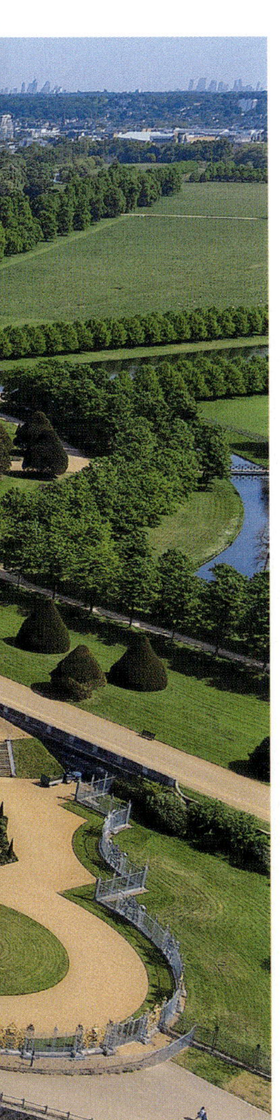

· 33 right: Henry VIII in the famous portrait by Hans Holbein the Younger (c. 1537). The king ascended the throne in 1509 at just 17 years of age. Thanks to a papal dispensation, he married his brother Arthur's widow, Catherine of Aragon, with whom he was unable to have any sons. This union, followed by five more marriages, was a source of momentous change for the country, led by a strong and equally contradictory personality.

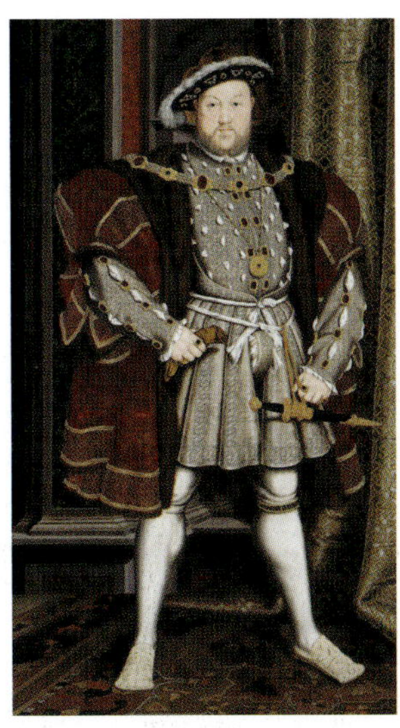

annullment of Henry's marriage to his first wife Catherine of Aragon, thus marking the beginning of his misfortunes. The luxurious complex was taken over by the king in 1528, who further embellished it, including the installation of the large astronomical clock dominating the Clock Court in 1540. The king demanded a huge extension of the kitchens and more space for his apartments. Specifically, he ordered the design of a three-story tower: the ground floor housed the treasurer's office with a small windowless room with thick walls next to it, which served as a vault, and the royal wardrobe. On the upper floor was the king's bedroom, flanked by a bathroom supplied with hot water and a study which, according to sources, was resplendent with works of art. On the top floor were his personal library, which was very rich and decorated with a wonderful gilded ceiling, and the secret room where precious objects were kept during the monarch's absence. The queen's apartments were a special case: their construction was delayed pending Catherine's divorce, but proceeded apace once Henry's union with Anne Boleyn was official. For the first time, the king and queen's chambers were placed next to each other, a custom that Henry repeated at all his future residences.

1485
Henry VII ascended to the throne of England and adopted the red-and-white Tudor rose as his emblem, representing the union of the Houses of Lancaster and York.

1509
Henry VIII was crowned king. He was assisted in his decisions by his adviser Thomas Wolsey, whom he appointed Lord Chancellor in 1515.

1514
Thomas Wolsey became Henry VIII's almoner. He settled at Hampton Court and began major work to turn it into a majestic residence.

1528
Cardinal Wolsey, having fallen into disgrace, ceded Hampton Court Palace to Henry VIII.

1529
Henry VIII initiated major changes, including the transformation of the kitchens, the royal apartments, the Great Hall, the Royal Chapel, and the tennis court.

1603
With the death of Elizabeth I, the Tudor dynasty came to an end. Her closest relative, James VI of Scotland, ascended the throne of England as James I Stuart and settled at Hampton Court.

1689
William III and Mary II, who came to the throne in 1689, commissioned Christopher Wren to design a new Baroque palace. To satisfy them, the architect demolished much of the Tudor castle.

1760
George III abandoned Hampton Court as his royal residence, preferring the nearby Kew Palace on the banks of the Thames.

1838
Queen Victoria opened the gardens and state apartments to visitors.

1986
In a terrible fire, the King's State Apartments suffered extensive damage.

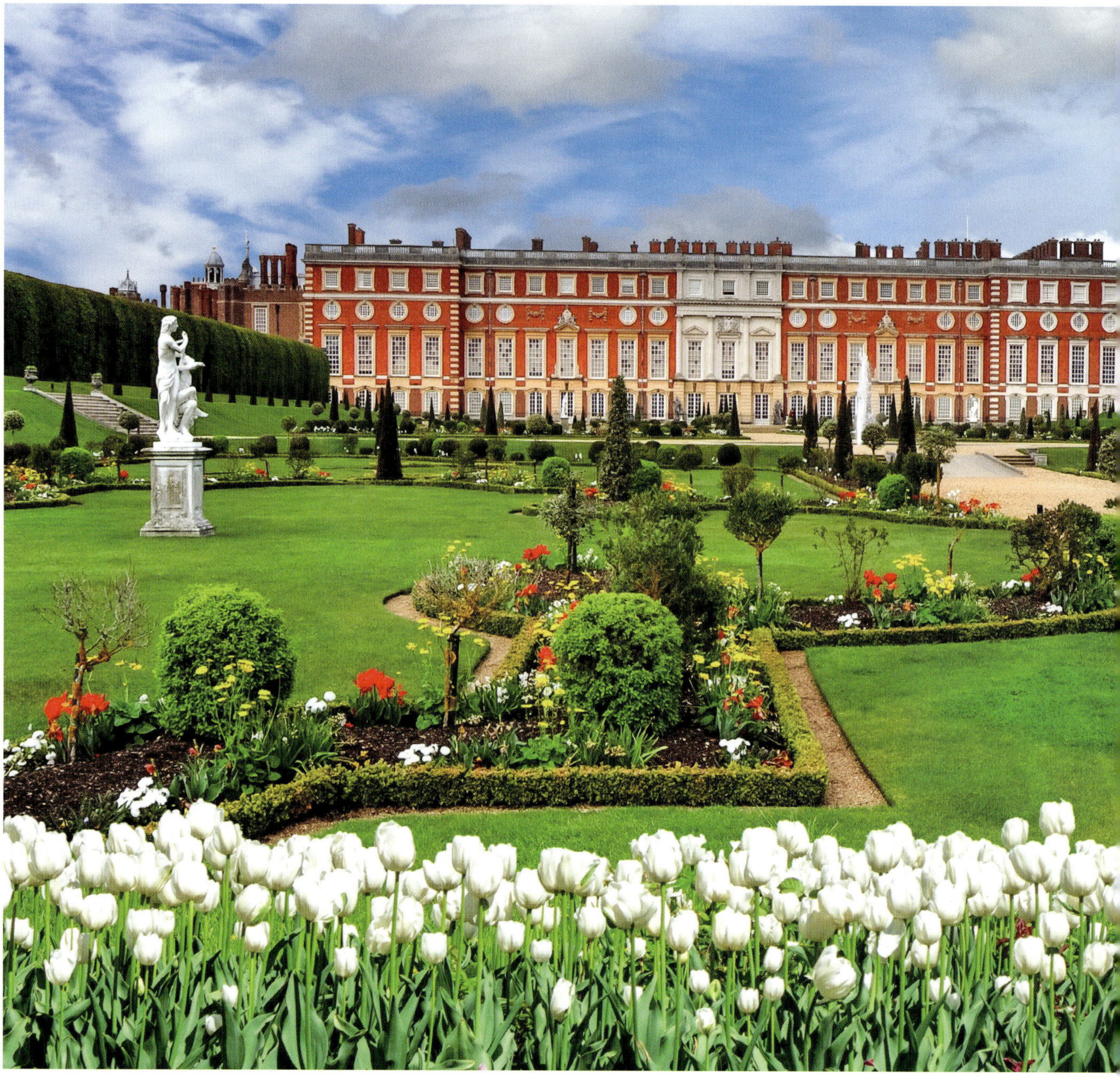

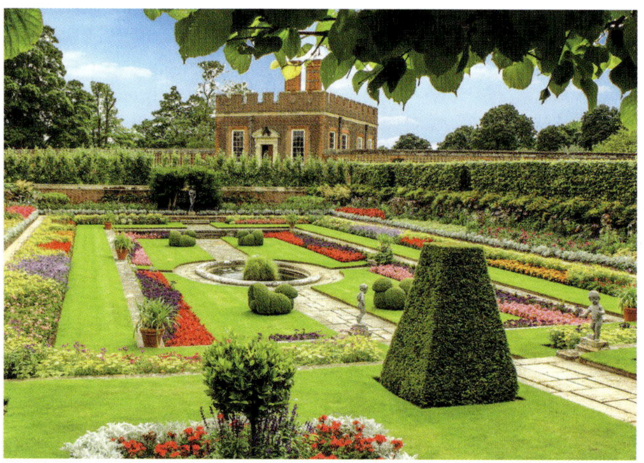

• 34–35: The southern front of the palace, with its pure, classical lines overlooking the vast and celebrated gardens designed by Christopher Wren in the 18th century.

• 34 bottom: The Hampton Court gardens date back to Henry VIII, but were further embellished and rearranged, particularly by Charles II and William III. Approaching the palace, you can admire the Privy Garden on its right side, enclosed by a splendid wrought-iron gate, and the Banqueting House, an 18th-century brick building with fresco cycles by Antonio Verrio (c. 1636– 1707), an artist from Lecce who moved to London and became a court painter.

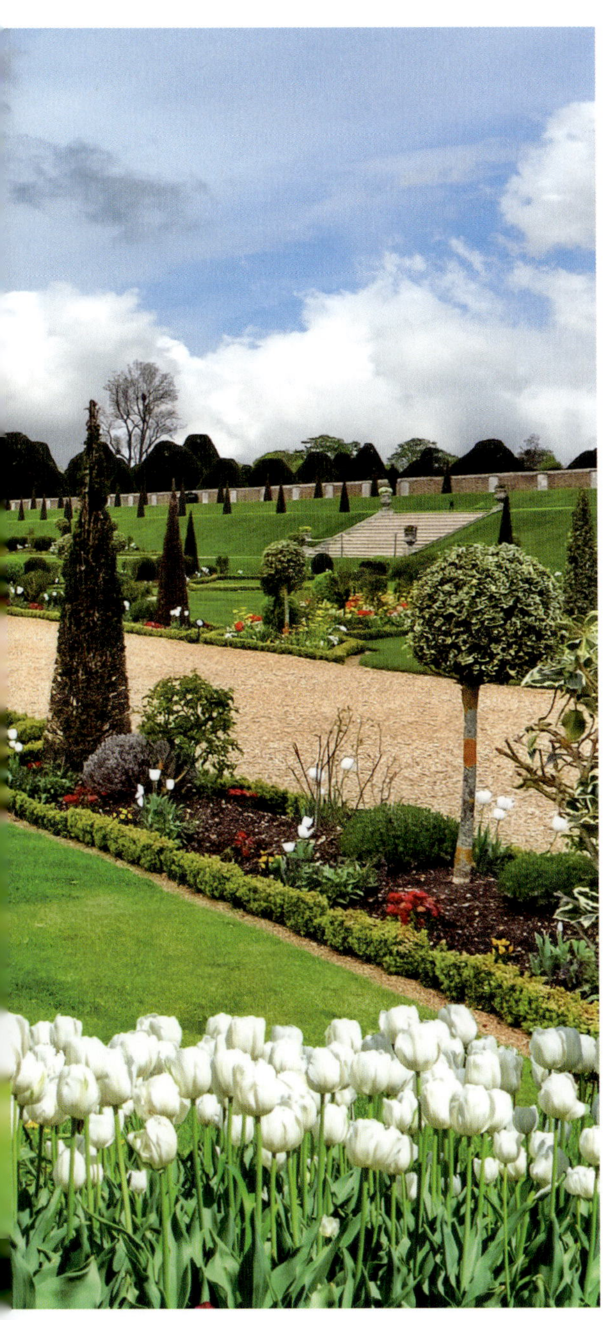

King Charles I (1600–1649) was responsible for the final layout of the court for playing jeu de game, the ancestor of modern tennis imported from France and very popular at the time, and for the acquisition of important works of art such as Andrea Mantegna's "Triumphs of Caesar." The last major alterations to the palace were ordered by William III of Orange, who, along with his wife Mary II, commissioned Sir Christopher Wren, the architect in charge of rebuilding London after the Great Fire of 1666, to design new rooms. Fortunately, the architect rejected his initial idea of demolishing the Tudor buildings to create a totally modern residence, an example of which is the southern front of the palace. The great architect's task at Hampton Court proved to be anything but simple: the financial difficulties of the monarchs and the poor condition of much of the structure, which was now dilapidated, forced him to design and redesign different and increasingly economical solutions. In the end, he decided to preserve from demolition some very important sections, such as the Great Hall and the Royal Chapel, while eliminating other rooms that were too compromised, including Henry VIII's apartments, or no longer suited to 18th-century residential and representative requirements, often resorting to architectural solutions of considerable ingenuity. Wren was also responsible for the redesign of the east entrance in line with the Long Water, the large water basin commissioned by Charles II, with the addition of a cloister around the Fountain Court, the adjustment of the different heights of the internal floors using a system of false ceilings and decorations to conceal structural problems, and the addition of a colonnade in the Clock Court, which proved to be a clear formal element of access to the Royal Apartments and, at the same time, an elegant cover to conceal the poor condition of the ancient walls.

• 35 bottom: The Base Court, the first courtyard accessed from the main entrance, features the tall Great Hall on the right and, in the center, by the passage known as Anne Boleyn's Gateway, which leads to the Clock Court behind it. Designed by the German mathematician and astronomer Nicolaus Kratzer, the clock, which is still in working order, was placed on the tower of the same name in 1540. It is still working, of course, according to a calendar that predates the Copernican revolution and Galileo's studies.

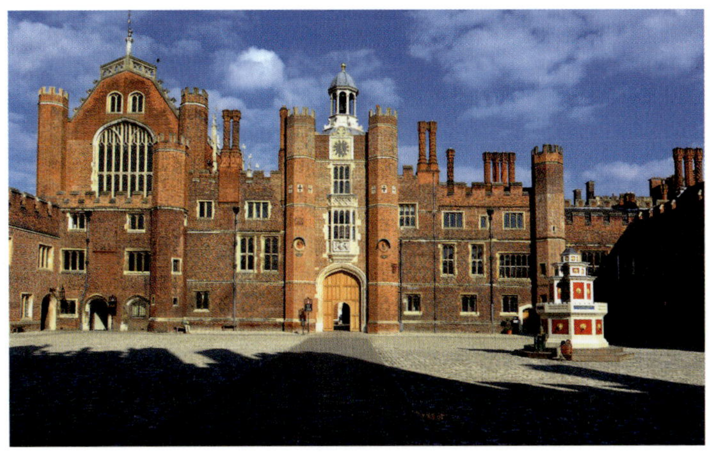

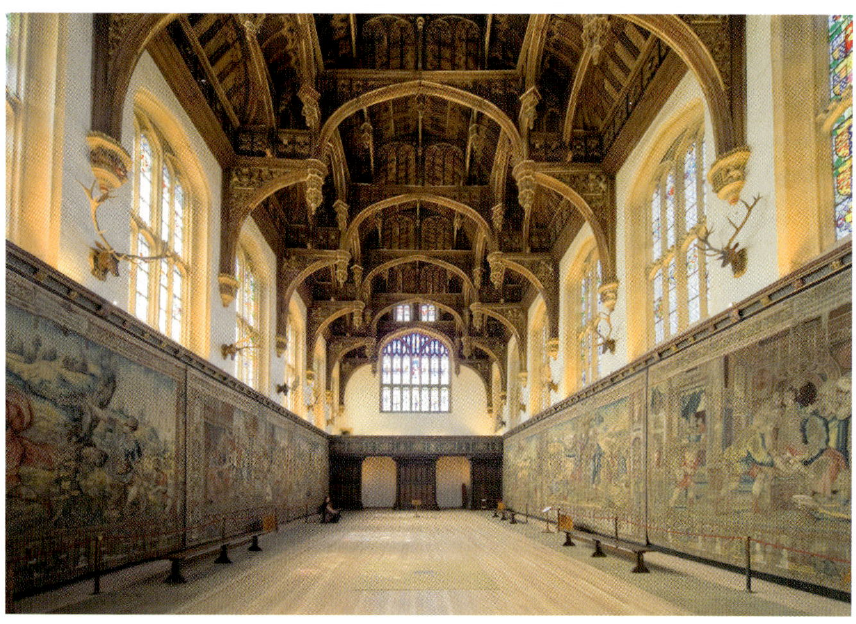

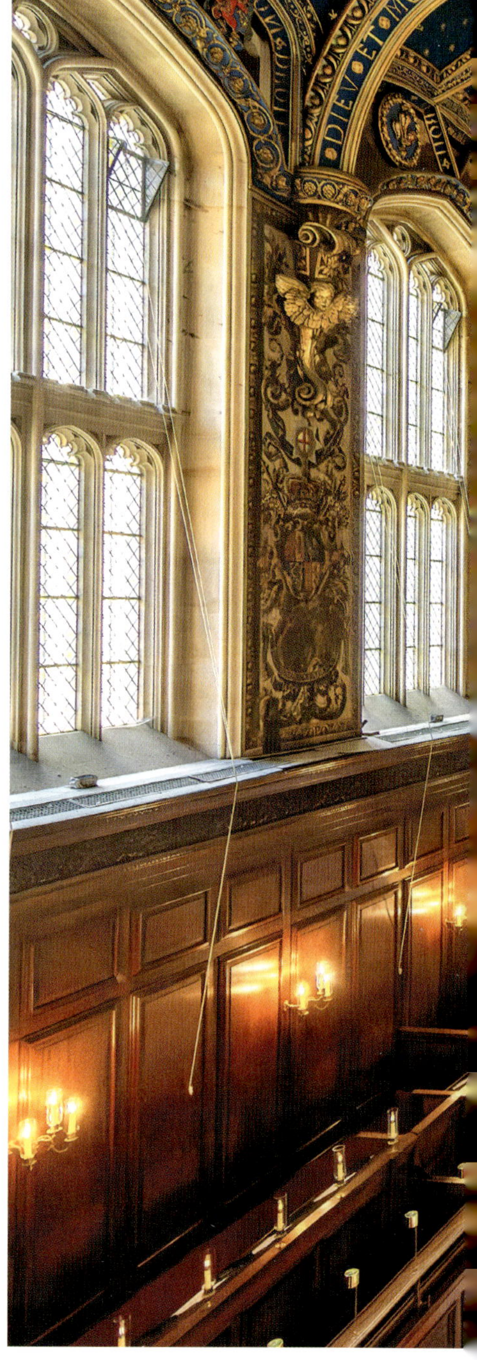

A passion for food

A notorious gourmet, Henry VIII displayed an immoderate passion for food and fine wine from a young age. While poor people's table was almost always made up of meager rations of bread and vegetables such as cabbage and turnips, with rare exceptions for poultry, rabbit, or fish, the tables of the aristocracy were essentially dominated by game, often with the addition of honey and plenty of fat. Henry was known for his fondness for veal and roast pheasant or turkey larded with bacon. These habits, as well as the introduction—already in the time of Henry VII—of a new, much more elaborate table ceremony, led to the sovereign's decision to expand the palace kitchens. Conceived as a sort of modern industrial production line, they were arranged along the entire length of the north side (the sunnier south side was reserved for the apartments), with a separate entrance through which huge quantities of provisions and waste passed. Each room was organized so as to be dedicated in the most efficient way to a specific type of preparation, in particular desserts, sauces, baked goods, and the presentation of dishes which, especially on important occasions, had to be spectacular and designed to impress guests: for example, by adding jewels or other precious surprises among the food. Over 200 people worked in Henry VIII's kitchens at Hampton Court, including head chefs, cooks, scullers, food attendants, pages, and supervisors, to serve over 800 meals a day to feed the royal family and the court, who were accustomed to sitting down at the table twice a day. Each person had a specific task, and the organization was subject to strict rules contained in the so-called Black Book. Three master chefs were responsible for roasting the meat: according to the inventories, over 1,200 oxen and 8,200 sheep were slaughtered each year.

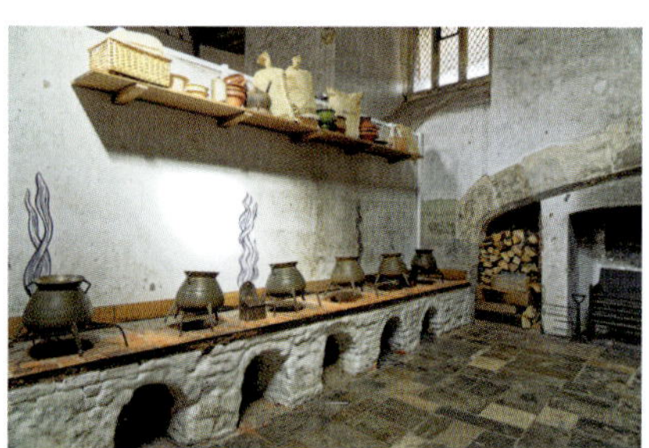

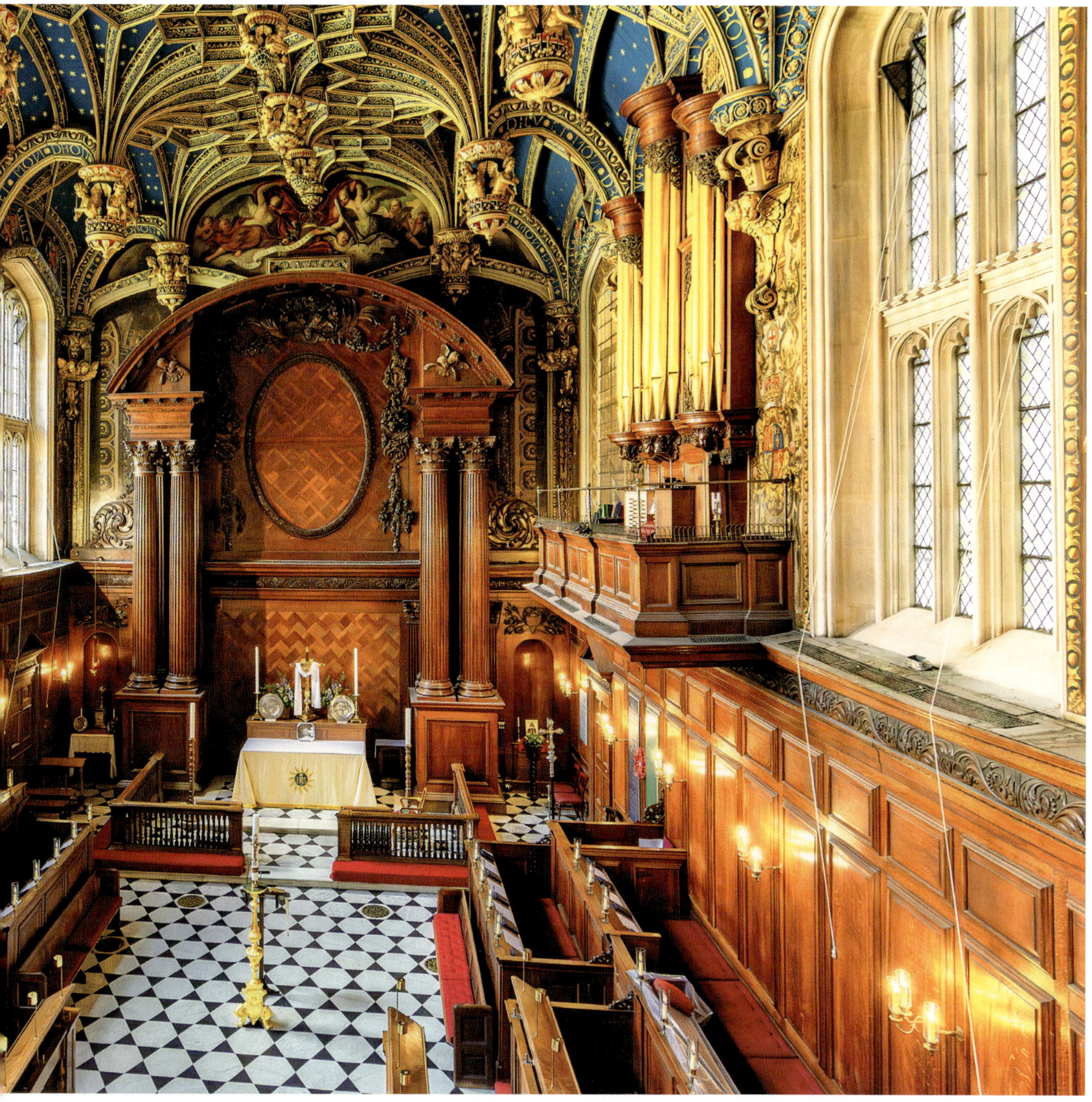

• 36 top: The Great Hall was built by Henry VIII at Hampton Court to impress guests and display power and magnificence. This large room was used as a dining hall for the lower ranks, with meals served at 10:00 a.m. and 4:00 p.m. The higher-ranking courtiers sat in another large hall in Henry VIII's apartments: it was accessed from the Great Hall, and a Yeoman checked those few who were allowed in. The carved wooden-truss ceiling dates back to the time of Henry VIII and is one of the wonders of the palace. The vast room is lit by warm light entering through large multi-light windows with stained glass (Victorian) decorated with coats of arms. Of great value are the 16th-century Flemish tapestries depicting stories of Abraham. Later used by Elizabeth I and James I Stuart, it was also used for theatrical performances: it is famous for having hosted William Shakespeare's company, which performed there in 1603–1604.

• 36–37 right: The Royal Chapel is one of the most famous rooms in the complex, a clear testimony to the splendor and opulence of the Tudors—although the wood paneling and furniture were redone in 1710 based on designs by Christopher Wren, and the sumptuous altar is the work of Grinling Gibbons. It was commissioned by Henry VIII in 1535, a year after the Act of Supremacy was passed, and was the only place in the palace intended for the spiritual needs of the court, under the complete control of the sovereign. The large, stunning blue-and-gold ceiling symbolizes the vault of heaven and bears the royal motto, "Dieu et Mon Droit" ("God and My Right"), already adopted by Henry V but which, at the dawn of the Anglican schism, took on a much more resolute meaning.

• 38-39: The ultimate expression of romanticism in Portugal, characterized by onion domes, Moorish stone portals, and crenellated towers painted pink and lemon yellow.

• 39 center: The Castelo dos Mouros, built by the Arabs in the 8th century, defended the entire region of Sintra from an elevated position chosen for its view. From this rocky outcrop, the Moors could watch over the coast and the surrounding area.

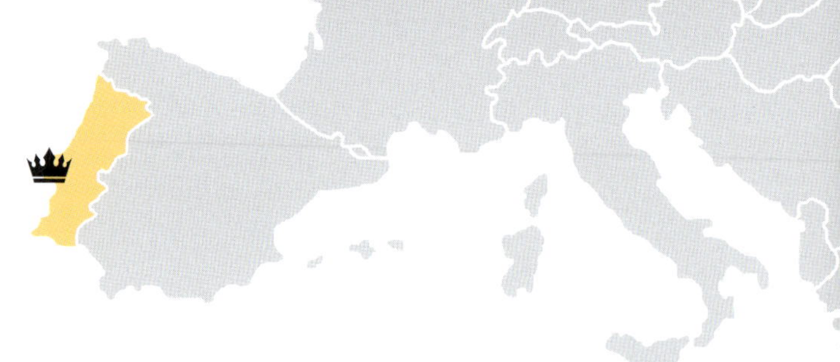

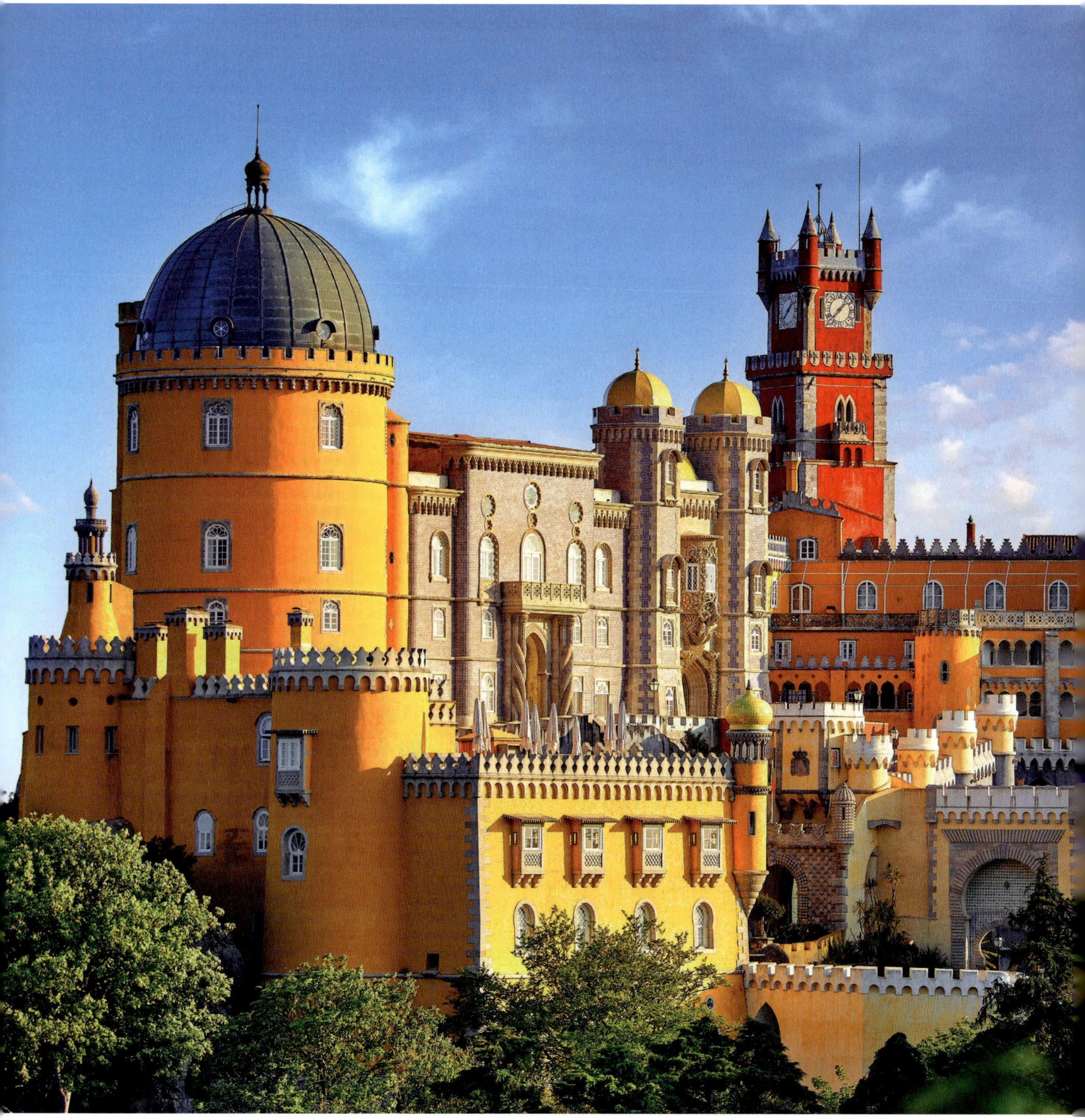

Palácio da Pena

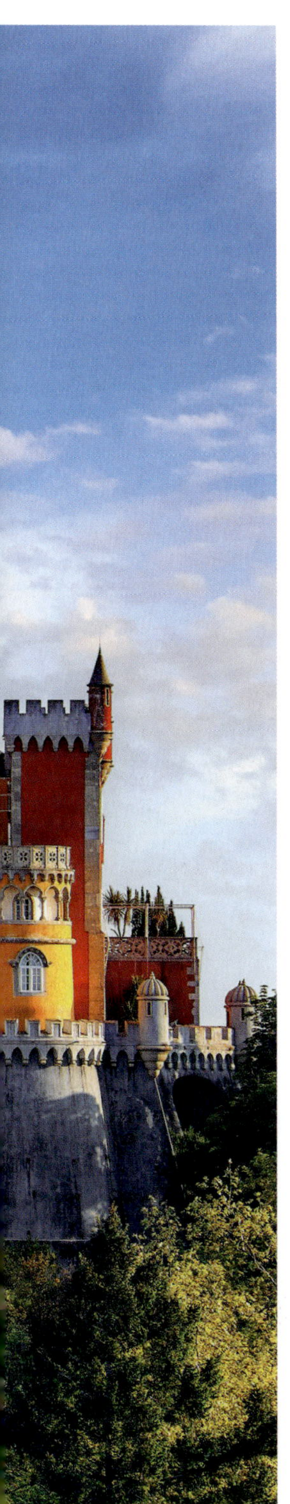

Immersed in a wooded landscape not far from the capital, Sintra is a town of undeniable charm that has enchanted many great figures from the past, from Hans Christian Andersen to Lord Byron and Richard Strauss. Attracted by the summer climate, milder than Lisbon's, as well as the panoramic location, with the Atlantic coast in the distance, Portuguese kings, aristocrats, and entrepreneurs built their holiday residences here, often hiding them amid lush gardens. However, the first to notice the strategic position of Sintra were the Moors, who in the 8th century built a fortress on high ground between the rocks and boulders of the Sintra Mountains, a fortress known

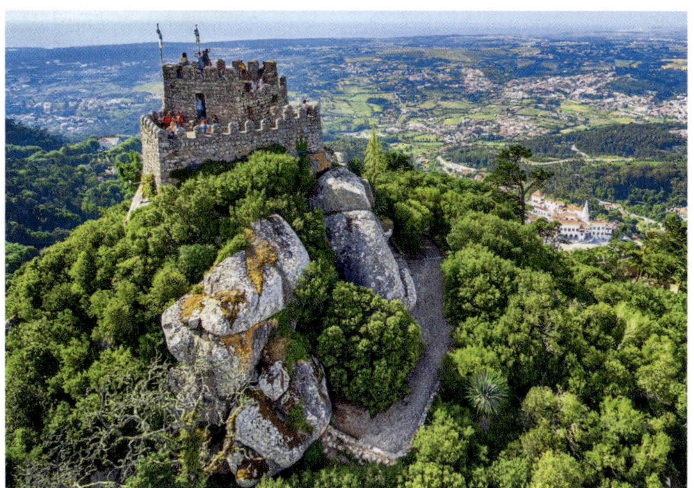

as "Castelo dos Mouros" was built to guard the main roads connecting Sintra with Lisbon, Cascais, and Mafra. The crenellated walls that still wind their way through the hills and valleys are extraordinary, thanks to the intervention of Ferdinand II in the 19th century, who fell in love with these places and decided to restore the ramparts, including the Torre Real, from which he enjoyed the wonderful view. In Sintra, the king decided to build his summer residence. Resembling a brightly colored fairytale castle, this unforgettable residence is the extravagant result of a combination of architectural and decorative styles ranging from neo-Manueline to neo-Gothic, neo-Renaissance to neo-Moorish, and even to Indian influences. It could easily have resulted in a chaotic ensemble, but instead it turned out to be a truly remarkable building, so much so that it has been voted

8th century
An Islamic army from Morocco landed in Andalusia and invaded the Iberian Peninsula. The area occupied by the Moors took the name of Gharb ("west of") al-Andalus. In Sintra, the Arabs built the Castelo dos Mouros.

1147
The King of Portugal, Alfonso I, managed to liberate the Castle of São Jorge and Lisbon. The Moorish castle in Sintra also surrendered to the Christians.

14th–15th centuries
King John I of Aviz began the renovation of another Moorish castle in Sintra, the future Palácio Nacional de Sintra.

1489–1520
Under King Manuel I, the Manueline wing of the Palácio Nacional de Sintra took shape.

1838
Ferdinand II of Saxe-Coburg-Gotha purchased an estate in Sintra that included the ruins of an ancient monastery. Construction began on the Palácio da Pena, designed by Wilhelm Ludwig von Eschwege.

1840
King Consort Fernando II and Queen Maria II of Braganza used the Palácio da Pena and its park as their summer residence.

1889
The Portuguese state purchased the Palácio da Pena from the heirs of King Louis I of Braganza, to whom Ferdinand II's second wife, Elise Hensler, Countess Edla, had sold it upon her husband's death.

1910
The Palácio da Pena was designated a National Monument and the most important center of the Cultural Landscape of Sintra, which includes the Castelo dos Mouros and the Palácio Nacional, as well as other palaces.

1995
Il Palácio da Pena, along with the entire cultural landscape of Sintra, became part of UNESCO's World Heritage.

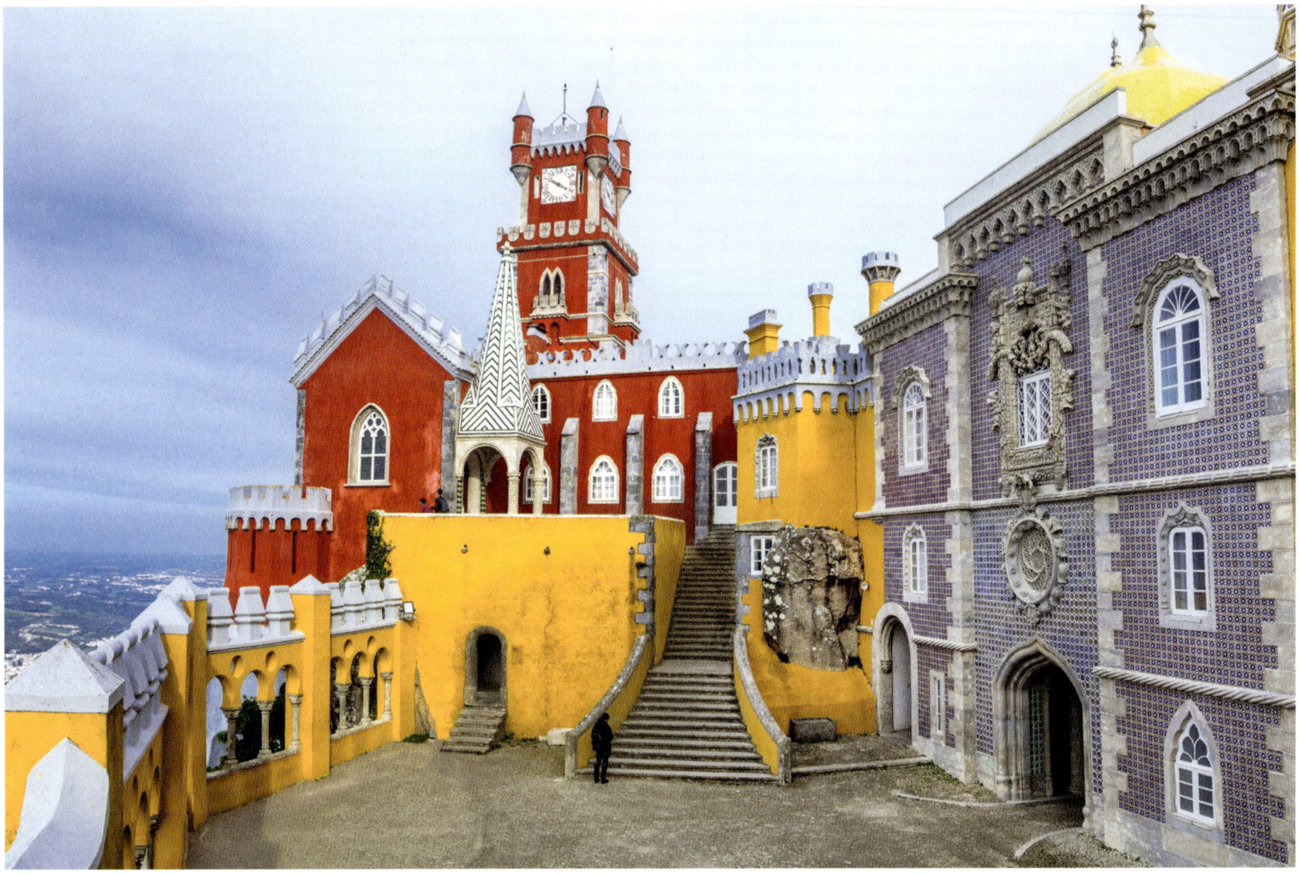

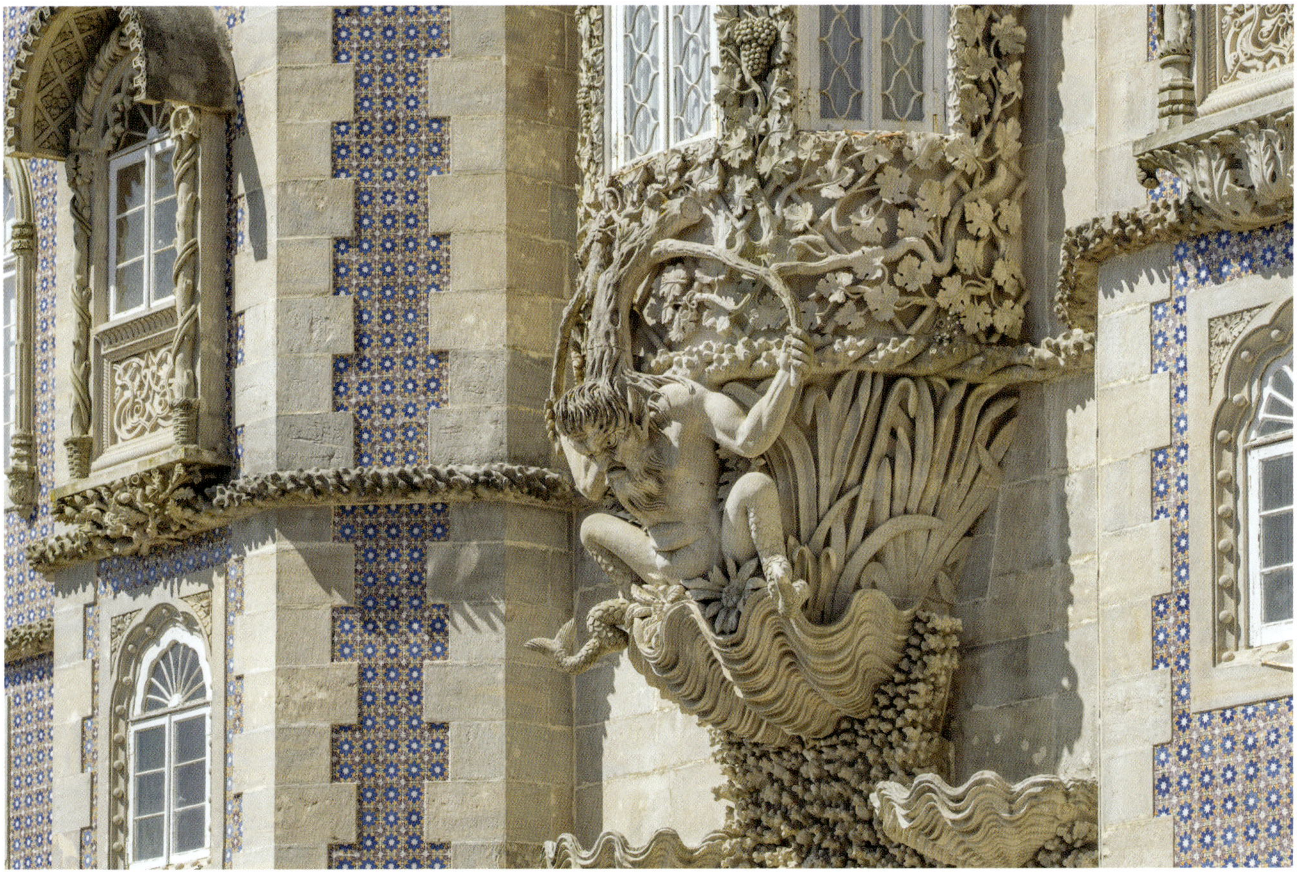

• 40 top: The Palácio Nacional da Pena is one of the seven wonders of Portugal. Its bright colors are the result of a restoration project in 1996 that replaced the previous, more subdued, colors.

• 40 bottom: The world of the sea is the protagonist of the Manueline style, which returns in a romantic reinterpretation in the Castle of Sintra. The sea monster surmounting the Arch of Triton is a creature half man, half fish. Below him are the depths of the sea, with shells and corals above the mainland, with branches of plants climbing up a bay window.

one of the seven wonders of Portugal and one of the thirteen most spectacular architectural works in the world. Within the castle walls, the passion for art of Queen Mary II's Viennese husband, Ferdinand of Saxe-Coburg-Gotha, is evident. He knew how to enhance what had previously stood in place of his summer residence. The history of the Palácio da Pena began before the 19th century. It was in 1506 when King Manuel I decided to found a monastery around a Romanesque chapel dedicated to the Virgin Mary and located on the highest hill in Sintra. The monastery, named after the one in Lisbon and dedicated to St. Jerome (Jerónimos), was damaged by the great earthquake of 1755 and then abandoned in 1834 with the dissolution of the monastic orders. A few years later, the king consort bought it and entrusted its restoration and transformation into a castle to the Prussian baron Ludwig von Eschwege, a renowned geologist and mineralogist who was fond of architecture and corresponded with some of the most interesting personalities of the time, including Johann Wolfgang von Goethe and Karl Marx. Eschwege worked in Sintra until 1855, the year of his death in Germany. Unfortunately, Queen Maria II never saw the complex completed because she died in 1853 while giving birth to her eleventh child. As a result, the palace was enjoyed mainly by her widower, Ferdinand, and his second wife, the Swiss actress and opera singer Elise Hensler.

The Palácio da Pena is surrounded by a 494-acre English-style park designed to suit the romantic tastes of Ferdinand II, simulating an almost perfect natural landscape with winding paths, ponds, and waterfalls immersed in lush, seemingly wild vegetation, consisting largely of exotic trees and shrubs imported from all corners of the world. Here and there, the landscape is enriched by fountains, gazeboes, belvederes, and small shelters, including the Alpine-style chalet built for his second wife, scattered throughout the greenery in an apparently random manner, but in reality designed to evoke awe and wonder.

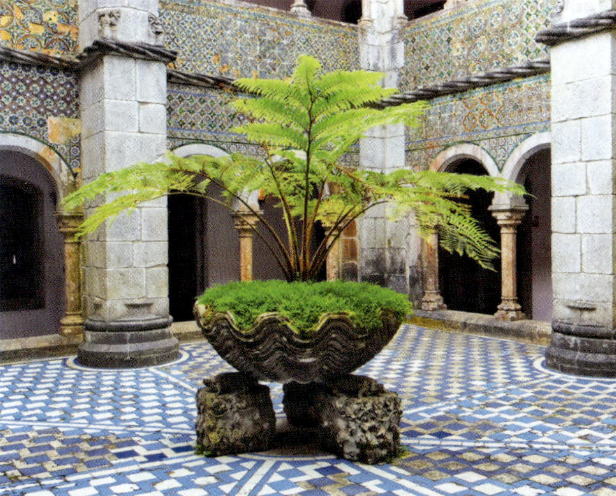

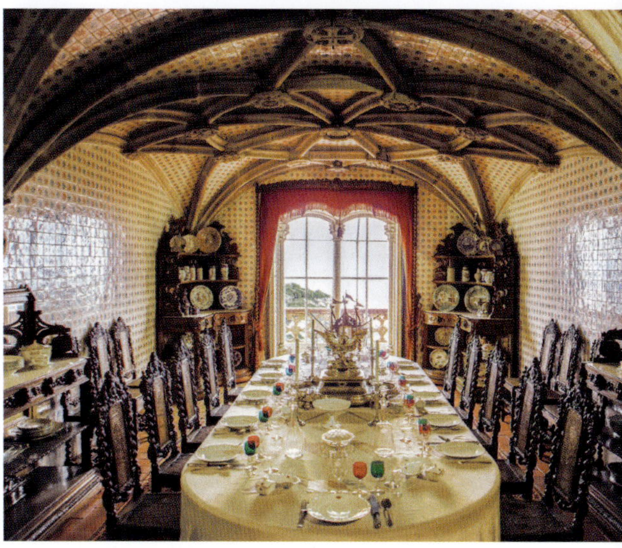

• 41 top: This cloister is one of the oldest areas of the palace: it corresponds to the courtyard of the 16th-century monastery founded by Manuel I. The Spanish-Arabic azulejos used to cover the walls are the original ones dating back to the early 16th century.

• 41 bottom: The dining room was converted from the refectory of the 16th-century monastery. The walls are entirely covered with azulejos. The table is set with original porcelain, crystal, and silverware.

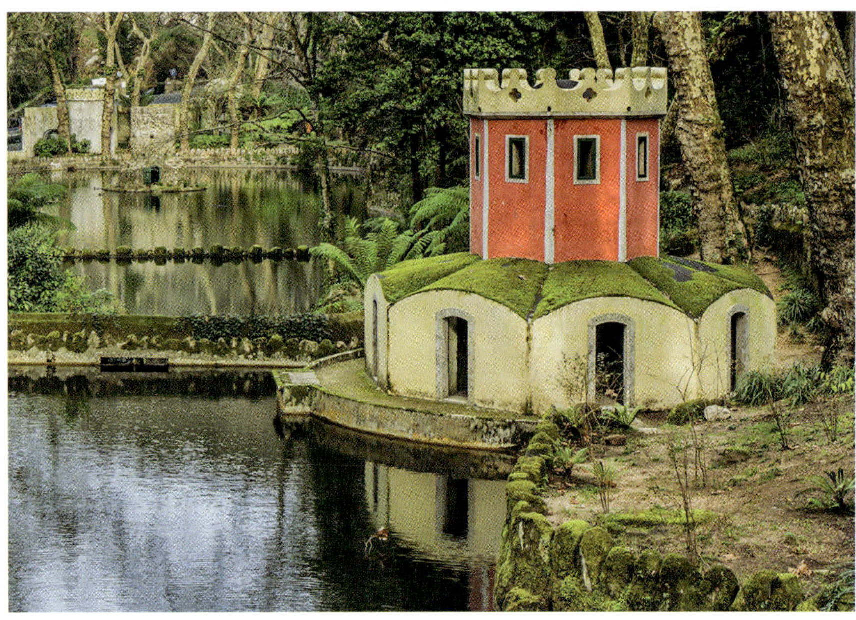

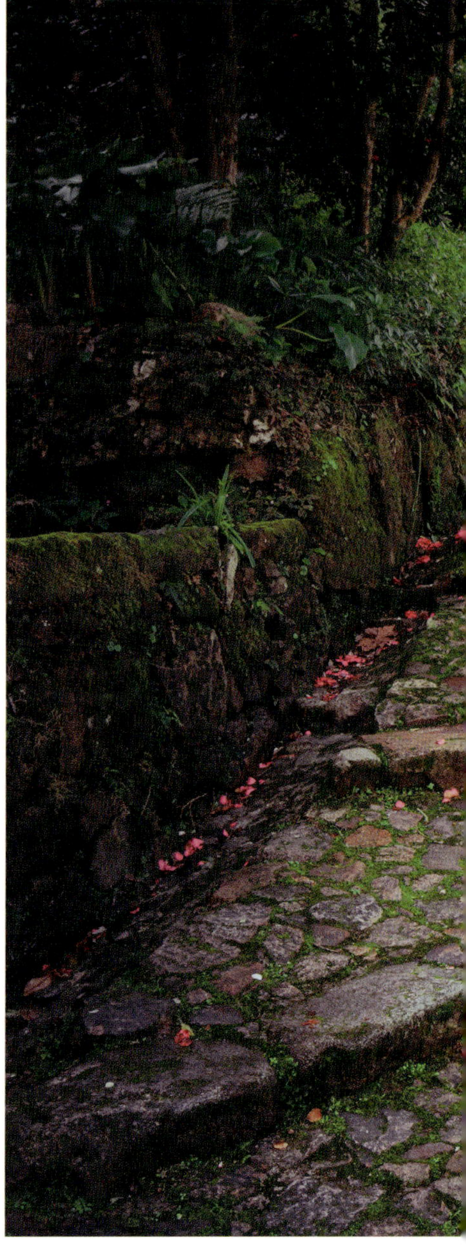

The National Palace of Sintra

Lower down than the Palácio da Pena, the historic center of Sintra-Vila is dominated by another royal residence, the Palácio Nacional de Sintra, easily recognizable by the two enormous fairy hat-shaped chimneys, 108 feet high, which surmount the kitchen chimneys. The palace was built on the ruins of a Moorish fortress, the first mention of which is found in a text by the Andalusian Arab geographer Al-Bakri (circa 1028–1094) and which passed into Christian hands in the 12th century with the Reconquista. More than a palace, it is a complex of buildings whose appearance is mainly due to King John I, who restored the central core in the Gothic-Moorish style in vogue at the time, and to Manuel I, who added a new wing in the Manueline style in the 16th century, in which decorative maritime elements are mixed with Arabic elements of the Mudejar style. This royal residence was decorated with gold from the Portuguese colonies and with magnificent azulejos created by Portuguese and Andalusian manufacturers. It is even said that an azulejo in the palace chapel is the oldest in Portugal.

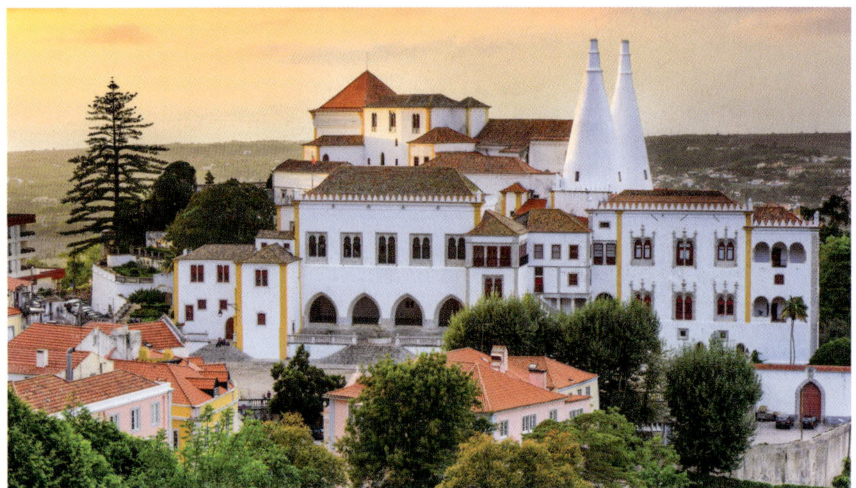

• 42 top: A small house in the shape of a crenellated tower for the swans and ducks that live in the park's artificial lakes. Everything was designed to impress visitors, such as the importation of exotic trees and shrubs from all corners of the world, such as giant North American redwoods, South American araucarias, Asian ginkgo biloba, and various species of ferns from Australia and New Zealand.

• 42 bottom: Towards the end of the Portuguese monarchy, the Palácio Nacional was the favorite summer residence of King Louis of Braganza's wife, Queen Maria Pia of Savoy, second daughter of King Victor Emmanuel II of Italy and therefore sister of Umberto I.

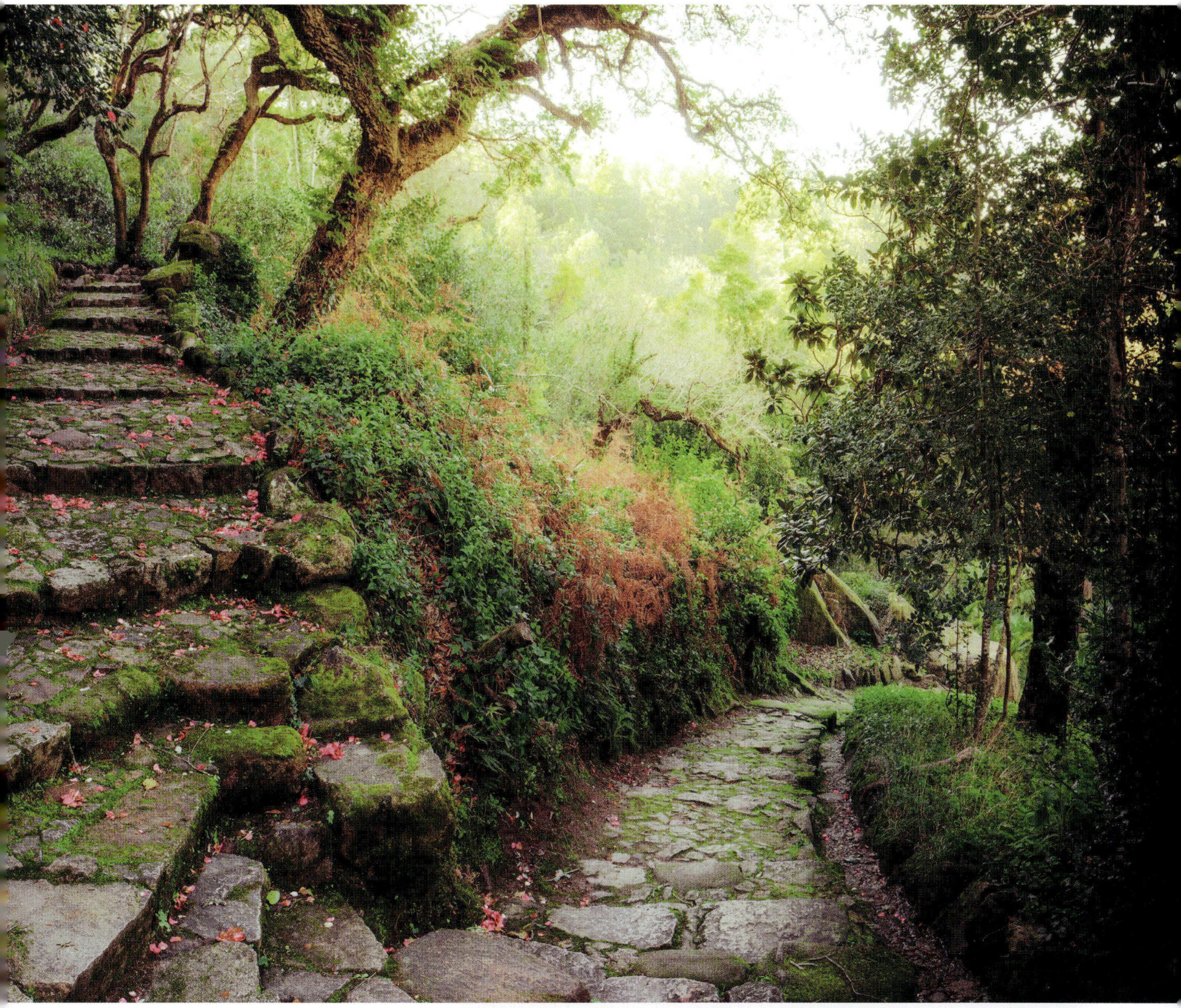

• 42-43: The layout of the park, commissioned by Ferdinand II, is decidedly romantic, with vegetation left to grow freely between the paths and ponds, without flower beds or trimmed hedges as in formal gardens.

• 43 bottom: Exotic plants and lush vegetation combine to create a magical atmosphere in the large English-style park surrounding the palace.

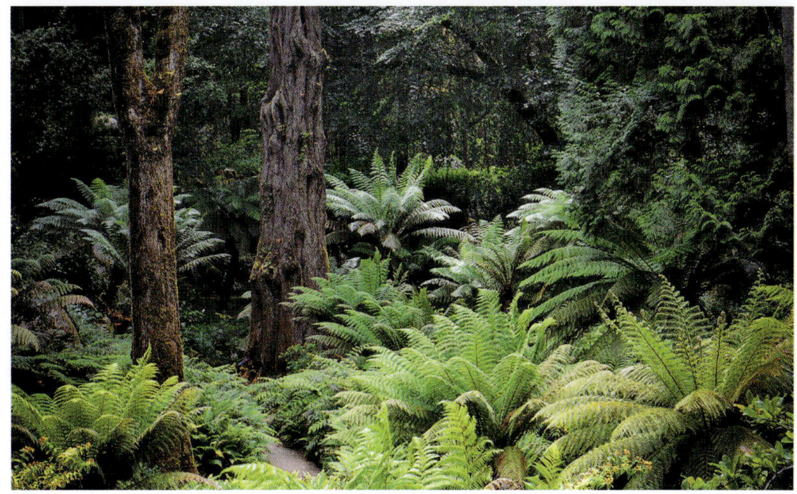

· 44–45: The ceremonial façade of the main body of the palace, designed by Mateus Vicente de Oliveira (1706–1785), as the backdrop to the Neptune fountain.

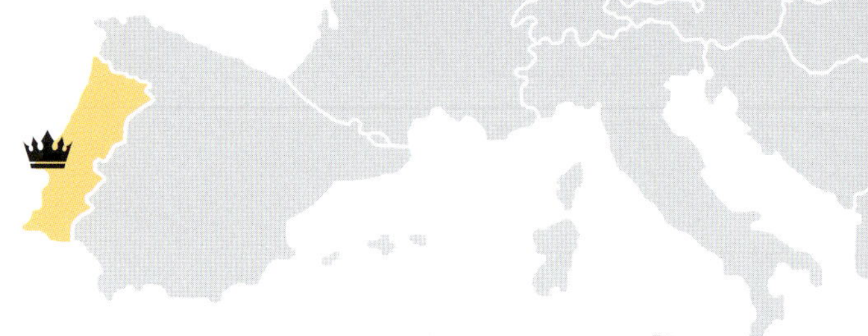

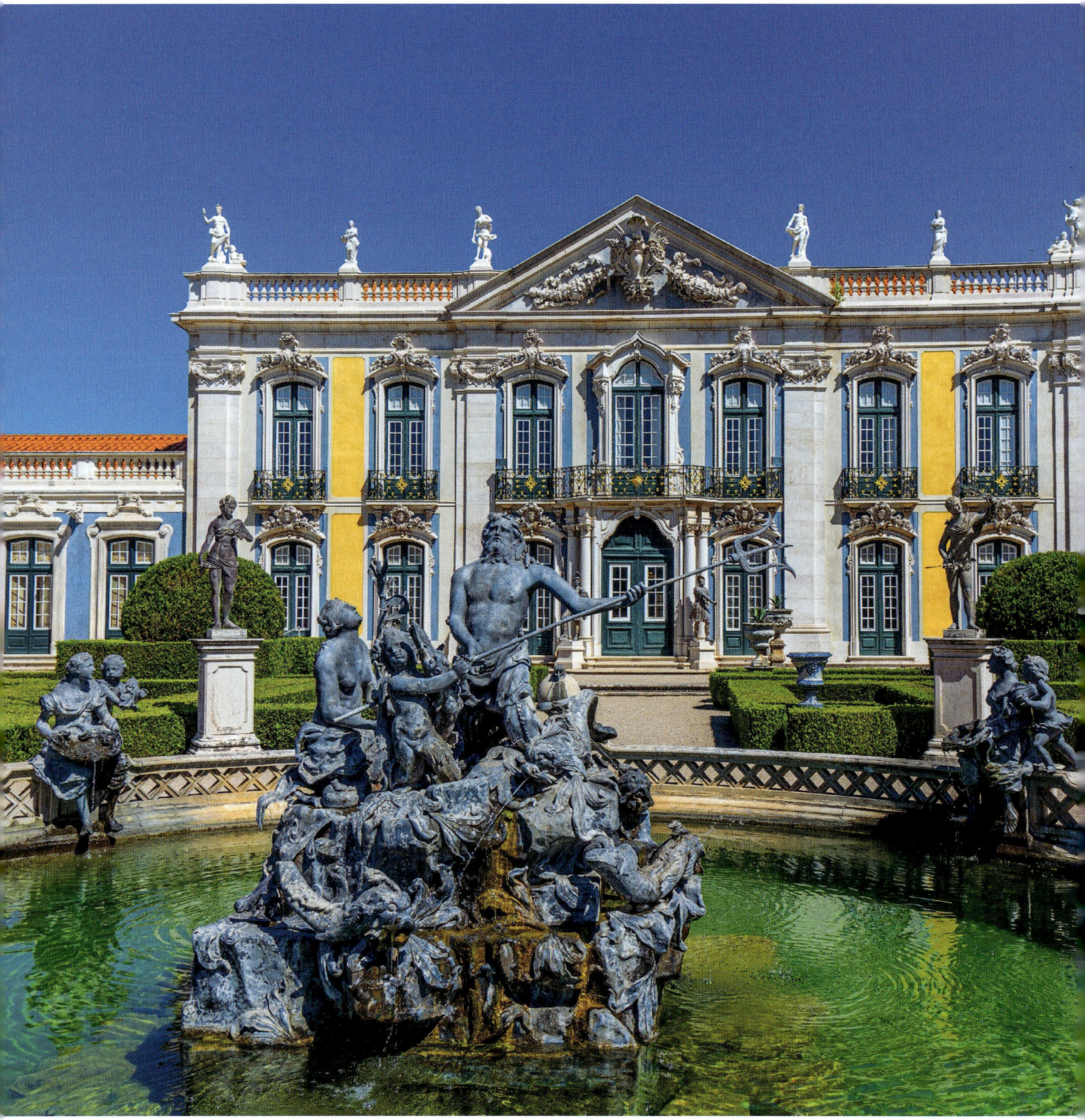

QUELUZ PALACE

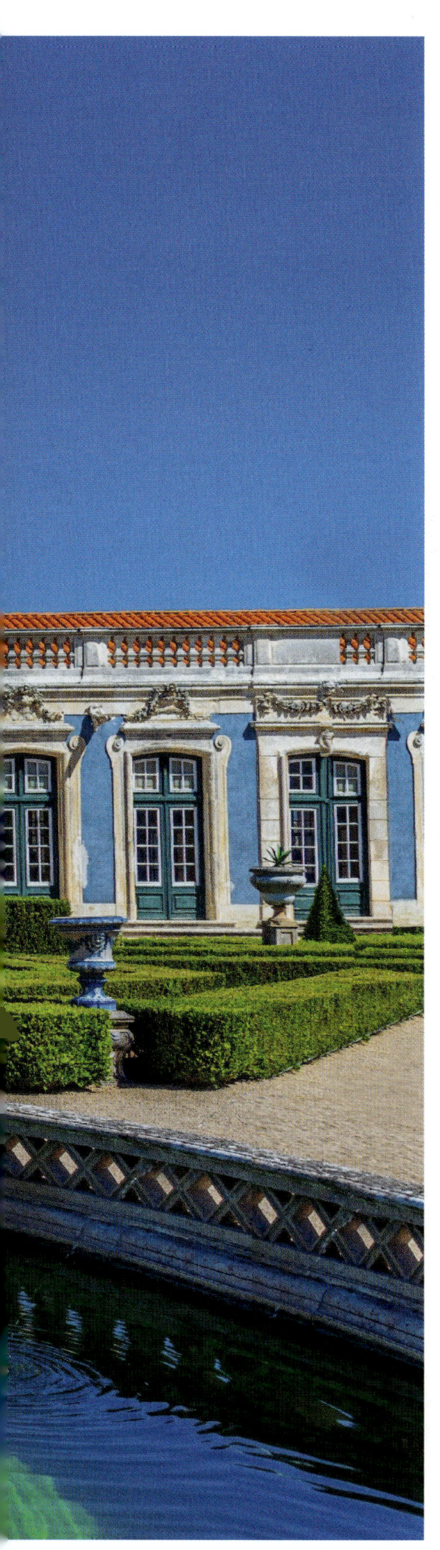

Immersed in gardens dotted with statues and fountains, the enchanting summer Palace of Queluz is one of the last examples of the great European Rococo style, a sort of Versailles, on a much smaller scale, less grandiose but no less elegant. Construction of the palace began on commission from Prince Peter of Braganza (who would later become King Peter III following his marriage to Queen Maria I, daughter of his brother), who asked for an existing 17th-century country villa to be enlarged. Work began in 1747 under the direction of the Portuguese architect Mateus Vicente de Oliveira. After an interruption due to the Lisbon earthquake of 1755, work resumed under the direction of Parisian Jean-Baptiste Robillon. When work restarted, a modified design was adopted to take into account the possibility of future earthquakes and prevent their terrible effects. This is why the palace is longer than it is tall, with low wings that increase its stability. When Peter became king in 1760 through his marriage to the heir to the throne, Maria I, further expansion work was undertaken to make the royal couple's residence suitable for their rank.

The interiors, designed to host parties and receptions, were elegantly decorated with allegorical frescoes and historical scenes along with azulejos, mirrors, carved wood, stucco, and boiserie. But concerts were the favorite entertainment of the owners. João de Sousa Carvalho, the best Portuguese musician of the Age of Enlightenment, who had trained in Naples in his youth, was often a guest at the court of Peter and Maria. For formal occasions held at Queluz, the royal couple commissioned ad hoc scores from him and other Portuguese composers, who were then invited to perform in the Royal Chapel for religious ceremonies or in the Music Room for family birthdays, name days, and other secular celebrations. Even today, the Music Room of the Royal Palace of Queluz is used as a concert venue, partly because of its extremely rare 18th-century Clementi piano.

1654
John IV established the Casa do Infantado, a complex of material assets that were an appanage of the second-born children of Portuguese nobles and monarchs, which included the future Palace of Queluz, often considered the Portuguese Versailles.

1747
Peter of Braganza, brother of King Joseph I, father of his future wife and heir to the throne, began construction of the sumptuous summer residence of Queluz.

1760
The palace was completed five years after the disastrous earthquake that razed Lisbon and other Portuguese towns to the ground.

1794
The royal family was forced to move to the Palace of Queluz due to a fire at the National Palace of Ajuda in Lisbon. They lived there until 1807.

1807
Following the invasion of Portugal by Napoleon's army, the Portuguese royal family was forced to flee to Brazil. The Palace of Queluz was abandoned.

1908
Following the assassination of King Charles I by two republican activists, the Portuguese state purchased the palace, which was partially destroyed by a fire 25 years later.

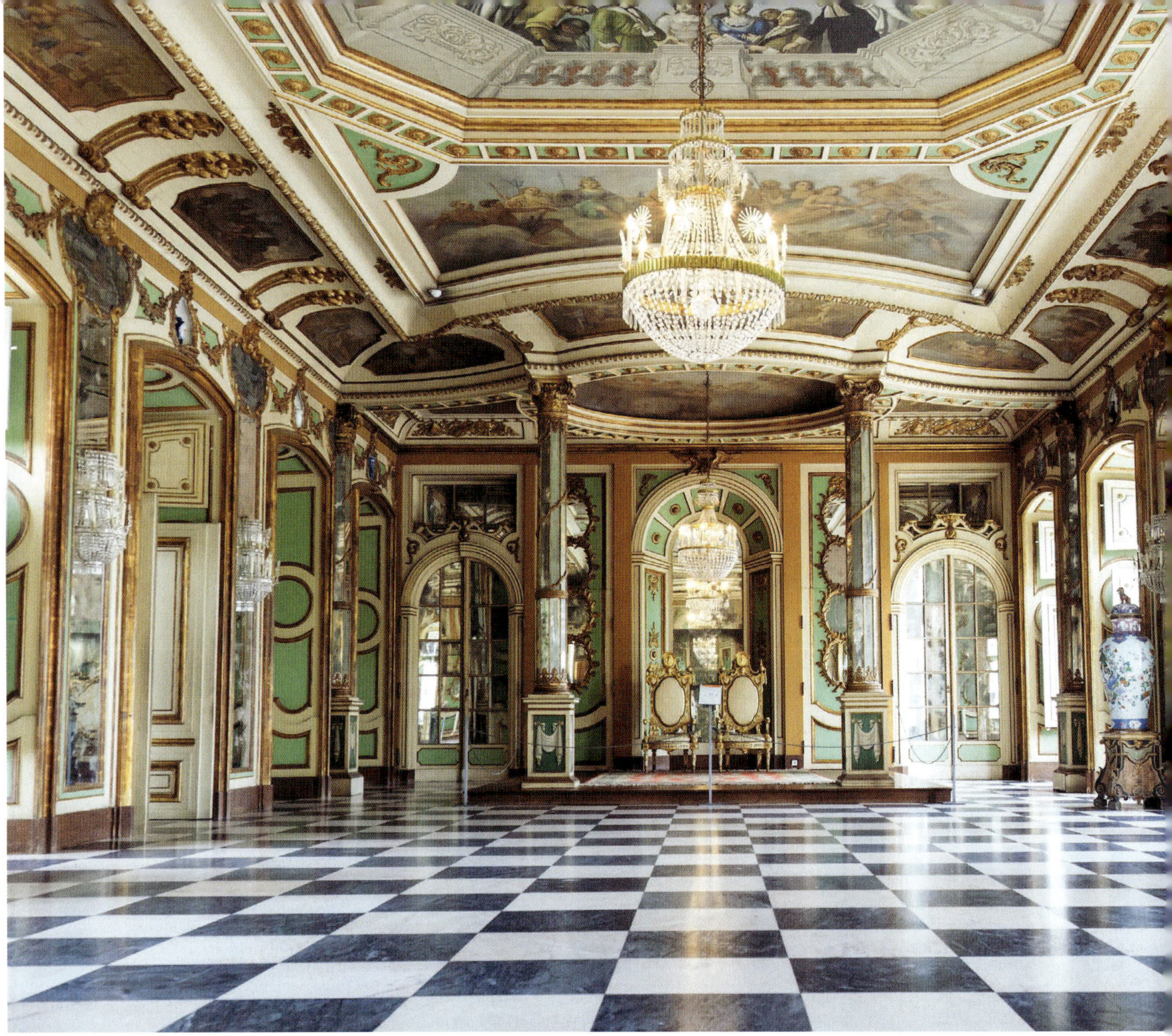

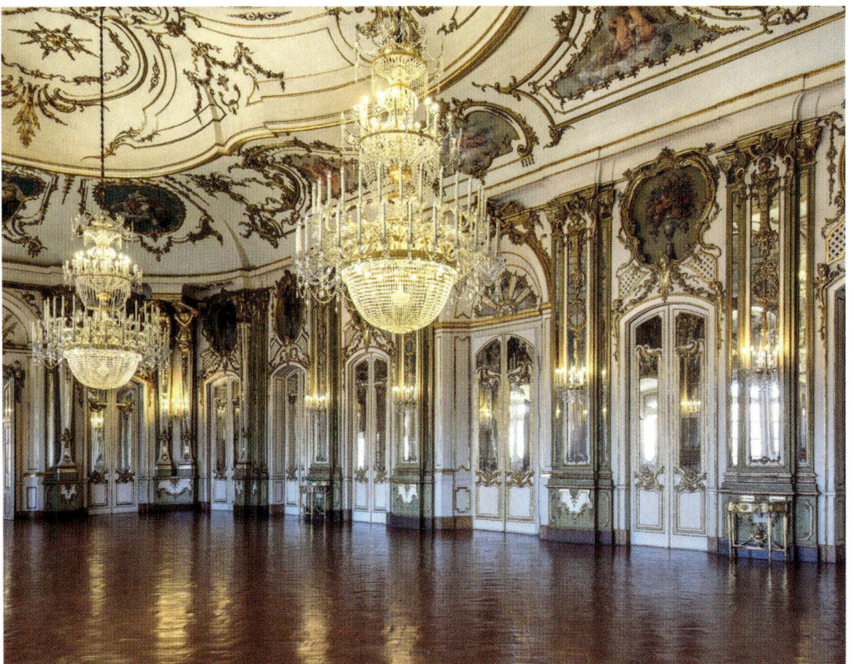

• 46-47: The Ambassadors' Hall, also known as the "Throne Room," is one of the largest rooms in the palace and is also very bright thanks to the large windows on the longer sides. On the ceiling, a fresco depicts Queen Maria and her family attending a concert.

• 46 bottom: The Ballroom is a Rococo jewel richly decorated in gilded bronze, with mirrors everywhere that amplify its magnificence in a blaze of light and that multiply the figures of the dancers, with remarkable effects, especially during masked balls and the most sumptuous parties.

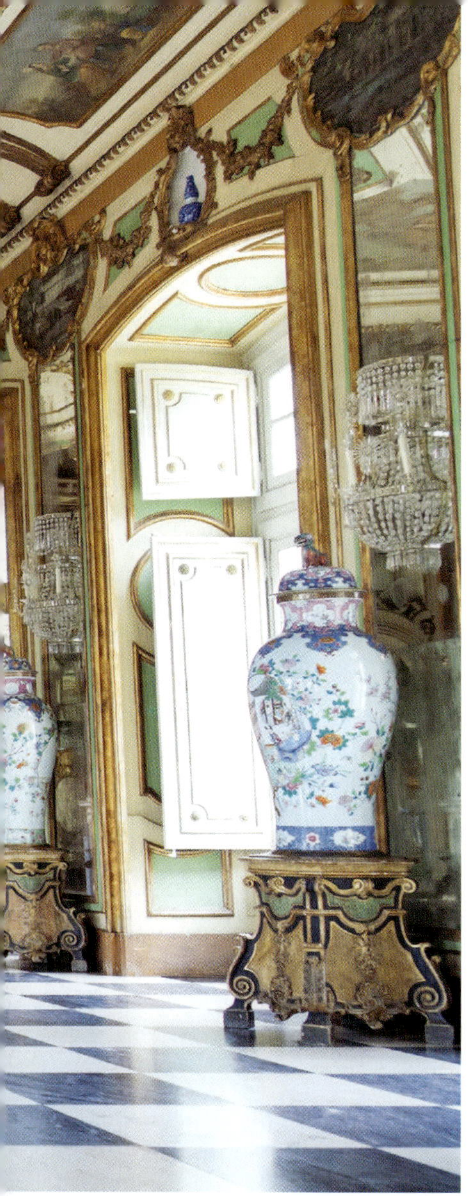

The queen's madness

At the time when the Palace of Queluz was built, Peter of Braganza was "just" the younger brother of the king of Portugal. He had been assigned the lands of Queluz with the ancient estate by virtue of his kinship. It was the powerful Marquis of Pombal, the most influential man in the country, who encouraged the marriage between the prince and his niece Maria. The wedding took place on 6 June 1760. Upon her father's death in 1777, Maria succeeded him to the throne and Peter became king consort. In order to govern freely, Pombal convinced the couple to move to the palace of Queluz to keep them away from Lisbon. When her uncle and husband died in 1786, Maria began to suffer from mental illness, which worsened over time. Forced to live in Queluz after the Royal Barraca de Ajuda was destroyed by fire in 1794, she forced those who cared for her to lock her discreetly in her apartments, from which her terrible screams could be heard. Whether this was an effect of porphyria, of incestuous ancestry, or of depression caused by the death of Peter and their first son, who died of smallpox at the age of 27, the fact remains that the queen's madness could not be ignored. Maria died in exile at the age of 81 in Rio de Janeiro, where the entire Portuguese royal family had taken refuge in 1809 upon the arrival of Napoleon's troops.

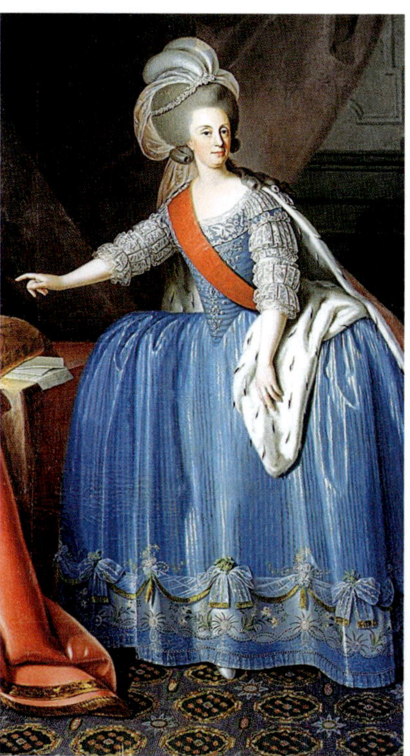

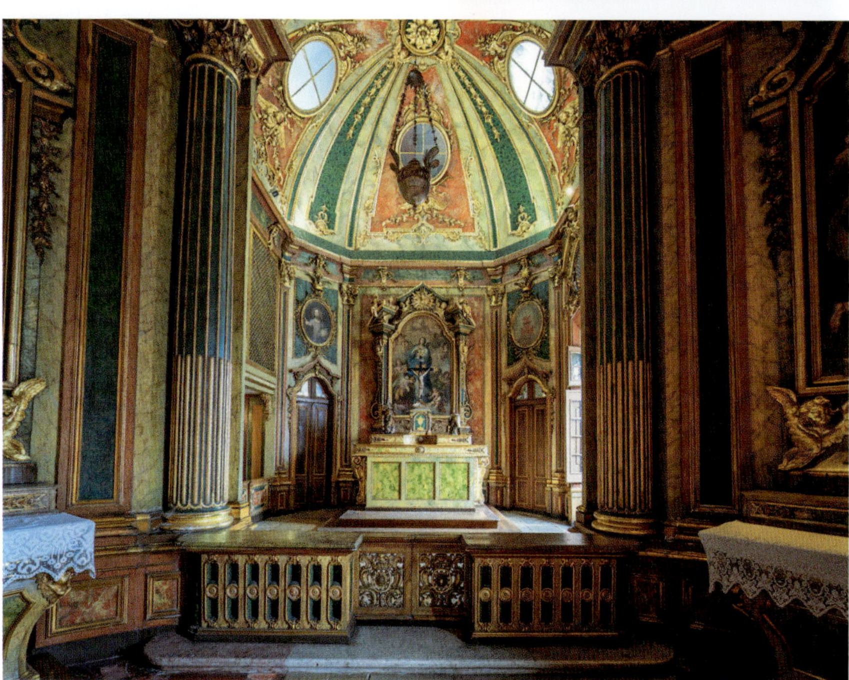

• 47 bottom: The chapel of the Palace of Queluz, dating back to 1752, was designed by architect Mateus Vicente de Oliveira, while the exquisite gilded carvings are the work of Silvestre Faria Lobo.

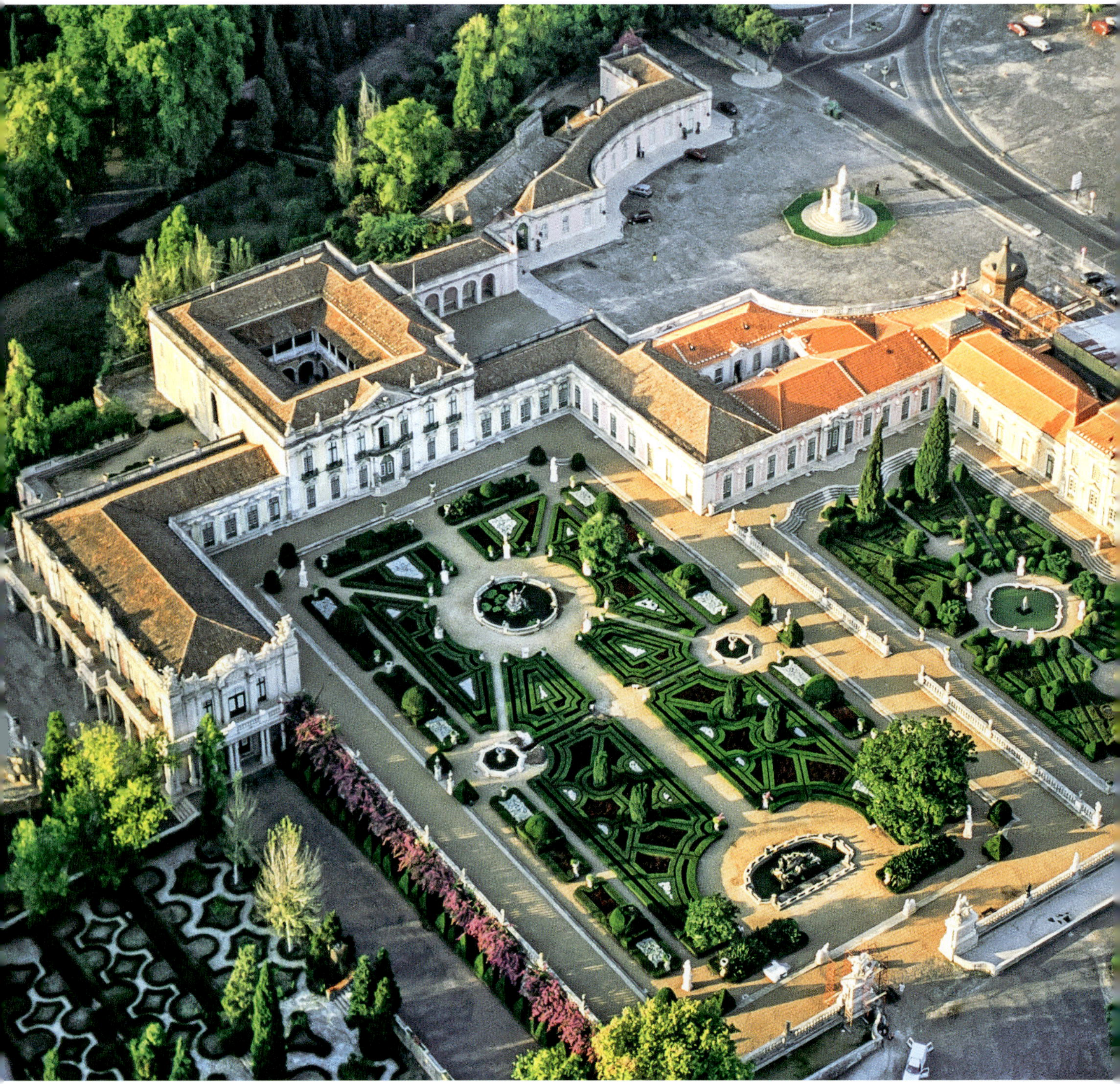

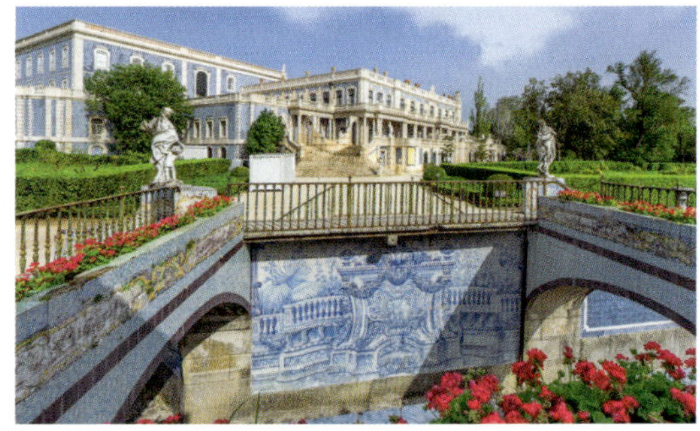

• 48-49: Aerial view of the Malta Garden: on the right is the wing of the palace that houses the Throne Room, the main room of the complex.

• 48 bottom: The gardens are crossed by a long canal that runs between two balustrades covered with azulejos. It was once filled with water, and the members of the royal family enjoyed traveling along it by boat or gondola.

• 49 center: Statues, fountains, large ceramic vases, and neatly trimmed box hedges create a perfect backdrop for the 18th-century façades of the Palace of Queluz.

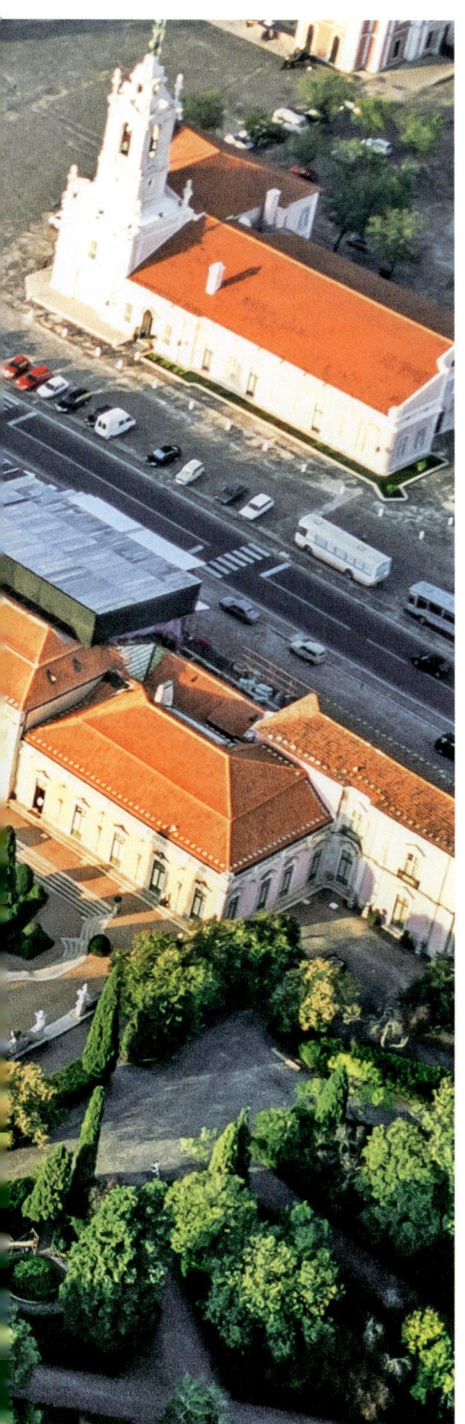

In the 18th century, the music for important social events, grand parties, and receptions was performed in the Ballroom or the Ambassadors' Hall by small ensembles playing waltzes and mazurkas amid a whirl of gala dresses, in candlelight enhanced by mirrors. Far from politics and court intrigues, and in possession of considerable wealth and refined habits, Peter III spared no expense. But it is the gardens that are the real highlight of this residence. For three generations of the Portuguese royal family, the sovereigns, their families, and the court spent long days in the green surroundings of Queluz, marking the time with walks, evening concerts in the open air, and firework displays. Decorated with statues inspired by classical mythology, crossed by wide avenues and enlivened by waterfalls, fountains, and water features, this 39-acre park is made up of a series of gardens. Closer to the palace are the formal French gardens, with topiary hedges and perfectly manicured geometric flower beds. In a distant corner, however, there is a botanical garden with greenhouses for exotic species and a central parterre with a collection of plants from every corner of the world. There is a large canal enclosed by

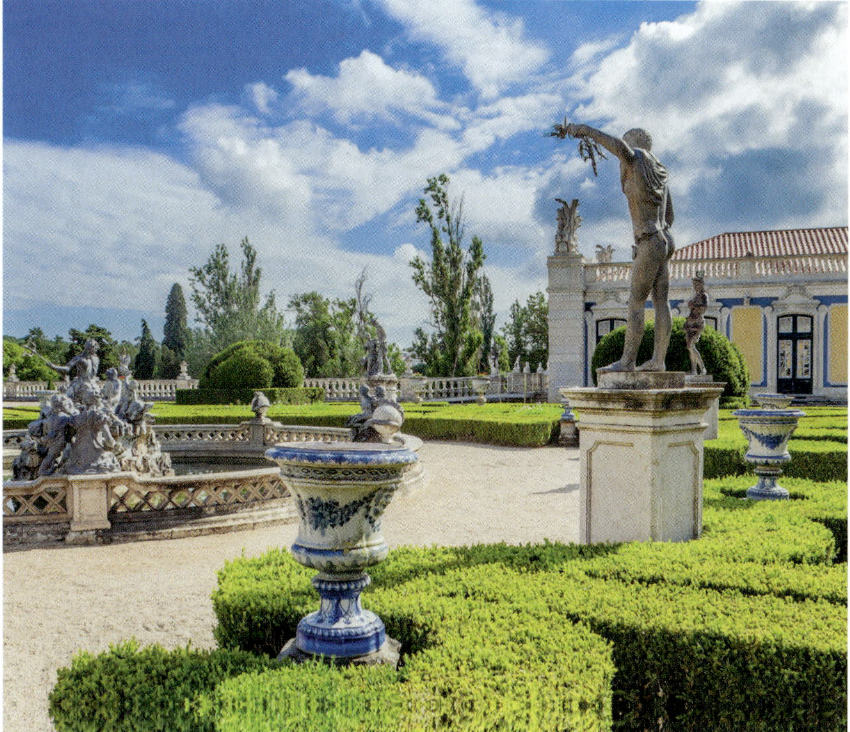

azulejos where the royals once enjoyed lazy rides in gondolas while listening to music played by a chamber orchestra set up in a nearby pavilion. For some time, there was even a cage where lions, tigers, monkeys, and other exotic animals were kept captive. The most spectacular feature, however, is the large waterfall in the center of the main axis of the garden, which was once decorated with stone and lead statues.

• 50-51: A view of the Alcázar of Segovia. In this image, the Spanish flag flies over the Tower of John II of Trastámara, named after the father of Henry IV and Isabella I of Castile. At the other end of the complex stands the Tower of the Homage.

• 51 center: After the Muslim conquest, Segovia was abandoned by many of its inhabitants. It regained its vitality thanks to Alfonso VI, who liberated it in the 12th century, repopulated it, and began construction of the Alcázar. In the stained-glass window of the Alcázar, the king of Castile is depicted together with the bishop of the city, Peter of Agén.

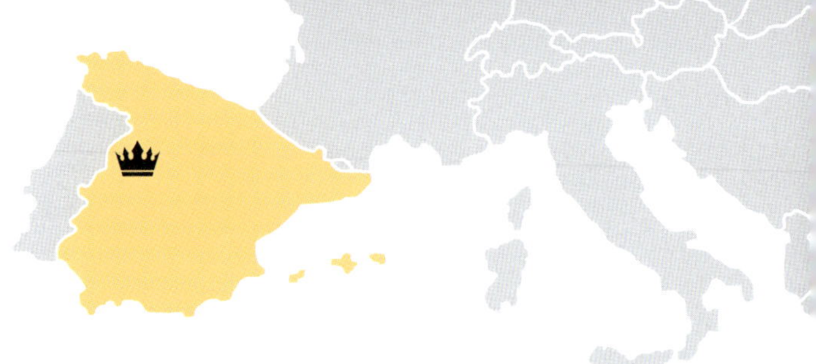

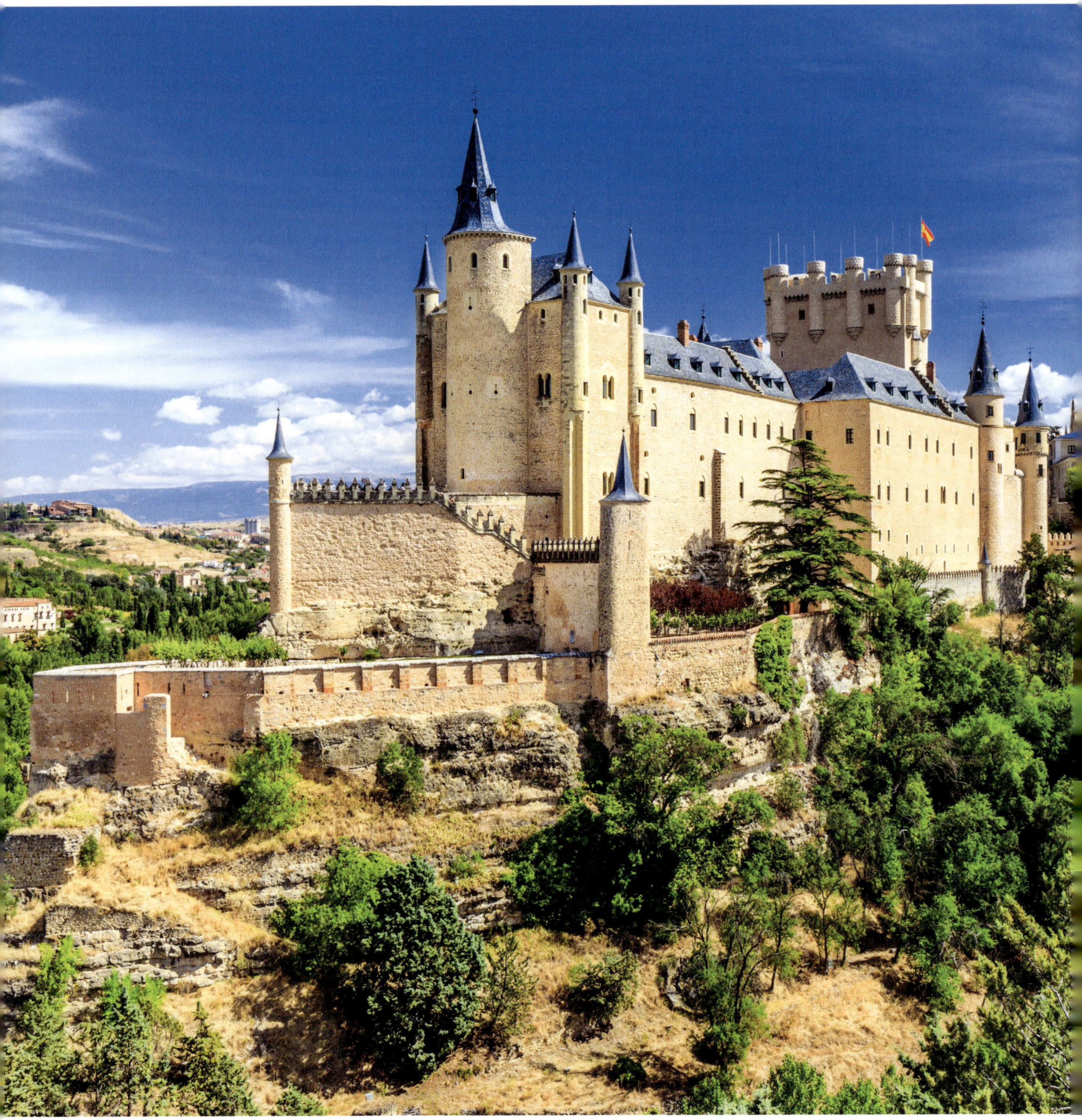

Alcázar of Segovia

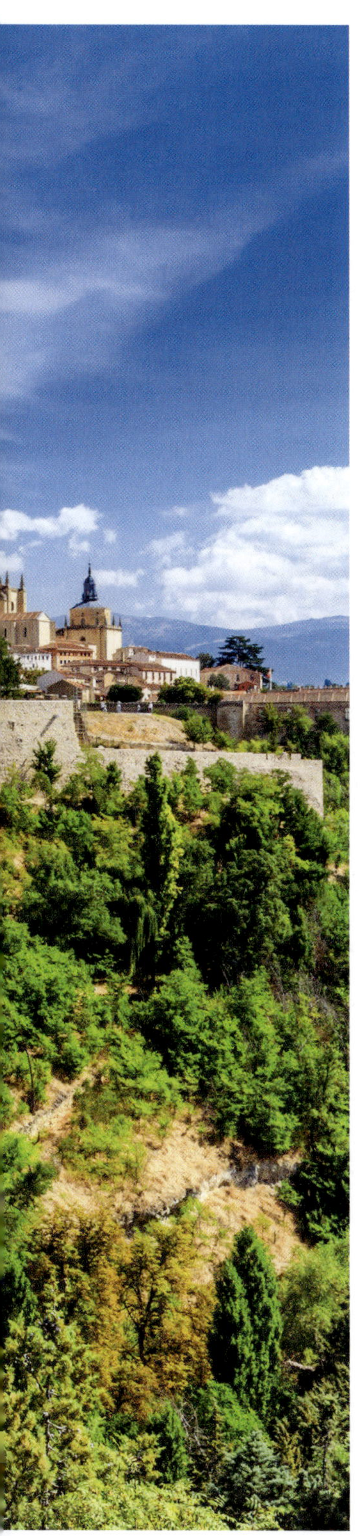

The Real Alcázar of Segovia is, along with the one in Seville, the best-preserved medieval fortress that has survived to the present day. The alcázares (from the Arabic al-qasr) were fortified residences of Moorish origin which, after the Reconquista of the Iberian Peninsula by Christian armies (that lasted from the 8th century until 1492 with the fall of the Sultanate of Granada, the last Muslim kingdom in Spain), became the seats of the restored Spanish power. As was characteristic of medieval architecture, these were buildings that grew and changed over time according to the needs and tastes of their owners: for example, with the addition of new apartments or the raising of towers. The Royal

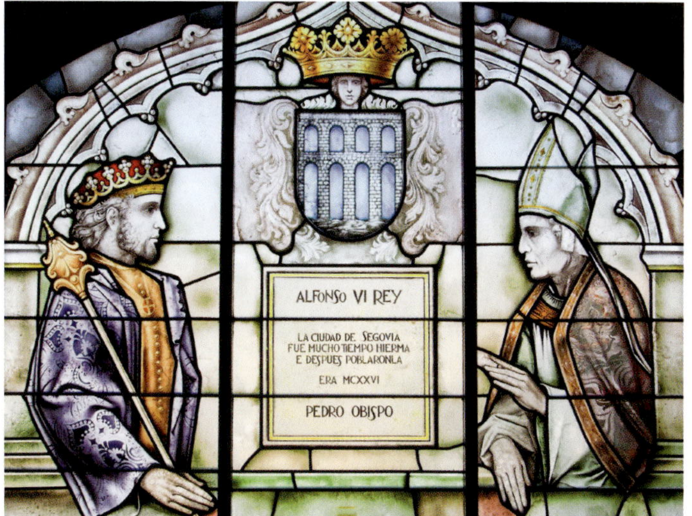

Alcázar of Segovia is no exception: it was built in the early part of the 12th century by order of Alfonso VI on the site of an Islamic fort that had been constructed on the remains of an ancient Roman fortification. It was later enlarged and restored by the kings of Castile, who ruled until modern times. Built on the edge of the Sierra de Guadarrama, on top of a high rocky spur shaped by the erosion of the Eresma and Clamores rivers, the Real Alcázar, which was fundamental for the control and domination of Castile, has the appearance of an austere military fortress on the outside, but its luxurious and opulent interiors were intended to reflect the immense wealth of the Castilian sovereigns.

722–732
The Battle of Covadonga, won in 722 by the Christians over the Moors, conventionally marks the beginning of the Reconquista of the Iberian Peninsula.

11th century
As the Christians reconquered the lost lands, they built fortresses or occupied those taken from the Muslims, including the castles of Cuéllar, in the province of Segovia, and La Mota in Medina del Campo.

12th century
The first written reference to the Alcázar of Segovia was in a document dated 1120, about 32 years after the Reconquista of the city.

1412–1474
With Catherine of Lancaster, John II, and Henry IV, the Alcázar reached its peak splendor.

1474
On December 12, at the Alcázar of Segovia, Princess Isabella of Castile received news of the death of Henry IV. The following day, she was proclaimed queen in the atrium of the Iglesia de San Miguel.

1570
The wedding of Philip II of Habsburg and Anna of Austria, daughter of Maximilian II of Habsburg, was celebrated In the chapel of the Alcázar.

1762
Charles III of Bourbon founded the Royal Artillery Academy in the Alcázar of Segovia.

1862
A fire destroyed the palace. Reconstruction began shortly afterwards.

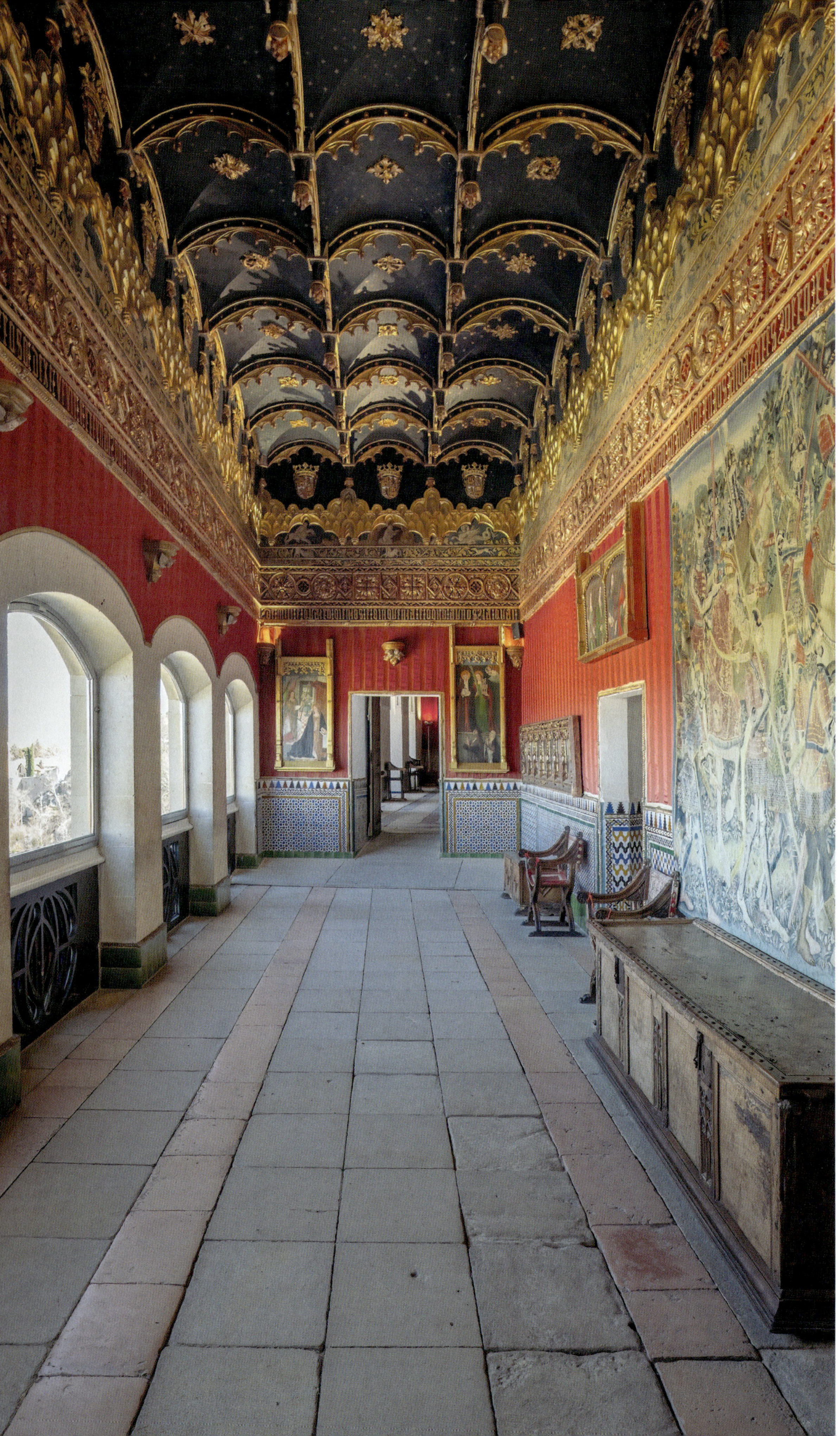

• 52: The Hall of the Cord is linked to a legend that features Alfonso X the Wise. It seems that the king had sinned greatly through pride during a speech to the Cortes in which he compared himself to God and that, as a sign of penance, he had a Franciscan cord made of stone in this room to remind him of his mistake forever.

• 53 top: The Mudéjar-style ceiling of the Hall of Kings is not the original one, which was unfortunately lost in 1862, but it is a faithful reproduction. This room, with good natural lighting and decorated only on the upper part of the walls, was intended to house the castle library.

• 53 left: The Sala della Galera or Sala degli Ambasciatori (Hall of the Galley or Hall of Ambassadors) was commissioned by Catherine of Lancaster, regent on behalf of her son John II between 1406 and 1418. The name of this room derives from the ceiling, which resembles the upturned hull of a galley. The original ceiling was destroyed by fire in 1862. The current ceiling is a reconstruction.

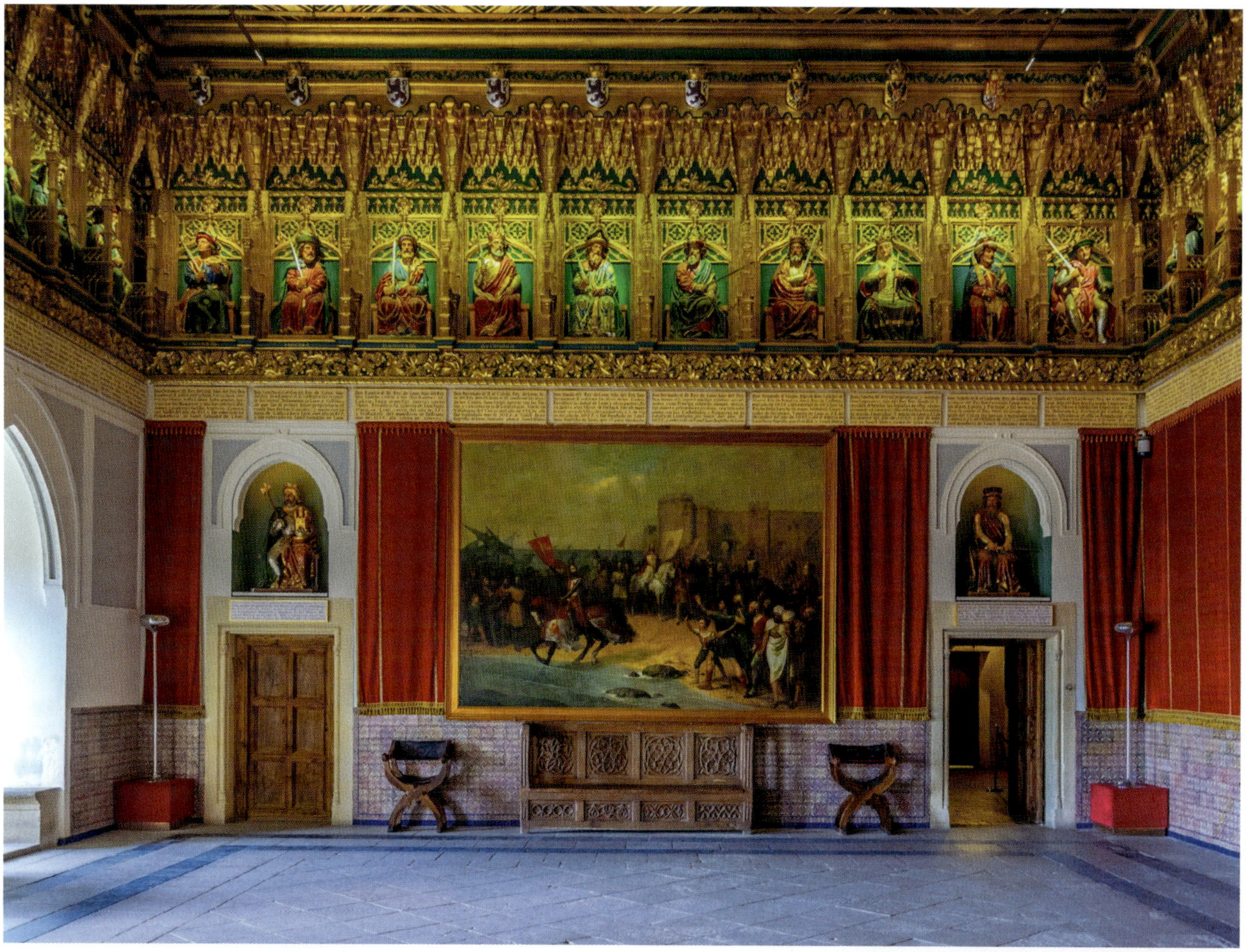

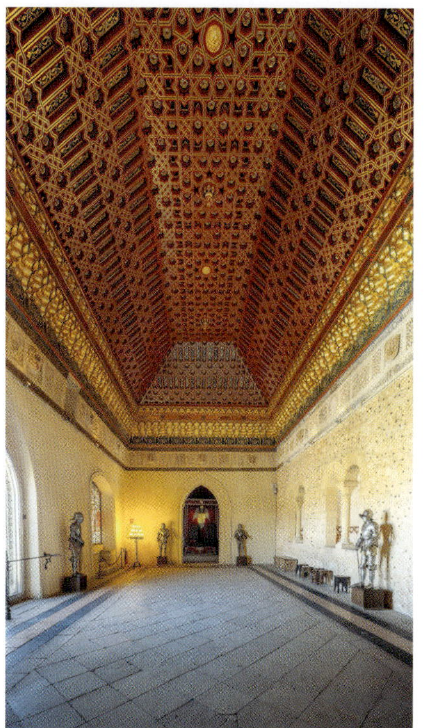

The Throne Room

The Throne Room or Solium was destroyed, like the other rooms, in the great fire of 1862. The flames burned all the furnishings and also engulfed the precious Mudejar wooden ceiling, which was irretrievably lost. Only the plaster frieze and the band of azulejos at the bottom survived. Today, the room looks as it must have in the time of the Catholic Monarchs, with two thrones placed under a canopy on which the heraldic motto "Tanto monta" ("They amount to the same") is prominent, with the initials I and F of Isabella and Ferdinand. The luxury of this room served to impress the ambassadors of the European courts who came to visit Spain and almost put them in a state of awe. Today, the drapes, tapestries, carpets, and cushions of yesteryear are no longer there, and the roof is no longer the original one, but the Moorish-style plaster frieze that runs around the ceiling and the plinth are still there. The azulejos baseboards on the walls still give an idea of the wealth of the Castilian court and, more interestingly, of the fact that Christians were fascinated by the beauty of Islamic craftsmanship.

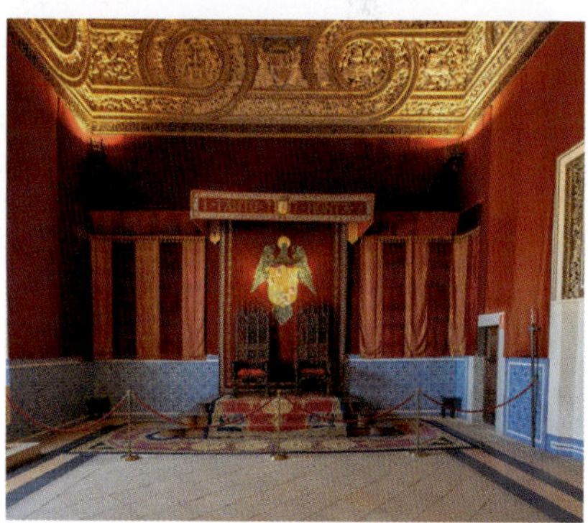

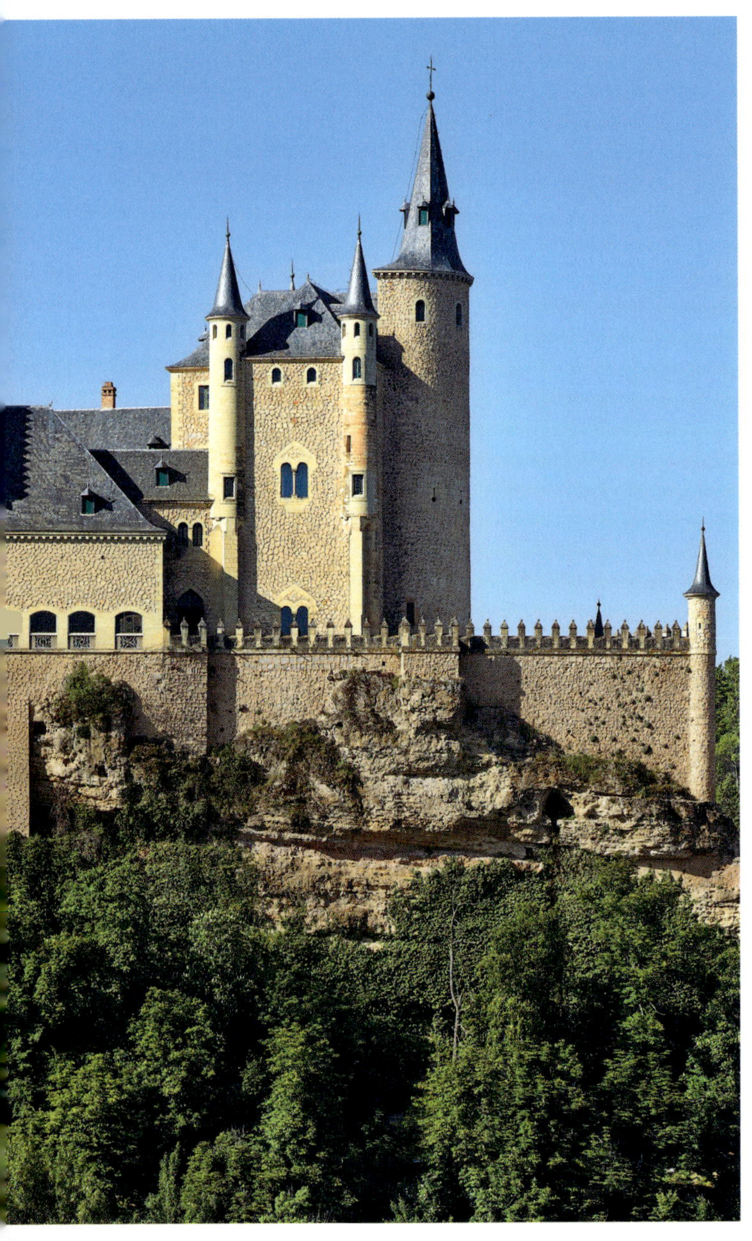

The favorite residence of Alfonso X the Wise (1221-1284), a man of such great culture that he was considered the founder of Castilian prose literature, reached its peak under the kings and queens of the Trastámara dynasty, becoming the seat of institutional power. Henry II, Catherine of Lancaster, wife of Henry III and mother of John II and Henry IV, half-brother of Isabella I the Catholic, made the royal palace one of the most sumptuous of its time with the addition of rooms (the Throne Room or Solium, the Hall of Kings, and the Hall of the Galley) richly decorated with Moorish-style plaster friezes, azulejos on the walls, and magnificent ceilings with gilded and painted wood carvings.

During the Habsburg reign in Spain (1516–1570), the royal residence was used for the wedding of Philip II to his fourth wife, Anne of Austria, in 1570. The king ordered major alterations to the palace, such as the conical slate spires that give it the typical appearance of central European castles, unusual compared to other Castilian fortresses. After the court moved to Madrid, the Alcázar lost its importance and was later used as a state prison. In 1762, Charles III of Bourbon founded the Royal College of Artillery in Segovia, which remained active until March 6, 1862, when a serious fire destroyed the roofs and the interior of the Alcázar along with most of the treasures contained in its halls, archives, library, and cabinets. What can be admired today is the result of careful reconstruction.

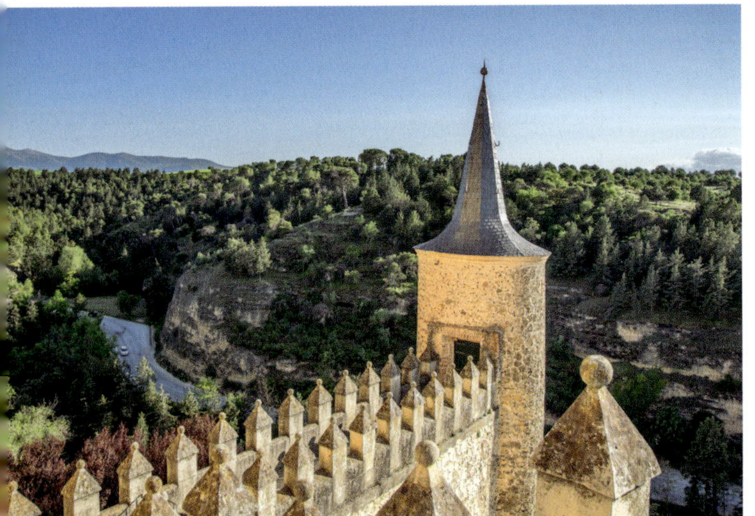

• 54 top: The Torre del Homenaje is characterized by a square keep with five turrets. It was here that the treasure of the Crown of Castile, which financed Christopher Columbus's voyage of discovery, was kept. Its slender appearance inspired Walt Disney for the castle in the animated film "Snow White and the Seven Dwarfs" (1937).

• 54 bottom: From the crenellated walls of the Alcázar, the view of the landscape surrounding Segovia is priceless.

• 55: The Tower of John II was built during his reign. This sovereign, who became king at the age of about two, was regent to his mother Catherine of Lancaster. The tower is about 262 feet high and overlooks the Patio de las Armas.

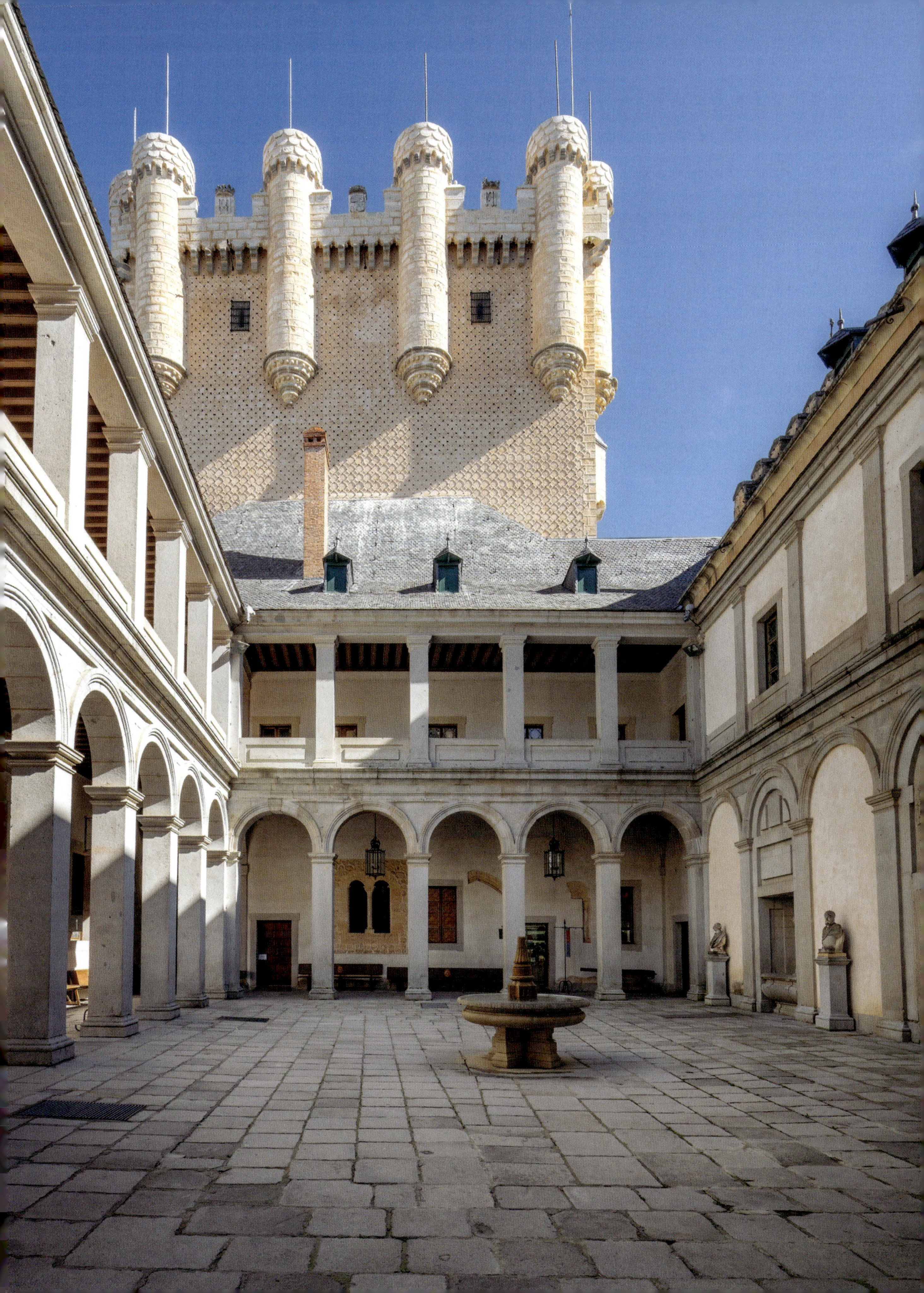

ROYAL PALACE OF MADRID

865
Emir Mohamed I of al-Andalus ordered the construction of a fortress on the site where, eight centuries later, the Royal Palace of Madrid would be built.

1083
Alfonso VI, known as "the Brave," king of León and later of Castile, reconquered Mayrit, which became a meeting point between two cultures, Eastern (Muslim and Jewish) and European.

1537
Charles V of Habsburg ordered the first expansion of the Real Alcázar.

1561
Philip II of Habsburg, King of Spain since 1556, moved the capital of his domains to Madrid. The Real Alcázar was enlarged and embellished.

1734
A fire destroyed the Real Alcázar. On the same site, Philip V commissioned the construction of the new Royal Palace.

1735–1764
Filippo Juvarra was commissioned to build the new palace, followed by Giovanni Battista Sacchetti, who was replaced in 1760 by Francesco Sabatini until the work was completed in 1764.

1764
Charles III of Bourbon was the first sovereign to take up residence in the palace, in 1764.

1930
Opposite the northern façade of the Royal Palace in Madrid, a park was created on the site where the stables designed by Francesco Sabatini stood in the 18th century.

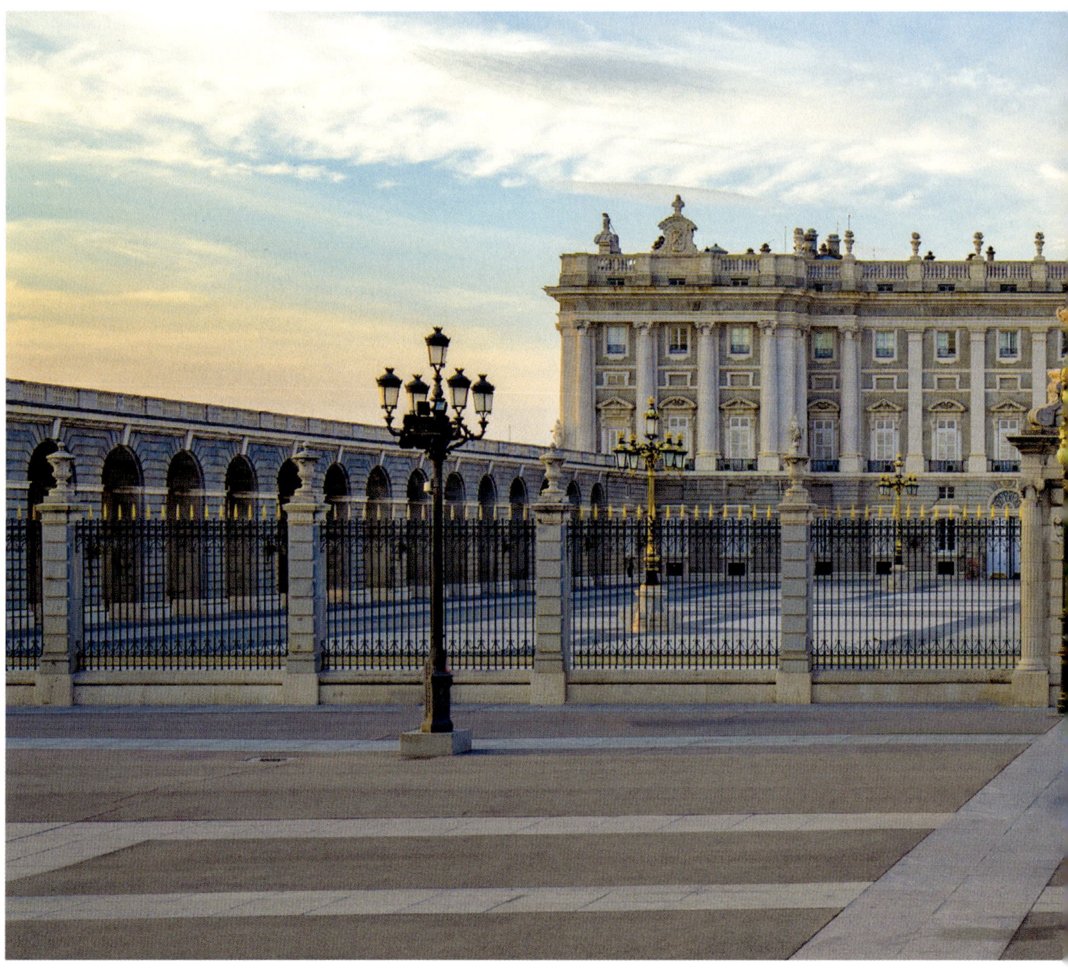

In 1561, when Philip II of Habsburg chose Madrid as the capital of the kingdom he inherited from his father Charles V—along with the Italian territories, the Netherlands, and the colonies in the New World—the city was nothing more than a provincial village dominated by the imposing fortress built by the Umayyad emir of Cordoba, Mohamed I. The election of this modest village (with no more than 10,000 inhabitants) located in the isolated heart of Castile as the capital was accompanied by a large influx of people, including members of the court, aristocratic families, officials, and religious figures, as well as merchants, artisans, and artists. Within a few years, the number of inhabitants multiplied and the capital of the kingdom was transformed into a single construction site, starting with the renovation of the Real Alcázar. However, despite the embellishments already

• 56–57: The Plaza de Armas and the main façade of the Royal Palace of Madrid, which show the styles of the architects who worked on its construction, from Filippo Juvarra to Giovanni Battista Sacchetti and Francesco Sabatini. The statues on either side of the clock represent, from left to right, the kings who built it: Philip V, Ferdinand VI, and their wives Maria Barbara of Braganza and Elisabeth Farnese.

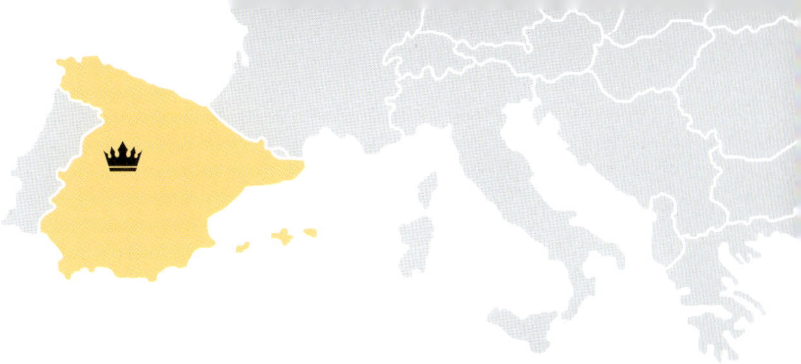

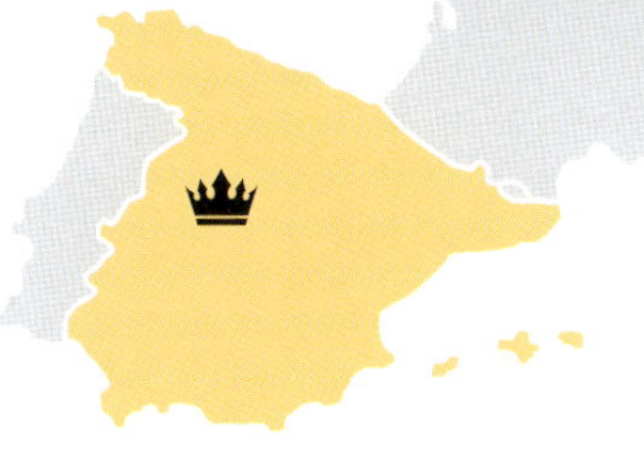

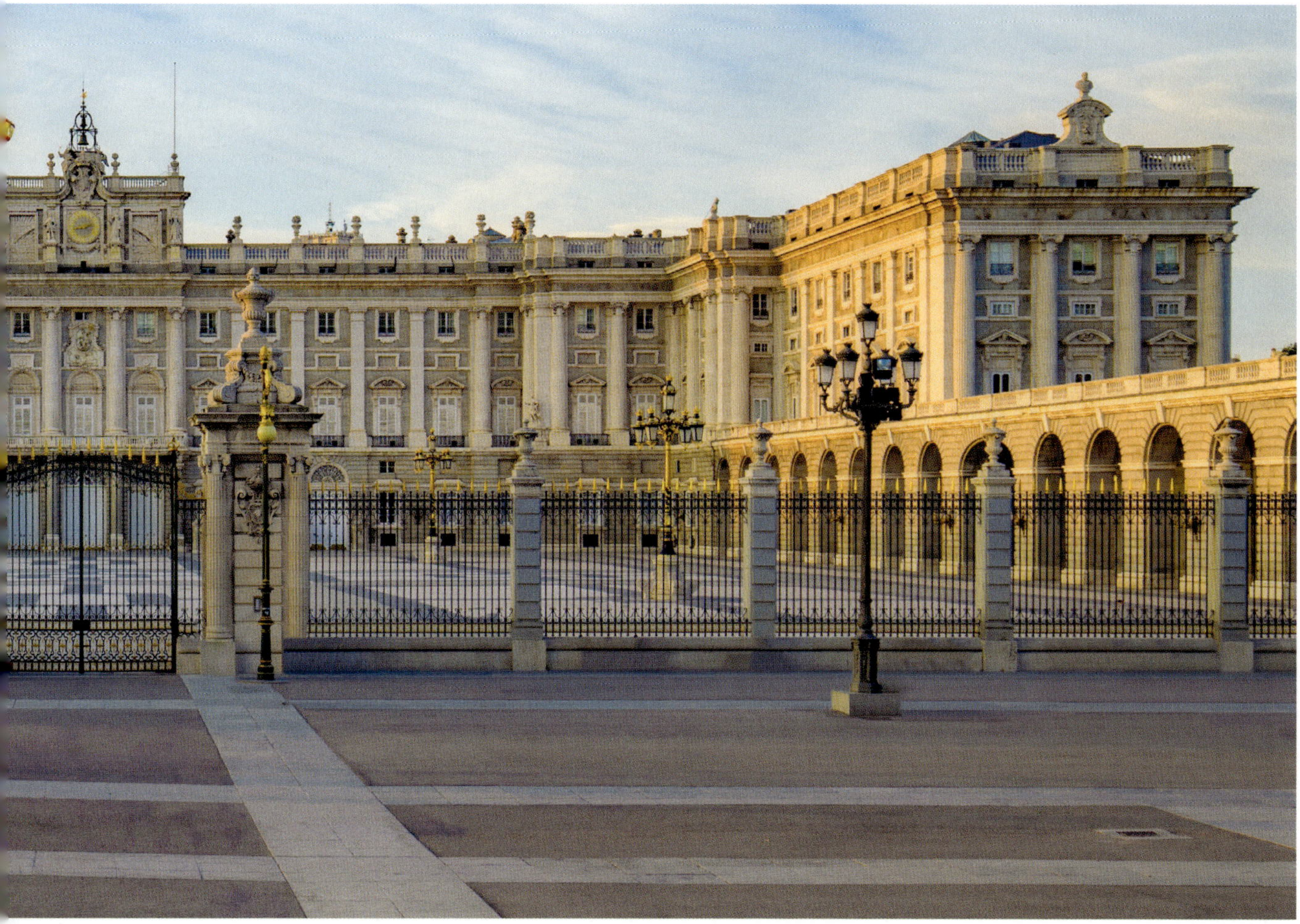

made by the rulers of the Trastámara dynasty and by Charles V to tone down its military-fortress look, the palace in Madrid still didn't look very harmonious and, according to visitors at the time, it was cramped and dark inside because there were few windows covered with wooden panels since glass was hard to find. Perhaps this is why, two centuries later, when a fire broke out on Christmas Eve 1734 and destroyed it, it was not a tragedy for Philip V, the first sovereign of Spain from the Bourbon dynasty, and his wife Elizabetta Farnese (1692–1766), Princess of Parma and Piacenza. The couple had never liked the austere building, which in its (apparently) solid appearance was the symbol of the centuries-old rule of the Habsburg dynasty in Spain. Furthermore, the palace had nothing to do with the splendor of Versailles, where the king, grandson of the Sun King, Louis XIV (1638–1715), was born and spent his youth. The fire, which some believed to be arson, was interpreted as an opportunity provided by fate to turn the page, but not entirely. The same site where the Real Alcázar stood was chosen for the construction of the new Royal Palace: it was necessary to give a sign of the continuity of the monarchy, but at the same time to emphasize the change of dynasty. Philip V expressly requested that the entire structure be built in stone, apart from the wooden doors and windows, in order to prevent

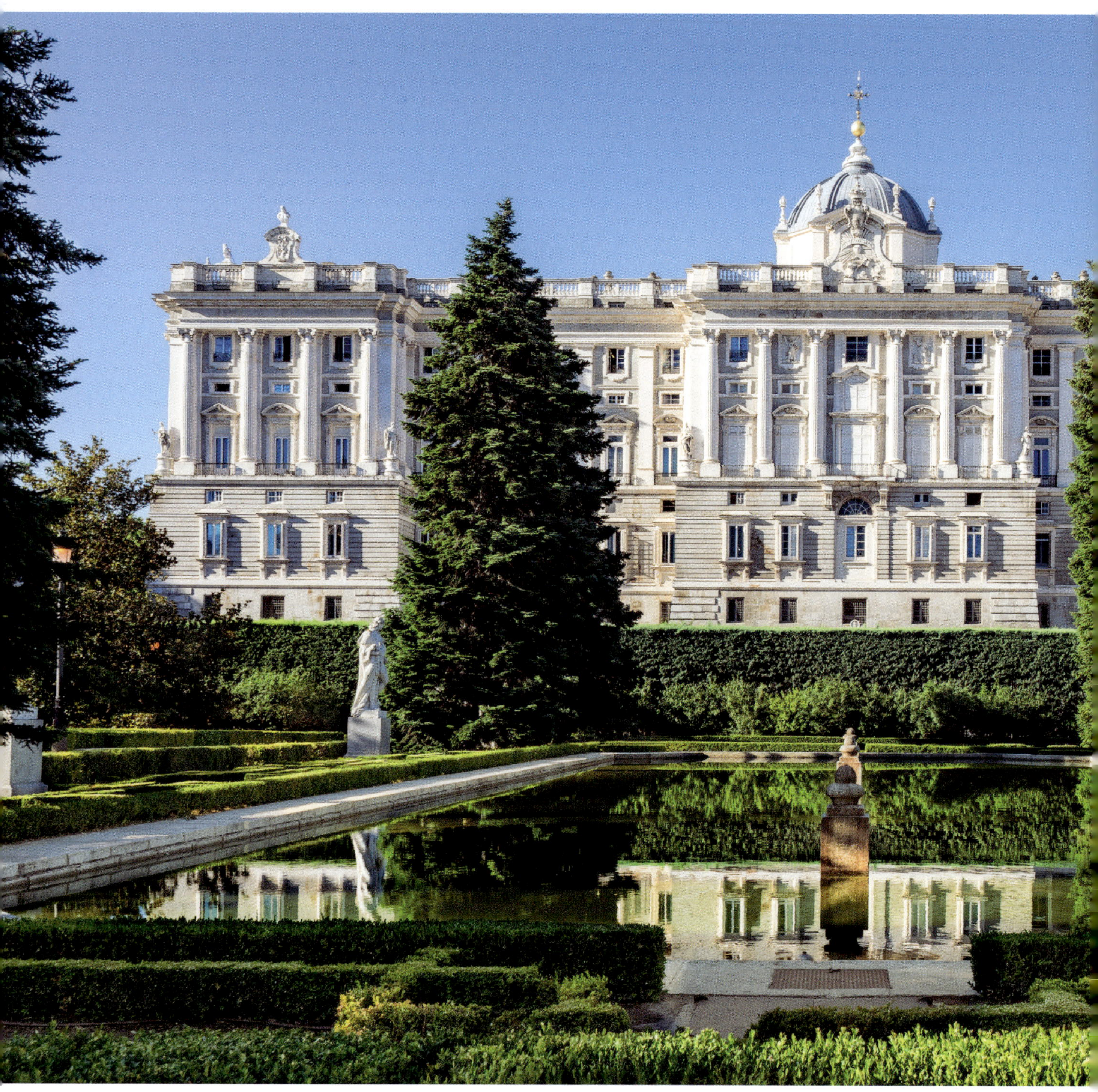

further fires. To build his palace, the sovereign called the greatest architects of the time to Madrid from Italy, preferring them to Spanish architects because Italian Baroque was the most fashionable style in all the courts of Europe. At the beginning of 1735, the first to be hired was Filippo Juvarra from Messina, who was chief architect to Vittorio Amedeo II of Savoy (1666–1732) and the designer behind the Basilica di Superga, the Palazzina of Stupinigi, and the façade of Palazzo Madama in Turin. However, Juvarra managed to build only the model of the palace before he died in January 1736; his work was continued by his pupil Giovanni Battista Sacchetti, who remained at court until 1760. The work was completed by Francesco Sabatini, commissioned by Charles III. It

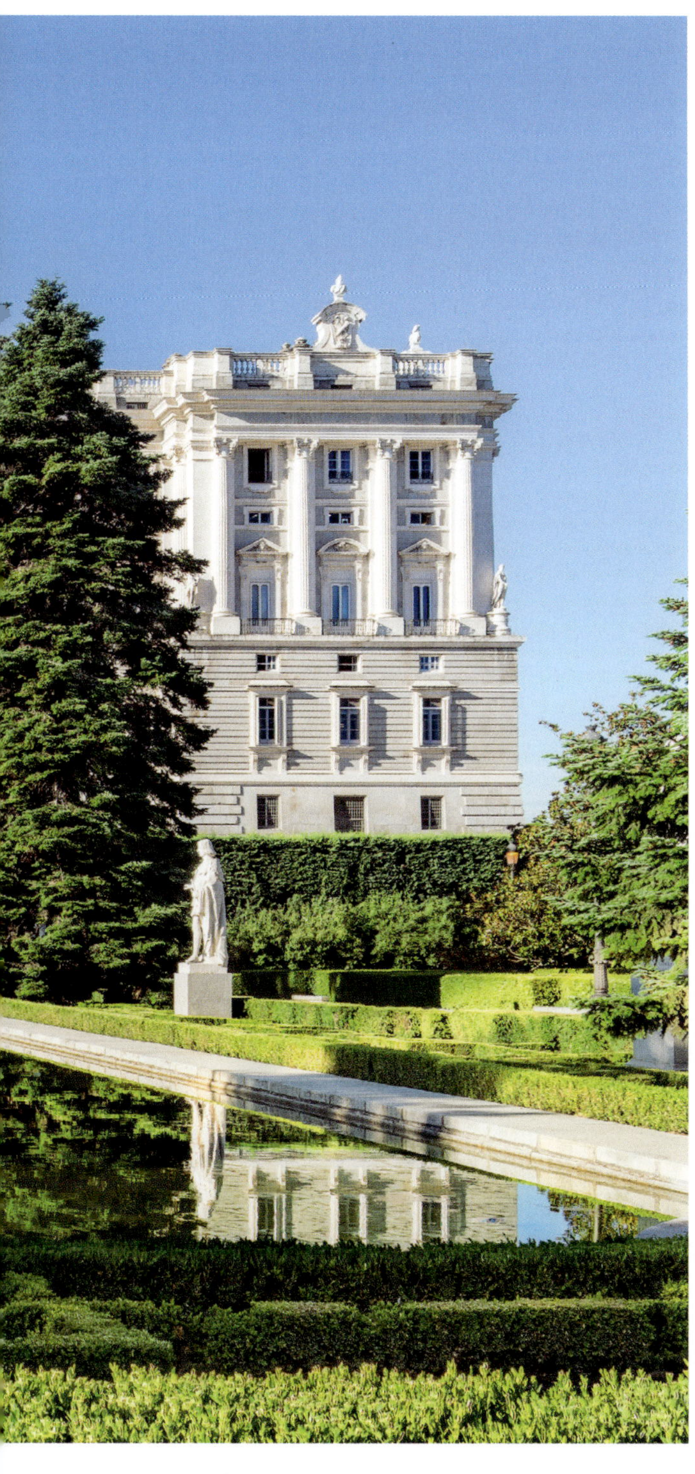

• 58-59: From the Sabatini Gardens, created in 1930 on land previously designated by the Italian architect for the court stables, the view stretches across the north façade of the Royal Palace, crowned by the dome of the Royal Chapel. Their completion, in the years after the Civil War, occurred in significant spatial and ornamental continuity with the Palace, as the Gardens were home to various statues initially designed for the cornice of the building itself.

• 59 center: The Campo del Moro garden was opened to the public in 1983. Over the centuries, the function of this land changed several times until, in the 18th century, various projects were proposed to Philip V to develop it. None of these were carried out until, during the reign of Isabella II, it was used as a playground for the young princes: all that remains of this arrangement are the spectacular straight avenues and the fountains aligned on the central axis, the Shells fountain and the Tritons fountain.

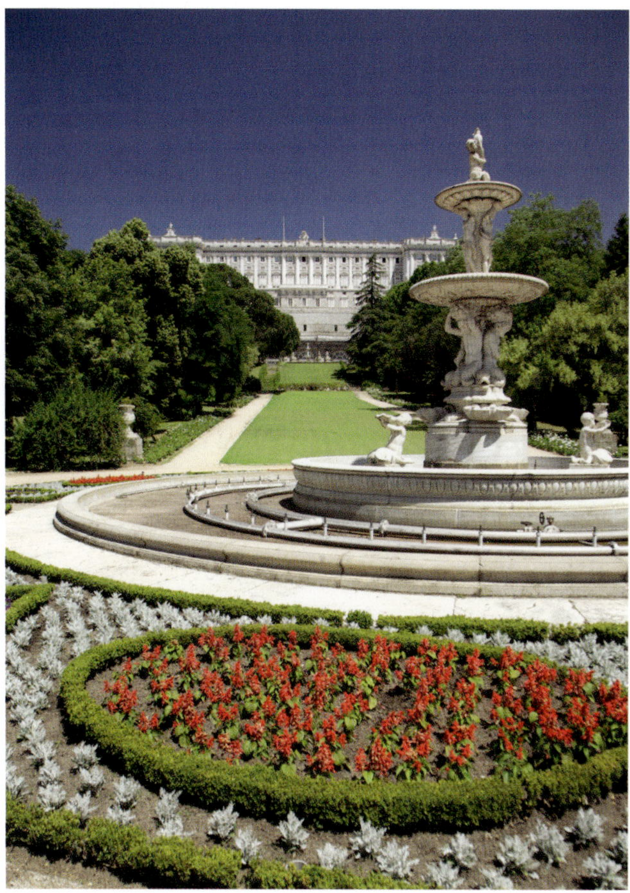

took 26 years: the imposing palace stood in the heart of Madrid; the outer walls, 459 feet on each side, enclosed a square courtyard, which was in turn surrounded by a loggia reminiscent of the Farnese Palace in Rome. Compared to Juvarra's design, Sacchetti had lightened it, while giving greater importance to the terrace on the third floor of the north façade, facing the gardens, and to the dome of the Royal Chapel. As for the interiors, the architect used a profusion of marble and ornamental stones, chosen for their color and rarity, but also to replace wood and prevent devastating fires. Today, the palace is used exclusively for ceremonies, conferences, and official events because the monarchs now live in the Zarzuela Palace on the outskirts of Madrid.

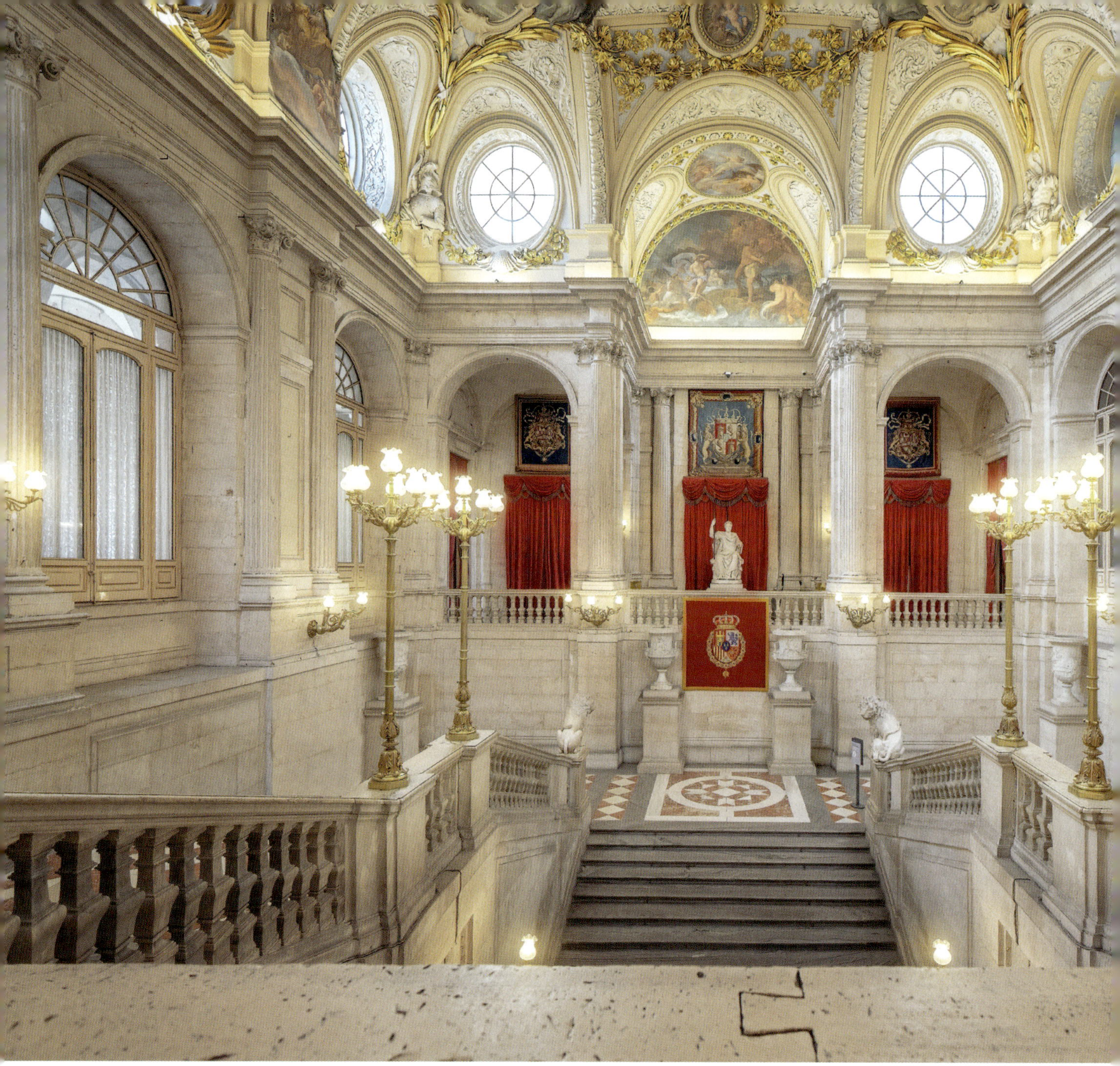

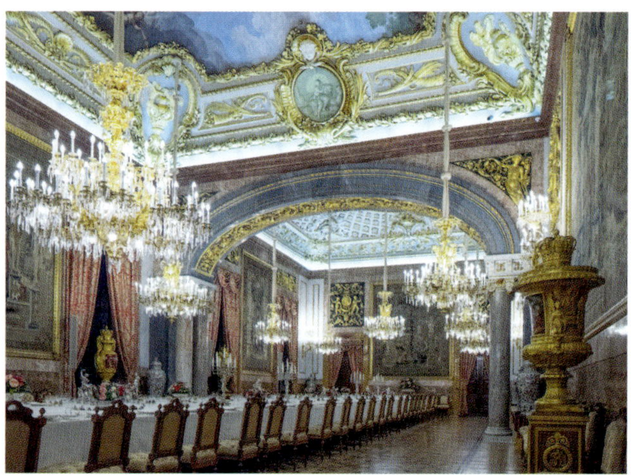

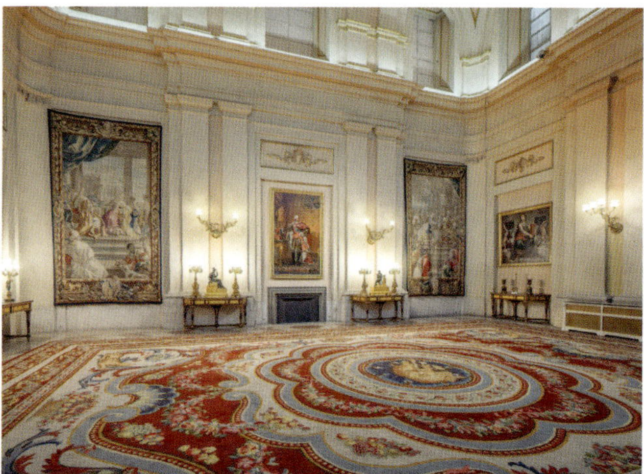

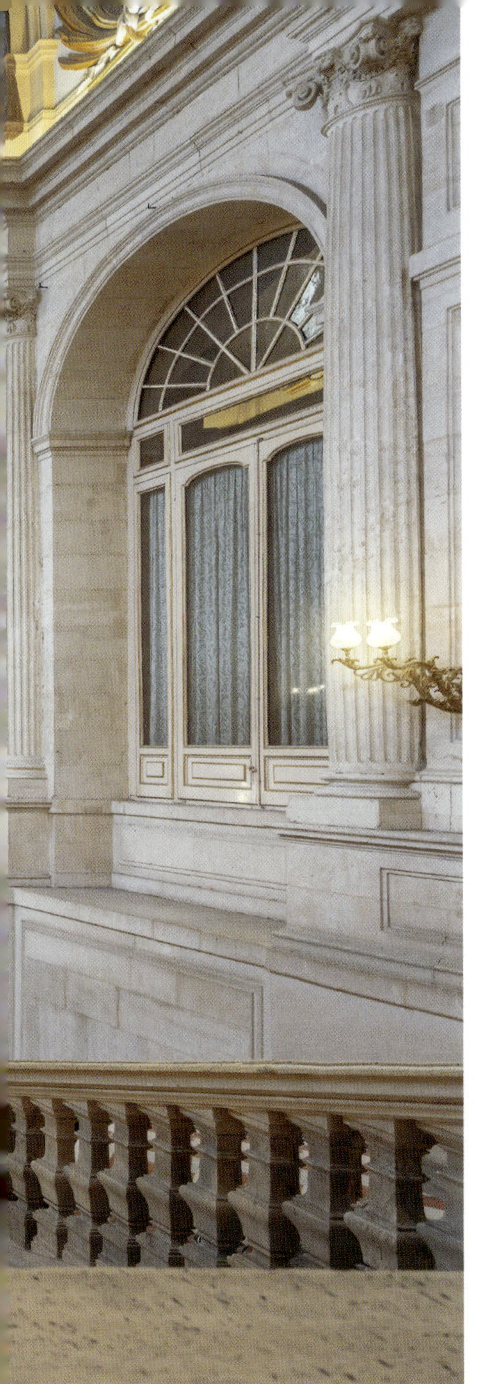

To each king his palace

The interior layout and decorations of the Royal Palace of Madrid have undergone changes over time according to the needs and stylistic preferences of its occupants. For example, Ferdinand VI and Maria Barbara of Braganza had no children, and therefore their apartments were spacious and on a par with those of the most opulent courts in Europe; however, Charles III and Maria Amalia of Saxony had eight children, and the architects had to divide the rooms. As for the decorations, Ferdinand VI, Giovanni Battista Sacchetti, and Corrado Giaquinto worked on the palace, giving it a baroque appearance rich in frills. On the contrary, Charles III showed a more sober and classicist taste, which was interpreted by Francesco Sabatini. The sovereign also commissioned other artists, such as Giambattista Tiepolo for the Throne Room, and Mattia Gasparini. In the 19th century, tastes changed again: Ferdinand VI preferred to see only one painting per wall hung on tapestry or wallpaper, and the masterpieces of his predecessors were transferred to the Prado Museum. The Empire style was imported from France by Joseph Bonaparte, while, during the Restoration period, the taste for Victorian royal residences characterized by interiors filled with furniture became widespread. An example of this is the Gala Dining Room, commissioned in 1879 by Alfonso XII from architect José Segundo de Lema (1823–1891).

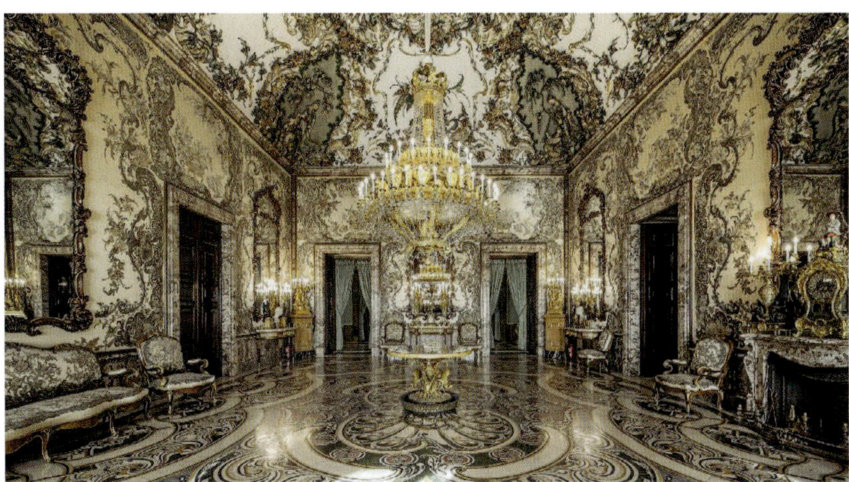

• 60–61: The main staircase of the palace was built in 1789 to a design by Francesco Sabatini for Charles III. Another staircase had originally been built by Sacchetti, but the king did not like it. It was therefore dismantled: Sabatini designed low, wide steps to make it easier to climb, especially for the sedan chairs used by the ladies to reach their apartments. Once you reach the large hallway of the main floor from the central staircase, you have an extraordinary view of the entire space.

• 60 left bottom: The Gala Dining Room, which was also used for balls, is surprising for its length. It is the result of the union of three separate rooms (once part of the Queen's Apartments) during the reign of Charles III and his successors. It was Alfonso XII who wanted to unite all the rooms to create a hall for lunches, dinners, and balls that could accommodate more than a hundred guests. The result was astonishing: the ceilings of the three different rooms feature 17th-century decoration, while the walls, the bronze ornaments, the Sèvres porcelain, the columns, and the chandeliers are indicative of the sovereign's preference for the French style.

• 60 right bottom: The Hall of the Halberdiers was designed by Sacchetti to host balls and parties, which explains the galleries at the height of the windows for musicians. When Charles III assigned it to the Guards, Sabatini decorated it in a sober manner, removing the ornaments planned by his predecessor. The richness of the room is nevertheless provided by the fresco by Tiepolo, Venus asking Vulcan for weapons for Aeneas, on the ceiling.

• 61 center: The Gasparini Room is a masterpiece of late Baroque taste: the artist to whom it is dedicated took care of every detail, from the inlaid marble floor to the Chinese-inspired plant decorations, the stucco vault, the silk wall coverings, and the fine wood furniture made by German cabinetmakers.

Alhambra of Granada

1237
The noble Muhammad ibn Nasr (1194–1273), founder of the Nasrid dynasty under the name Muhammad I, conquered Granada and made it the capital of his sultanate.

1238
Muhammad I began construction of the Alhambra. The 9th-century Alcazaba was surrounded by a new circle of walls and became the military zone of the palace.

1273–1302
Under Muhammad II, the Alcazaba was enlarged and construction of the Generalife began.

1314–1325
During the reign of Ismail I, the Mexuar Palace is built, designed to house audiences and administer justice. The sultan began construction of the Palace of Comares and expanded the Generalife.

1354–1391
With Muhammad V (1338–1391), son of Yusuf I, Nasrid architecture reached the height of its splendor with the Palace of the Lions.

1492
On January 2, the last sultan of Granada, Boabdil, officially surrendered his kingdom to the Catholic monarchs Ferdinand of Aragon and of Castile.

1527
Emperor Charles V, grandson of Ferdinand and Isabella, demolished parts of the Nasrid palace. In their place, the architect Pedro Machuca, a pupil of Michelangelo, began the construction of a large Italian-style building with a circular courtyard that would not be completed until the 20th century.

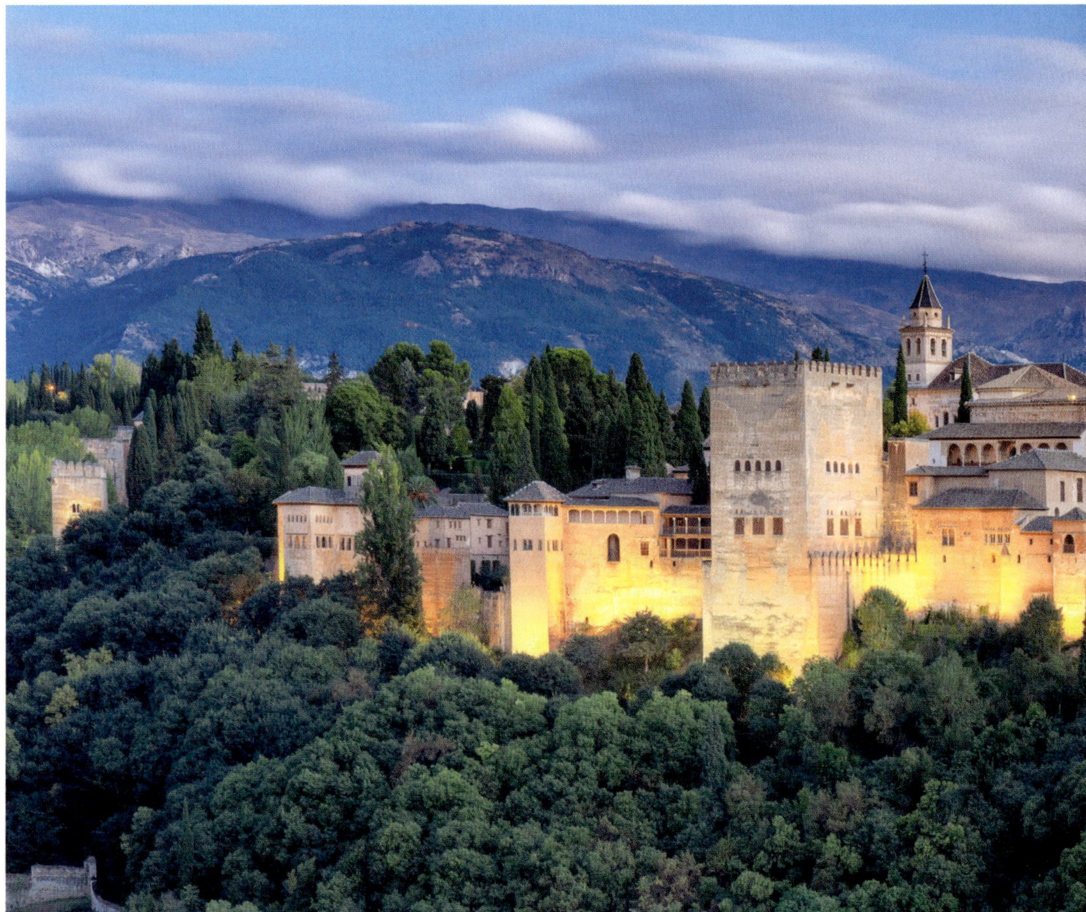

In the 10th century, the Berbers who ruled the Taifa (independent kingdom) of Granada did not choose the Sabika Hill at random to build a fortified citadel (al-Qaṣbah, in Spanish Alcázaba): from its heights, it dominates Granada and the valley of the Darro River. This was the first nucleus of the Alhambra, the magnificent city-palace built by the Nasrids between the 13th and 14th centuries, whose name derives from the Arabic Al-Qalah al-Hamra, the Red Fortress, perhaps because of the reddish hue of its severe ramparts at sunset—or perhaps because, as one of the wisest men in Granada, the poet and vizier Ibn al-Khatib (1313–1375) said, during its construction the building sites were active even at night, when work continued feverishly by torchlight, casting red glows on the sun-dried bricks of the outer walls. Although the origin of the name is uncertain, we know for sure that the first stone was laid in 1238 by the order of Muhammad I, founder of the Nasrid dynasty and founder of the Kingdom, or Sultanate, of Granada. The Muslim prince wanted a palace that would be both a private residence and a place from which to exercise his power and govern his domain. The successors of Muhammad

• 62-63: View of the entire Alhambra complex from the Albaicín, the old Arab quarter of Granada located on the hill opposite the Alhambra. On the right is the terrace of the Torres Bermejas ("vermilion towers"); in the center is the Alcázaba dominated by the Towers de la Vela and de Homage; around the imposing Comares tower are the Nasrid palaces and, behind them, the imposing Palace of Charles V.

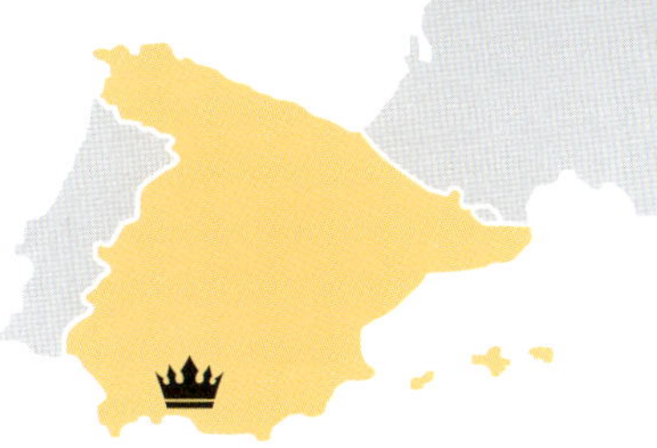

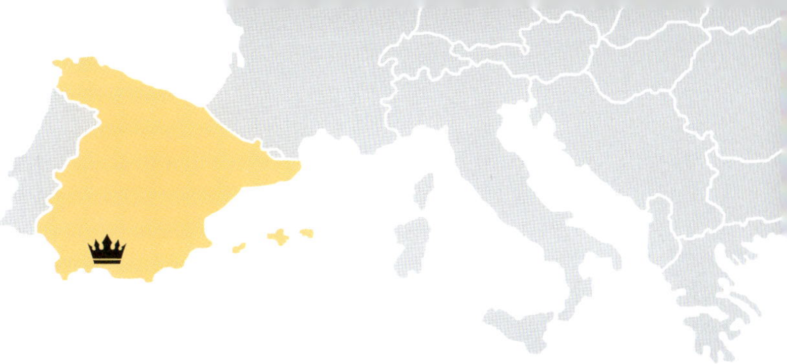

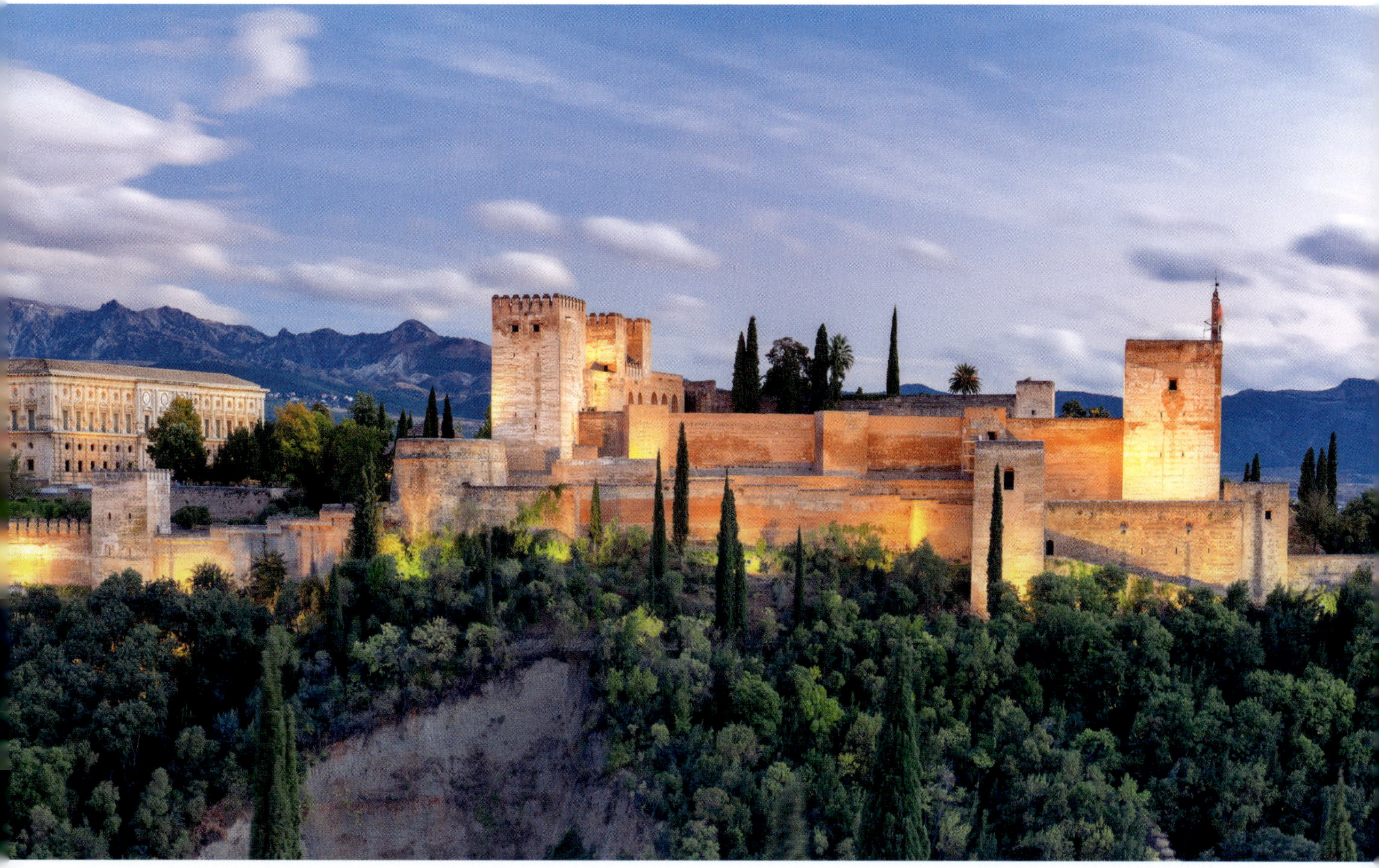

I added several elements of great artistic value to the palace, making it a marvelous center of beauty and harmony that inspired the Arab poets of the Nasrid era to compare it to a shining diadem. The palace complex was divided into three parts. On the western tip of the Sabika Hill stood the Alcázaba fortress, a veritable fortress with armories and provision stores and the quarters of the soldiers responsible for the sultan's security: its presence was tangible proof of a world that feared not only external enemies but also internal ones.

Outside the military area, but still within the walls, was the actual palace, with buildings constructed in several phases by the sultans: it seems that before part of the complex was demolished in the 16th century to make way for the enormous Renaissance palace of Charles V, there were as many as seven. Finally, inside the walls, was a small medina with the homes of courtiers and servants, shops, workshops, a mosque, and a cemetery. As for the heart of the Alhambra, the palace, it is not easy to distinguish what exactly belongs to each of the sultans who succeeded to the throne of Granada, among the clusters of palaces, terraces, gardens, courtyards, and covered passageways connected to each other. However, it is known that it was the founder of the dynasty, Muhammad I, who took care to bring water to the complex, where there were no springs, in order to irrigate the vegetable gardens and orchards and to supply the buildings, fountains, pools, and channels

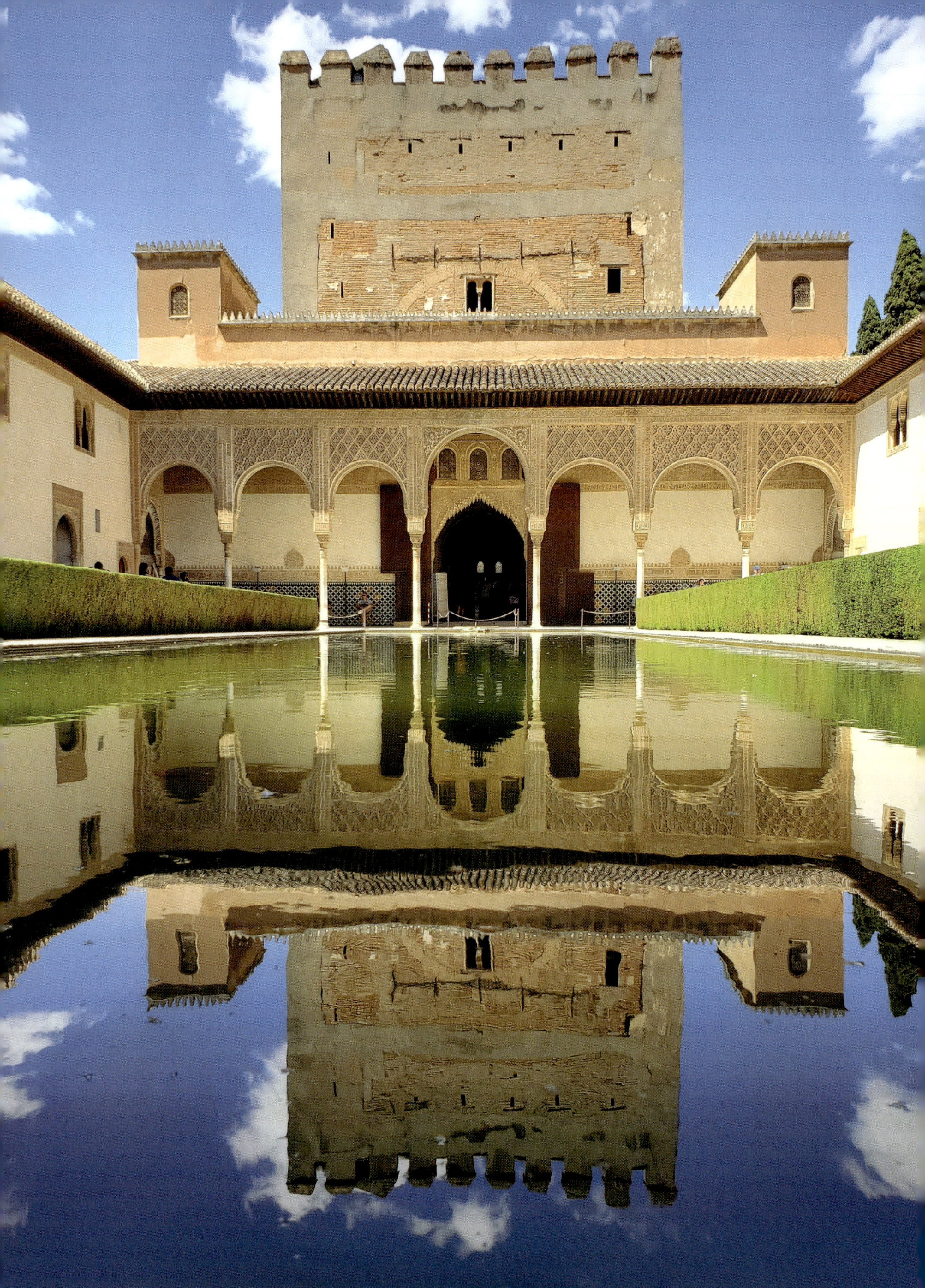

that divided the courtyard gardens into four, symbolizing the Islamic paradise.

It is also known that two rulers who lived in the 14th century, Yusuf I and his son Muhammad V, were responsible for the most beautiful parts of the Alhambra. The former had the Throne Room or Hall of Ambassadors built, a magnificent room carved out of the Comares Tower and overlooking the Patio de los Arrayanes (Patio of the Myrtles), where every inch of space is covered with incredible decorations: floral arabesques, endlessly repeating geometric patterns, and stucco engraved with star motifs. There is also a cedar wood ceiling which, due to its symbolic representation of the universe, is considered one of the greatest masterpieces of Moorish art. We owe the Patio de los Leones to Muhammad V. It is a rectangular open space surrounded by a portico around which were arranged the private apartments of the sultan and his harem—i.e., the rooms shared with his three wives (his fourth wife, who was his favorite, lived separately from the others, probably in the Tower of the Captive).

With the Reconquista, the fall of the fortress in 1492, and the expulsion of the last sultan, Boabdil, the Castilian monarchs, enchanted by the beauty of the complex, decided not to raze it to the ground but to make it their residence during their stays in Granada. When Isabella died on December 18, 1504, she was in the Alhambra. Her tomb and that of her husband Ferdinand, who died 12 years later, are housed in the crypt of the Royal Chapel of Granada, the city that symbolizes the Reconquista. In the 16th century, however, an entire section was demolished to make way for the enormous Italian-style Renaissance palace of Emperor Charles V, who entrusted the design to a Spanish pupil of Michelangelo, Pedro Machuca. However, the emperor's residence remained unfinished, and the entire Andalusian palace fell into a state of neglect that lasted until the 19th century, when it was finally rediscovered thanks to the publication in 1832 of the book "Tales of the Alhambra" by the New York writer, journalist, and traveler Washington Irving (1783–1859).

• 64: The Patio de los Arrayanes, overlooked by the Comares Palace, is the largest courtyard in the Alhambra. It was designed by Nasrid architects to take advantage of the open space during the summer months. The delicate plasterwork provided protection from the sun while allowing air to pass through. Water flows silently into a rectangular pool, reflecting the myrtle hedges, arrayanes, and architecture like a mirror. All around are doors leading to the private quarters of the sultans' wives and concubines.

• 65 top: The stunning muqarnas stucco ceiling in the Sala de las dos Hermanas, or Hall of the Two Sisters (a room in the Palacio de los Leones): it is said that this may have been the room reserved for the sultans' favorites. The Muqarnas are a decorative motif in the form of niches or honeycomb cells, found throughout Islamic architecture. They are reminiscent of the stalactites in the cave where Muhammad received inspiration for the Koran from the archangel Gabriel.

• 65 bottom: The Torre de las Damas. The pool and the loggia are all that remains of the Partal Palace, built at the behest of Sultan Muhammad III near the Palace of the Lions between 1302 and 1309: it is therefore the oldest palace still standing in the Alhambra.

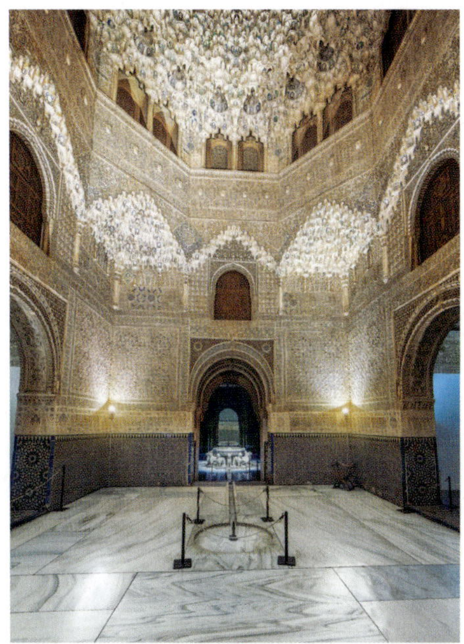

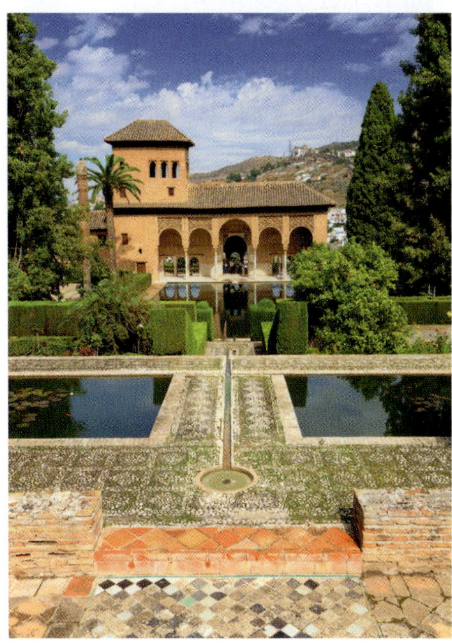

• 66-67: The magnificent courtyard of the Palacio de los Leones measures 115 feet long by 66 feet wide and is surrounded by a gallery supported by 124 slender, finely decorated white marble columns. What makes it a masterpiece, in addition to its perfect proportions and the beauty of the Fountain of the Lions, is the refinement of the ornamental decorations similar to lace, among arabesques and calligraphic inscriptions of verses by Ibn Zamrak. The water flowing from the fountain is a fundamental element: from here, channels carried it throughout the palace to cool the rooms. The 12 lions symbolize the signs of the zodiac and the months of the year.

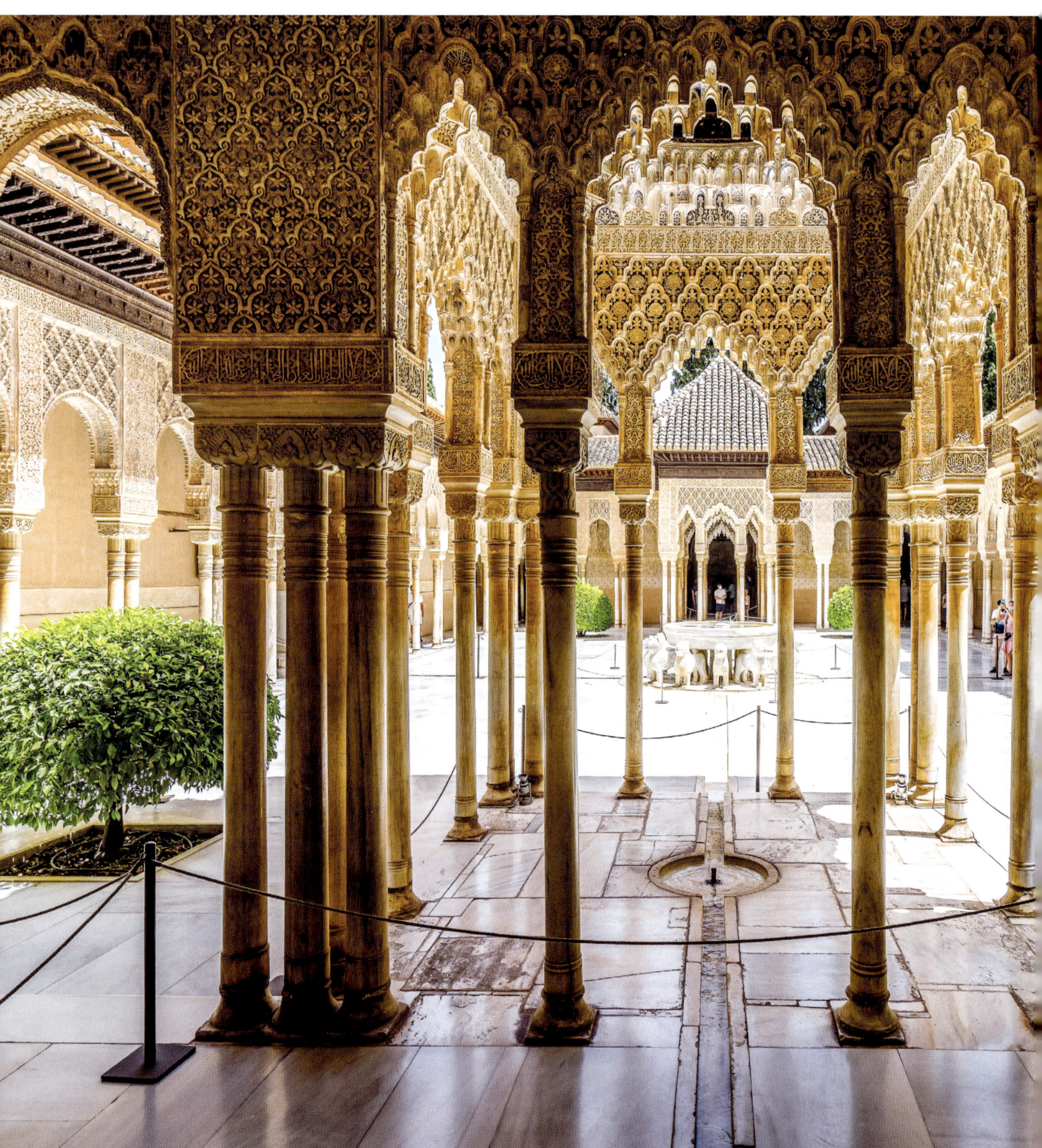

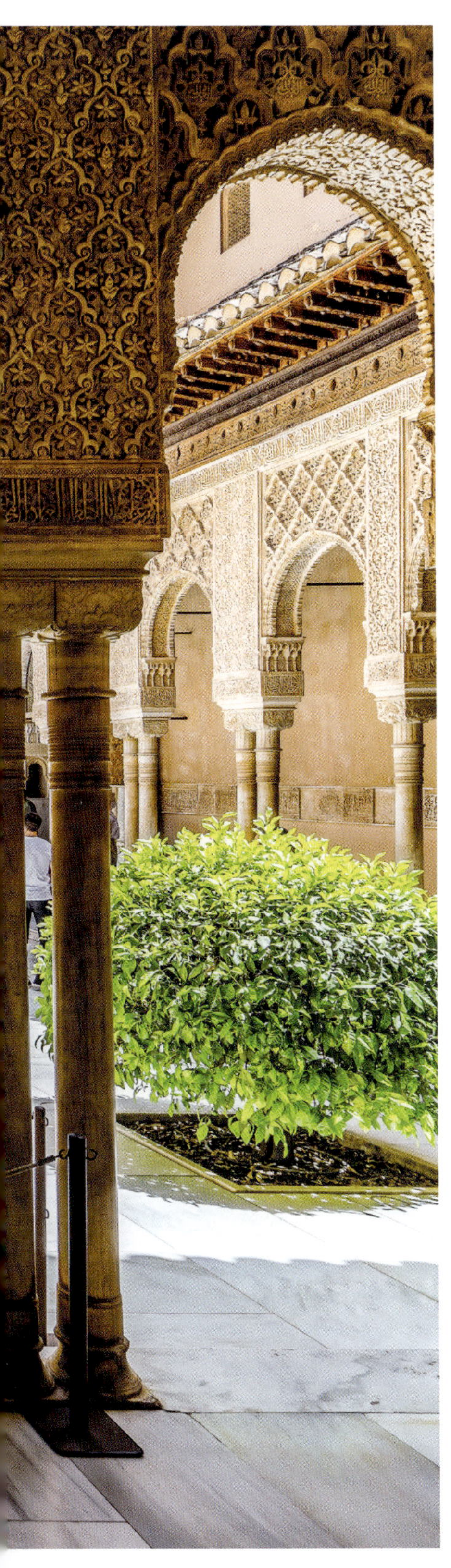

Words in stone

Ibn Zamrak was an Arab-Andalusian poet who lived at the court of Granada during the reign of Muhammad V, of whom he was private secretary and later vizier. Several calligraphic inscriptions visible in the Alhambra reproduce his verses. On the dodecagonal basin of the Fountain of the Lions, for example, there is a qasida ("poem") that provides some interesting information. The first verse invokes Allah's blessing on Muhammad V, who commissioned the work between 1370 and 1390. Other verses provide information, through a beautiful poetic image, about a technical detail: "Do you not see how the water overflows beyond the edges and how the pipes hide it in an instant? In the same way, a lover whose eyelids are swollen with tears, struggles to hold them back for fear of being observed." From the fountain, water gushes from the mouths of 12 stone lions, feeding four channels carved into the white marble that intersect at this point, dividing the courtyard into four sections in a symbolic representation of the Koranic Paradise.

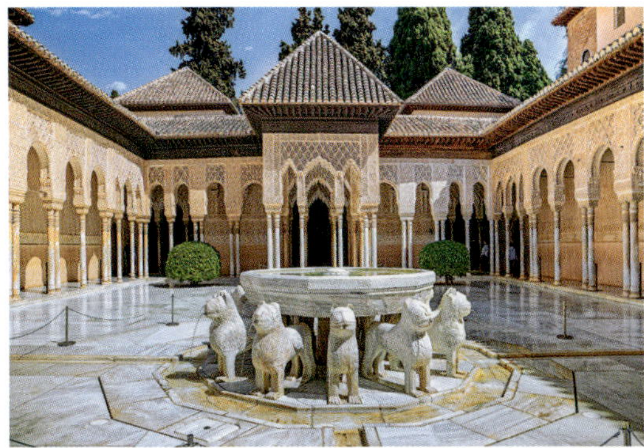

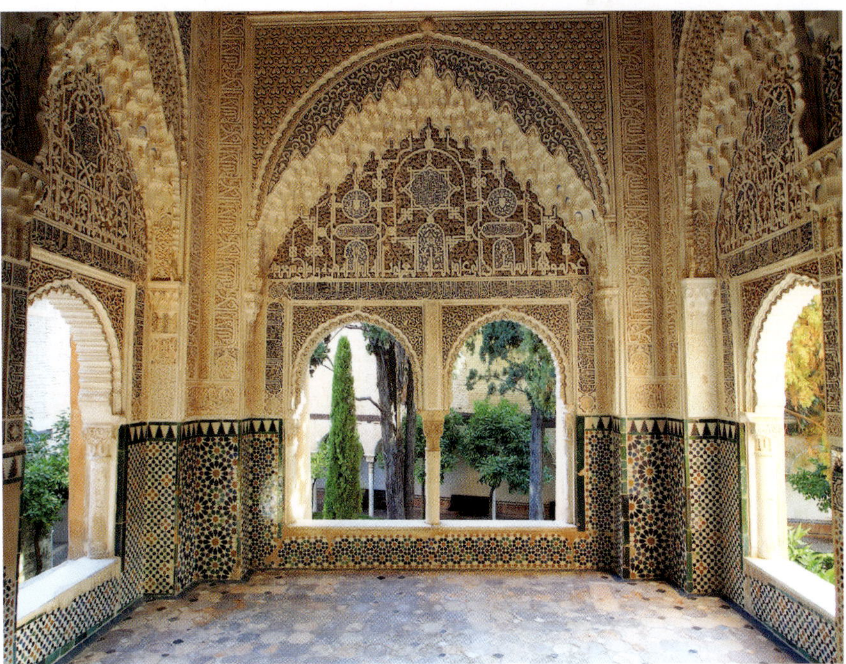

• 67 bottom: A corner of the Alhambra decorated with a mosaic or alicatados. The aliceres, small glazed tiles, were fixed together with white stucco to bring out the beautiful colors of the final mosaic.

Palace of Versailles

1607
The future King Louis XIII reached the woods around the village of Versailles during a hunting trip for the first time.

1623–1631
Louis XIII had a hunting lodge built in Versailles. In the following years, the property was enlarged, and in 1631 the hunting lodge was replaced by a small castle.

1651
Louis XIV's frequent visits to Versailles began with a hunting party.

1654–1666
Louis Le Vau was appointed chief architect. The work on enlarging Louis XIII's old castle began in 1661.

1657
Gardener and landscaper André le Nôtre was appointed controller general of buildings, arts, and manufacturing in France.

1681
The design and construction of the Palace continued under the direction of Jules-Hardouin Mansart.

1682–1710
The Sun King moved the court from Paris to the Palace of Versailles, where the future Louis XV was born in 1710.

1715–1722
With the death of Louis XIV, the court abandoned Versailles, and the Palace entered a period of neglect that ended in 1722 with the return of Louis XV, who took it upon himself to complete his great-grandfather's work. He commissioned the construction of the Petit Trianon and the Opéra.

1774
On May 10, 1774, Louis XV died in Versailles and his grandson Louis XVI ascended the throne. The Hameau de la Reine was commissioned for the queen, a sort of small rural village not far from the Petit Trianon.

1789–1793
The revolution of 1789 led to the arrest of the sovereigns. The palace was abandoned and emptied of its treasures.

1837
King Louis Philippe I decided to transform the Palace of Versailles into the Museum of the Glories of France.

The name "Versailles" refers to the activities of farmers, as it derives from the Latin verb vertor, "to turn the earth." And this was Versailles at the beginning of the 17th century, a small farming village 15.5 miles from Paris, surrounded by farmland and a wooded area where Henry IV went hunting for deer. Louis XIII was only six years old in 1607 when he arrived at Versailles to hunt with falcons. Between hunts, the young king fell in love with the place and decided to make it a game reserve. Tired of having to return to the Louvre palace in Paris or Saint-Germain-en-Laye to spend the night, in 1623, after purchasing some land, the king decided to commission the construction of a hunting lodge on the site of the future palace. In 1632, however, the modest pavilion was demolished to make way for a building in red brick, white stone, and slate consisting of a main central body flanked by two lower wings and small detached pavilions: the first nucleus of the future palace. Following the death of Louis XIII in 1643, the palace of Versailles was forgotten: the new king, Louis XIV, was only a child, and France would be plagued by foreign wars and internal struggles for several years. However, 1661 proved to be a favorable year for a change of course, and the king's dream of owning a residence that would exemplify his power began to take shape. For a time, he was content with his father's palace, having just the park landscaped by André Le Nôtre. The major works began in 1666 when the king's mind conceived the ingenious plan that would lead him to subjugate the court, depriving it of its freedom of action and forcing it to live in Versailles, far from Paris, thus laying the foundations for absolute monarchy. The first court architect to make changes to the old palace was Louis Le Vau, the inventor of French Baroque classicism, which took the name "Louis XIV style." In Versailles, he had a first Orangery built in 1663, which was then rebuilt in 1684 by his colleague Jules Hardouin-Mansart, two new wings for the kitchens and stables, the Porcelain Trianon (a pavilion covered with blue and white majolica in the Delft style), and the Ambassadors' Staircase. Above all, however, he devoted himself to the Enveloppe (the "envelope"), a large building with its façade facing the gardens, which, following their perimeter, incorporated the old castle of Louis XIII facing Paris on either side. In 1670, the architect died, leaving the task of continuing the work and delivering future projects to François d'Orbay. In 1674, the palace designed by Le Vau was completed. Now it was necessary to bring the interiors up to the same standard as the exteriors, taking care of every little detail, and for this, generations of painters, plasterers, cabinetmakers, and glassmakers were employed. Among them, the name of Charles Le Brun stands out.

• 68–69: The façade of the palace facing Paris corresponds to that of the castle built by Louis XIII between 1631 and 1634 on the site of the former hunting lodge. Louis XIV never demolished his father's castle, but instead asked his architects to give it a monumental appearance. The Marble Court is the oldest part of the Palace of Versailles. Louis XIV kept the building constructed by his father with its red bricks and slate roofs; but between 1661 and 1682, the three façades were redesigned and embellished. Before the construction of the Opera House several years later, concerts featuring works by his favorite musician (and dancer) Jean-Baptiste Lully were held in the Marble Court.

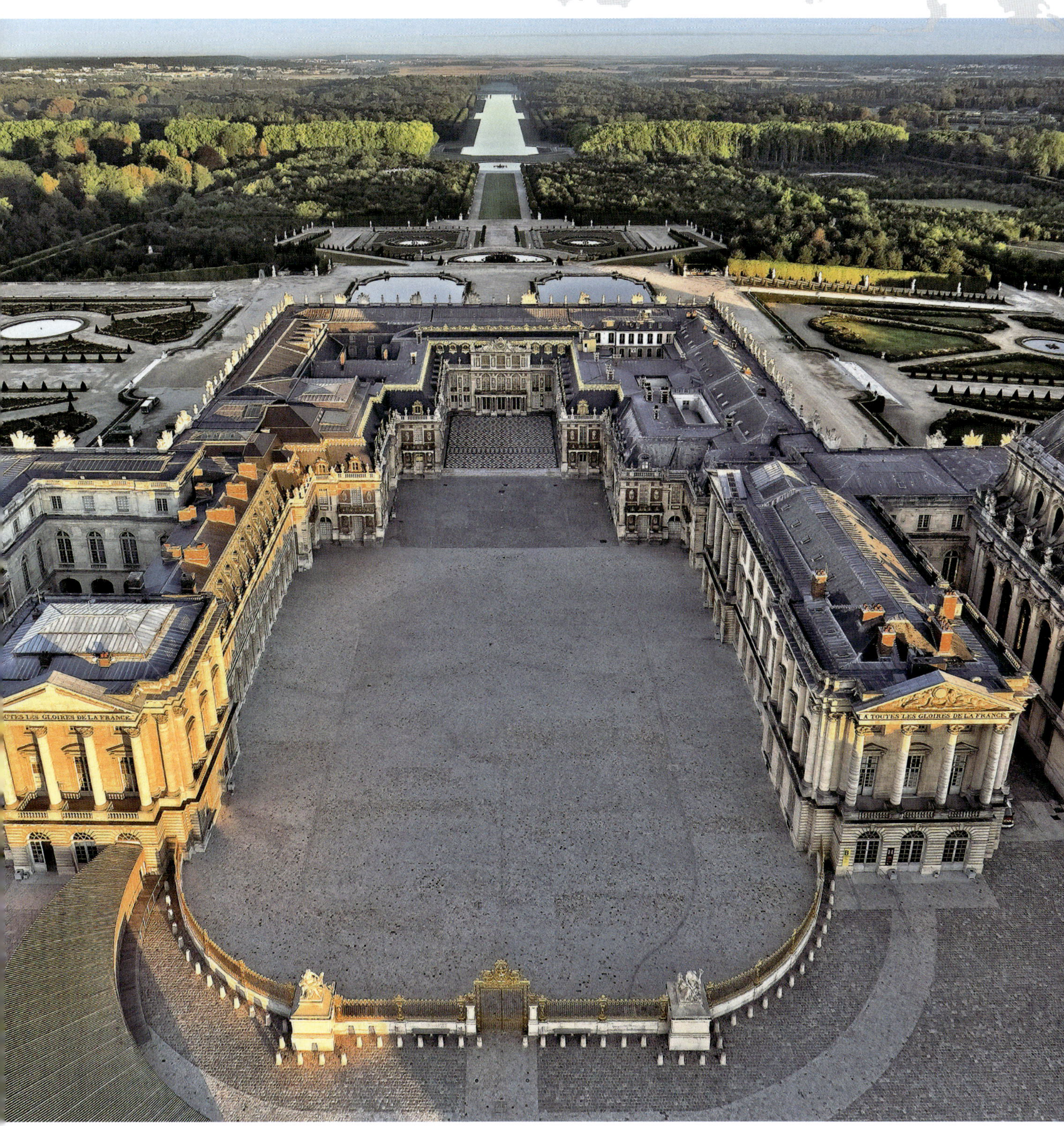

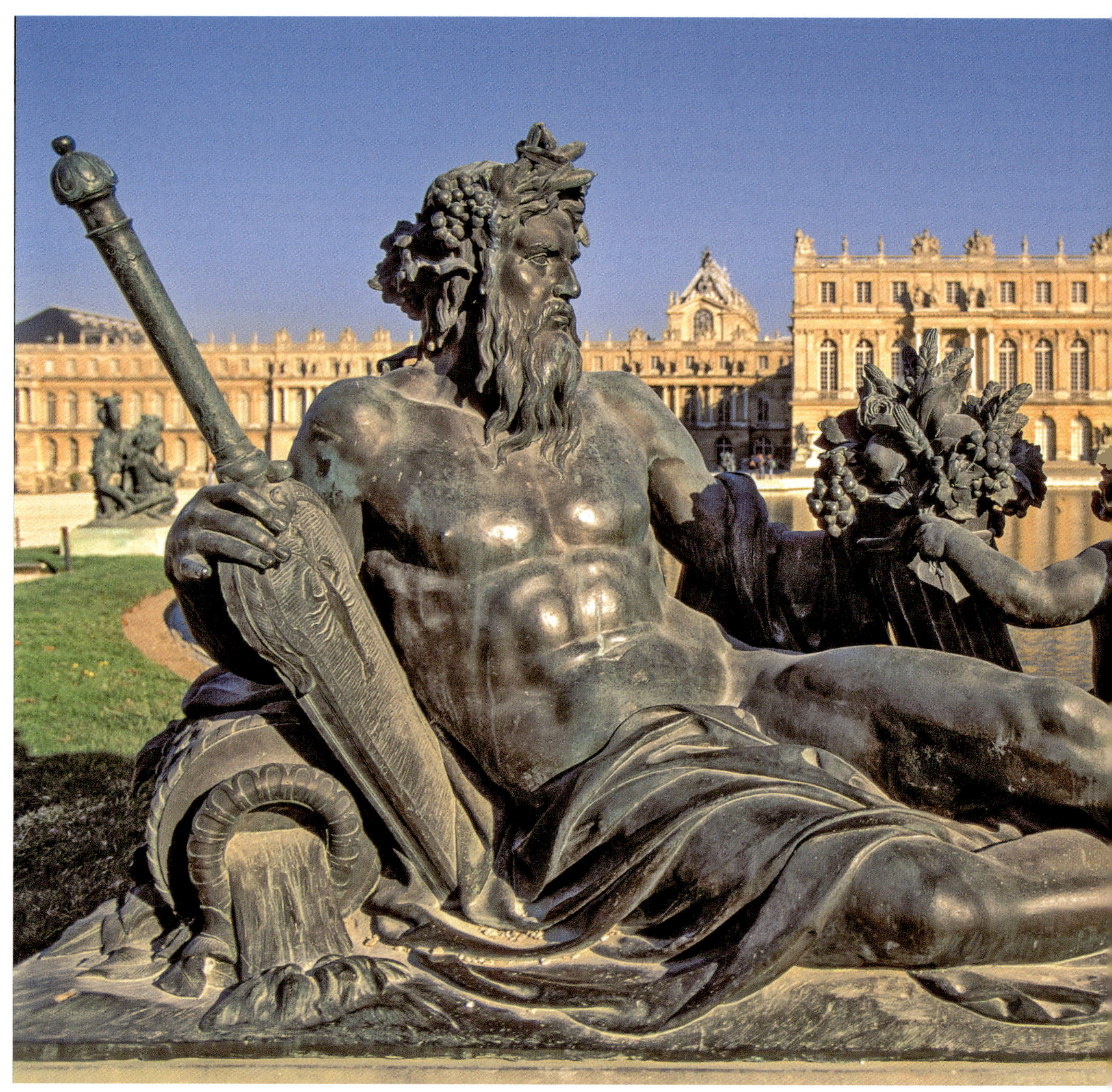

Jules Hardouin-Mansart, an ambitious man and excellent courtier, was ultimately responsible, among other things, for the construction of the Grand Trianon, the pavilion where Louis XIV used to rest after long days spent in the Palace, the Hall of Mirrors, and finally the fifth version of the Royal Chapel. With the death of the Sun King, the palace of Versailles emptied. The valets, servants, ministers, ladies, and courtiers who had crowded the corridors during the king's illness disappeared. All that remained were the miasmas caused by the poor hygiene of the multitude of people who had lived there from 1682. Nothing remained of its former glory. Only on special occasions were the doors reopened: for example, in 1717, Tsar Peter I of Russia stayed at the palace. Versailles was later inhabited again and returned to being the center of the French monarchy from 1722 to 1789, when it all came to an end. The last royal residents were Louis XVI and Archduchess Marie Antoinette of Habsburg-Lorraine. During the short period when they lived in Versailles, the queen ordered the construction of a sort of farm in the

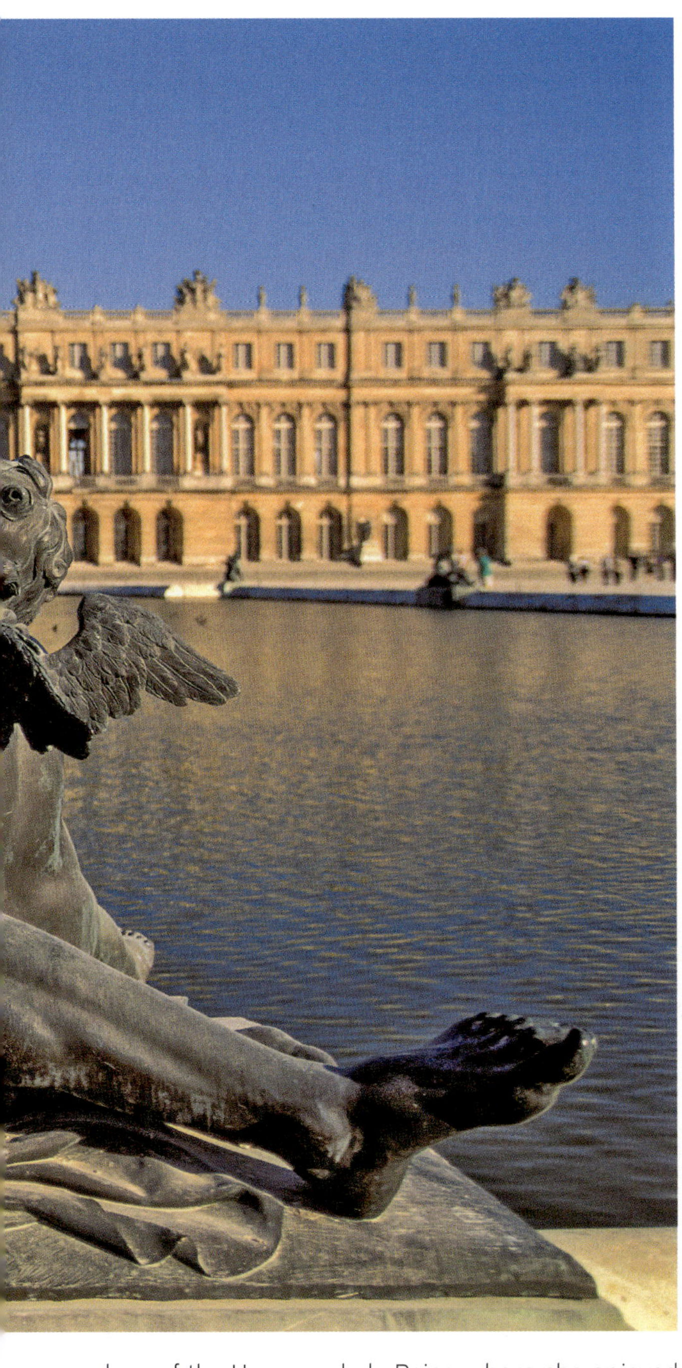

• 70-71: The façade of the Palace of Versailles facing the gardens was designed by Le Vau between 1678 and 1684. Jules Hardouin-Mansart then took over, closing Le Vau's long porticoed terrace, which was considered impractical due to its exposure to the elements, and creating the Hall of Mirrors.

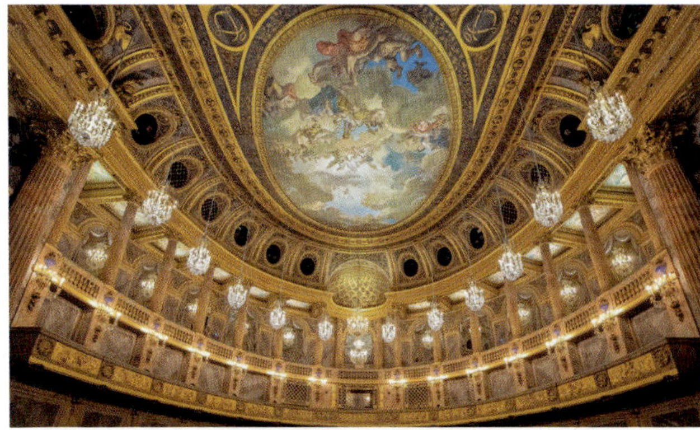

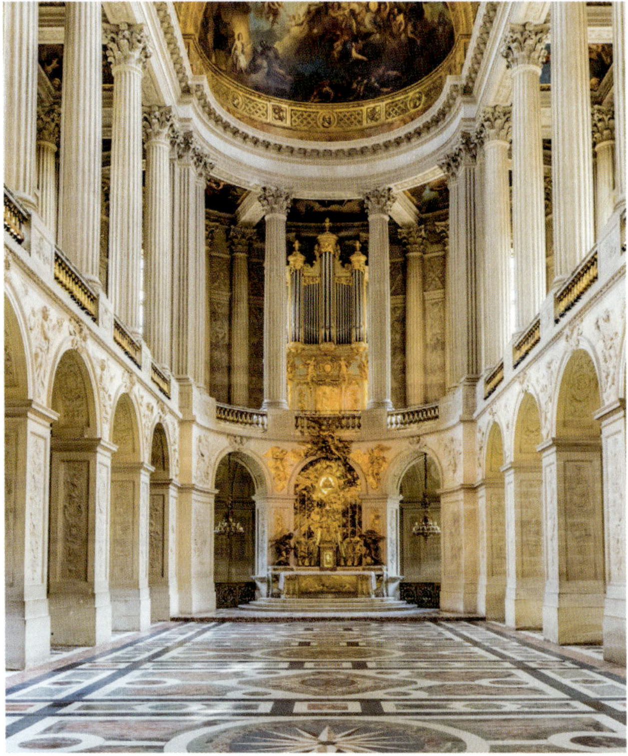

meadows of the Hameau de la Reine, where she enjoyed a peaceful country life among roses to cultivate and animals to feed. Yet only a few years remained before the decline and end of the Ancien Régime. With the forced return of Louis XVI and his family to Paris, the gates of Versailles were closed, at least to the royal family. The palace was closed and in 1792 the National Convention, the executive and legislative assembly in power during the Revolution, ordered all the paintings and sculptures in the palace to be transferred to the Louvre, which meanwhile had been

• 71 top: The Opera Royale in Versailles has an oval layout. The orchestra floor was mobile and could be raised to the level of the auditorium, doubling its size: the theater was also used for parties, as a ballroom, and even for banquets. The bas-reliefs decorating the interior were created by Augustin Pajou, while Louis Durameau painted Apollo crowning the arts on the ceiling.

• 71 bottom: Dedicated to St. Louis IX of France, patron saint of the French branch of the Bourbons and venerated by the king himself, the fifth Royal Chapel was the largest ever built at Versailles and was also the only building whose high vaults broke the regular horizontality of the palace roofs, so much so that the Duke of Saint-Simon described it as an "enormously large catafalque." The interior, with three naves, is dominated by a women's gallery with Corinthian columns. On the steps leading to the altar stands the crowned monogram "L," alluding to both Saint Louis and the sovereign.

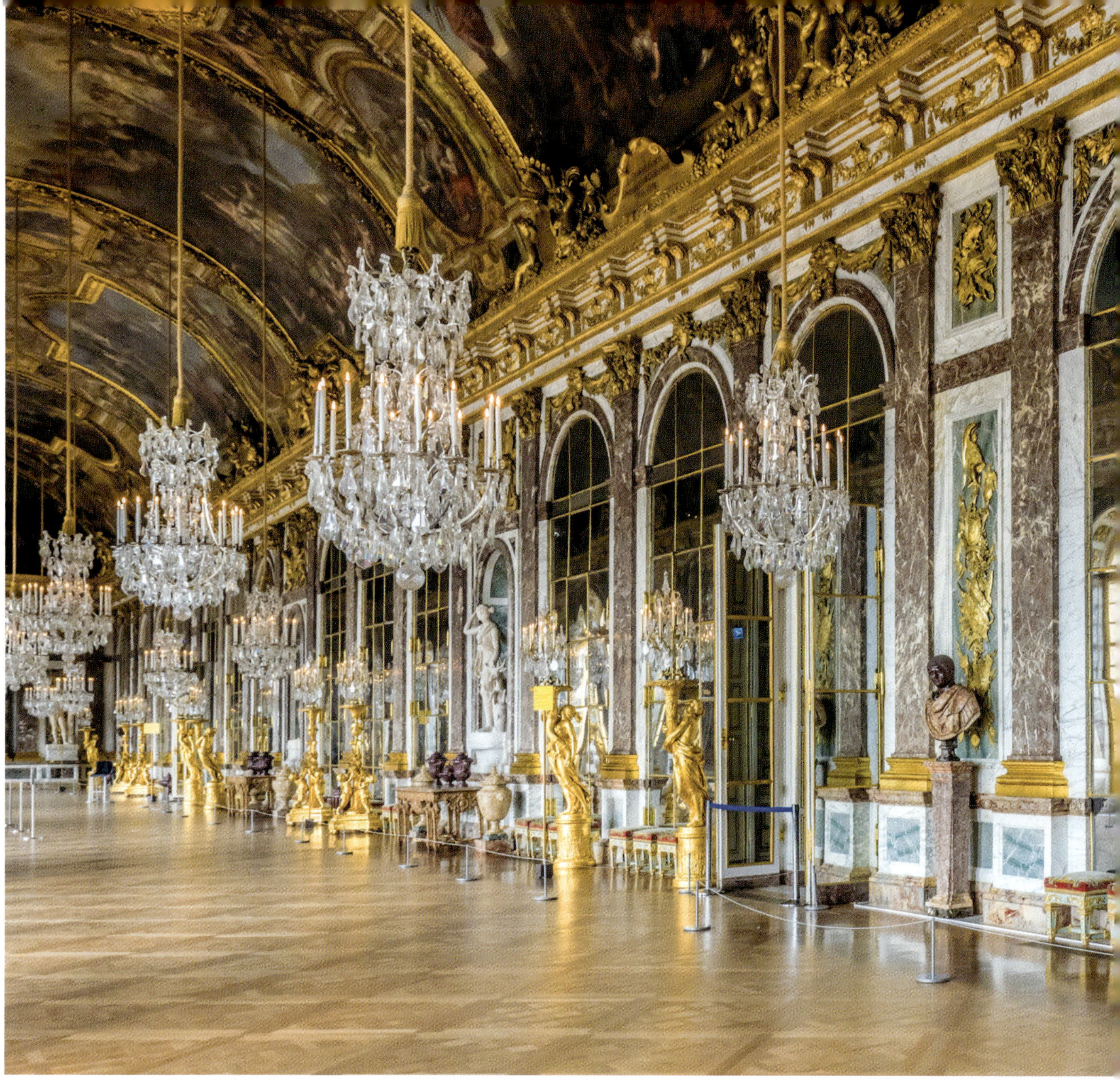

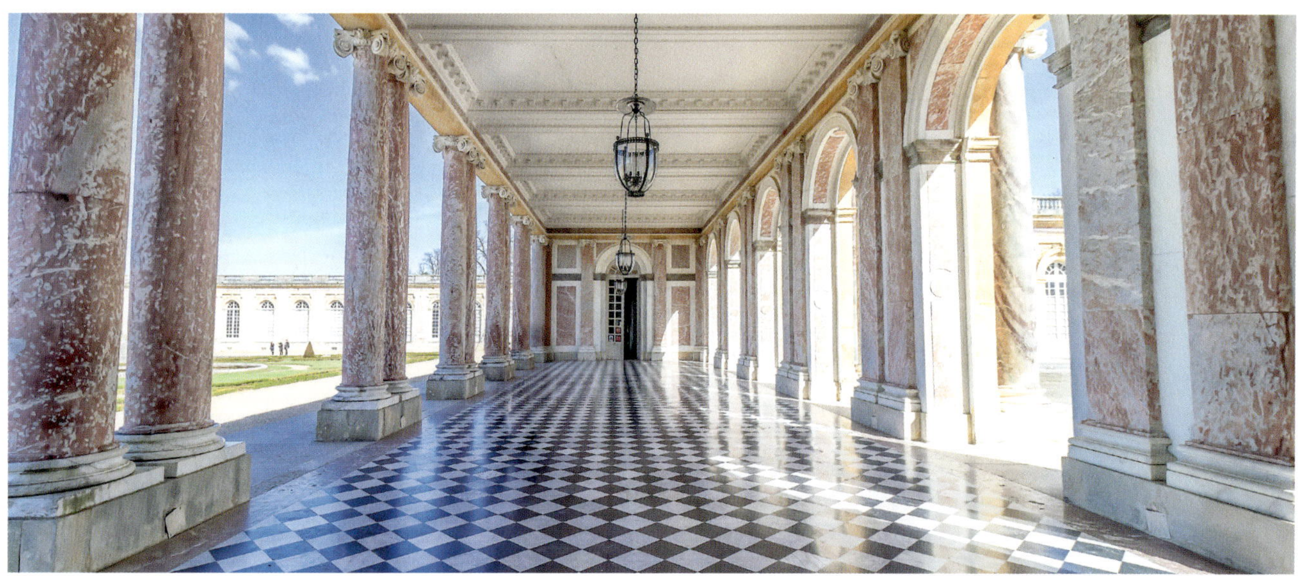

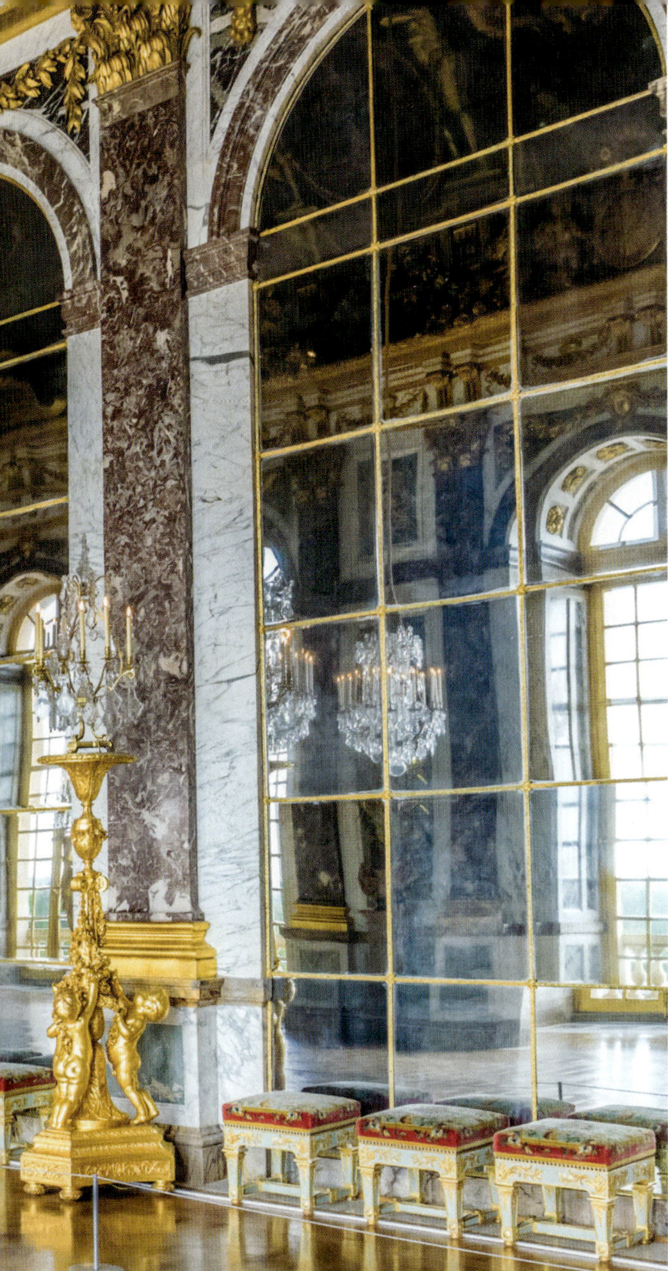

• 72–73: The most spectacular room in the palace, the perfect setting for the daily display of the Sun King's grandeur, occupies the entire west façade facing the gardens, with a length of 239 feet, and separates the King's Apartments from those of the Queen. The Hall of Mirrors was built to a design by Jules Hardouin-Mansart, while the pictorial decorations were entrusted to Charles Le Brun. Light passes through 17 windows; on the opposite side, the same number of mirrors of the same size, the work of Venetian artists, had a decorative and perspective function: they both created the illusion that the space was larger and amplified the light. The original candelabra, before being melted down to pay for the war, were made of silver and sometimes solid gold, then replaced by gilded bronze.

• 72 bottom: The Grand Trianon, where Louis XIV went to escape court rituals, was built to a design by Jules Hardouin-Mansart on the site of the former village of Trianon (demolished in 1670) northwest of the park of Versailles. It replaced the "porcelain" Trianon. Covered in marble, it was inaugurated in the summer of 1688 by Louis XIV and Madame de Maintenon, the king's last favorite, who succeeded Montespan (of whom she had been the governess) and took care of some of the king's seven children.

• 73 bottom: The Hall of Mars served as a link between the Hall of Venus and the Hall of Diana (each of the rooms in the Grand Apartments of the King was dedicated to a planet associated with the name of a Roman god) and was used as a guard room, providing access to the Grand Apartments of the King. Louis XIV had designated the Hall for card games, placing several tables there. There were also two galleries, later removed by Louis XV, which had been built to accommodate musicians.

The monopoly of mirrors

The use of mirrors emphasized France's wealth, as in the 17th century these objects were produced in limited numbers and only in Venice, which held the international monopoly. To produce mirrors in France and reduce costs, the king's finance minister, Jean Baptiste Colbert, offered large sums of money to Venetian masters to persuade them to settle in Saint-Gobain, a small town not far from Paris, where the Manufacture Royale de Glaces de Miroirs was founded. Venice's reaction was immediate, and it used every means at its disposal—eventually even threats—to bring its glassmakers back. By then, however, the French had also learned the techniques for making high-quality mirrors and, by the end of the reign of Louis XIV, were rivaling the monopoly on this luxury item.

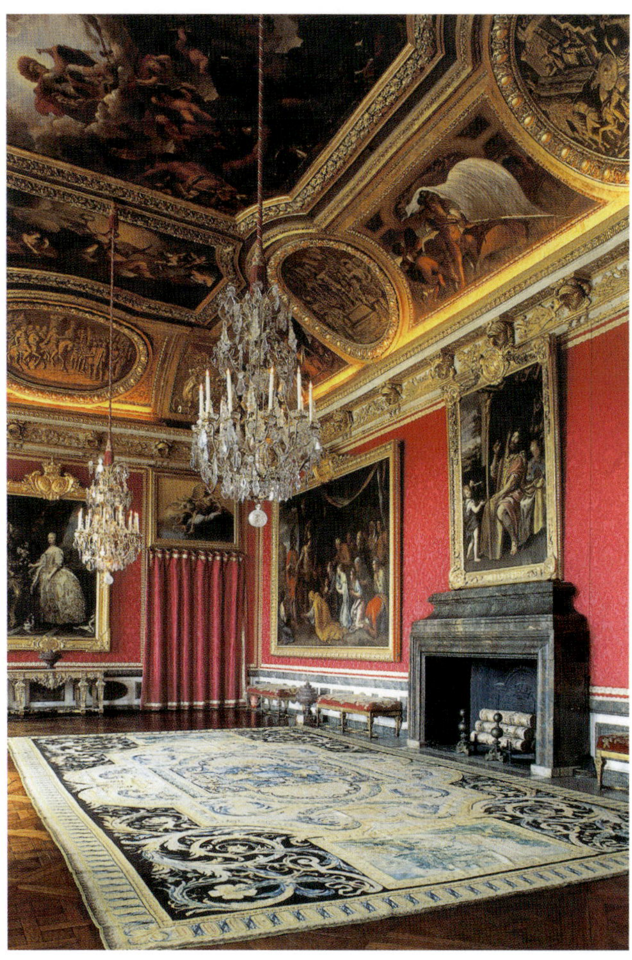

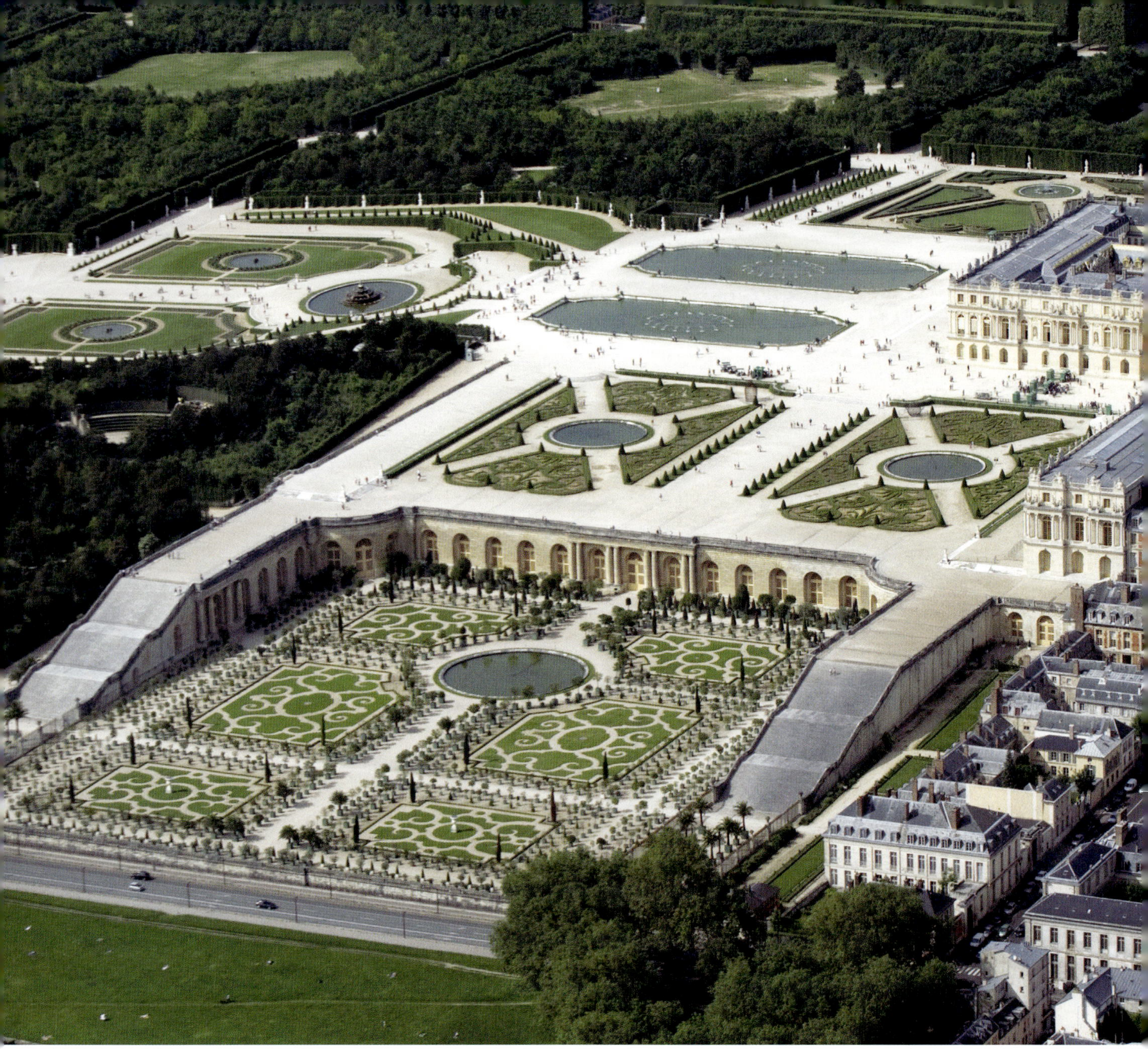

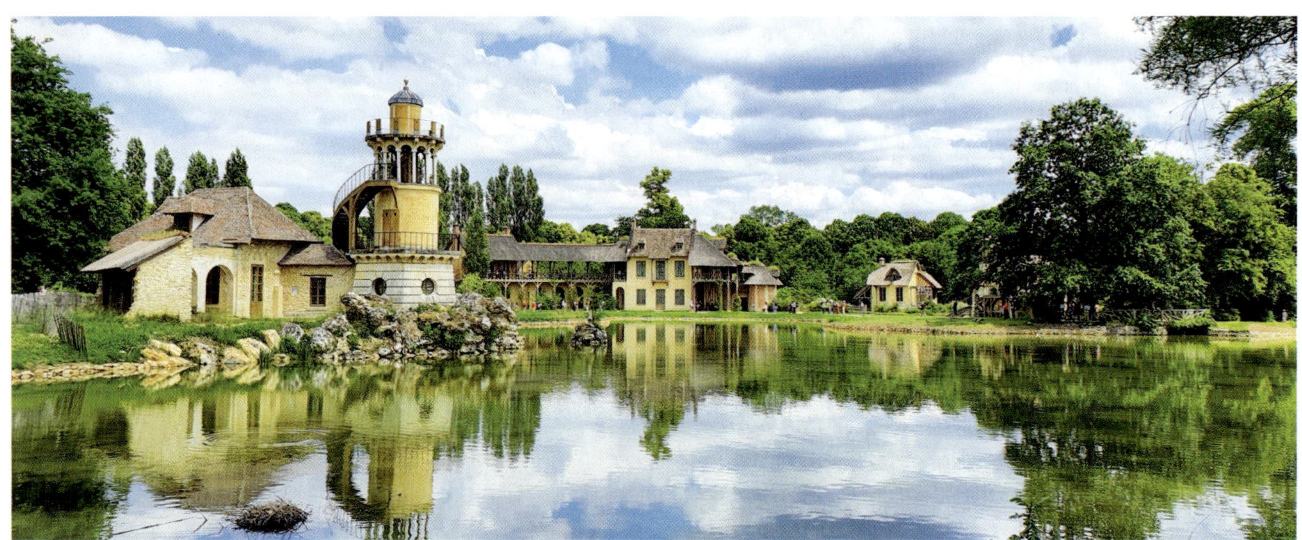

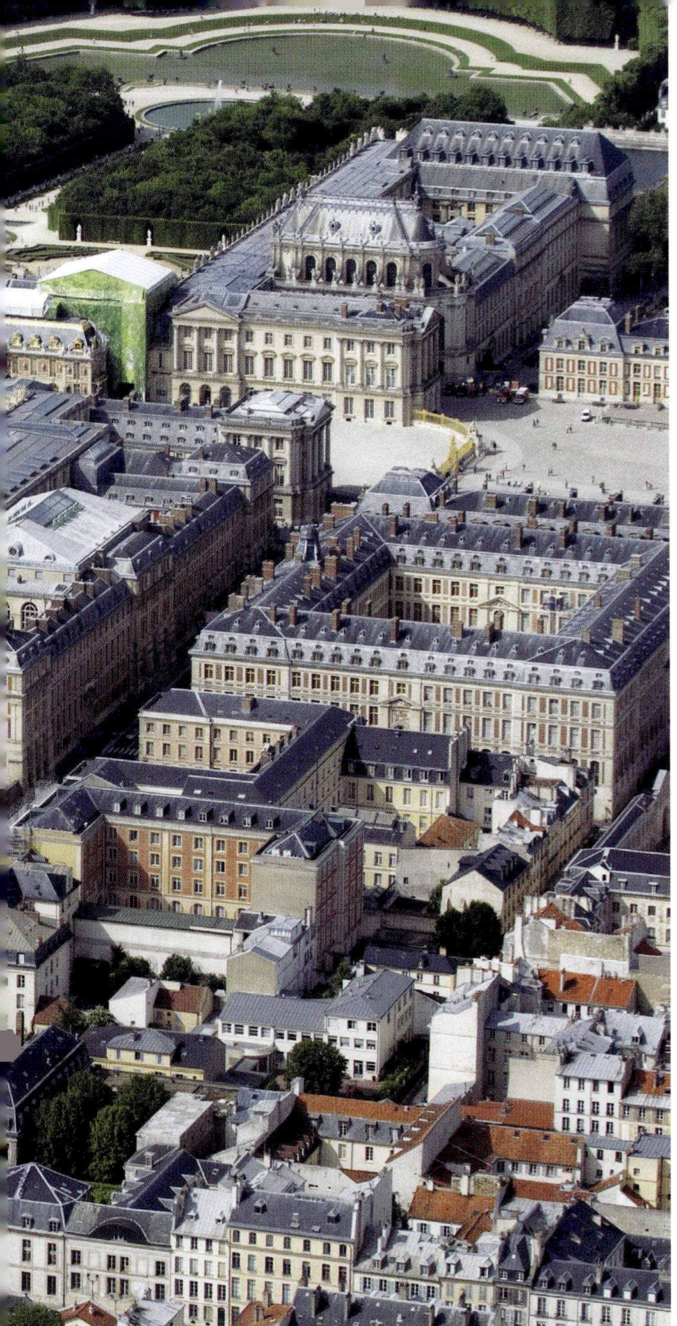

transformed into a public museum. The following year, the king and queen were guillotined and the monarchy abolished: most of the Bourbon properties were sold at auction. The palace was now an empty shell and was converted into a warehouse where valuable items confiscated from the French nobility were stored. In 1804, Napoleon Bonaparte, who had become emperor, considered making Versailles his new residence, but the cost of renovation was too high, forcing him to settle for the Grand Trianon. With the Restoration, neither Louis XVIII, the younger brother of the guillotined king, nor Charles X returned to Versailles. It was not until the Duke of Orleans, Louis Philippe I, the last king of France (ruled 1830–1848), ascended the throne that the castle was restored to its former glory. He did not return to live in the castle, but he is credited with transforming the complex into a huge museum, the Musée de l'Histoire de France, dedicated to celebrating "the glories of France."

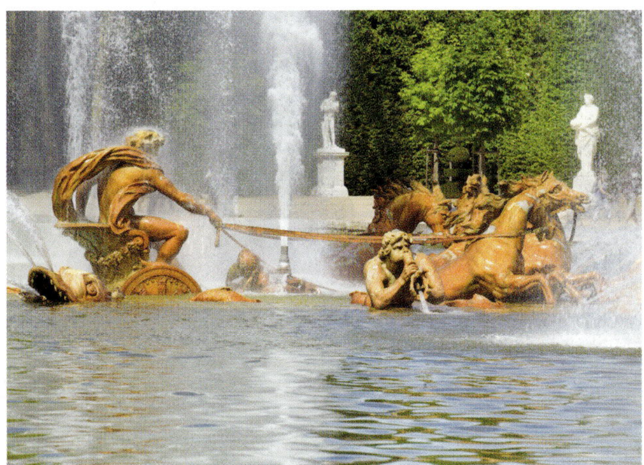

• 74-75: The park is André Le Nôtre's masterpiece and was laid out before the palace was built because the king loved to entertain his entire court outdoors with games, night parties, concerts, and theatrical performances directed by Molière himself and enlivened by the music of Jean-Baptiste Lully, in which the king actively participated. The landscape architect had shrubs and mature trees brought in from all over France to recreate a real forest. Over the years, the gardens took shape, embellished with marble, stone, and bronze sculptures, hidden corners, groves, paths, and streams. The new Orangery, which still stands today, was created under the so- called Parterre du Midi by Jules Hardouin-Mansart between 1684 and 1686, twice the size of the one previously designed by Le Vau. The south-facing exposure, thick walls, and the gardeners' ingenuity in insulating the windows with straw made it possible to preserve hundreds of potted plants and shrubs suitable for mild climates in winter, such as orange trees, whose fruit was much loved by Louis XIV, and palm trees. From May to October, the pots were transported outside to the Parterre Bas. The central gallery, 508 feet long, is flanked by two side galleries: light enters through large arched windows. The Enveloppe surrounds the old castle and continues with two symmetrical wings overlooking the orderly French gardens.

• 74 bottom: Le Hameau de la Reine was a sort of rural village built around a small artificial lake. The queen would go there to escape the constraints of court life, to lead a rustic lifestyle and to organize theatrical performances and parties. The architect Richard Mique had twelve buildings constructed, surrounded by vegetable patches, orchards, and gardens, with wooden walls and thatched roofs, inspired by Norman architecture.

• 75 center: The Latona Fountain was designed by André le Nôtre and built between 1668 and 1670. It depicts the episode from the Metamorphoses by Ovid, contained in Book VI. Latona asks Jupiter for help, who intervenes by turning the Lycians into frogs. This episode was not chosen at random, it was an allegory of the unrest caused by the Fronde when Louis XIV was still a child: the message sent to the courtiers and all the French people was clear: the king would not tolerate another revolt.

Fontainebleau Castle

12th century
The Château de Fontainebleau was built as a hunting lodge for French monarchs, possibly by Louis VI, but more likely by his son Louis VII.

14th century
Used until the 14th century, the castle was abandoned during the Hundred Years' War.

1528–1540
Francis I began the transformation of the castle into a Renaissance palace.

1532–1539
From 1532, under the direction of Rosso Fiorentino, the Gallery of Francis I, completed two years earlier, was decorated. This period saw the birth of the artistic movement known as the "First School of Fontainebleau," which introduced Italian Mannerism to France.

1548–1589
During the reign of the Valois in Fontainebleau, architects Philibert Delorme, Francesco Primaticcio, Baptiste Androuet du Cerceau, and his son worked in succession.

1645–1646
Louis XIV stayed from time to time in Fontainebleau and the castle was renovated. The Garden of Diana was landscaped by André Le Nôtre who, along with Louis Le Vau, also modified the Parterre. The king ordered the construction of a theater.

1814
With the signing of the Treaty of Fontainebleau, Napoleon Bonaparte was forced to abdicate. On April 20, he left the Fontainebleau Castle.

1981
The castle became a UNESCO World Heritage Site.

The history of the Château of Fontainebleau has ancient roots linked to a passion shared by most of the kings of France: hunting. The dense forest of Fontainebleau, where it was possible to hunt wild boar and deer, attracted French sovereigns starting with Louis VII, sixth ruler of the Capetian dynasty and probably the first king to live in Fontainebleau. A simple hunting lodge was first built on the site, which was then enlarged under Louis IX to become a residence worthy of its inhabitants.

The foundations and the donjon, a massive square keep without buttresses, partly rebuilt in the 16th century, remain as evidence of those ancient times. Louis IX, the saintly king, loved to retreat to his "beloved deserts of Fontainebleau" to devote himself to prayer. In 1328, with the death of Charles IV, the Capetian dynasty died out and was succeeded by the Valois, who began to frequent the castle less assiduously. However, due to its isolated position, it served as a refuge for the royal family during the first epidemics of the plague. During the Hundred

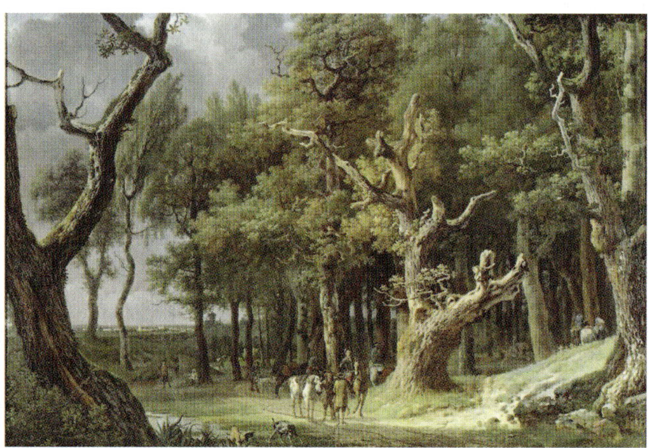

Years' War, the court moved to the Loire Valley and, in the meantime, the medieval castle of Fontainebleau remained empty and protected by its forest. It was not until around 1530 that Francis I returned to the manor because he wanted a Renaissance palace modeled on the princely courts that he had frequented in Italy since

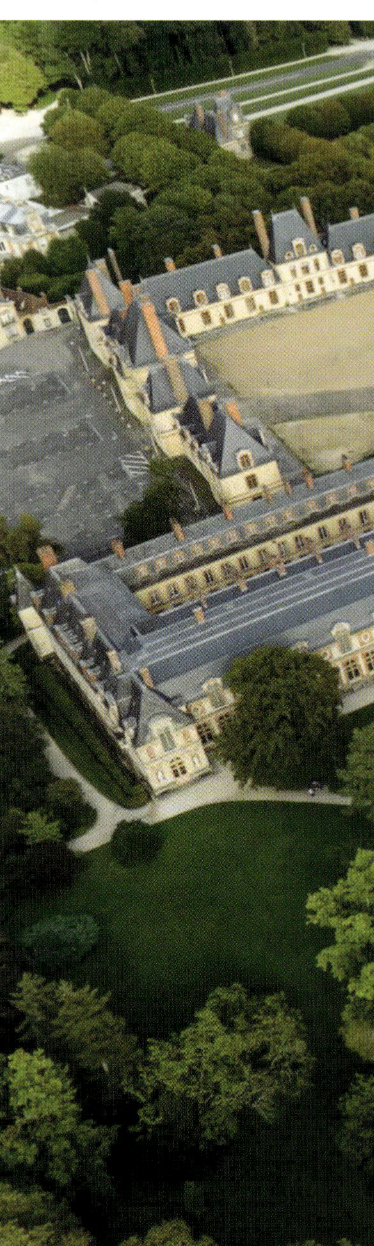

• 76 left: A view of the forest of Fontainebleau in a painting by Jean-François Hue from 1782.

• 76-77: Located about 37 miles from Paris, immersed in the forest of the same name, Fontainebleau is the only French castle to have been inhabited by all the monarchs of France from the 12th to the 19th century. The aerial view highlights the irregular layout that took shape under Francis I through the connection of the castle walls with the religious buildings built by Louis IX. In the foreground is the Courtyard of the White Horse with the Horseshoe Staircase, followed by the Courtyard of the Fountain overlooking the Garden of Diana, the Oval Courtyard (overlooking the Parterre), the Courtyard of the Princes to its left, and finally the Court of the Offices.

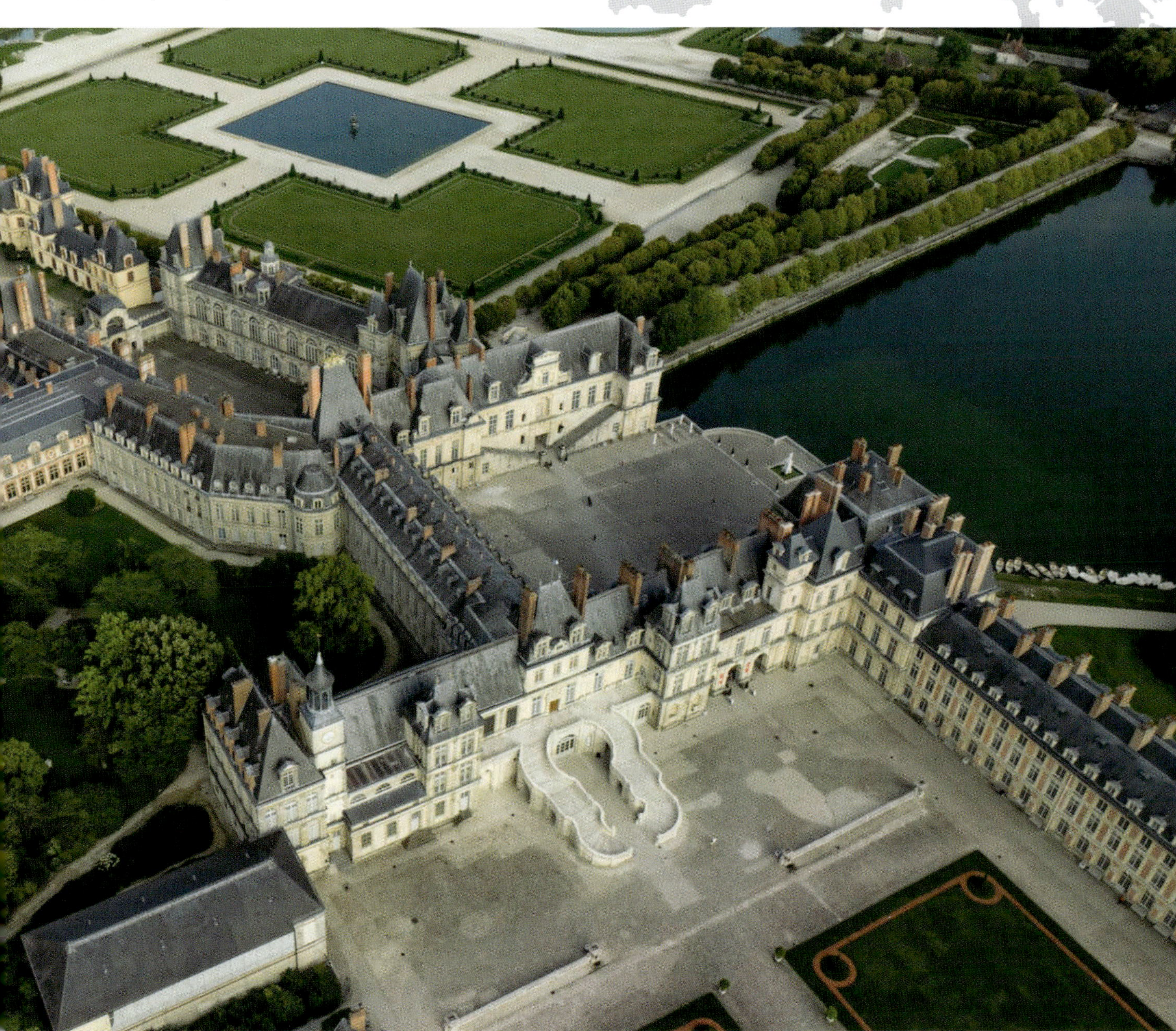

1515, when he had just become king. He chose the castle of Fontainebleau, which he had been fond of since his youth, neglecting the castles of Amboise (where he had hosted Leonardo da Vinci from 1516 to 1519), Chambord, and Blois, which he had built on the Loire.

With a series of interventions, new buildings were added to the medieval structures, along with a series of wings and pavilions facing the garden, giving shape to the irregular and unusual layout of the current castle. The king entrusted the project to the master builder of Paris, architect Gilles Le Breton, who used sandstone as the building material.

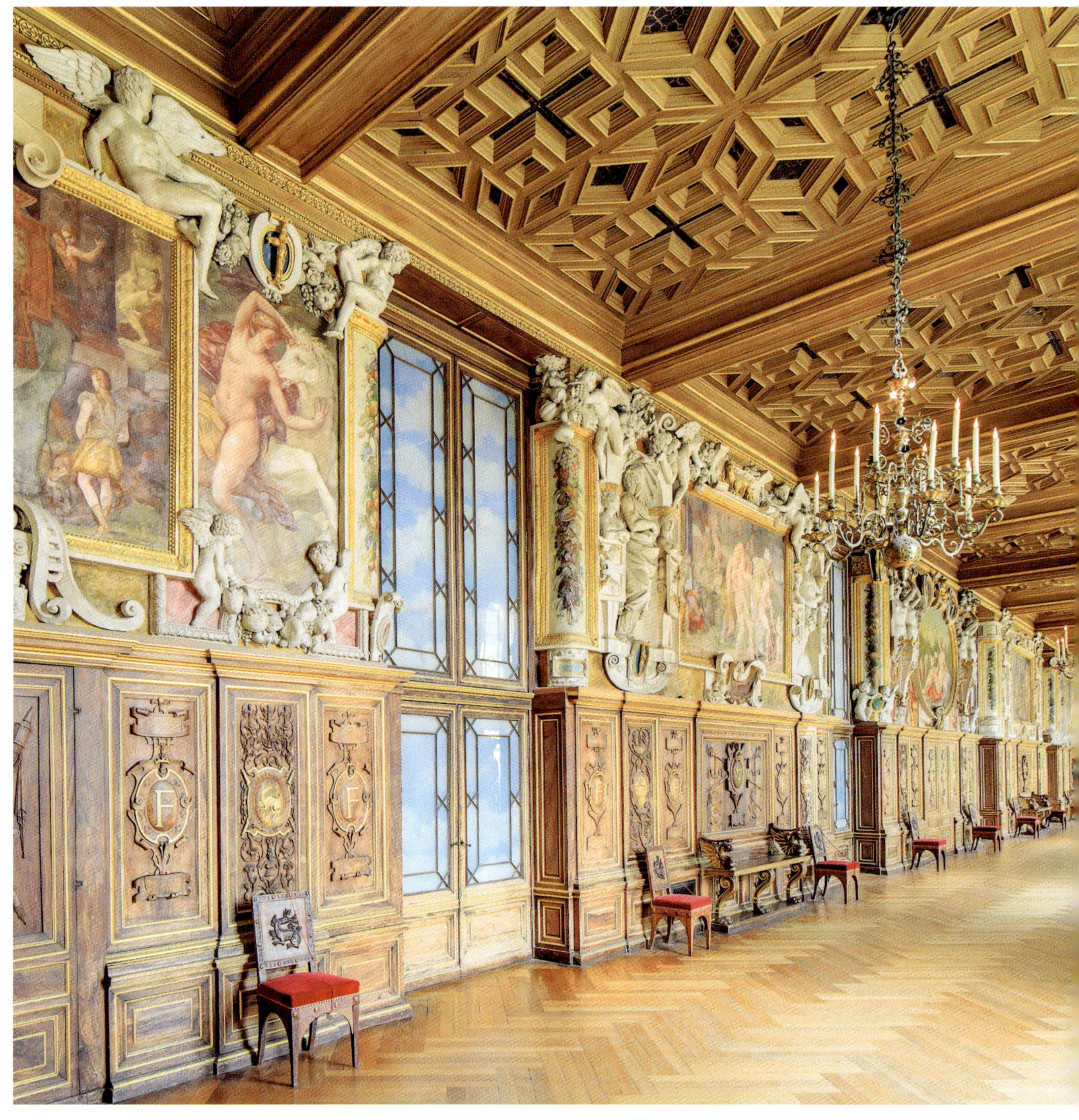

Soon, the construction site, which attracted the greatest Italian artists of the time, found itself at the center of a fundamental renewal in the arts and culture, and from there spread an artistic fervor attentive to the Italian Renaissance known as the "School of Fontainebleau." The ultimate expression of that era is the Gallery of Francis I, a true masterpiece built between 1532 and 1539. It was not a necessary passageway between rooms, and was used only by the king: Francis kept the key to the Gallery and only opened it to important visitors.

The walls covered with oak and walnut panels and the carved ceiling are the work of Italian furniture maker Francesco Scibec da Carpi (who arrived at court in 1530). The former are engraved with the king's initials, a crowned F, and his emblem, the salamander. After the death of Francis I, his son Henry II entrusted the work still in progress to Philibert Delorme, who, in particular, turned the Courtyard of the White Horse from a service

• 79 top: The Royal Elephant, decked out with the salamander and a caparison decorated with the lilies of France and an "F," is an allegorical representation of the king and his qualities: greatness, power, goodness, temperance, and generosity.

• 79 bottom: During the reign of Francis I, what became the King's Staircase in the 18th century (commissioned by Louis XV) was the bedroom of the favorite Anne de Pisseleu. The frescoes allegorically depict the love affairs of Alexander the Great.

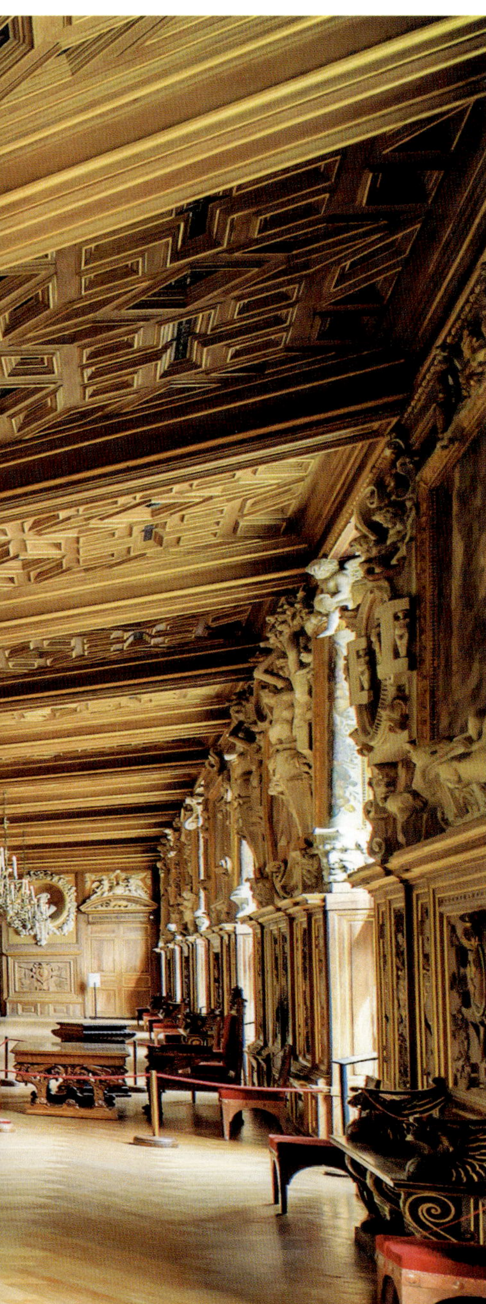

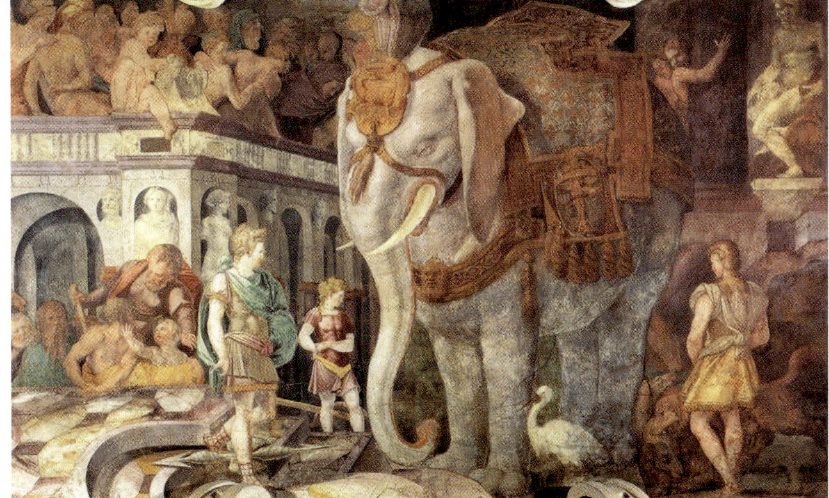

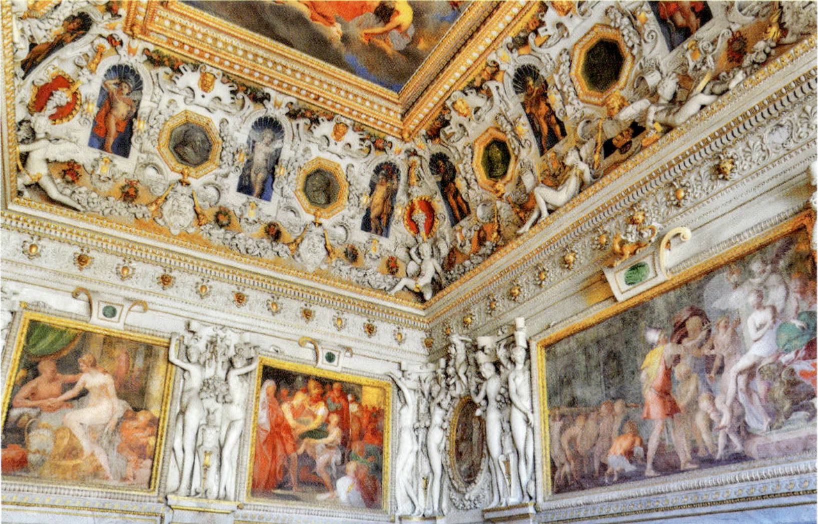

• 78–79: The Gallery of Francis I connected the king's rooms to the ancient convent church, and it was precisely this function as an ideal connection that determined the iconographic plan of Rosso Fiorentino's decoration, whose meaning can only be understood when viewed as a whole. Above the main frescoes stands the salamander, while at the bottom center of the main scene there is always a cartouche with another symbolic or narrative image commenting on the whole. In general, the theme of the frescoes is an allegorical celebration of the king's life and virtues.

area into the main courtyard of the castle. However, the architect's luck, supported by Henry II's favorite Diane de Poitiers, declined with the death of the king: two days after his death, his wife Catherine de Medici dismissed him and appointed Francesco Primaticcio as superintendent. However, the days of the Italian queen's memorable parties and banquets were coming to an end with the outbreak of the Wars of Religion (1562–1598), which did not spare the Île-de-France region, bringing destruction to the Château de Fontainebleau. The Valois' successors, the Bourbons, generally preferred other residences, with the exception of Henry IV who ordered new work to

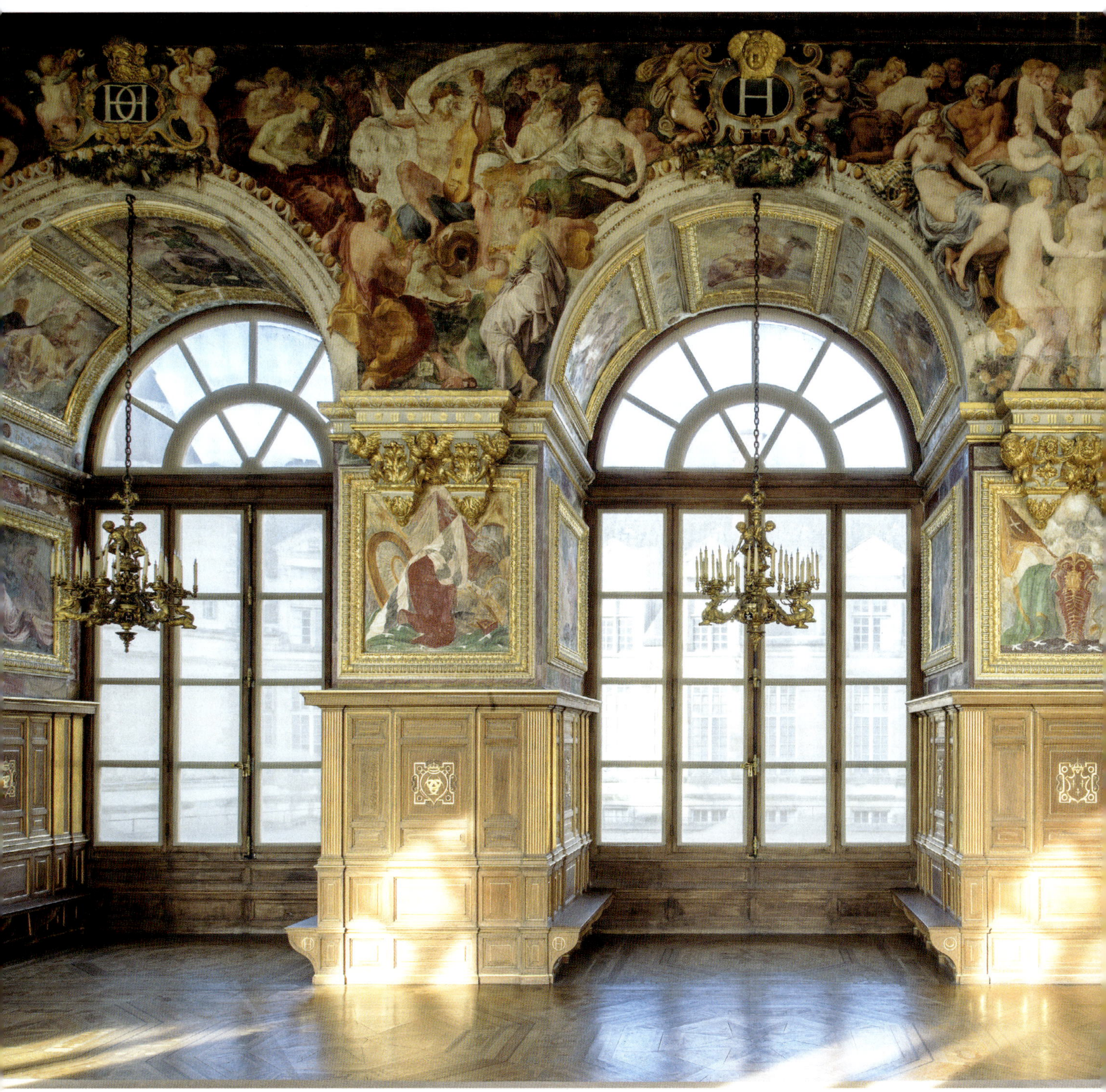

be carried out, surrounding himself with numerous artists, so much so that some art history critics speak of a Second School of Fontainebleau. The last royal resident was Napoleon Bonaparte. The emperor called the palace the "house of centuries" because it had welcomed the Capetian, Valois, and Bourbon kings since the Middle Ages. In 1804, he gave instructions to restore the castle to its former glory: new furniture was brought from Paris and the old one restored in homage to the splendor of the Ancien Régime. On April 20, 1814, one year and one day after the fateful and decisive battle of Leipzig, Napoleon was at Fontainebleau: after receiving news of his dismissal, before leaving for his exile on the island of Elba, he saluted the men of the Imperial Guard, the elite military unit he himself had created on May 18, 1804, who had gathered in the Courtyard of the White Horse (then called the "Courtyard of Farewell").

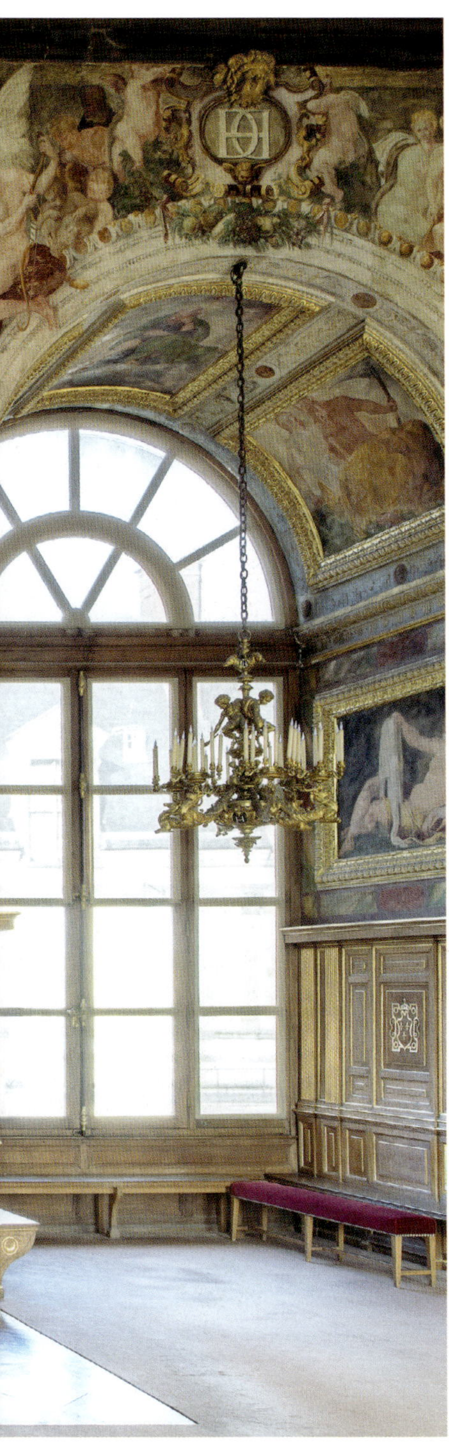

• 80–81: The Ballroom, overlooking the gardens and the Oval Courtyard, was designed by Philibert Delorme starting in 1548. The wood paneling was done by Scibec da Carpi, while the paintings were started in 1554 by Francesco Primaticcio, assisted by Niccolò dell'Abate. At the end of the room, Delorme installed a monumental fireplace, completed in 1556. The room contains several references to Diane de Poitiers, who is portrayed in two frescoes above the fireplace. In the 19th century, King Louis Philippe had the elaborate wooden floor added, which copies the original designs of the ceiling coffers.

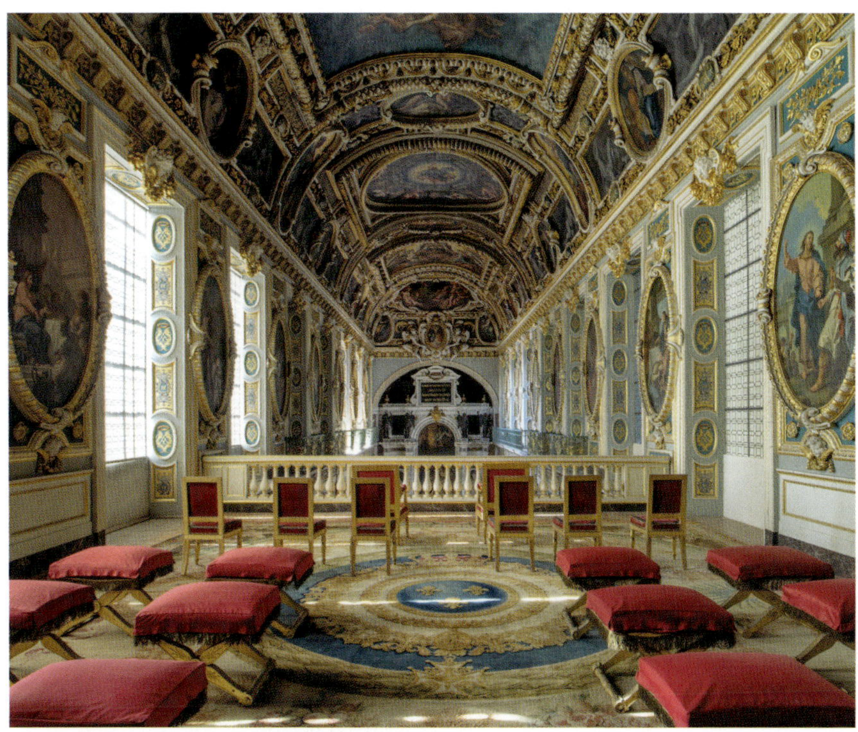

• 81 top: The castle's royal chapel, dedicated to the Trinity, is considered Martin Frèminet's masterpiece. Richly decorated with gold and stucco, the church has two levels that allowed the royal family to attend services from a gallery. The ceiling features a series of paintings by Ambroise Dubois in the Mannerist style.

The Salt Cellar

Preserved at the Kunsthistorisches Museum in Vienna, the Salt Cellar of Francis I, made of ebony, gold, and enamel, is a masterpiece of goldsmithing. It was the king himself who asked Benvenuto Cellini (1500–1571)—writer, sculptor, goldsmith, and a rebel—to create a salt cellar to be used during royal banquets. The Salt Cellar consists of a small sculpture resting on an oval base and is 10 inches tall. Standing out are two figures: Neptune, god of the sea; and Gaia, goddess of the earth, crowned with a garland of flowers and fruit, sitting on a crushed elephant as a cushion, adorned with a blue cloth with golden lilies, the emblem of the French crown. In front of the two figures is a boat that serves as a container for salt, while next to Gaia a small temple serves as a container for pepper.

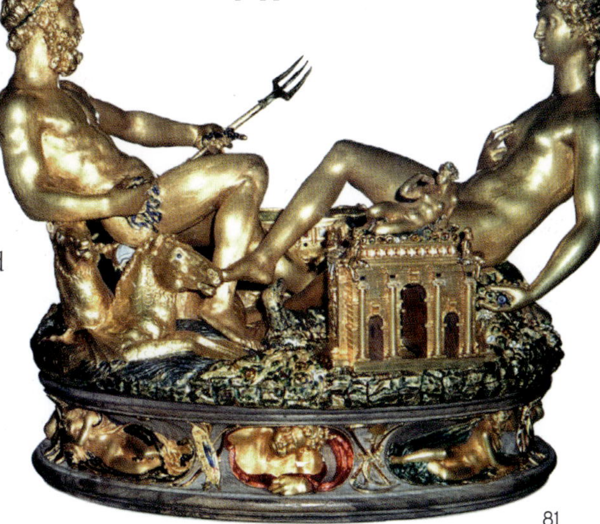

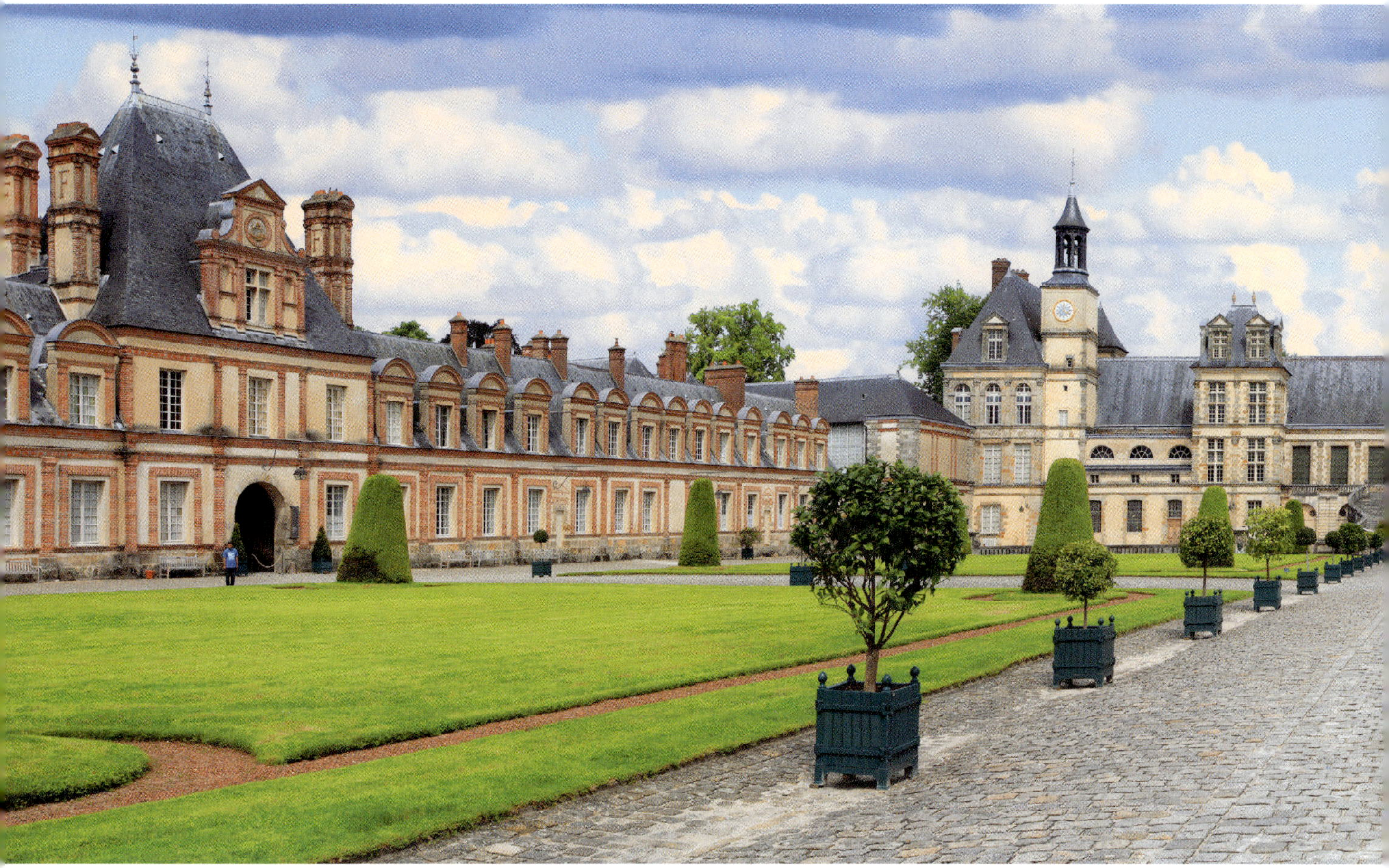

• 82-83: In the 16th century, the Courtyard of the White Horse became the castle's court of honor. The large external staircase, whose construction was entrusted to architect Philibert Delorme around 1558, was designed to provide a majestic entrance to Henry II's apartment. However, it disappeared less than a century later, replaced by the famous Horseshoe Staircase. The courtyard is a group of buildings constructed over a period spanning five centuries, which is why they feature different styles. On the left stands the Clock Tower, behind which is the Trinity Chapel. Also on the left are the buildings of the north wing: built around 1530 and known as the Ministers' Wing, it was extensively restored in the 19th century. The central building is decorated with a salamander, and the chimneys bear the initials of Francis I. On the opposite side, the 18th-century wing of Louis XV stands in place of the Gallery of Ulysses, which had been decorated by Primaticcio. In the time of Francis I, the ground floor housed the shops of wealthy merchants who lived at court.

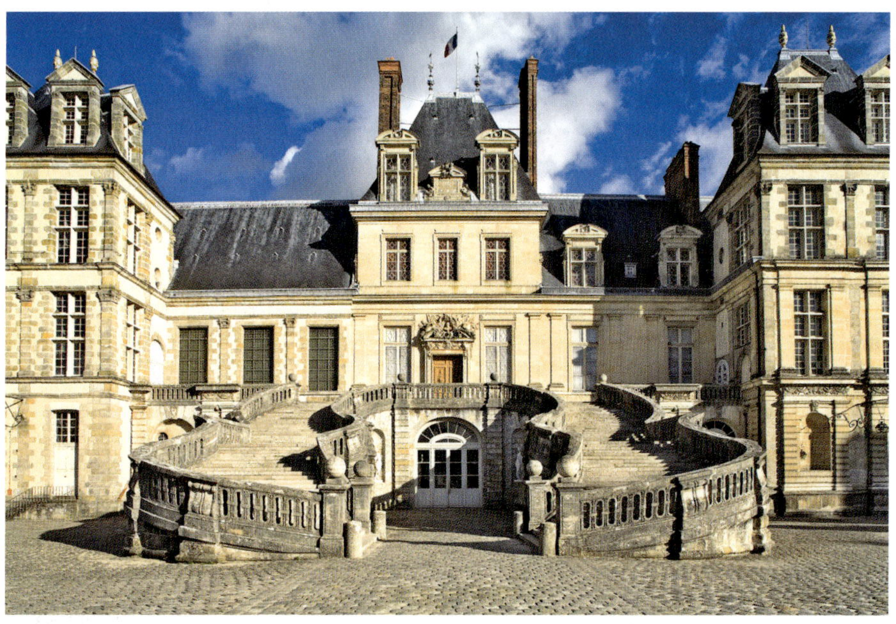

• 82 bottom: The horseshoe staircase was designed by architect Jean Androuet du Cerceau for Louis XIII in 1632.

• 83 bottom: View of the Garden of Diana, which at the time of Francis I was called the "Queen's Garden." Redesigned by Catherine de Medici, Henry IV, who added an orangery, Louis XVI, and even Napoleon, it was transformed into an English garden by Louis Philippe in the 19th century.

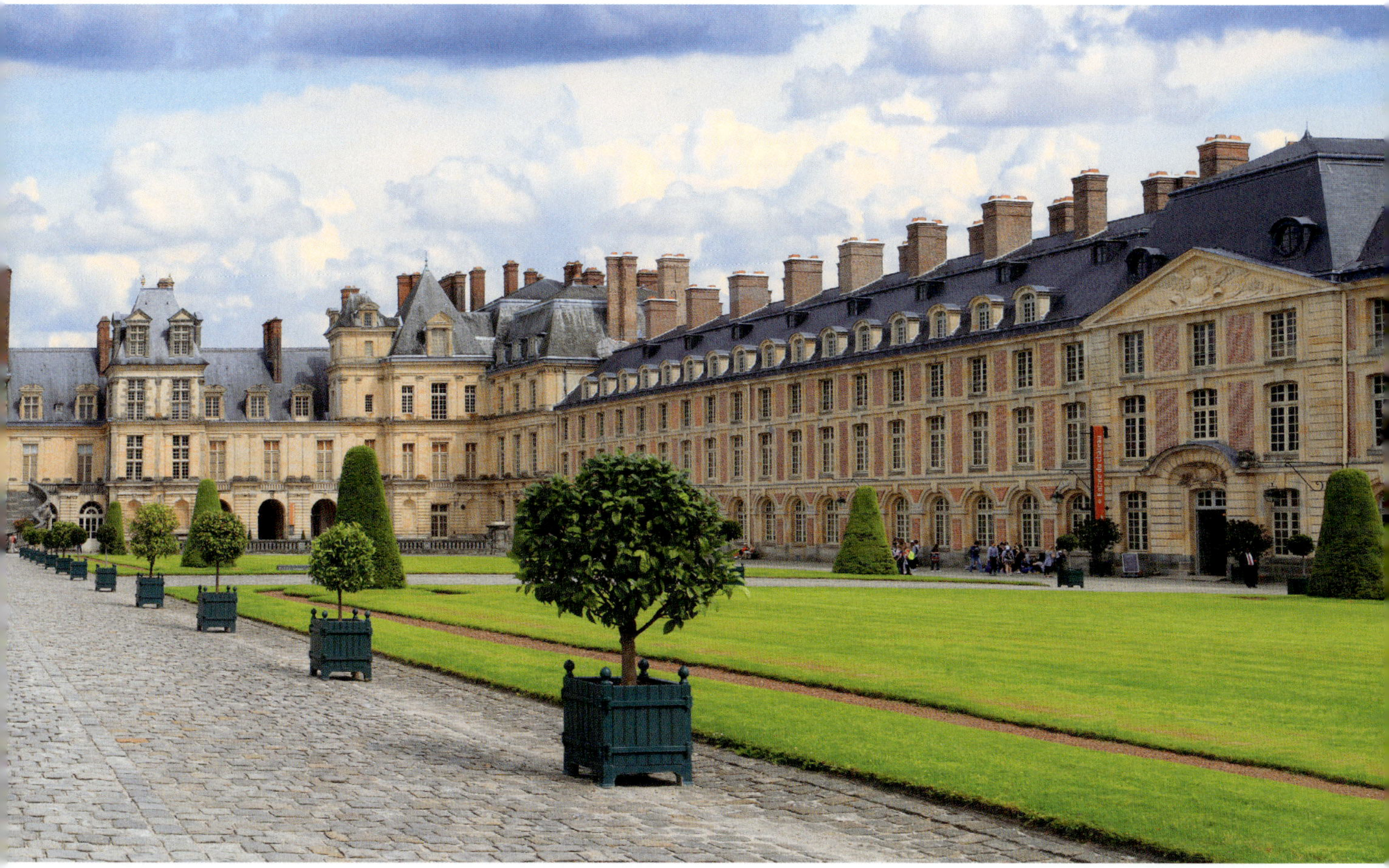

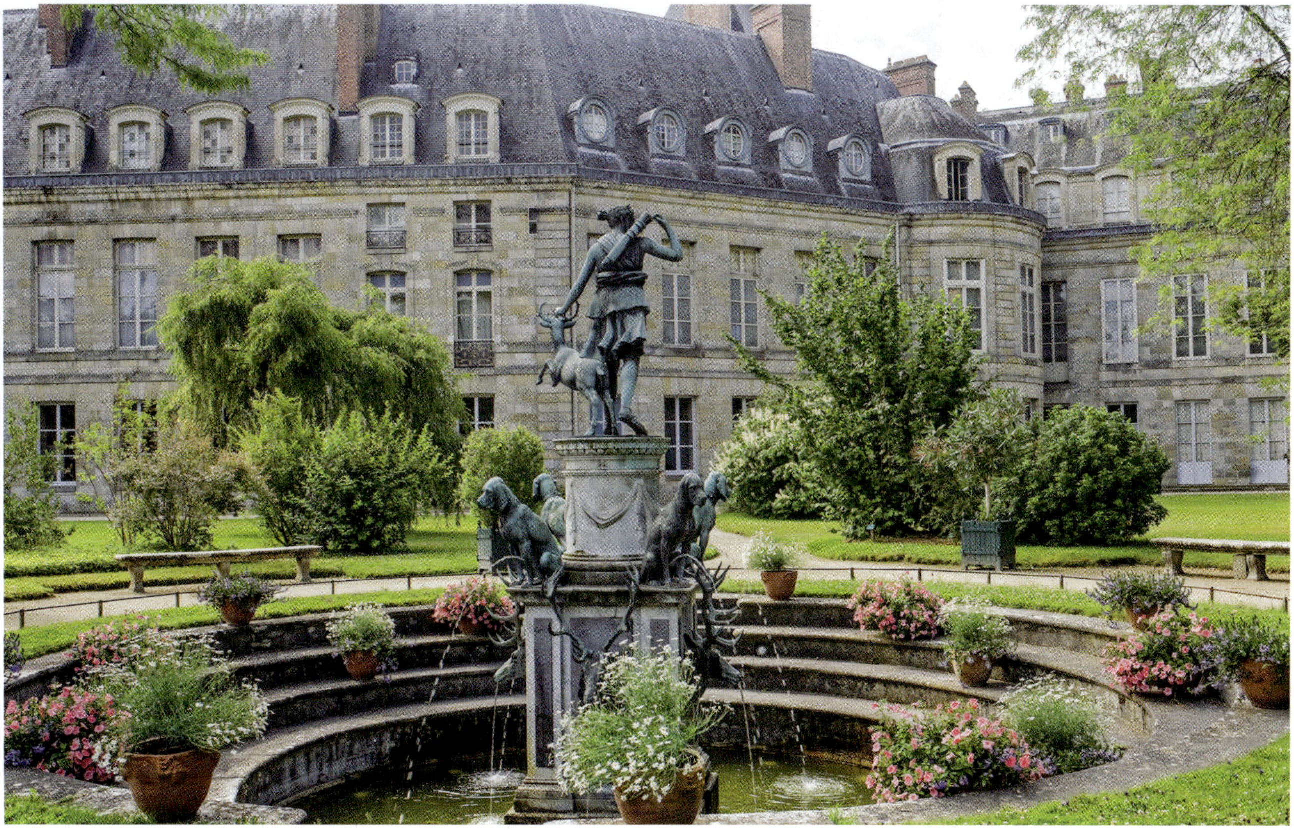

Chaumont Castle

11th century
In Chaumont-sur-Loire, around the year 1000, Odo I, Count of Blois, founded a fortress to defend the county from attacks by the Count of Anjou.

1037
The property passed to the Norman Gelduin the Younger. His son Geoffroy left it to his niece Denise de Fougères, wife of Sulpice I of Amboise.

1465
The King of France, Louis XI, burned down Chaumont Castle to punish Pierre I d'Amboise, who was involved in a revolt of nobles.

1467-1475
Pierre I regained possession of the estate. His heirs began rebuilding the castle, which was completed in 1511.

1550
Catherine de Medici bought Chaumont Castle.

1560
Diane de Poitiers obtained Chaumont Castle from Catherine de' Medici in exchange for Chenonceau Castle.

1750
The aristocrat Jacques-Donatien Le Ray bought the castle and proceeded to renovate it.

1803
The property passed to Le Ray's son.

1875
After a series of changes in ownership, Chaumont Castle was purchased and renovated by Marie-Charlotte Constance Say, wife of Henri Amédée de Broglie.

1884
The landscape architect Henri Duchêne created the park.

1938–2008
Marie-Charlotte Constance Say sold the castle to the French state. Since 2007, the estate has belonged to the Centre region and, in October 2008, it became a cultural meeting center.

Around the year 1000, Odo I, Count of Blois, had the Châteaude Chaumont-sur-Loire built to control the border between the counties of Blois and Anjou. To express his gratitude for the help with thwarting the attacks of the Count of Anjou, Odo granted the castle to the Norman knight Gelduin, who in turn passed it on to his son Geoffroy. The latter, having no direct heirs, decided to leave the fortified manor to his grand-niece Denise de Fougères, who in 1054 married Sulpice I of the Amboise family, occupying the castle for almost five centuries—despite disputes with King Louis XI of France during the 15th century—until Catherine de Medici purchased it in 1550.

The noble family, which takes its name from Amboise, a town in Touraine, included prominent figures in the history of the Kingdom of France, who had to rebuild the Château de Chaumont after Louis XI's guards destroyed it in 1465 to punish the count for leading a revolt. During this period, the manor was refined in its forms, with Italian taste influencing new architectural elements, such as sculptures with

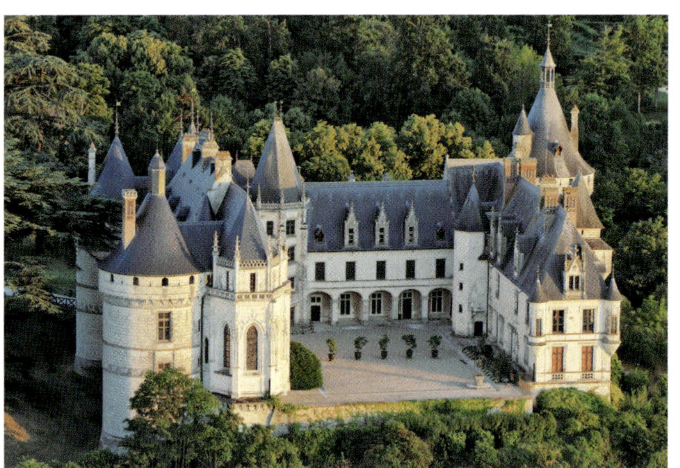

arabesques and shells, which were integrated into the original Gothic forms. On March 31, 1550, Catherine de Medici purchased the castle of Chaumont for 120,000 liras from Charles-Antoine de la Roche-Foucauld and his wife Antoinette d'Amboise.

Upon the death of her husband Henry II, lover of Diane

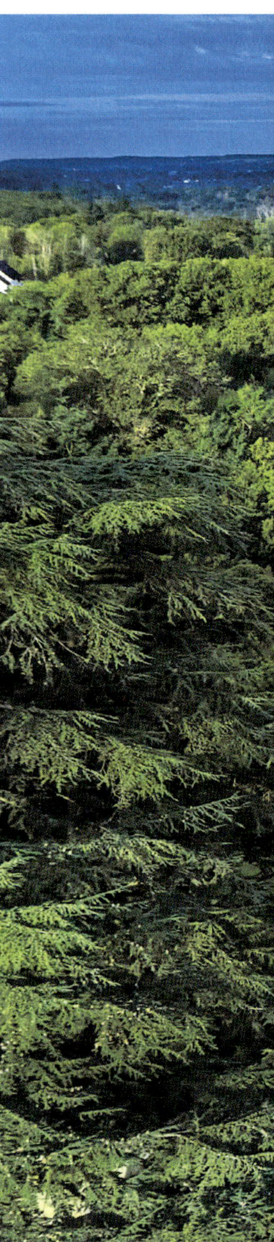

• 84 center and 84-85: Views of the Castle of Chaumont-sur-Loire, which in 2000, along with the entire Val de Loire, became a UNESCO World Heritage Site.

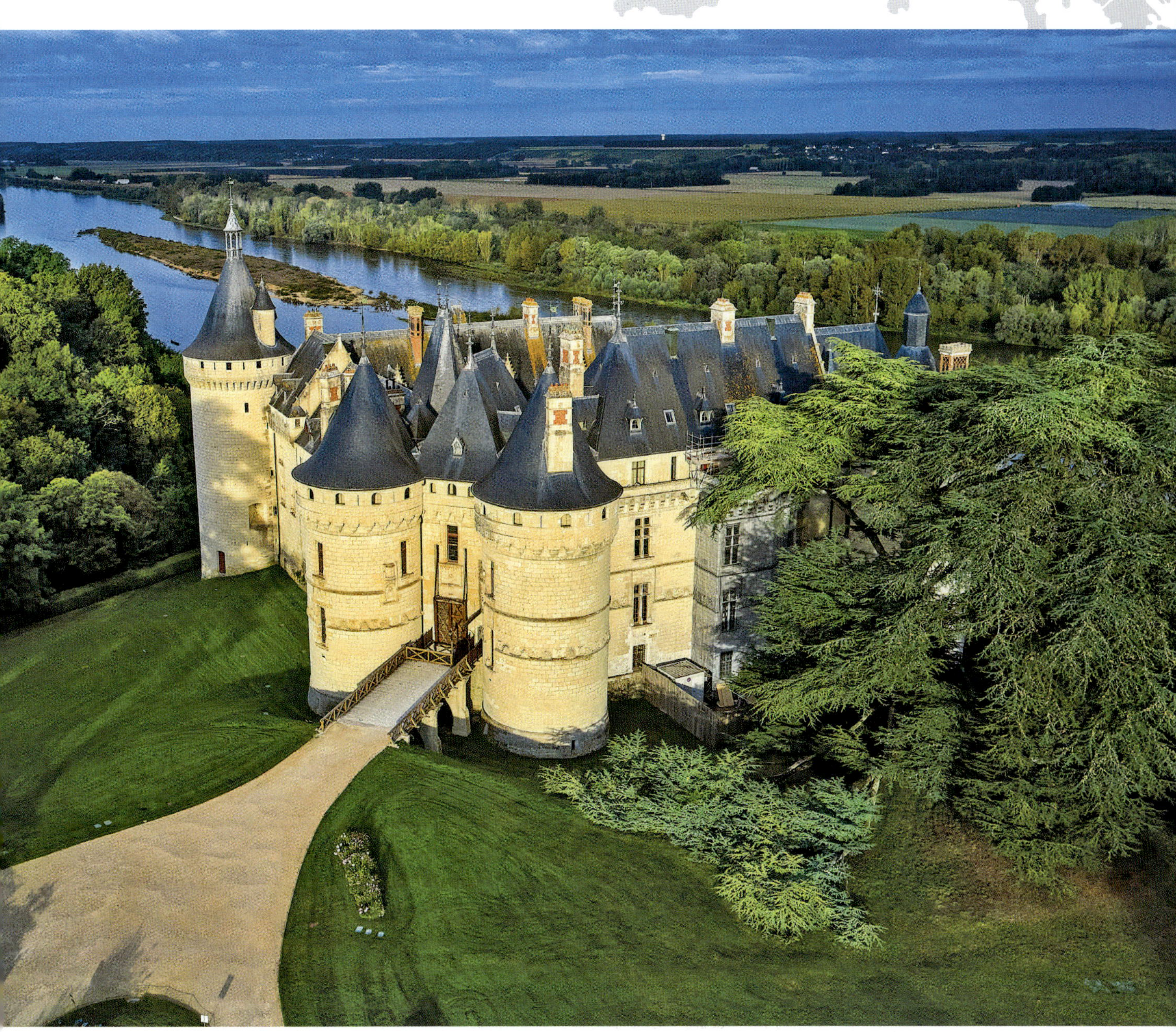

de Poitiers, she forced the king's historical favorite to accept the estate in exchange for the more prestigious but less profitable Chenonceau Castle: the vast domain of Chaumont was worth twice as much due to its extensive agricultural land and because boats passing through the Loire had to pay a toll. Negotiations began three months after the king's death. Bent by the decision, Diane, who was very attentive to the condition of her residence, had some work done at Chaumont and had her two emblems affixed above the leaded windows of the walkway. However, she spent only short periods of time at the castle.

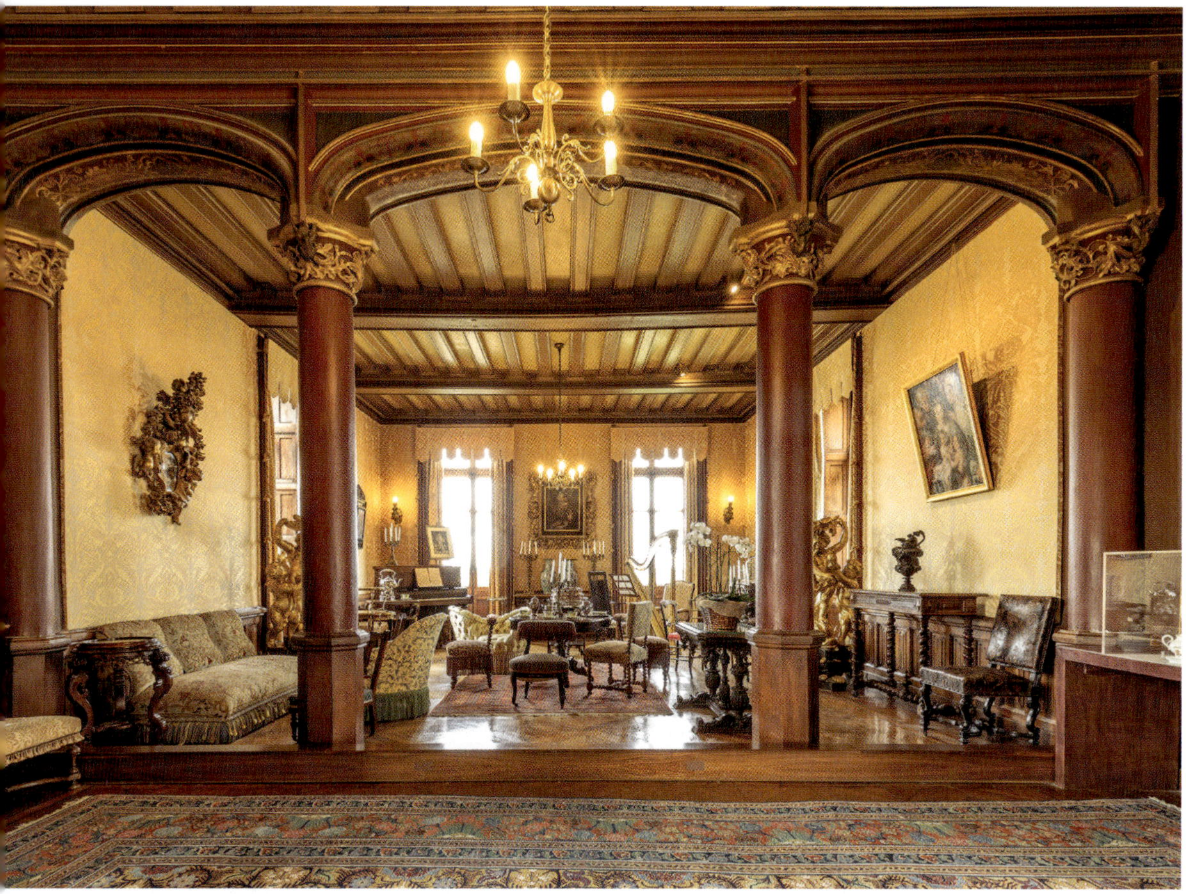

• 86 top: The Great Hall was furnished by Jules-Édouard Potier de la Morandière, architect to Viscount Joseph Walsh, whose family owned the Chaumont estate before the de Broglie family. At that time, the fireplace was designed as inspired by those of the Château de Blois. This hall was used for receptions by the de Broglie couple.

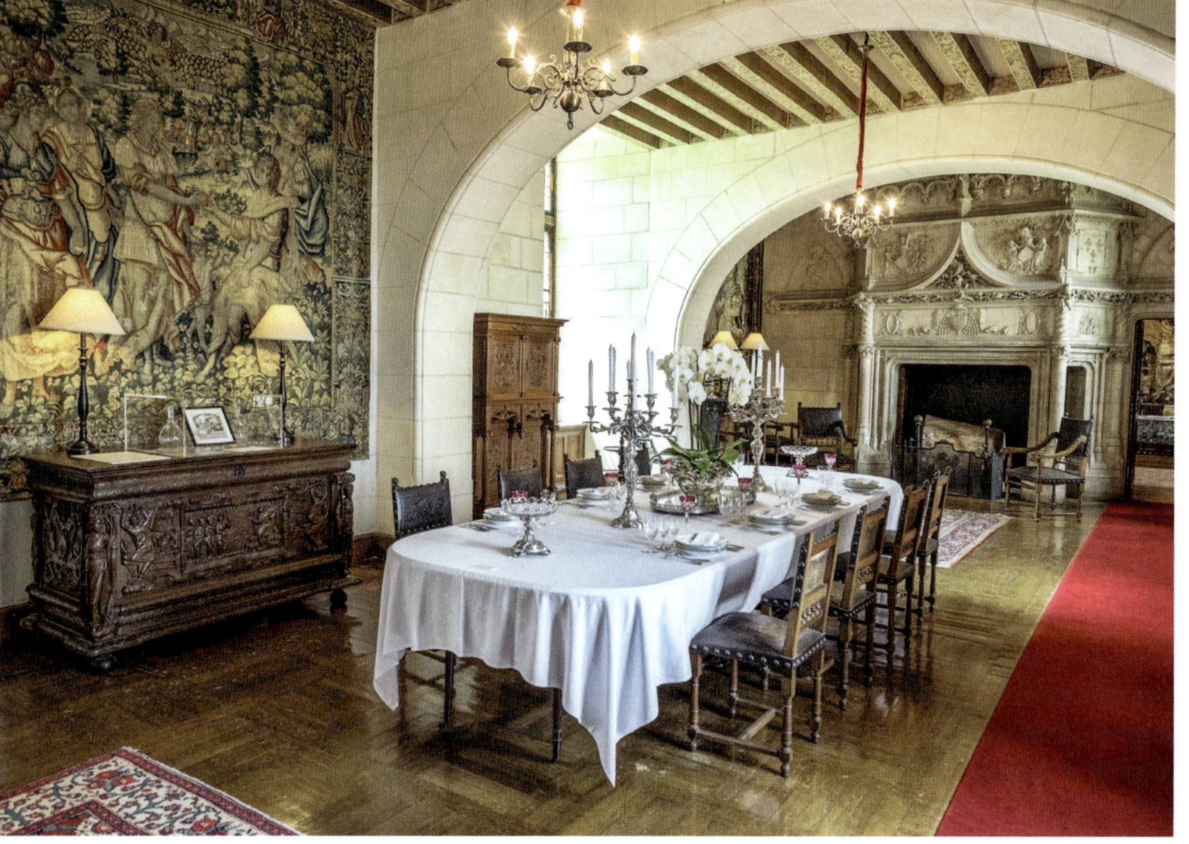

• 86 bottom: The Chaumont dining room could be considered the center of the princess's social life. This room, 56 feet long, was originally used as a kitchen. It was the de Broglie family who transformed it into a dining room, renovating it in Renaissance style with a large fireplace and polychrome ceiling.

Between the end of the 16th century and the middle of the 18th, the castle passed through the hands of various owners. In 1750, it was purchased by Jacques-Donatien Le Ray de Chaumont, who had the disrepaired north wing demolished to open up the main courtyard towards the Loire. Upon his death in 1803, the estate passed to his son James Le Ray, who spent most of his life overseas. It was during his absence that Germaine de Staël, forced into exile from Paris by Napoleon Bonaparte, was hosted in the castle. Chaumont then welcomed famous guests such as Madame Récamier, Benjamin Constant, the writer François-René de Chateaubriand, and the British poet George Byron. After a series of changes in ownership, in 1875 Chaumont was bought by Marie-Charlotte Constance Say, heiress to the wealthy Say sugar cane plantation and wife of Prince Henri-Amédée de Broglie. The couple modernized the property, installing electricity, running water, and central heating with stoves. The "historic" rooms, such as the Council Chamber and Catherine de Medici's bedroom, were redecorated. Due to a series of bad investments and the stock market crash, in 1938 the princess, now ruined, was expropriated by the French state, which took possession of the estate and the collection of tapestries and historic furniture.

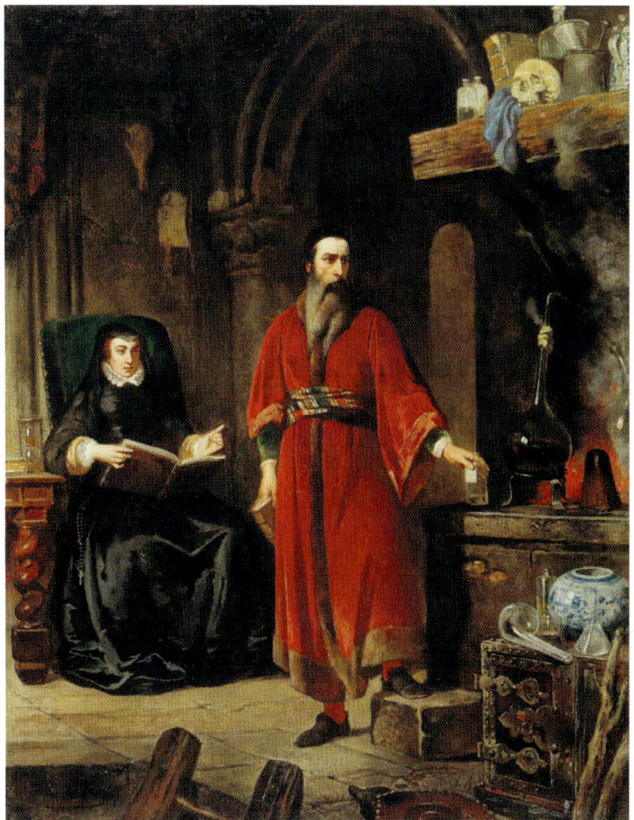

The queen's trusted necromancer

If the Florentine astrologer Cosimo Ruggieri—pictured here with the queen—had limited himself to reading the stars, he would not have fueled the malicious rumors circulating about him. However, in addition to being the confidant of the future queen Catherine de' Medici, with whom he had arrived in France with his brother Tommaso, Ruggieri was also able to make predictions by reading animal entrails, and he practiced spells with pins stuck into wax figurines (in 1598, he avoided an arrest after the discovery of puppets depicting Henry IV) as well as making distilled poisons. Among the many legends about his sinister magic was one that claimed that the magician had kidnapped a Jewish baby, beheaded him, and, using black magic, asked the head to reveal secrets that would make him powerful. The queen, who was somewhat afraid of Ruggieri, but also attracted by the occult and esotericism, availed herself of his talents and hosted him at Chaumont.

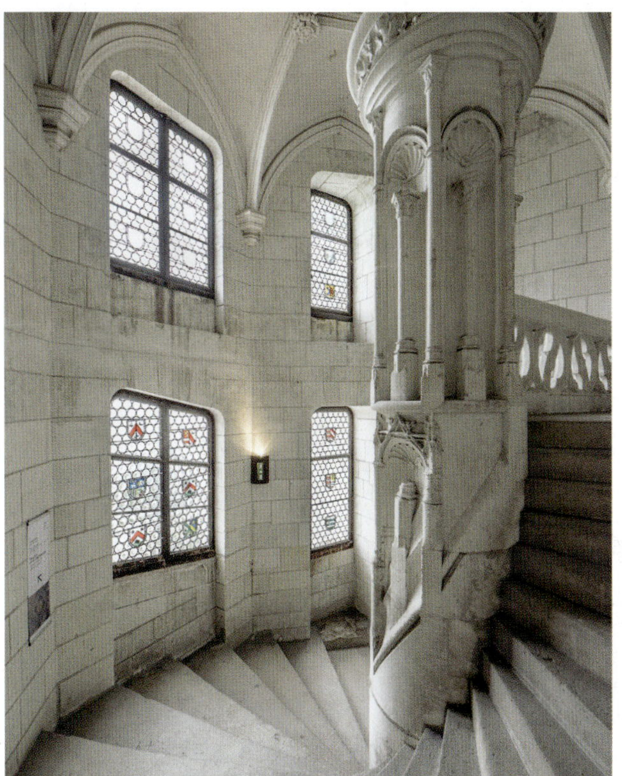

• 87 bottom: The grand staircase at Chaumont was built in the early 16th century. Its spiral is housed inside a polygonal tower. Originally, the tower protruded from the façade and was open on three sides. The decoration features both Gothic and Renaissance elements, such as shells, an ornament of Italian inspiration. The window panes are decorated with coats of arms created by the master glassmaker Pierre-Georges Bardon for the Prince de Broglie.

Amboise Castle

1434
The medieval castle of the Amboise family's fiefdom was confiscated and became part of the French crown's possessions.

1470
The King of France, Charles VIII, was born in Amboise.

1492
Charles VIII promoted the renovation of the castle, gathering a group of Italian artists, including architect Domenico da Cortona, humanist Fra Giocondo, and landscape gardener Pacello da Mercogliano.

1498
Charles VIII died in Amboise. He was succeeded by his cousin Louis XII, who had a wing built perpendicularly to the Charles VIII wing in the Renaissance style.

1499
Louis XII ceded the castle to Louise of Savoy. Her children, the future King of France Francis I and Marguerite d'Angoulême, grew up there.

1515
Francis I became king: renovation work continued at Amboise with the reorganization of the Louis XII wing.

1516–1519
Francis I gave Leonardo da Vinci the manor house of Clos-Lucé in Amboise, where the artist died on May 2, 1519.

1700–1800
Amboise lost its importance and Louis XIV turned the castle into a prison.

Located in the town of the same name in the Indre-et-Loire department, Amboise Castle is one of the most important castles in France. Owned by the lords of Amboise for four centuries, the manor passed to the French crown in 1434. From that moment on, it became a royal residence and French sovereigns worked to renovate and expand it. King Louis XI of Valois (1423–1483) was the first to live there with his royal family and considered it a safe residence in which to raise the Dauphin, the future Charles VIII, who was born within the castle walls. He was the initiator of the changes made to the original medieval fortification, as is evidenced by the tower. Upon his return from the war in Italy, he introduced changes that would transform the castle into a magnificent Renaissance palace like those admired in Italy. The king brought numerous artists from across the Alps to Amboise, including Domenico da Cortona and Fra Giocondo. Day and night by candlelight, in summer and winter, many masons, laborers, carpenters, and joiners worked for the monarch. When the work was completed, the castle became the center of the French monarchy. The days followed a more or less set schedule: they began with mass, walks in the garden, followed by consultations on affairs of state, and then leisure activities: billiards, marbles, hunting trips for the king, and card games for the queen. But the most popular pastime at the time was jeu de game, and there were two courts in Amboise. On the morning of April 7, 1498, while on his way to attend a tournament, the king lost his life when he hit his head on a door lintel. His widow, in accordance with the marriage contract, married his cousin, Louis d'Orléans, who became king under the name Louis XII. It was January 8, 1499.

The renovation work begun by the late sovereign was completed, particularly that relating to the construction of the second tower, the Heurtault, and the

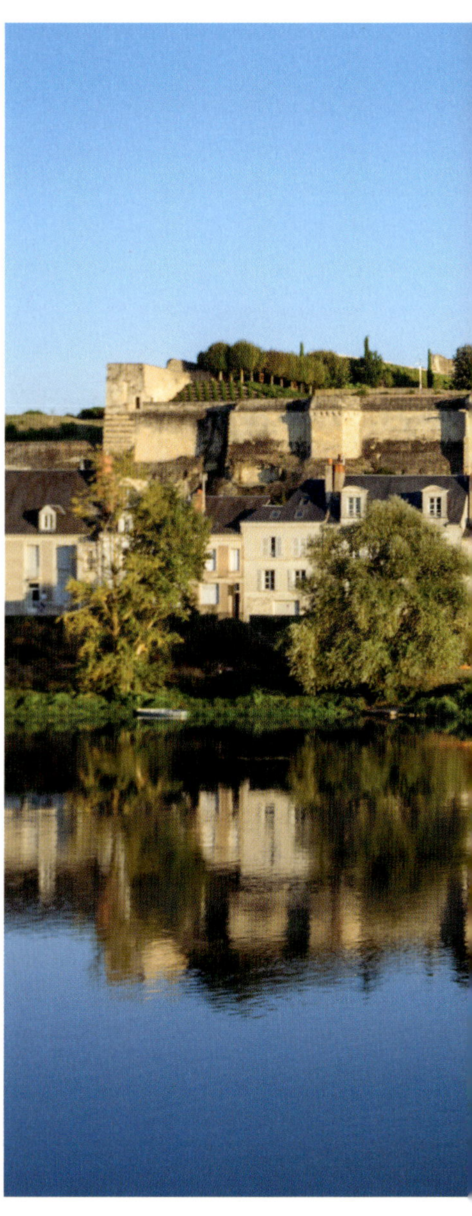

· 88-89: The Château d'Amboise is located on a rocky outcrop, and its ramparts offer a magnificent view of the Loire Valley. In the photo, in the center, the Minimes Tower stands in front of the Gothic wing built under Charles VIII. Like the Heurtault Tower opposite, it is large, with a gentle slope and a series of curves that allowed knights to climb the ramp to the castle terraces.

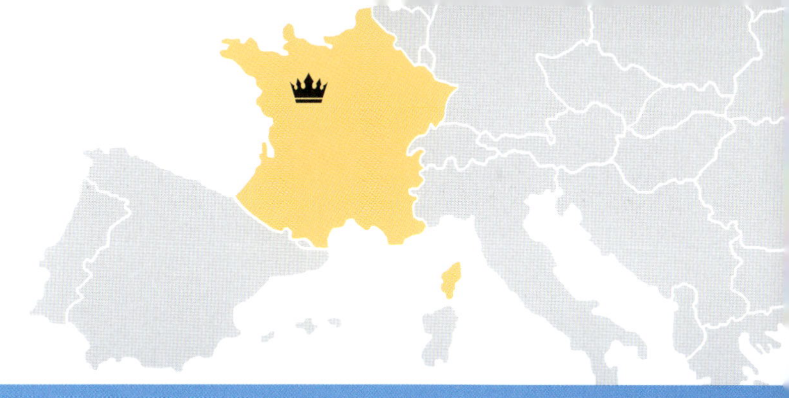

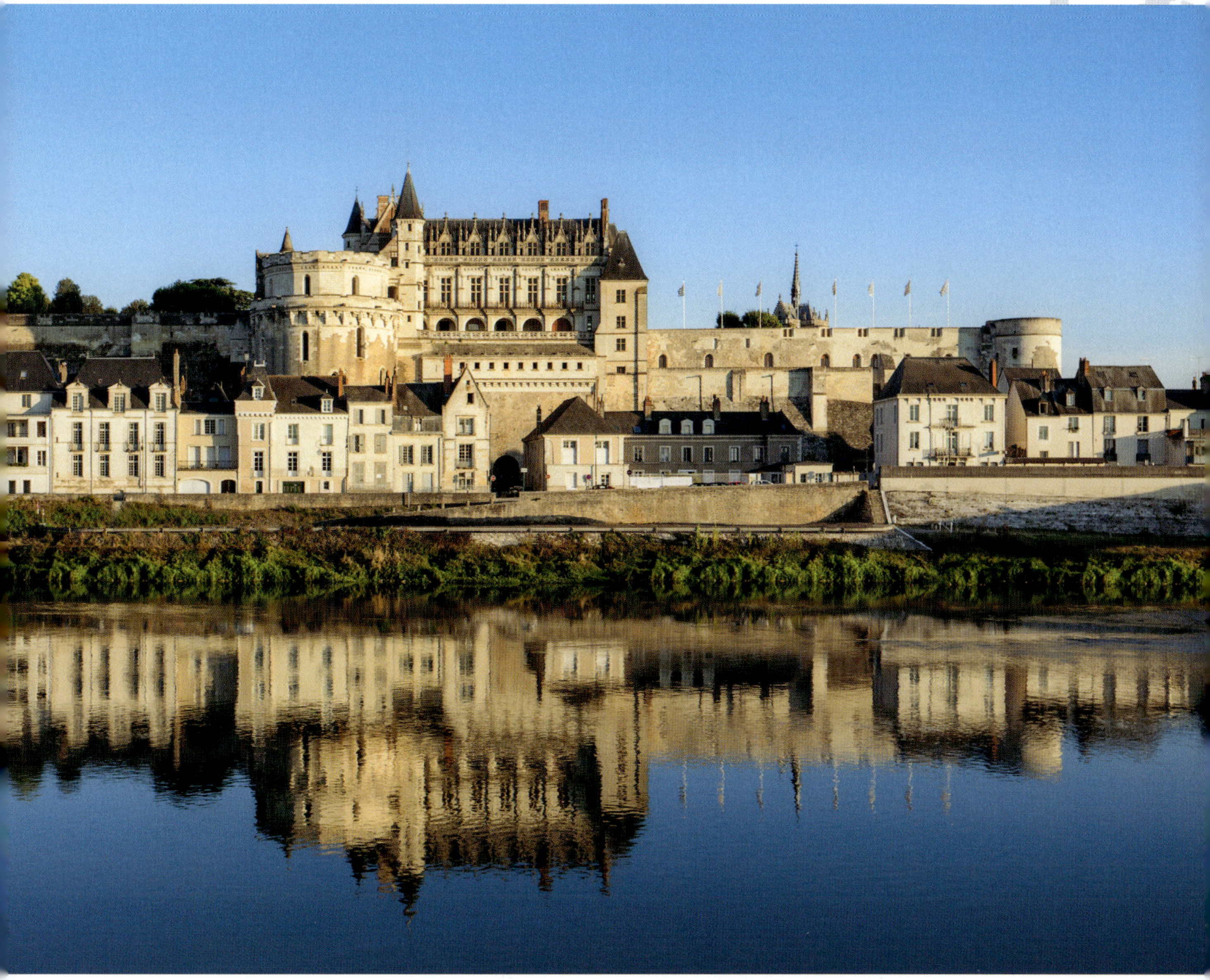

gallery that bordered the garden designed by the horticulturist Pacello da Mercogliano. Louis XII did not settle in Amboise, but moved to his family residence in Blois with the intention of turning it into a proper royal palace. The castle of Amboise was granted to Louise of Savoy, who moved there with her children, Francis and Marguerite d'Angoulême.

In 1515, having become king through his marriage to the eldest daughter of Louis XII, Francis I began to neglect Amboise, both because his wife preferred to move to the castle of her childhood in Blois and because other commitments kept him away. The castle gates were only opened for celebrations and special banquets, shows, wild-boar hunts, and jousting tournaments. It was in this environment that, in 1516, as part of Francis I's entourage, Leonardo da Vinci arrived (along with his pupil Francesco

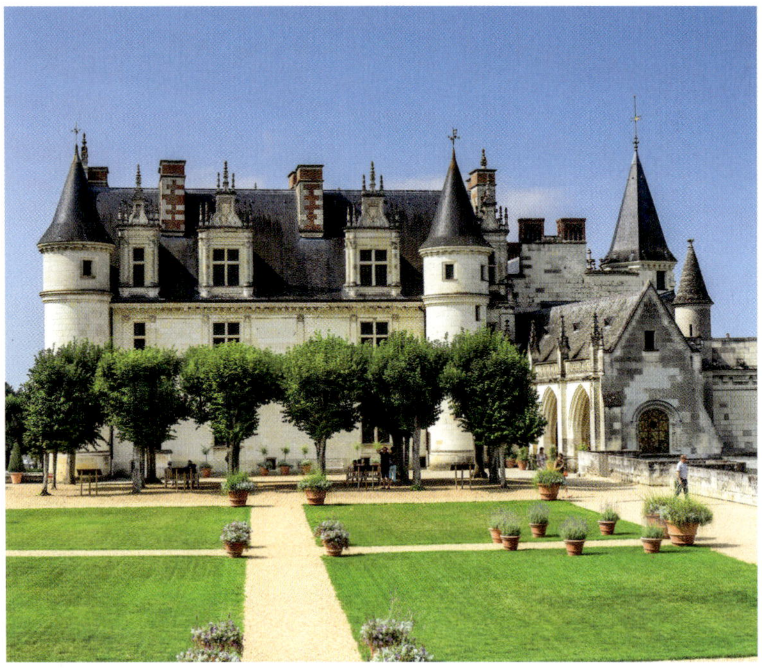

Melzi). It was here, in the small manor house of Clos-Lucé, not far from the castle, that the artist died on May 2, 1519. The king had him buried in the collegiate church of Saint-Florentin at the foot of the Amboise Castle. Henry II, son of Francis I, continued the expansion of the palace by ordering the construction of new buildings on the eastern side: these were the last changes made to the residence, which, century after century, through various changes of ownership and functions, fell into oblivion and was only restored at the beginning of the 20th century.

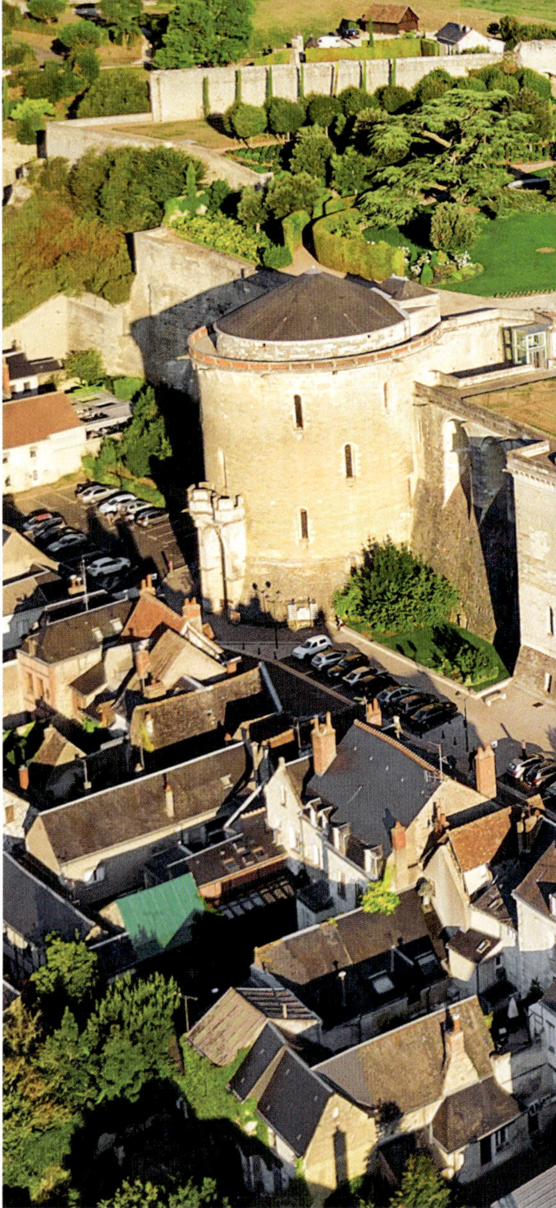

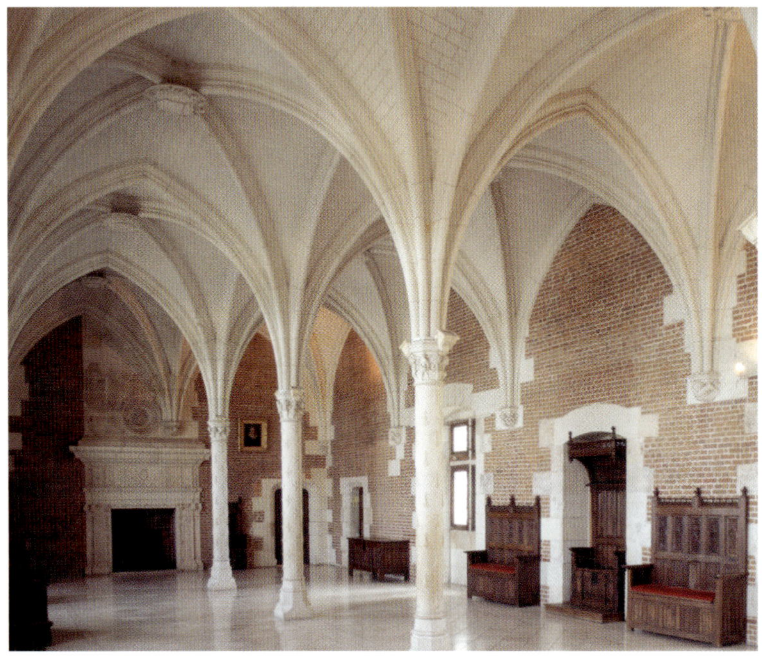

• 90 top: View of the Louis XII wing of the Château d'Amboise from the gardens, "the terrace of Naples," redesigned by Pacello da Mercogliano. A ménagerie, or a sort of ménagerie, was also created where, according to the fashion of the time, wild animals were kept, including three lions.

• 90 bottom: The Council Chamber is characterized by the coexistence of Gothic style—the cross vaults, the fireplace with its trapezoidal hood—with the Renaissance style. The hood of the Gothic fireplace is carved with ermine spots (symbol of Brittany) and lilies of France. The same emblems decorate the columns and stained-glass windows overlooking the Loire. In the large Council Hall, the king would meet to discuss affairs of state with governors, officers, and members of the clergy.

• 90–91: This striking aerial view shows the entire Amboise Castle complex, embellished with beautiful gardens. In the center, protected by a semicircular hedge, you can see the bust of Leonardo da Vinci.

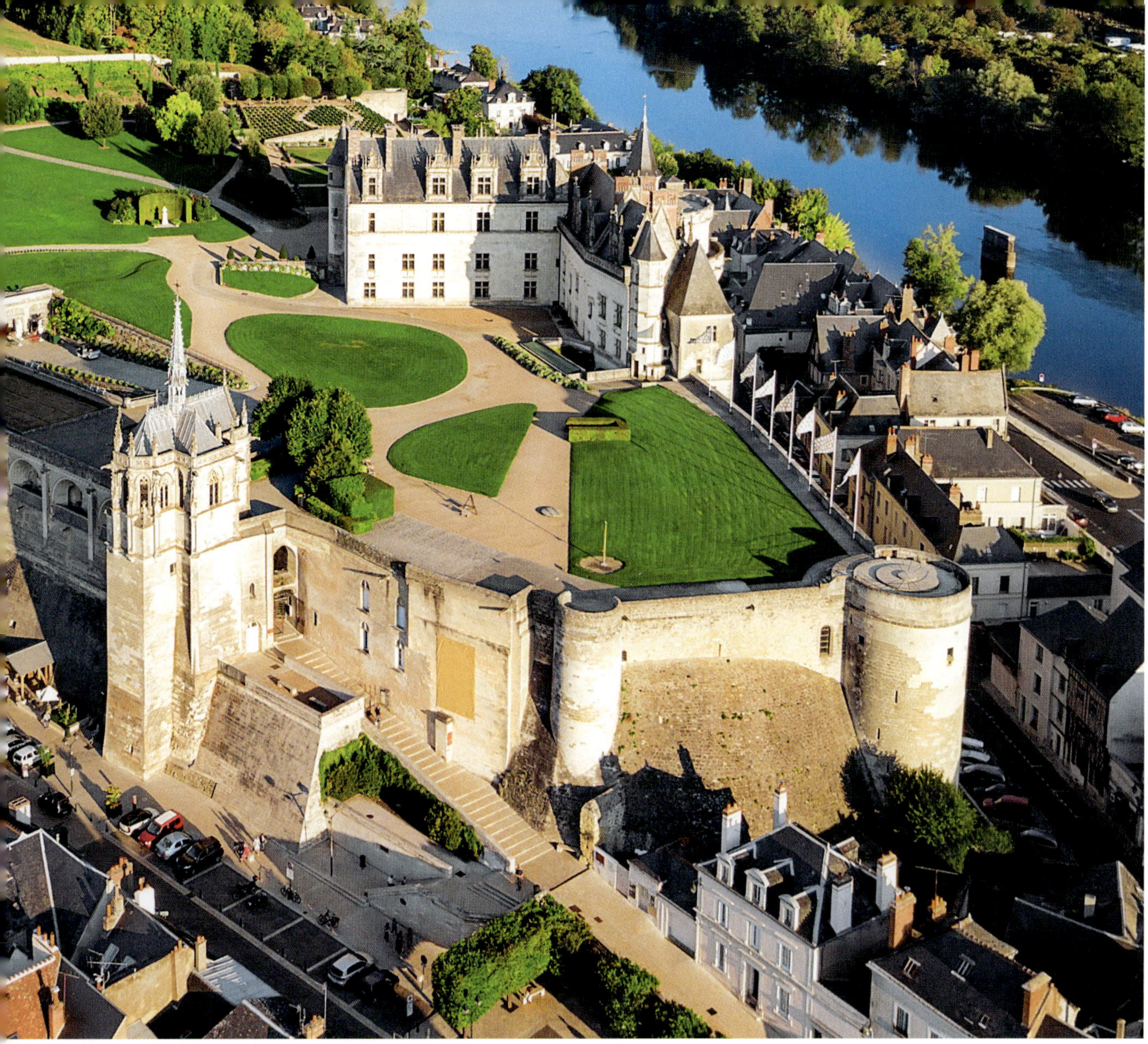

Leonardo, the king's guest

In 1516, during the period when Francis I had moved his court to Amboise, the king welcomed the elderly Leonardo da Vinci at the Château du Clos-Lucé. The small manor house, restored in the style of Louis XII, was located a short distance from the royal castle: according to a legend (never confirmed), the two residences were connected by an underground passage that allowed Leonardo to visit the king whenever he wished. The Renaissance genius spent the last three years of his life at Clos-Lucé. Named chief painter, engineer, and architect of the king, he was granted a pension of 2000 ecussoleil. During this period, Leonardo worked on a series of "visions" for the king, such as further renovations to Amboise, but above all a new castle in Romorantin, a place dear to the king because it was where his mother, Louise of Savoy, lived. He also devoted himself to perfecting his inventions and had the opportunity to showcase his skills as a director in staging wonderful shows to entertain the sovereign and his courtiers. In the basement of the castle, numerous models based on the artist's sketches are now on display, including a tank, a siege bridge, and the precursor to a helicopter. The park also features several life-size works based on Leonardo's drawings.

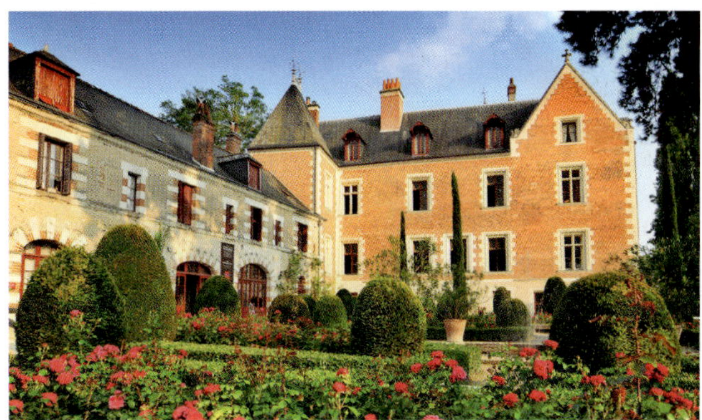

CHENONCEAU CASTLE

1514–1521
The noblewoman Katherine Briçonnet, wife of Thomas Bohier, secretary general of the finances of the King of France, supervised the reconstruction of Chenonceau Castle.

1526
After Katherine Briçonnet's death, the castle passed to the French crown as payment for the family's debts.

1547
Henry II of Valois gave Chenonceau to his favorite, Diane de Poitiers.

1551–1559
Diane de Poitiers undertook a series of works to embellish the manor. She commissioned the magnificent bridge from the architect Philibert de L'Orme.

1560
Catherine de Medici (1519–1589), widow of Henry II, took the castle away from Diane de Poitiers and made it her home.

1561–1589
Under Catherine de Medici, work resumed on the construction of the bridge over the Cher River featuring a gallery. The queen also had new gardens laid out.

1589
Upon the death of Henry III, son of Catherine de Medici, Chenonceau passed to his wife Louise of Lorraine-Vaudémont.

1601
After the death of Louise of Lorraine-Vaudémont, the residence was inherited by Charles of Bourbon, son of Henry IV, and remained the property of the Dukes of Vendôme until the beginning of the 18th century.

1733
On June 9, financier Claude Dupin purchased Chenonceau. His wife, Madame Louise Dupin, restored the castle to its former glory.

1864
The chemist Théophile-Jules Pelouze purchased Chenonceau for his wife Marguerite, who led a series of renovations.

1913
In 1913, the castle passed to the chocolate-manufacturer family Menier. During the First World War, the residence became a military hospital.

The history of Chenonceau Castle, nestled on the banks of the River Cher, is marked by a succession of women. Each of them, starting with the first lady of the house at the start of the 16th century, contributed to embellishing it and make it the perfect setting for romantic encounters, parties, and literary symposiums. The first owner of the Chenonceau estate, which included a fortified mill and the remains of an ancient castle, was the wife of Thomas Bohier in the early 16th century. It was given to her by her wealthy husband, who had taken advantage of the financial difficulties of the previous owner, Pierre Marques, to take possession of the estate. In place of the old manor house (only the moat and keep were retained), the Bohiers had a new residence built over a period of six years starting in 1514, modeled on a Venetian palace. Although it did not yet have the famous bridge, the Gothic elements added in this first phase of construction foreshadowed the splendor of the final building. Upon the death of the Bohier couple, the property passed to the crown and was taken over by Governor Anne de Montmorency on behalf of King Francis I, whose attention at that time was focused on the construction of the nearby Château de Chambord, only 37 miles away. In 1547, upon the death of Francis I, his son ascended to the throne of France and took the name Henry II. The young king had been married since 1533 to Catherine de Medici, a descendant of the wealthy Florentine banking family. Although his wife was educated, intelligent, and respectful, from the year after their wedding the king began to prefer Diane de Poitiers, to whom, despite being twenty years his senior, he remained faithful throughout his life. As a token of his love, Henry II gave her the Château de Chenonceau. In the few years that Diane was the mistress of the house, in addition to reorganizing the magnificent gardens, she commissioned the architect Philibert de L'Orme to build the most amazing feature of the castle: the arched bridge connecting it to the opposite bank. The woman's fortune waned in 1559 with the death of the king: Catherine de Medici immediately demanded the castle back, giving Diane the castle of Chaumont in exchange. Although

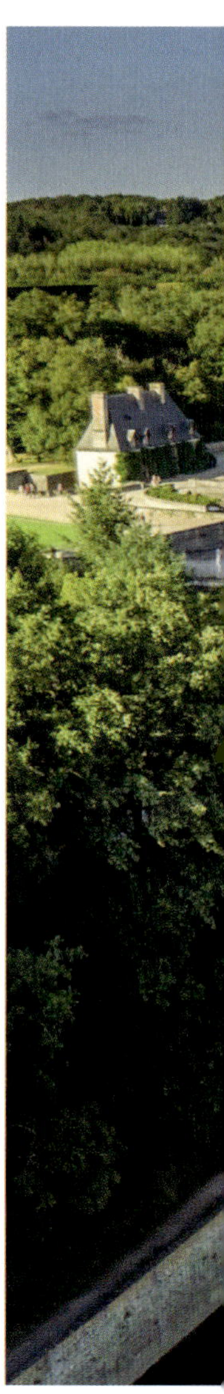

• 92-93: A magnificent view of Chenonceau Castle, which seems to float above the Cher River. The bridge over the Cher was designed in 1559 on the orders of Diane de Poitiers. When Catherine de Medici forced Diane to leave the castle, only the arches, designed by Philibert de L'Orme, had been completed. The gallery was redesigned in 1576 by Jean Bullant. On the left, on the terrace above the River, Diana's geometric French garden extends for 130,000 square feet, while on the opposite side Catherine de Medici had her garden laid out, bordering a park with centuries-old trees.

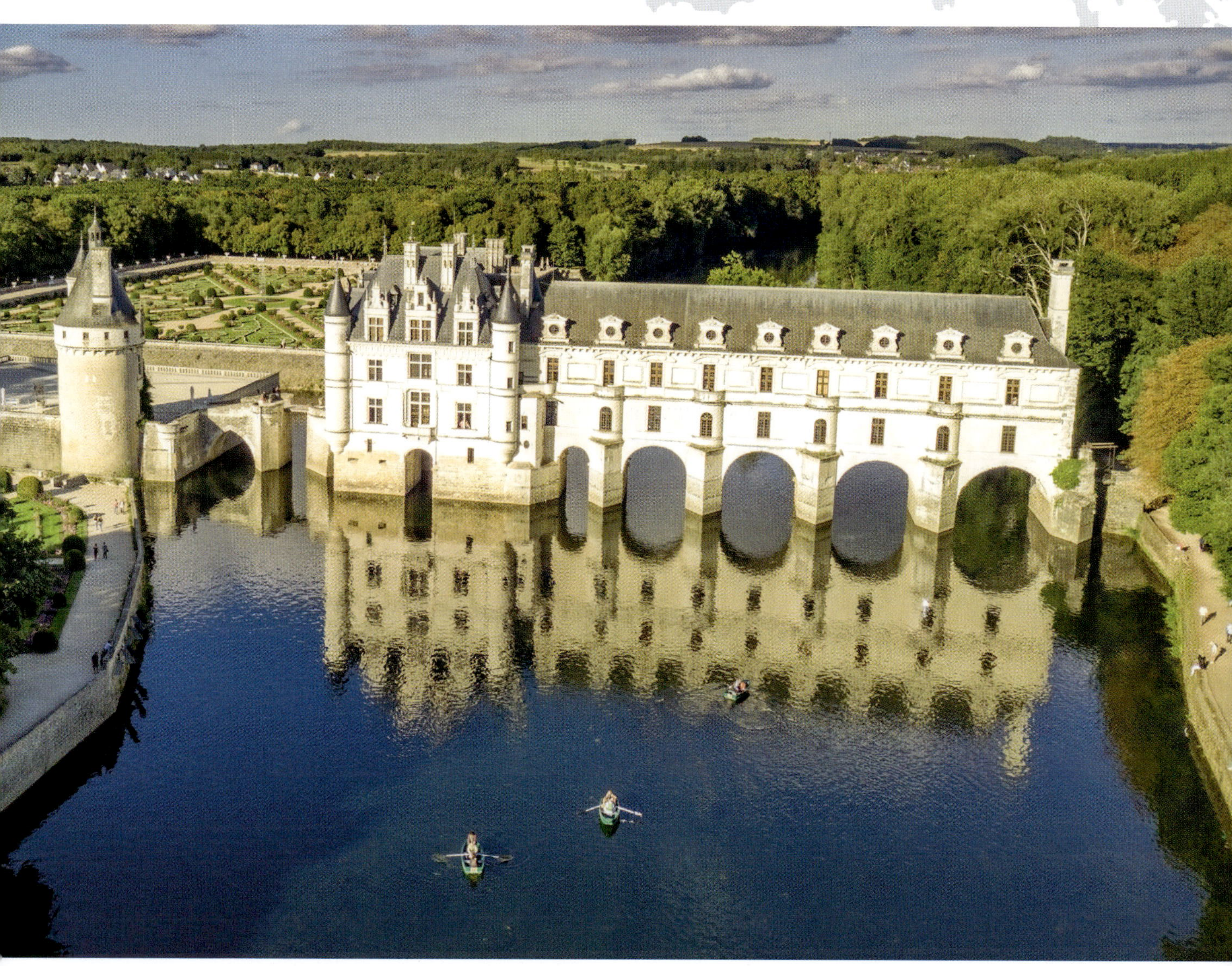

France was in a complicated situation due to the clashes between Catholic and Protestant forces, Catherine spared no expense in organizing parties and entertainment that took place on the richly furnished upper floor on the magnificent covered gallery above the castle bridge: an elongated two-story wing, characterized by façades animated by ingenious avant-corps, eighteen windows, and nine dormers on each side. Meanwhile, her sons succeeded her on the throne of France: the frail Francis II, who died in 1560, and Charles IX. Upon his death in 1575, his brother Henry, a complex and extravagant personality, became king. He died only four years later, leaving his widow, Louise de Vaudémont, Princess of Lorraine, without heirs. She remained at Chenonceau, in the castle inherited from Catherine de Medici. From that moment on, she wore the white mourning dress of queens and shut herself away for eleven years in her simple apartments, whose walls she had painted black.

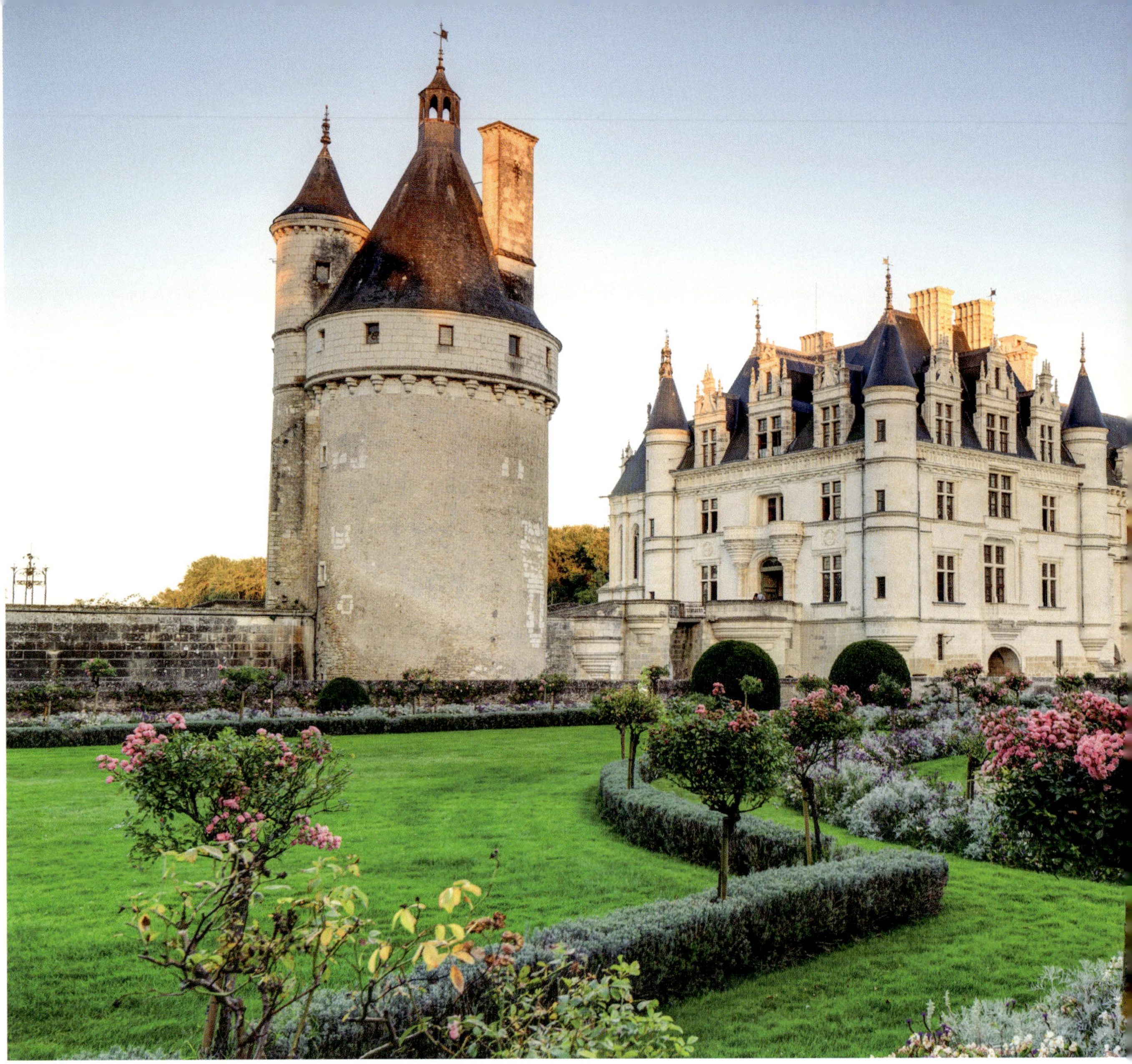

The masterpiece of the favorite

At the beginning of the 16th century, the castle garden was nothing more than a large plot of land used mainly as a vegetable garden. In 1551, work began on the construction of a French-style garden to the east of the castle, which was to be the most beautiful in the region. Various workers were hired, including carpenters, masons, diggers, and stonecutters, who were tasked with building a terrace raised above the river. To protect it from flooding, stone walls were erected around the garden and a moat was built, into which the waters of the Cher poured through a sluice. A wooden bridge connected the garden to the castle entrance. After two years of intense work, the green area, a square space of 5 acres, was completed. At the center of this rigorous geometric layout, there is still a fountain with a high jet of water, as was customary in the Renaissance.

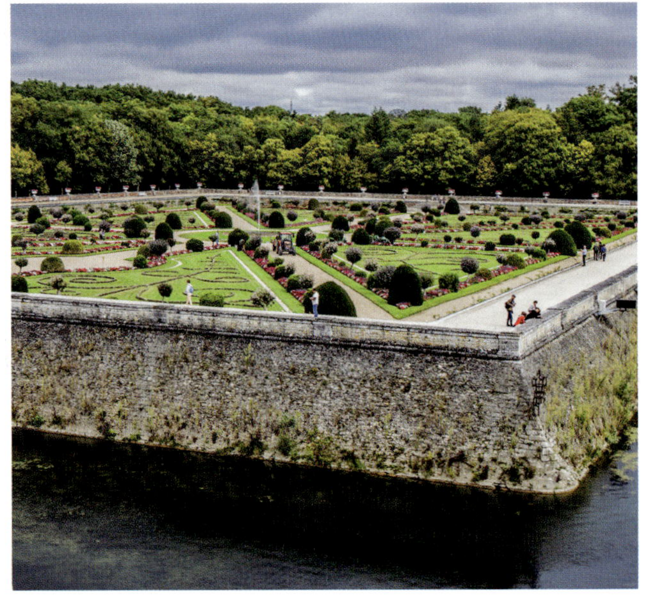

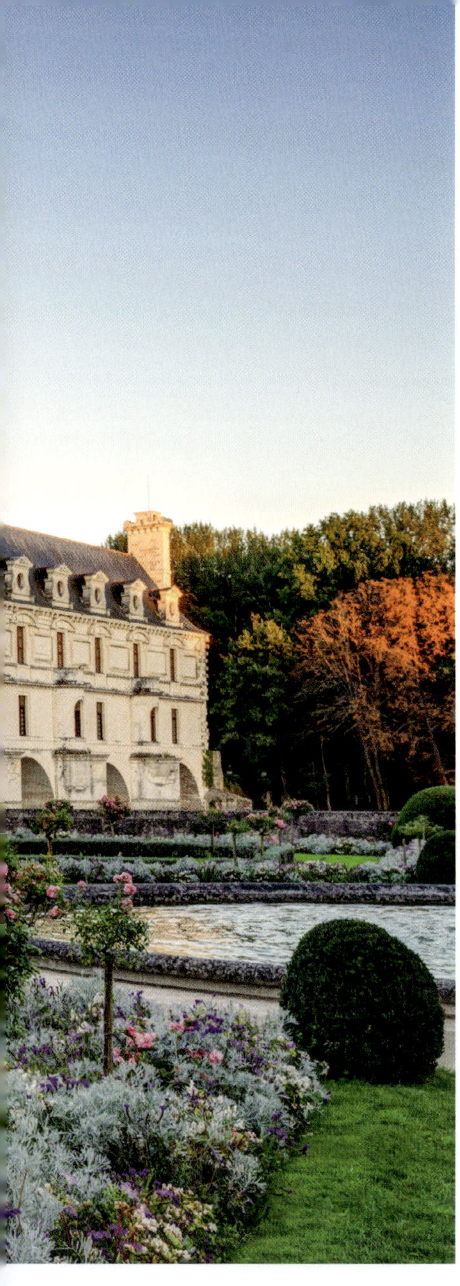

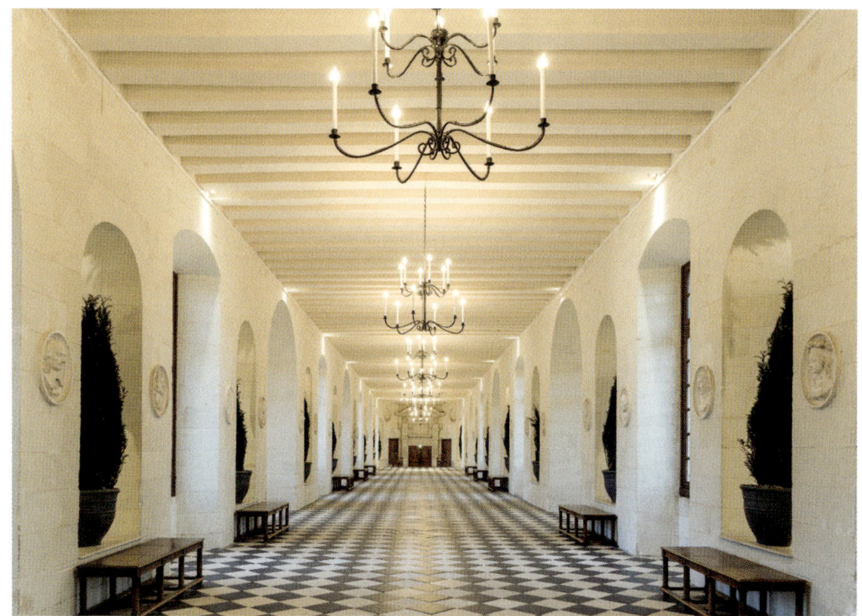

After his death, the castle passed from owner to owner until 1733, when it was purchased by the ambitious Claude Dupin, whose wife Louise, a beautiful, intelligent, and progressive woman, used to entertain the leading figures of the Enlightenment in her salon, from Voltaire to Montesquieu, Bernard le Bovier de Fontenelle, Pierre de Marivaux, and the young Jean-Jacques Rousseau. The last lady to live in the castle was Marguerite Pelouze, who spent a fortune restoring it to its former glory during the time of Diane de Poitiers. A political scandal led to her ruin, and Chenonceau continually changed hands until 1913, when, during World War I, the two galleries were converted into a hospital run and subsidized by Simone Menier at the expense of her family (chocolate producers), who were the last owners of the manor.

• 94-95: From Catherine's garden, there is a magnificent view of the west façade of the castle. The structure consists of five grass-covered panels gathered around an elegant circular pool.

• 95 top: Catherine de Medici's Gallery, inaugurated in 1577 with a spectacular celebration, is 196 feet long and features a tuff and slate floor. At each end are two large Renaissance fireplaces.

• 95 bottom: In Diane de Poitiers' room, the initials of Henry II and Catherine de Medici stand out on the coffered ceiling and fireplace: an H and a C intertwined to form the D of Diane. Sixteenth-century Flemish tapestries cover the walls.

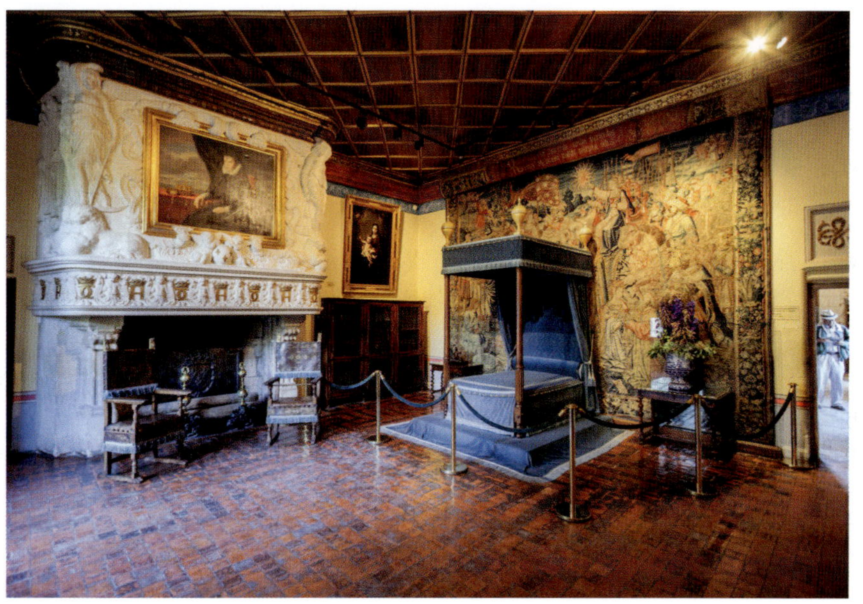

Fénis Castle

25 BC
After defeating the Salassi, the Roman emperor Augustus (63 BC–14 AD) founded *Augusta Prætoria Salassorum*, now known as Aosta.

774–904
After the fall of the Western Roman Empire (476), the Aosta Valley became part of the Lombard Kingdom in 568. With the defeat of the Lombards, the territory became part of the Carolingian Empire (800–887) in 774, before being annexed to the Kingdom of Burgundy in 904.

1032
Umberto Biancamano (c. 970–1047 or 1048), the alleged founder of the Savoy dynasty, obtained the title of Count of Aosta: his descendants would strengthen their power over the territory in the following centuries.

10th–12th century
Towers and fortified houses were built on the mountains and in strategic positions by the local lords who ruled on behalf of the Savoy family: the d'Avise and the Châtelard families as well as the Sarriod de la Tour (or de Bard) and, above all, the Challant family.

1340–1421
Aimone di Challant (c. 1305–1387) began the renovation of the first 14th-century nucleus of Fénis Castle in 1340. This was completed by his son Bonifacio. The manor served as the administrative headquarters of the Challant-Fénis family.

1895–1898
After years of neglect and changes of ownership, in 1895 Fénis Castle became owned by Alfredo de Andrade (1839–1915), who undertook a restoration campaign aimed at stopping its deterioration.

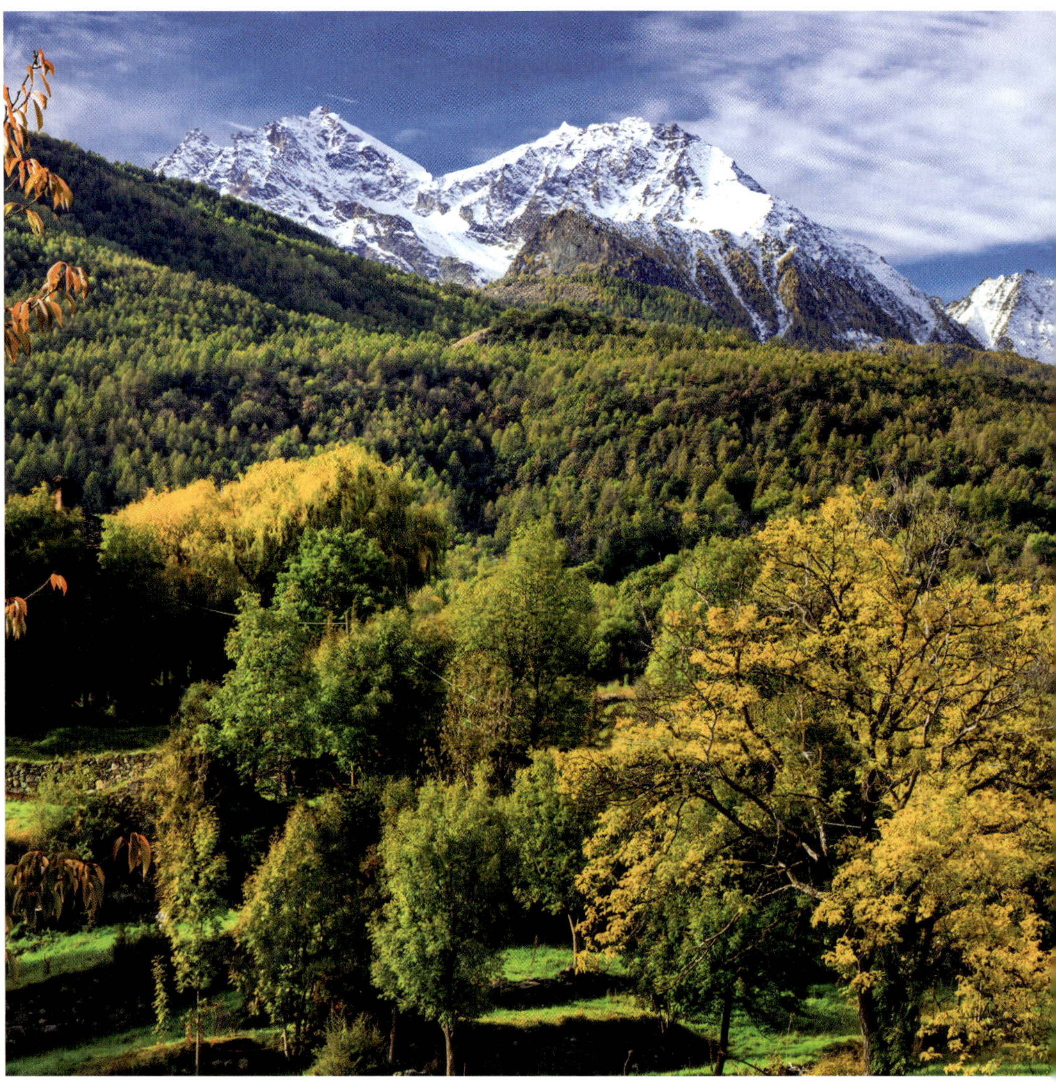

Starting in the 12th century, the noble Challant family enjoyed great power throughout the Middle Ages and the Renaissance thanks to the support of the Savoy family, the counts of Aosta. The founders of the dynasty had several cadet branches, which often fought among themselves and with other noble families in the valley, to obtain temporal and spiritual offices and to defend their fiefdoms. The castles of Fénis, Verrès, Ussel, and Issogne bear witness to the predominant presence of the family in the Aosta Valley. Among the members of the family who achieved a position of prestige thanks to their loyalty to the Savoy family was Aimone di Challant, founder of the Challant-Fénis,

• 96-97: Fénis Castle, one of the symbols of the Aosta Valley, is located on a plateau just over 18 miles from the capital.

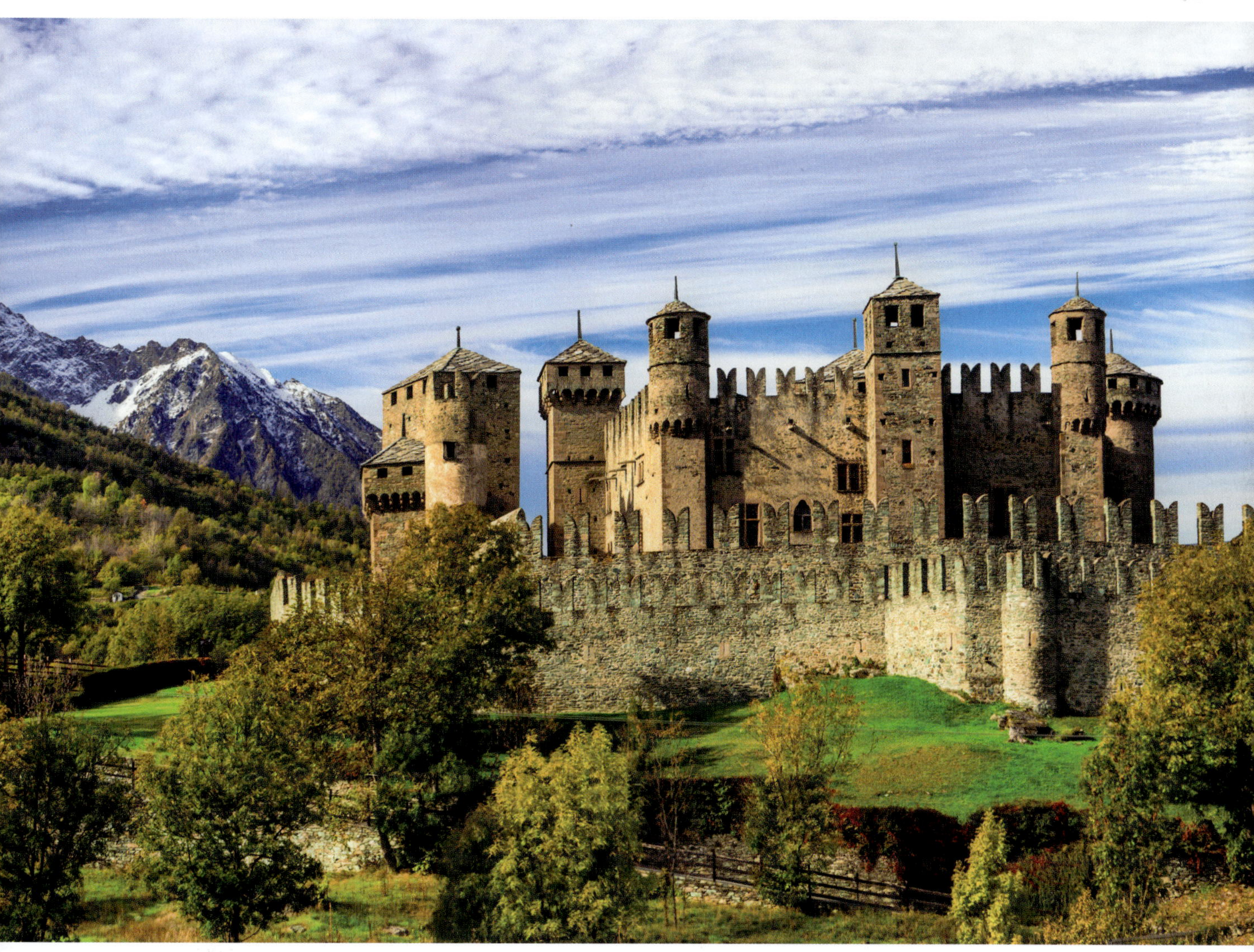

born at the beginning of the 14th century. To demonstrate the power he had gained through various military and diplomatic positions, he ordered that the Castle of Fénis, at the time a simple tower, be enlarged, rebuilding the central body in its current pentagonal shape, incorporating existing buildings, and extending and strengthening the crenellated walls. Although the castle was still adorned with military and defensive elements, it was beginning to take on the appearance of a prestigious residence for the Challant family. It could accommodate about 60 people, including the feudal lord, his family, servants, and military garrison. Upon the death of Aimone di Challant, the fiefdom and castle of Fénis passed to his eldest son Bonifacio, who continued the renovation work in 1392, transforming the manor into a comfortable residence, embellished, in accordance with the fashion of the time, with paintings evoking the spirit of the court. It was during this period that a new building was constructed to the west, giving the inner courtyard its current appearance, with two floors of wooden balconies and a large semicircular stone staircase.

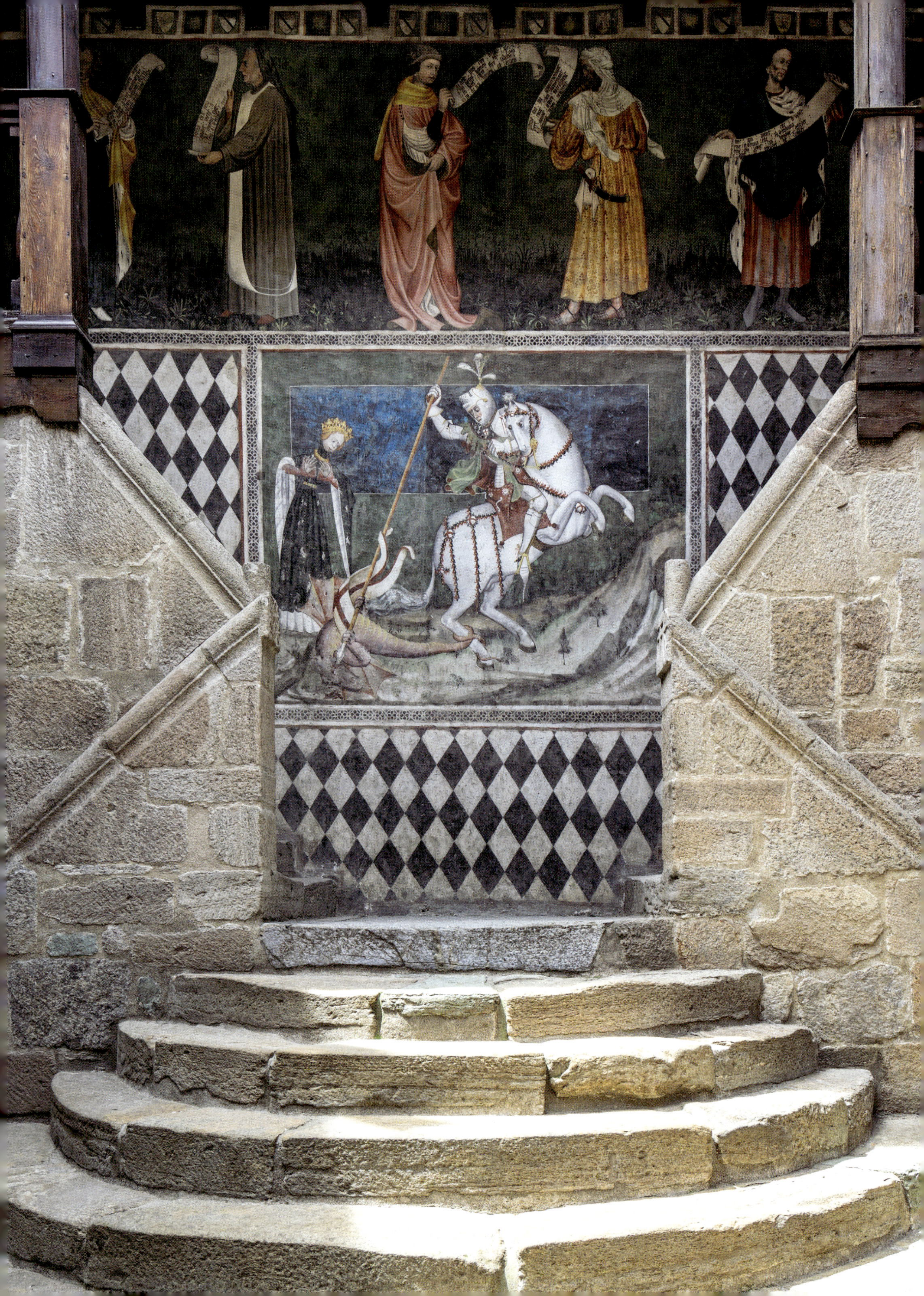

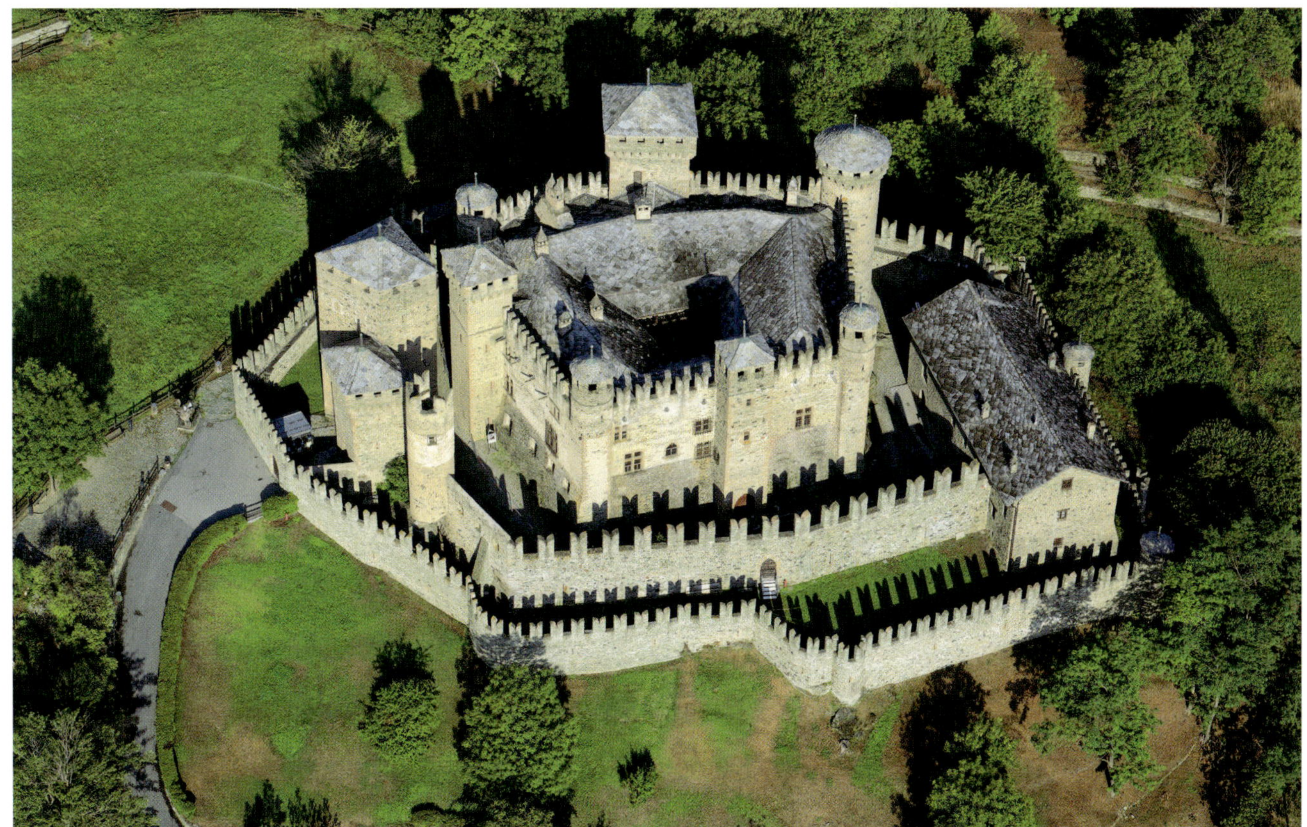

Unlike other medieval castles located on hilltops or built next to a river to take advantage of natural defenses, this castle stands in the middle of a gentle grassy hill. The double walls that characterize its structure were built precisely to make it more secure. The outer part has an irregular plan with several guard towers connected by a walkway. The interior is a sort of labyrinth with the heart of the castle at its center: a small but charming courtyard with its wall paintings and semicircular staircase. The underground rooms housed the cellars and prisons, while the ground floor contained the service rooms and kitchens. The reception rooms and the apartments of the feudal lord and his family occupied the first floor. The castle remained in the Challant family's possession until 1716. After the death of the last descendant of the family, the castle passed from owner to owner until it fell into a state of neglect. It was even used as a stable and barn. Alfredo d'Andrade bought it at the beginning of the 20th century and, after extensively restoring it, donated it to the state. Today it is owned by the Aosta Valley Region.

• 98: The fresco on the staircase depicts Saint George slaying the dragon and freeing the princess. Attributed to Giacomo Jaquerio (1375–1453) and his workshop, it was painted around 1415. On the walls of the courtyard, other paintings feature rows of saints, sages, and philosophers.

• 99 top: The castle was built on a fortification first mentioned in a document from 1242 as the property of the Viscount of Aosta, Goffredo of Challant, and his brothers. At that time, there was a single wall surrounding the castle, with a building in the center.

Fénis at the Valentino

During the Italian Artistic and Industrial General Exhibition held in Turin in 1884, Alfredo d'Andrade, an expert in medieval architecture, was inspired by Fénis and Verrès castles in the Aosta Valley, as well as other manors in Piedmont, to design a medieval village within the Valentino Park that would stand the test of time, unlike the other pavilions built for the occasion and demolished at the end of the event. The village overlooks the River Po and looks like a typical 15th-century fortified village, with houses, churches, squares, and fountains reconstructed along a main street. The courtyard of the fortress, which dominates the small urban center, is a faithful reproduction of that Fénis Castle, with its semicircular staircase, fresco of St. George slaying the dragon, and wooden balconies.

Royal Palace of Turin

1563
Duke Emanuele Filiberto of Savoy (1528–1580) moved the capital of the Duchy from Chambéry, in Savoy, to Turin. The court settled in the Bishop's Palace, which became the Royal Palace.

1584
The Royal Palace was designed by Ascanio Vitozzi (1539–1615), an architect and military engineer from Orvieto. Partially built, it was only completed after the civil war (1639–1642).

1684
As part of the expansion of the residence commissioned by Duke Vittorio Amedeo II (1666–1732), the Palace Gallery, known as the "del Daniel," was created by architect Daniel Seiter (1647–1705).

1713
Filippo Juvarra (1678–1736) arrived in Turin at the court of Vittorio Amedeo II. The architect proposed a grandiose urban redevelopment project for the capital, in addition to the renovation of the Royal Palace.

1832
Pelagio Palagi (1775–1860) was called to Turin by King Carlo Alberto (1798–1849), who commissioned him to renovate the rooms of the Royal Palace, intervene in the Royal Gardens, and solve the problem of the closure of the Piazzetta Reale.

1861–1946
Vittorio Emanuele II of Savoy (1820–1878) was the first king of Italy, and Turin was the capital of the Kingdom until it was moved to Florence in 1865. With the referendum of June 2, 1946, the Italian people voted in favor of the Republic, putting an end to the monarchy in Italy.

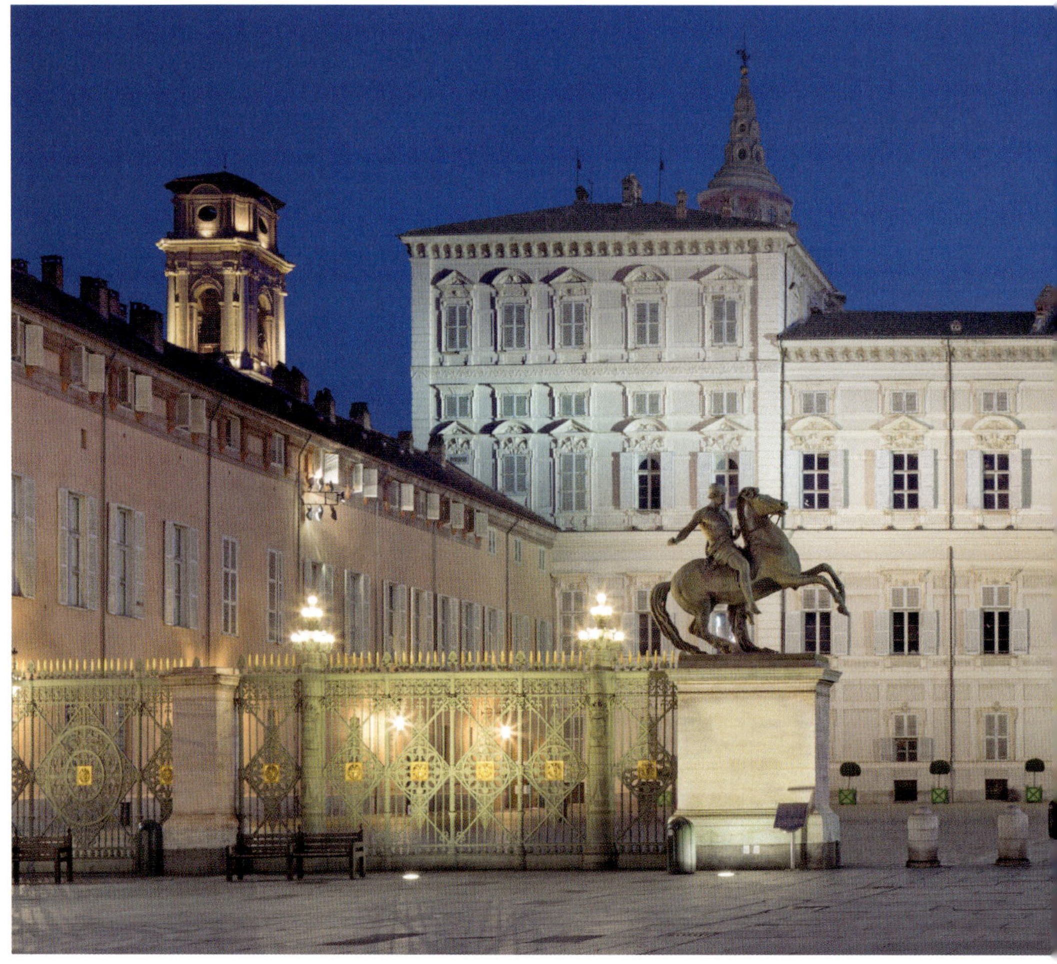

The current Royal Palace of Turin is the result of long transformations that took place at different times, following the needs of those who had lived there since the 16th century, the changing tastes of the time, and the architects called upon to work on it. Very little remains of the bishop's residence that Emanuele Filiberto chose as the seat of the ducal court when he moved the capital of the Duchy of Savoy from Chambéry to Turin. Upon the death of his father, Carlo Emanuele I (1562–1630), finding the austere palace unsuitable as a royal residence, he began the construction of a new residence, part of an ambitious project destined to profoundly change the architecture of the square and the city itself, which was to be worthy of its role as the capital of a European state. The task was entrusted to the court architect Ascanio Vittozzi, but construction went through various phases, and it wasn't

• 100–101: The façade of the Royal Palace is 426 feet long and 98 feet high. Despite its austere and imposing look, it is perfectly in line with the sobriety of the entire square in front of it and with the image that the Savoy family wanted to project to the world.

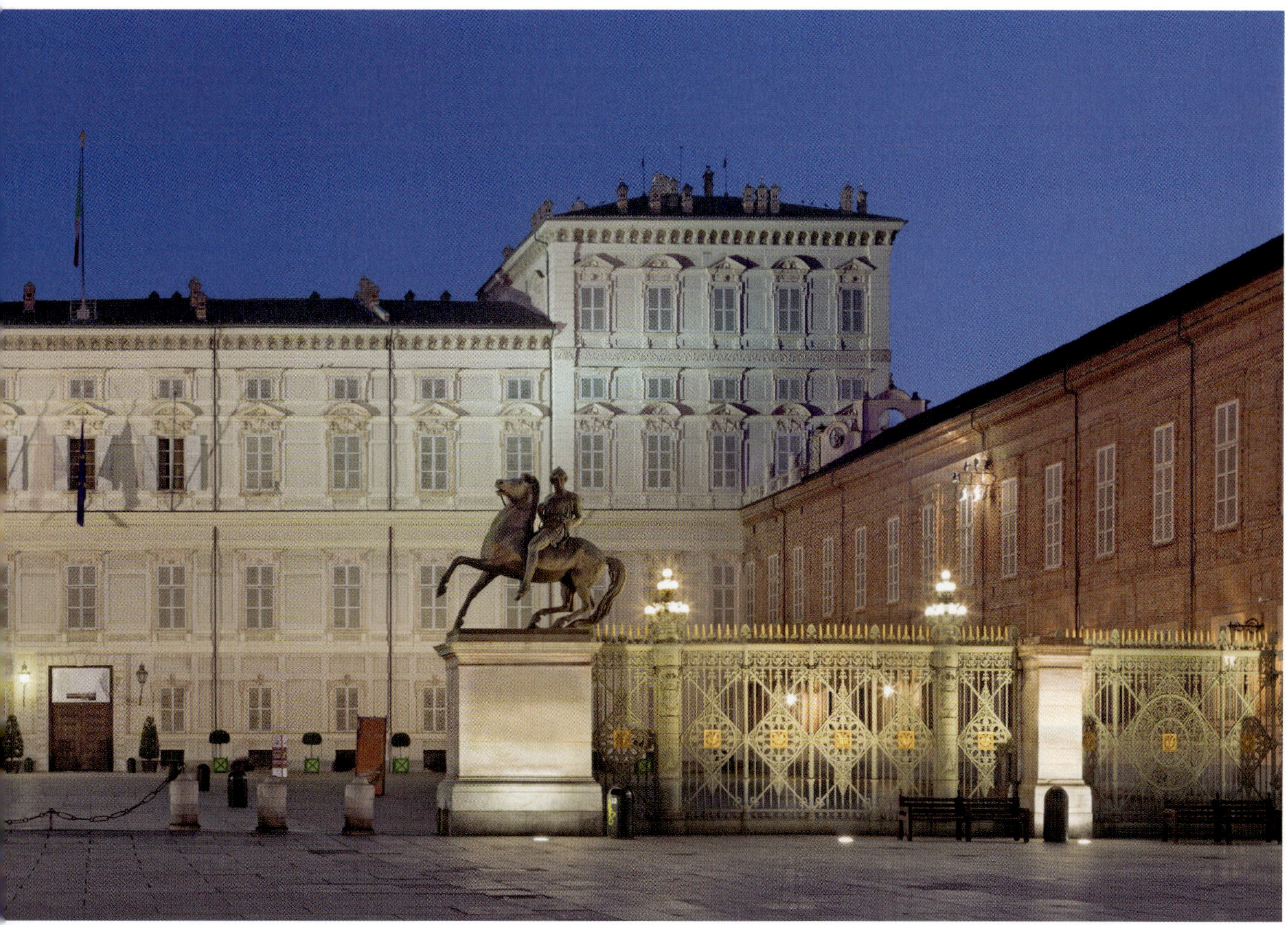

until the second half of the 17th century that the work on the so-called "Palazzo Novo Grande" was completed. In the following centuries, the leading court architects made further changes and additions to meet the representational needs of the Savoy family. In 1663, for example, for the marriage of Carlo Emanuele II to Françoise Madeleine d'Orléans, the rooms on the main floor were rearranged and divided into two apartments, one facing the square for the duke and the other facing the courtyard for the duchess. The most significant alterations to the palace, both in terms of style and layout, were carried out under Vittorio Amedeo II, who, during his long reign (from 1675 to 1730), transformed Savoy politics, claiming, with the outbreak of the War of the Spanish Succession, the full autonomy of the Duchy from the influence of Spain and France, eventually acquiring the coveted royal title. Although his reign was certainly not characterized by peace, the monarch did not fail to call great artists to court, including Filippo Juvarra, who was appointed His Majesty's Chief Architect. In the Royal Palace, he devoted himself to renovating the refined and luxurious interiors; his most famous work is the Scala delle Forbici (Scissors Staircase), designed with four flights. When Juvarra left for Madrid in 1735, the position of Chief Royal Architect passed to Benedetto Alfieri (1699–1767), who, among other works, designed the Teatro Regio.

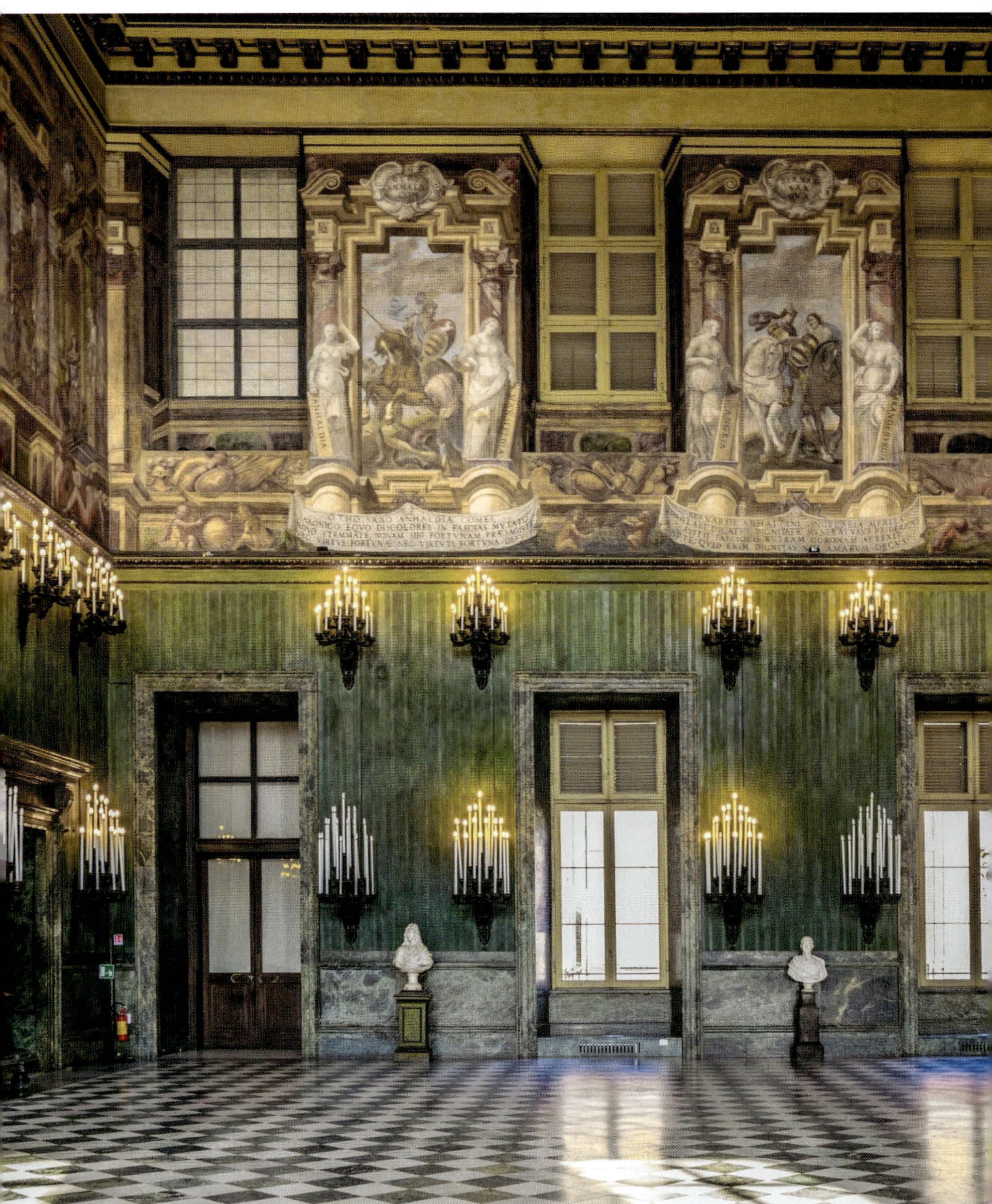
OTHO SAXO ANHALDIÆ COMES
EQVO DISCOLORES IN FASCIAS
STEMMATE NOVAM SIBI FORTVNAM PRÆSAGIV

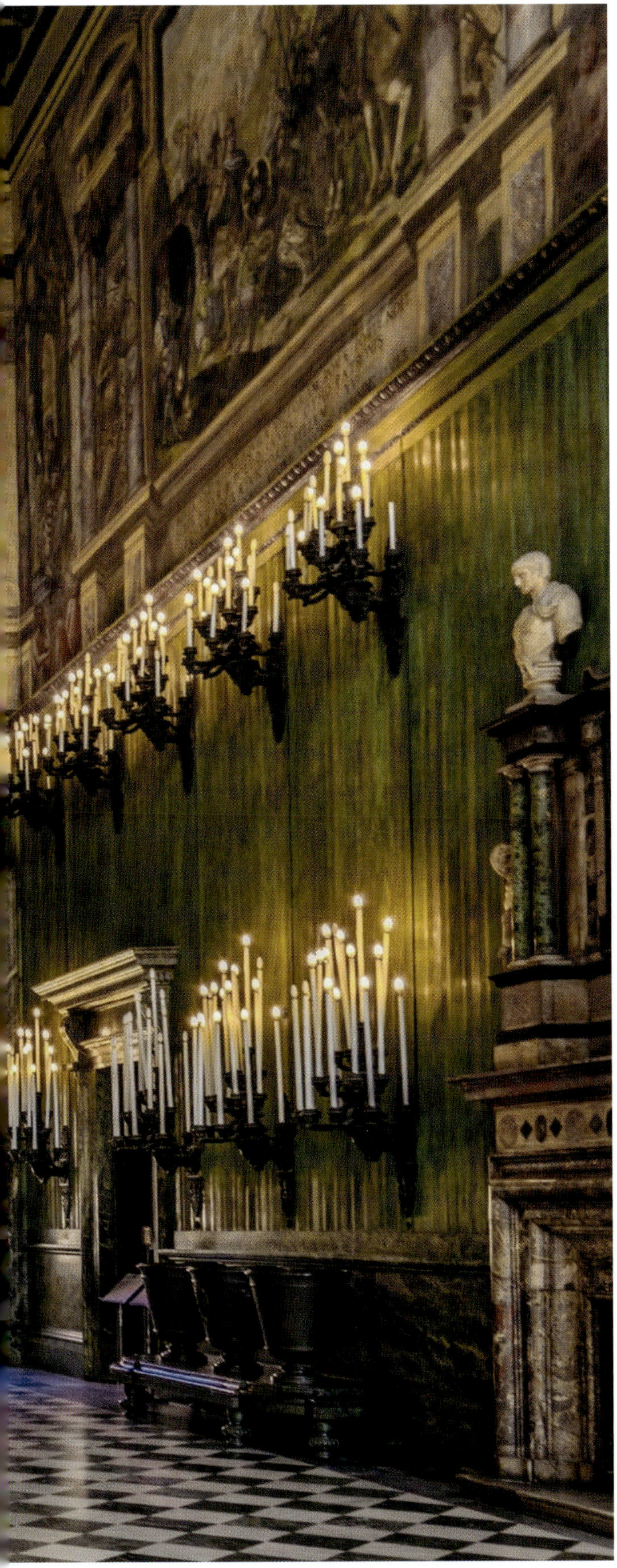

At the Savoy table

Lunch time at the Savoy court was all a matter of strict etiquette. While in the 17th century meals were always held in public, in the 18th century, under Vittorio Amedeo II, ordinary lunches were held in private in the king's apartment. The task of serving them fell to the Grand Chamberlain, assisted by two Gentlemen of the Chamber. Obviously, the protocol was much more complicated for official lunches and left no room for error. It was the court chamberlain's job to make sure that the customs of the Savoy court were honored along with those of the guest, who would sit next to the king at the center of the long side of the table with his wife opposite him; the least important guest sat at the head of the table. The menu was agreed upon by the Chamberlain with the Chief Steward, who coordinated the kitchens, as well as the choice of wines. The white wine from the Rhine was very popular. As it was unfiltered, it had a cloudy appearance and left a residue at the bottom of the glass: this inelegant inconvenience was overcome by using colored glasses.

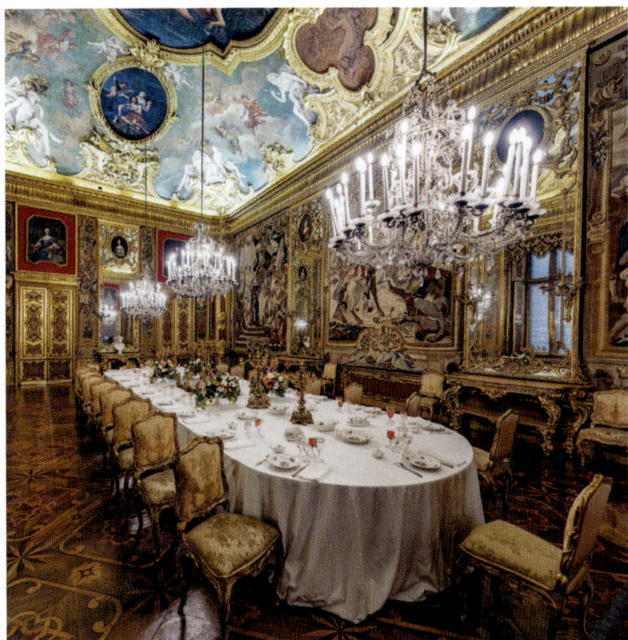

• 102–103: The grand staircase leads to the Hall of the Swiss Guards, where they were stationed. For this vast room, the Savoy family wanted a horizontal meridian line, about 39 feet long, placed diagonally on the floor. Through a hole in the upper part of the south wall, next to the central window, the sun's rays are projected along the line drawn on the floor, marking local noon.

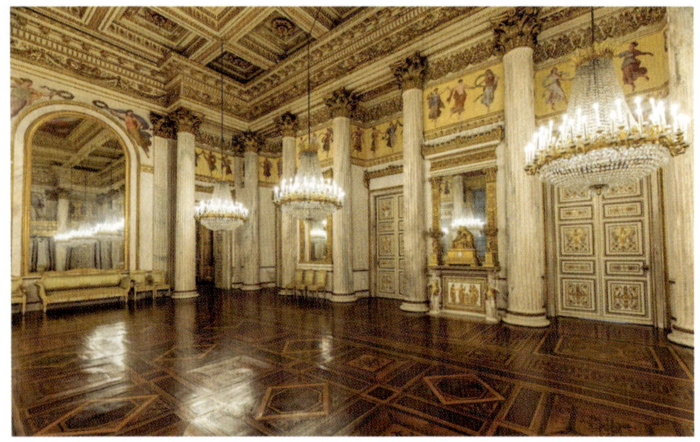

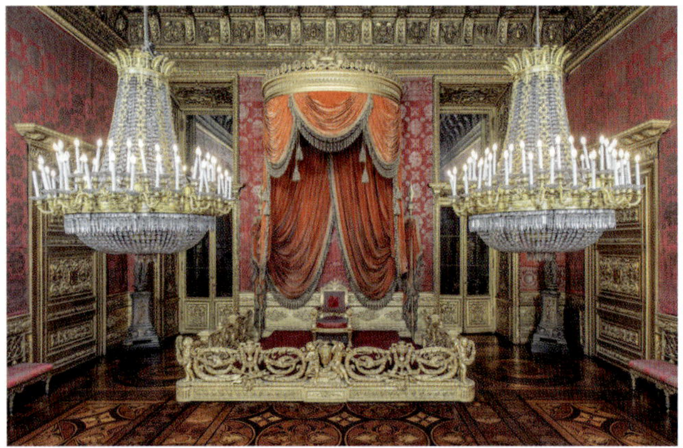

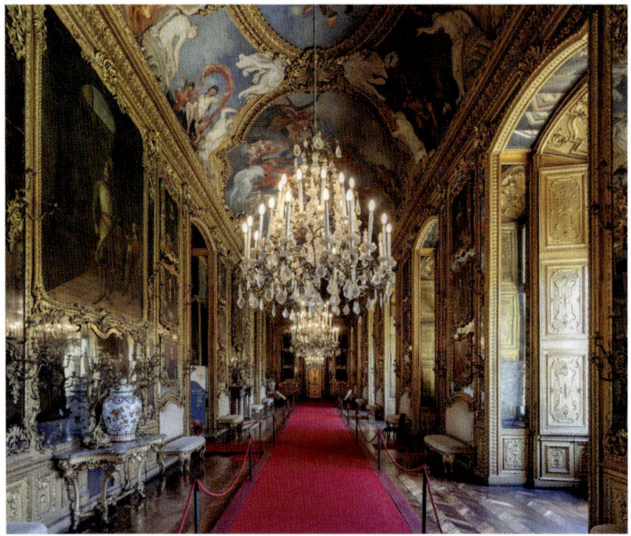

Difficult years followed: Vittorio Amedeo III (1726-1796) found himself reigning during the French Revolution and the First Italian Campaign led by General Napoleon Bonaparte, who forced the king to sign the disastrous Treaty of Paris in 1796, which established French hegemony over the Savoy state. The Savoy family would not return to Turin until May 20, 1814. Carlo Alberto of the cadet branch of the Carignano family had the task of restoring the dynasty to its former glory, starting with the refurbishment of the rooms of the Royal Palace. Pelagio Palagi was commissioned for the task and called to court in 1832. The architect and painter satisfied the sovereign with his choice of neoclassical style, which was very popular in European courts during the Restoration, with its abundant use of marble and stucco. In 1861, the Savoy family, with Vittorio Emanuele II, obtained the crown of the Kingdom of Italy. To celebrate the birth of the nation and make the palace worthy of its new role, the king commissioned architect Domenico Ferri to design a monumental marble staircase to replace the existing one. The work had not yet been completed when, with the transfer of the capital to Florence, Vittorio Emanuele II and his wife Maria Adelaide moved to Palazzo Pitti in 1865 and then to Rome, where they chose the Quirinale as their residence. The Royal Palace in Turin became the place to stay during visits to the city. After the referendum of June 2, 1946, in which the Italians decreed the end of the monarchy in favor of the Republic, the Royal Palace, which became property of the State, underwent a period of decline from which it rose again as a museum after major restoration work.

• 104 top: Commissioned by Carlo Alberto, the Ballroom surprises visitors with its size and rich decorations. Particularly spectacular are the eight imposing chandeliers in Bohemian crystal and gilded bronze.

• 104 center: The Throne Room is dominated by an imposing red velvet baldachin adorned with golden silk pendants. The balustrade surrounding the throne is made of carved and gilded wood.

• 104 bottom: Used for court celebrations, the Galleria del Daniel, by Daniel Seiter, is one of the most sought-after rooms in the palace and is every bit as impressive as the Hall of Mirrors at Versailles. The splendid crystal chandeliers date back to the 18th century, while the bronze wall lights, the clock, and the candelabra decorated with hunting scenes were created by sculptor Francesco Ladatte.

• 105: The Grand Staircase, made entirely of marble and designed by Domenico Ferri, is enriched with decorative vases and statues of the most important members of the House of Savoy.

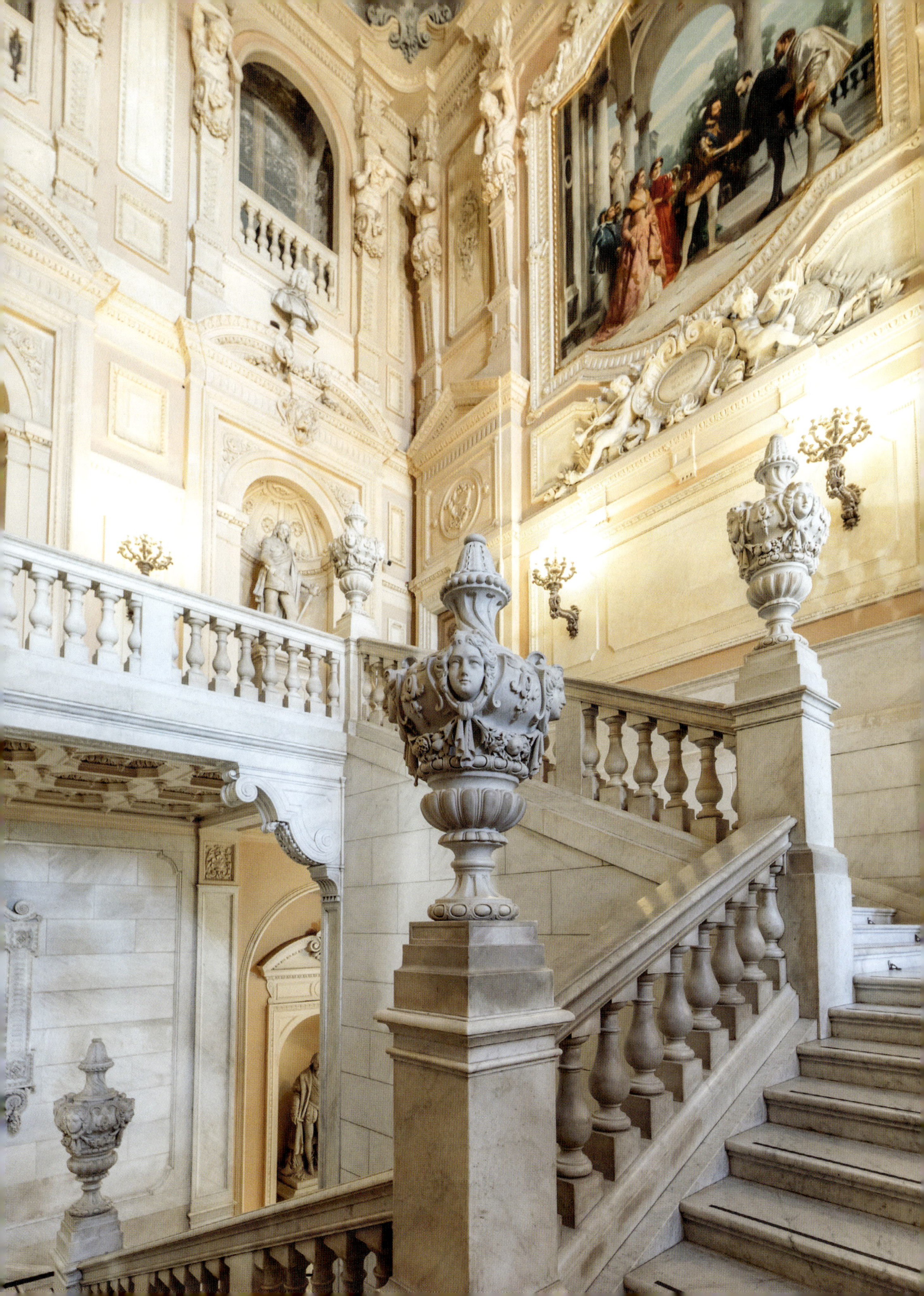

Royal Palace of Caserta

1734
Charles of Bourbon ascends to the throne of the Kingdom of Naples and Sicily. He was the one who commissioned the palace.

1752
The first stone is laid on January 20, marking the start of construction of the Royal Palace of Caserta and the Royal Park.

1762–1770
The Caroline Aqueduct is inaugurated. It supplied water to the park and the English garden. In 1764, the Royal Palace was partially habitable.

1773–1789
Carlo Vanvitelli was responsible for the English Garden. In 1774, the Belvedere di San Leucio was renovated.

1806–1815
Gioacchino Murat took the furniture from the Royal Palace of Portici and furnished the Royal Palace of Caserta.

1825–1830
Francis I was appointed King of the Two Sicilies. He lived in the palace with a multitude of servants.

1830–1859
On October 4, 1839, the first Italian railway line, the Naples–Portici, was inaugurated, and it was later extended to Caserta.

1859–1861
In 1861, after the annexation of the Kingdom of the Two Sicilies to the Kingdom of Italy, the palace was abandoned.

On January 20, 1752, Charles of Bourbon, King of Naples and Sicily, began construction of the Royal Palace, which would become the symbol of the Bourbon dynasty and the masterpiece of its architect, Luigi Vanvitelli. The choice of Caserta was not accidental: first of all, the king needed to move away from the sea because of the danger posed by attacks by the English fleet; secondly, he harbored the grandiose dream of founding a new capital where the old Caserta once stood, which would grow around the palace. Finally, there was one thing that perhaps attracted him more than anything else: the estate included several hectares

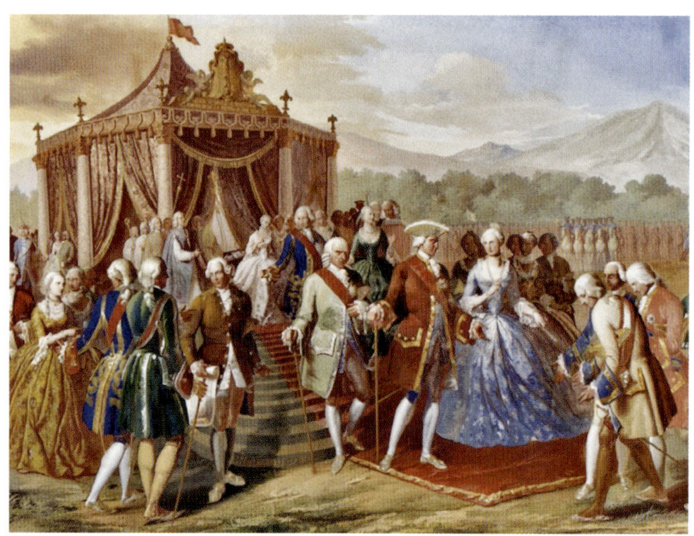

of gardens and dense woods where he could indulge in his favorite activity, hunting. Thousands of men worked under the watchful eye of Luigi Vanvitelli; camels and pack animals roamed the construction site, causing more amazement at the beginning of the project than the palace itself. The architect supervised the excavations, made calculations, and decided which artists to call upon for the interior decorations. However, the work continued well beyond 1759, when Charles of Bourbon was forced to return to Spain to occupy the vacant throne. Luigi Vanvitelli died without seeing his work completed, apart from the Court Theater: the palace was inhabited from 1780, but was not finished until the mid-19th century during the reign of Ferdinand II of the Two Sicilies.

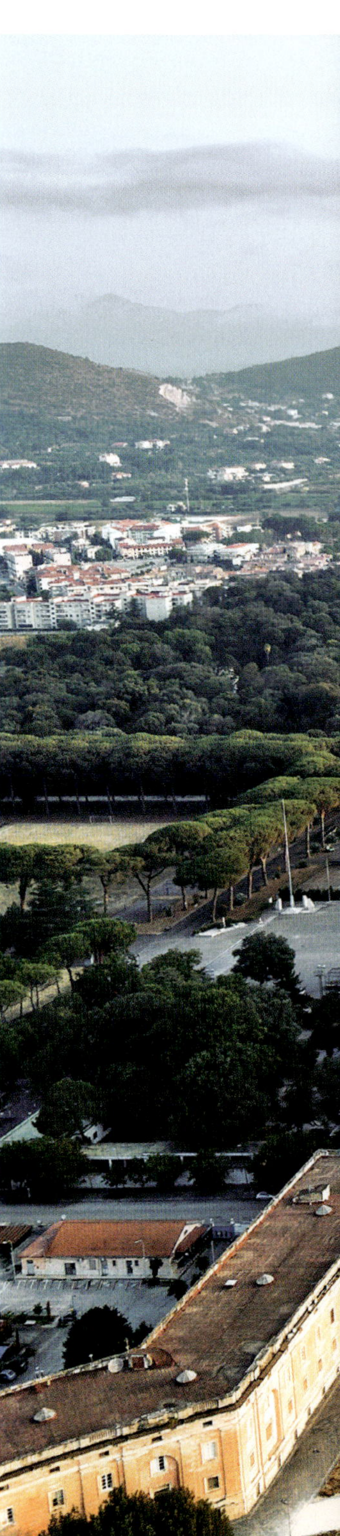

• 106 center: The ceremony of the laying of the first stone (1844) was painted by Gennaro Maldarelli on the vault of the Throne Room.

• 106-107: Aerial view of the Royal Palace of Caserta. The rectangular plan (810 feet by 623) designed by Luigi Vanvitelli divides the interior into four courtyards by means of two buildings intersecting at right angles.

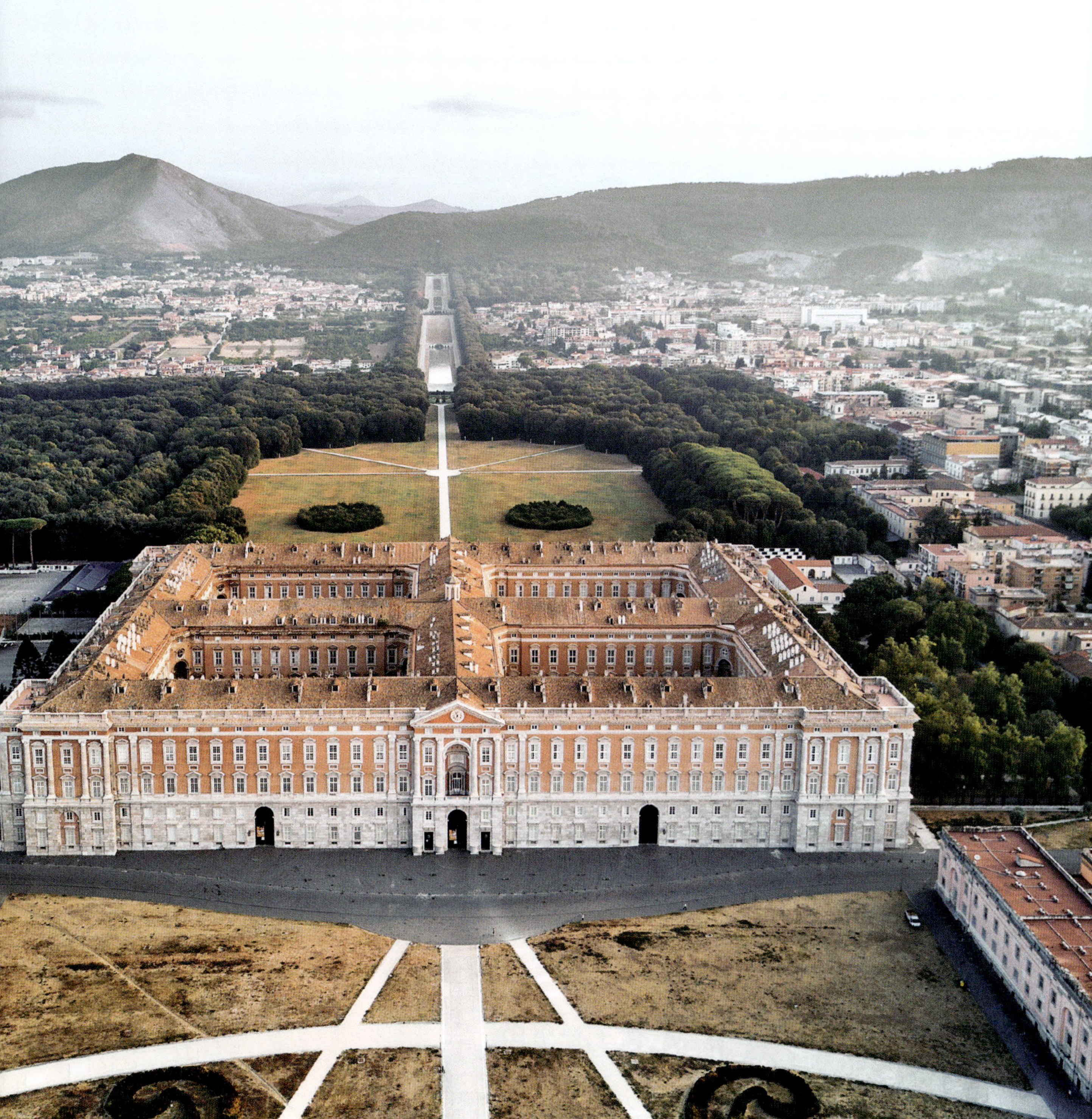

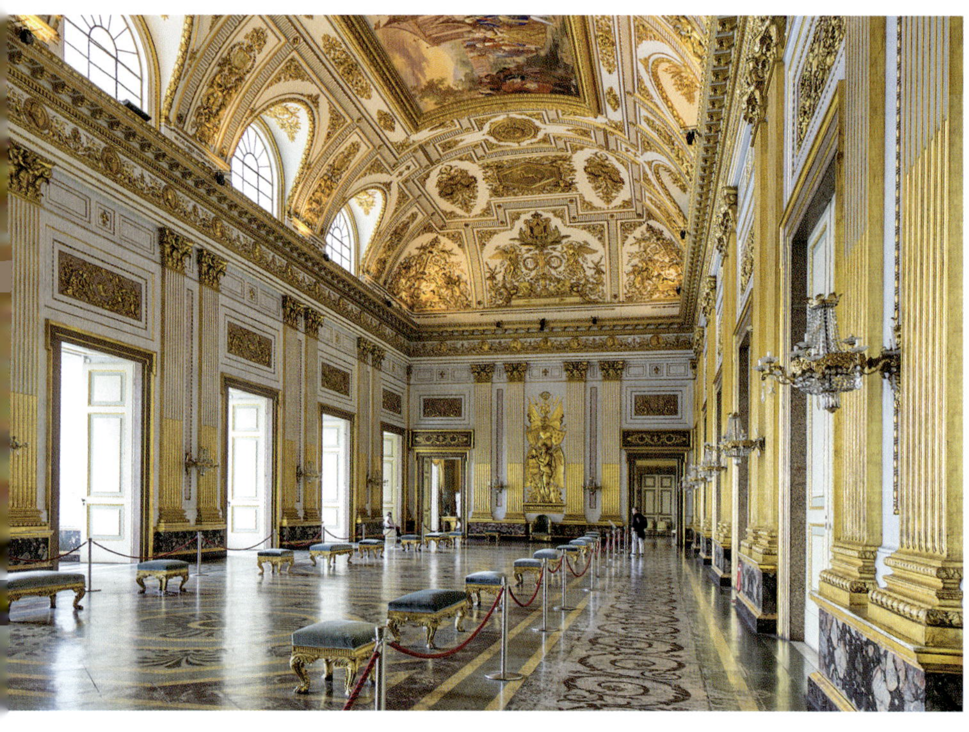

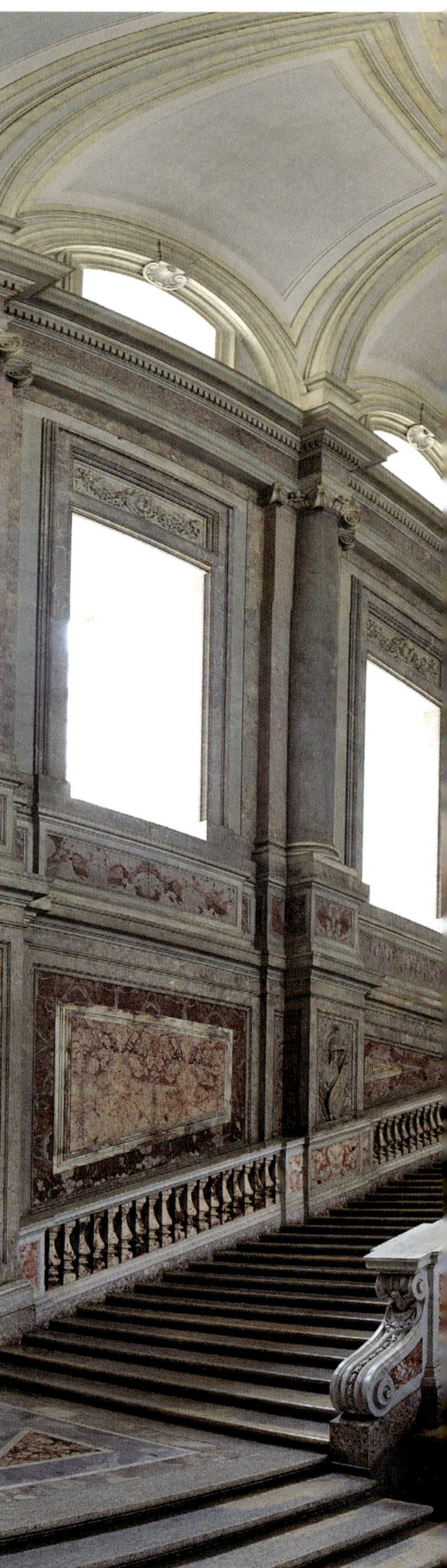

The Bourbon Nativity

Starting with King Charles of Naples and Sicily, the Bourbon monarchs contributed to the establishment of the nativity-scene tradition. The Royal Nativity Scene, on display in Caserta in the Elliptical Hall, was created by court artists, the king himself (who is said to have designed some of the models for the shepherds) and Queen Maria Amalia, along with other ladies who made the shepherds' clothes. The figurines were partly made of terracotta (head, hands, and feet), while the body was made of tow and wire. Ferdinand VII was also a keen collector of nativity scenes and had one set up every Christmas in the royal palaces where the royal family spent the holidays. It was great fun to recognize famous people or beloved dogs in the figurines. The image shows a detail of the mid-18th-century Court Nativity Scene.

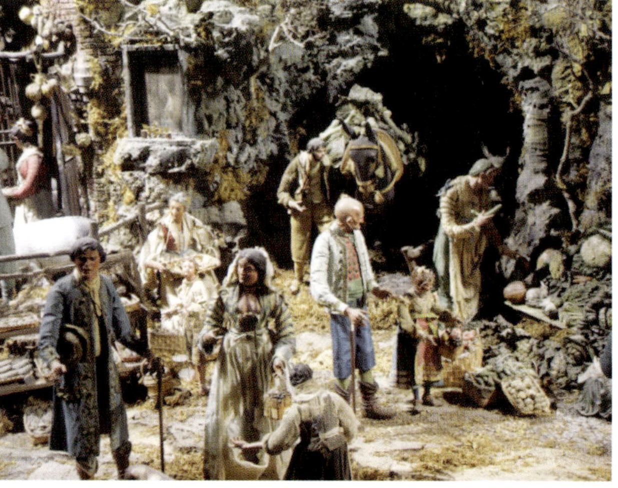

• 108 top: The Throne Room, more than 131 feet long and lit by six windows, is decorated with gilded stuccoes that give it a majestic appearance. Everything is a celebration of the Bourbons.

• 108–109: The Grand Staircase of the Royal Palace, a masterpiece by Luigi Vanvitelli, leads to the floor where the Apartments and the Palatine Chapel are located. At the top of the central ramp are two lions, symbolizing the power of reason and arms, alluding to the virtues of King Charles.

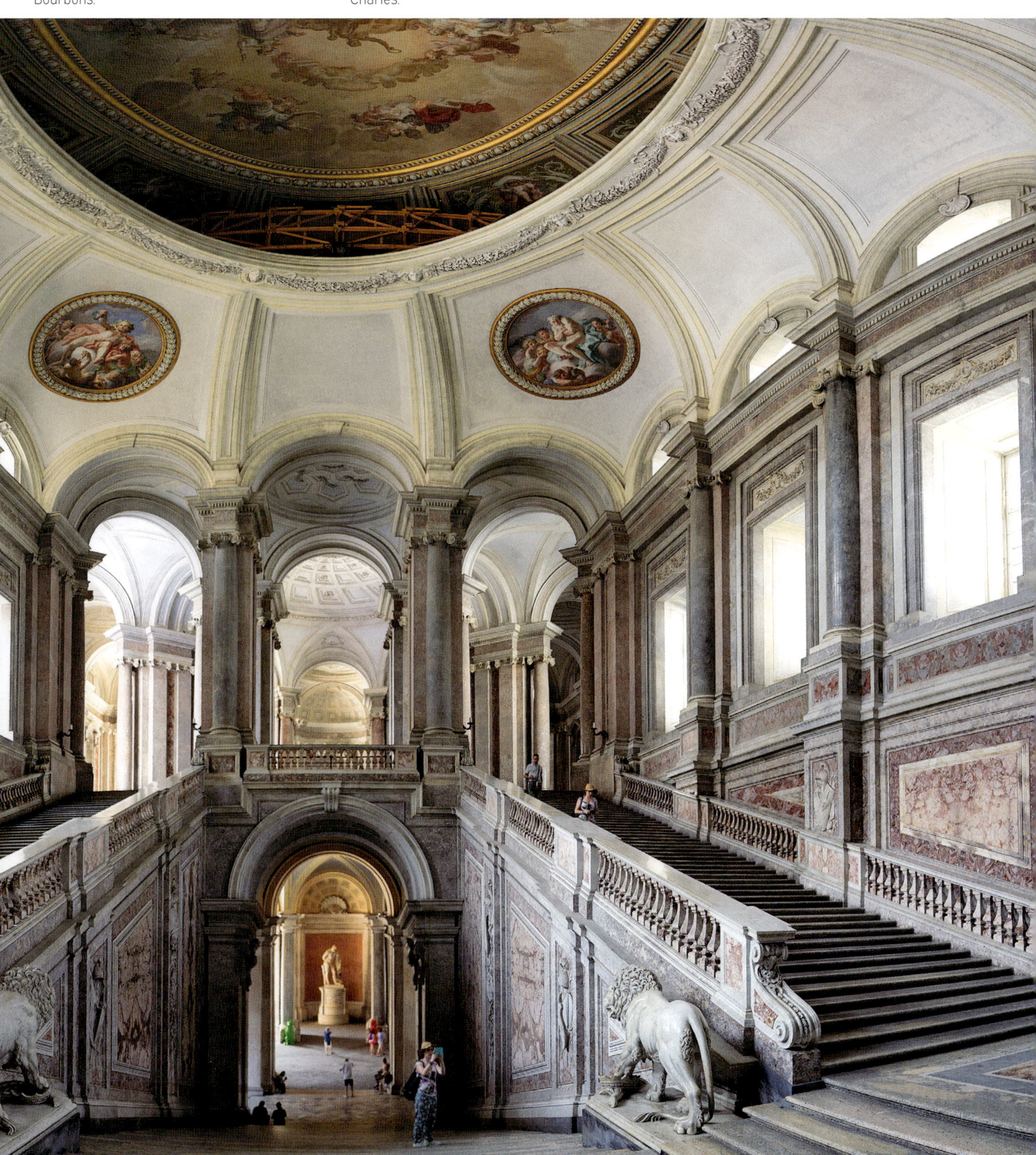

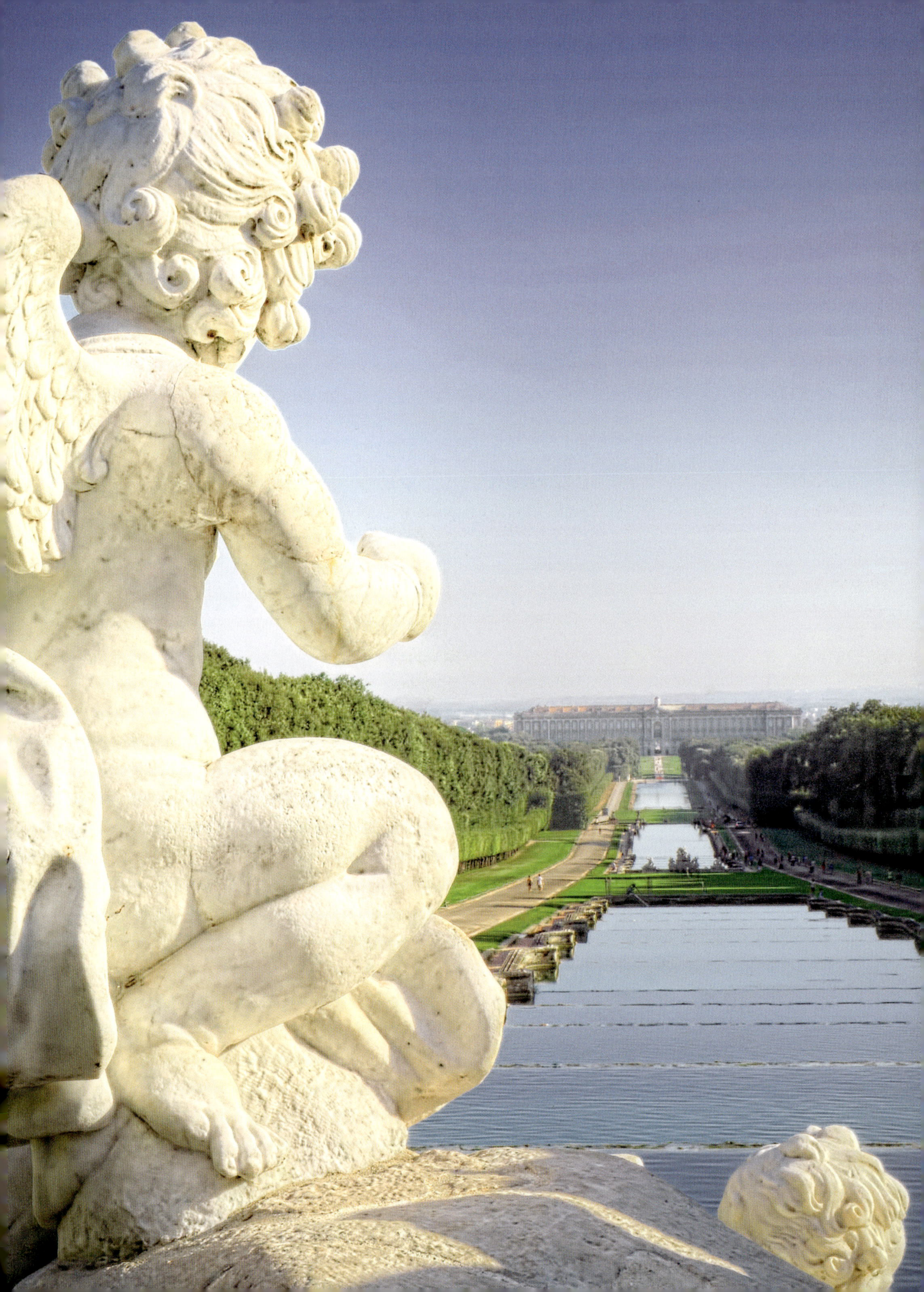

All the rooms in the palace and the magnificent park seem to have been designed to rival the palace of the Sun King in Versailles. Luigi Vanvitelli created the perfect residence for the Bourbon court, starting with the Grand Staircase, a perfect synthesis of classicism and theatrical scenography. But one of the most representative examples of the architect's art is the Palatine Chapel, inaugurated in 1784. Built in neoclassical style, it has a single nave richly decorated with marble and columns. Throughout the Royal Palace, built over two centuries, you can see the signs of the passage of time and changing of fashions, from Charles to Ferdinand IV, the two French sovereigns and then again the Bourbons with Francis I, Ferdinand II and Francis II, King of the Two Sicilies. The apartments are characterized by overlapping styles: large and redundant in detail in the Baroque style; austere and rich in references to ancient Rome in the Neoclassical style; affected and flowery in the Rococo style, and with stucco applications in the Empire style.

As for the park, in his early designs, Luigi Vanvitelli had conceived it as symmetrical and orderly, in the French style; but over time, the artist abandoned that idea, giving the whole a more compact and regular appearance, in the Italian style, with lawns and square flower beds alternating with pools and water features. With a colossal architectural work, the Caroline Aqueduct, he managed to convey water from the Fizzo to Caserta (he had ridden for days to find a suitable source for the undertaking) to fill the magnificent fountains of the Via d'Acqua, designed so that all the basins were clearly visible from the lower vestibule of the Royal Palace. Starting in 1786, Queen Maria Carolina wanted to create a landscape garden on the eastern side of the park, the so-called "English garden," which was very different from the geometry of formal Italian and French gardens. At the end of the 18th century, before the sovereigns fled to Sicily to escape the revolutionary uprisings, the garden was almost complete with the addition of false ruins, but with some authentic elements from the excavations in the Vesuvian area of Herculaneum and Pompeii.

• 110: The Park of the Royal Palace of Caserta was a royal delight suitable for the entertainment of the Neapolitan court. It covers an area of about 296 acres.

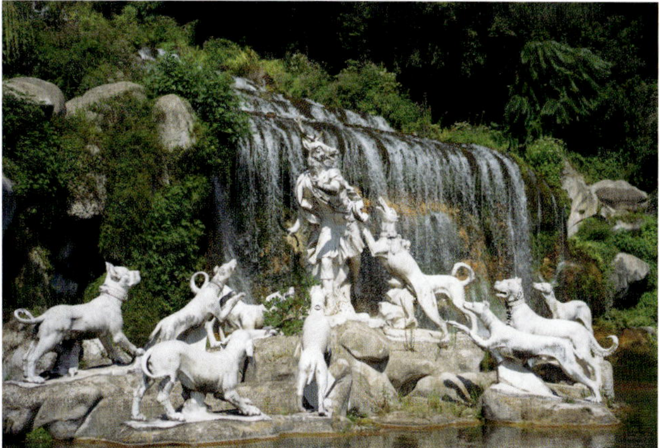

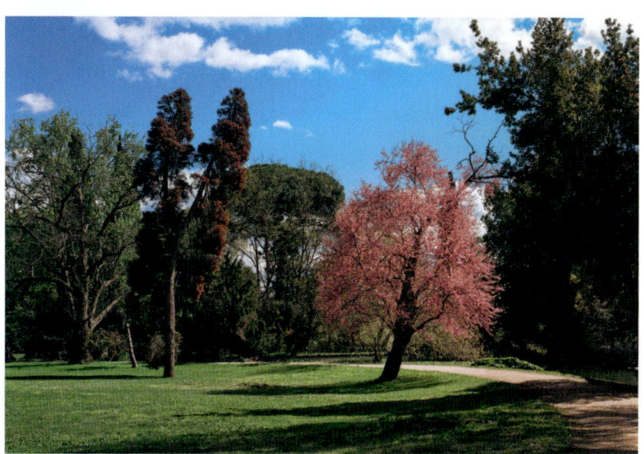

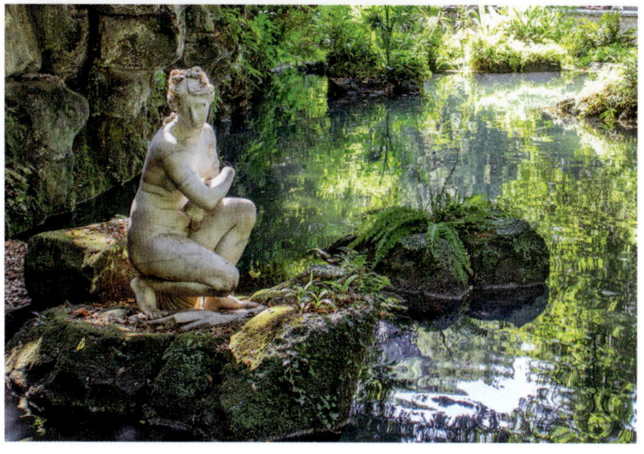

• 111 top: The last fountain on the Via d'Acqua is the *Fountain of Diana and Actaeon*, built between 1786 and 1789.

• 111 center: The English garden commissioned by Queen Maria Carolina.

• 111 bottom: The sculptural group *Bath of Venus* is reflected in the pond in front of the Cryptoporticus. The work was created by Tommaso Solari in 1762.

Castel del Monte

1194
The future Frederick II of Hohenstaufen was born in Jesi to Constance of Hauteville (1154–1198) and Emperor Henry VI of Swabia (1165–1197). He would unite the crowns of the Holy Roman Empire and the Kingdom of Sicily.

1229
Frederick II was in Jerusalem on a crusade and admired the Dome of the Rock, which was probably the inspiration for Castel del Monte.

1240
In a document, the only certain evidence on the subject, dated January 29, Frederick II writes of Castel del Monte, which at that time was already in an advanced stage of construction.

1463
In a decree dated December 1, the "Castello di Santa Maria del Monte" is referred to for the first time by the name by which it is known today: Castel del Monte.

17th–18th century
Abandoned, the castle was plundered and stripped of its furnishings and marble wall decorations. It was used as a prison, and a shelter for shepherds, brigands, and political refugees.

1876
The castle was purchased by the Italian state, which arranged for its restoration.

1996
Castel del Monte has been included in the UNESCO World Heritage Site List.

The history of Castel del Monte is inextricably linked to that of Frederick II of Hohenstaufen, known by the epithets *Stupor mundi, Puer Apuliae, and Immutator saeculi* ("Wonder of the World," "Son of Apulia," and "He Who Changes His Age") in the chronicles of his contemporaries, who were enchanted by his personality. Celebrated for his culture, knowledge, and tolerance towards the Arab and Jewish worlds, controversial in his conflicts with the Papacy and in his choices of government, he was head of the Holy Roman Empire, King of Sicily, and King of Jerusalem, succeeding in his intent to create a true myth around himself.

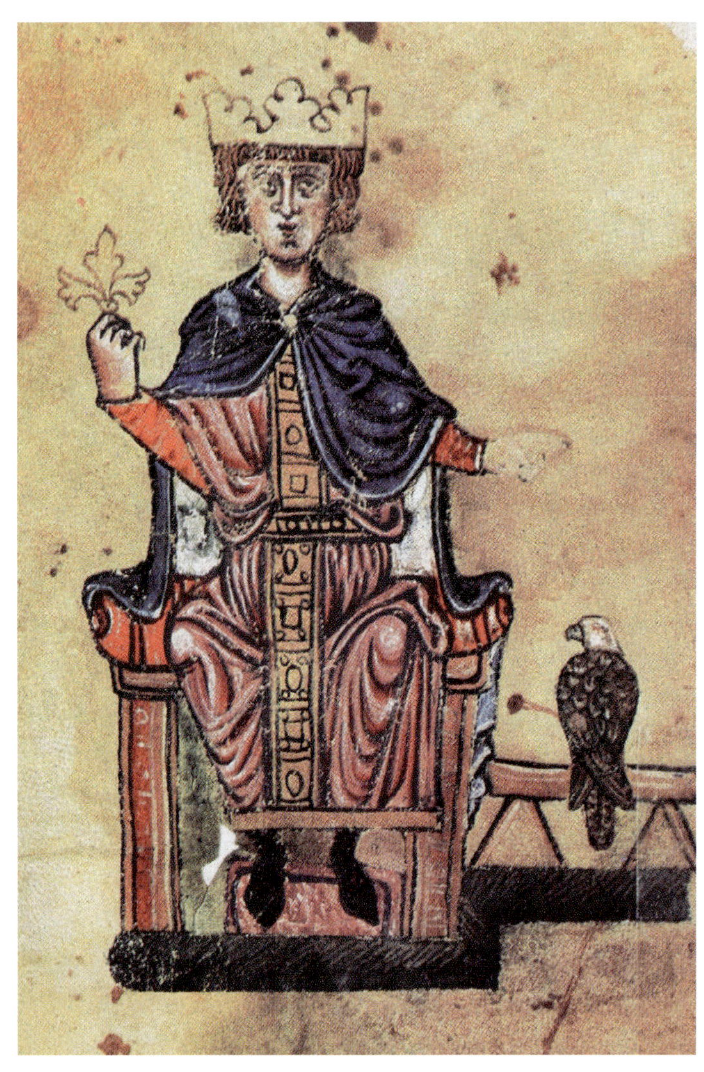

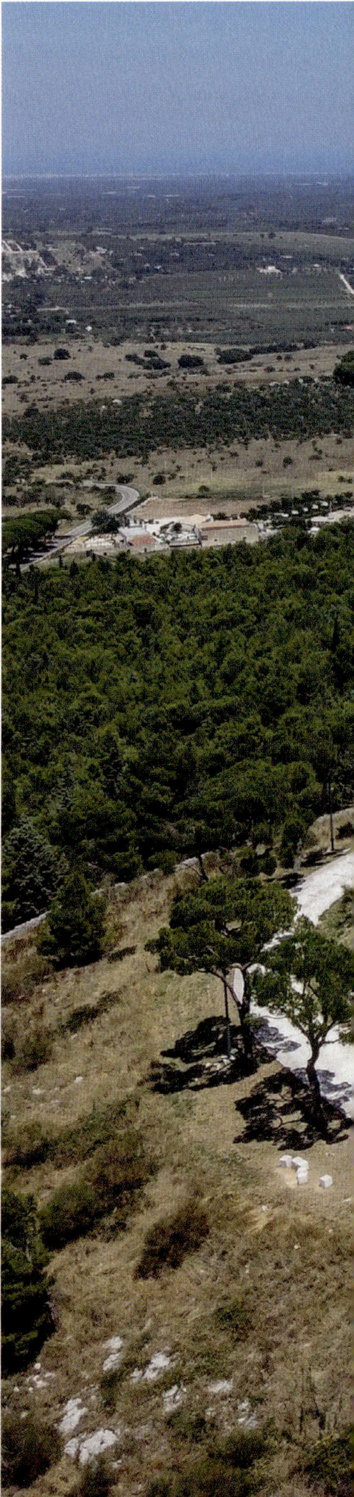

• 112 bottom: Emperor Frederick II depicted with one of his favorite falcons in his *De arte venandi cum avibus* (The Art of Hunting with Birds), now in Rome, Vatican Library, codex Pal . lat. 1071, fol. 1, from the late 13th century.

• 112–113: View of the Apulian plateau of the northern Murge from the top of the hill where Castel del Monte stands, the most famous manor built by Frederick II of Swabia, the puer Apuliae, in the 13th century.

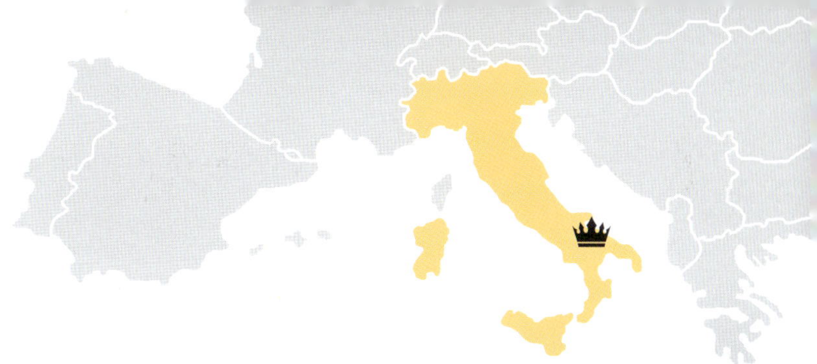

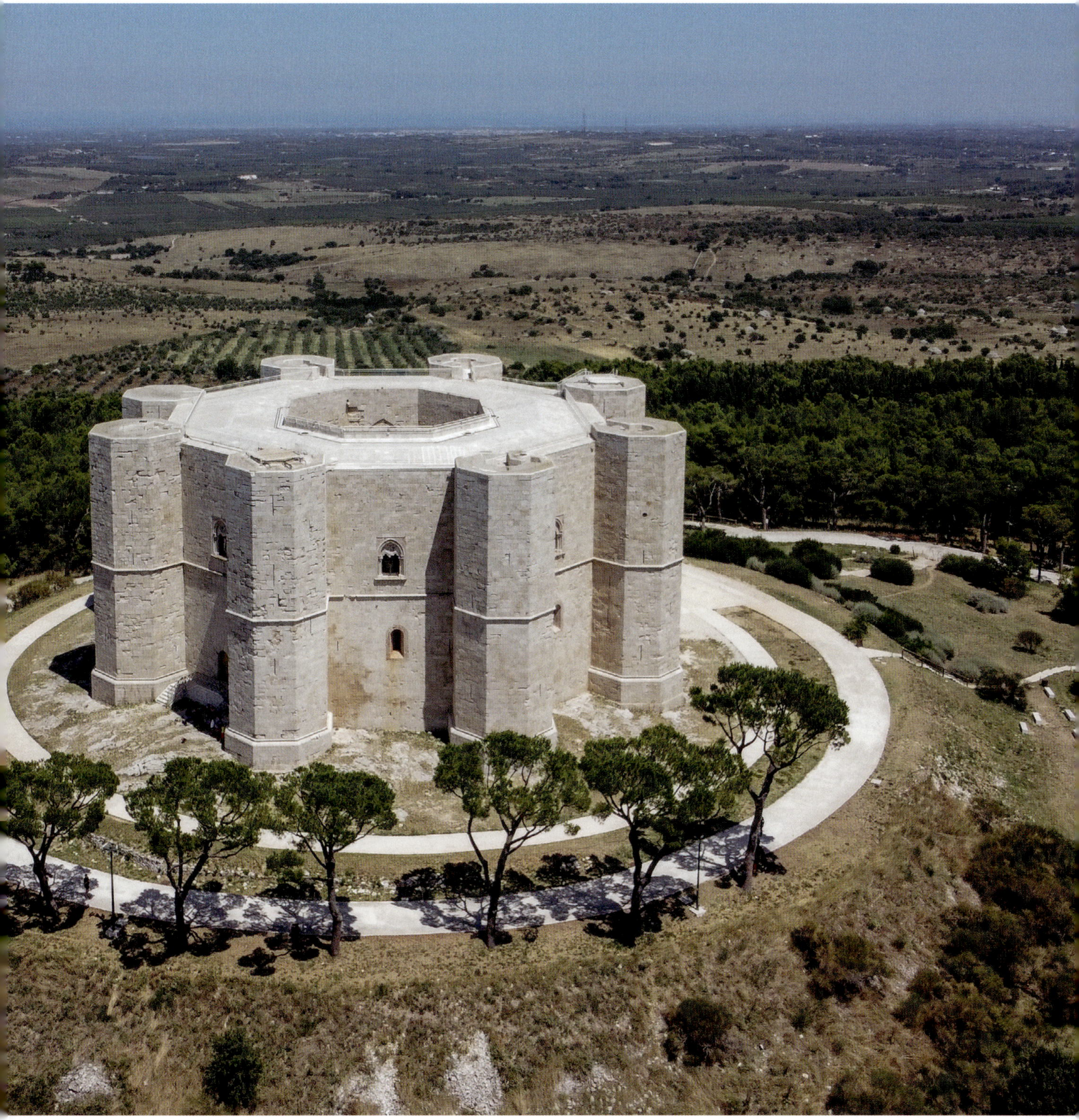

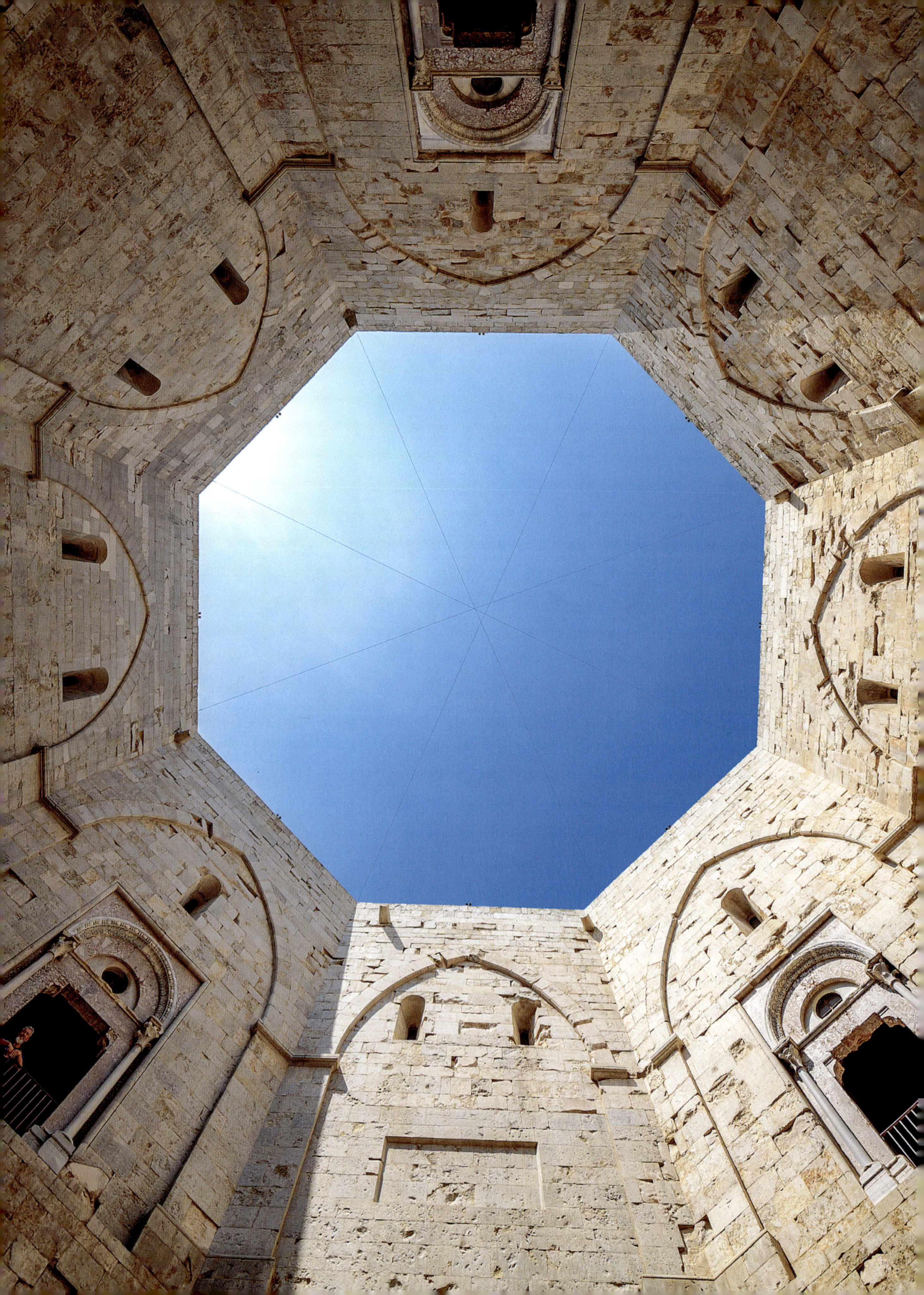

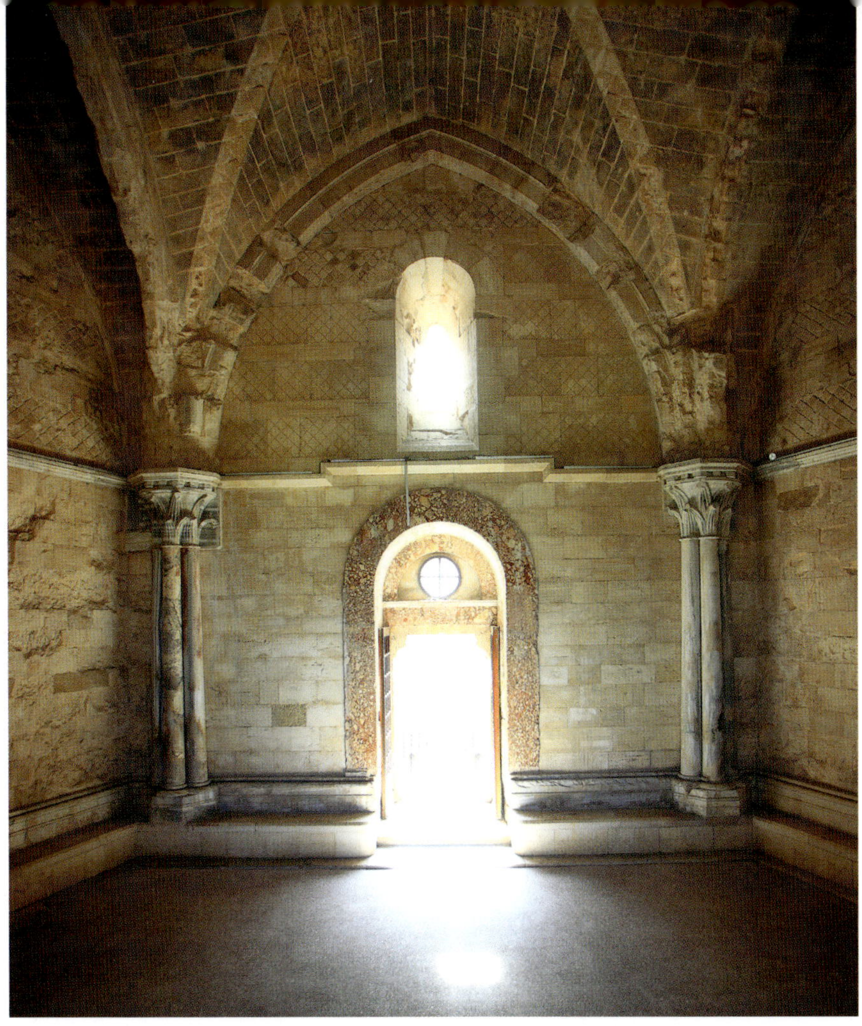

• 114: The central courtyard, which echoes the octagonal shape of the exterior, has a cistern for collecting rainwater in the center. Looking up, it feels as if you are at the bottom of a well, a symbol of knowledge in the Middle Ages.

• 115 top: The interior of the castle is divided into two floors, similar in proportion and shape but very different in overall effect: while the ground floor is supported by sturdy columns and dimly lit by tall, narrow windows, the upper floor is airy and flooded with light filtering through large double and triple windows facing the outside. The precious multicolored marble, mosaic-adorned walls, original paintings, and tapestries have been lost over the centuries.

A shrewd administrator, he commissioned the construction or refurbishment of several castles and fortresses, symbols of his absolute power, to keep his dominions in southern Italy under control. The most famous of all is Castel del Monte, which dominates the surrounding plain at Andria in Puglia from an isolated hill. It was designed with an octagonal plan, and it is almost certain that Frederick II never saw it completed or resided there, while, due to one of the frequent reversals of fortune in 1266, his young grandsons Henry, Frederick, and Enzio, sons of his son Manfredi (1232–1266), the last Hohenstaufen ruler of the Kingdom of Sicily, were imprisoned there by Charles I of Anjou. The precise purpose for which this solid and massive building was constructed has not yet been identified, and there are many interpretations. In fact, considering the dense woods that once surrounded it, some believe it was built as a base from which to hunt with falcons, which the emperor loved so much that he dedicated a treatise to them, *De arte venandi cum avibus*. Other scholars argue that it was a representative castle or a sumptuous private residence, a place of delight. Finally, given the size of the complex, some have argued that it was more likely to have been used as a defensive structure. It was certainly not a permanent residence: except for the lost palace in Foggia, built in 1223 as a true imperial residence, and the Magna Curia in Palermo, Frederick used to move frequently between Italy and Germany and the various seats of his kingdom.

The recurring number eight

The castle has an octagonal layout and is surrounded by eight towers of the same geometric shape; there are eight rooms on the lower floor and the same number on the upper floor; the inner courtyard is octagonal, as was apparently the basin carved from a single piece of marble that stood in the center. It is clear that the number eight is a recurring theme in the construction of the building, which leads one to esoteric interpretations given the highly magical and symbolic nature of the number, which horizontally is the symbol of infinity—and in Greek, Latin, and Arabic cultures, it symbolized eternity. The number eight also represents the day of the Resurrection (after the seven days of creation).

Royal Palace of Palermo

c. 850
Arabs from North Africa conquered Palermo and built a fortress, *qasr*, on the site where the Royal Palace of Palermo now stands.

1061
Roberto and Ruggero d'Altavilla landed in Messina, beginning the conquest of Islamic Sicily.

1072
Ruggero d'Altavilla conquered Palermo after a four-month siege.

1130–1131
Ruggero II founded the Kingdom of Sicily on the ruins of the ancient *qasr* and began construction of the Royal Palace.

1140
On April 28, the Palatine Chapel was consecrated.

1194–1250
The Altavilla dynasty was replaced by the Swabian dynasty. Frederick II made the palace his imperial residence.

1266–1282
Upon the death of the last Swabian sovereign in 1266, the Kingdom of Sicily was assigned to the Angevins. After the Sicilian Vespers revolt, the Aragonese took power.

1553–1570
After a period of neglect, the palace was chosen as the residence of the viceroys of Spain.

1798
Ferdinando IV of Naples and Maria Carolina of Habsburg-Lorraine moved from Naples to the Royal Palace in Palermo.

The monumental complex of the Royal Palace of Palermo, known as the "Palazzo dei Normanni," is the result of construction, demolition, and superimposition that took place over approximately 250 years, and even longer if we consider the changes made during the Spanish rule of Sicily (16th–17th centuries) and during the Bourbon rule between the 18th century and 1816. Today, it is the seat of the Sicilian Regional Assembly. The history of the royal residence began in 1072 with the arrival in Palermo of the brothers of the Norman dynasty of Altavilla, Roberto Guiscardo and Ruggero, who forced the Muslims to surrender. At the time, the city was a thriving commercial center that attracted merchants from all over the Mediterranean. The mighty walls of Balarm protected the districts that made up the city: in the central district, al-Qasr, the sultan, lived in his fortress, surrounded by al-Khalesa (Kalsa), the district in the port area. The first to move the court from Messina to Palermo in 1112 was Adelasia del Vasto, mother of the future Ruggero II, who in that same year was knighted in the ancient palace of the emirs and took the reins of government, proving himself as wise and authoritative as his father Ruggero I. During his reign, Palermo became Christianized with the construction of wonderful churches, from Martorana to San Cataldo to San Giovanni degli Eremiti, while some neighborhoods remained reserved for Muslims, who continued to control part of the trade. Even before ascending to the throne, Ruggero II began to devote himself to the construction of a sumptuous residence for his dynasty: the Royal Palace, or Palazzo dei Normanni, which in the following decades became the political and administrative heart of the short reign of the Altavilla family. For his residence, the sovereign chose to renovate the old Qasr, which had been built by the emirs on the remains of ancient Punic and Roman fortifications. The new Norman fortress was equipped with four towers: Greca, Pisana, Gioaria, and Chirimbi. Only two remain (Pisana and Gioaria): the others were demolished by the Spanish viceroys. In the center was a royal hall where audiences and banquets were held. There were staircases, loggias, terraces, fountains, and lush gardens shaded by palm trees, in a style that would not have displeased the previous Saracen rulers of Palermo. And of course, to describe it in the words of French author Guy de Maupassant (1850–1893), there was the magnificent place where the royal family gathered in prayer: "The Palatine Chapel, the most beautiful in the world, the most precious religious jewel dreamed of by the human mind and executed by the hand of an artist."

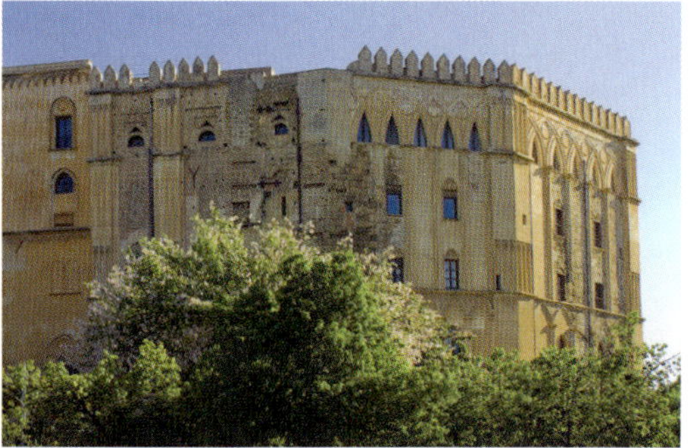

• 116 bottom: The southwest corner of the palace is one of the oldest parts of the complex, along with the Pisana tower, the Gioaria tower, and the Palatine Chapel. The fan-shaped rooms probably housed the Norman political prisons.

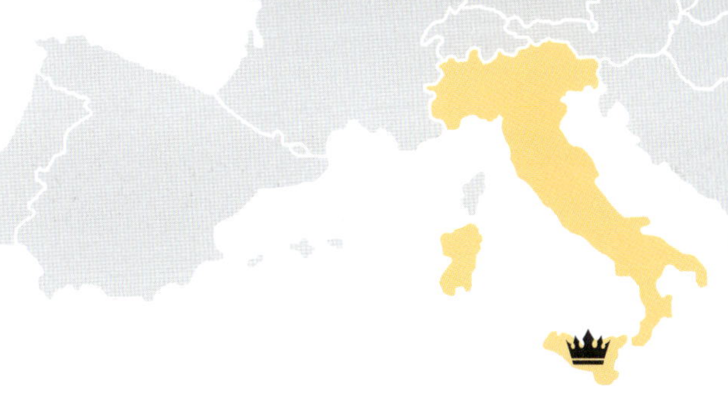

· 117: The Pisana Tower, or Santa Ninfa Tower, is the oldest wing of the palace and one of the few parts of the complex that has retained any of its original Norman appearance, visible in the blind arches of the façade. In 1786, an astronomical observatory was placed on top of it: today it is one of the national headquarters of the Institute of Astrophysics.

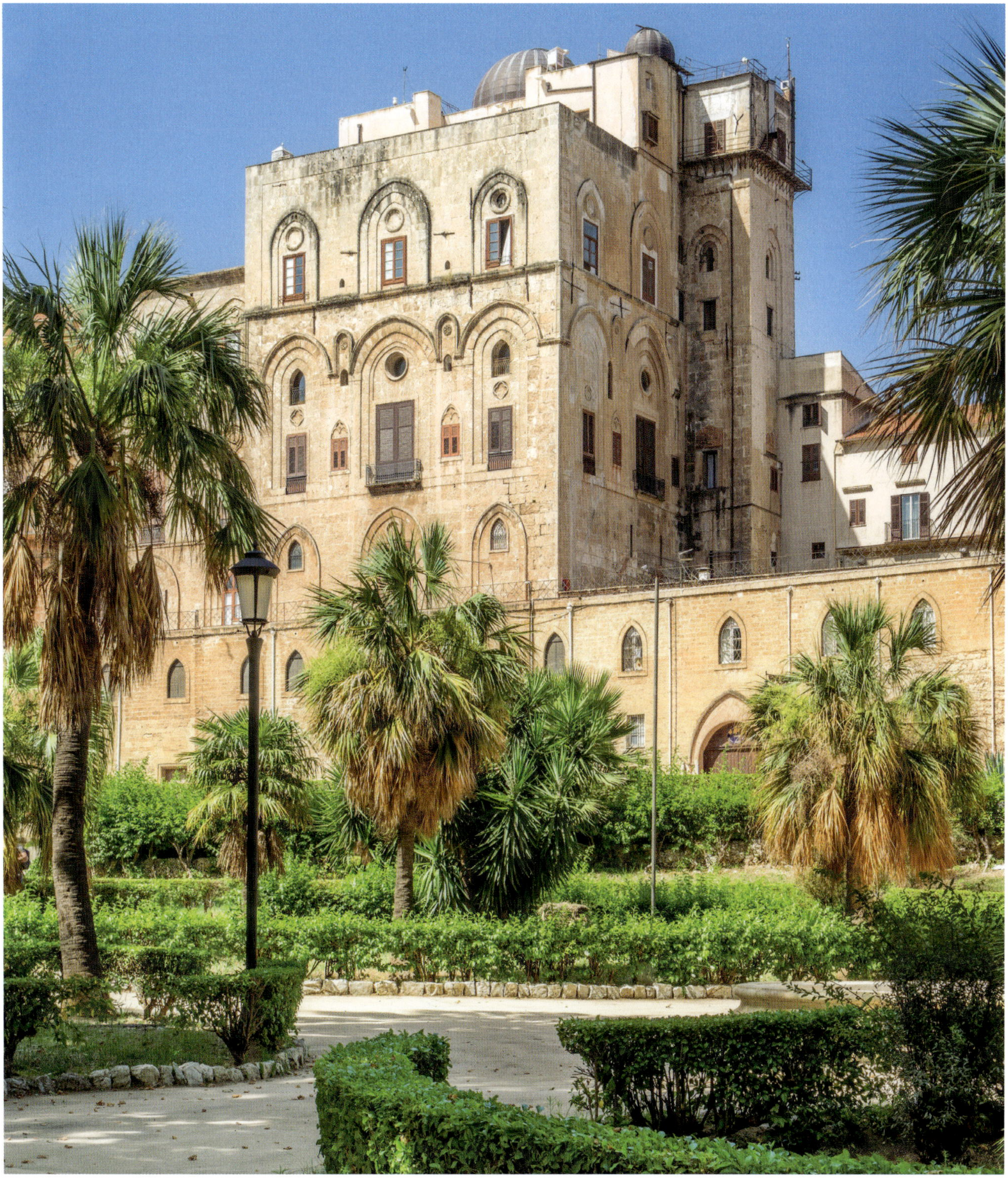

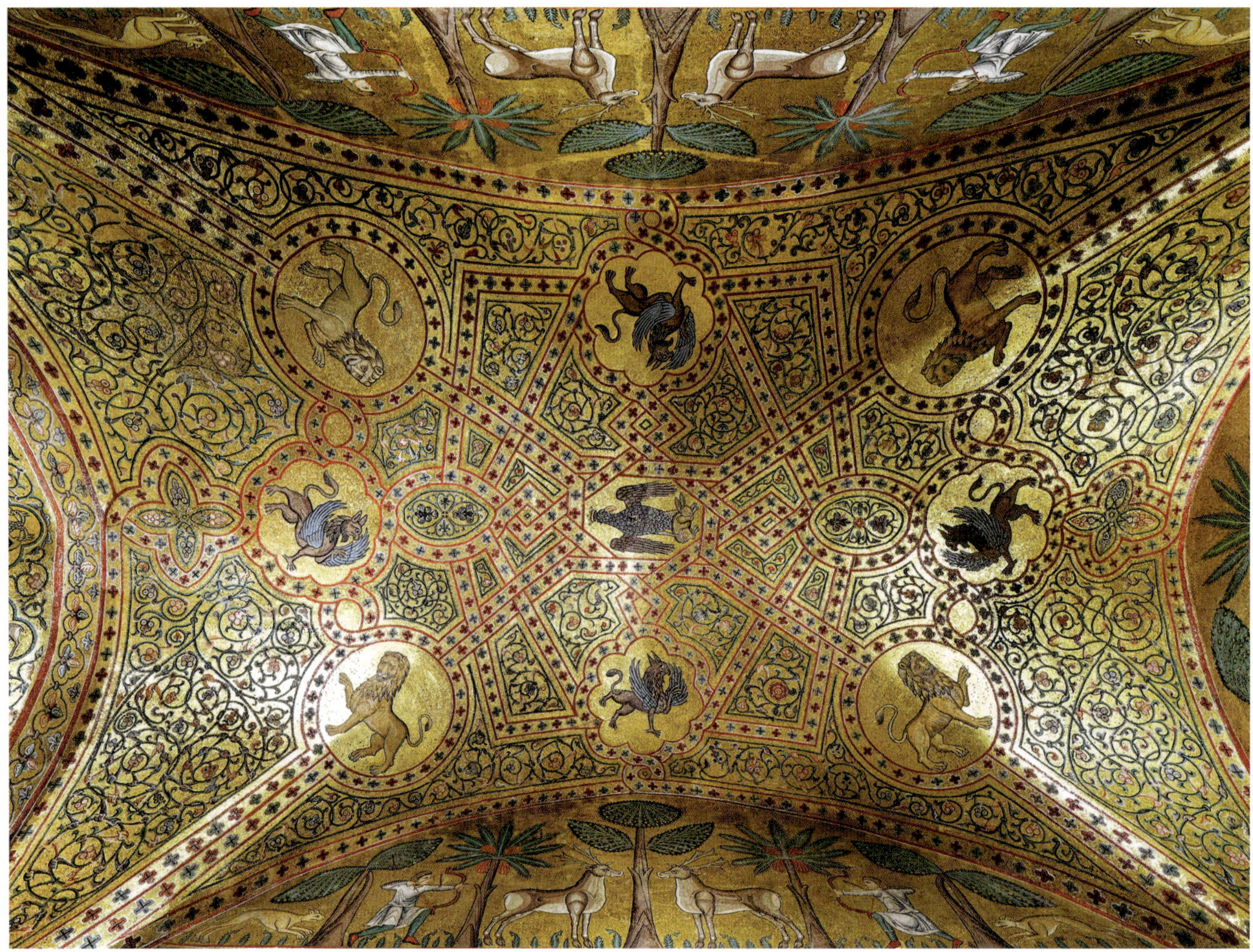

• 118 Top: In the cross vault, arabesques intertwine with floral motifs and geometric decorations, but there are also medallions with phoenixes and lions, and in the center is an eagle clutching a rabbit with its talons. According to tradition, this subject was added to the original mosaics by Frederick II of Swabia, who had adopted this bird of prey as the symbol of the Holy Roman Empire. The eagle alludes to nobility and courage, while the rabbit represents cowardice. The Norman lion, on the other hand, was the symbol of the Altavilla dynasty.

• 119: The Room of Ruggero (the name has nothing to do with the first king of Sicily) is located in the Gioaria tower: this small room was built around 1170, when his son Guglielmo I (1120–1166) had recently died and Guglielmo II's (1153–1189) mother was regent. Its purpose is unknown: given its location in the royal apartments, it was certainly for private use, perhaps a bedroom or dining room. Rectangular in plan, the room features rich mosaic decoration, executed by Byzantine-trained masters, which surrounds it on all sides above a marble plinth about 6.6 feet high.

At the court of the Altavilla

Chronicles, miniatures, and ancient travel accounts provide glimpses of life within the walls of the Royal Palace inhabited by Norman rulers and their families: so austere on the outside, the interior appears to have been covered in shining gold and gems. In the time of Ruggero II, the treasure was kept in the Pisana tower, while the sovereign rested in the Gioaria or Joharia tower (from the Arabic *al-jawhariyya,* meaning jeweled), the representative building that overlooked the city. The remaining spaces housed the apartments of the women and eunuchs who served the king and queen. The palace also housed the workshops of *the Tiraz,* the royal manufactory.

The chronicles report that some of the emirs' customs, such as frequenting *the harem* or *the hammam,* were not rejected by the Norman kings. Islamic doctors and scholars, poets, artists, and scientists from the Eastern world were welcome at court, including the geographer al-Idrisi. During the reign of Ruggero II, the palace became the most active intellectual center of the kingdom, taking full advantage of Sicily's role as a cultural crossroads. It should not be forgotten that Ruggero had received a refined education from Greek and Islamic tutors, learning Greek and Arabic in addition to the French he spoke at home.
The "voluptuous" idleness of the Altavilla family was ultimately fueled by banquets, dances (depicted on the ceiling of the Palatine Chapel), music, and theater performances.

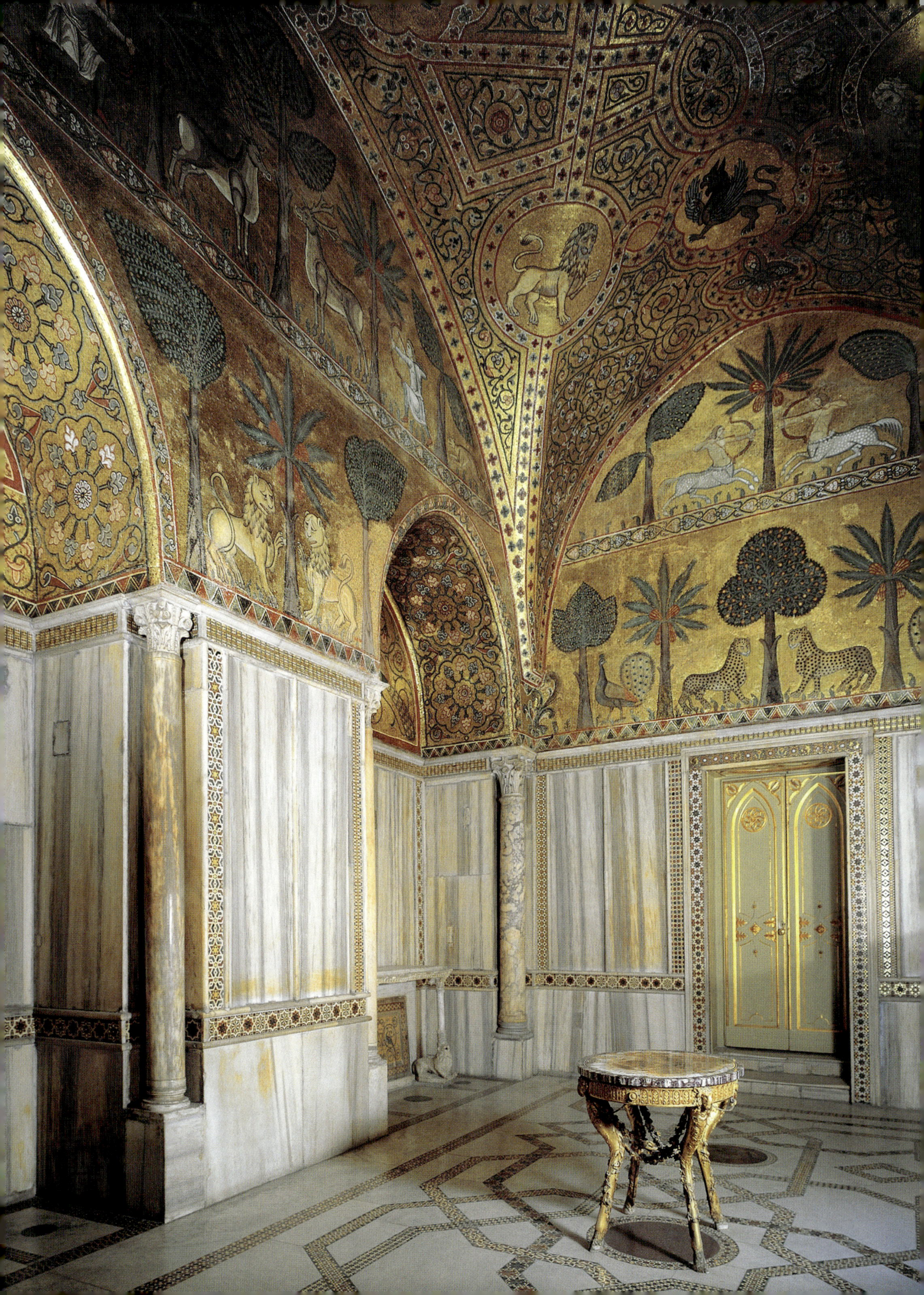

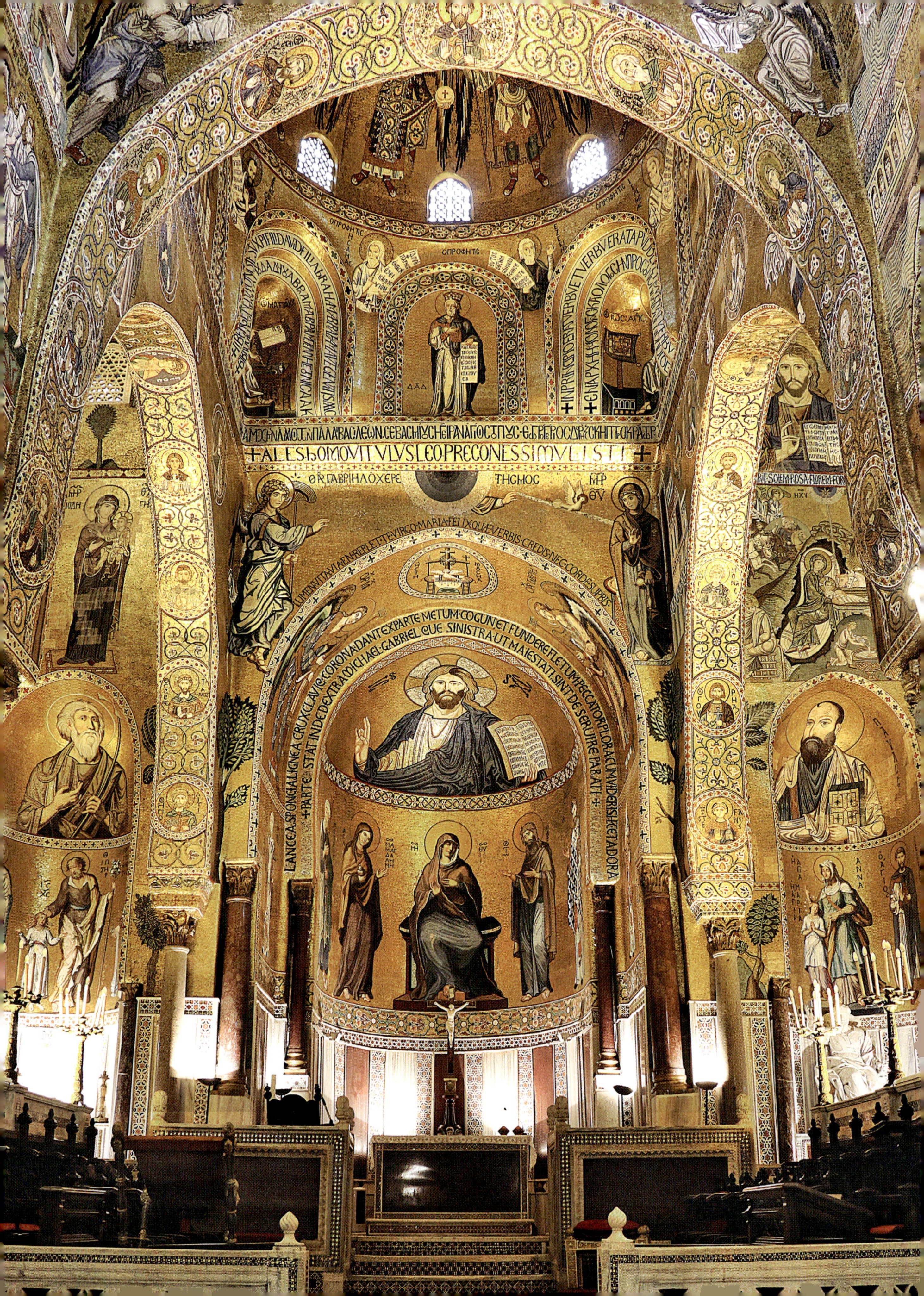

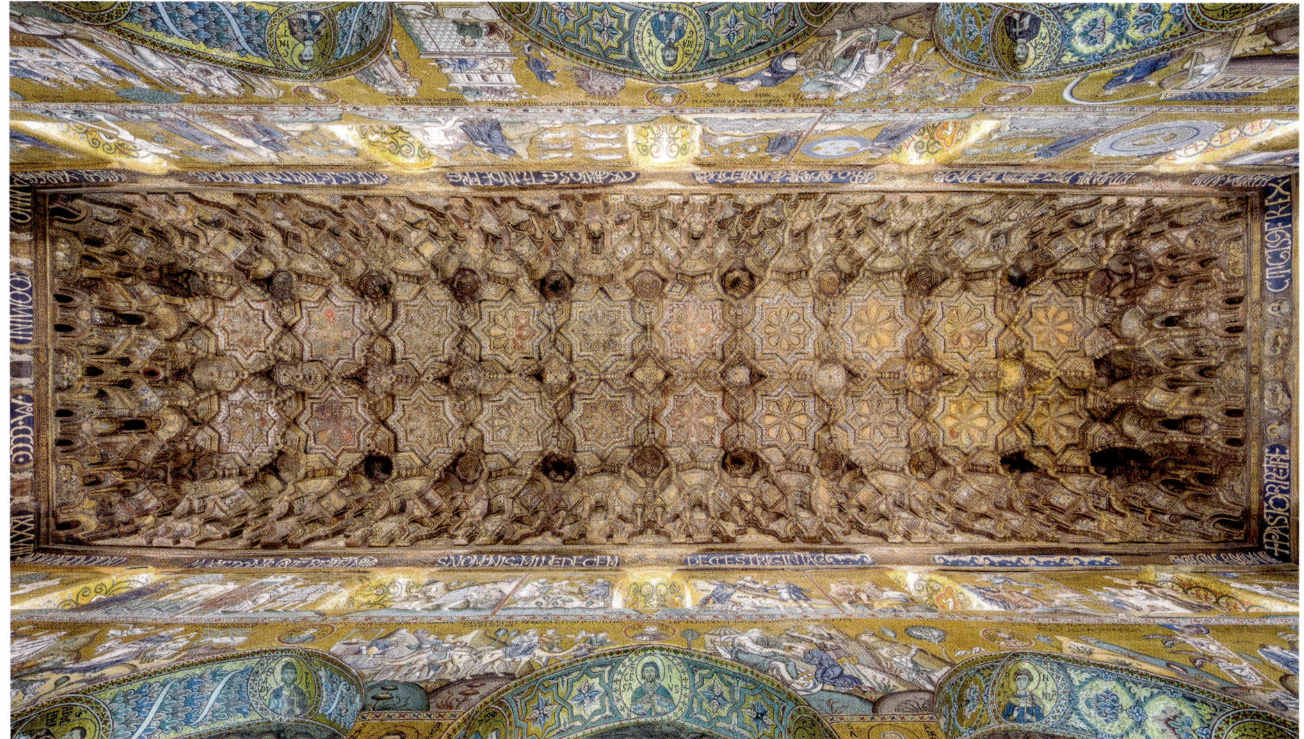

The heart of the Palermo palace is the Palatine Chapel, the private church of the royal family, which during celebrations took place in the tribune located in the transept: Ruggero II had begun its construction in 1129, even before ascending to the throne, on top of a preexisting church (the crypt of the current church). At its inauguration in 1140, with the work largely completed, prelates from all over the kingdom attended. Originally, the Chapel was an independent building, separate from the Palace, with its own façade, but over time it ended up being incorporated into it. The plan is divided into three naves separated by rows of cipollino marble and granite columns, with the three apses facing east, as was typical of Byzantine churches. Greek, Arab, and Norman-Latin craftsmen worked on it at the request of the sovereign of Altavilla. The splendid mosaics on a gold background that glisten in the apses, dome, transept, and naves are in Byzantine style, the work of masters from Constantinople and skilled local craftsmen who had trained at their school. During the Bourbon period, the Palatine Chapel was restored and new mosaics were added to the exterior walls.

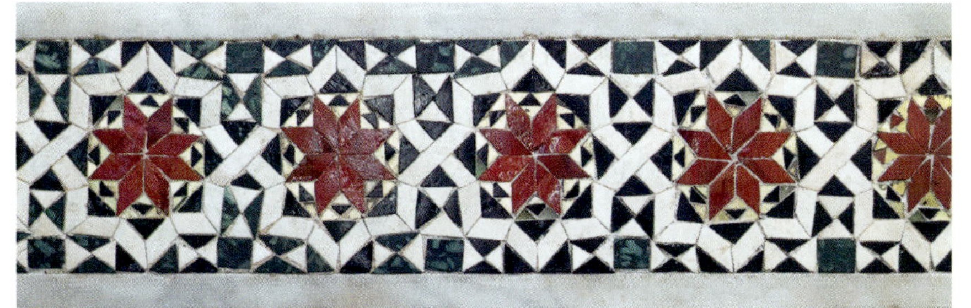

• 120: The spectacular interior of the Chapel shines with gold, precious stones, and marble, such as the extremely expensive and rare Egyptian red porphyry. The gold, scattered so profusely, does not symbolize the wealth of the king, but the light of Paradise. The mosaics in the nave, which are later than those in the presbytery, depict biblical scenes and date back to the period between 1160 and 1200.

• 121 top: The *muqarnas* motif on the sides of the ceiling was made with very thin panels of fir wood from the Nebrodi Mountains. The central part is decorated with eight-pointed star polygons containing small human figures; each polygon is framed by beautiful calligraphic inscriptions in the Kufic style. The complexity of this masterpiece is such that it is impossible to appreciate it with the naked eye from below.

• 121 bottom: In the floor of the Chapel, *the opus sectile*—the use of marble tiles of different sizes, colors, brightness, and shades—in the Byzantine tradition and Cosmatesque style, is mixed with the intricate geometric patterns typical of Islamic craftsmanship. The floor is made of white marble, antique yellow, serpentine, and Egyptian red porphyry, the latter being particularly precious not only because the quarries had been exhausted for centuries and scrap material had to be used, but also because its color was a prerogative of Eastern emperors and an expression of royalty: Ruggero II did not choose it by chance.

• 122–123: Chillon Castle, near Montreux, stands on a limestone rock overlooking Lake Geneva. While the north façade with its loopholes bears witness to the castle's defensive function, the south side, facing the lake, with its magnificent Gothic windows, is an example of a princely residence.

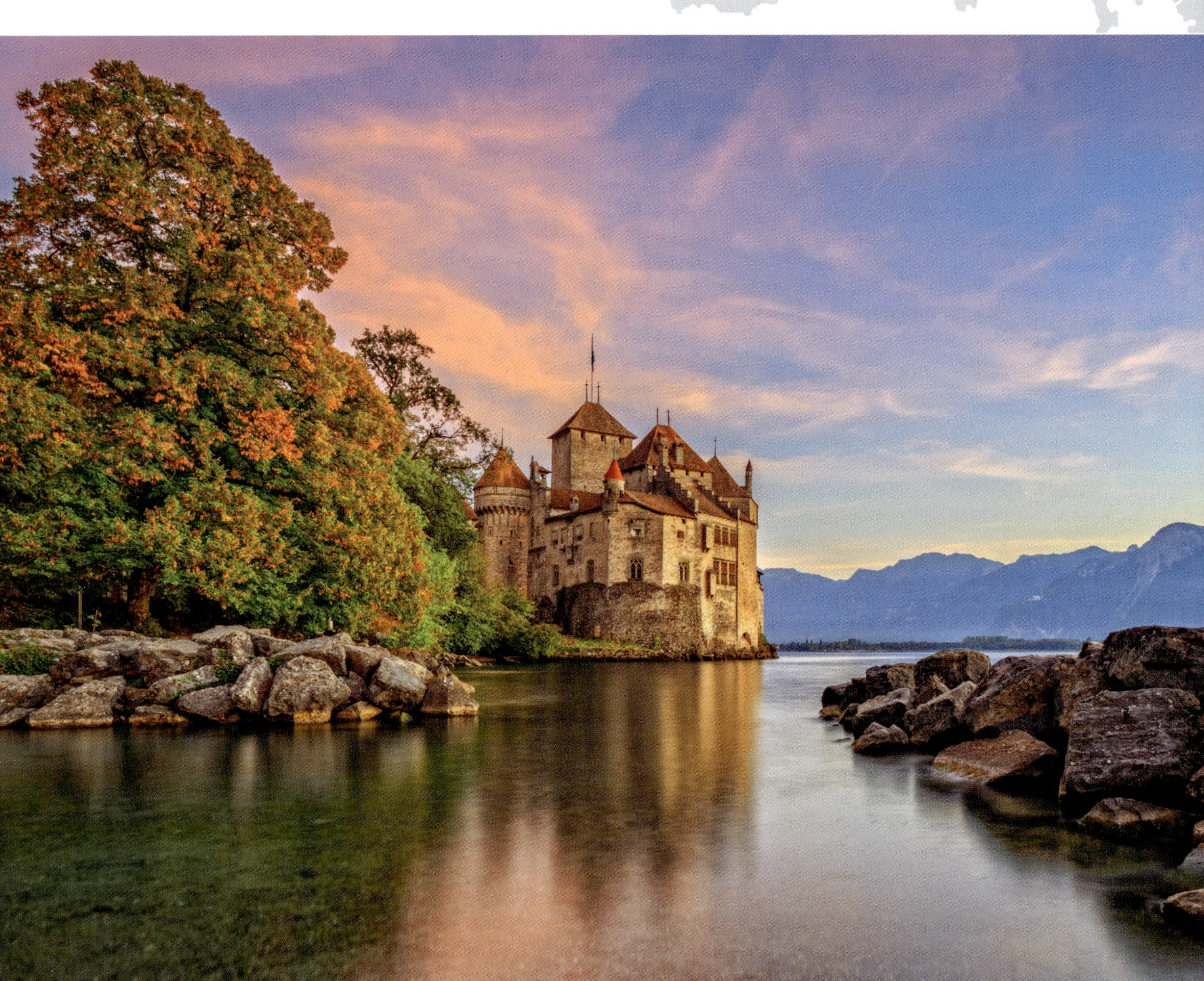

Built around the 10th century as a fortress perched on a rocky outcrop on the shores of Lake Geneva, surrounded by the Alps, Chillon Castle is one of Switzerland's most-visited historical sites. Its history has deep roots: excavations carried out since the end of the 19th century have established that the site has been occupied since the Bronze Age. From the 12th century, the ancient castrum was chosen as their seat by the Counts of Savoy, who were engaged in the conquest of the Canton of Vaud, a strategic passage close to the mountain passes and crossed by the main communication routes, including the Via Francigena. From Chillon, the Savoy family controlled the passage of travelers, merchants, and pilgrims to Italy and demanded payment of a toll in exchange for security and maintenance of the road. The castle as it

CHILLON CASTLE

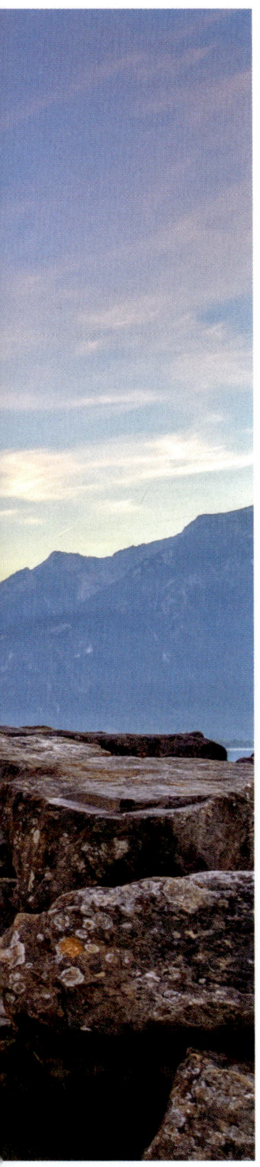

appears today is the result of expansions and renovations that began according to the needs of the times and of its owners, starting with those requested by Count Peter II of Savoy, who made the manor his summer residence. The architect Jacques de Saint-Georges, who was also active in North Wales at the court of Edward I of England, was commissioned with the project. The most evocative rooms of the manor date back to that period, including the Castellano Hall, with its two oak columns decorated with crochet capitals, the Hall of Justice, characterized by black marble columns and windows overlooking the lake, and the underground passages with Gothic vaults where, in the 16th century, François Bonivard, a nobleman and prior who fought for Geneva's independence from the Duchy of Savoy, was imprisoned for six years. Around 1340, Count Aimone of Savoy had his bedroom (Camera Domini), connected to the chapel by a secret staircase, frescoed with floral motifs by a certain Jean de

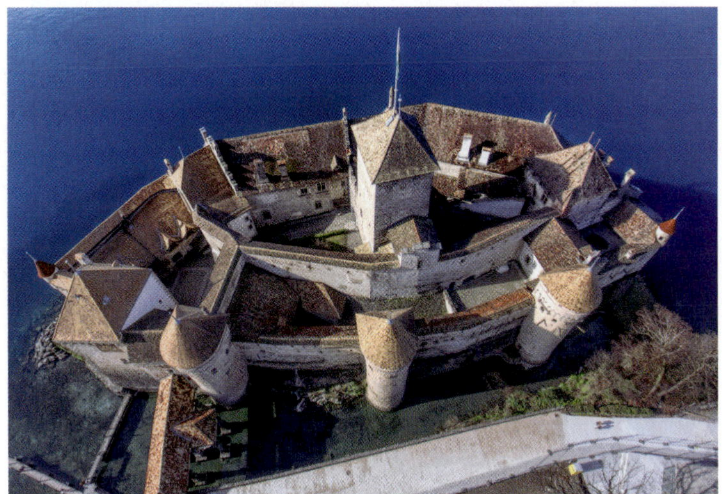

Grandson. The chapel dedicated to St. George also dates back to the period when it belonged to the Savoy family: inside, visitors can admire a series of 14th-century paintings. Over time, however, the Chillon residence was neglected by the Savoy family, who were forced to move constantly to control their vast duchy. The manor remained in the hands of a castellan until it was abandoned in 1536, when the Bernese claimed the fortress after a three-week siege.

• 123 center: The fortress, built on a real island, is oval in shape and measures approximately 328 x 164 feet. The interior of the castle was organized around courtyards that served for the castellan and the prince's residence.

1150
On the shores of Lake Geneva, near Montreux, the Savoy family gained control of the fortress of Chillon, beginning the conquest of Vaud.

1214
Thomas I of Savoy founded the town of Villeneuve, 1.24 miles upstream from the village of Chillon.

1255–1268
Peter II, Count of Savoy, made Chillon Castle his summer residence and began work to enlarge and embellish it.

1436
Amedeo VIII (the last antipope, known as Felice V) ordered major changes to the defensive system, but they remained unfinished. The castle was destined to be abandoned.

1530–1536
François Bonivard, a Protestant prior and opponent of the Catholic Savoy family, was imprisoned for six years in the castle dungeons because of his religious opinions.

1536
With the reconquest of Vaud, the Bernese occupied Chillon Castle, which became the permanent residence of the bailiff until 1773.

1798
On January 10, the Bernese left Vaud to the cities of Vevey and Montreux. Chillon Castle became the property of the Canton of Vaud. It was used as an artillery depot and state prison.

1816
Lord Byron visited the castle.

19th century
Restoration work on the manor house began, initiated by archaeologist Albert Naef. Restoration campaigns are still ongoing today.

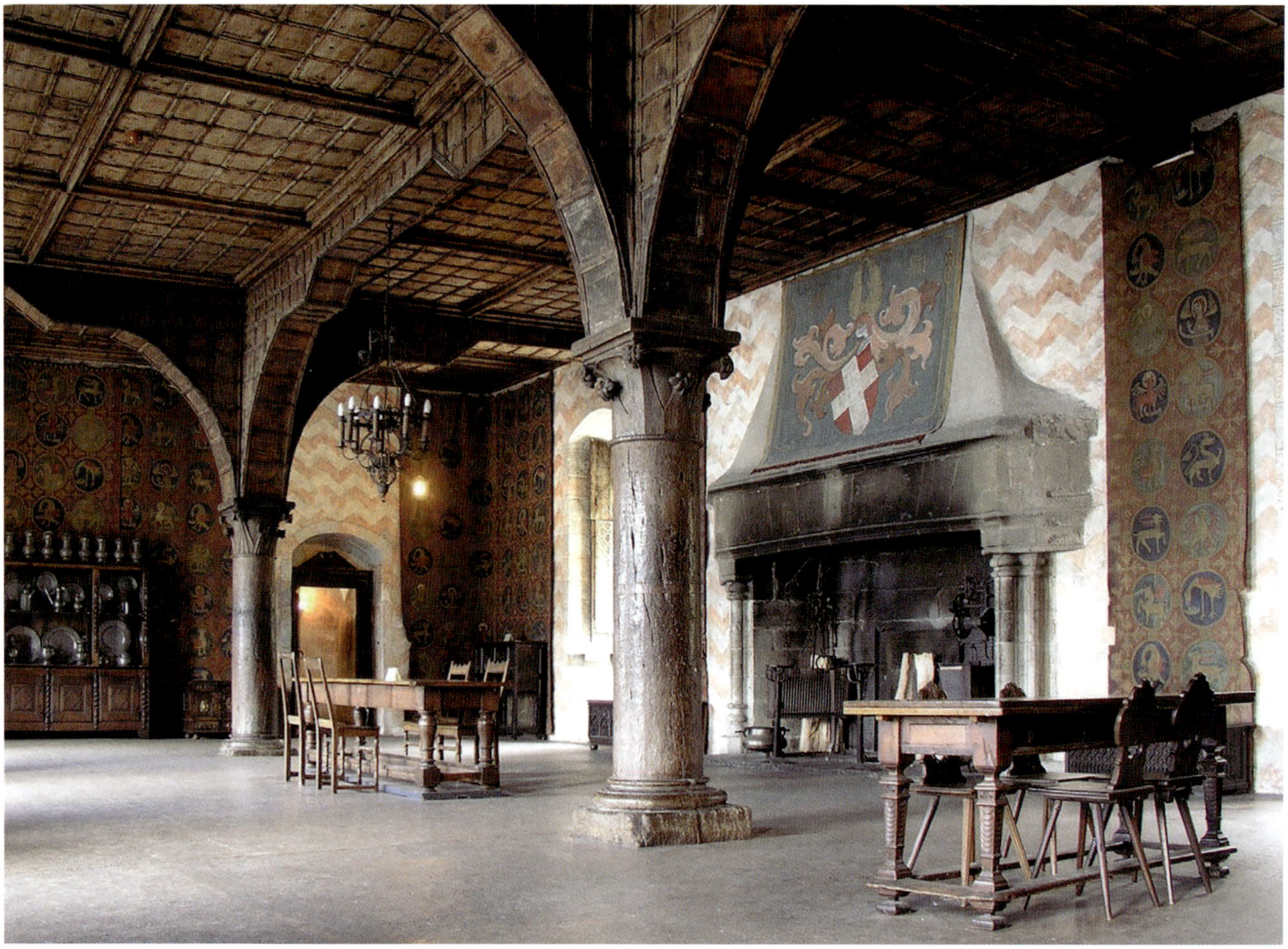

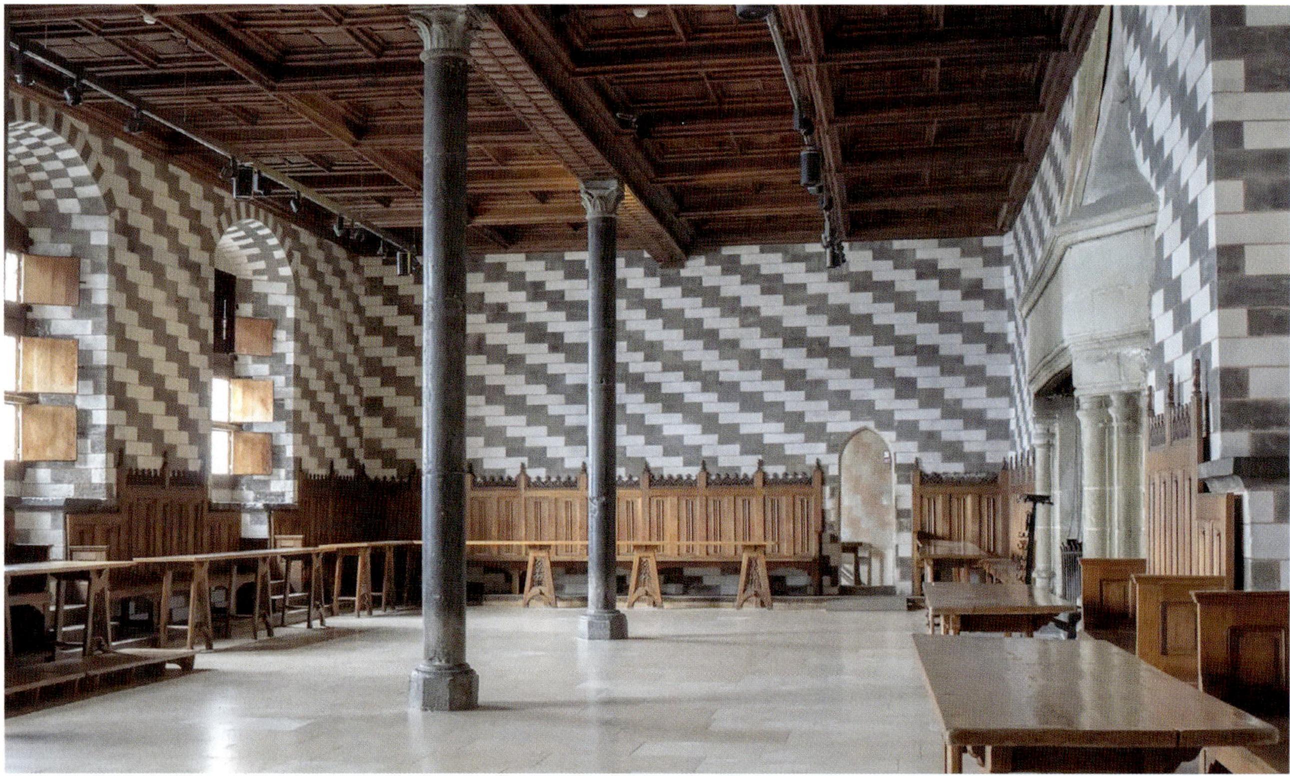

The new owners made the castle the permanent residence of a bailiff belonging to a patrician family from Bern until 1733, when the administrators preferred a more comfortable residence in Vevey. During the Bernese period, the castle's defenses were adapted to the defensive requirements dictated by new firearms. At the end of the 18th century, the patriots of Vevey and Montreux obtained the castle from the Swiss without opposition. Becoming a state prison and arsenal, the building attracted the attention of the first Grand Tour travelers. The Genevan Jean-Jacques Rousseau made it the setting for "Julie, or the New Heloise" (1761), describing it as built "on a rock that forms a peninsula on the lake." Lord Byron dedicated a poem to the prisoner François Bonivard in 1816, and the Castle was referenced also by Victor Hugo (in "Le Rhin," a travelogue in epistolary form written during his trip to Switzerland), Alexandre Dumas, and others.

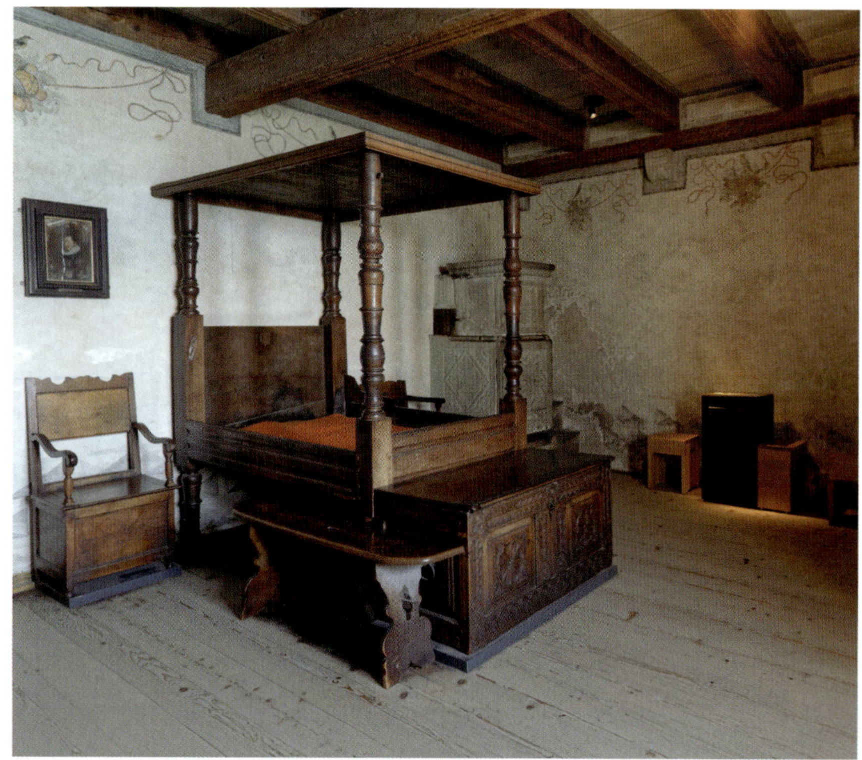

• 124 top: The Castellano Hall with wooden capitals commissioned by Peter II, and the 15th-century coffered ceiling. The insignias of the numerous bailiffs who succeeded one another from 1536 to 1733 bear witness to the castle's Bernese period.

• 124 bottom: The Hall of Justice was built by Peter II of Savoy. This is where vassals were received and justice was administered; it also served as a hall for parties and banquets..

• 125 top: The bedroom of the Counts and Dukes of Savoy (Camera Domini) dates back to the 13th century, but a century later it was decorated with drawings of animals, flowers, and fruits.

Lord Byron at Chillon

In June and September 1816, Lord Byron visited Chillon Castle: the poet and writer had been forced to leave England because of his behavior, which was unacceptable to conservative English morals. During his first visit, accompanied by his friend Percy Bysshe Shelley, Byron, after reading Jean-Jacques Rousseau's novel *Julie, or the New Heloise,* he wanted to visit the places where the story had taken place. It was then that his descent into the gothic dungeons of the castle where the Savoy family had held François Bonivard prisoner inspired him to write the poem *The Prisoner of Chillon.* A year later, an autograph engraved by Byron was reported in the underground prison, but its authenticity was immediately disputed. What is certain is that the inscription was a great success and a sort of myth grew up around it, so much so that Alexandre Dumas, Victor Hugo, Charles Dickens, Mark Twain, and many others mentioned it in their diaries, letters, and travel writings. Among them was Gustave Flaubert, who wrote in 1845: "Amidst so many obscure names scratching and cluttering the stone, it shines alone in a line of fire. I thought more of Byron than of the prisoner."

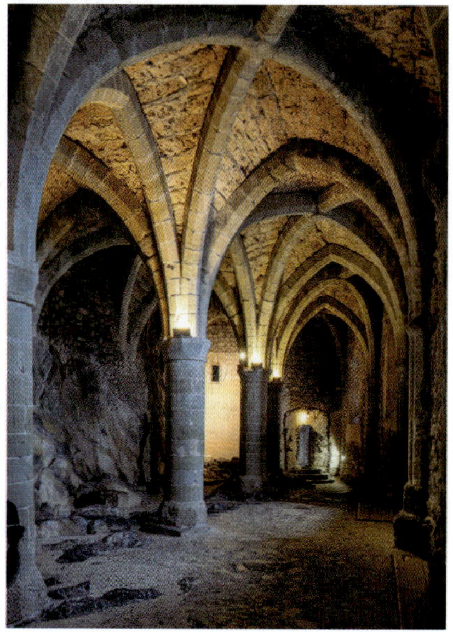

• 126-127: Aerial view of Hofburg Castle: in the foreground, the arched façade of the Michaelertrakt, immediately behind the courtyard where the Amalia Palace is located. On the left, the Prunksaal building, which has housed the Court Library since the early 18th century.

• 127 center: The massive arched building of the Neue Burg was added to the Hofburg complex between 1881 and 1913.

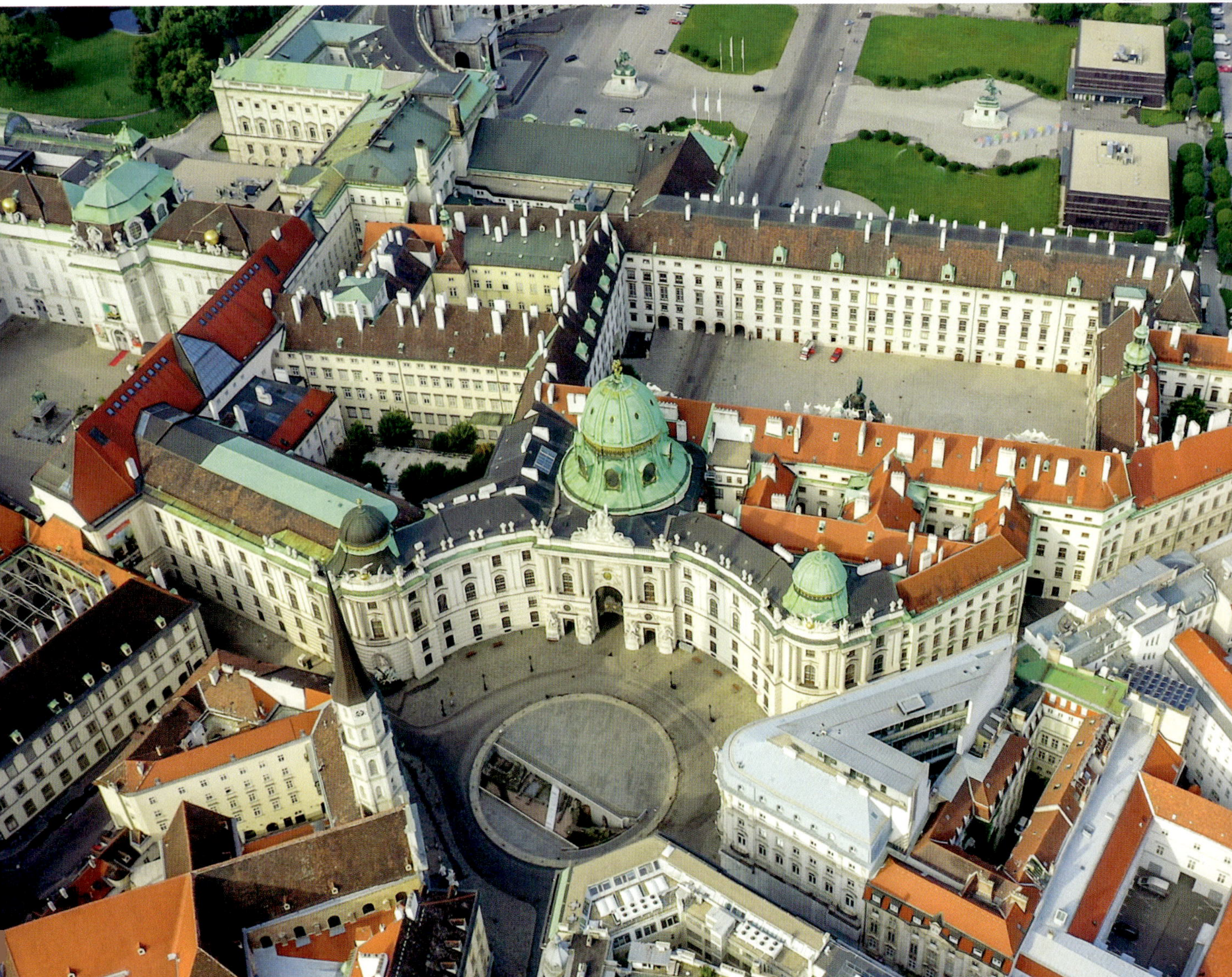

When Rudolf I, the first Habsburg to be elected Holy Roman Emperor in 1273, settled in Vienna six years after his accession to the throne, the complex of today's Hofburg, in the heart of the Austrian capital, was little more than a rectangular courtyard with four corner towers, now known as the Swiss Courtyard. It was not until Charles V ascended the throne three centuries later that the first work began on modernizing the fortress, which not only involved strengthening the defensive structures but also adapting them to the changing needs of the court. This work was continued by his son Ferdinand I. During their reigns, the existing wings were raised by several floors and a fourth wing was built, in which the famous Swiss Gate was opened, probably the work of architect Pietro Ferrabosco. Dating back to this period. were also

Hofburg Palace in Vienna

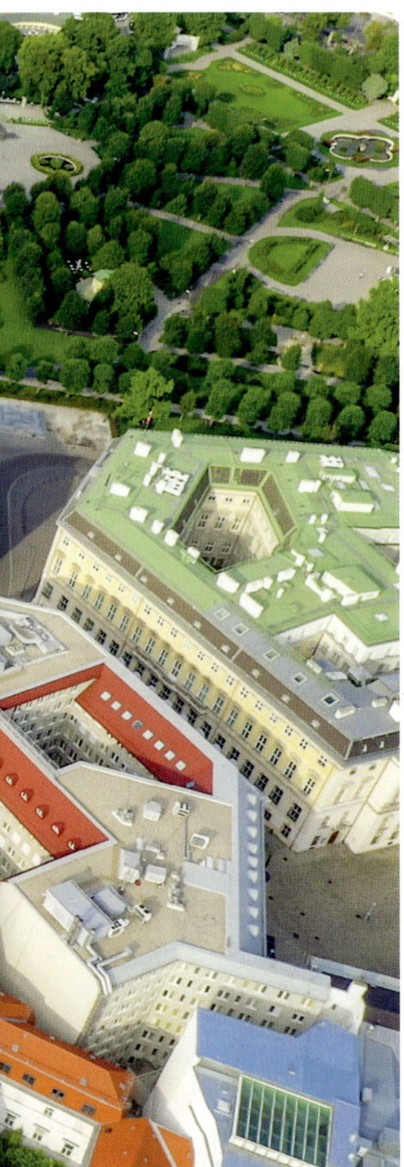

the Kinderstöckel, or palace for the offspring, the Court Chancellery, the Kunstkammer for the art collection, and a new Ballhaus, a building intended for a kind of tennis game, later transformed by Maria Theresa into the Imperial Theater, or Hofburgtheater. Starting in 1559, several isolated buildings were added to this initial nucleus, including the current Lipizzaner stables and the so-called "Amalia Palace." The Thirty Years' War broke out in 1618, interrupting the work, which only resumed in 1660 under Emperor Leopold I. His plans included transforming Vienna into a modern Baroque capital and the castle into a structure that would represent the empire in all its magnificence. To this end, he sought to give greater architectural uniformity to the Hofburg, which was still composed of several separate buildings. After him, Charles VI, who arrived in Vienna in 1711, completed what his father had begun. He endowed the Hofburg with the monumental entrance on Michaelerplatz

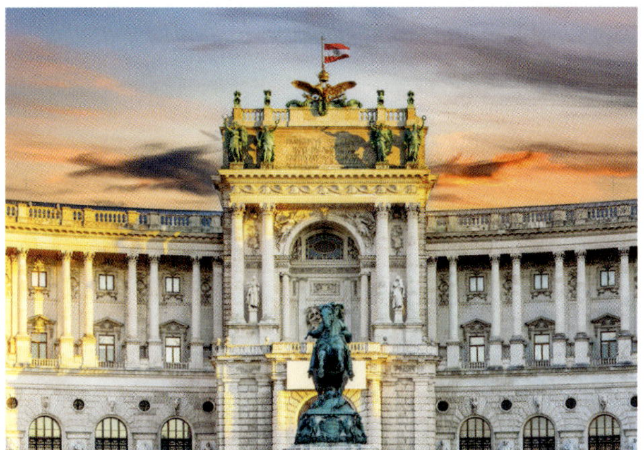

with its famous dome-covered rotunda (completed only in 1893 when it was decided to demolish the Hofburgtheater, which prevented its completion) and the wing of St. Michael. He also had the imperial stables built (now the Museums Quartier) and, between 1729 and 1735, in a splendid Baroque building, he rebuilt the Spanish Riding Winter School, the oldest in the world and the only one dedicated to teaching horsemen and horses (the

1275
Ottokar II, King of Bohemia and Duke of Austria, built the original core of the Hofburg, now the Swiss Courtyard, on the site where Henry II of Babenberg had built a first fort.

1519
Emperor Charles V began renovating the Hofburg. The Swiss Gate was opened.

1556
Ferdinand I continued the transformation of the Hofburg, building, among other things, the Kinderstöckel (children's building), the Court Chancellery, the Kunstkammer (art chamber) for the imperial art collection, and a new ballroom.

1559
Leopold I began a renovation plan of the Hofburg: a first step towards the creation of the imperial palace as it appears today.

1711
Charles VI transformed the Hofburg into a Baroque imperial palace, including the monumental entrance on Michaelerplatz.

1740
Maria Theresa, daughter of Charles VI and wife of Francis I, ascended the throne. She was responsible for transforming the Ballhaus into the Imperial Theater or Hofburgtheater, as well as the renovation and expansion of the Imperial Library.

1848–1870
Franz Joseph was elected emperor, married Elisabeth of Bavaria in 1854, and in 1870 began construction of the Imperial Forum.

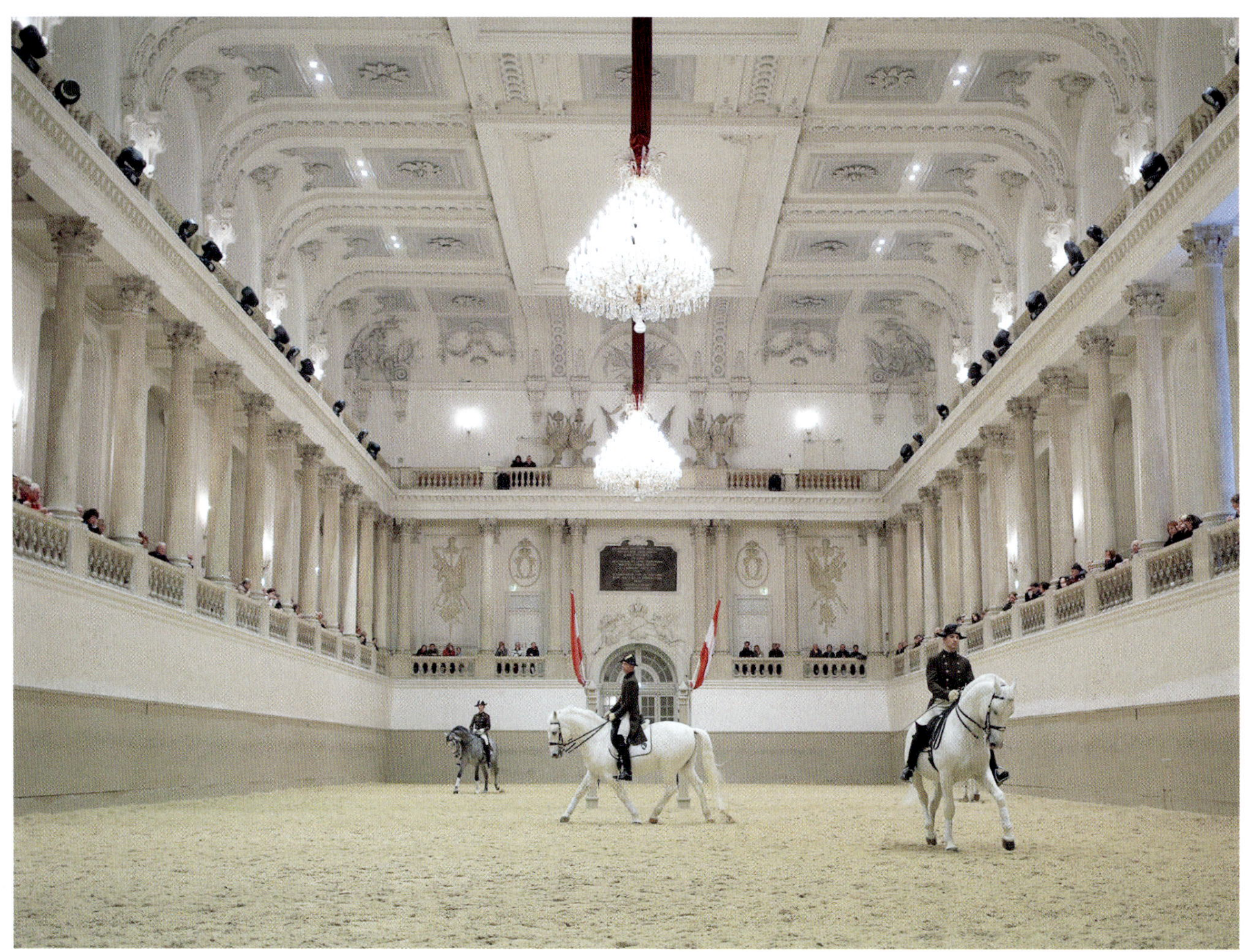

Lipizzaner horses) "the classical art of riding" for five centuries. Charles VI was also responsible for the construction of the Imperial Library, begun in 1722, a jewel of early 18th-century architecture. In particular, the Gala Hall or Prunksaal, covered by a 98-foot-high dome, is considered one of the most extraordinary Baroque library rooms in the world: the emperor's daughter and heir, Maria Theresa, had it renovated by Nicolò Pacassi. During the reign of Franz Joseph, who ascended the throne in 1848, the Hofburg underwent its final transformation. The emperor ordered the demolition of the surrounding walls, clearing a large area that would become the present-day Ringstrasse. This marked the start of a major program of architectural and urban renewal of the former rampart area between the imperial stables and the Hofburg, with the construction of the so-called Imperial Forum, consisting of the twin buildings of the Museum of Fine Arts and the Natural History Museum, facing Maria-Theresien-Platz, which in the original design were to be connected to the Hofburg by two wings extending from the throne room towards the Ringstrasse. In 1898, following the tragic death of Empress Elisabeth of Bavaria, better known as Sissi, Franz Joseph lost all interest in the project, of which only the Neue Burg (or New Palace), the wing facing the garden, had been built, but was left incomplete.

• 128 top: The spectacular covered riding arena of the Hofburg, built in Baroque style. Lipizzaner horses have been trained and have performed here since the 18th century.

• 129: The gala hall of the former Habsburg court library is almost 262 feet long and 98 feet high and is crowned in the center by an enormous dome frescoed by Daniel Gran. It depicts the apotheosis of Emperor Charles VI, who commissioned the construction of the library in 1722. In the center of the hall stands a statue of Charles VI by court sculptor Antonio Corradini, dating from 1735..

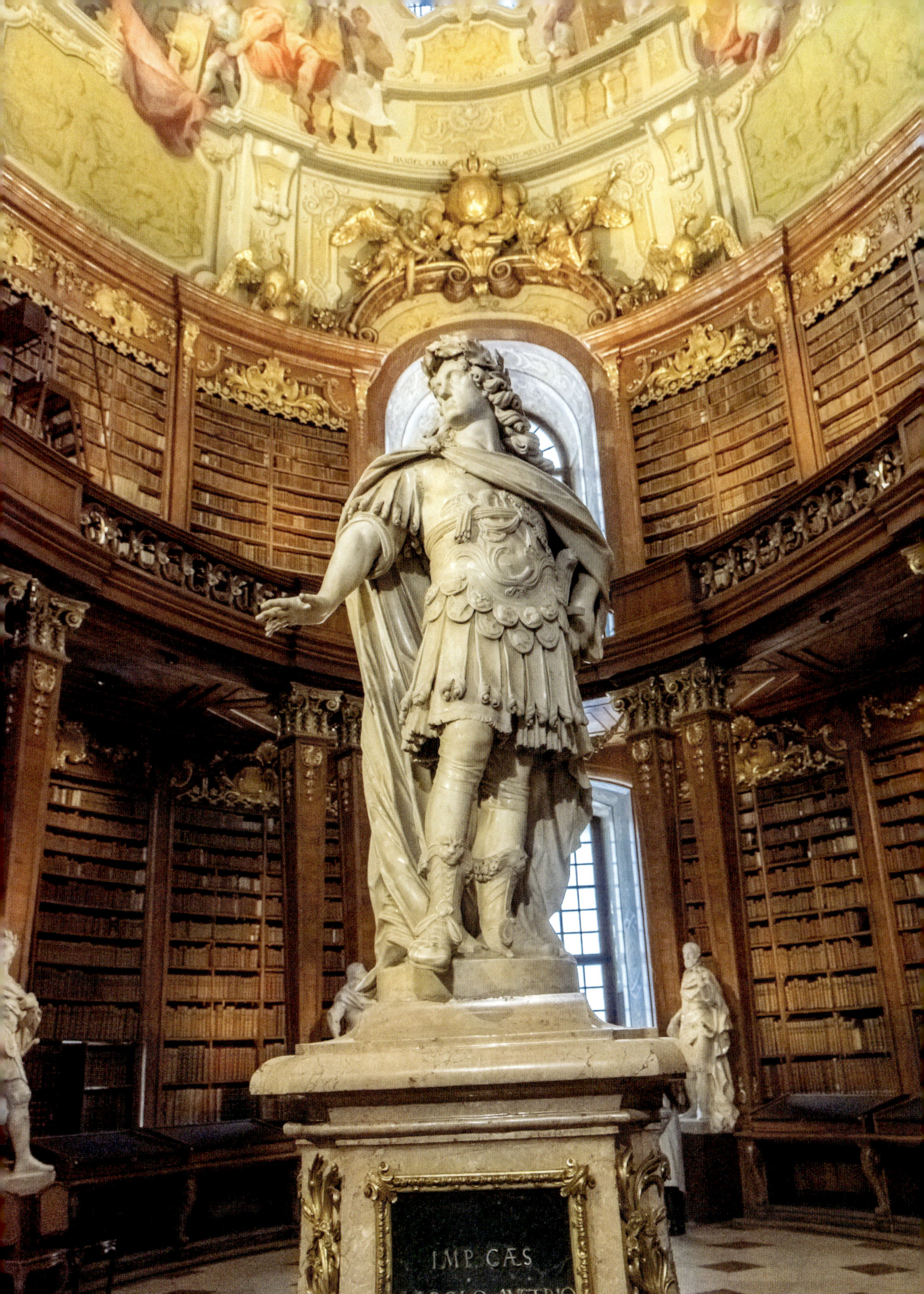
IMP. CÆS

Sissi's apartments

Elisabeth of Bavaria married Emperor Franz Joseph on April 24, 1854. Independent and unconventional, Sissi, as she was called in her family, rarely stayed in Vienna, preferring the landscapes of Hungary and traveling throughout Europe, which allowed her to escape the oppressive court environment and rigid ceremonial protocol. During the rare moments when she resided in the imperial capital, she had an apartment at her disposal, now a museum dedicated to her, on the main floor of the Amalia Palace in the Hofburg, adjacent to the emperor's apartment and furnished in a sober neo-rococo style. In her bedroom, which was also used as a sitting room, Sissi had a healthful iron bed, in keeping with the obsession with health, beauty, and physical fitness that seems to have accompanied her throughout her life. Her beauty treatments began at six in the morning in her dressing room and gym with adjoining bathroom equipped with a zinc-plated copper bathtub, a small sink, and a dolphin- shaped toilet. Elisabeth would reach her apartment via the Eagle Staircase, Adlerstiege, in the Leopoldina wing and used the large salon for receiving visitors. The spacious antechamber and the small adjoining salon were the family's gathering place before court balls.

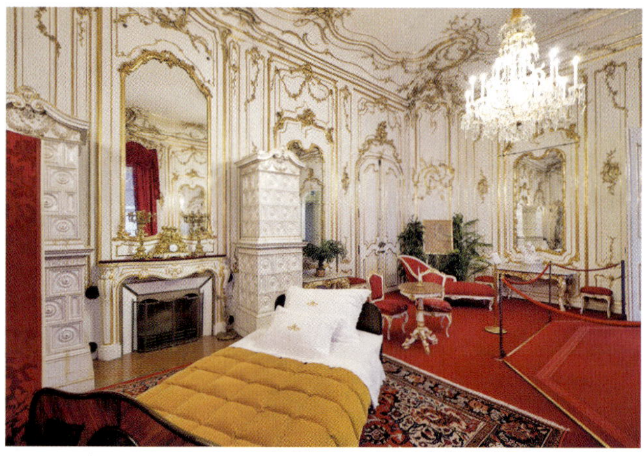

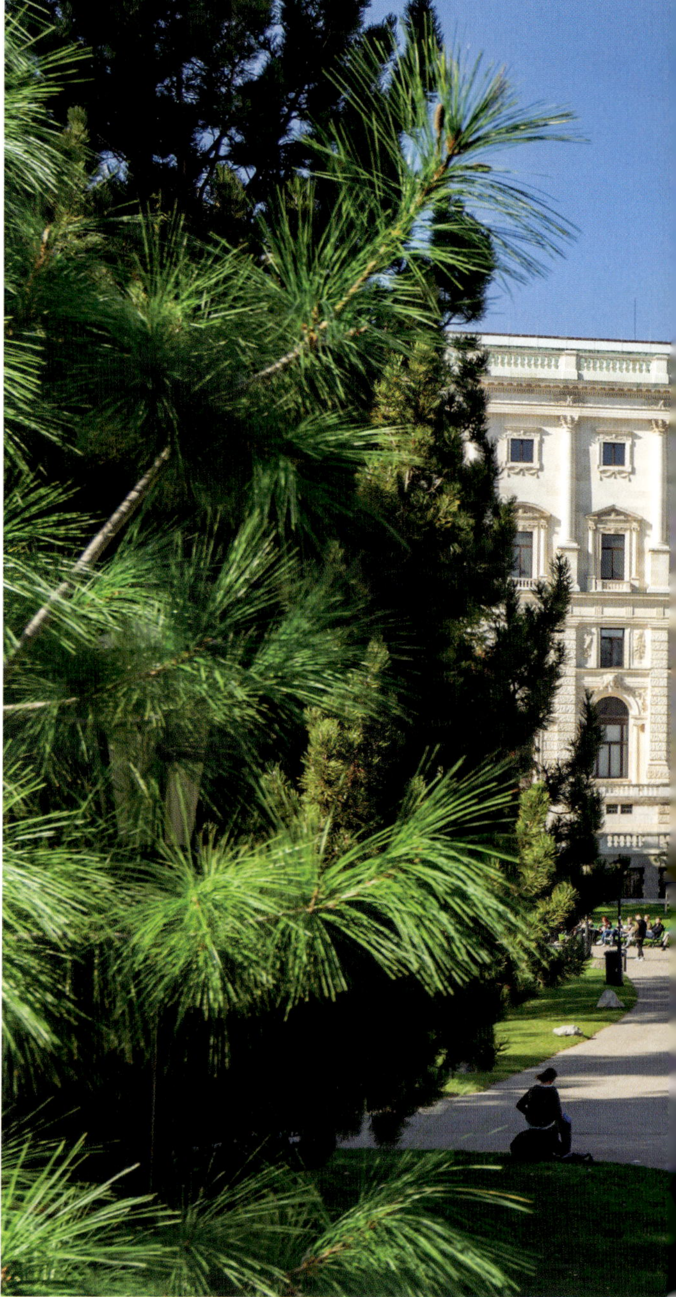

• 130 center: Empress Sissi's bedroom with adjoining sitting room.

• 130–131: The Jugendstil greenhouse in the Burggarten, known as the "Palmenhaus," was built by Friedrich Ohmann between 1902 and 1906. With its 590-foot length and 42-foot width, it was constructed using a combination of stone and glass elements, housing plants from all over the world and a large number of birds and monkeys. Closed in the 1980s, today it is a place to relax, a greenhouse, and a butterfly house.

• 131 bottom left: The emperor's bedroom was furnished with only a few essential items. Among the simple furnishings were a folding washbasin and a kneeler. The emperor used to wake up at 3:30 in the morning. At that time, a folding rubber bathtub was placed in the bedroom and the emperor took a bath. After getting dressed, he entered his study to begin reading his papers at 4 o'clock sharp.

• 131 bottom right: The emperor's study served as a sitting room. Among the numerous family portraits here is the famous portrait of the empress with her long hair let loose by Franz Xaver Winterhalter, which can be seen reflected in the mirror..

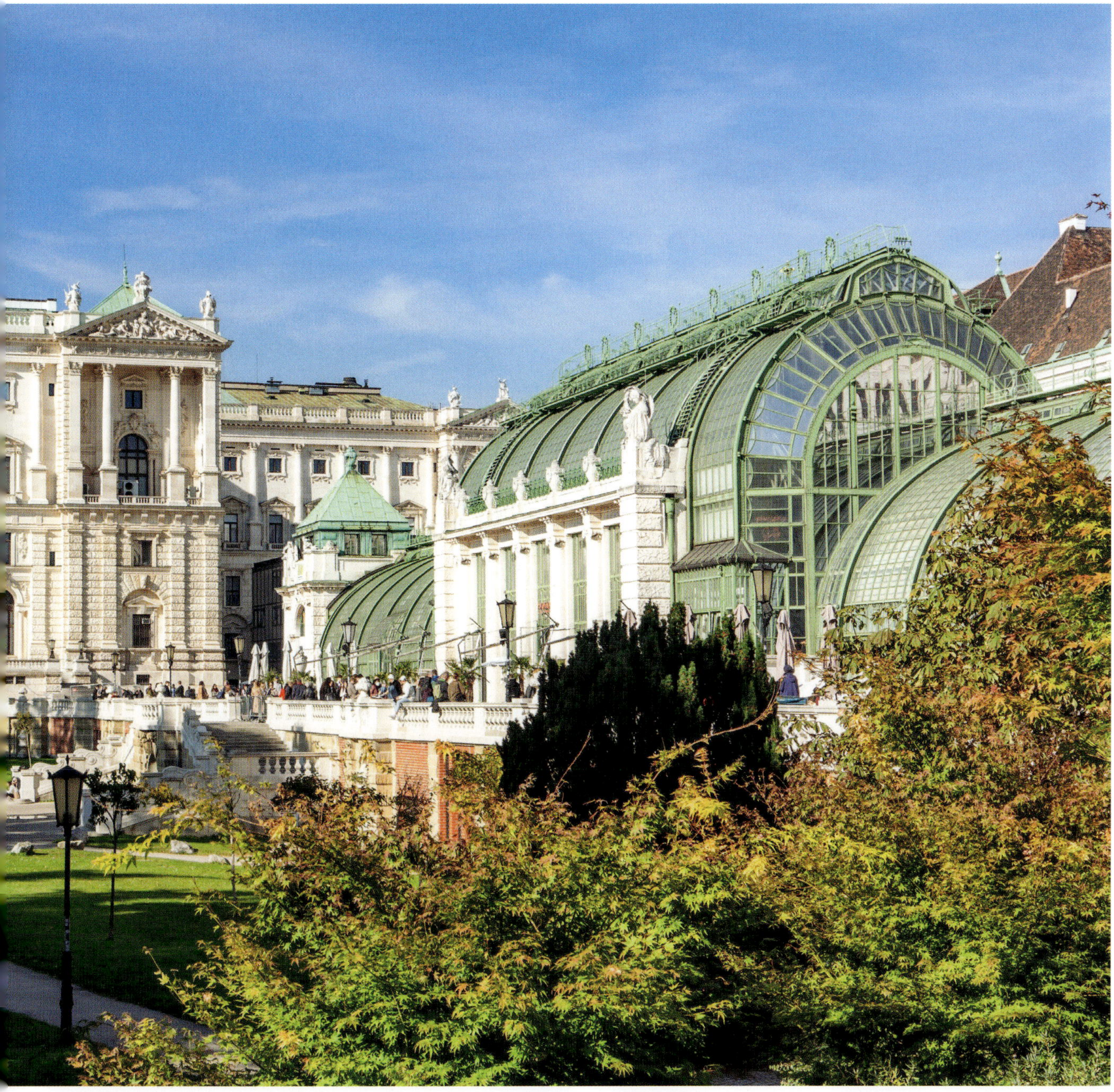

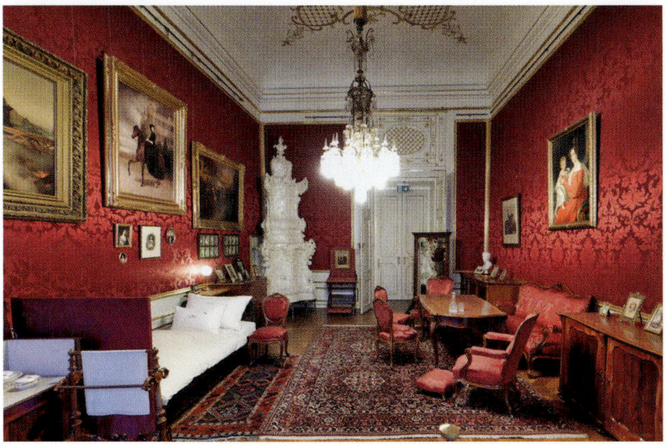

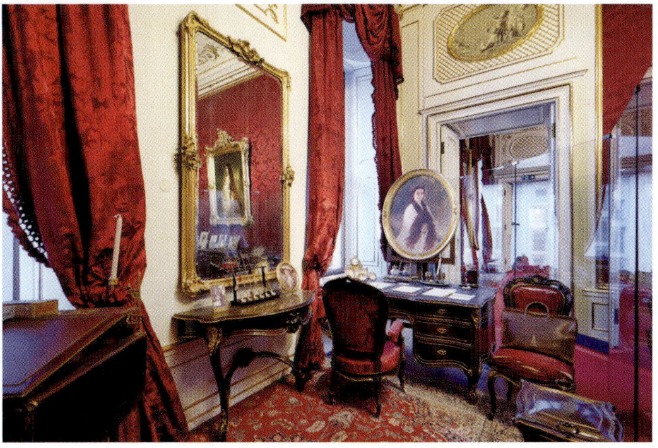

Belvedere Castle

1712–1723
Prince Eugene of Savoy Soissons commissioned architect Johann Lucas von Hildebrandt to build Belvedere Castle, a masterpiece of Baroque architecture.

1752
Belvedere Castle was purchased by Maria Theresa and in 1896 it became the official residence of the heir to the throne, Franz Ferdinand.

1770
Maria Theresa organized a grand reception in the castle for the wedding of her daughter Marie Antoinette to the Dauphin of France, Louis XVI.

1776
Maria Theresa and her son Joseph II moved the Imperial Art Gallery, or Gemäldegalerie, from the Hofburg to Belvedere Castle, opening it to the public in 1781, thus making it one of the first public museums in the world.

1891
The collection from the Gemäldegalerie was transferred to the new Museum of Fine Arts, the Kunsthistorisches Museum.

1903
Belvedere Castle housed the State Gallery of Modern Art. It was the first museum dedicated to new trends in Austria, with a particular focus on the Viennese Secession.

In the 18th century, the political, economic, legislative, and cultural center of the Austrian monarchy was the Hofburg in Vienna; but not far away, the countryside surrounding the capital at the end of the 18th century saw the start of construction of Belvedere Castle in the early 1700s, one of the most beautiful princely residences in Europe. A masterpiece of Baroque architecture, the castle was commissioned to Johann Lucas von Hildebrandt by Prince Eugene of Savoy-Carignano Soissons, an Italian nobleman, lover of luxury and ostentation, and passionate art collector who, after renouncing the ecclesiastical life, embarked on a brilliant military career, first at the court of Louis XIV of France and, from 1679, in the service of Emperor Leopold I of Habsburg. Distinguishing himself in the Battle of Vienna in 1683 against the Ottoman armies, he rapidly earned a career in the imperial army, becoming one of the most powerful and richest men in the empire. Hildebrandt designed a complex consisting of two opposite buildings, the upper Belvedere, used for representative purposes, and the lower one, the prince's private residence, built in the style of French country castles and completed in 1716. Seven years later, the work on the upper Belvedere was also completed, resulting in a building possibly even more refined and grandiose than the first. Here, the Savoy family received statesmen and diplomats in the marvelous setting of the double-height marble hall, the Marmorsaal, decorated with frescoes, stuccoes, marble, chandeliers, and trompe l'oeil decorations, emblematic of the opulence and wealth that the leader could display, both as a war hero and as a patron of the arts. From the windows of the upper Belvedere, in an elevated position, there was a unique panorama stretching from the historic center of the city, with a privileged view of the Hofburg, to the wooded hills around Vienna, as well as the magnificent garden that gently slopes down to connect the two buildings of the complex. Designed by landscape architect Dominique Girard, a pupil of André Le Nôtre, it is a perfect example of a French Baroque garden with descending terraces developed around a central axis, ornamental flowerbeds bordered by box hedges, finials symbolizing power and wisdom guarding the entrance avenue, ancient sculptures lining the avenues, fountains, and water basins that reflected the castle. A lover of exotic animals and rare plants, the prince also had a menagerie, a winter garden, or orangery, and a greenhouse, which has unfortunately been lost.

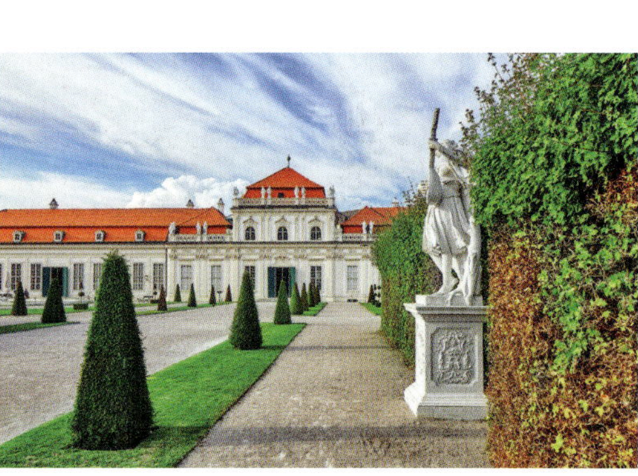

• 132 bottom: The lower Belvedere was built in the style of French country castles and was completed in 1716. As a Baroque masterpiece of rooms that follow one after the other, it was the prince's private residence.

• 133: Aerial view of the Belvedere Castle complex. The lower Belvedere can be seen in the foreground, while the upper is in the background. In the center are the French gardens. A great example of a Baroque garden, the Belvedere park is characterized by flowerbeds with intricate hedges arranged to form a pattern of volutes and racemes imitating precious brocades.

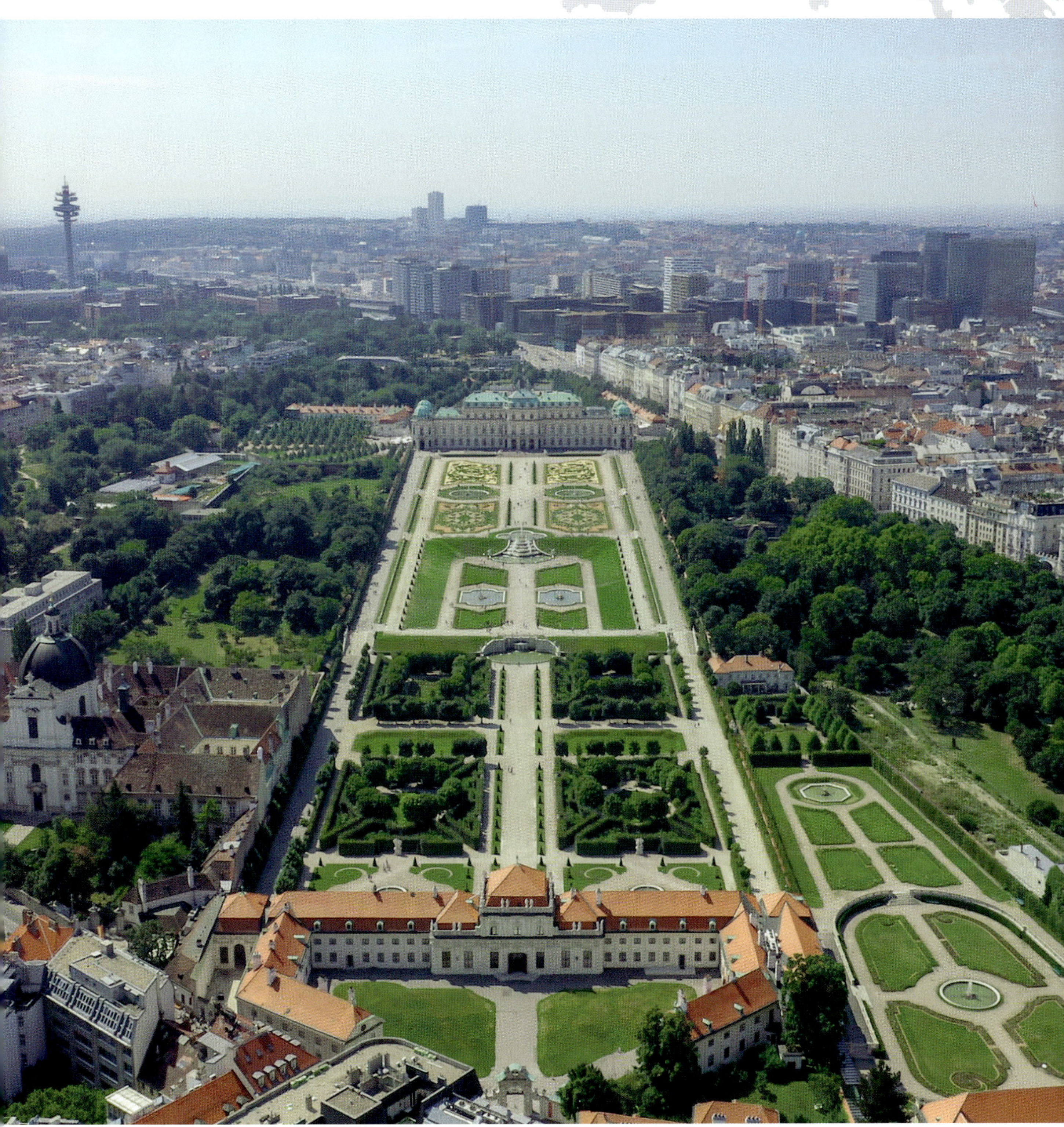

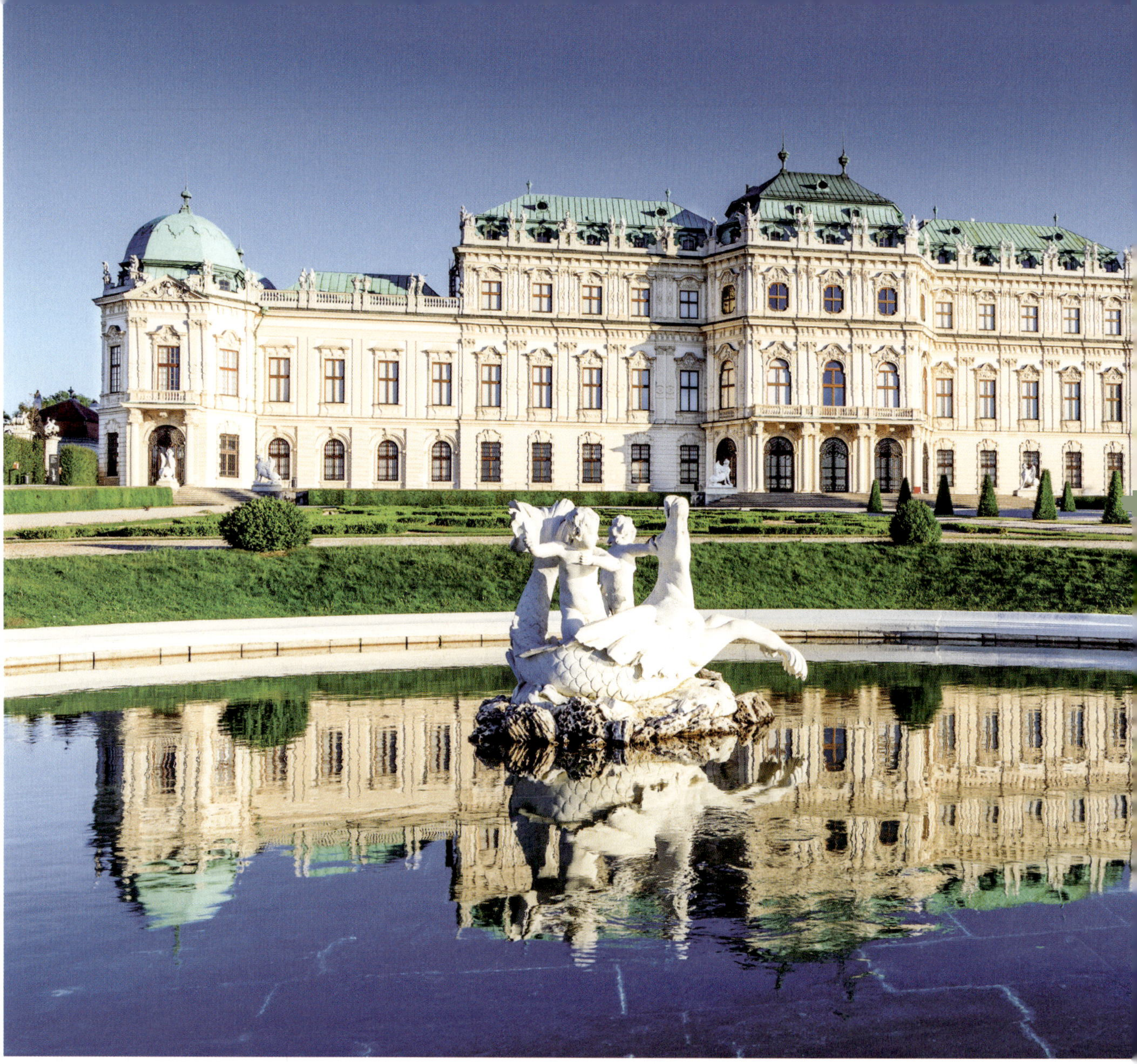

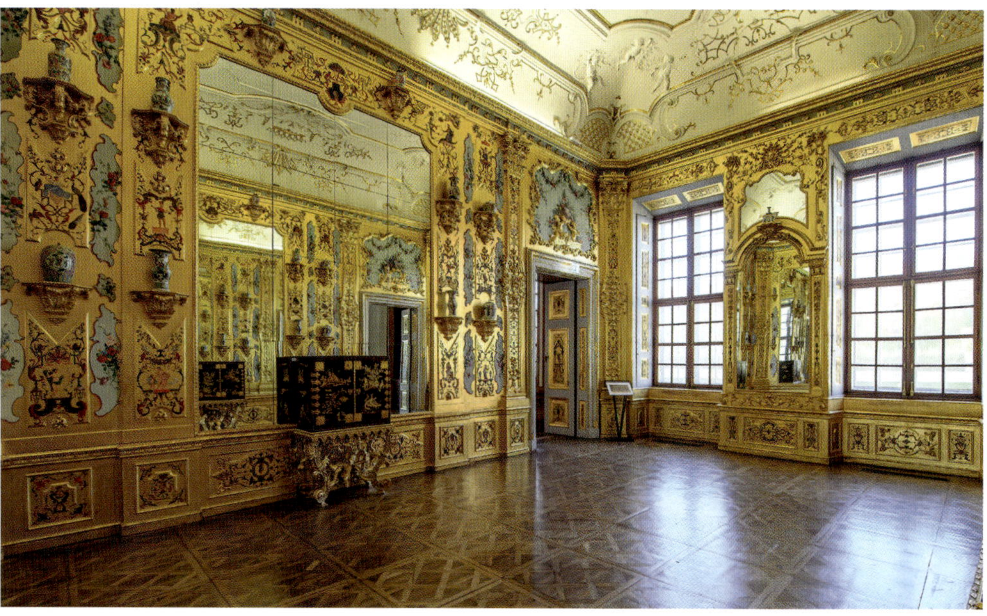

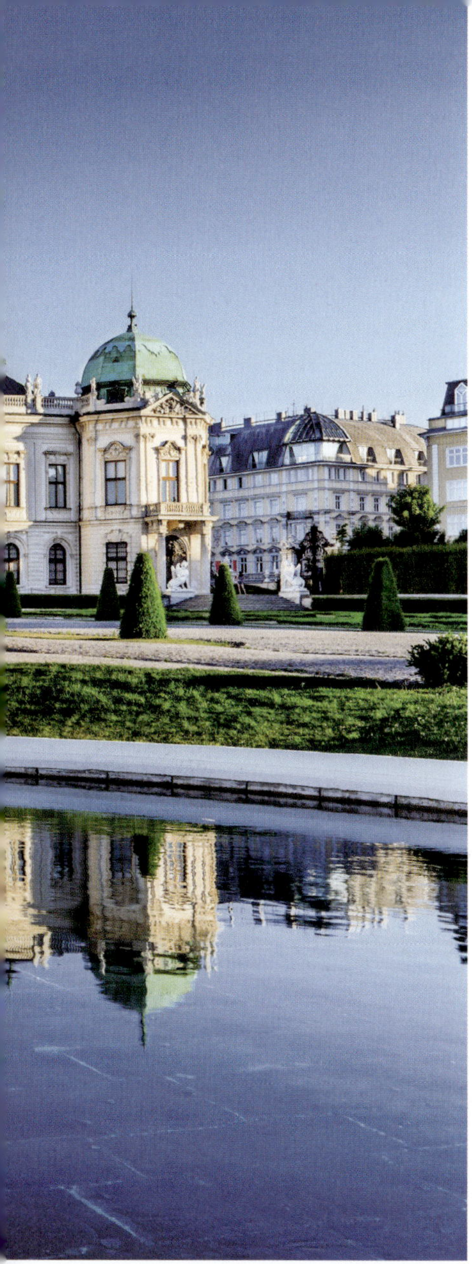

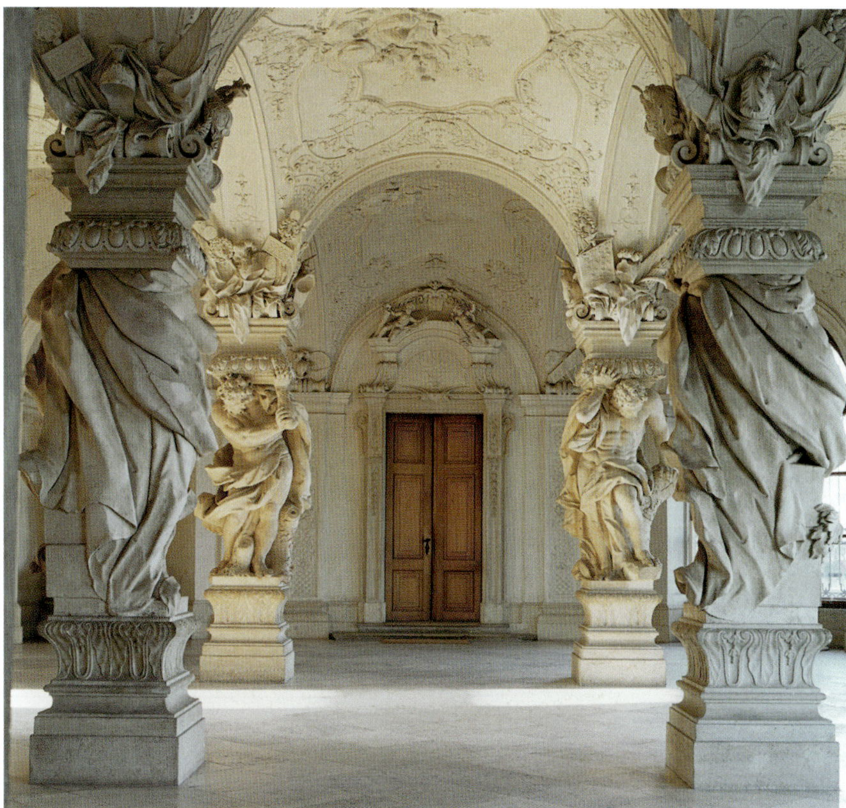

An important marriage

In 1752, Maria Theresa purchased Belvedere Palace, but she never lived there. In the 1780s, she moved the imperial picture gallery there, now part of the collections of the Museum of Fine Arts, and opened it to the public. Previously, the Belvedere had only been open occasionally for receptions.

In 1770, the most sumptuous masked ball in the history of the palace was held in its halls. The occasion was the marriage of Marie Antoinette to the Dauphin of France, Louis XVI; and the guests were so many that the Silver Chamber ran out of tableware and had to borrow from the nobles. For lighting, over ten thousand candles were lit and as many glass balls were lit with oil. Today, Belvedere houses the largest collection of Austrian art, ranging from the Middle Ages to the modern age.

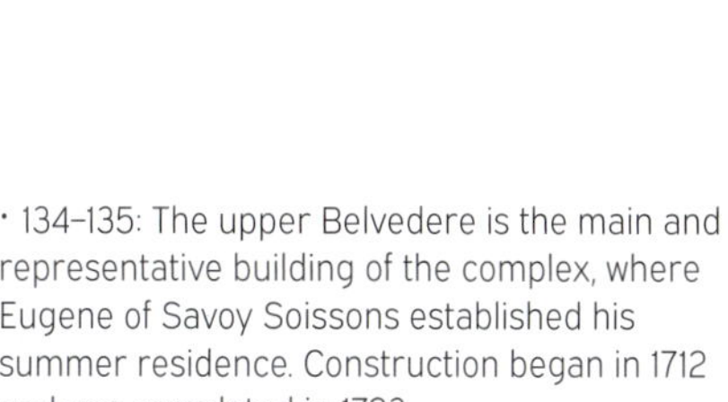

• 134–135: The upper Belvedere is the main and representative building of the complex, where Eugene of Savoy Soissons established his summer residence. Construction began in 1712 and was completed in 1723.

• 134 bottom: The Golden Room in the lower Belvedere is characterized by typical Baroque opulence. Maria Theresa had this room renovated and adorned with mirrors and porcelain, transferring most of the decorations from Prince Eugene's city palace in Himmelpfortgasse.

• 135 top: Evocative image of the Sala Terrena in the upper Belvedere.

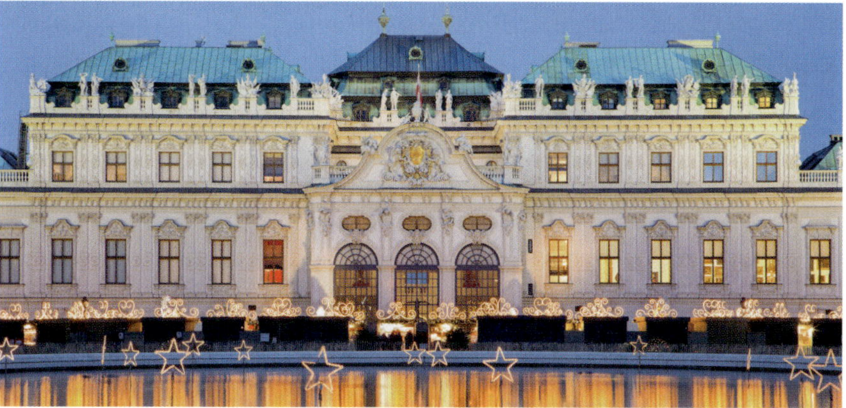

• 136-137: View of Schönbrunn Palace from the side of the Court of Honor with one of the two fountains that adorn the large space.

• 137 center: View of Schönbrunn Palace overlooking the Grand Parterre with flower beds whose decorations change with the seasons. At the rear, the Court of Honor, with its two symmetrical fountains, is surrounded by service buildings, along with the one that houses the court theater (to the left of the entrance).

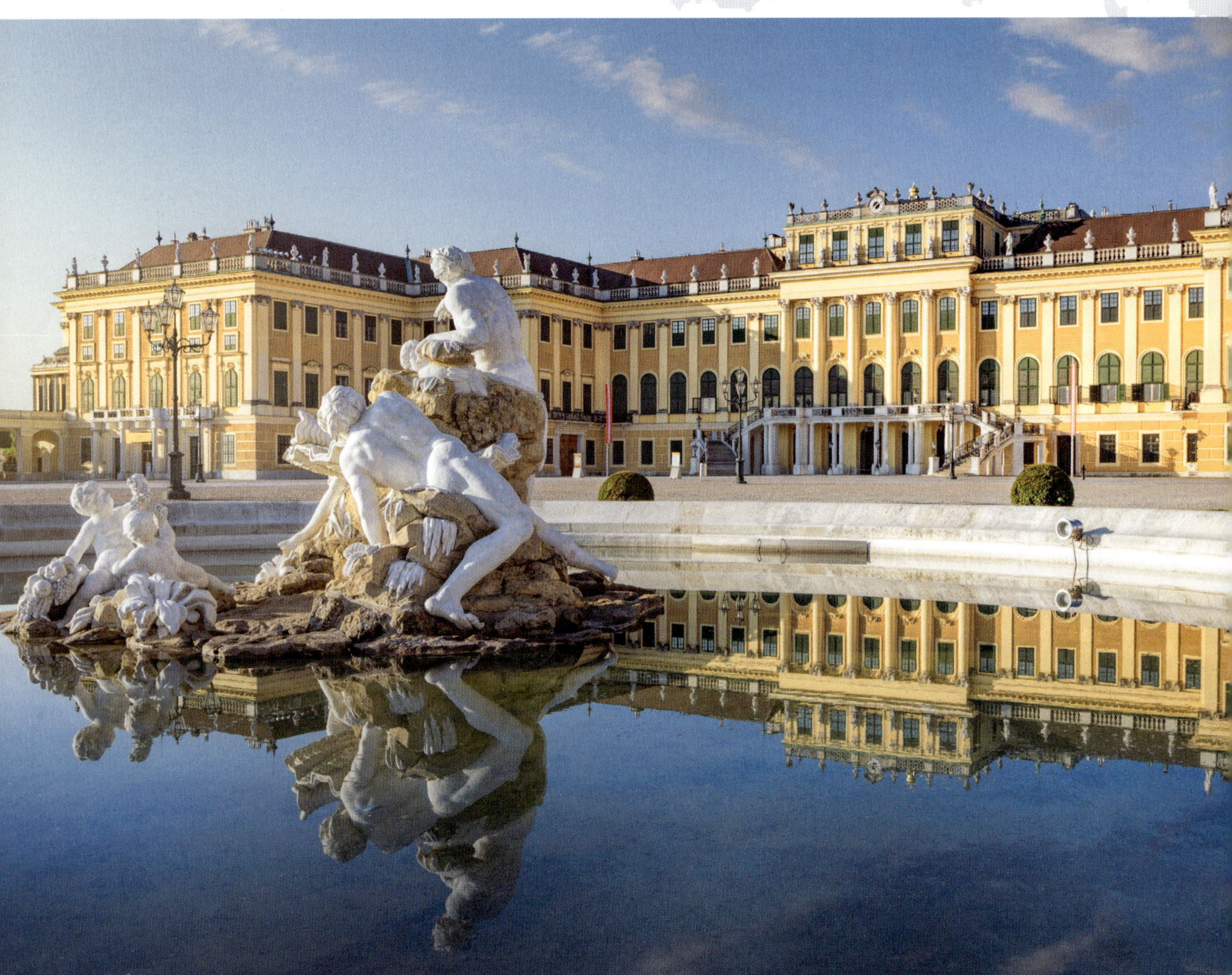

Built in the 18th century in the open countryside, now on the outskirts of Vienna, Schönbrunn Palace is the masterpiece of Empress Maria Theresa of Habsburg, who transformed what was once a hunting lodge donated in 1736 by her father, Emperor Charles VI, into a summer residence. It's a Baroque masterpiece by architect Nicolò Pacassi, used by the Holy Roman Emperors to host the court and for their leisure time until the end of the Holy Roman Empire in 1806, and subsequently as a permanent residence until 1918. During the reign of Maria Theresa and her husband Francis Stephen of Lorraine, under the direction of Pacassi, the castle took on its present form: the service quarters were created and the interiors were redesigned, and both the private apartments of the sovereigns and those of their numerous children—16 in total—were built and redecorated. Magnificent state rooms were created with rocaille motifs, frescoes, and mirrors that reflected the light from

Schönbrunn Palace

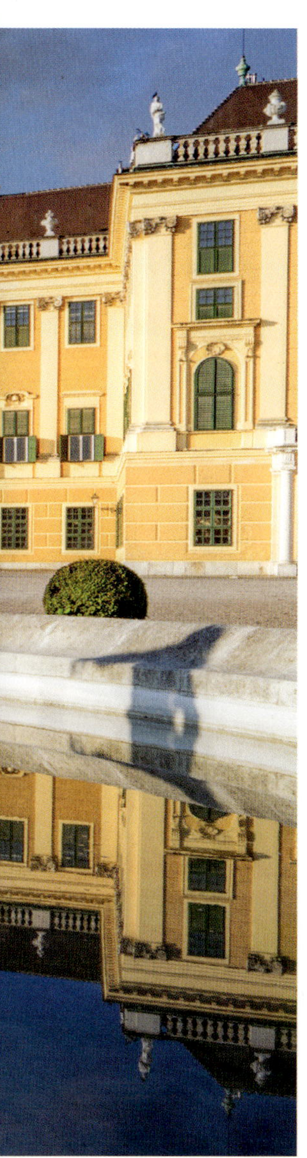

the big chandeliers and enlarged the spaces, and paintings were hung on the walls in frames decorated with gilded stucco. The so-called "Maria Theresa style" became popular at that time, a distinctive feature of the empress's palaces, of which the Grand Gallery on the main floor is a magnificent example. Intended to host balls, official lunches, and court ceremonies, it is the heart of the palace, overlooking the Courtyard of Honor on one side and directly connected to the Small Gallery overlooking the garden on the other. The façades overlooking the Courtyard of Honor and the garden were also redesigned by Nicolò Pacassi in a refined and elegant Rococo style, but between 1817 and 1819 they were revised in favor of more sober lines, taking on the classic "Schönbrunn yellow" color, which became a distinctive feature of the castle. In 1747, the imperial residence was also equipped with a theater: the empress was passionate about Italian opera and French comedy and often performed in plays with her children. A small jewel of the palace

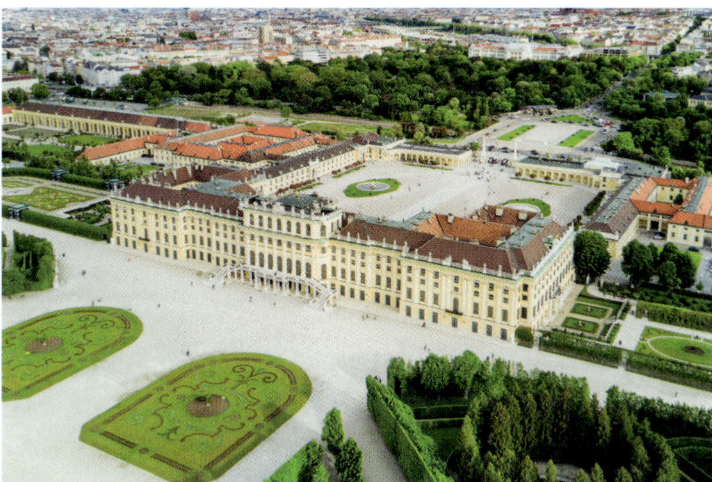

are the apartments for Maria Theresa and her two children who still lived at court, created between 1769 and 1770 in the southeast corner on the ground floor. They are known as the "Bergl Rooms," named after the painter Johann Wenzel Bergl who decorated them. The artist, with his highly personal Rococo style, created trompe-l'œil illusions that made the rooms seem idyllic, as if immersed in nature, surrounded by animals, exotic plants, and architectural elements that accentuated the perspective. After Maria Theresa's death in 1780, Schönbrunn Palace remained uninhabited.

1569
Maximilian II purchased the Katterburg estate on which Schönbrunn Palace would be built. Years later, his son Matthias II discovered the spring that would give the estate its name: Schöner Brunnen, "Beautiful Spring."

1693
Johann Bernhard Fischer von Erlach was commissioned by Leopold I to renovate Schönbrunn Palace.

1743
Maria Theresa of Habsburg, Empress since 1740, transformed the hunting lodge into a magnificent Baroque residence, entrusting the work to Nicolò Pacassi.

1751–1752
In the Schönbrunn park, Emperor Francis Stephen I, husband of Maria Theresa, inaugurated the construction of the oldest zoological garden still active in the world.

1772–1780
Maria Theresa commissioned architect Johann Ferdinand Hetzendorf von Hohenberg to redesign Schönbrunn Park.

1805–1810
Napoleon Bonaparte entered Vienna and set up his headquarters in Schönbrunn Palace.

1882
The Palmenhaus, a super-modern greenhouse made of iron and glass, was opened in the gardens of Schönbrunn.

1916
On November 21, Franz Joseph, the last absolute ruler of Austria, died in Schönbrunn.

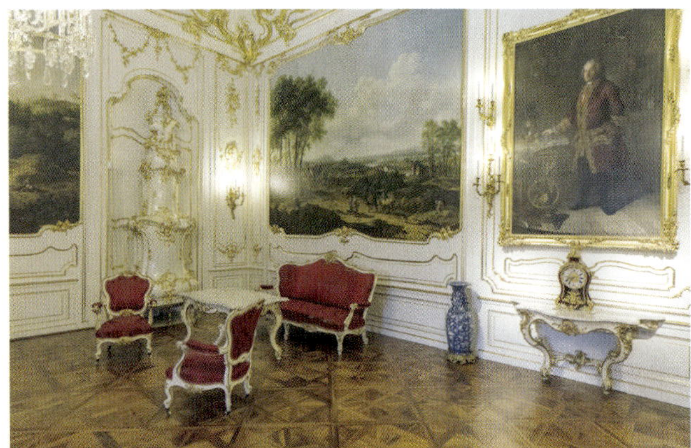

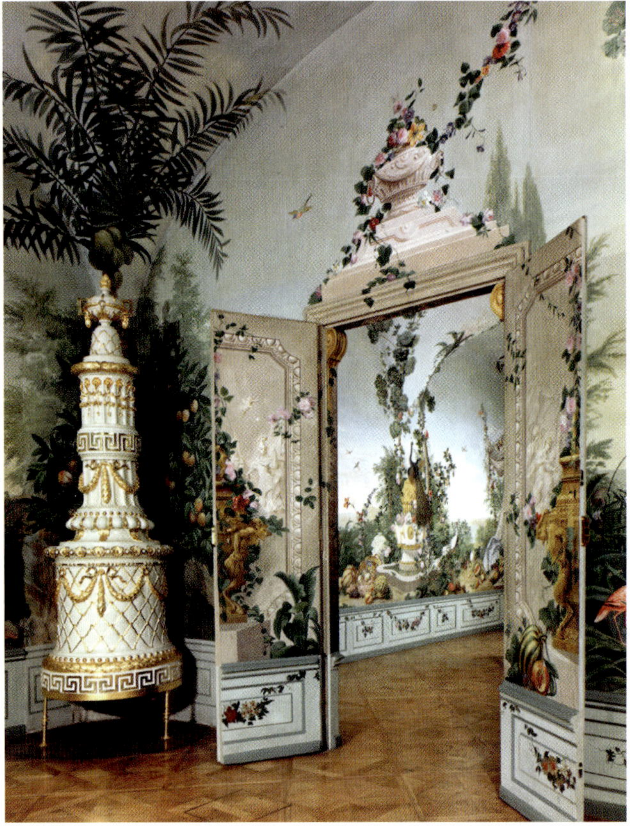

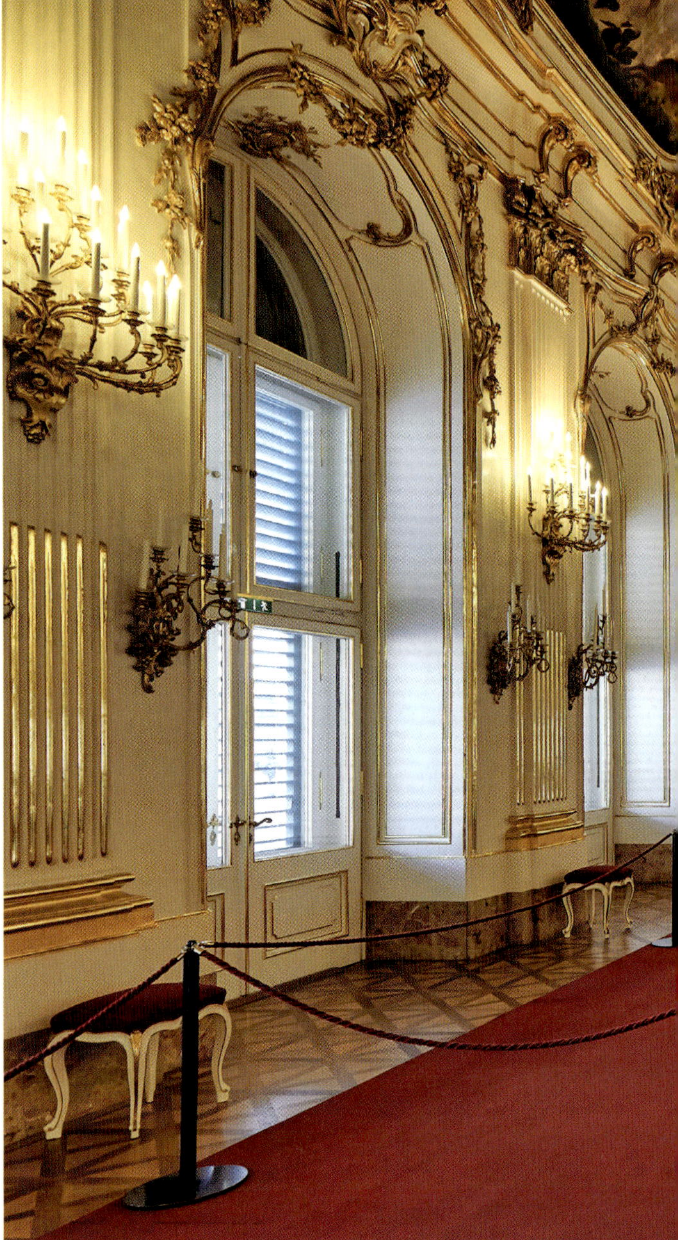

A few years later, Napoleon Bonaparte disrupted the geopolitical order of Europe and occupied Vienna in 1805. On October 14, 1809, Francis II of Habsburg signed the peace treaty at Schönbrunn, where the French emperor had set up his headquarters. Once the Napoleonic storm had passed, the Viennese court returned to its old habits, spending only the summers at Schönbrunn, where Franz Joseph was born in 1830. When he ascended the throne in 1848, a new era of splendor began for the palace beloved by the emperor, who spent much of his lifetime there with his wife Elisabeth of Bavaria (1837–1898), better known as Sissi.

• 138 top: The Grand Rose Salon, with two smaller adjoining rooms, takes its name from Joseph Rosa or Roos, who Maria Theresa commissioned to paint fifteen idyllic landscapes of Italy and the Alpine regions in the style of the second half of the 18th century.

• 138 bottom: The first of the Bergl Rooms in Maria Theresa's summer apartment, also known as the "Goëss" apartment after the court lady of Empress Elisabeth of Bavaria who lived there in the second half of the 19th century. The idea was to create a seamless transition between the interior spaces and the garden.

• 138–139: The Grand Gallery, in "Maria Theresa style," is located on the main floor of the building, above the carriage passageway commissioned by the empress. It is 141 feet long and almost 32 feet wide, with a ceiling frescoed by Gregorio Guglielmi, who depicted the imperial couple, Maria Theresa and Francis Stephen I, surrounded by the personifications of the virtues: Wisdom, Power, and Justice.

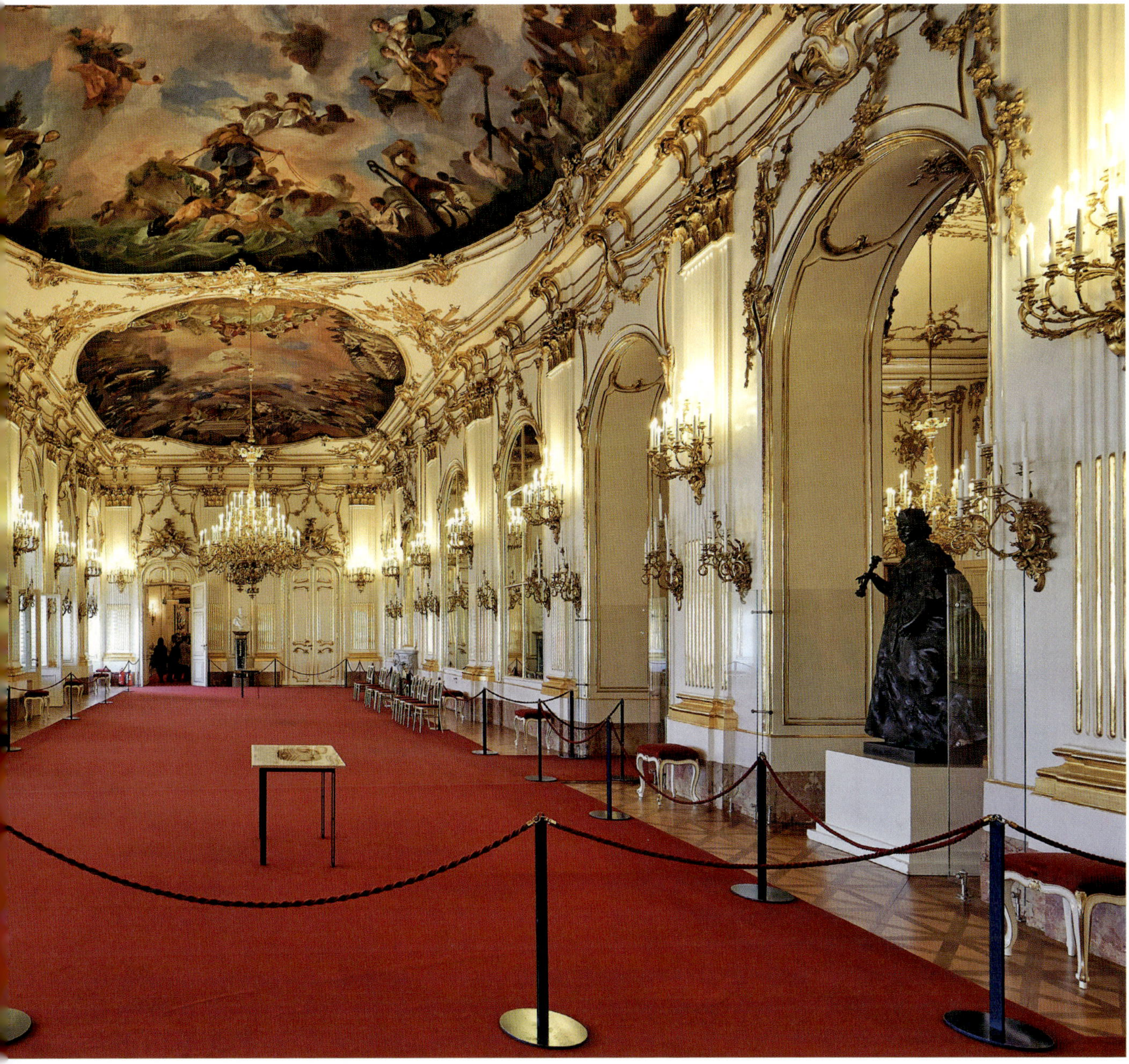

At the table

In Franz Joseph's private dining room, on the main floor of the west wing, private family lunches were served, cooked by the so-called "secret kitchen" and not by the court kitchen. The emperor sat at one side of the table, in the center, with Sissi opposite him and the archduchesses and archdukes next to her. The strict court protocol required the table to be laid with linen purchas\ed from Austrian factories in Silesia and embroidered with the imperial insignia. The cutlery was placed to the right of the plate along with the napkin, while the glasses were arranged in a fan shape in front of each place setting. There were between three and six courses: the emperor preferred boiled beef, Tafelspitz, while Sissi preferred French oysters, fish, roasts, vegetables, and ice cream for dessert.

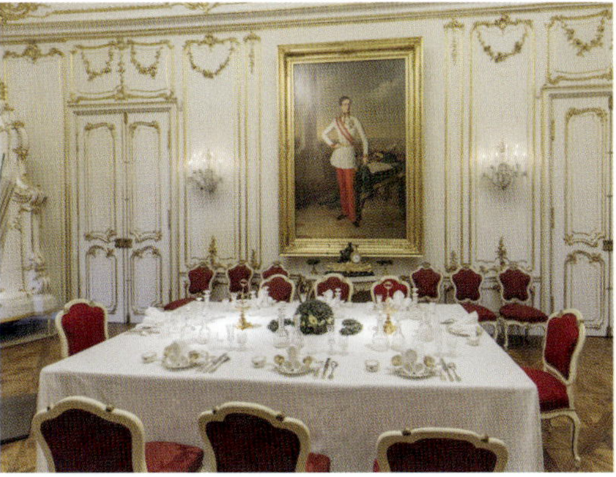

The palace and park at Schönbrunn form an inseparable whole, constantly reflecting each other. Empress Maria Theresa commissioned landscape architect Johann Ferdinand Hetzendorf von Hohenberg to give the park a spectacular appearance, with the Grand Parterre laid out symmetrically along the central axis. This leads the eye to the top of the garden where the Gloriette stands, a triumphal arch of classical inspiration that serves as the backdrop to the garden. The work was completed in 1780, shortly before the death of the sovereign who had loved the place so much.

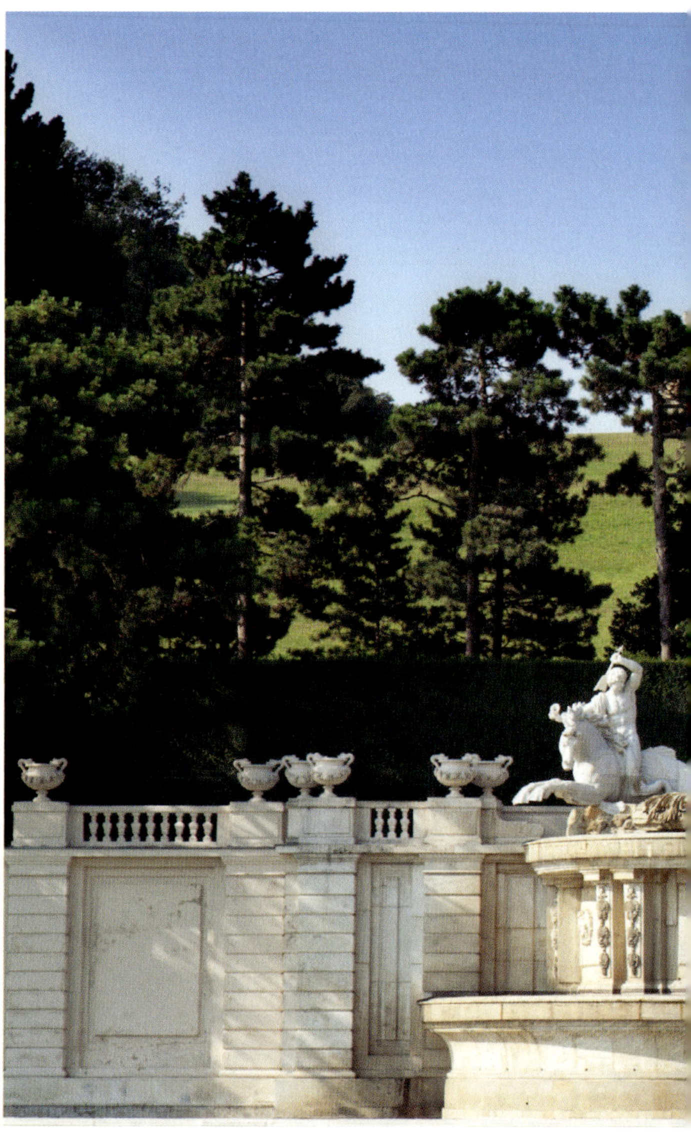

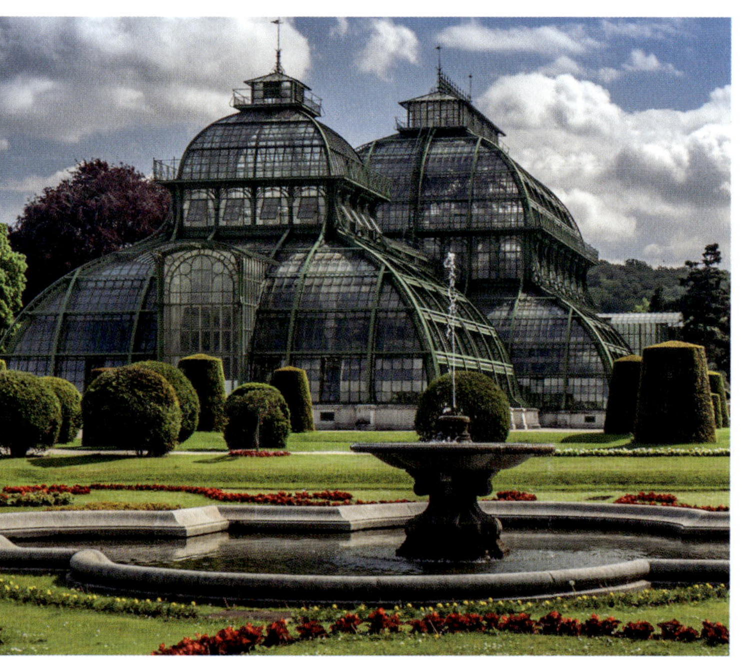

Water is an essential element in the Schönbrunn gardens, featuring large pools, fishponds, and monumental fountains that von Hohenberg placed at the focal points of the garden as the final setting for the perspective of an avenue or an open space, such as the Neptune Fountain, which closes the perspective of the Grand Parterre, with the group of the sea god rising, trident in hand, on a high rocky background. The passion for science and botany of many members of the Habsburg dynasty found free expression in the Schönbrunn Park, where buildings were specially constructed to cultivate all kinds of plants, from the Orangery, built in 1754 by Jean-Nicolas Jardin for Emperor Francis Stephen I, to the 19th-century rose garden and the karesansui, the Japanese garden, which was restored to its former glory in 1996. There is also a Tyrolean corner with a cottage in the woods of Schönbrunn Hill, a place of rest and recreation, far from the constraints of court life. The future Emperor Franz Joseph spent his childhood here, and in 1895 a farm was set up to supply Empress Elisabeth of Bavaria (1837–1898) with fresh milk every day. However, the most interesting building in the park is the large Palm House, built by Franz Joseph's younger brother, Archduke Ferdinand Maximilian of Habsburg-Lorraine, who was passionate about science and wanted to preserve and cultivate the rare and exotic plants he imported from his travels, many of which were still unknown in Europe.

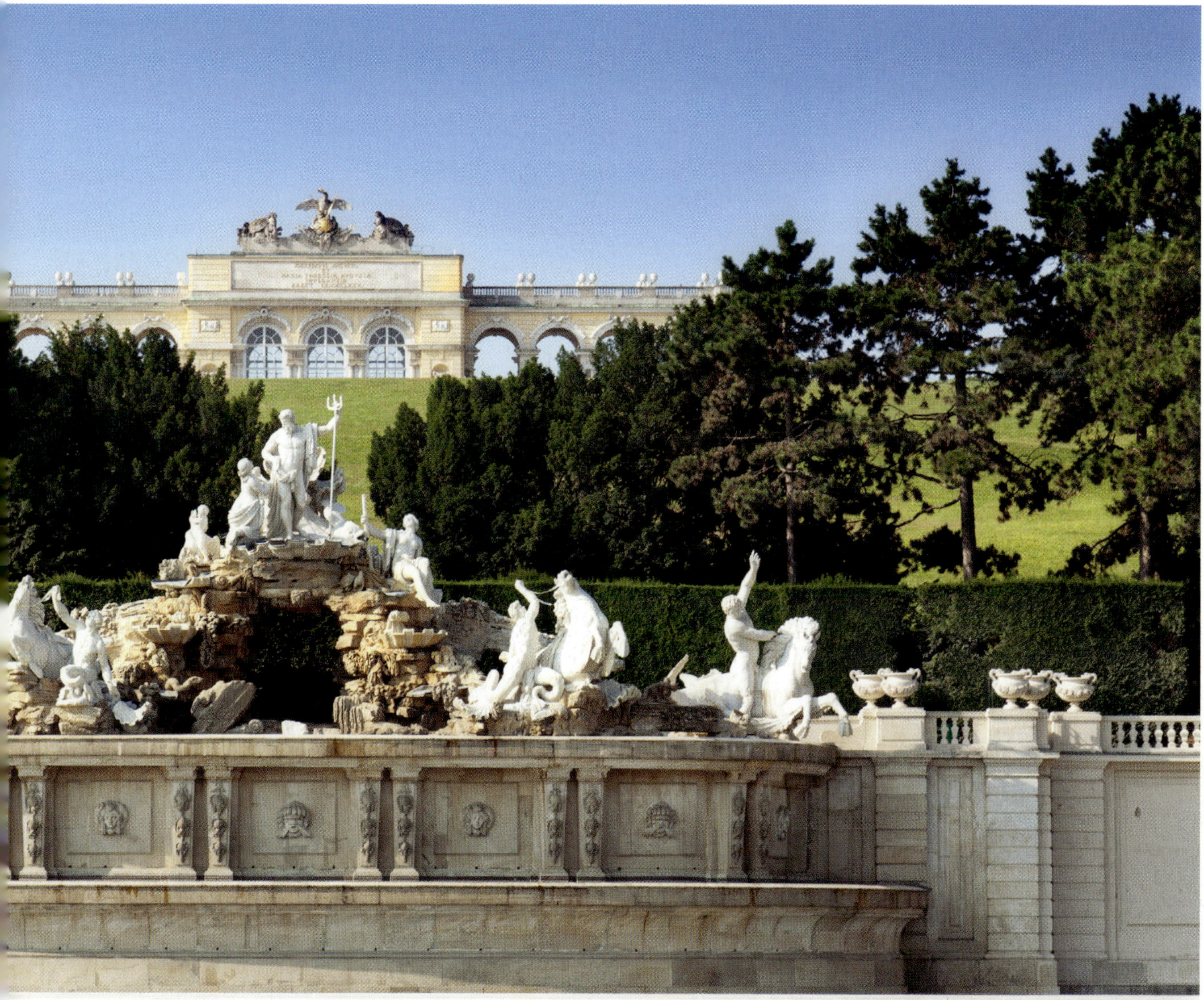

• 140 center: The main structure of the Palmenhaus in Schönbrunn Park, in its central, highest part, reaches a height of 91 feet. Each pavilion is climate-controlled differently: the first reproduces cold climates, the second temperate climates, and the third the hot and humid climates typical of tropical areas. The greenhouse was inaugurated on June 19, 1882, by the Emperor. Alongside the Palmenhaus, the surrounding garden was also landscaped with geometrically designed parterres, fountains, and topiary trees.

• 140–141: The Neptune fountain with the sculptural group by Johann Wilhelm Beyer in the center and, in the background, the Gloriette, the classic-style pavilion that closes off the view of the Grande Parterre. The central part of the building is designed to imitate an ancient triumphal arch crowned by the imperial eagle. The two symmetrical side wings are porticoed and topped by a belvedere terrace protected by a balustrade.

The maze

The maze, already present in 1720, originally consisted of four square elements with winding paths that stretched for a total length of 2.4 miles. In the center stood a pavilion, from which one could have a bird's-eye view of the whole maze. In the following century, the maze was gradually abandoned because its dense covering could encourage behavior contrary to the morals of the time. In 1990, it was partially restored to its original design, and today visitors can explore over 1,970 feet of winding paths through hedges with dead ends.

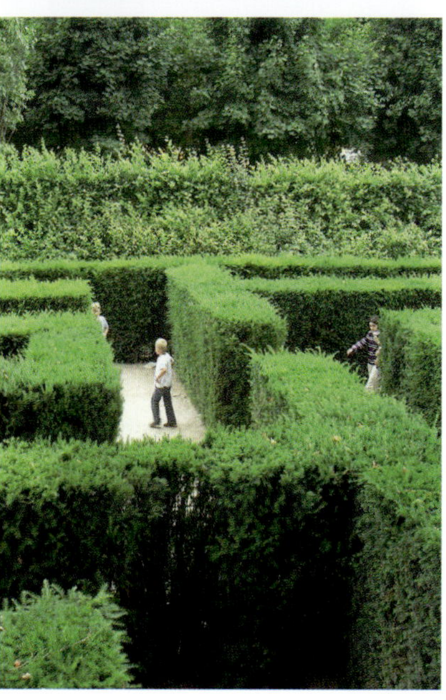

Sanssouci Palace

1713
With Frederick William I, king from 1713, Prussia became a major European power and prepared for its great rise thanks to the unscrupulous foreign policy of alliances and economic and commercial reforms of the king's son and heir, Frederick II, known as "the Great."

1745–1747
In Potsdam, the capital of Brandenburg, Frederick II collaborated on the design of a Rococo-style summer residence: Sanssouci Palace, surrounded by a beautiful Baroque ornamental garden.

1763–1769
The Neues Palais was built in Prussian Baroque style in the palace grounds to host royalty and important dignitaries.

1764
At the behest of Frederick II, the park was enriched with the Neue Kammern (New Chambers), which served as guest quarters, and the Bildergalerie (picture gallery) to house the king's art collection.

1841
At the behest of Frederick William IV, Sanssouci Palace was enlarged with the addition of two side wings.

1873
The first emperor of Germany, William I, opened the doors of Sanssouci Palace and made it accessible to visitors as a museum.

1990
In 1990, the Sanssouci complex was included in the UNESCO World Heritage List.

Sanssouci Palace is located in Potsdam, the capital of Brandenburg, less than 25 miles from Berlin. It is the masterpiece of Frederick II, the favorite retreat that the king had built for himself to devote his time to his passions when discipline did not call him to the battlefield as the commander of an army that led Prussia to rival the great European powers. Frederick II ascended the throne in 1740 after a troubled childhood divided between the wishes of his father, Frederick William, who wanted to turn him into a soldier, and those of his mother, Sophia Dorothea of Hanover, daughter of George I of Great Britain, with whom he shared artistic and intellectual interests. He quickly learned to govern Prussia, adopting the good and useful lessons he had learned from his parents. Once he became king, at the age of only 28,

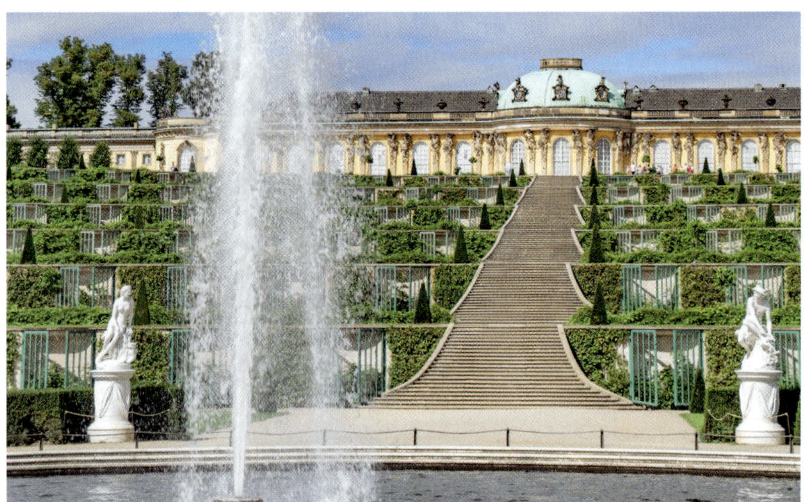

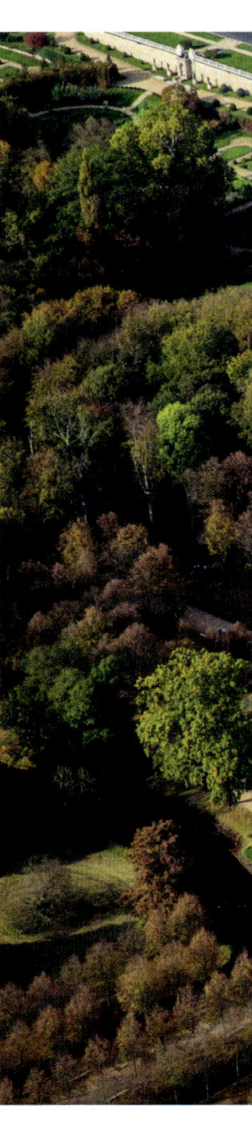

his resourcefulness and his skills amazed the leaders of other European powers: after three months as sovereign, he had already occupied Silesia in the context of the War of the Austrian Succession (1740–1748) and, with his victory, he had overturned the European balance of power, putting an end to the Franco-Habsburg rivalry and allying himself with Great Britain. The new balance of alliances would lead to the Seven Years' War (1756–1763), considered by historians to be the first world conflict, from which he would emerge victorious. If at war the King of Prussia made good use of the rigor and discipline inherited from his father, together with an exceptional army, it was during times of peace that he allowed himself to be guided by the indolence inherited from his mother, earning himself the nickname "philosopher king." He spent his life surrounded by intellectuals,

• 142 center: The building designed by Georg Wenzeslaus von Knobelsdorff is topped by a dome: an idea taken by the king from the Pantheon in Rome. After the death of Frederick II, the building was enlarged with the addition of two side wings at the behest of Frederick William IV, and new buildings were constructed in the garden, such as the Orangery.

• 142–143: A view from above of Sanssouci Palace, a masterpiece of Berlin Baroque, surrounded by the greenery of Brandenburg.

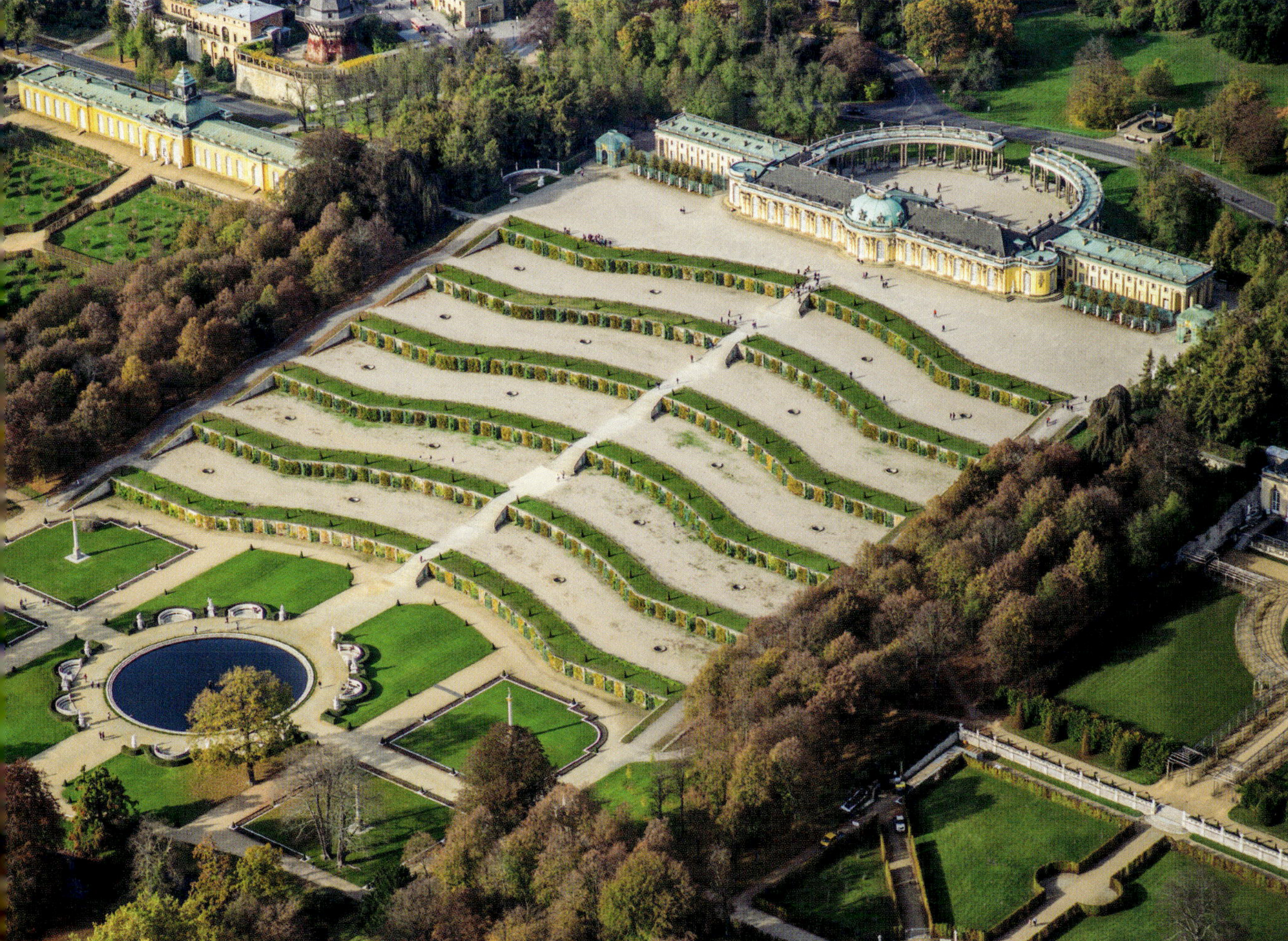

writers, and musicians; a voracious reader, he was always up to date on everything that was published In France, the country he considered culturally superior. In order to cultivate his interests, he set himself the task of finding a place to settle far from Berlin and the obligations of the court. Just as the King of France had chosen Versailles and Maria Theresa had chosen Schönbrunn, Frederick the Great chose Potsdam, initially the old city palace, which was embellished for the occasion. In the meantime, however, he ordered the construction of his own summer residence, a place where he could live in peace, free from the obligations imposed by etiquette. To emphasize his desire for carefree living, the king named the residence "Sanssouci," which translates as "without worries." The first stone of Sanssouci Palace was laid on April 14, 1745, and, in record time, Frederick II's summer residence, five hours by carriage from Berlin, was finished after two years of intense work. The king was directly involved in the project, producing drawings and sketches to be submitted to the architect Georg Wenzeslaus von Knobelsdorff, a former captain in the Prussian army, who had to curb all his ideas of grandeur in order to build not a stately palace but a single-story residence. In front of it, the eccentric king had extraordinary terraces planted with vineyards.

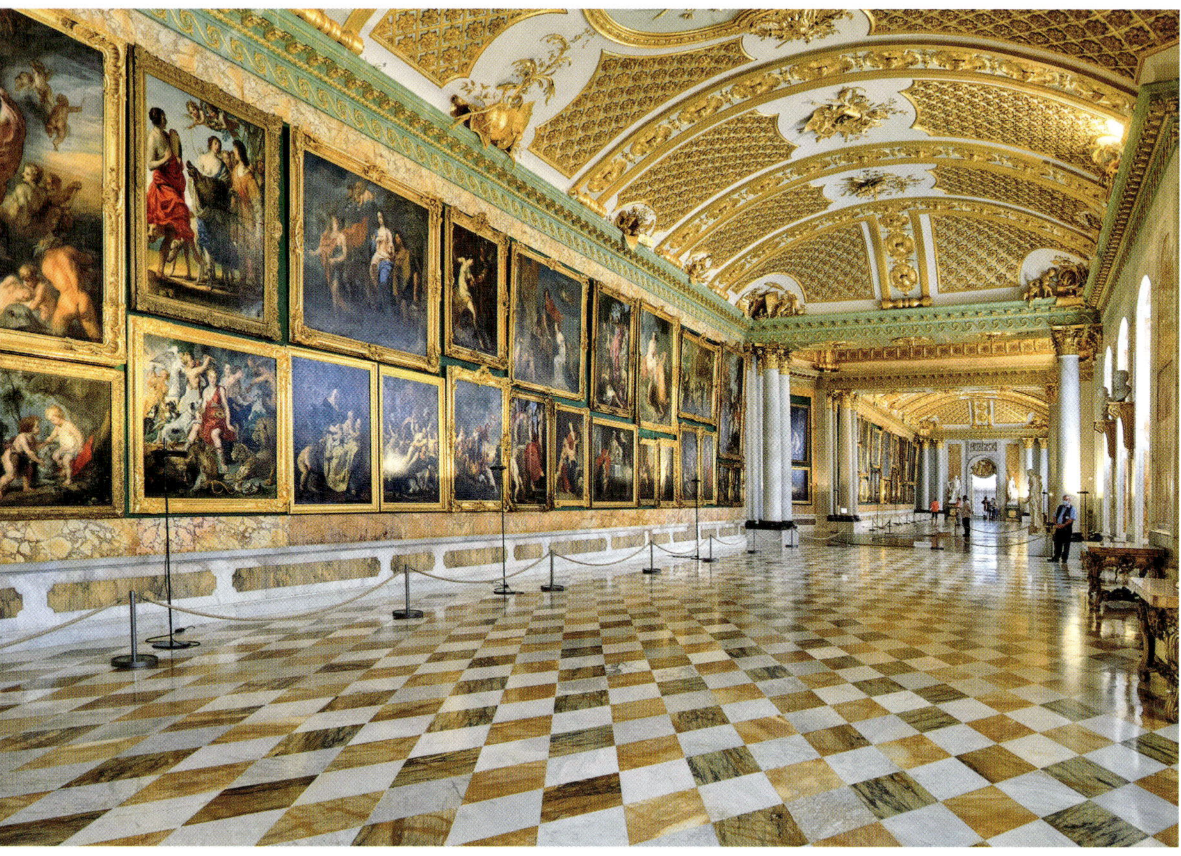

• 144 top: The Gallery is located behind the king's apartment. The wall of the narrow, long room is divided by niches, in which are marble sculptures of Greek and Roman deities. On the walls are paintings by Nicolas Lancret, Jean-Baptiste Joseph Pater, and Antoine Watteau. Antoine Pesne also worked on the decoration of the room.

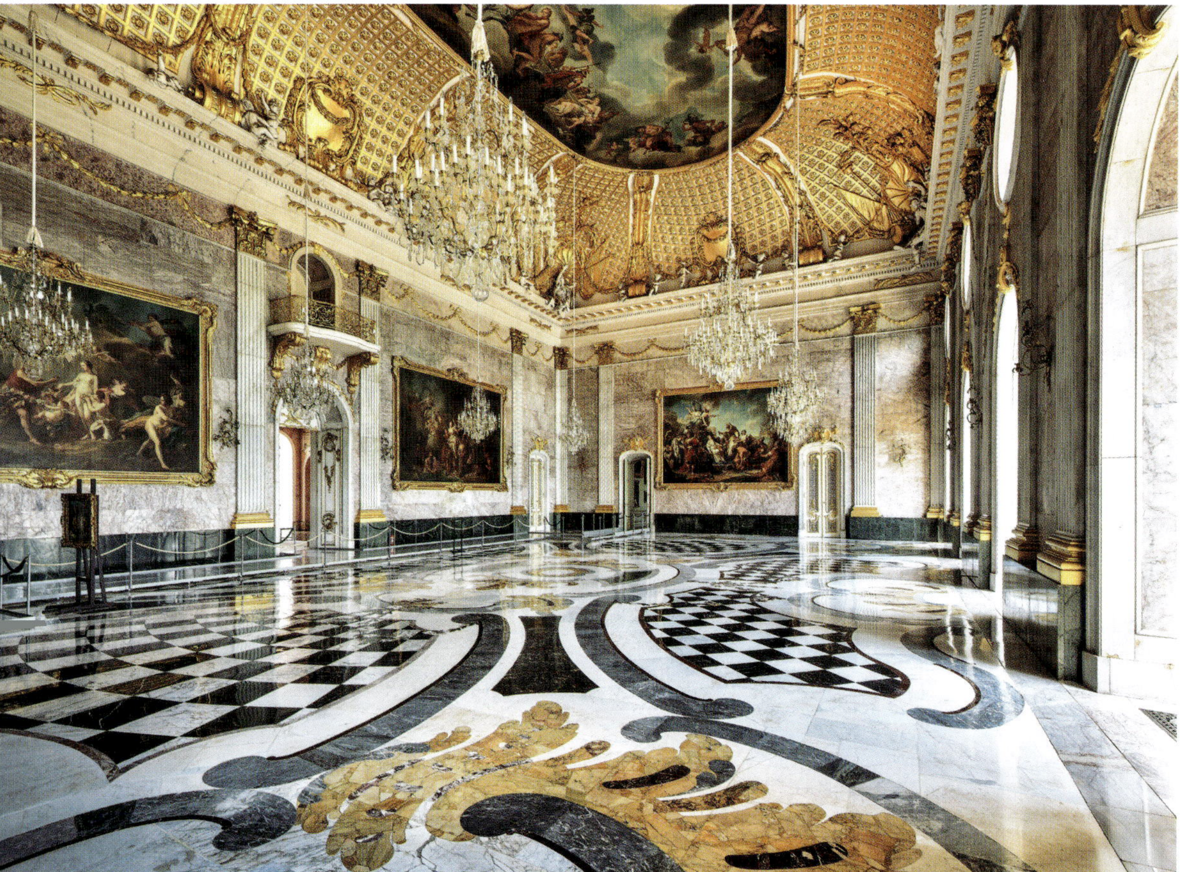

• 144 bottom: For the design of the Marble Hall (Marmorsaal), located in the center of Sanssouci Palace under the green-oxidized dome, architect Knobelsdorff, at Frederick II's request, was inspired by the Pantheon in Rome. Light entered through an oval window in the vault. The name of the room comes from the columns and decorations on the walls and floor being made of Carrara and Silesian marble.

A day in the philosopher king's life

With a damp cloth on his face: this is how Frederick II began his day at around 3 or 4 a.m. after 6 hours of sleep. Immediately, discipline and duty called him to his daily work: reading correspondence, petitions from peasants, requests from his subjects, official dispatches, and military matters. Then it was time for breakfast: the king drank water and coffee (with mustard in his later years), nibbled on pieces of chocolate, and was fond of fruit, especially cherries. By 9 a.m., he had already played the flute for a couple of hours: this was his time for reflection. There is little to say about the king's attire because he always wore the same worn uniform jacket and a battered tricorn hat over his gathered hair. After reviewing his troops on horseback and sometimes taking part in drills regardless of rain, snow, or scorching sun, at noon the king would enjoy a four-hour lunch along with his guests.

Refined dishes were served, often foreign and spicy foods prepared by the 12 Italian, French, and Russian court chefs, who received a rating from the sovereign every day. After the meal, the king played the flute again, then concentrated on the affairs of the kingdom until tea time, served in the late afternoon. Towards evening, he devoted himself to music again, accompanied by other performers, sometimes professionals called to court, sometimes guests who could play an instrument.

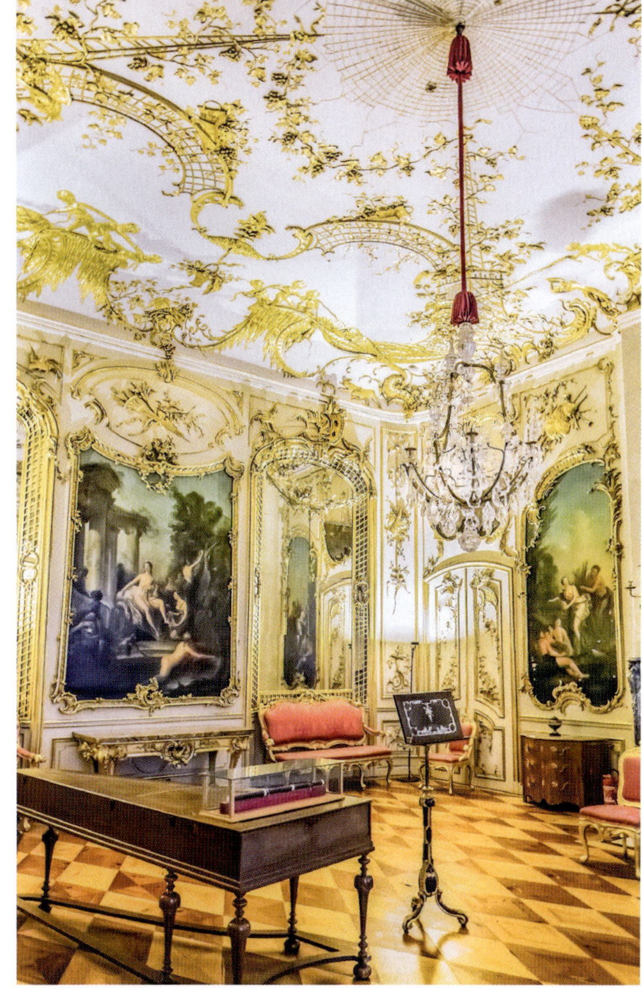

The palace was inaugurated with a banquet for 200 guests and a concert by the royal orchestra. Frederick invited his intellectual friends and numerous musicians, including Johann Sebastian Bach, to his palace. He collected works of art, paintings, objects, and even precious Silbermann fortepianos, and was never separated from his greyhounds. The interiors were designed by Georg Wenzeslaus von Knobelsdorff himself. The architect was influenced by French classicism and by painter Antoine Pesne, but above all by King Frederick the Great himself, the greatest promoter of the so-called Frederician Rococo style that developed in Prussia in the 18th century, of which Sanssouci Palace is the finest example. Frederick II was involved in everything, both administratively and artistically. He drew the sketches himself, as well as the layout of the rooms, the interior decorations, and the statues in the garden. The style took its name from the artists involved: the brothers Johann Michael and Johann Christian Hoppenhaupt, Johann Friedrich and Heinrich Wilhelm Spindler, Johann August Nahl, and Johann Melchior Kambly were all inspired by his sketches. Walking from room to room in Sanssouci Palace, it is clear that the king was not particularly interested in luxury or the trends of his time, but rather sought beauty interpreted according to his own needs.

• 145 top: The Concert Hall at Sanssouci Palace is a Rococo masterpiece. Rocaille decorations adorn the ceiling and walls, together with paintings and mirrors that fit perfectly into the overall design. The wooden frames come from the workshop of sculptor Johann Michael Hoppenhaupt. The paintings on the walls, created in 1747 by Antoine Pesne, depict themes from mythology. The fortepiano was built in 1746 by the renowned German organ builder Gottfried Silbermann. Frederick II's music stand, made in 1767 by the woodcarver Johann Melchior Kambly, emphasizes the function of this room.

Sanssouci Palace is located between the Bilder-galerie building to the east, which houses a rich collection of paintings, and the Neue Kammern to the west, originally an orangery that was later converted into a guest wing and ballrooms. The picture-gallery building was commissioned by Frederick himself to replace a pre-existing greenhouse used for growing tropical plants. The work, under the direction of architect Johann Gottfried Büring, took place in the 1760s. The sovereign had collected his first works of art in Rheinsenberg: they were paintings by his favorite painters Nicolas Lancret and Antoine Watteau and depicted bucolic scenes. Serenades, romantic

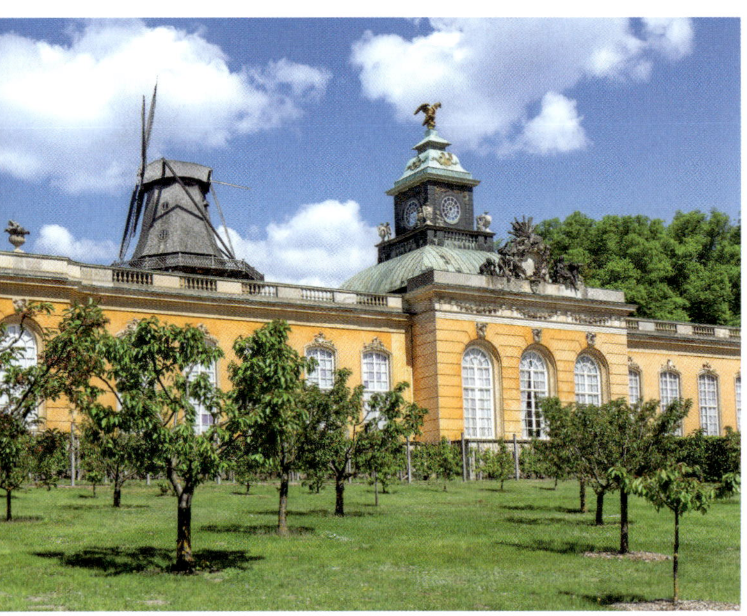

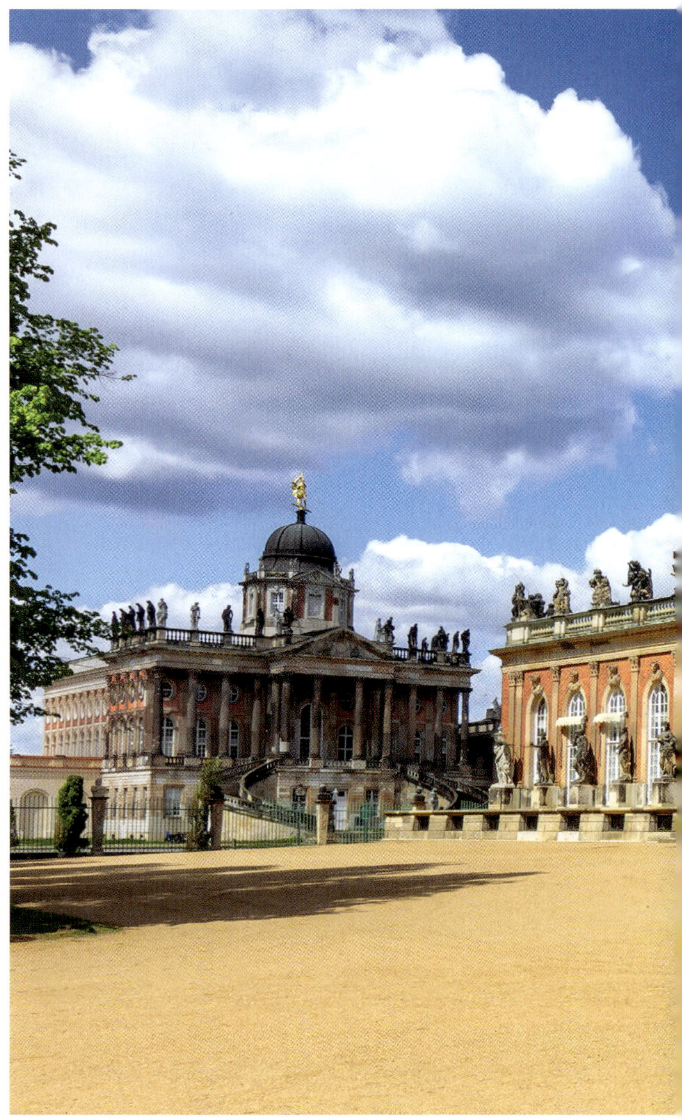

encounters, and classic fêtes galantes centering around music, conversation, and flirtation reflected the spirit of the king during those carefree years. When in Potsdam, in his new palace, he was persuaded by his friend the art collector Francesco Algarotti, and the philosopher Jean-Baptiste de Boyer (who was marquis d'Argens, his chamberlain and, for a time, director general of the Academy), to abandon the frivolous art of the French painters and buy paintings by Italian and Flemish artists. Thus, in 1754, when someone offered him a Lancret, the king replied that he had had "enough of that kind." He sent his trusted men around Europe to buy paintings by Raphael, Titian, and Correggio.

• 146 center: The Neue Kammern building is 360 feet long and 21 feet high and was built to a design by Georg Wenzeslaus von Knobelsdorff in the same style as the king's palace. In summer, the empty rooms of the orangery served as a theater, banquet hall, and concert hall. After the orange trees were moved to another location, the Neue Kammern changed function between 1771 and 1775 and was converted into a palace for guests and entertainment.

• 146–147: The magnificent façade of the Neues Palais is topped by a dome with a golden royal crown, supported by a sculpture of three nymphs. Hundreds of sculptures adorn the building designed by Johann Gottfried Büring, Jean-Laurent Le Geay, and Carl von Gontard.

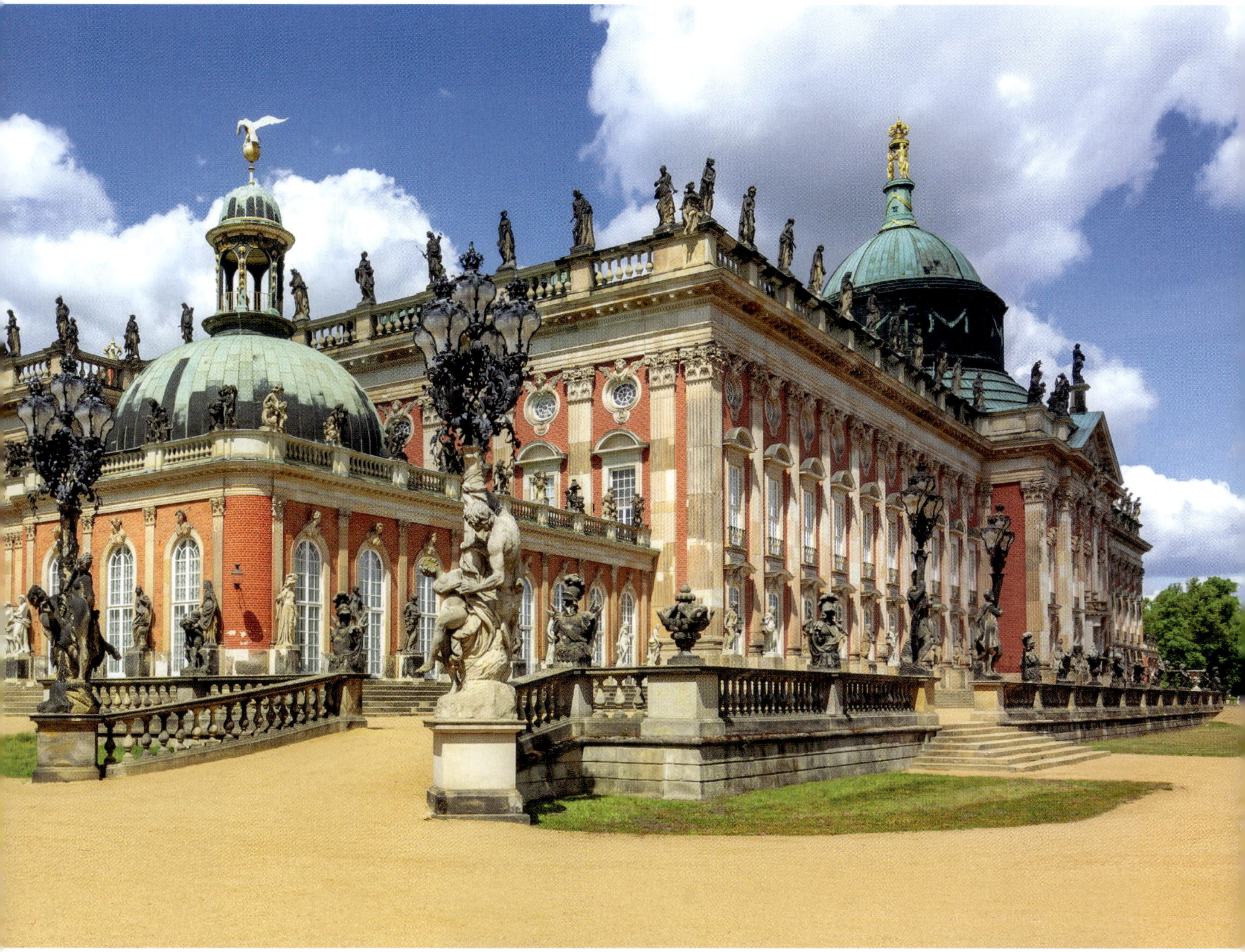

• 147 bottom: The Chinese Tea House is a small pavilion in Sanssouci Park. It was built in 1757 by Johann Gottfried Büring. The building reflects the passion for the East that spread in the 18th century, becoming a true fashion. Outside the tea house, there are several statues representing typical characters such as mandarins.

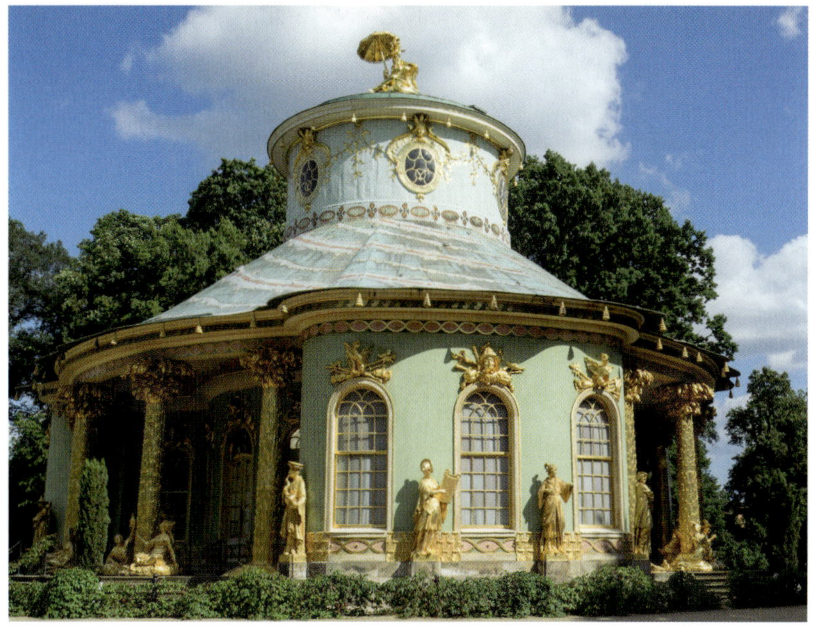

Hohenzollern Castle

Perched on a hill overlooking the town of Hechingen with a magnificent view of the Black Forest, Hohenzollern Castle was the cradle of the namesake family, which throughout history included princes, kings of Prussia, and emperors. The family split into two branches in the 13th century: the Swabian branch remained Catholic during the Protestant Reformation and died out in 1848, becoming cadet to the second branch of Franconia. The union of the vast domains of the latter would lead in the 18th century to the creation of the Kingdom of Prussia and subsequently to the unification of Germany and the formation of the German Empire in 1871. The dynasty remained in power until the end of World War I, when the third and last German emperor, William II (1859–1941), was deposed. But we must go back to the year 1000 to find out more about the origins of the family, about which there is little certainty. In a document dated 1770, Frederick II of Prussia (1712–1786), known as "the Great," wrote: "The house of Hohenzollern is so remote that its origins are

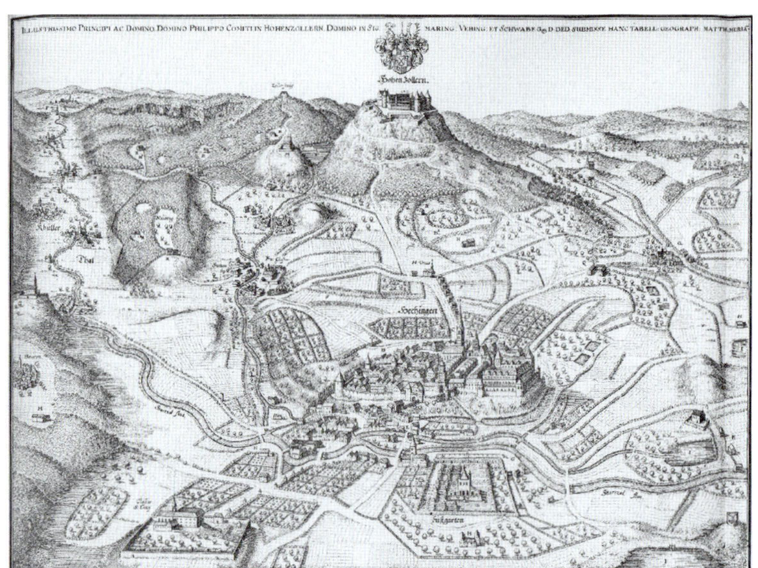

lost in the mists of antiquity. We could cite fairy tales and conjectures about its derivation, but fairy tales are currency that has no value among the sensible and enlightened public of our times. Tassillon is the first count of the Hohenzollerns known in history, and he lived in the year 800." The family takes its name from the historic region

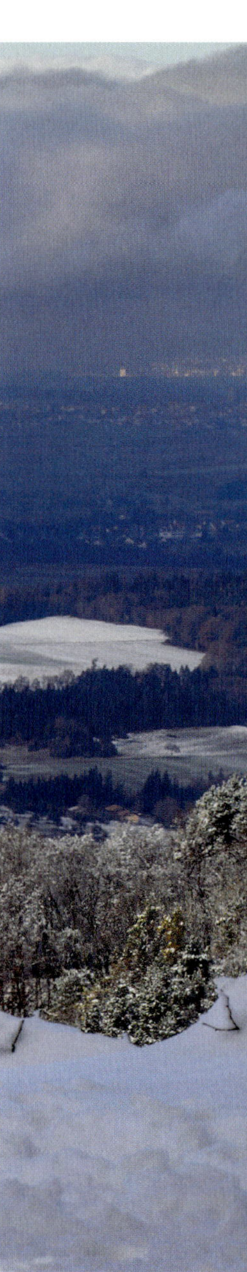

11th century
On top of Mount Hohenzollern, at an altitude of 2805 feet, not far from the city of Tübingen, stood the first Hohenzollern Castle. Only the chapel remains of the whole original medieval building.

1061
Burcardo I, first Count of Zollern, considered the founder of the Hohenzollern dynasty and lord of the castle on top of Mount Hohenzollern, died. His successors, loyal to the Hohenstaufen imperial family, expanded the borders of the dynasty's possessions.

1423
Due to a conflct between the Hohenzollerns and Württemberg, the first Hohenzollern castle was completely destroyed during an attack by the union of the Swabian imperial cities.

1454–1461
The manor was rebuilt and its defenses strengthened: the Hohenzollern family took refuge there in times of danger.

18th century
The castle was abandoned and fell into ruin.

1846–1867
The King of Prussia, Frederick William IV, commissioned architect Friedrich August Stüler to rebuild Hohenzollern Castle in neo-Gothic style to celebrate the prestige of the family.

• 148 bottom: Hohenzollern Castle with the village of Hechingen at its feet in an engraving by Matthäus Merian from around 1650.

• 148-149: A magnificent view of Hohenzollern, built above the town of Hechingen in Baden-Württemberg (southern Germany).

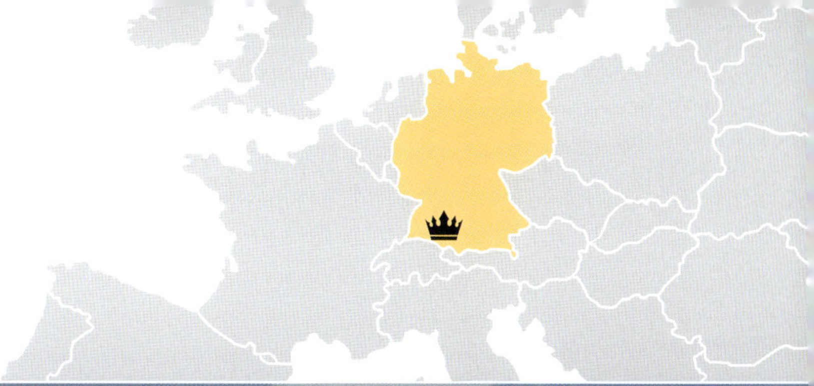

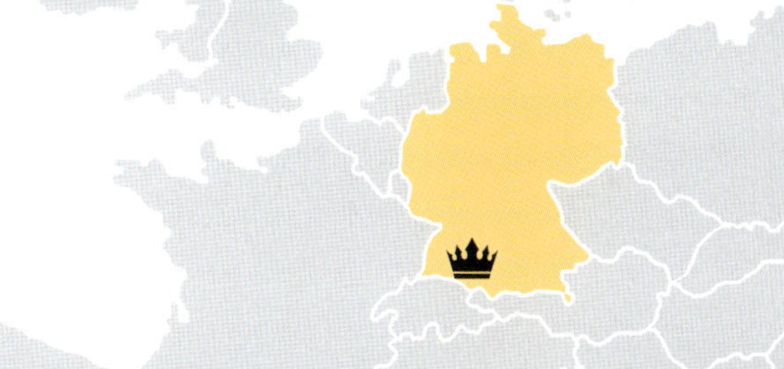

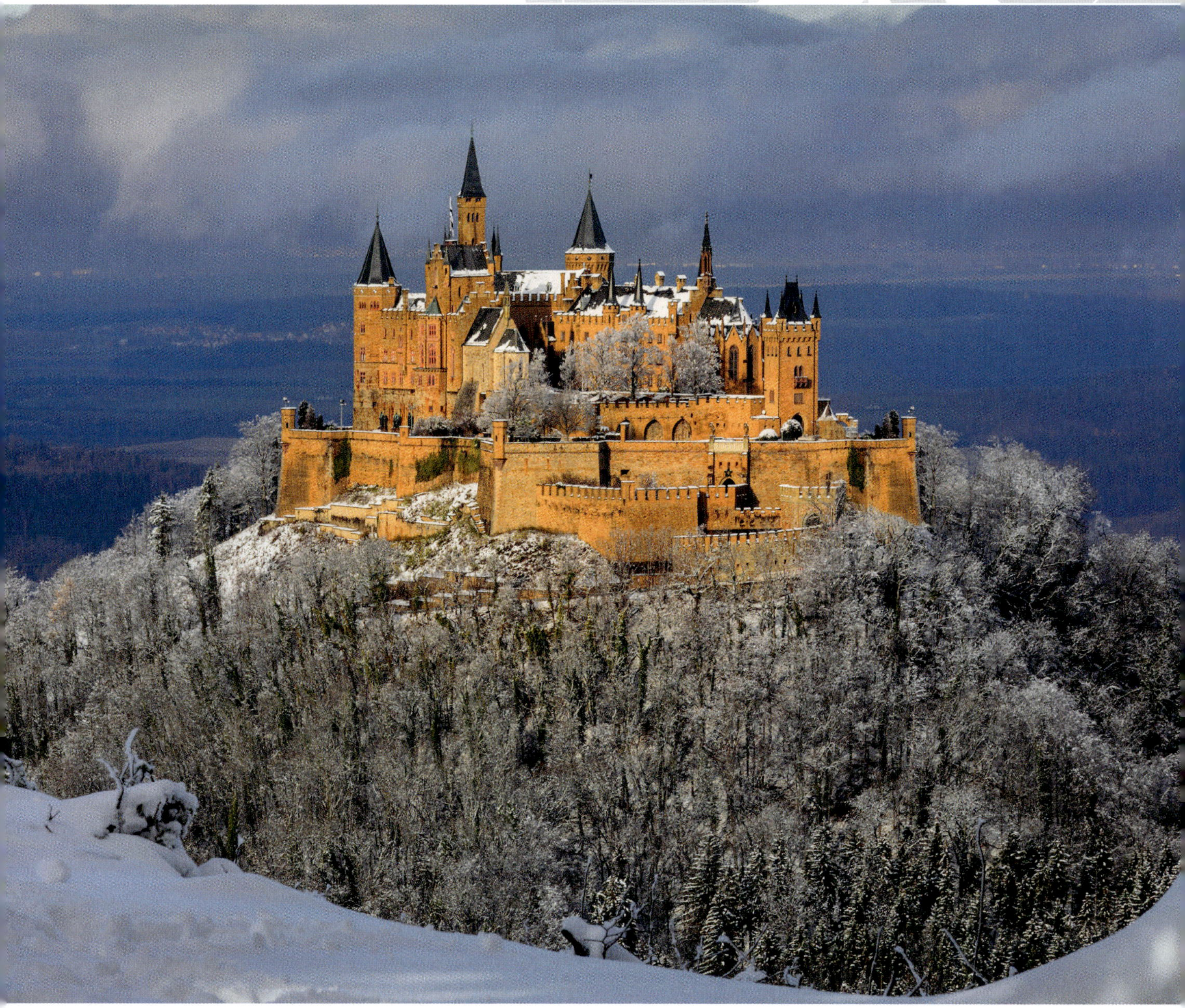

of Swabia, now part of the state of Baden-Württemberg, where Zollenberg Castle was built on a hill in the 11th century. The first reference to the fortress on the conical hill of Mount Hohenzollern, at an altitude of 2805 feet, dates back to 1061 and coincides with the death of Burcardo, king of the castle. There is no information about what the manor looked like, but it must have been imposing, fortified, and luxuriously furnished: a contemporary source described it as "the crown of all the castles of Swabia" and "the most fortified house in Germany."

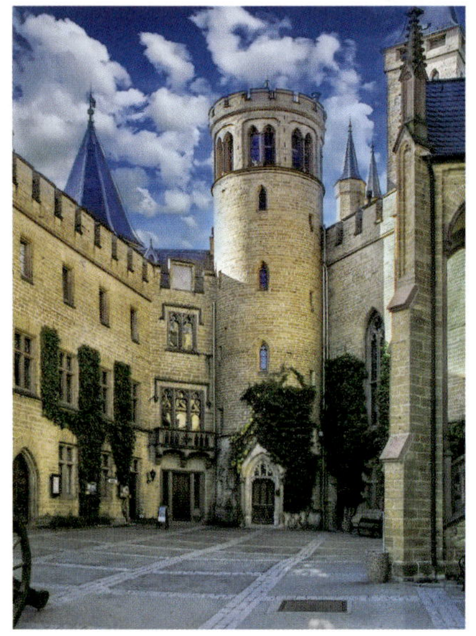

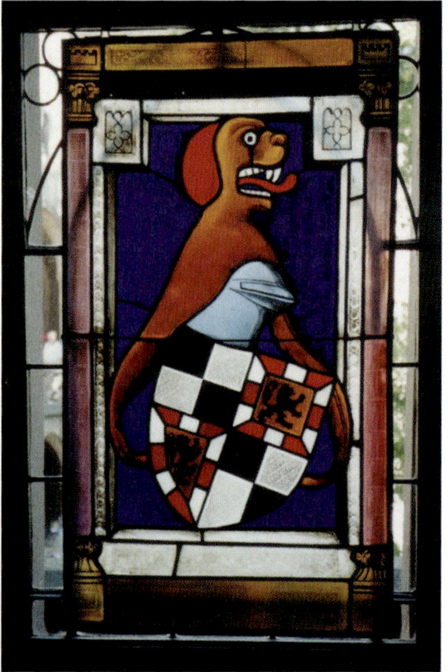

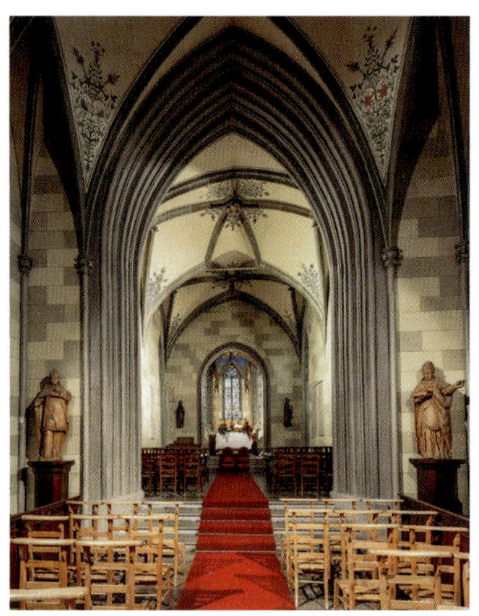

The rise of the family, allies of the Hohenstaufen emperors, began with Count Frederick III when he became burgrave of the city of Nuremberg in 1191. In 1423, the residence of the first Hohenzollern counts was completely destroyed. With the division of the family into two branches, the Swabian and the Franco-Brandenburg, the castle remained in the hands of the members of the former, who were Catholic. In 1454, they ordered its reconstruction, and the castle was transformed into a fortress that proved to be a useful refuge during the Thirty Years' War (1618–1648). Subsequent historical events led to the ruin of the manor until the crown prince, the future King Frederick William IV, decided to have the ancestral seat of the House of Hohenzollern rebuilt in neo-Gothic style. The work, entrusted to the architect Friedrich August Stüler (1800–1865), began around 1850 and was completed in 1867. Today, as the king wished, the castle dominates the Swabian plain and is one of Germany's major tourist attractions, not least because it houses several masterpieces linked to the history of Prussia, from paintings by famous artists to a collection of gold and silverware from the 17th to the 19th centuries.

• 150 top: The inner courtyard of Hohenzollern Castle.

• 150 center: Coat of arms of the Hohenzollern family as burgraves of Nuremberg in a stained-glass window at Hohenzollern Castle. The family motto is "Nihil sine Deo" ("Nothing without God").

• 150 bottom: St. Michael's Chapel, built in the 15th century, is one of the few remaining parts of the old castle.

The reconstruction by Frederick William IV

Described as "a romantic on the throne," the Prussian king Frederick William IV was still crown prince when in 1819 he first visited Hohenzollern Castle, which had fallen into ruin. Poetically and sentimentally attached to the Middle Ages, the era of his ancestors' rise to power, the sovereign began to dream of rebuilding it. In a letter dated 1844, he wrote: "The memories of the year 1819 are extremely dear to me and, like a pleasant dream, it was above all the sunset we watched from one of the castle ramparts . . . now this adolescent dream has turned into a desire to make Hohenzollern Castle habitable again. . . ."

The famous Berlin architect Friedrich August Stüler fulfilled the king's wish by creating a medieval castle in neo-Gothic style in the 19th century. The building has 140 rooms, including the library with its important frescoes, the king's bedroom, the family tree room, the "Blue Salon," and the queen's chamber. The chapel dedicated to St. Michael, the only remaining building from the previous 15th-century castle, was integrated into the new construction.

• 151: Defended by turrets and battlements, Hohenzollern Castle stands almost 2952 feet above the conical massif of the Swabian Jura.

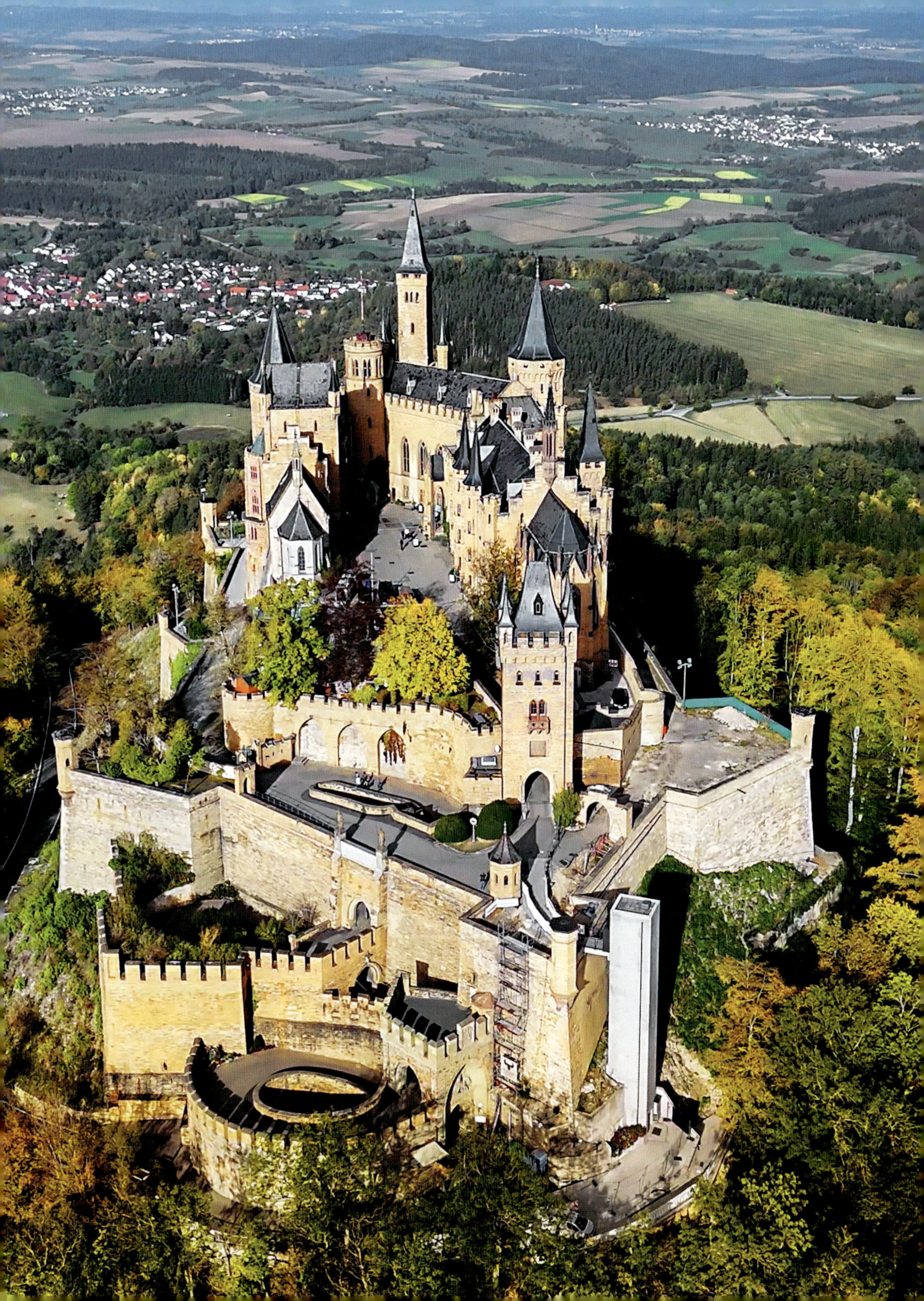

Neuschwanstein Castle

1832–1836
In 1832, the Crown Prince of Bavaria, Maximilian Wittelsbach, purchased the ancient Hohenschwangau Castle and had it rebuilt in neo-Gothic style. The royal family used the residence as a hunting lodge and summer retreat.

1845
On August 25, Ludwig von Wittelsbach, the eldest son of Crown Prince Maximilian and Princess Marie of Prussia, was born in Nymphenburg Castle near Munich.

1848
On March 20, King Ludwig I of Bavaria abdicated in favor of his eldest son Maximilian: Ludwig became crown prince at only two and a half years of age.

1864
On March 10, Maximilian II died and Ludwig was proclaimed king, taking the name Ludwig II.

1869
On September 5, work began on the construction of Neuschwanstein Castle, inspired by the ideas of the painter and theater set designer for Wagner's "Lohengrin," Christian Je, based on designs by Eduard Riedel and Georg von Dollman.

1870–1886
Ludwig had Linderhof Castle, designed as a copy of Versailles, built in southern Bavaria.

1878–1886
Despite financial difficulties, Ludwig ordered the construction of Herrenchiemsee Castle on an island in Lake Chiemsee, inspired by the Palace of Versailles. The work was never completed.

1886
On June 13, Ludwig II drowned in the waters of Lake Starnberg under circumstances that remain unclear.

Dukes, princes, and sovereigns of the ancient Wittelsbach dynasty built palaces, churches, and theaters over the centuries to beautify the land of Bavaria. Ludwig I, for example, transformed Munich by building palaces with classical façades and wide boulevards. In general, the members of the noble family focused their efforts on public works. Ludwig II, the most famous king of the dynasty due to his eccentric behavior, took a different approach: apart from an attempt to build a theater in Munich to stage Richard Wagner's operas (which was eventually built in Bayreuth), he devoted himself to grandiose and extravagant architectural projects for his own personal use. As a child, he had wandered in awe through the residences of his father, King Maximilian II of Bavaria: the austere one in Munich and the summer residence in Nymphenburg. But above all, Hohenschwangau, near the village of Füssen, nestled in the magnificent scenery of the Bavarian Alps, had sparked his imagination. It was an ancient medieval fortress that Maximilian II, despite being a pragmatic ruler, had restored in neo-Gothic style. Artists and writers had been hosted within its walls, including Hans Christian Andersen, the famous Danish author of fairy tales set in castles that could well have looked like those of Bavaria. It was in Hohenschwangau that Ludwig spent the summers of his childhood, and it was probably here that his imagination was shaped. The castle had belonged to the Knights of Schwangau, and it was here that he learned the legends of the swan knight, Lohengrin. Like his father, Ludwig initially thought of rebuilding an ancient castle in ruins nearby, but since it was nothing more than a ruin, the sovereign commissioned Christian Jank, a German painter and architect, to design the façade of a new castle, which was to be a sort of "temple for his divine friend," inspired entirely by Norse mythology.

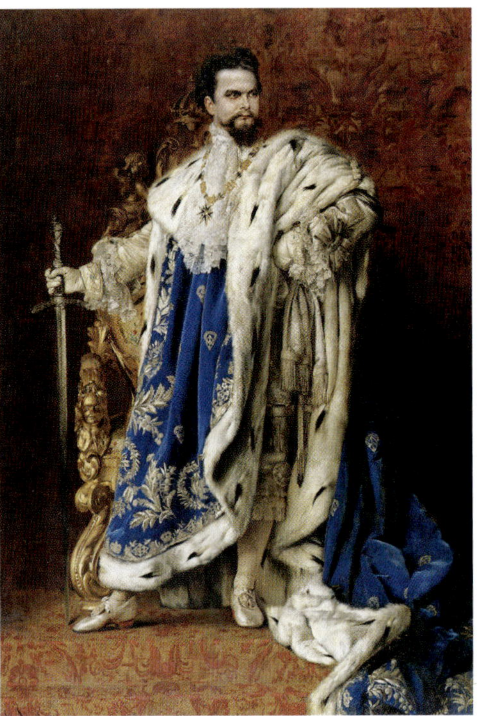

• 152 left: Ludwig II, dressed as Grand Master of the Order of St. George, in a portrait by Gabriel Schachinger, completed in 1887. The painting is clearly inspired by the portrait of Louis XIV by Hyacinthe Rigaud, a copy of which is on display in Herrenchiemsee Castle.

• 153: Neuschwanstein Castle set in the magnificent scenery of the Bavarian Alps.

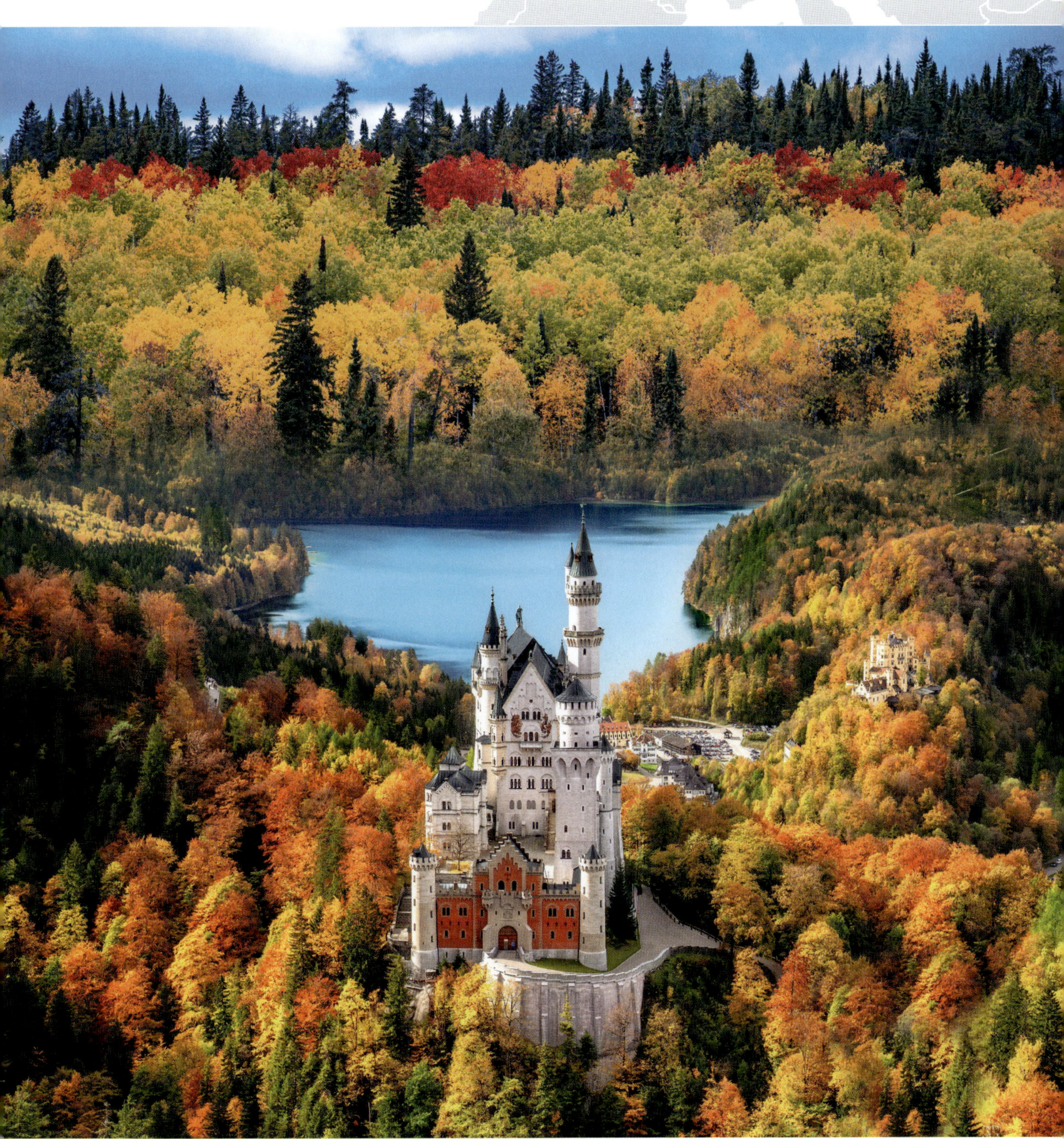

The actual project was entrusted in 1867 to architect Eduard Riedel, who was succeeded in 1874 by Georg von Dollmann. The king ordered that the castle be built "in the authentic style of the ancient fortresses of the German knights," while taking into account the innovations and advances made in the arts since the Middle Ages. The castle was to have "numerous guest rooms, comfortable and welcoming, from which one can enjoy a wonderful view of the majestic Säuling mountain, the Tyrolean mountains, and the vast plain." Work began in 1869: more than 300 workers were hired and worked day and night. The machinery used was state-of-the-art: a steam crane was indispensable for lifting the heavy blocks of white sandstone with which the castle was built. A carriage road was built to reach the construction site, connecting it to the nearest village's railway station. The interiors did not reflect the simplicity of the exterior: Hyacinth Holland and Peter Herwegen had designed the building in a neo-Gothic style (the former had to promise the king that only the two of them would understand certain esoteric meanings of the decorations), while Eduard Ille, Georg von Dollmann, and Julius Hofmann, who took over from him, added Byzantine-style modifications. The king himself supervised the work: he watched the castle grow from Hohenschwangau with binoculars and gave his opinion on every detail concerning the frescoes, the furnishings, the accessories, and the decoration of the rooms. Inside the residence there are more than 200 rooms, but only 14

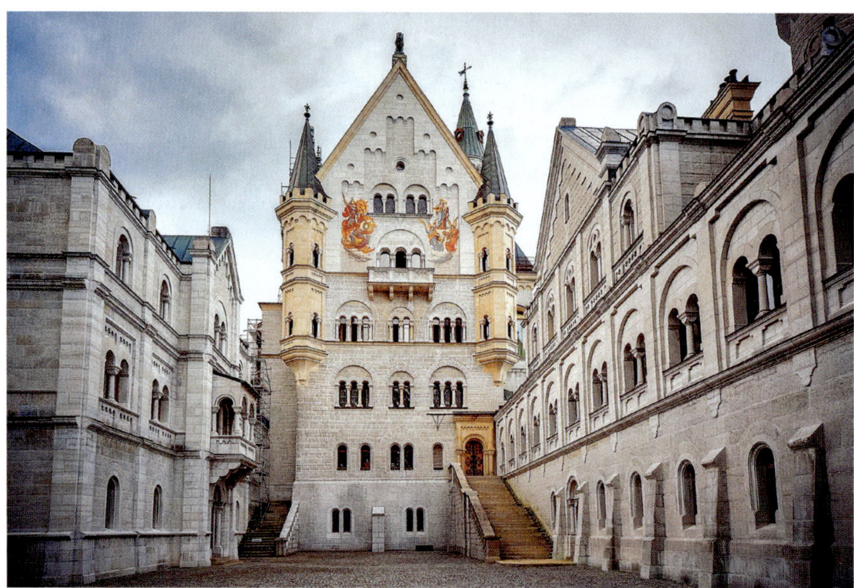

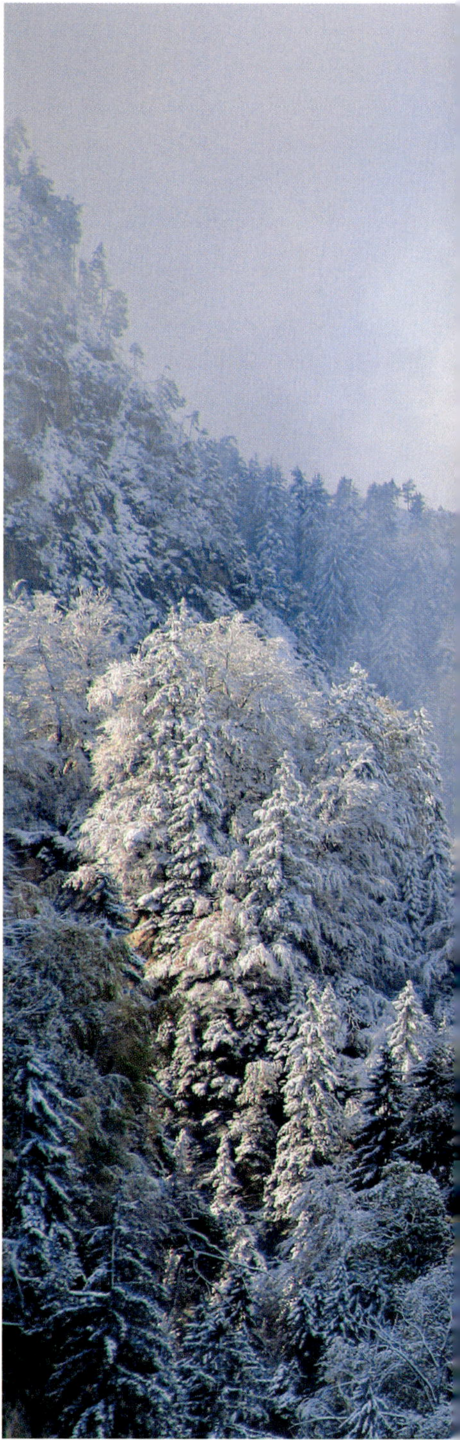

were completed before the king died in circumstances that have never been clarified. Wagner's works provided the subjects for the decorations, and three characters in particular recur: the poet Tannhäuser, the swan knight Lohengrin, and his father, the king of the Holy Grail, Parsifal. The heart of the castle was the Throne Room, the only room built in Byzantine style. The king was inspired by the Church of Saint Sophia in Constantinople.

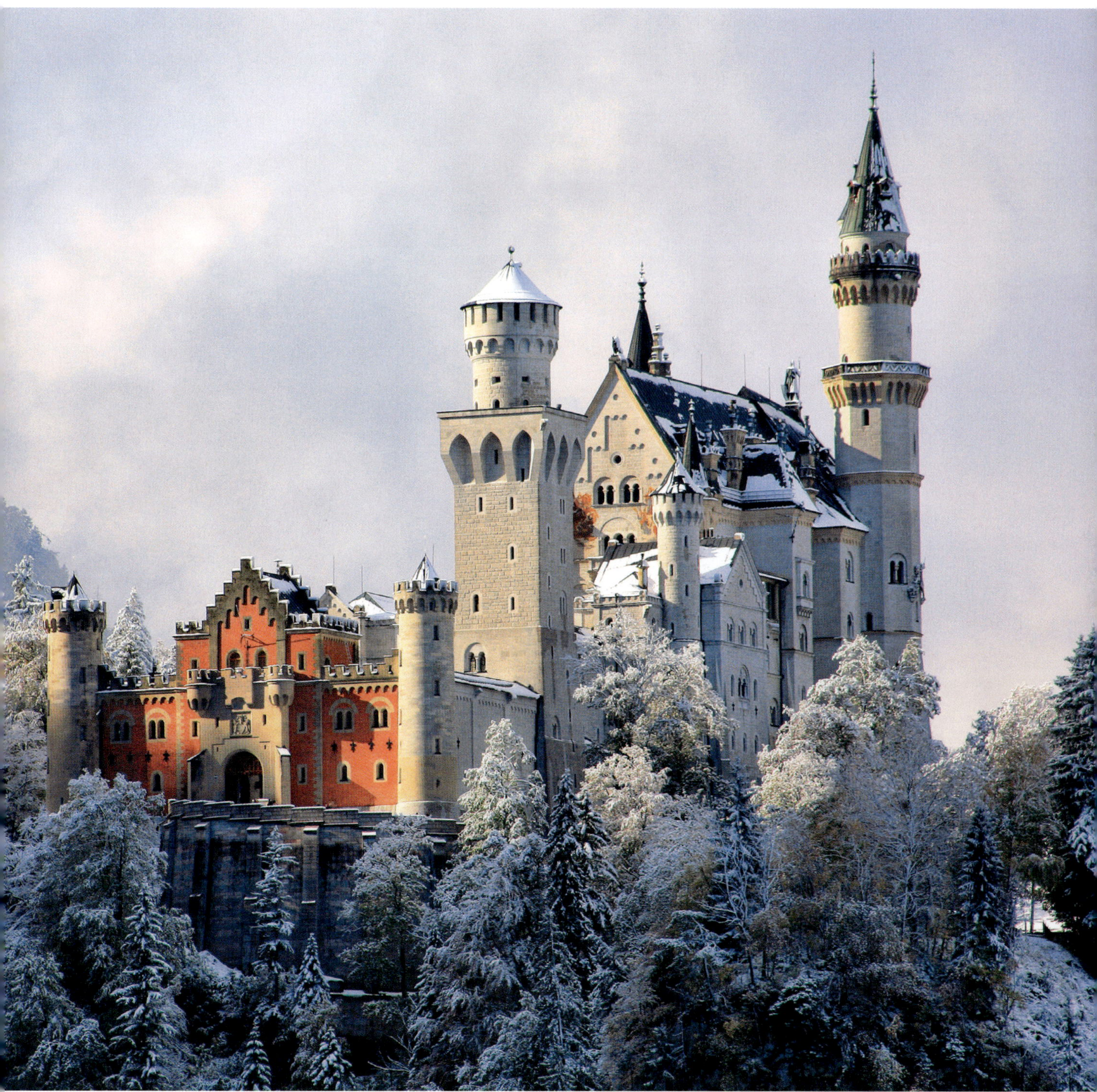

• 154 center: The frescoes above the façade overlooking the courtyard of honor, painted in a romantic style, depict Saint George slaying the dragon and the Patrona Bavariae, the patron saint of Ludwig's kingdom.

• 154-155: This evocative image of Neuschwanstein Castle on a winter's day, after a recent snowfall, accentuates its fairy-tale appearance, which seems to have been taken from one of Andersen's stories.

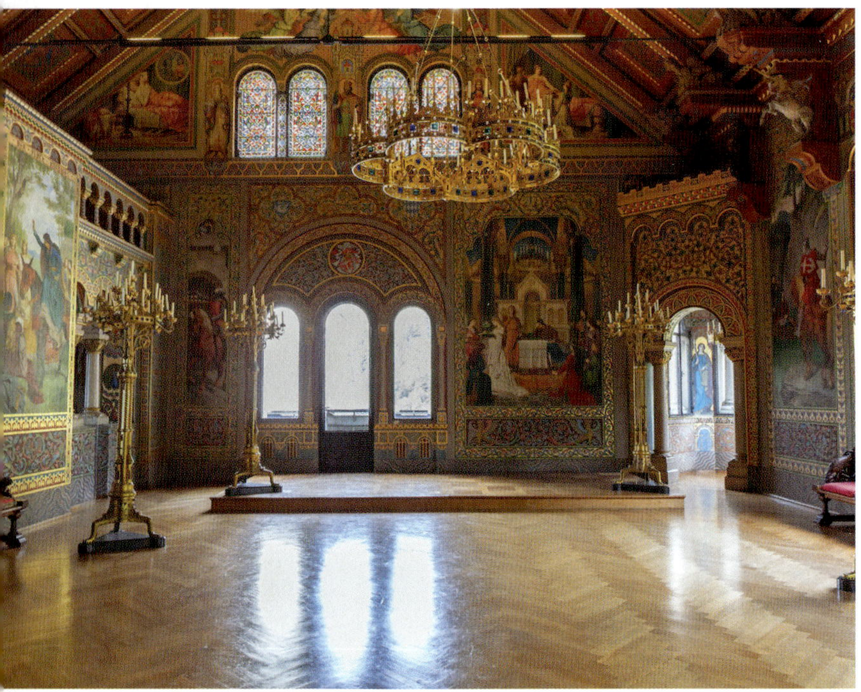

• 157: The Throne Room resembles a sacred place: in the northern apse, a throne was to be placed in place of the altar, but it was never built due to the death of the sovereign. With this room, Ludwig wanted to emphasize his role as King of Bavaria and the fact that he had been invested by divine grace. The gilded bronze chandelier in the Throne Room, shaped like a Byzantine crown, illuminated the room with 96 candles.

The comforts of Ludwig II

Despite its neo-Gothic appearance, Neuschwanstein Castle, like Linderhof and Herrenchiemsee, was equipped with all the comforts and technological innovations known at the end of the 19th century, which fascinated the king. For example, the fireplace in the Neuschwanstein kitchen had two automatic spits that were powered by the heat rising through the hood, and the hot air was also used to heat the castle. For the latter, there were five boilers on the ground floor which heated water to produce hot air that rose to the upper floors through a complex system of pipes and ducts. Mechanical lifts carried food from the kitchen on the ground floor to the dining room on the second floor. At Linderhof and Herrenchiemsee, the dining table was "retractable": to please the king, who wished to eat alone, the table was lowered through the floor between courses using a sophisticated lift, set in the kitchen, then hoisted up, already laid, into the dining room. An elaborate system of bells ensured the servants' diligence, and there was a telephone. Even the toilet was equipped with innovative comforts for those times, such as a flush toilet and running hot water.

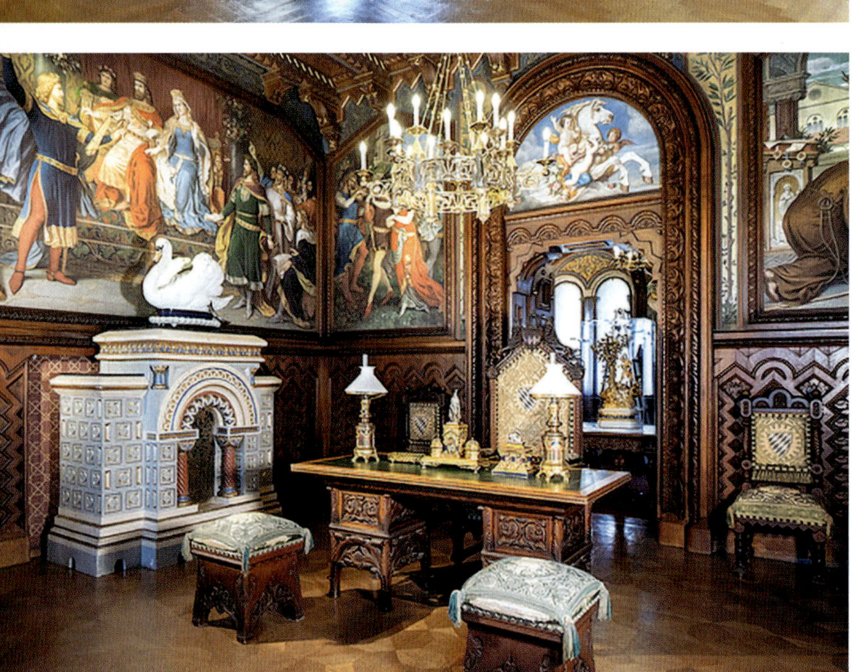

• 156 top: The Singers' Hall, on the fourth floor of the castle, clearly shows the influence of the Wartburg Hall in Eisenach, where the famous singers' contest, central to Richard Wagner's opera "Tannhäuser," is said to have taken place. However, the walls of the hall are decorated with the saga of Parsifal and the Holy Grail and his son, the swan knight Lohengrin. The high coffered ceiling reproduces the signs of the zodiac.

• 156 bottom: Ludwig II's study is located on the third floor of Neuschwanstein Castle. The walls were covered with oak panels. The murals depict the Tannhäuser saga. The king worked at the large table on which his writing set still stands. A white swan rests on the tiled stove.

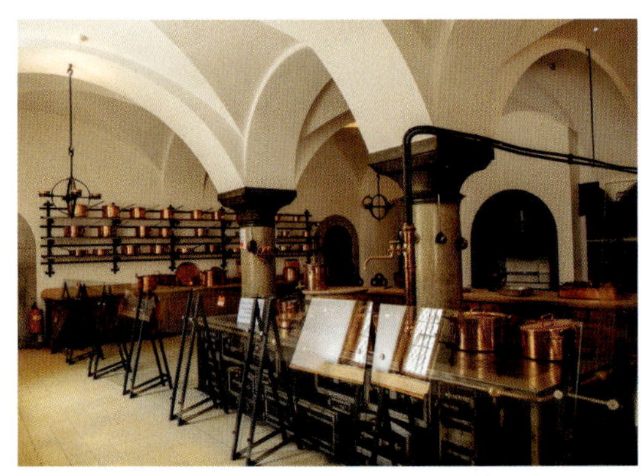

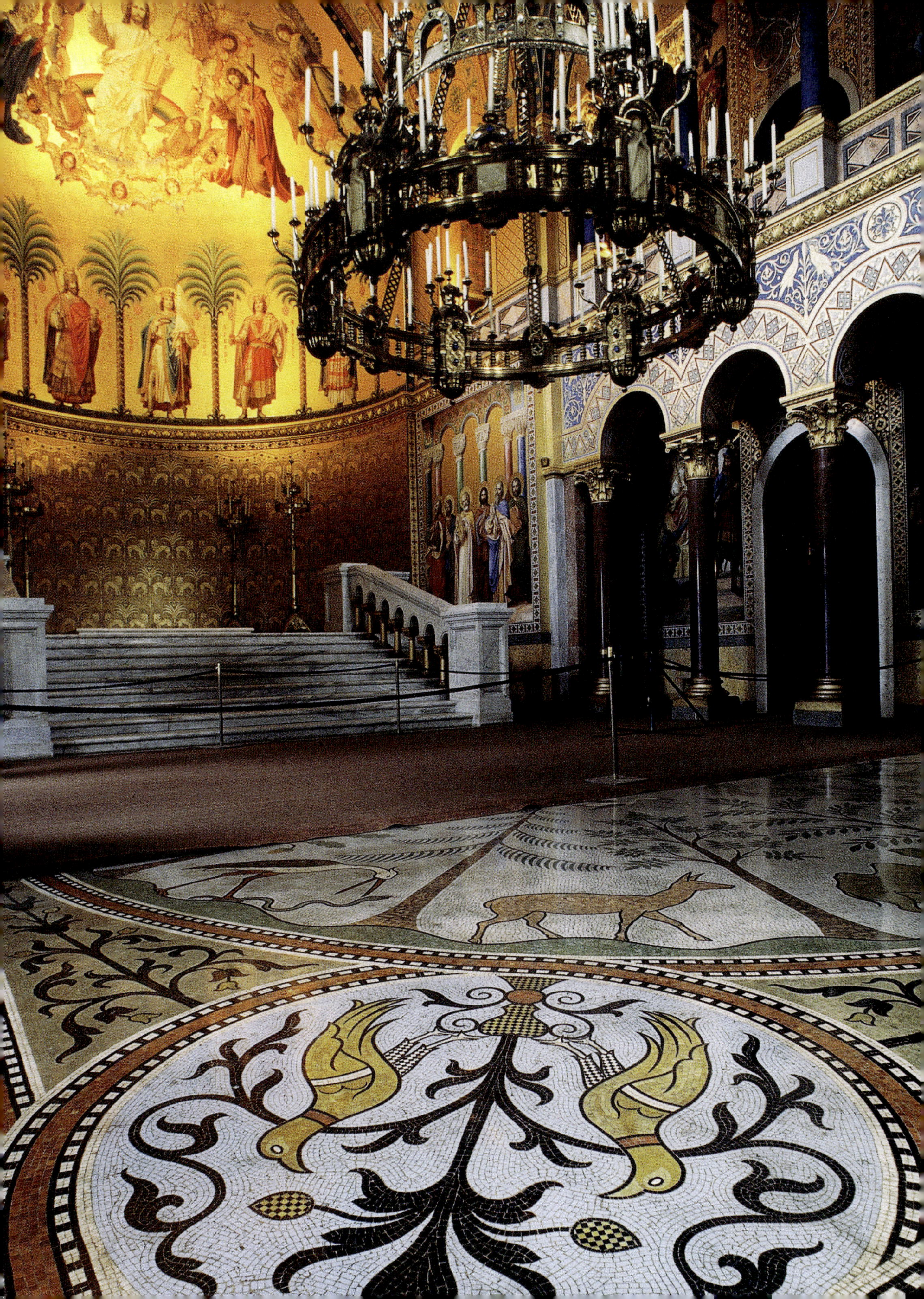

• 158-159: With its elegant appearance, immaculately manicured gardens, and beautiful park, De Haar Castle is one of the most beautiful castles in the Netherlands.

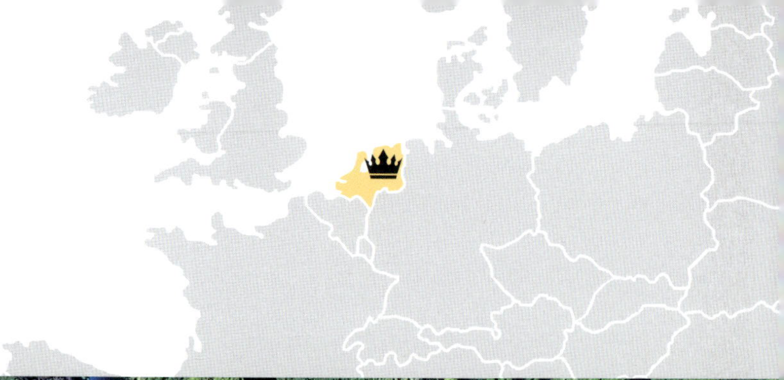

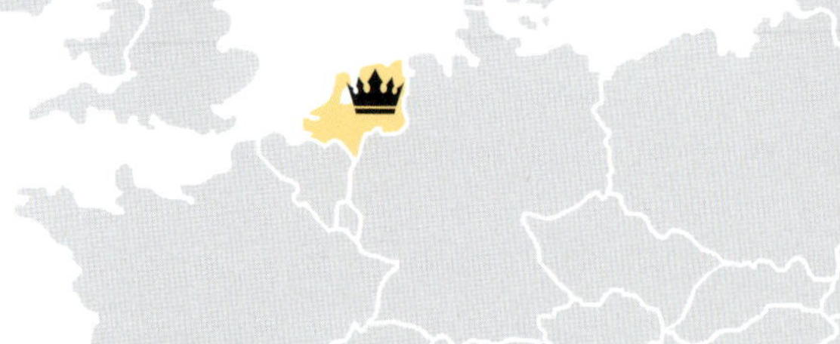

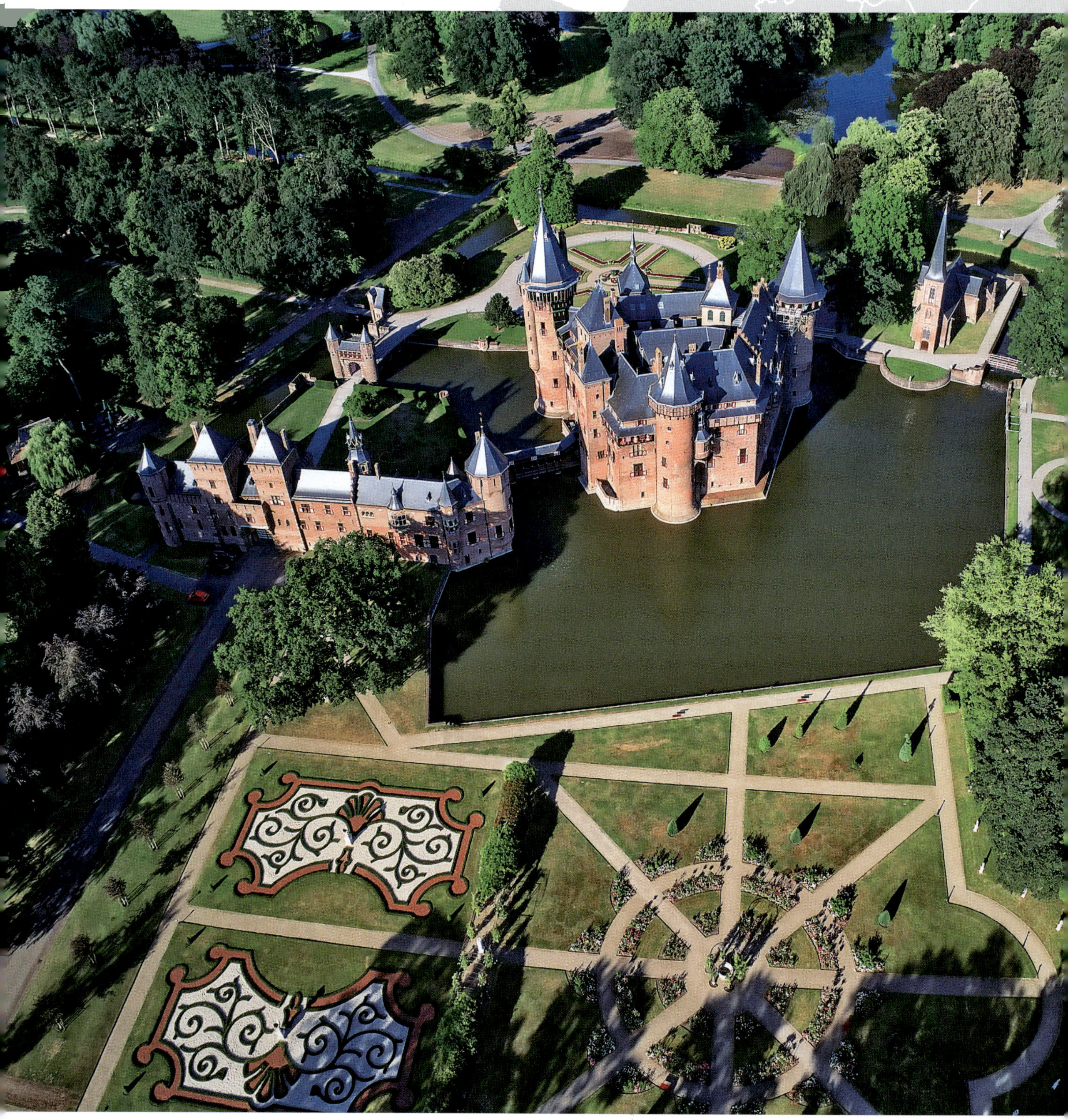

De Haar Castle

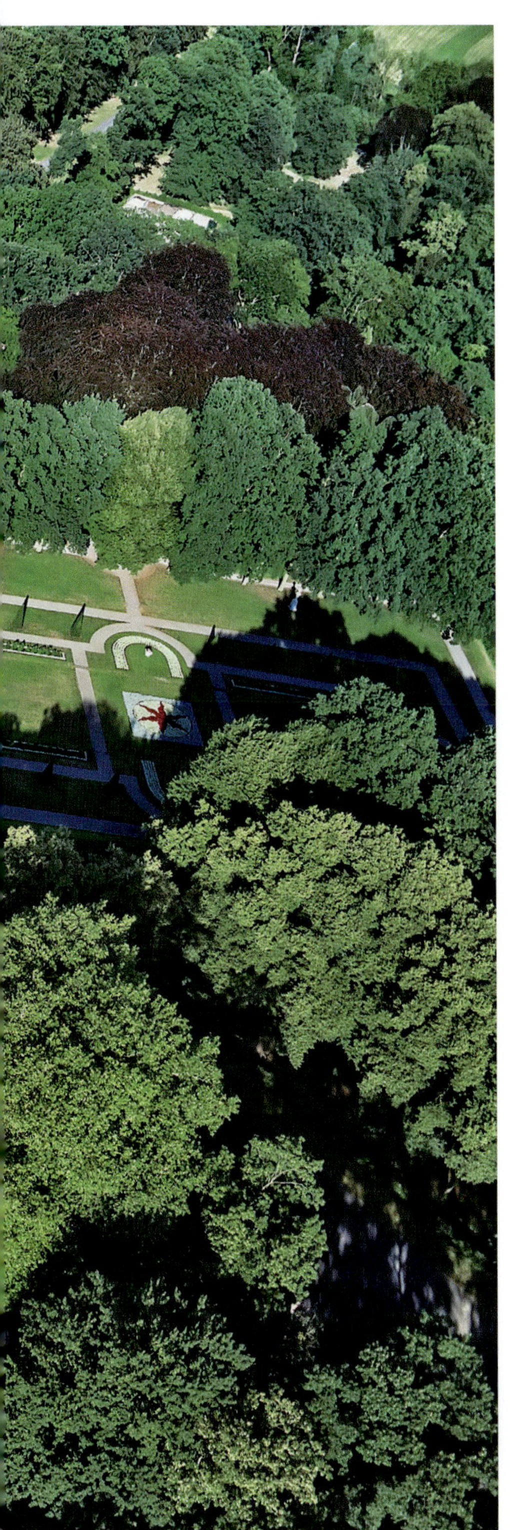

De Haar Castle is located in the village of Haarzuilens, a few miles from the center of Utrecht. Although it was first mentioned in a document dating back to 1391, it is very likely that it is at least a hundred years older. When, many centuries later, the property was inherited by Baron Étienne van Zuylen van Nijevelt van de Haar, the manor was in a state of serious disrepair. It was saved from demolition when the baron decided to renovate it, restoring it to its former glory, if not improving it. It was a financially burdensome task, but Étienne van Zuylen could also count on the capital of his wealthy wife, the heiress Hélène de Rothschild, who belonged to the famous dynasty of influential bankers. The renovation, which lasted twenty years from 1892 to 1912, was entrusted to Pierre Cuypers, considered the Dutch version of Eugène Viollet-le-Duc, the French architect famous for his restoration of medieval buildings, particularly Notre-Dame Cathedral in Paris, and for the reconstruction of the citadel of Carcassonne, also in France. Pierre Cuypers had already designed the Rijksmuseum and the central station in Amsterdam. The result of his work is the impressive neo-Gothic castle that can now be admired in all its splendor, with towers and moats, ramparts and drawbridges standing out against the backdrop of the large park. But that's not all: all the interior rooms of the castle, the chapel, and even the houses in the nearby village of Haarzuilens, which were demolished to make way for the park and rebuilt a mile away, bear the signature of Pierre Cuypers. Today, De Haar Castle belongs to a foundation, but the descendants of the family continue to spend their vacations there in September, when the property is closed to the public.

13th century
The first building was probably built in the 13th century on an embankment near the village of Haarzuilens.

1391
A written source confirmed the existence of a fortified house (whose appearance is unknown) owned by a member of the Van der Haar family, vassals of the Prince-Bishop of Utrecht.

15th century
The castle passed to the Van Zuylen family through the marriage of Josina van de Haar to Dirk van Zuylen.

1482
Due to a dispute between the bishop and the city of Utrecht, the castle was damaged and later rebuilt in its characteristic pentagonal shape.

19th century
Étienne van Zuylen inherited the De Haar estate, which was by then in a state of neglect. Along with his wife Hélène de Rothschild, the baron decided to rebuild the manor as a tribute to his glorious family.

1892–1912
Pierre Cuypers oversaw the reconstruction of the castle, giving it the neo-Gothic appearance that characterizes it today.

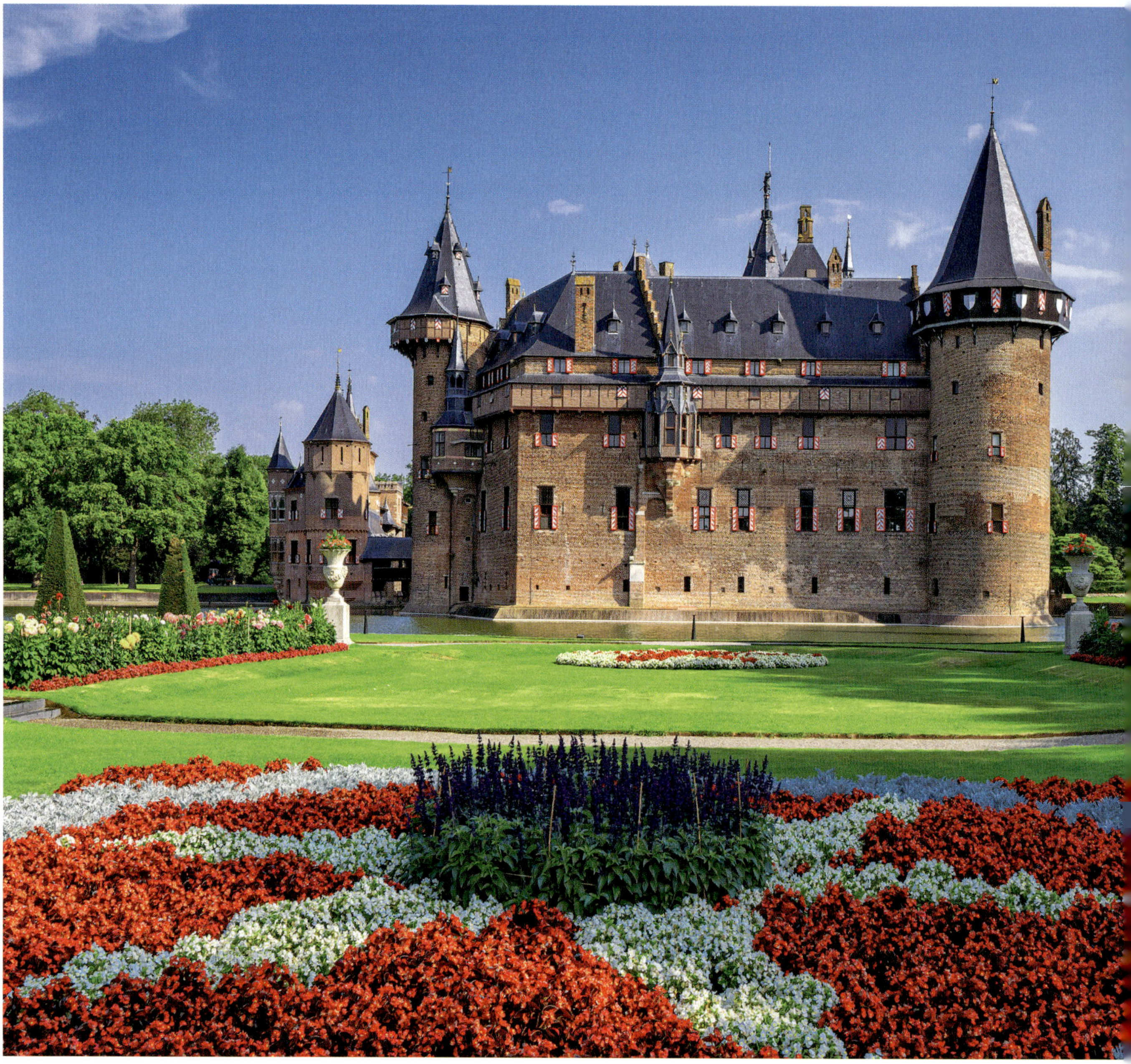

The castle kitchen

In the basement of Haar Castle are the service rooms, the kitchens, the pantry, and even a room used as a butcher's shop because Baron and Baroness van Zuylen loved to spoil their guests with refined meat dishes, from duck à l'orange to stuffed chicken and venison steak. In 1898, a French company installed an innovative and enormous coal stove (measuring approximately 20 feet in length). The grates on the floor around the stove were used to supply air to the two coal fires, while the smoke was discharged underground. Hanging on the walls is a gleaming copper kitchen set consisting of 150 pieces. In his quest for perfection, Cuypers apparently even designed the tableware.

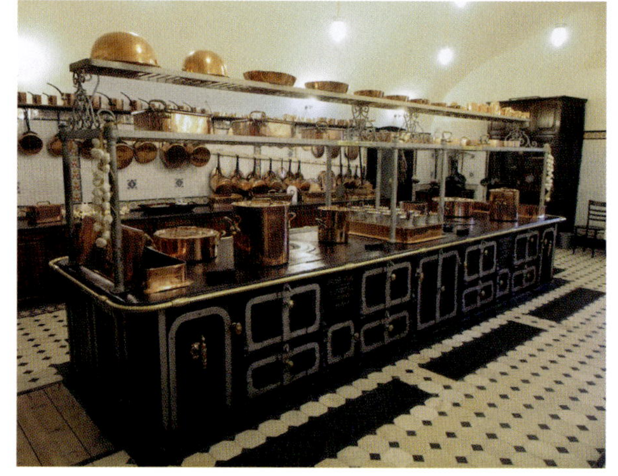

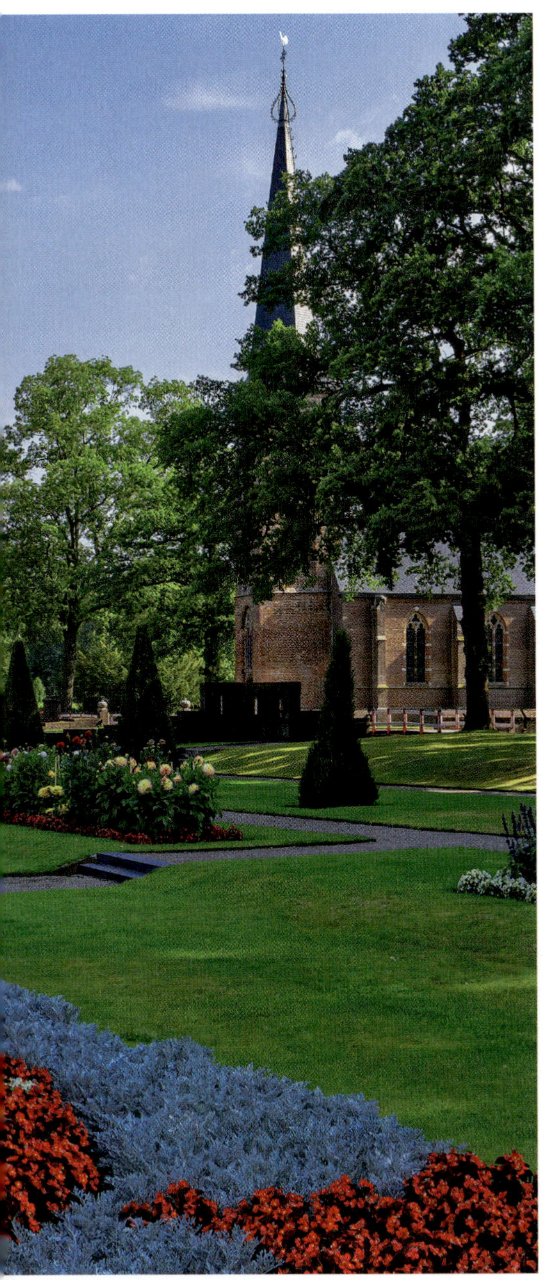

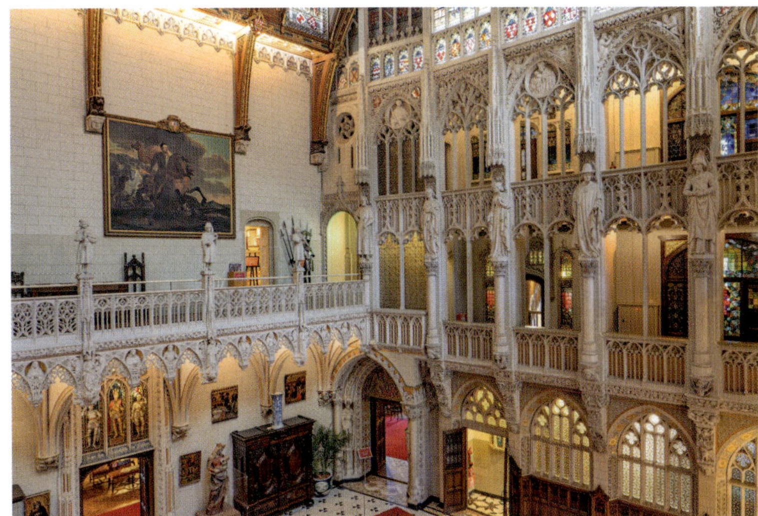

The Baron and Baroness van Zuylen lived in Paris, on Avenue du Bois de Boulogne, and also had a villa in Nice. Although they rarely visited Holland, they spared no expense in renovating the castle. The main hall, designed by Pierre Cuypers, amazed the couple's guests with its exquisitely neo-Gothic appearance, reminiscent of a 14th-century cathedral, complete with statues and stained-glass windows. The interiors were equipped with every comfort, including central steam heating and electric lighting, supplied by a generator. The rooms were furnished with period furniture, Persian carpets, huge tapestries, antique paintings, and precious Chinese and Japanese porcelain from the Rothschild collections. The whole complex was designed as a holiday residence where the couple and their descendants could relax in luxury, surrounded by every comfort, enjoying moments of leisure in the company of their friends. Baron van Zuylen spared no expense in landscaping the park and gardens around the castle, even going so far as to purchase, demolish, and then rebuild the farmhouses in the nearby village of Haarzuilens a little farther away in order to make room for his private green space. The project, entrusted to landscape architect Hendrik Copijn, included plans for the manor to be surrounded by trees: van Zuylen scoured the entire province of Utrecht to buy 7,000 trees, either centuries old or at least well-established, capable of framing the building and highlighting it with their mature foliage, as well as sheltering it from the wind. The result was a beautiful English-style landscape park with winding paths, ponds, canals, and romantic bridges. French-style Baroque gardens inspired by those of Versailles were also created, as well as a Roman Garden with boxwood trees skillfully shaped into cones.

• 160–161: The formal gardens near the castle were created by restoring the original gardens and expanding them to their current size. In the vast green spaces surrounding the manor, you can stroll along canals and moats shaded by centuries-old trees reflecting in the water.

• 161 top: The main hall was used for lavish receptions, such as masked balls. According to a family legend, the baron and baroness met at a masked ball in Paris in 1886. He, a young cavalry officer at the time, was dressed as Hercules.

Frederiksborg Castle

1560
King Frederick II acquired the fiefdom of Hillerødsholm and three small islands in Lake Slotsø, in the center of the town of Hillerød, and began renovating an old manor house.

1600–1620
Christian IV demolished his father's old manor house and built the current Renaissance castle of Frederiksborg. Hans van Steenwinckel the Younger was responsible for the work.

1693
King Christian V dedicated the castle chapel to the Danish orders of knights, the Order of the Elephant and the Order of Dannebrog.

1720
The Sparepenge pleasure palace near Frederiksborg Castle was demolished and replaced by a beautiful Baroque garden.

19th century
After years of neglect, Frederick VII moved to Frederiksborg and, with his morganatic wife Louise Christine Rasmussen, had it renovated.

1859
A fire destroyed much of the castle's interior.

1878
The castle was restored and transformed into the Danish National History Museum, which tells the story of 500 years of Danish history through a collection of paintings, portraits, and historic vehicles.

Between the ends of the 15th and 17th centuries in Denmark, as in the rest of Northern Europe, the kings and aristocratic families of the country built castles and residences, mostly in the Flemish Renaissance style, characterized by austere lines, softened by elaborate spires and pinnacles. Much of this historical period corresponds to the accession to the throne of Christian IV, who was crowned at the age of only 19 in 1596. During this golden age, the kingdom of Denmark and Norway reached the height of its influence in Northern Europe. Thanks to an impressive fleet, in the early ears of his reign the king reaffirmed Danish supremacy over the Baltic Sea. However, participation in the Thirty Years' War in 1625 proved to be a trap for the ambitious sovereign, who fell prey to diplomatic and geopolitical choices that led Denmark to lose its supremacy in Scandinavia to Sweden. Starting at the end of the 15th century and commissioned mainly by this sovereign, a patron of the arts and aware that the "façade" of his country had to correspond to the manifestation of his power, architectural masterpieces were built in Copenhagen and elsewhere in Denmark which still today bear witness to that period of great prosperity. About 19 miles away, in Hillerød, the king wanted to restore the ancient Frederiksborg Castle where he was born. His father, Frederick II, had purchased the manor in 1560 from a Danish admiral and then had it rebuilt. Between 1600 and 1620, Christian IV decided to demolish part of the old building because he wanted his court to live in a residence worthy of the princes of the time. During the years when the Flemish architect Hans van Steenwinckel the Younger worked at Frederiksborg with workers and craftsmen called from all over Europe, the royal family lived in a pavilion called "Sparepenge," on the eastern shore of the lake, opposite Frederiksborg: the king continued to use the pavilion when he wanted to get away from the court, for example, to drink with his closest friends.

• 162 top: The symbol of the Kingdom of Denmark: the three crowned lions.

• 162–163: View of Frederiksborg Castle, the most impressive Renaissance castle in Scandinavia. It stands on three small islands in Lake Slotssøen, about 30 kilometers from the Danish capital.

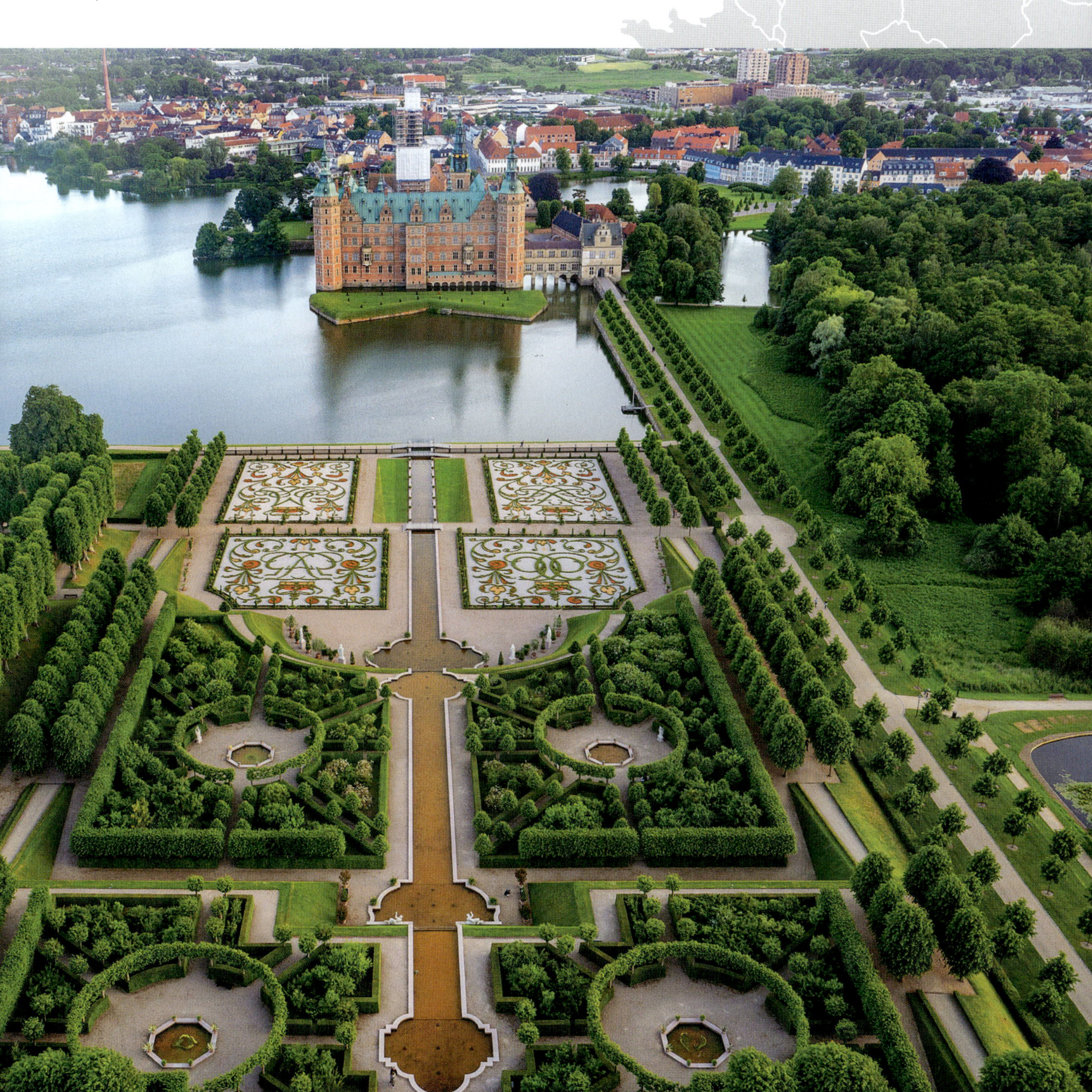

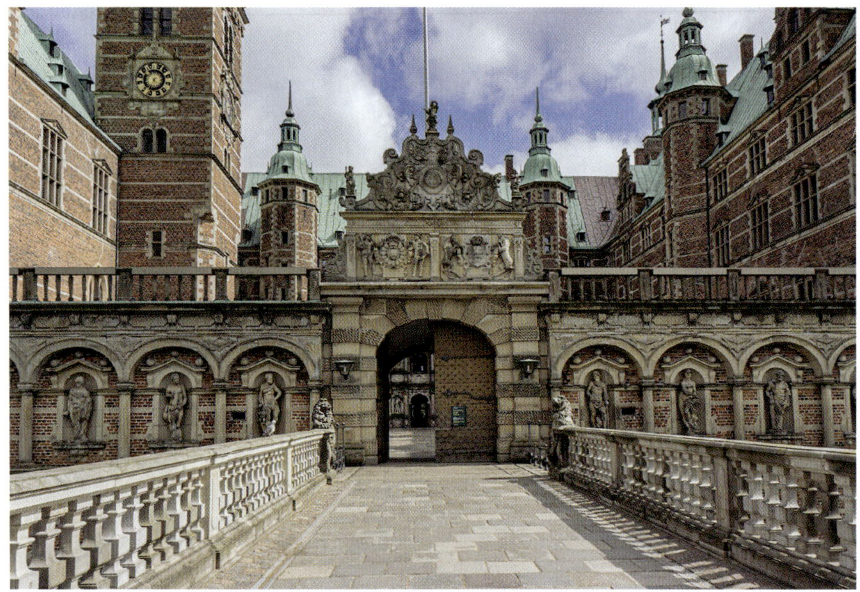

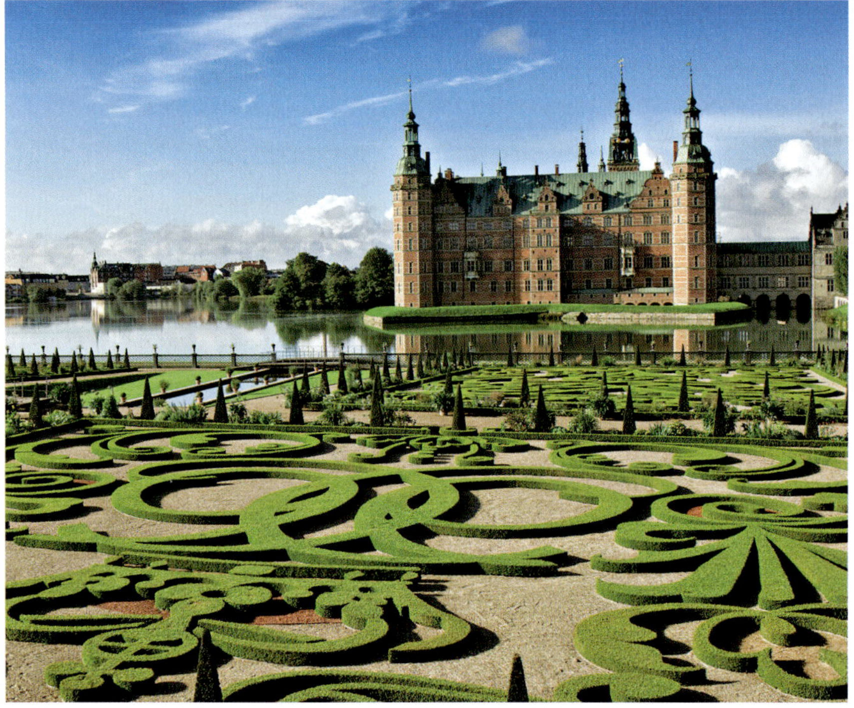

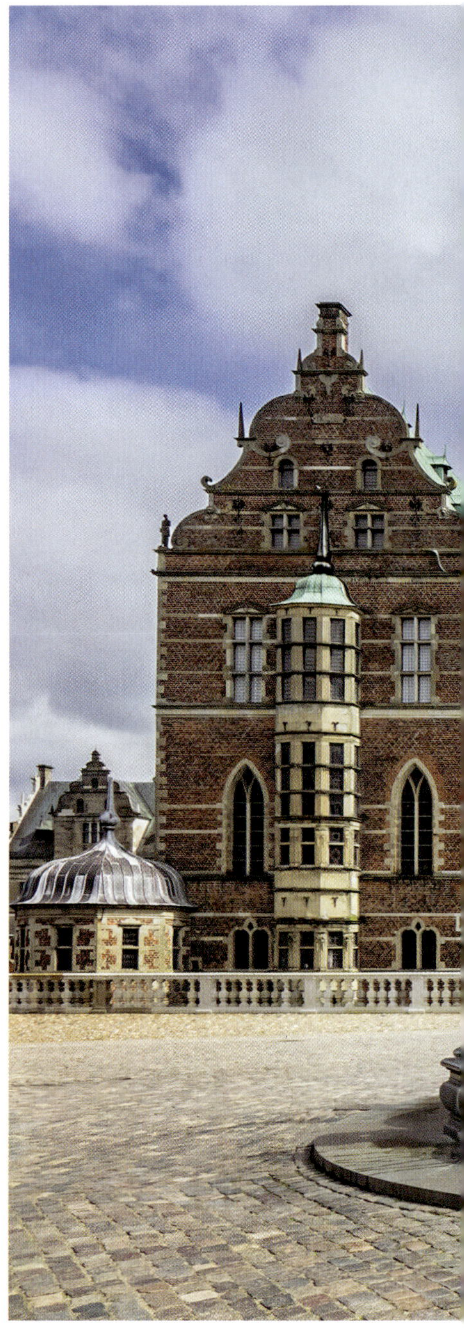

Frederiksborg was rebuilt according to the canons of late Flemish and Dutch Renaissance architecture, in transition to the Baroque style. Every detail in the castle, an expression of the power of the Danish monarchy in the early 17th century, exuded wealth both inside and out: Christian IV enlisted the help of the greatest artists of the time, such as the Dutch Mannerist sculptor Adriaen de Vries, who had already worked at the court of Rudolf II in Prague and in the service of General Albrecht von Wallenstein, and who created the Neptune fountain in the center of the main courtyard. The gardens, which are still one of the main attractions today, were laid out later, when in 1720 the landscape architect Johan Cornelius Krieger was

• 164 top: Frederiksborg Castle is richly decorated because it was intended to showcase Christian IV's position as a powerful European monarch. The construction of the palace is attributed to Hans van Steenwinckel the Younger, who was responsible for most of the royal projects. However, the extent of his involvement is unclear, both because many people contributed to the design of the building, including the king himself, and because it took several years and many rethinkings before the work was completed.

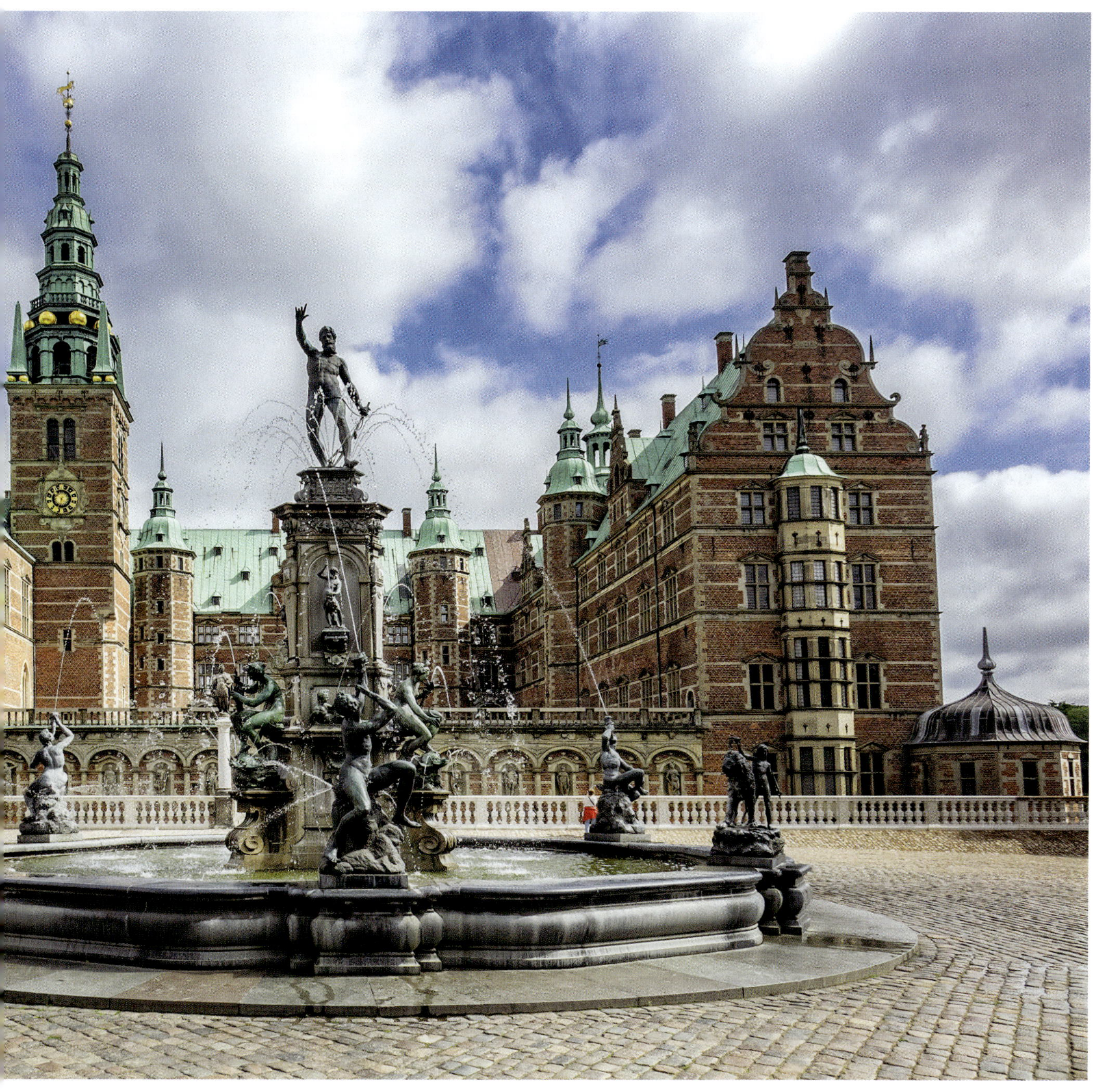

commissioned to create a new one to replace the Sparepenge leisure palace, which had been demolished. Influenced by the formal French garden style of André Le Nôtre, Krieger created a beautiful Baroque garden that unfolds in four terraces sloping down to an oval pond and moat. One of the parterres is occupied by carefully pruned royal monograms (of Frederick IV, Frederick V, Christian VI, and Margaret II). Next to the Baroque garden is the English garden, where nature expresses itself in all its beauty without human intervention. It was created in the 19th century around the Badstueslottet, a romantic building: the ground floor served as baths and a sauna in Frederick II's time.

• 164 bottom: View of the magnificent Baroque or formal garden of the castle. Fallen into ruin at the end of the 18th century, it was recreated according to the original plans in the 1990s.

• 164–165: The Neptune Fountain in the main courtyard, designed by sculptor Adriaen de Vries, was built between 1620 and 1622. The numerous bronze statues depict the sea god Neptune, placed in the center (an allegory of the king's supremacy over the sea), surrounded by tritons.

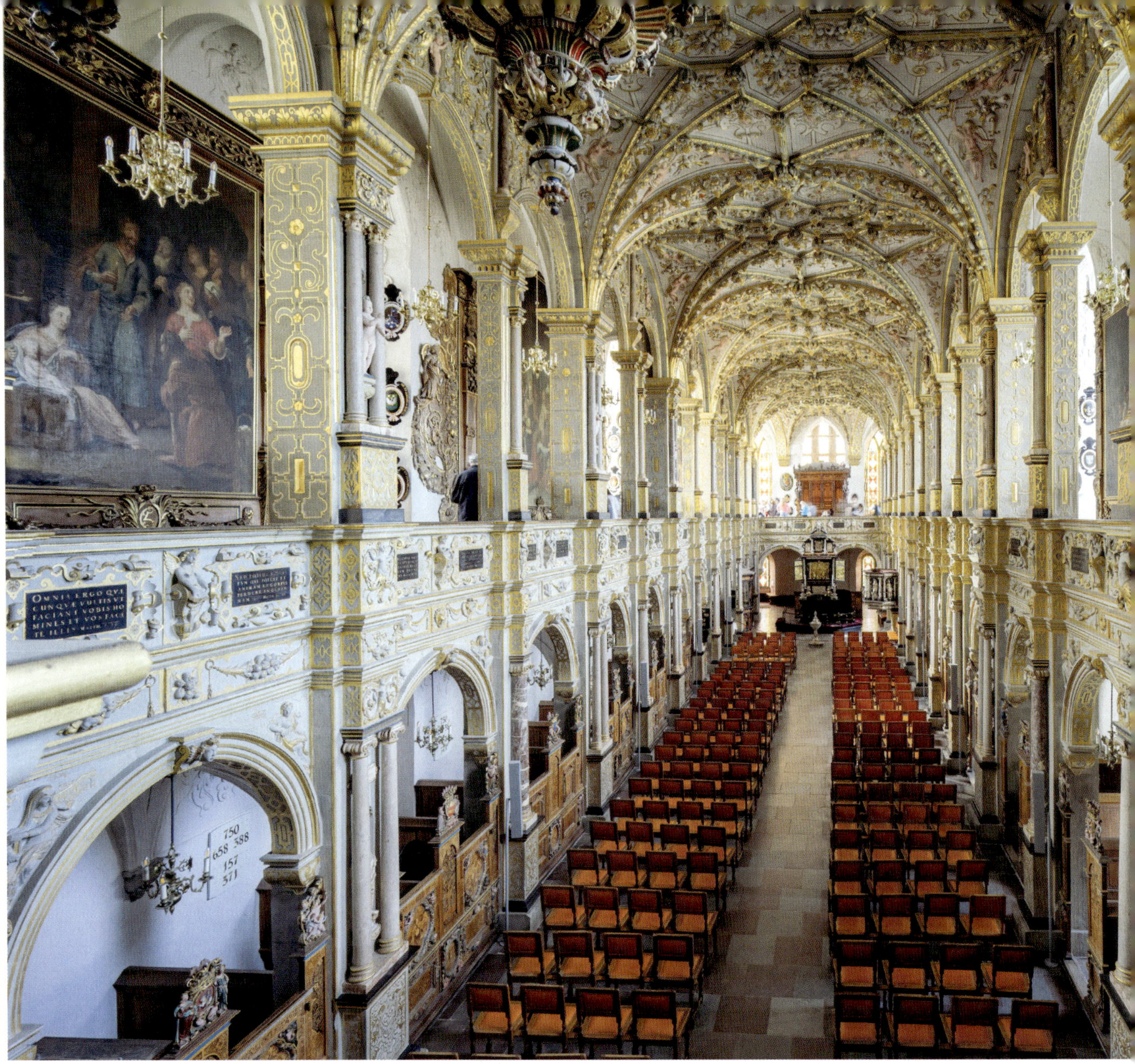

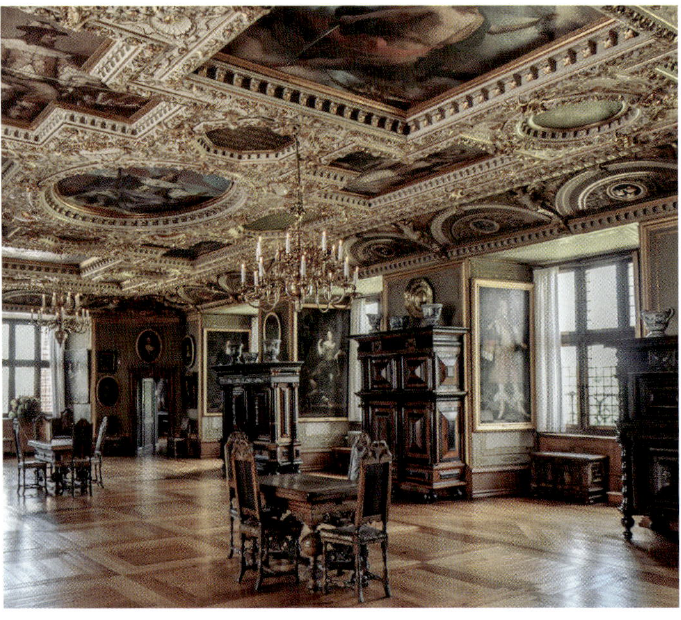

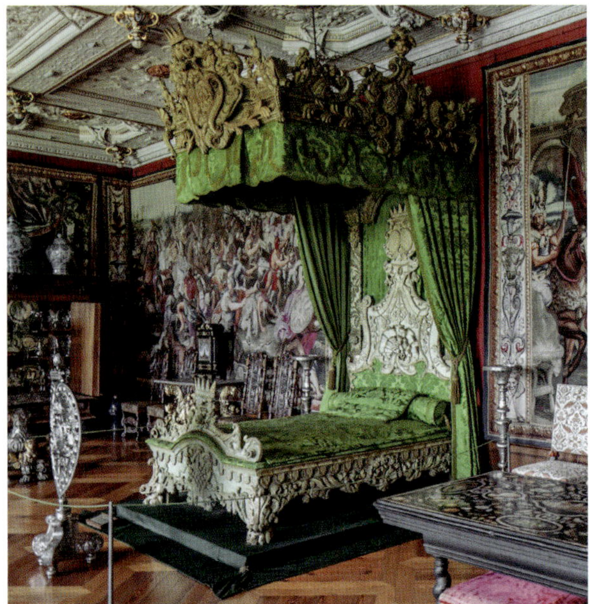

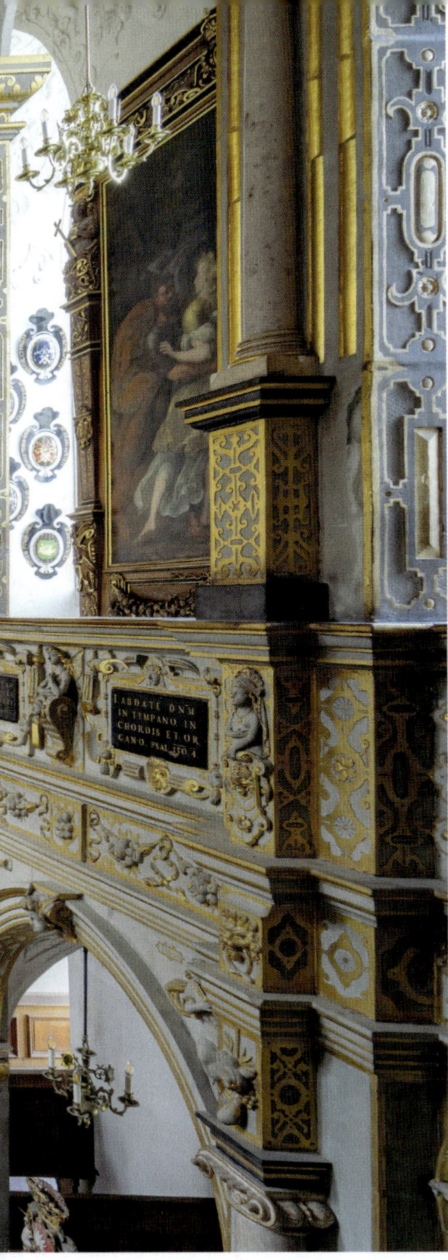

· 166–167: The luxurious bedroom from the period of absolute monarchy. Note the precious tapestries made at Louis XIV's Les Goblins factory in Paris and the four-poster bed, also from the early 18th century.

· 167 center: The Great Hall (called "Riddersalen," or Knights' Hall, since the 18th century) is a faithful reconstruction of the ballroom from the time of Christian IV. Official receptions and banquets were held here and it was lavishly decorated to impress guests. This hall was destroyed by fire in 1859. The meticulous restoration work was completed in 1880.

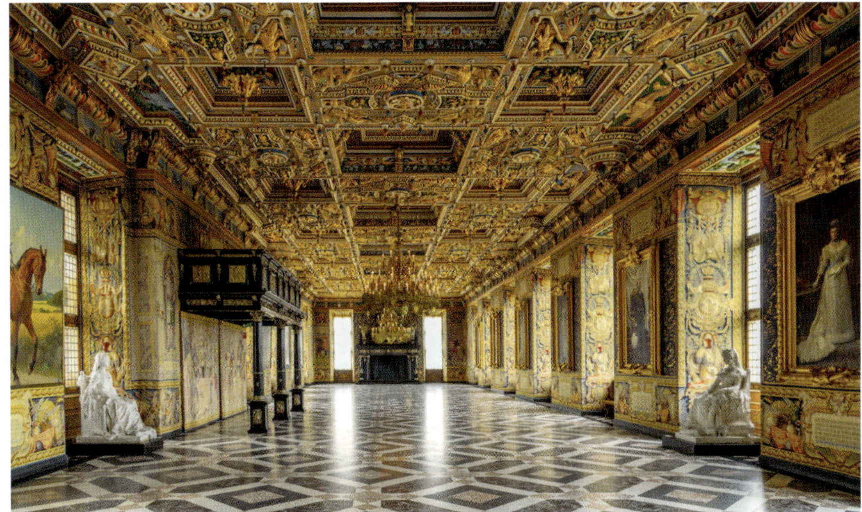

The Compenius organ

In the gallery at the southern end of the chapel is the ancient Compenius organ, which has been in operation for more than 400 years. Even today, every Thursday at 1:30 p.m. its notes ring out from the wooden pipes throughout the church for thirty minutes, recreating a Renaissance atmosphere. The instrument was built in 1606 at the request of the German Lutheran bishop Henry Julius of Brunswick-Lüneburg, a nobleman and lover of the arts, husband of Elizabeth of Denmark, sister of Christian IV.

To create the instrument, which was intended to demonstrate the excellent functioning of wooden pipes, leading German organ builder and organist Esaias Compenius was hired, assisted by composer and music theorist Michael Praetorius.

Upon the death of the Duke of Brunswick-Lüneburg in 1613, the project was continued by his brother-in-law, King Christian IV, and the organ was installed in the Frederiksborg Chapel in 1617.

The organ was built without regard to expense, using ivory to cover the pipes and fine woods. The 1001 pipes are made of walnut, pear, oak, ebony, and maple. The stops are operated by levers decorated with small silver human heads.

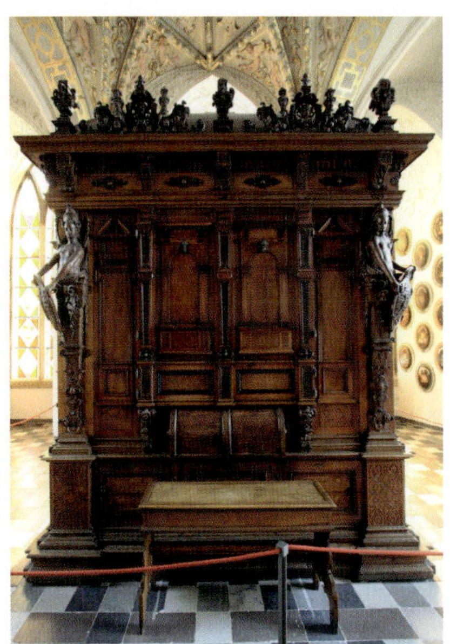

· 166 left bottom: The Renaissance chapel built by Christian IV, seen from the gallery. It is adorned with the coats of arms of the Knights of the Order of the Elephant and the Order of Dannebrog, as well as other emblems from more recent times. During the years of absolute monarchy, sovereigns were crowned here.

· 166 right bottom: The Rose or Knights' Hall served as a dining room reserved for ladies and gentlemen of the court. The name of this room, where courtiers exchanged confidences, perhaps refers to the Latin expression "Sub rosa," short for "Sub rosa dicta velata est" ("What is said under the rose is secret"). In ancient times, when a rose was placed on the table, those who had heard or said something undertook to maintain the strictest confidentiality. After the fire of 1859, the room was restored to its original appearance.

• 168–169: Drottningholm Palace, or "Queen's Hill," surrounded by its magnificent park and Baroque garden. In 1981, the royal family moved there, making it their permanent residence. The rooms in the south wing are reserved for the king and his family, while the rest of the building and gardens are open to visitors all year round.

• 169 center: Queen Louise Ulrike of Prussia received the Chinese Pavilion, located in the area farthest from the castle, as a gift from her husband Adolf Frederick. At that time, everything Chinese was considered fashionable. The gardens around the Chinese Pavilion were created in the mid-18th century on the orders of Louise Ulrike and are characterized by groves and more secluded corners than the rest of the park.

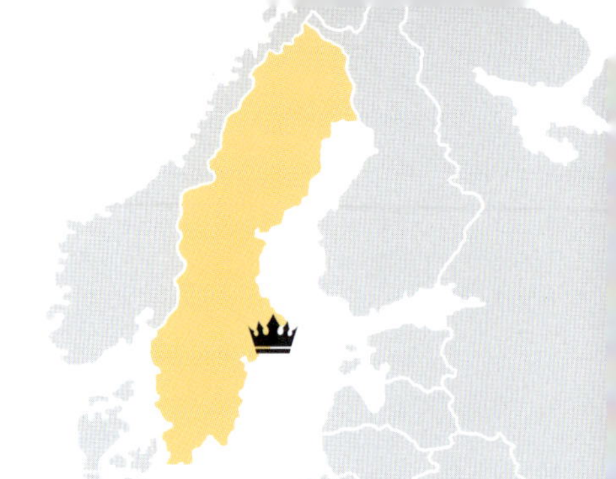

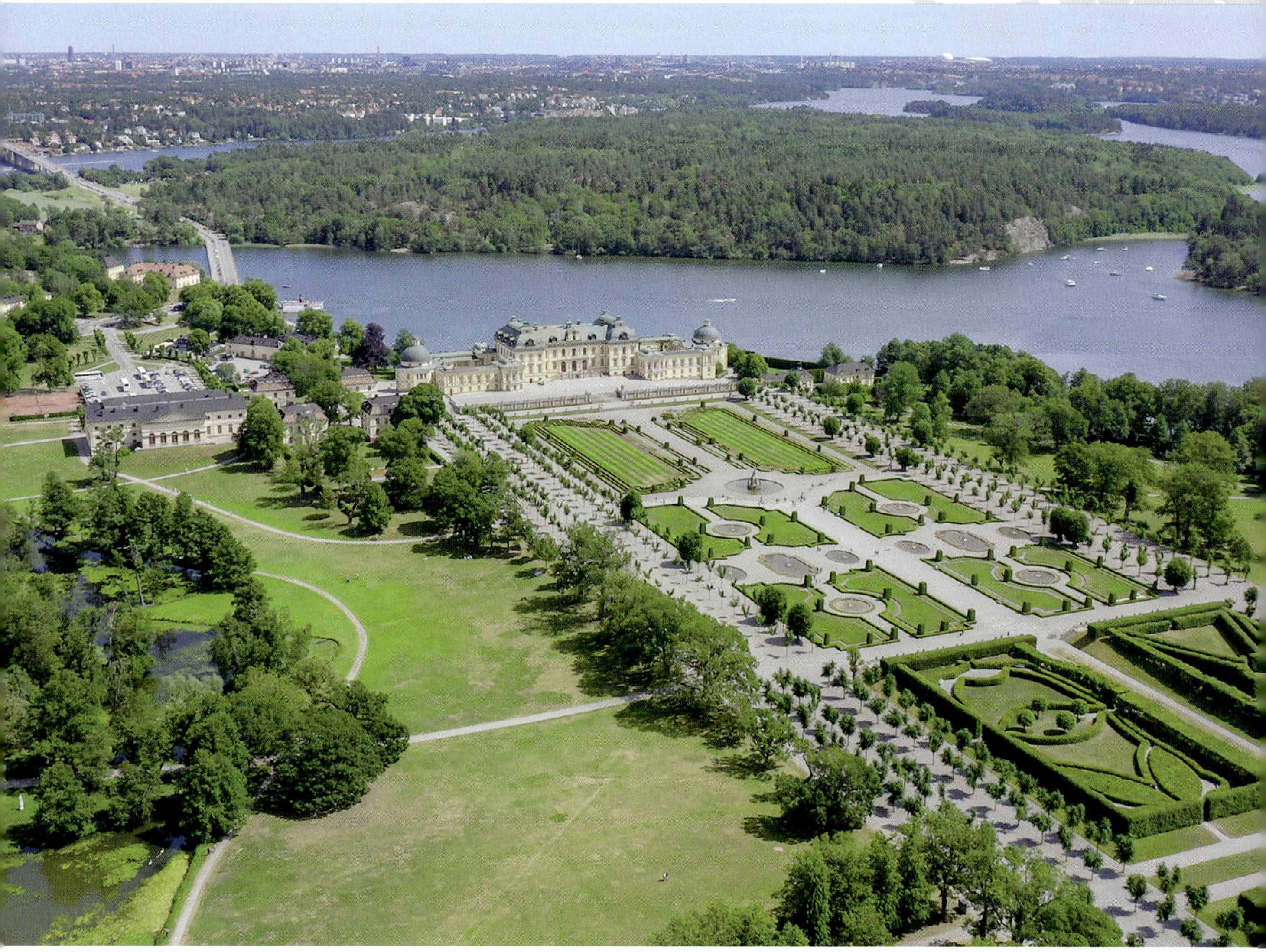

Less than 10 miles from the center of Stockholm, romantically nestled on Lake Mälaren, Drottningholm Palace and Gripsholm Castle face each other across two inlets. The former, residence of the royal family since the 1980s, boasts a history dating back to the 16th century, when the current Baroque palace was replaced by an earlier Renaissance-style royal palace. Its current appearance dates back to the late 17th century when, with an eye on the majestic palaces of the European courts, the castle was built between 1662 and 1686 on the orders of Hedwig Elizabeth Charlotte of Holstein-Gottorp. The queen, who was widowed by Charles X and regent on behalf of Charles XI, needed a prestigious residence near Stockholm to accommodate the court. So when the old Renaissance palace burned down in a fire, the sovereign commissioned architect Nicodemus Tessin the Elder to design a building in the French Baroque style. Her son would take care of the interior. The two architects also designed the Baroque garden adjacent to the palace, a green space surrounded by four

DROTTNINGHOLM CASTLE

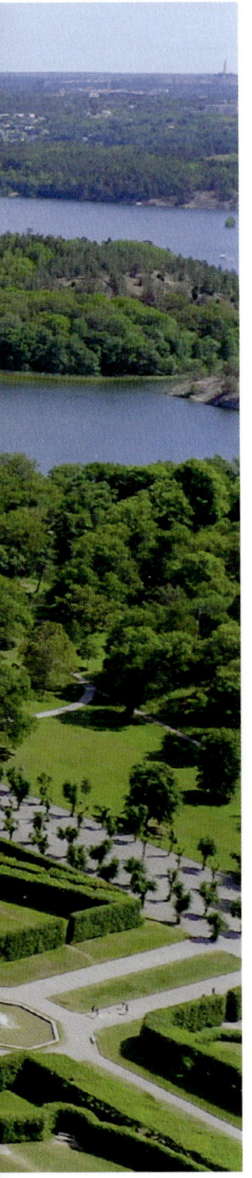

rows of lime trees, clearly inspired by the parks of French residences, where rigor, order, and symmetry reigned supreme. From then until 1792 (the year of Gustav III's death), Drottningholm served regularly as a residence for the court, and the various royal dynasties that lived there adapted the palace to their personal tastes, calling the country's leading artists and craftsmen to the court. Chronicles from the time show that although Drottningholm was a country residence, guests were subject to rules of conduct linked to the weather. During the reign of Gustav III, if the sun was shining, the day was spent in the park and the Chinese Pavilion, and guests could dress informally. In bad weather, however, the elegantly dressed guests remained in the palace.

The king himself decided whether the weather was good or bad by hanging a playing card on the door of the Audience Hall every morning: if it was a heart, the

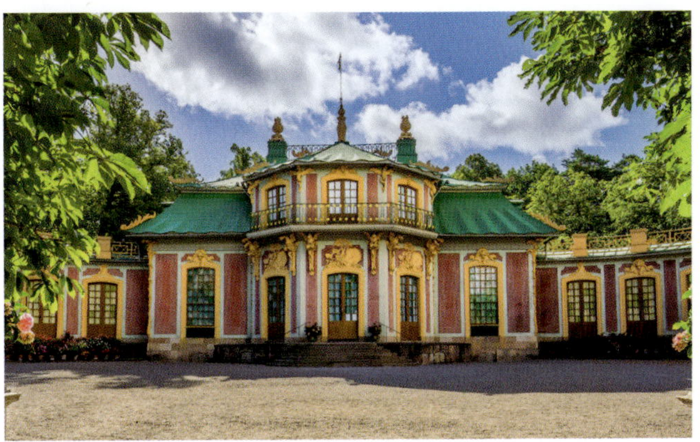

weather was officially fine; if it was a sword, the king announced that there would be bad weather. Gustav III was the last king to live in the palace; after him, only the kings of Sweden visited it occasionally. After a period of neglect lasting about a century, the palace was restored to its original splendor to welcome Swedish sovereigns once again.

16th century
In Drottningholm, John III Vasa commissioned architect Willem Boy to build a two-story Renaissance palace with a tower as a gift for his wife, Queen Catherine of Austria.

1661
Queen Hedwig Eleonora Charlotte of Holstein-Gottorp, widow of Charles X, acquired the Drottningholm estate from politician and military leader Magnus Gabriel de la Gardie, but the palace was destroyed by fire in the same year.

1662
On the orders of Hedwig Eleonora, work began on the construction of Drottningholm Palace on the ruins of the palace under the direction of architect Nicodemus Tessin the Elder.

1681
On the death of Nicodemus Tessin the Elder, the task of completing the palace was passed on to his son Nicodemus Tessin the Younger. The Charles XI Gallery dates from this period.

1744
The heir to the Swedish throne, Adolph Frederick, King of Sweden from 1751, gave Drottningholm Palace to his bride, Princess Louise Ulrike of Prussia, as a wedding gift.

1751–1771
Queen Louise had the rooms of the palace, including the library, decorated in the French Rococo style. The theater was built.

1777
The palace was sold to the Swedish state, but Gustav III continued to live there and had the interior renovated.

1792
With the death of Gustav III, the splendor of Drottningholm Palace began to fade and the residence was virtually abandoned throughout the 19th century.

1907
The palace was restored to its former glory after years of renovation work. Since 1981, it has been the permanent residence of the Swedish royal family, who occupy the south wing.

1991
The castle and its grounds were listed as a UNESCO World Heritage Site.

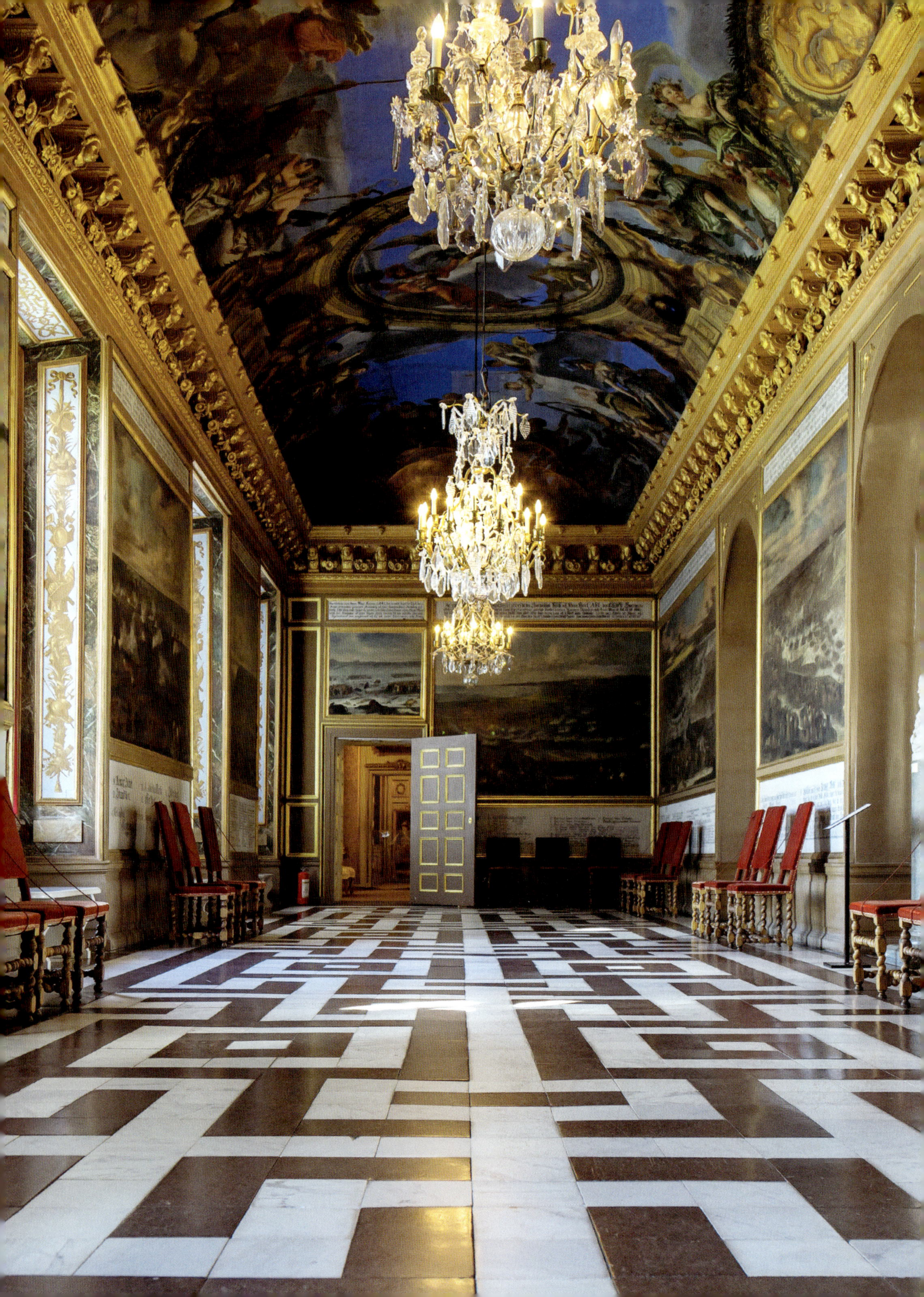

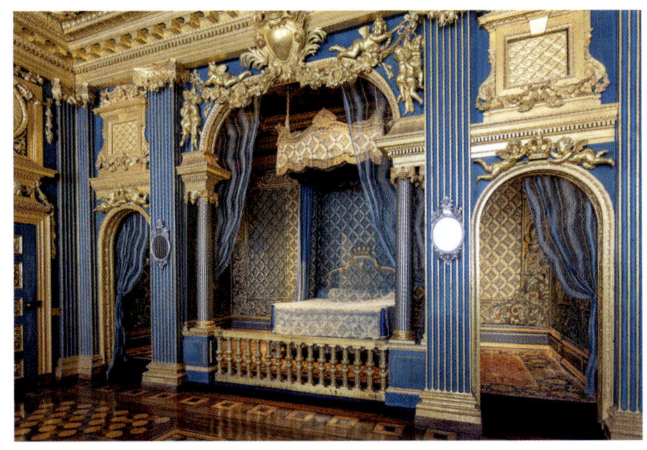

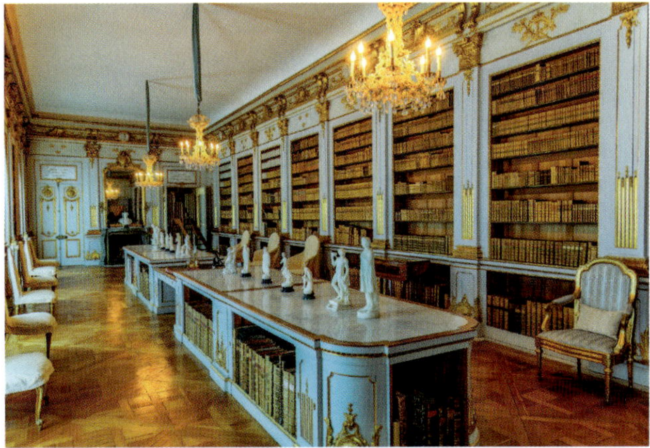

The coffee experiment

Coffee was imported to Sweden in the second half of the 17th century, becoming very popular in the salons of the Swedish aristocracy despite the enactment of an edict in 1746 to regulate its consumption and the high taxes levied on its purchase: failure to pay the duty resulted in fines and the confiscation of cups and saucers. The reason for this aversion was the belief that the substance was harmful to health. Gustav III was convinced of this and, to confirm his theory, he ordered an experiment. Two twins, who had been sentenced to death, were spared so that one could drink three cups of coffee a day for the rest of his life, while the other would drink the same amount of tea. Two doctors were appointed to supervise the experiment, whose verdict disproved the king's fears. Gustav III died before any of them, at the hands of his assassin on March 16, 1792. He was followed into the afterlife by the two doctors and finally, by natural causes, the twins—and, in any case, the one who had drunk tea died first. The government later tried again to ban coffee consumption, but never succeeded in persuading the Swedes to give it up.

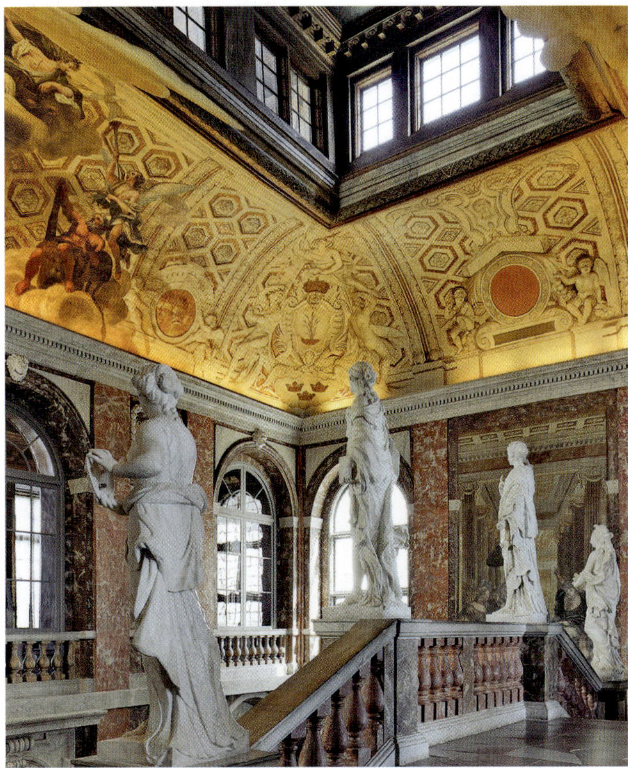

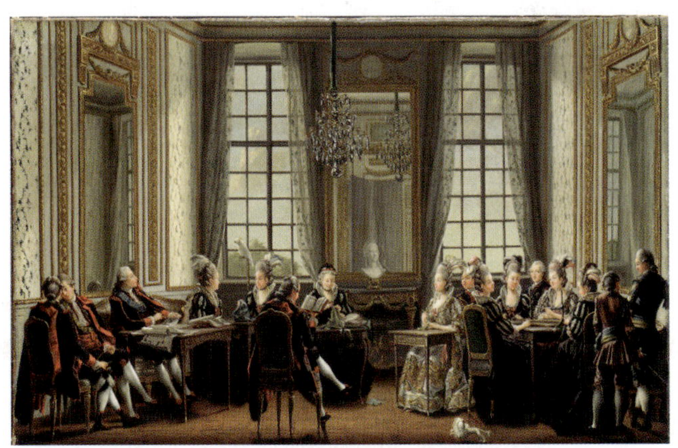

• 171 left bottom: A moment of leisure in Drottningholm during the reign of Gustav III in a painting from 1779 by Pehr Hilleström.

• 170: Charles XI's Gallery, decorated with paintings depicting the Scanian War (1675–1679).

• 171 left top: Queen Hedwig Elizabeth's luxurious state bedroom is one of the most important rooms in Drottningholm Palace. It was designed by some of the country's most skilled artists and craftsmen.

• 171 right top: The library of Louise Ulrika of Prussia, wife of Adolf Frederick, the first king of Sweden from the House of Holstein-Gottorp. The queen loved art and culture and led a brilliant social life. The current room was originally designed as a picture gallery, but was converted into a library in 1760.

• 171 right center: A detail of the palace staircase, the most magnificent and sumptuous ever designed by Nicodemus Tessin the Elder, the architect responsible for the castle's design.

Wilanów Castle

1596
The capital was moved from Krakow to Warsaw. Sigismund III Vasa had the ancient building of the Dukes of Masovia (14th century) renovated by several architects.

1674–1696
The King of Poland and Grand Duke of Poland, Jan Sobieski, nicknamed "The Lion of Lehistan" by the Turks, purchased an estate on the outskirts of Warsaw, in Wilanów, and had a Baroque summer residence built. The work was entrusted to Agostino Vincenzo Locci.

1696–1730
After the death of John III Sobieski in Wilanów in 1696, the palace passed into the hands of his sons and then, from 1720, to the famous magnate families of Sieniawski, Czartoryski, Lubomirski, Potocki, and Branicki.

1730–1733
After becoming the property of King Augustus II the Strong of Poland, the Wilanów residence and its gardens were renovated in the fashion of the time.

18th century
The palace passed from one noble family to another and, in 1778, from Countess Maria Zofia Czartoryska to Princess Izabela Lubomirska, who had some of the interiors renovated in the neoclassical style.

1805
The art collection of Count Stanisław Kostka Potocki was exhibited in Wilanów: it was one of the first public exhibitions in Poland.

1939–1945
The palace was damaged by German forces during World War II.

1962
The Wilanów Palace was opened to the public after being restored.

In 1674, John III Sobieski, hero of the Battle of Vienna (September 11–12, 1683)which was fought alongside the Habsburgs against the Turks, was appointed ruler of the Polish-Lithuanian Commonwealth. A cultured man and patron of science and the arts, he had a palace built in the countryside outside Warsaw as his summer residence. The design of what was supposed to be a simple country residence, so much so that a farm and a hunting reserve were planned near the main building, bears the signature of the architect and set designer Agostino Vincenzo Locci, who followed in his father's footsteps, as his father had been the court architect of the Vasa family. It was the king's successors, in particular King Augustus II, who transformed the Baroque palace into a luxurious residence, enlarged and decorated by the best artists of different eras. This is why the complex seems to have several souls, combining the typical style of Italian country villas with that of Polish Baroque palaces and 18th-century French palaces. The oldest part of

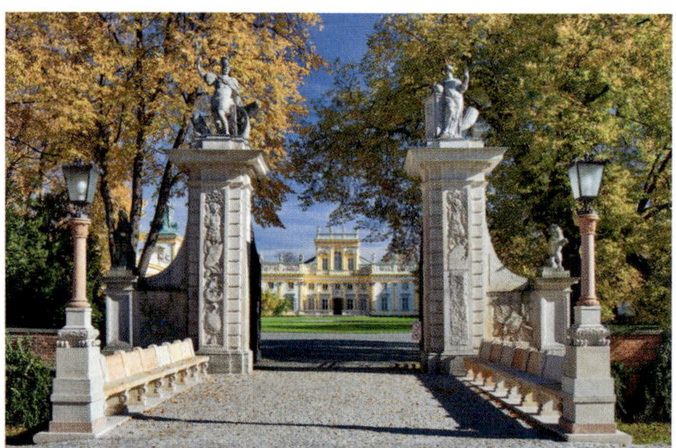

the palace consists of the Royal Apartments (including the antechambers of the king and queen, the bedrooms, the Great Vestibule, the Dutch Cabinet, and the Royal Library) furnished during the reign of John III and his wife Maria Casimira Luisa de la Grange d'Arquien, and richly decorated with gilded

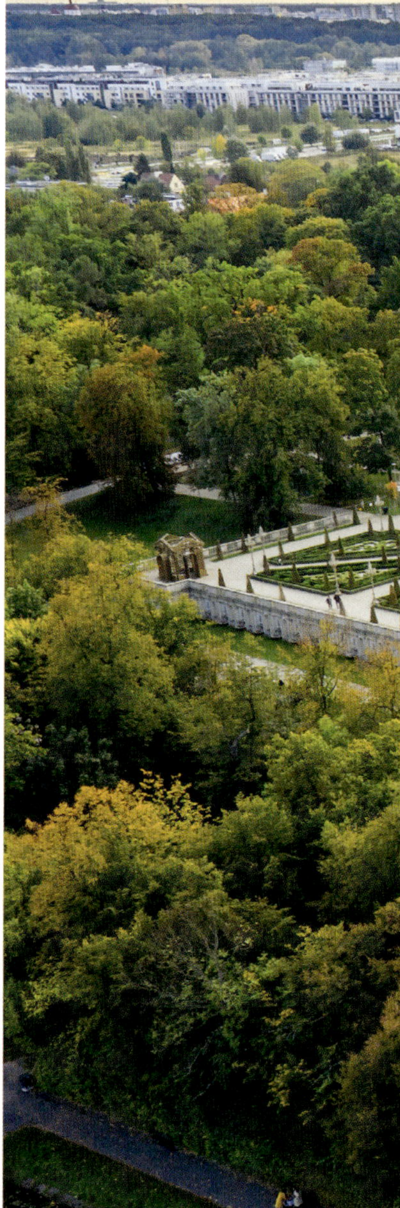

• 172 bottom: The entrance to Wilanów Palace preceded by the garden. The latter is an important feature of the palace, as recalled by the inscription on one of the gates, which quotes Horace: "Ducite solicitae quam iucunda oblivia vitae" ("Forget your daily worries and relax in the garden").

• 172–173: View of the Wilanów complex and its park. At the time of Jan III Sobieski, the northern garden was occupied by an orchard; vegetables and aromatic herbs were also grown there. Today, the garden surrounding the palace is laid out on a terrace designed by Agostino Vincenzo Locci and is arranged in the French style typical of the Baroque period.

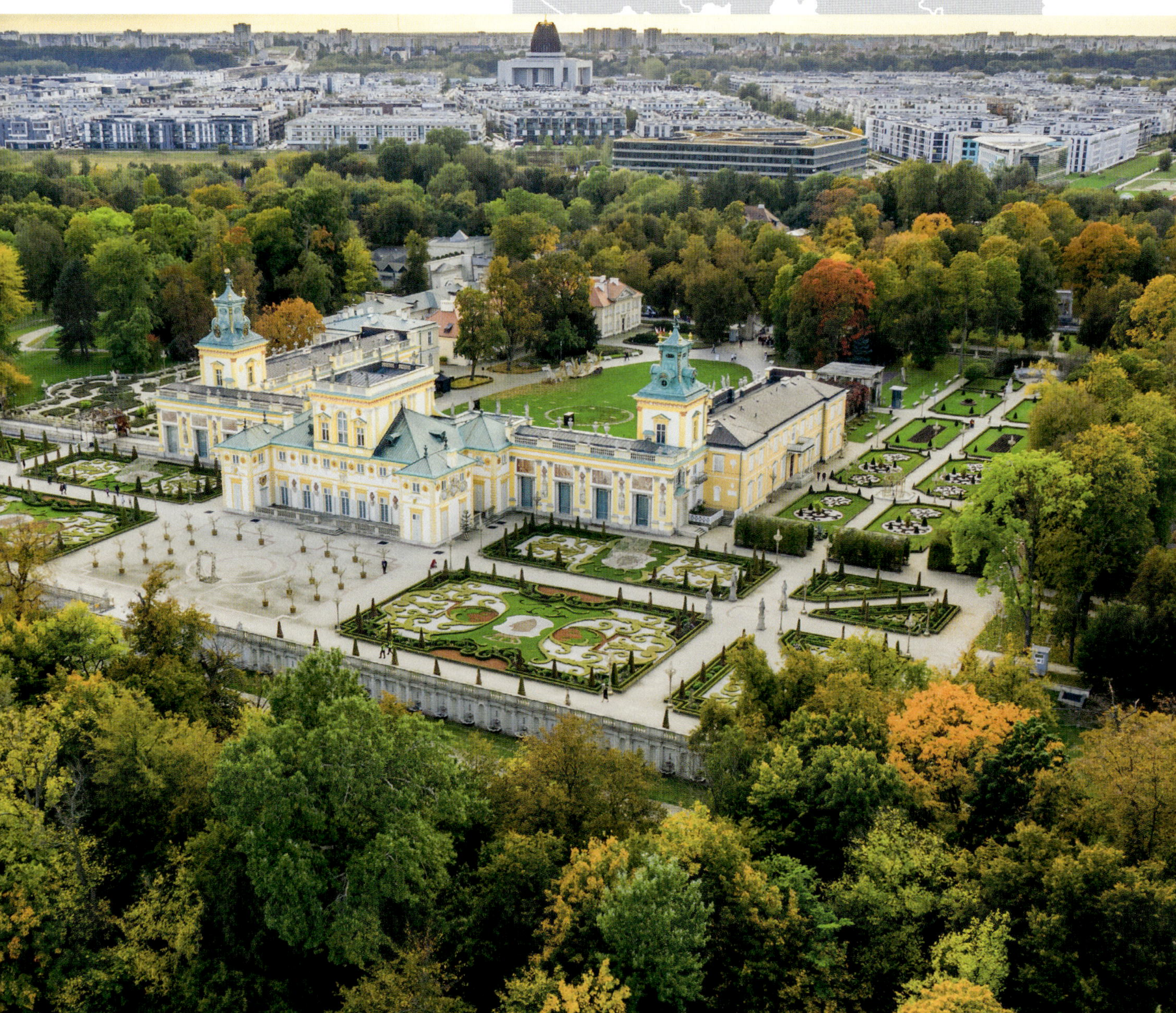

stucco, paintings, and precious tapestries. Walking from one room to another, you can discover the habits of the palace's first owner: the antechamber, for example, was a reception room where guests waited to speak to the king. According to the custom of the time, John III granted audiences in his bedroom, seated on the ceremonial bed, while visitors remained standing. Only the closest family members and the most distinguished guests were allowed to sit in the company of the sovereign. However, the queen's bedroom is the most sumptuous room in the entire palace. From Baroque to Neoclassical, visitors can explore the apartments of Princess Izabela Lubomirska, née Czartoryska, in the south wing of the palace. The furnishings and interior decorations reflect the artistic inclinations and passion for collecting of the refined lady of the house, who gathered objects during her travels in Europe. The furnishings range from French Aubusson furniture to early 18th-century English desks, from mirrors to Meissen porcelain. The bathroom, added to the palace in the last quarter of the 18th century, is the most interesting room: it was in fact a sort of living room used not only for its intended purpose but also for meetings and leisure. This dual function is demonstrated by the presence of a bathtub resting on six lion's paws and a chaise longue with an ostrich feather canopy. Finally, the Chinese and hunting rooms, furnished over time with a series of themed objects, were inhabited at the end of the 19th century, reflecting the owners' passion for Oriental fashion and hunting.

The garden painted by Canaletto

In 1766, Bernardo Bellotto left for St. Petersburg to work at the court of Catherine II. On the way, he stopped to visit King Stanislaus Augustus Poniatowski with the intention of obtaining credentials to better present himself to the tsarina. He enjoyed his stay at the Polish court so much that he decided to stay, and two years later he was appointed court painter. He received a salary of 400 ducats a year for his work, plus another 430 for personal expenses. Thanks to Bellotto's almost photo-realistic technique, it has been possible not only to reconstruct what Warsaw must have looked like before the bombings of World War II, but also other places, such as the park of the Wilanów Palace. The splendor of the garden laid out by John III is brought back to life in the views painted in 1777 at the request of Stanislaus Augustus. In Canaletto's painting, kept at the Royal Castle Museum in Warsaw, you can see that the garden was laid out on two levels with a terrace in front of the palace that served as an extension of the interior. Accessible via a staircase, the lower terrace extended where, at the time of John III, there were probably symmetrical ponds, replaced by flower beds.

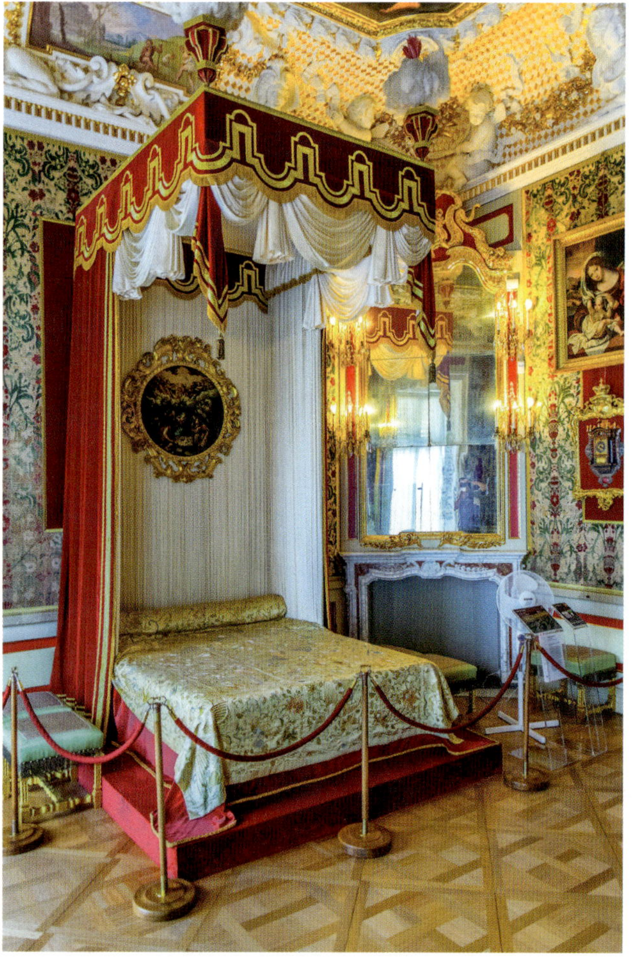

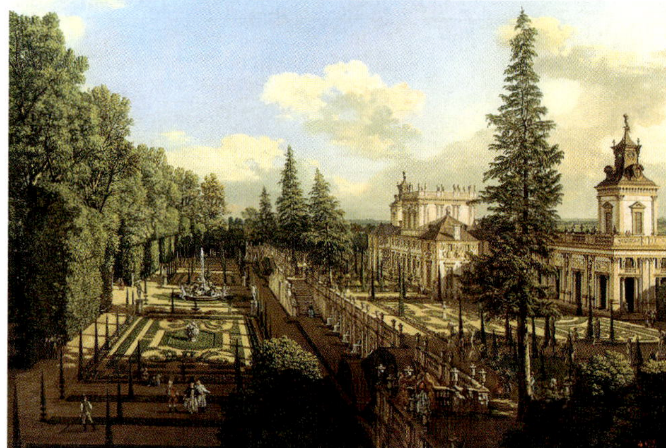

• 174 left: The private apartments are lavishly decorated with precious fabrics, frescoes, and works of art.

• 175 top: A wing of the Wilanów Palace overlooking the Baroque garden with its typical broderies (flower beds bordered and decorated by low hedges on a gravel or sand background). The presence of statues, fountains with water features, and grandiose perspectives, as well as the symmetrical arrangement of the parterres, is typical of the Baroque period.

• 175 bottom left: The Chinese rooms bear witness to the castle owners' passion for Eastern culture, which is revived here through a rich art collection.

• 175 bottom right: Princess Izabela Lubomirska's bathroom was not only used for its specific purpose but also as a private sitting room, as can be seen from the furnishings.

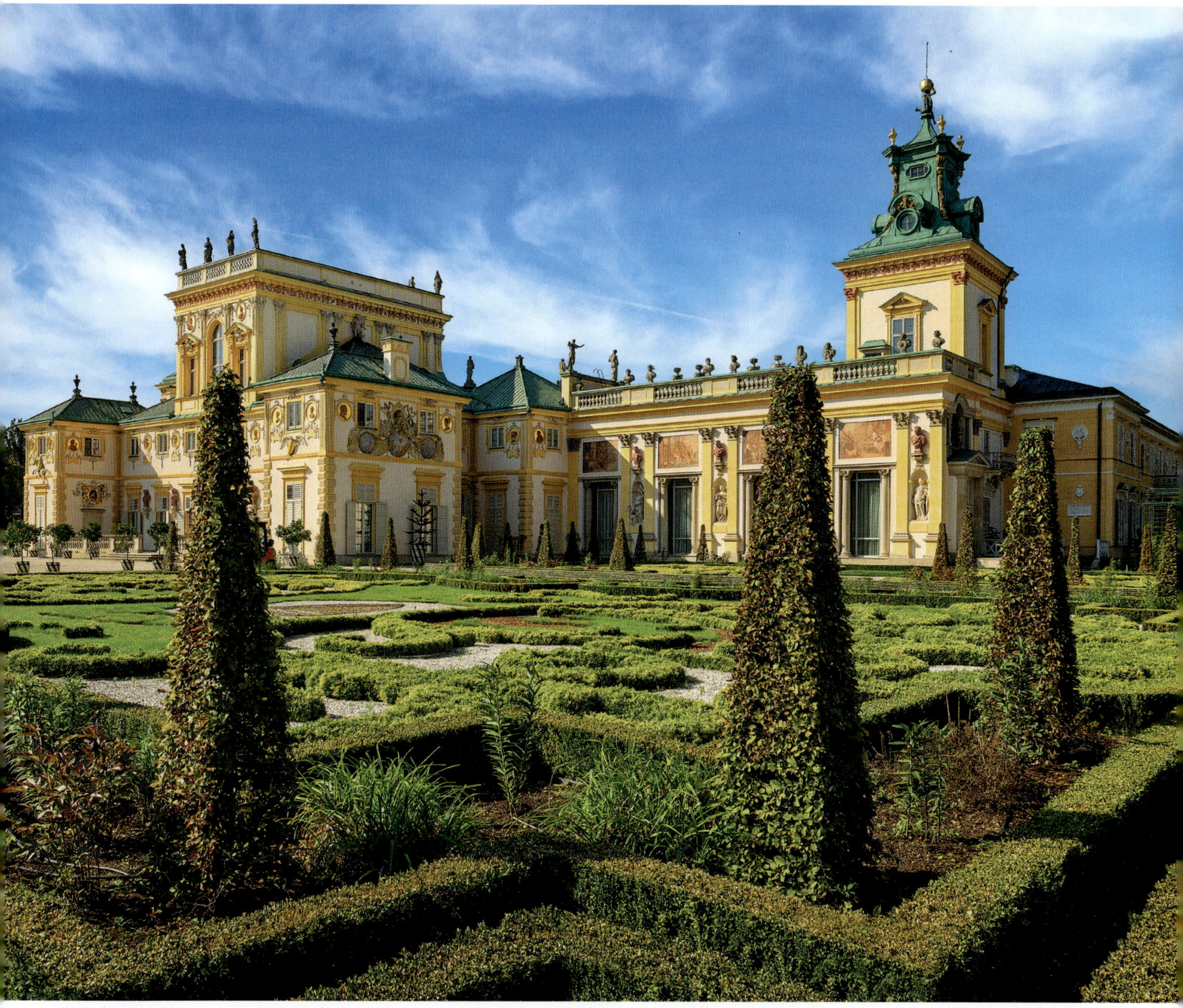

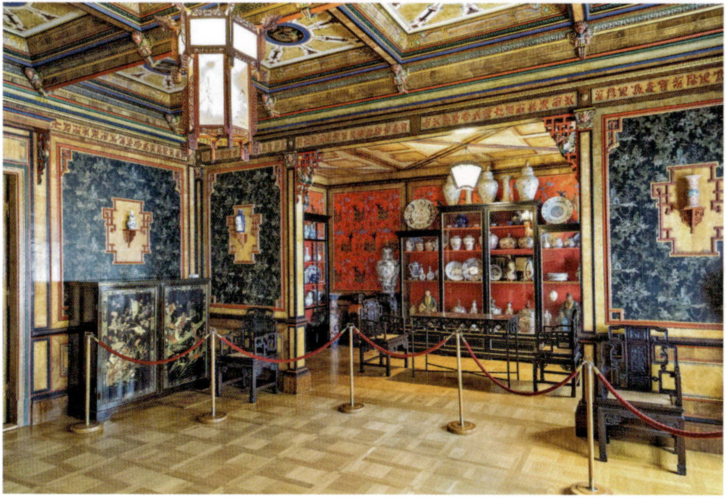

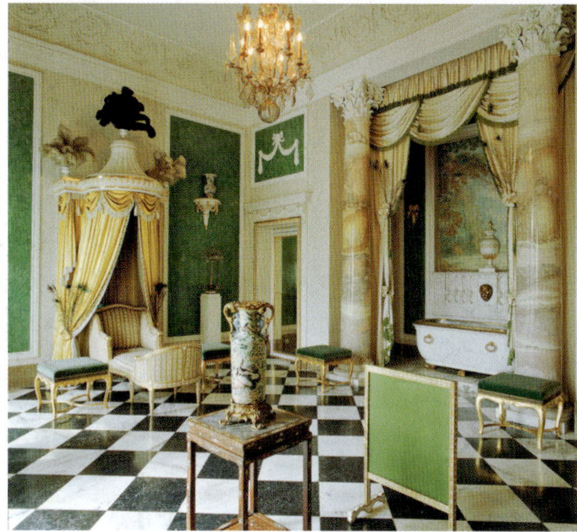

Wawel Castle

1000
Bolesław I of Poland, known as "the Brave," was crowned the first king of Poland in the year 1000. During his reign and that of his son, construction began on a cathedral and a Palatium on ancient fortifications on Wawel Hill in Krakow.

14th century
Casimir III the Great, the last monarch of the Piast dynasty, transformed the medieval Palatium on Wawel Hill into a royal castle in the Gothic style.

1390
Ladislaus II Jagiellon had the walls surrounding Wawel Hill reinforced.

1499
A large fire destroyed most of the castle built by the Piasts and the first Jagiellonian kings.

1502–1536
Elected King of Poland in 1501, Alexander Jagiellon undertook the reconstruction of Wawel Castle, calling on Italian architect Francesco della Lora, who introduced the Renaissance style to Poland.

1520–1536
The work continued under Sigismund I, king from 1506, and Sigismund II Augustus. After the death of Francesco Fiorentino in 1516, Bartolomeo Berrecci completed the work in 1536.

1537
In 1536, a fire destroyed part of the newly completed castle. The following year, reconstruction work began under the supervision of Bartolomeo Berrecci and Nicola Castiglione until 1545, and then Matteo l'Italiano from 1545 to 1549.

1596
With the transfer of the capital from Krakow to Warsaw, the Wawel Royal Castle began to lose importance and throughout the 17th and 18th centuries it suffered attacks, fires, and looting.

The noun "Poland" began to circulate in the rest of Europe through chroniclers only at the end of the 10th century, but Slavic tribes from the east, from present-day Ukraine and Belarus, had settled in the region since the 6th century. The Vislani had occupied the upper Vistula area near Krakow, while the Polani—from whom the name of the nation derives—had set up their camps in what is now Wielkopolska, Greater Poland. In 900, the rise of the Piasts began: probably of Polanian origin, they united and conquered the peoples of the territory, giving rise to the nucleus of the future Polish state; and in 1000 Bolesław the Brave was elevated by Emperor Otto III of Saxony (980–1002) as the first king of Poland. From that period onward, Wawel, the hill overlooking the Vistula River that dominates Krakow from a height of 748 feet, became the center of the Piasts' temporal and religious power. On the hill, even before the construction of various fortifications and the Palatium (the ancient residence of the first Polish kings, whose remains can be found in the northern wing of the present castle), the first religious buildings appeared, including a stone church, which was replaced three centuries later by the magnificent cathedral that stands today. Over time, the princely residence was enlarged by Casimir III the Great. The king en-

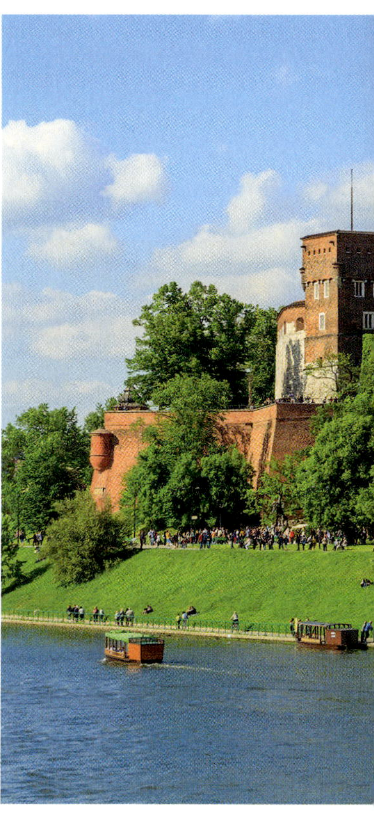

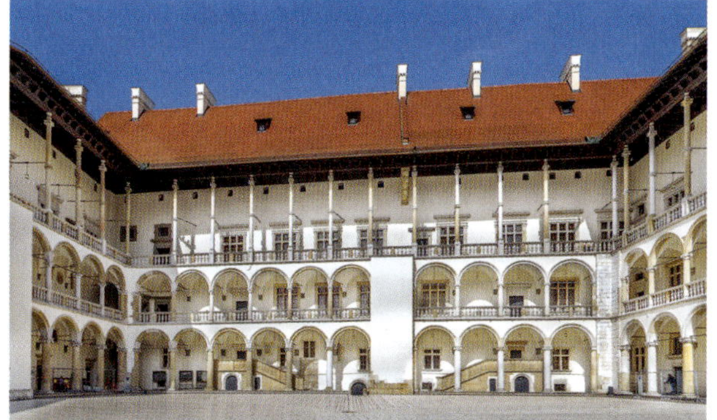

• 176 center: The large courtyard of Wawel Castle, with its slender arched columns reminiscent of Italian Renaissance cloisters, is the most characteristic part of the residence. It was built in several successive stages under the expert supervision of Polish and Italian architects and artists. It had a dual function, both representative and practical. It was intended to impress visitors, but also to be functional for court life, transforming into an open space capable of hosting ceremonies. The porticoes on the top floor served to connect the various rooms of the castle.

• 176–177: A striking image of Wawel Hill from the Vistula River. On the left, you can see the Thieves' Tower, below which were the underground prisons, while on the right is the Sandomierz Tower, built in 1460 and recognizable by its cylindrical shape. These two towers, together with the Senators' Tower, are the oldest elements of the Wawel complex: i.e., the 15th-century fortifications.

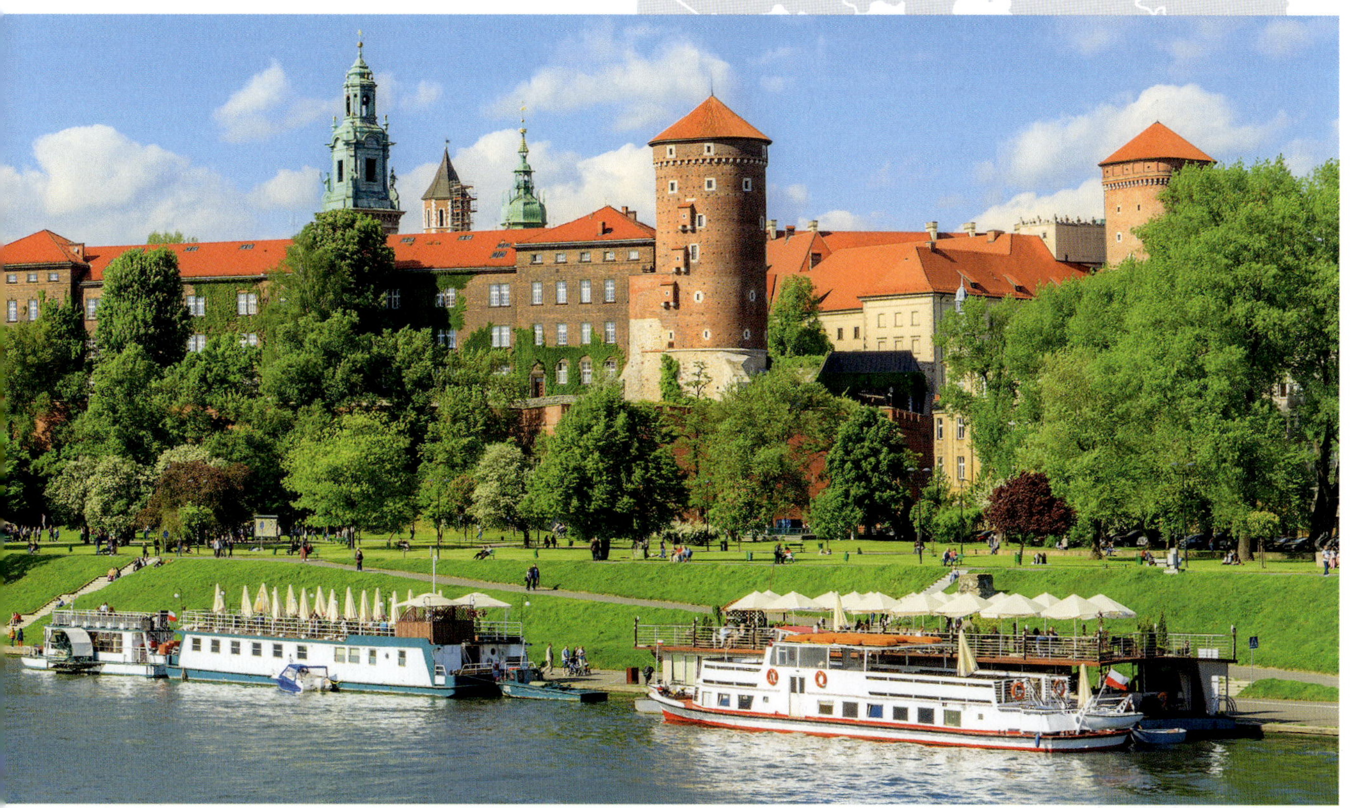

trusted the project to Wacław of Tenczyn, who designed it in the Gothic style, inspired by other royal palaces on the European continent. The palace was used and adapted to the new needs of the court by all the kings of the Piast dynasty, who ruled until 1370, and by the Jagiellonian rulers, the royal dynasty originally from Lithuania, who ruled Poland from 1386 to 1572. After a serious fire in 1499 destroyed most of the buildings constructed in the Middle Ages during the reign of Piast King Casimir III the Great, the castle was rebuilt and transformed into a magnificent Renaissance residence with the help of several Italian artists. The palace was built by the rulers of the Jagiellonian dynasty, Alexander, Sigismund I, and Sigismund II, who had been educated in the spirit of humanism by Filippo Buonaccorsi. The Florentine architect Francesco della Lora worked on the project of the king and his wife Bona Sforza, daughter of Gian Galeazzo Sforza, Duke of Milan, and Isabella of Aragon, along with Bartolomeo Berrecci. The residence was completed in 1536, but in the same year it suffered another fire. Reconstruction began in 1537 and lasted a year under the supervision of Bartolomeo Berrecci, who was succeeded by Nicola Castiglione until 1545 and Matteo l'Italiano from 1545 to 1549. Impressed by the beauty of the castle, magnates and nobles who frequented the king's court soon began to build similar palaces and public buildings. In 1596, with the move of the capital from Krakow to Warsaw, the palace fell into disrepair, although coronations and official celebrations continued to be held there. The oldest part of the complex, dating back to the 15th century and still visible today, corresponds to the fortifications surrounding the Renaissance castle and cathedral.

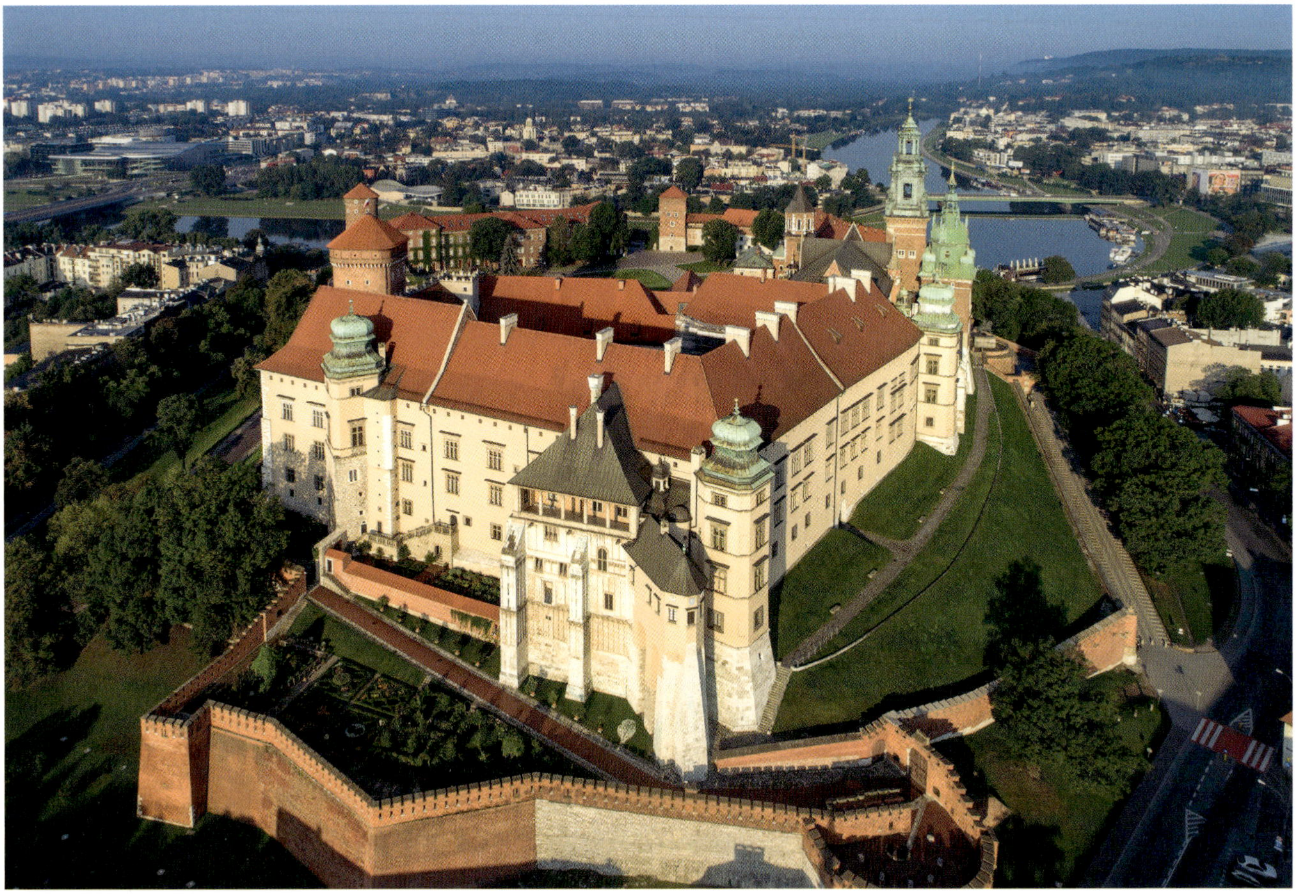

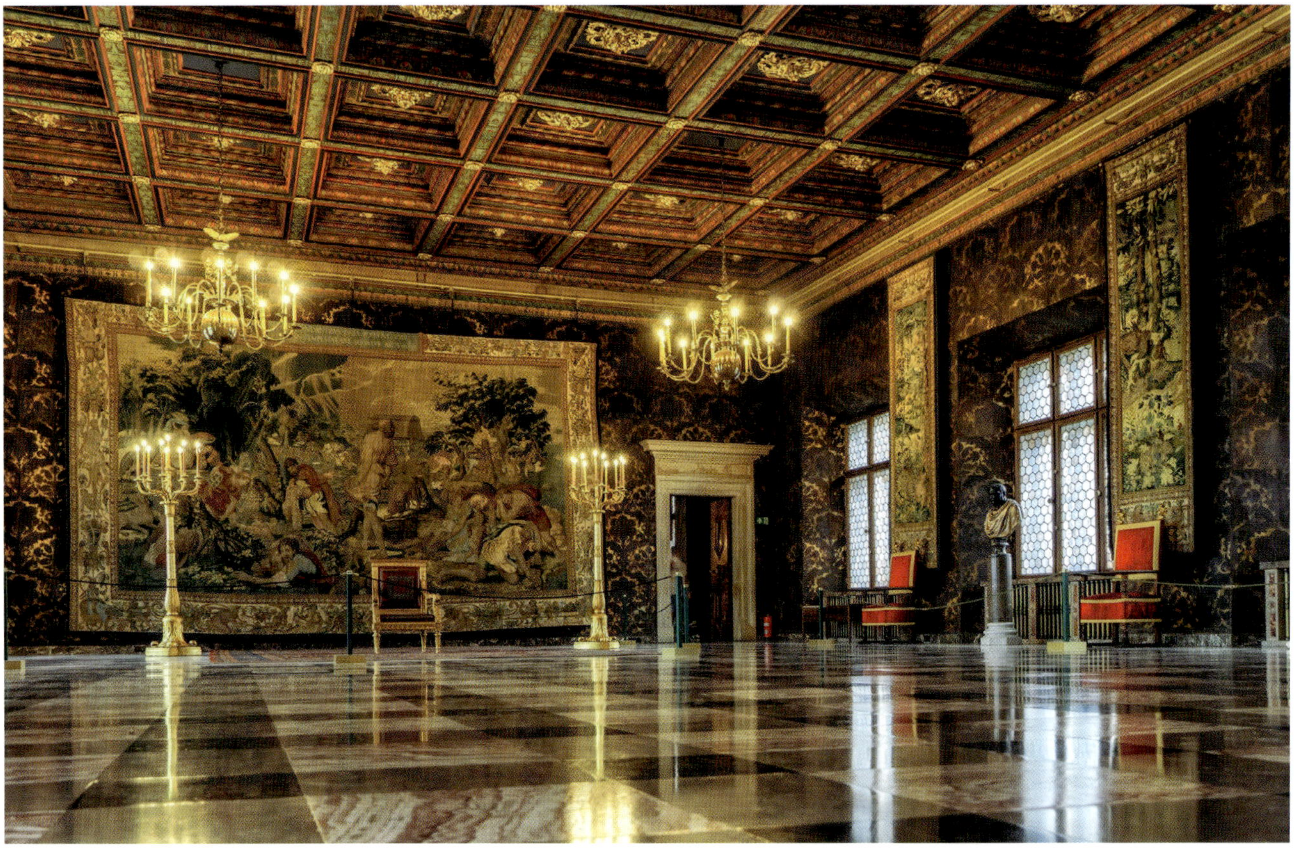

• 178 top: View of the Renaissance castle on Wawel Hill. You can admire the terraced royal gardens, reconstructed as they would have appeared in the 16th century. Spread over two terraces, they were embellished with grassy and floral beds in geometric patterns, as was customary in the Renaissance. There was also a small orchard and a gazebo.

• 178 bottom: The Senators' Hall is the largest room in the castle. Today it takes its name from the Senate meetings that were held there. In the 16th century, it was used for theatrical performances and dances organized for royal weddings, such as that of Bona Sforza and Sigismund I in 1518. The musicians' balcony was added in 1592.

• 179 top: Among the reception rooms, the Hall of Birds is one of the most sumptuous, so much so that it served as the throne room and audience chamber. Built after the fire of 1595, it owes its name to the sculptures of birds in flight suspended from the ceiling, which decorated the hall around 1600. Today, the name refers to the frieze decorating the room, with drawings of birds in each panel.

• Center right: Under the ceiling of the Hall of Deputies, there is a frieze painted between 1529 and 1534 by Hans Dürer, brother of the more famous Albrecht, in collaboration with Anton da Breslavia. On the walls hang tapestries woven between 1553 and 1571 in Brussels.

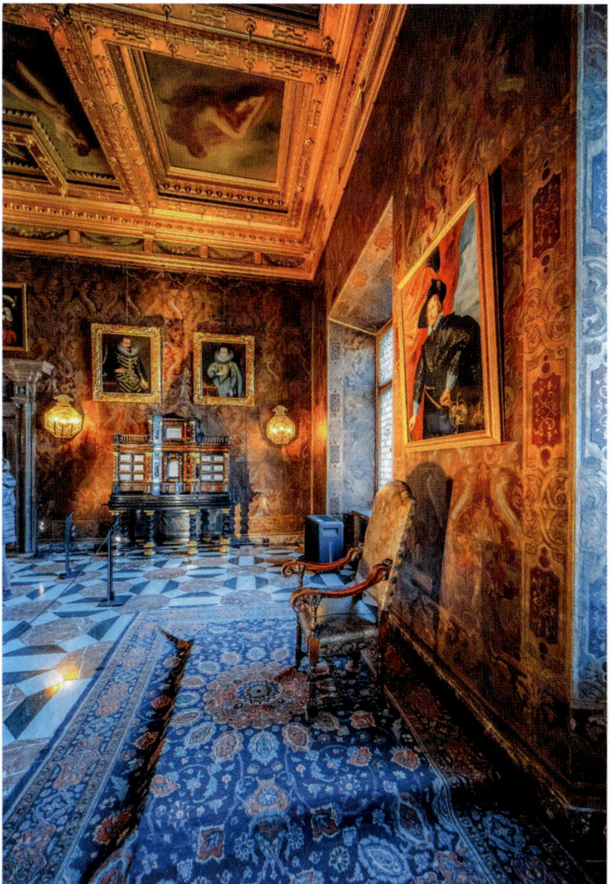

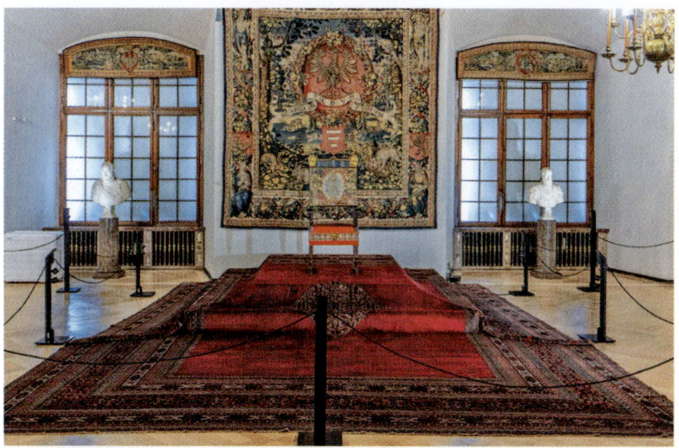

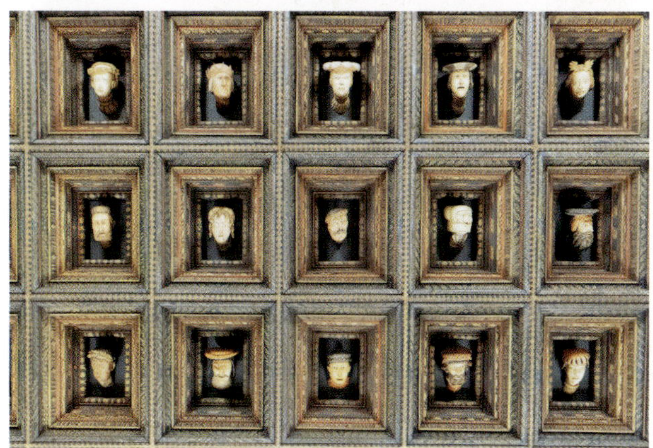

The castle tapestries

The centuries-old seat of kings and symbol of the Polish state, in 1930 the Castle became one of the country's most important museums, housing a valuable collection of paintings, sculptures, textiles, goldsmiths' work, weapons, porcelain, and furniture. Particularly valuable are the Jagiellonian tapestries, or Wawel tapestries, a collection originally comprising 365 pieces gathered by the kings of

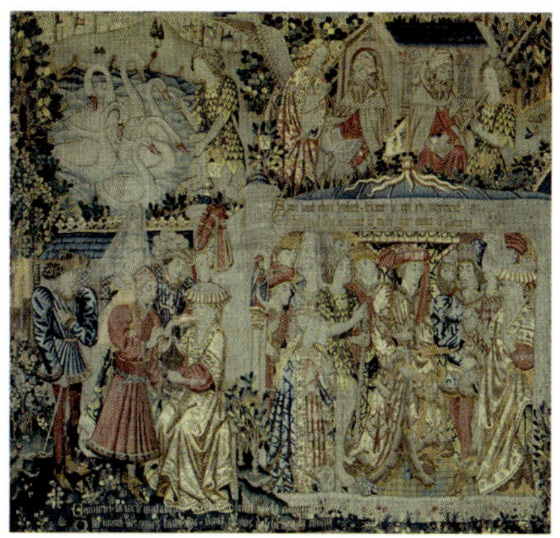

the dynasty to decorate the interior of the castle (but not only that, as hanging on the walls they also served to prevent the heat produced by the fireplaces from escaping). Today, 136 remain. The first tapestries, among which the History of the Knight of the Swan stands out, a masterpiece from the workshop of Pasquier Grenier in Turnai, Burgundy, were part of Bona Sforza's dowry. Others were commissioned by Sigismund I in Antwerp and Bruges, while others were ordered by Sigismund Augustus in Brussels between 1550 and 1560. Plundered in 1795 by the Russians, the collection was recovered in the 1920s.

• 179 bottom: The most interesting feature of the Hall of Deputies or Hall of Heads is the coffered wooden ceiling dating back to 1531–1535 and decorated with thirty polychrome heads of Polish kings.

PRAGUE CASTLE

882–884
On one of the hills overlooking Prague, Hradčany, Bořivoj I, founder of the Přemyslid dynasty, built the first nucleus of the future castle.

915–935
During the reign of Vratislaus I and his son Wenceslaus I, the castle became the seat of the Bishop of Prague. Two churches were built, St. George's and St. Vitus's Basilica.

1085
On June 15, Vratislaus II was crowned King of Bohemia. He chose Vysehrad as his royal residence instead of Hradčany Castle.

12th century
Soběslav I, son of Vratislav II, ordered the construction of the Romanesque part of the Royal Palace in Hradčany.

13th century
Ottokar II expanded the castle, turning it into a splendid royal residence (all of which was later lost).

1346–1378
After becoming King of Bohemia in 1347 and Holy Roman Emperor in 1355, Charles IV of Luxembourg gave a strong artistic and architectural boost to Prague and the Royal Palace, which became the imperial residence.

1378–1419
Charles IV's son, Wenceslas IV, continued the work of embellishing the Royal Palace in Prague, but it was abandoned after the Hussite Wars.

1471–1516
After becoming King of Bohemia in 1471, Vladislav II Jagiellon reestablished himself in Hradčany Castle. He ordered new fortifications, buildings, and rooms.

1526
With Ferdinand I of Habsburg, elected King of Bohemia in 1526, and Rudolf II, Prague became the capital of European culture and the castle was transformed into a Renaissance residence.

1649
At the end of the Thirty Years' War, the Habsburgs moved the capital to Vienna and Prague began an inexorable decline.

1753–1775
Maria Theresa of Austria commissioned court architect Nicolò Pacassi to rebuild the castle buildings in the neoclassical style.

1918–1993
After the founding of the Czechoslovak Republic in 1918, the castle became the seat of the head of state. In 1920, it was renovated by Jože Plečnik.

The first ruling dynasty of Bohemia was the Přemyslids. From the 10th century, the princes settled in a fortress perched on a hill overlooking the Vltava River in Vysehrad. On the other side of the river, there was another fortress on a hill called "Hradčany," a term that meant "Castle Quarter," but which also came to refer to the castle itself. It was only after the coronation of Vladislav II of Bohemia in 1140 that the Royal Palace began to gain importance, and Vyšehrad was abandoned within two centuries. More than a castle in the true sense of the word, Prague Castle is a complex of buildings added and renovated over the centuries. The complex includes the old and new Royal Palaces; St. Vitus Cathedral in the third courtyard; the basilica and monastery of St. George, the oldest building in the complex; the palaces belonging to the nobility, renovated in the 18th century; the Chapel of the Holy Cross, designed by Nicolò Pacassi in the second courtyard; and the Royal Gardens and the charming Golden Lane, with its small houses built against the rampart wall to house the castle guards and, during the reign of Rudolf II, the alchemists in search of the philosopher's stone. Today, apart from St. Vitus Cathedral, whose construction began under Charles IV in 1344 and was completed in the 19th century, and the Old Royal Palace with its famous Vladislav Hall, the buildings that make up the Castle all seem to belong to the same century, the 18th century, elegantly standardized by Maria Theresa of Habsburg's court architect Nicolò Pacassi in a sort of functional Classicism that anticipated the geometric rigor of Neoclassicism. The Romanesque part of the Royal Palace was mostly destroyed by frequent fires and sieges during the site's troubled history. However, something remains of the Renaissance castle.

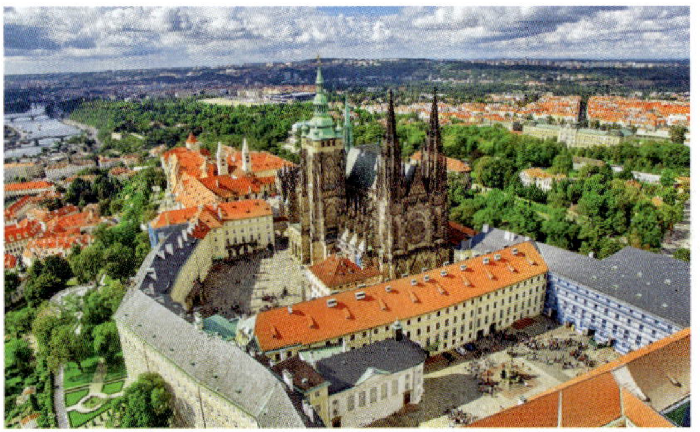

• 180 bottom: Aerial view of the Prague Castle complex. The photograph shows how the New Royal Palace, designed by Nicolò Pacassi, replaced the ramparts protecting St. Vitus Cathedral, located in the third courtyard.

• 181: In the background is Prague Castle and, behind it, the towering St. Vitus Cathedral. Until the end of World War I, the castle was the residence of the rulers of Bohemia, whose crown passed from the Premyslids to the House of Luxembourg and then, in 1471, to the Jagiellonian dynasty. The Habsburgs maintained power over Bohemia from 1526 to 1918, the year the Czechoslovak Republic was founded.

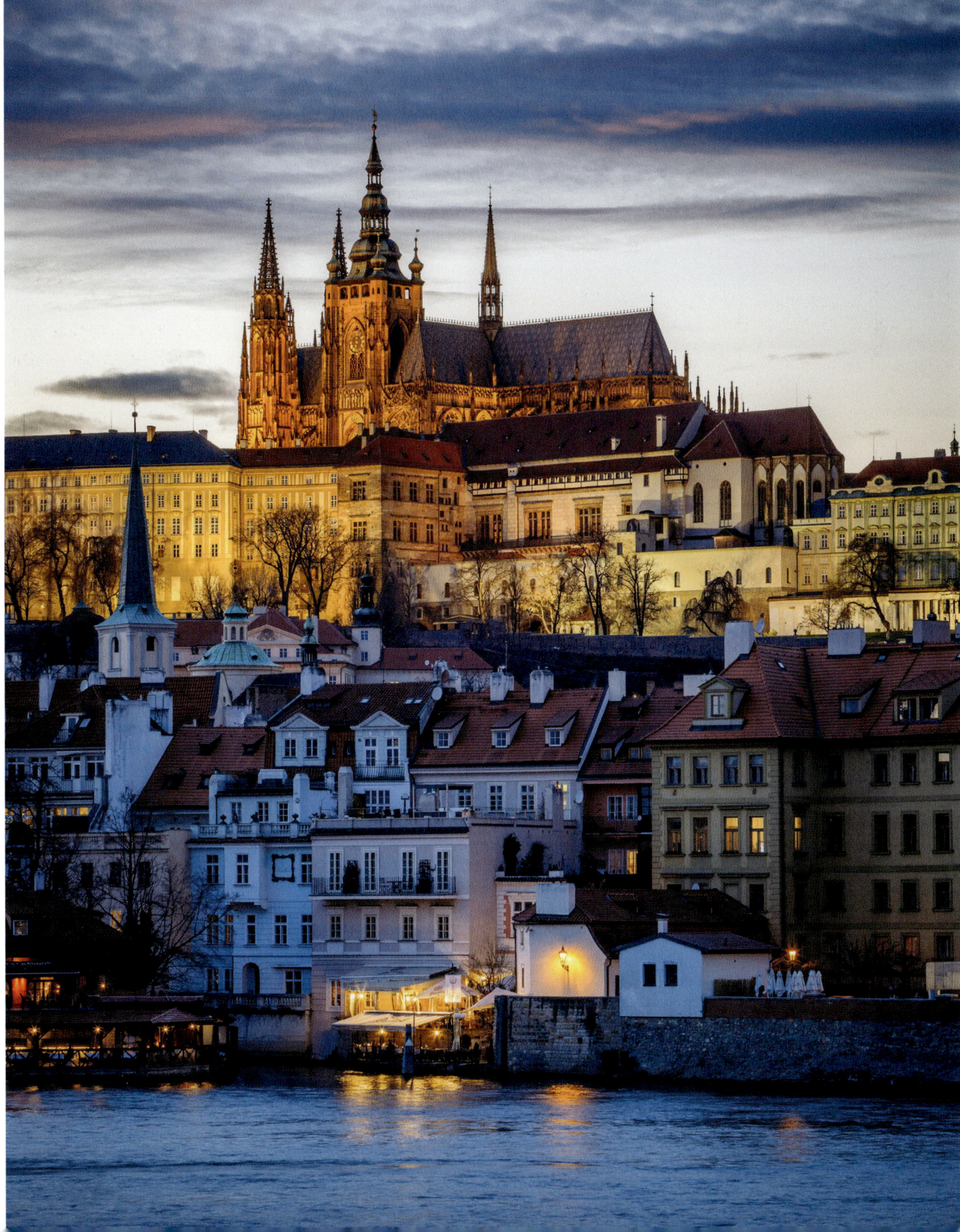

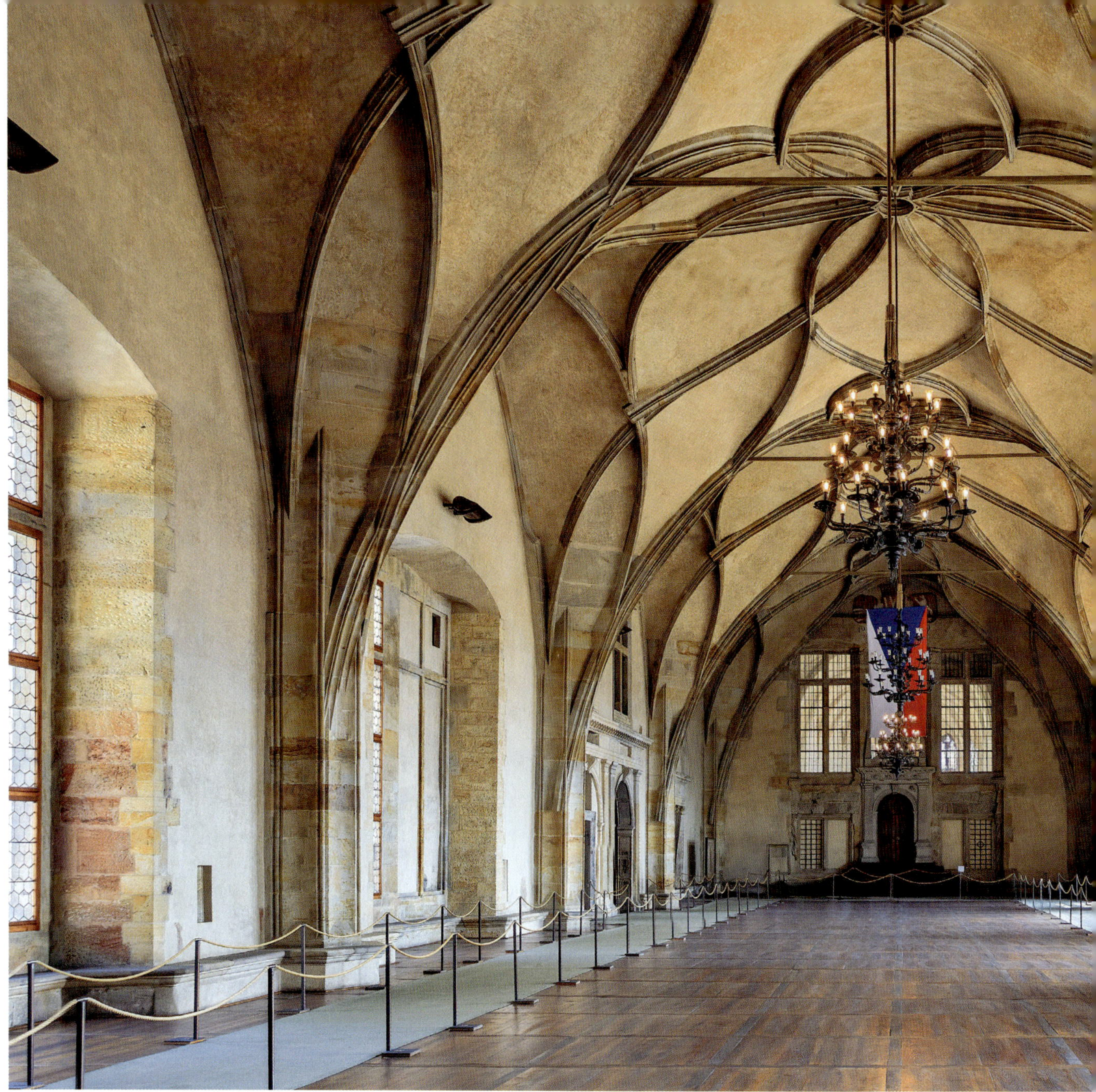

With the arrival of the Habsburgs on the imperial throne and in Bohemia, the most famous occupant of Prague Castle was Emperor Rudolf II, an avid collector and lover of art and science. After moving the capital from Vienna to Prague, he found himself having to rebuild the castle, which had been devastated by fire in 1541. The sovereign summoned architects and builders, mainly Italian, from Vienna to the court to turn the Royal Palace into a splendid residence. A new wing was built on the northern side of the castle, overlooking the Second Courtyard. On the ground floor were the stables for the magnificent Spanish horses (now used as exhibition spaces and to host temporary exhibitions); above them, between 1602 and 1606, the immense Spanish Hall was built, intended for large receptions, equestrian games, and musical and theatrical performances. The current appearance of the room is not what it was in the time of Rudolf II, when the ceiling was coffered, life-size terracotta and stucco statues by Adriaen de Vries were displayed in the niches, and the walls were decorated with pilasters and stucco reliefs, some of which have survived. The Hall, damaged during the Prussian bombing of Prague Castle in 1757, was restored by Nicolò Pacassi. Today it is part of the State Rooms and is used to receive official guests of the President of the Czech Republic.

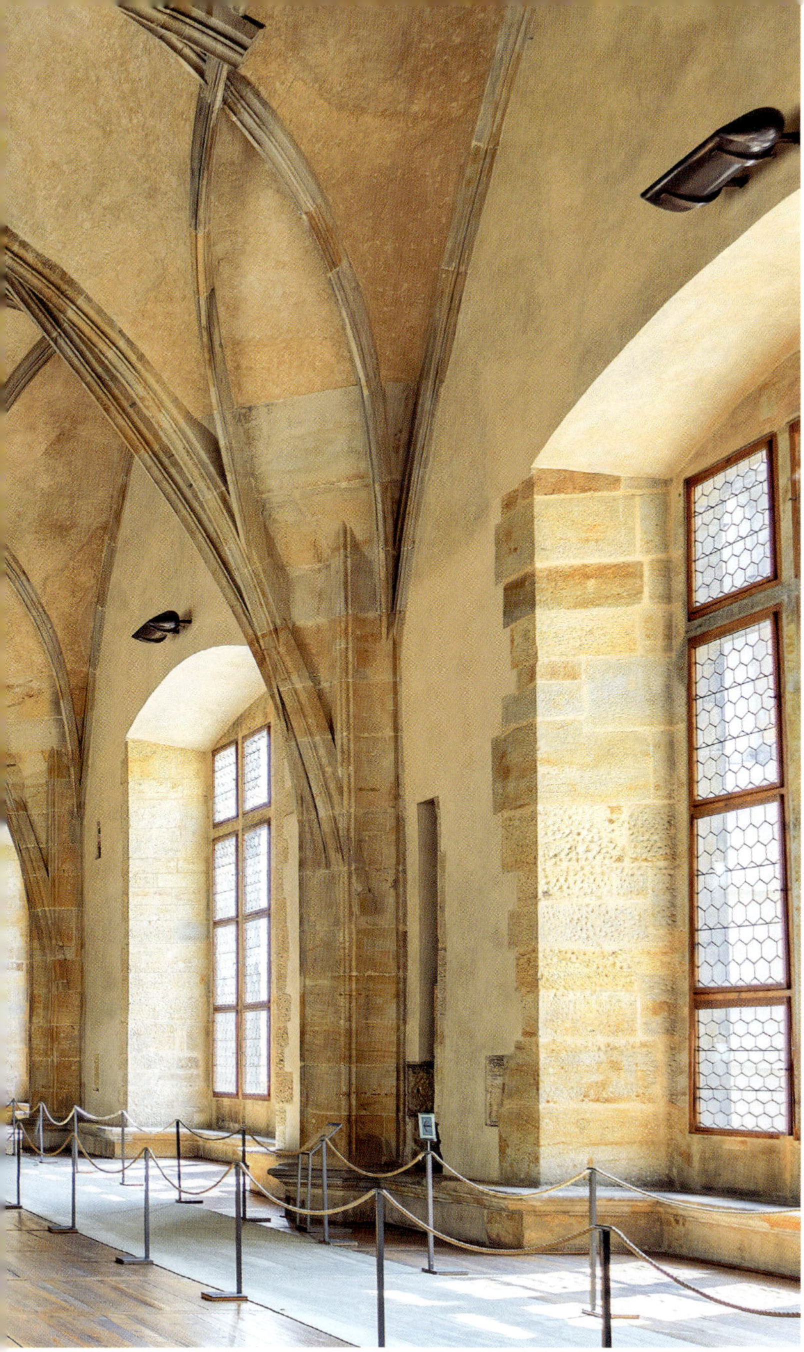

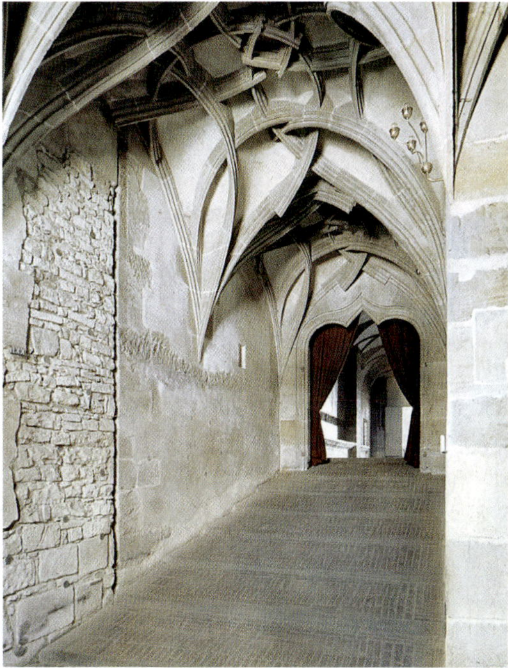

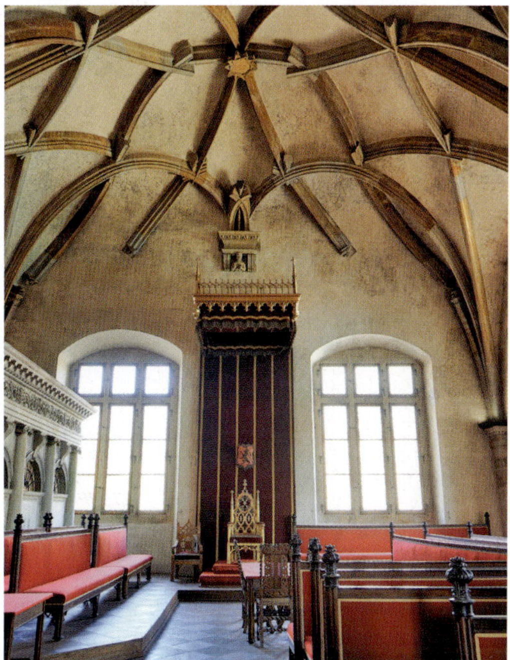

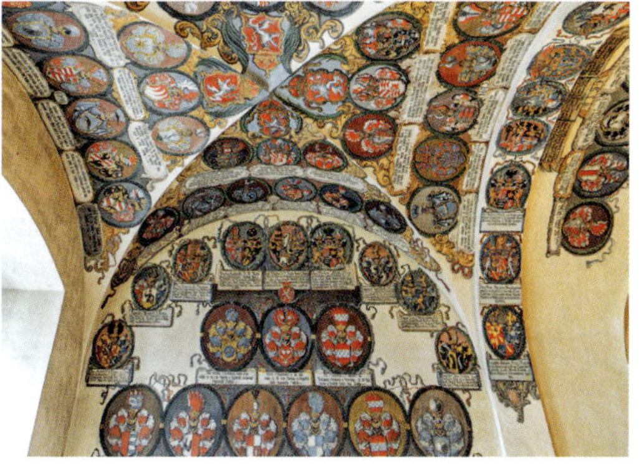

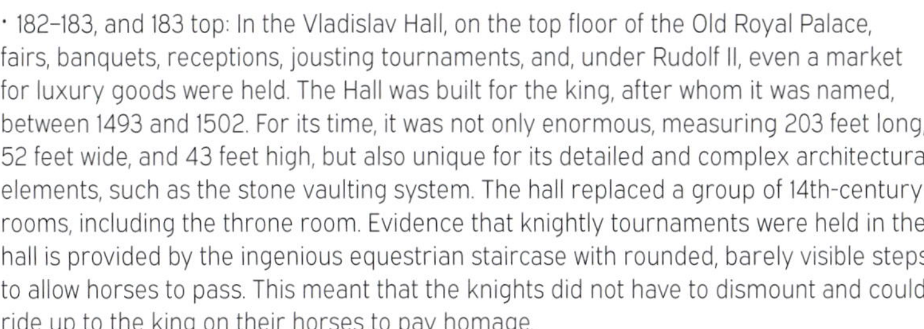

• 182–183, and 183 top: In the Vladislav Hall, on the top floor of the Old Royal Palace, fairs, banquets, receptions, jousting tournaments, and, under Rudolf II, even a market for luxury goods were held. The Hall was built for the king, after whom it was named, between 1493 and 1502. For its time, it was not only enormous, measuring 203 feet long, 52 feet wide, and 43 feet high, but also unique for its detailed and complex architectural elements, such as the stone vaulting system. The hall replaced a group of 14th-century rooms, including the throne room. Evidence that knightly tournaments were held in the hall is provided by the ingenious equestrian staircase with rounded, barely visible steps to allow horses to pass. This meant that the knights did not have to dismount and could ride up to the king on their horses to pay homage.

• 183 center: The Diet Hall with the throne and 19th-century furnishings is located in the north wing of the palace from the time of Wenceslas IV. Renovated by Vladislav II, it was destroyed by fire in 1541 and then rebuilt.

• 183 bottom: The spectacular ceiling of one of the four rooms of the New Land Registry. The coats of arms depicted are those of the officials who worked there from the 16th to the 18th centuries.

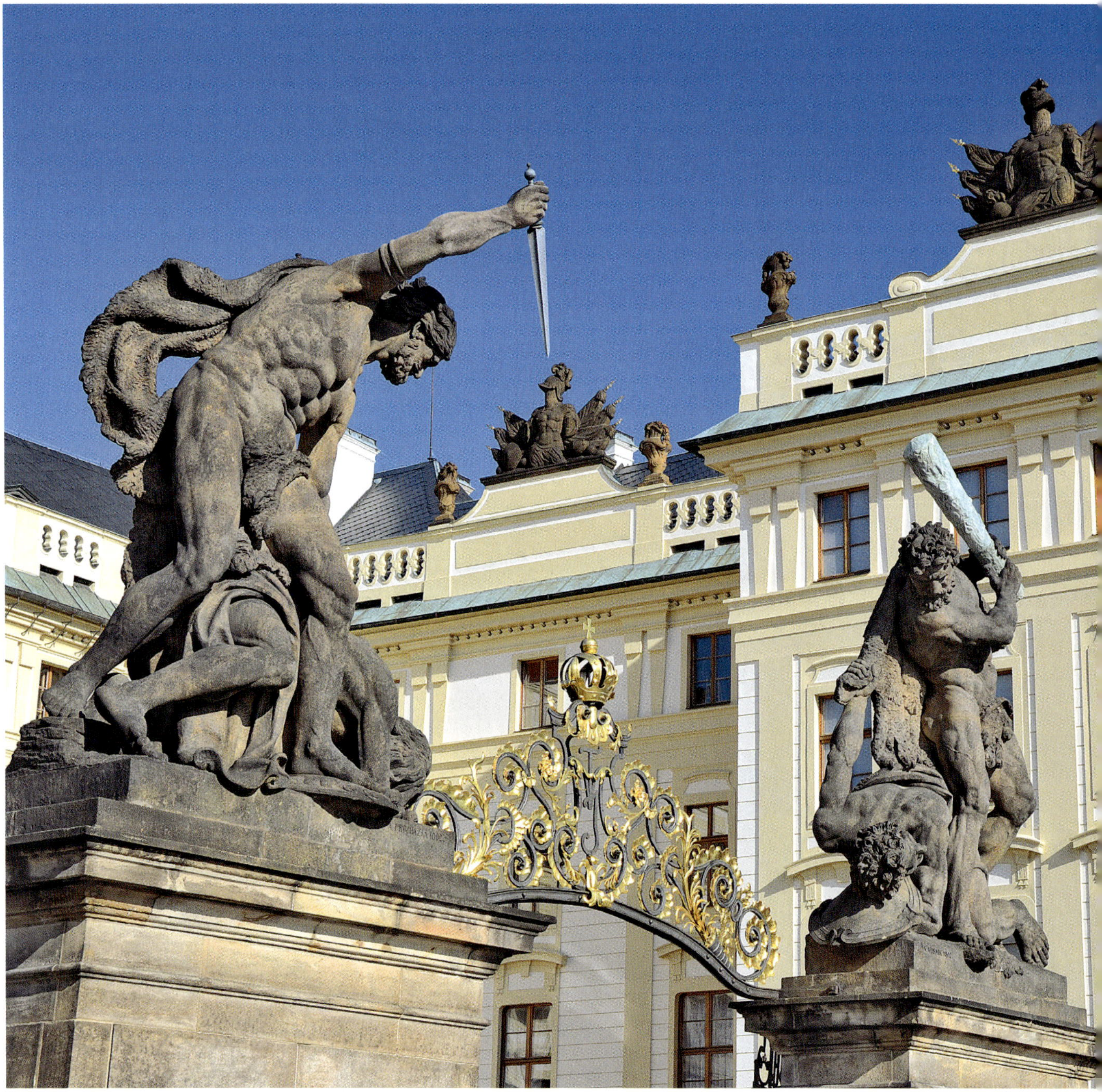

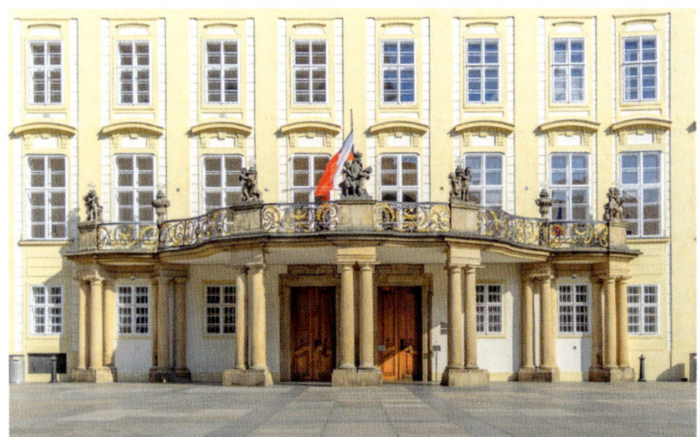

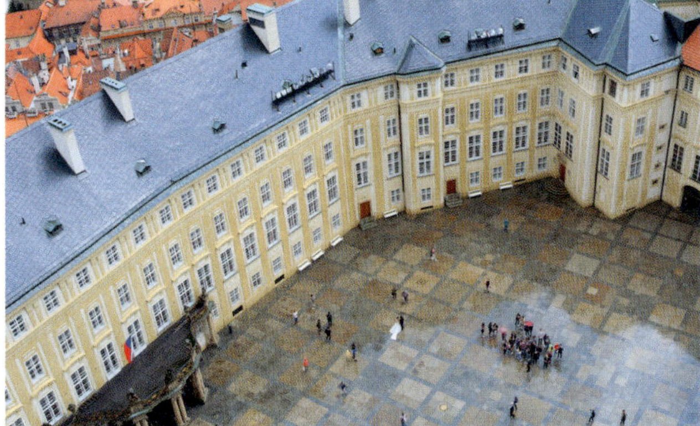

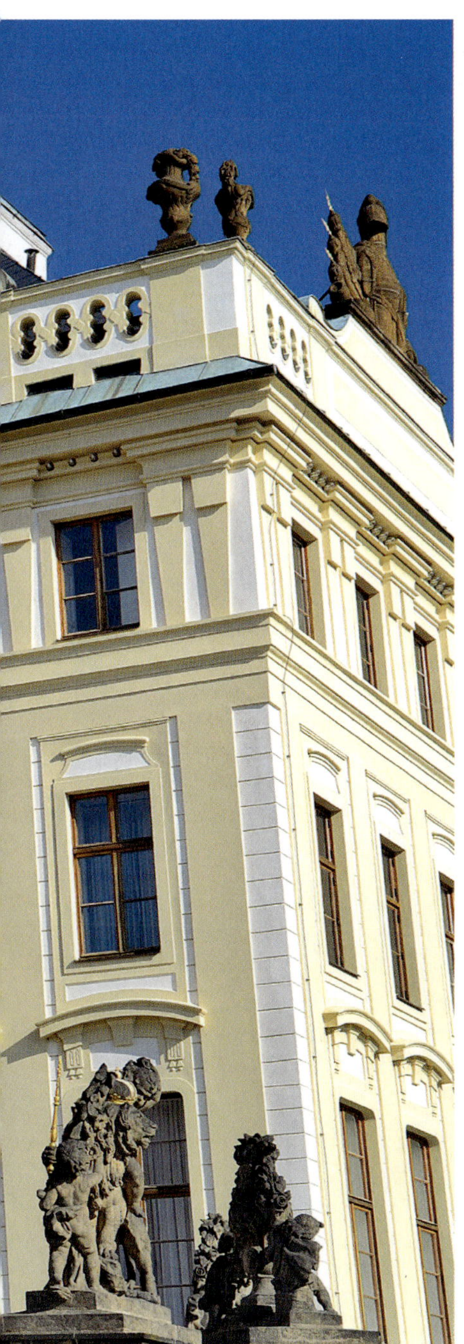

The successors of Rudolf II of the Habsburg dynasty added their own touches to the castle until the 17th century, when Leopold I laid the first stone for the Baroque completion of St. Vitus Cathedral in 1673. However, the most extensive work was carried out by Maria Theresa of Austria, who commissioned Nicolò Pacassi to unify the buildings facing the three courtyards of the castle complex, giving them a uniform and imposing appearance. In an area of the castle where residential buildings stood in the 13th century (destroyed by fire in 1541), the adjacent Rosemberg and Lobkowicz palaces are located: inside the complex, they overlook St. George's Square and, outside, the southern gardens. The former now hosts exhibitions and cultural events, while the neighboring Lobkowicz palace displays valuable works and objects that belonged to the family that still owns the palace. Among the most interesting pieces are works by Pieter Brueghel the Elder, Cranach, Velázquez, Canaletto, and Rubens. The collection also includes a library of rare books from Central Europe and a music archive that includes scores by Mozart, Beethoven, and Gluck. In the 20th century, the complex, which had fallen into decline, was restored and modernized by Jože Plečnik, the Slovenian architect who was commissioned to carry out the work. He was responsible for the granite monolith in the center of the third courtyard, erected in 1928 to celebrate the tenth anniversary of the Czech Republic.

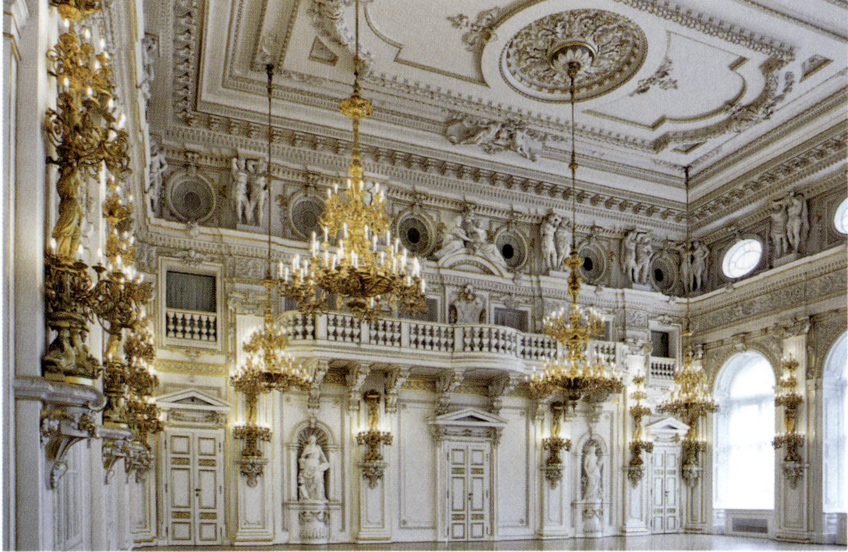

· 184–185: The Giants' Gate, so called because of the colossal statues copied from originals by Ignaz Platzer, leads to the First Courtyard.

· 184 bottom left: The façade of Rosenberg Palace. The flag of the Czech Republic, the same as that of Czechoslovakia, flies from the balcony.

· 184 bottom right: View from above of the Third Courtyard, showing the architectural uniformity of the buildings, designed by Nicolò Pacassi in the 18th century.

· 185 center: The Spanish Hall, dating back to the 17th century, was renovated several times in the 18th and 19th centuries, finally taking on a Baroque appearance much later than the style of the period in which Rudolf II had it built. The late-19th-century renovations were carried out in preparation for the coronation ceremony of Franz Joseph I as King of Bohemia, an event that never took place.

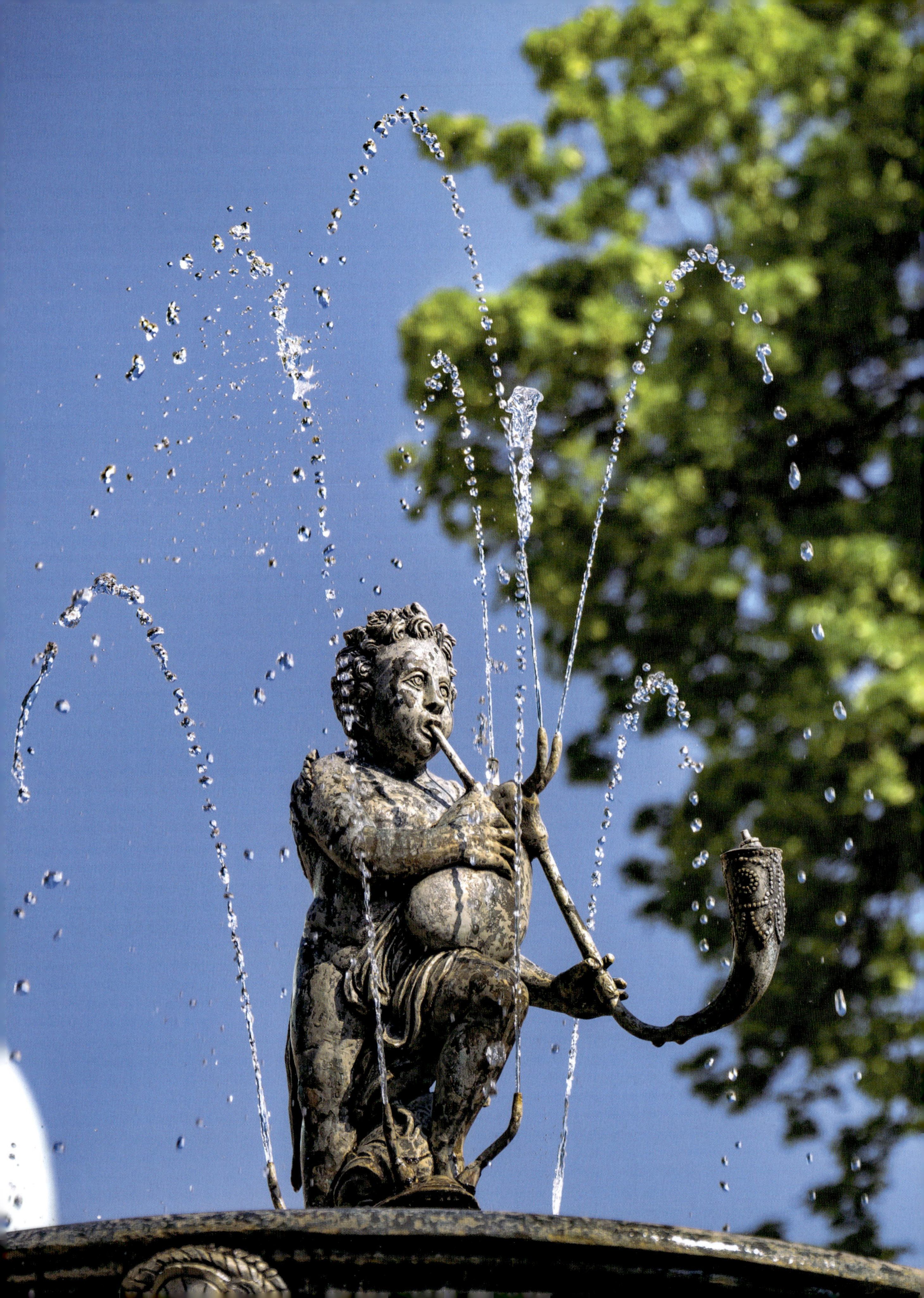

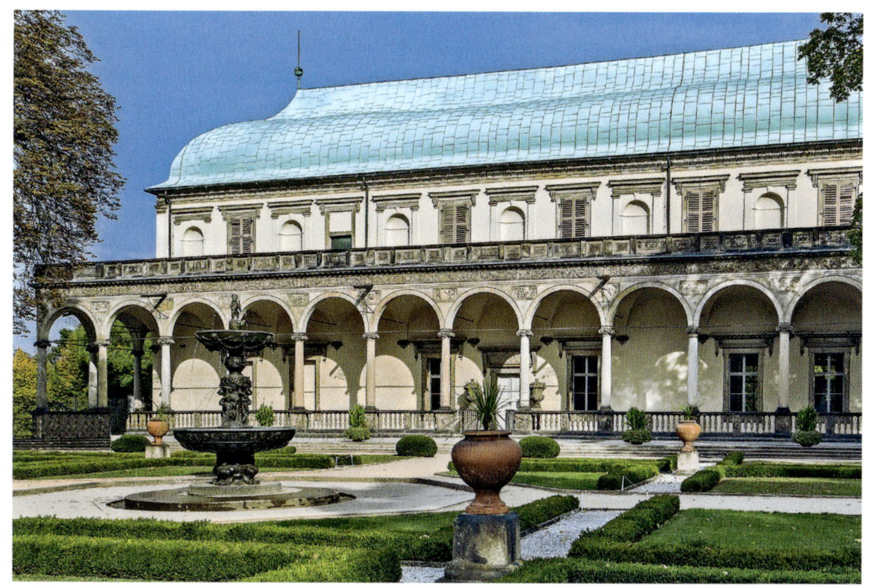

In the lush Royal Garden, separated from the Castle by the Deer Moat (originally built as a defensive barrier but transformed into a hunting reserve by Rudolf II), Italian Renaissance architecture bursts forth alongside nature. This green area was laid out by Ferdinand I of Habsburg in the first half of the 16th century on the site of medieval vineyards. The king also ordered the construction of a series of buildings for the entertainment of the court, including a pavilion—later converted into a ballroom—originally intended for the game of jeu de game, which was very popular at the time. The Belvedere Palace was also built in Renaissance style for his wife Anna Jagiellon. Rudolf II, motivated by his love of nature, also took an interest in the castle's grounds: he wanted a symmetrical Italian garden and had hundreds of trees, shrubs (including rare and unknown species), and boxwood bushes planted to form a maze. There was also a pheasantry, a menagerie for exotic animals, a pond, a riding school, a court for playing jeu de game, and even a sort of arena where Spanish courtiers could watch bullfights. The sovereign was also attracted by the idea of creating a hanging garden and consulted Vincenzo Gonzaga on this subject, asking him to send him the plans for the one he had designed for his palace in Mantua. The Belvedere Palace was used to house part of his art collection and as a study for the famous mathematician and astronomer Tycho Brahe.

• 186, and 187 top: In front of the Belvedere Pavilion is the Singing Fountain (Zpívající fontána), so called because the water produces a melodious sound as it falls into the copper basin. The Royal Gardens were famous for their variety of plants and flowers, including tulips, which were loved by Rudolf II and imported from Istanbul. From here, they were exported to Holland.

The menagerie fashion

Even before Ferdinand I had the Royal Gardens laid out, Bohemian kings kept lions—the animal that features prominently in their coat of arms. The first evidence dates back to 1280: a document reports that a Venetian merchant asked Wenceslaus II to pay the debt for a pair of lions. A century later, Charles IV even appointed a lion keeper, the custos leonum. The Prague menagerie enjoyed its golden age under Rudolf II, who enlarged the Royal Gardens to accommodate various animals in enclosures, cages, and pavilions. In 1592, 12 lions lived in the castle with an Indian keeper and, in 1599, according to reports, the first lion was born in the Czech lands. Rudolf II's magnificent menagerie was famous and, as was customary at the time, visitors from other kingdoms brought animals from their own countries as gifts to the emperor.

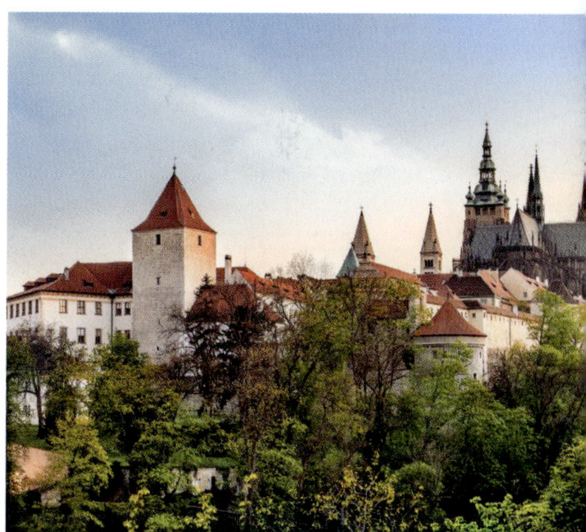

• 187 bottom: The Deer Moat beneath the castle, created during the reign of Ferdinand I as a defensive barrier. Rudolf II had it converted into a hunting reserve where, in addition to deer, other animals such as roe deer, elk, and perhaps even reindeer lived.

Eszterházy Castle

1720
Architect Anton Erhard Martinelli built a 22-room hunting lodge for Count József Eszterházy in Fertőd, the original nucleus of Eszterházy Castle.

1762
Upon the death of his brother Antal Pál Eszterházy, Nicholas I Eszterházy inherited the ducal title, becoming the fifth Prince Eszterházy.

1763
In the town of Fertőd, Prince Nicola I Eszterházy commissioned Johann Ferdinand Mödlhammer, and later Melchior Hefele, to build a sumptuous hunting lodge known as the "Hungarian Versailles."

1766
The Eszterházy Castle, not yet completed, was inhabited for the first time.

1768–1773
The castle's opera house was completed. The composer Franz Joseph Haydn lived, composed, and performed his concerts here until 1790. Five years later, work on the puppet theater was also completed.

1784
With the construction of the monumental fountain at the entrance to the complex, the Eszterházy Castle was completed.

In the town of Fertőd, approximately 124 miles west of Budapest, stands what is known as the "Hungarian Versailles," a sumptuous palace, one of the most magnificent examples of Hungarian Rococo architecture, built by Prince Nicholas I Eszterházy in the second half of the 18th century as a summer residence and hunting lodge for his family, who lived permanently in Vienna. The Eszterházy dynasty was one of the oldest Hungarian families, whose roots dated back to the 13th century, and had always been linked to the Habsburgs, of whom they had been a loyal and valuable ally. In 1623, Prince Miklós Eszterházy (1583-1645) and his private army pushed back the Turkish army on the banks of the Nyitra River, setting an example for other nobles eager to replicate his exploits. They also sided with the emperor during the Thirty Years' War, the Napoleonic Wars, and even when the Hungarian War of Independence broke out in 1848. Rewards in terms of wealth, titles, and honors were not long in coming, making the Eszterházy family the most powerful aristocratic family in the nation. It is therefore not surprising that when Nicholas I, who detested the formal life of Vienna, decided to build himself a luxurious retreat in Fertőd, transforming the hunting lodge that had been built by his grandfather in 1720 to a design by Anton Erhard Martinelli, he spared no expense: the prince spent 13 million guilders or Austrian florins. In order to build the palace on solid foundations, it was necessary to reclaim the marshy land on which it was to stand. Partially habitable as early as 1766, Prince Nicholas I held court in the Eszterházy Palace for most of the year, organizing grand hunts in the reserve surrounding the castle—which was guarded, it is said, by 150 bodyguards in the prince's pay. However, the residence soon became not only a popular place of entertainment for the Hungarian aristocracy, but also an important cultural and musical center with a library that still contains 22,000 volumes and a gallery that housed about 650 paintings, including Raphael's "Madonna Eszterházy" (1508), the court theater inaugurated in 1768 by Franz Joseph Haydn with the opera "Lo speziale" ("The Apothecary"), and a puppet theater whose construction was completed in 1773. In 1781, on the occasion of a grand concert by Haydn held on May 30 in the Sala Terrena, the guests included Archduchess Maria Christina of Habsburg with her husband, Duke Albert of Saxony-Teschen. The golden age ended with the death of the prince in 1790, and it was not until the early 20th century that another Eszterházy, Nicholas IV, took up residence within those walls. He and his wife, the beautiful Margit Cziraky, devoted themselves to renovating the castle and gardens. At the beginning of the 20th century, the park was rebuilt in the style of the time. After World War II, in 1945, the castle was expropriated by the state. Today, after extensive restoration, it has been reopened to the public and hosts exhibitions and cultural events.

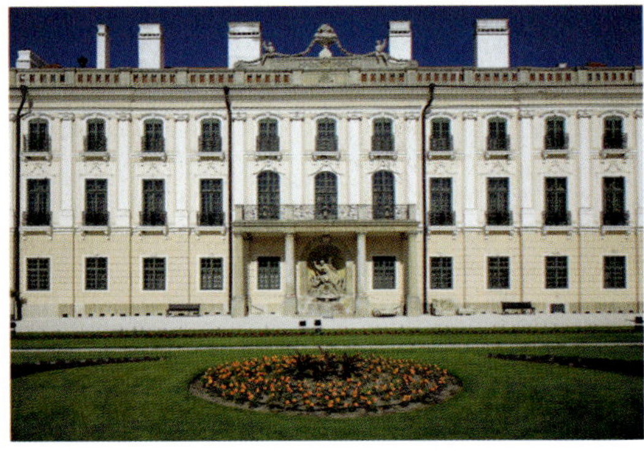

• 188 bottom: The Eszterházy Castle in Fertőd was designed by Johann Ferdinand Mödlhammer, who was replaced in 1765 by Melchior Hefele. Although the building initially seems to have been modeled on the Palace of Versailles, the result shows many similarities with Schönbrunn Palace in Vienna.

• 189: The Eszterházy park, which extends on three sides, dates back to the first half of the 18th century with a typical Baroque garden with a geometric layout dotted with statues. In the second half of the century, it was transformed into a hunting park extending over an axis almost 1.3 miles long.

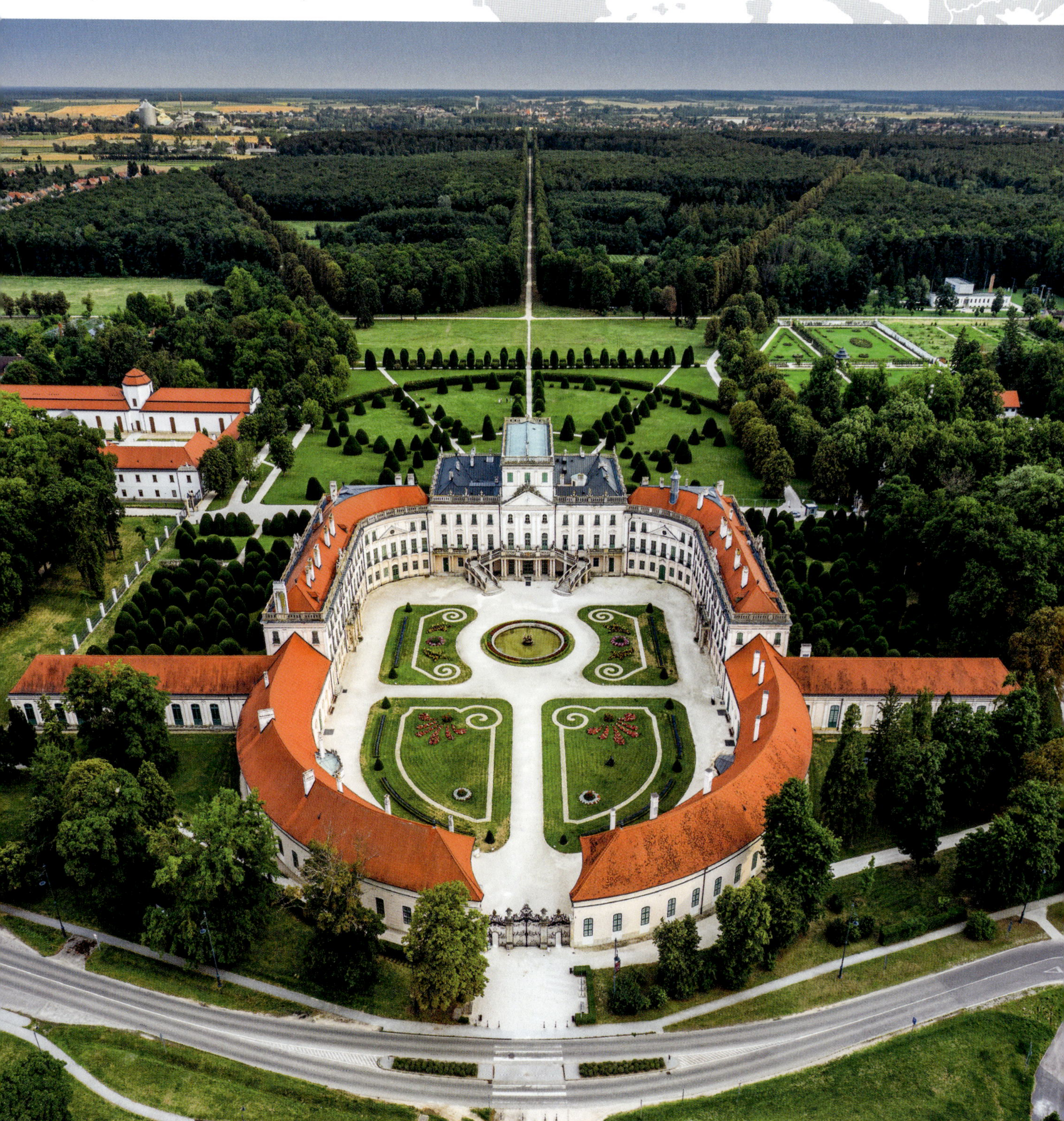

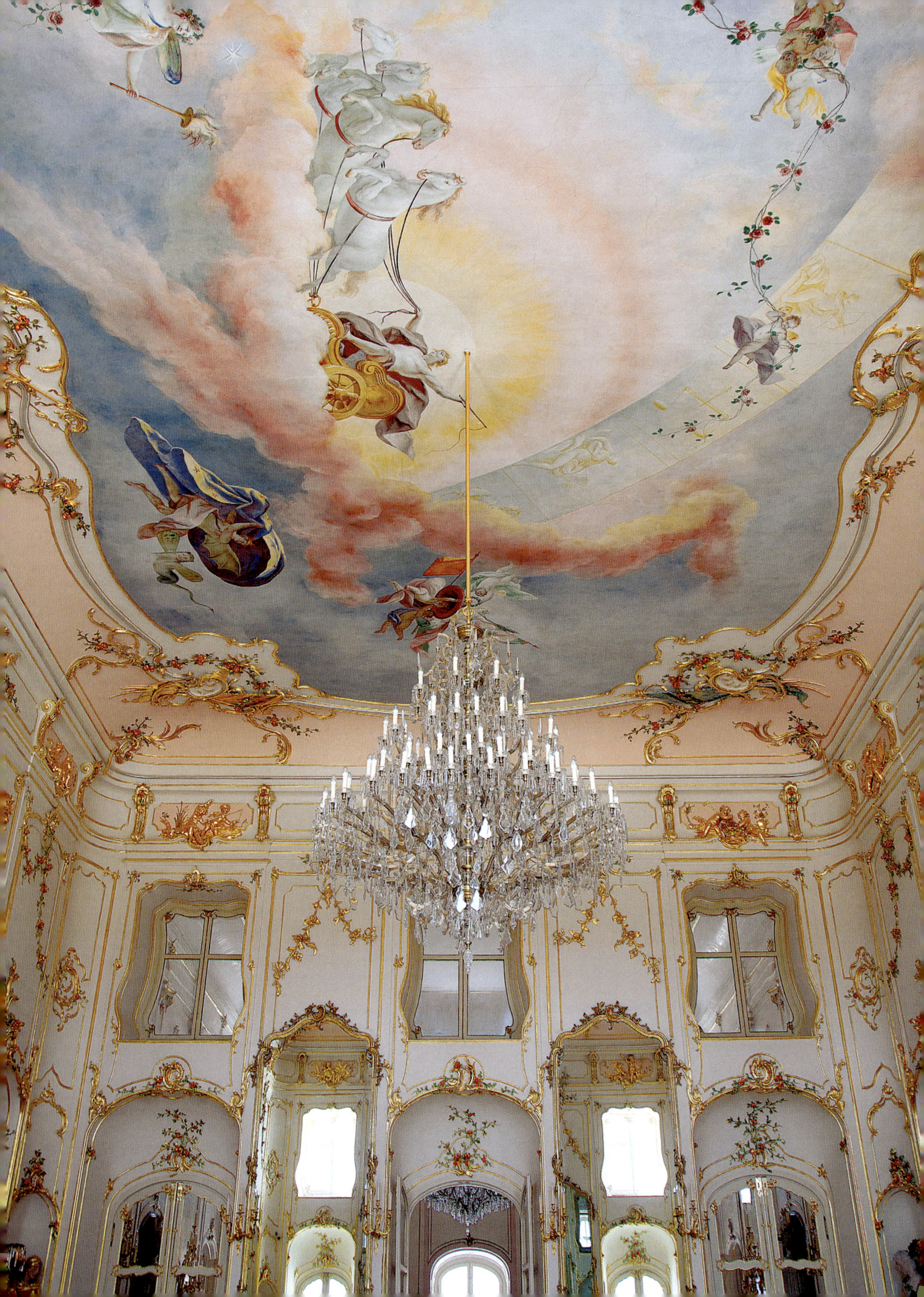

• 190: The rich rocaille decoration in gilded stucco adorning the hall of the Eszterházy Palace is reminiscent of the state rooms of Schönbrunn Palace.

• 191 top: Among the 126 rooms of the palace, the largest is the Sala Terrena, designed in the form of a grotto with a vaulted ceiling, originally decorated with dancing angels carrying E-shaped garlands of flowers, a reference to the owner's name.

• 191 center: The Great Hall of the Esterházy Palace was built by Prince Paul I Esterházy in the second half of the 17th century to a design by architect Carlo Martino Carlone. It is decorated in the Baroque style; the subjects of the ceiling frescoes are an apology of the Esterházy family. Renovated at the end of the 18th century with the neoclassical restructuring of the palace, it is still used today as a concert hall due to its excellent acoustics. Since the 20th century, it has been called the "Haydn Hall" in honor of the composer who lived at court for thirty years.

• 191 bottom: In the image, Franz Joseph Haydn in a 1792 portrait by Thomas Hardy, kept at the Royal College of Music Museum in London.

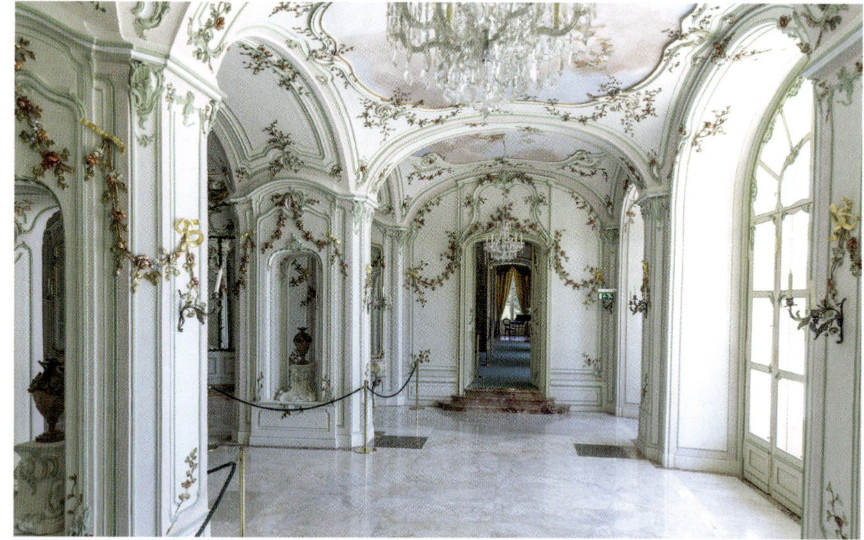

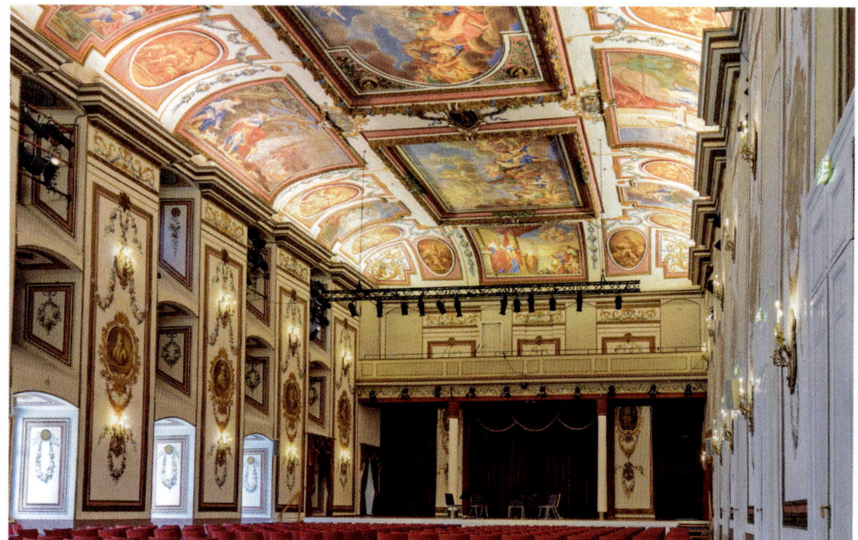

Music at court

Between 1766 and 1790, German composer Franz Joseph Haydn lived at the court of the Eszterházy family. In Fertőd, he had a four-room apartment in the servants' quarters, and it was within those walls that he wrote most of his symphonies, which he conducted himself in the court theater in the presence of numerous guests. The theater, unfortunately destroyed by fire in 1779, could seat up to 400 spectators. In the quiet of this isolated place, the composer wrote up to a hundred works a year, but, as he wrote to his Viennese musician friend Marianne von Genzinger, sometimes the isolation of the place and the distance from everything weighed heavily on him. This melancholic feeling was also reflected in his music, as was the case in 1772 when he staged the Farewell Symphony, dedicated to Prince Nicholas I. During the performance of the final adagio, the musicians took turns stopping playing, extinguishing the candles on their music stands and leaving the hall, leaving only two violins, played by Haydn himself and the first violinist Luigi Tomasini, to finish the concert. It was a message to the prince, who had prolonged his stay at the castle of Fertőd beyond measure, and the members of the orchestra were eager to return to their families.

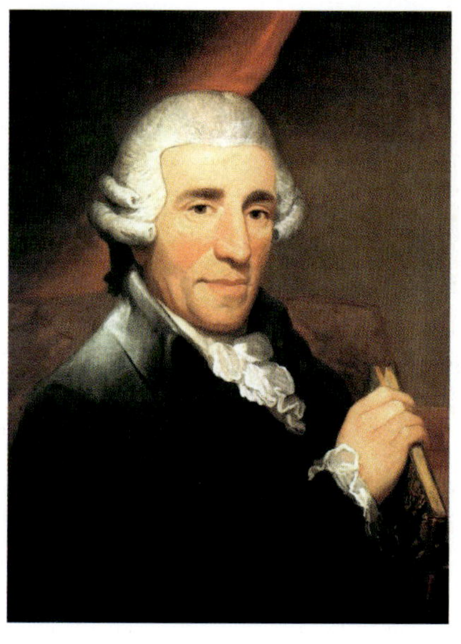

BRAN CASTLE

1211–1226
The Teutonic Knights built a wooden fortress to defend the border of Transylvania and control the passage of merchants. The structure was abandoned in 1226.

1377–1388
Louis I of Hungary granted the people of Brașov permission to build a stone fortified structure at their own expense, which would later become Bran Castle.

1407
The manor was ceded by the King of Hungary, Sigismund of Luxembourg, to Mircea I of Wallachia. The property subsequently passed to the princes of Transylvania and served as a bulwark against attacks by the Ottoman Empire.

1448
The voivode (prince) of Wallachia, Vlad III, gained control of Bran Castle. From there, in 1459, he attacked Brașov and its surroundings and ruled with cruelty. Upon his death, the castle was given to the inhabitants of Brașov and abandoned.

1651
The prince of Transylvania, György II Rákóczi, bought the castle.

18th–19th centuries
Despite being restored on two occasions, the castle remained largely uninhabited for two centuries.

1920
After the union of Transylvania with Romania on December 1, 1918, Bran Castle passed to the sovereigns of the Kingdom of Romania, who used it as a summer residence until 1932. Queen Marie of Romania, wife of King Ferdinand I, began major restoration work.

1948
The communist government nationalized the castle: the Romanian royal family was forced into exile and their residence was turned into a museum.

2009
After lengthy negotiations, the entire property was returned to the heirs of the Romanian royal family.

Located on the border between Transylvania and Wallachia in Romania, the eerie Bran Castle has always been considered the home of Prince Vlad III, who lived there in the 15th century and was identified four centuries later as the character Dracula in the namesake novel by Bram Stoker (1847–1912); in truth, the voivode—a title corresponding to a prince—only visited the castle occasionally as an outpost to control the borders and, according to some studies, may have spent a period there imprisoned by Matthias Corvinus before being taken to Visegrád where, from 1462, he remained for 12 years. However, it is not surprising that the manor, and Transylvania, inspired the imagination of the Irish writer and, before him, that of Jules Verne (1828–1905). Although neither of them had ever set foot in Romania, they drew on ideas that had spread in the 18th century, according to which Eastern Europe was an area where the most disturbing legends about the undead, vampires, and werewolves could find a basis in a fascinating, if distressing, truth. The little-known nature of Transylvania and the presence of isolated castles and fortresses that were in a state of neglect at the end of the 19th century seemed perfect for setting Gothic novels. Thus, through the words of Bram Stoker and, 100 years later, in the images shot by director Francis Ford Coppola, Bran Castle became the symbol of Transylvania. The history of the manor began in 1211 when a first fortified outpost was built by the Teutonic Knights, on the orders of King Andrew II of Hungary (1326–1382), to control the border between the historic regions of Wallachia and Transylvania from incursions by the Cumans and Pechenegs. More than a century later, in 1377, the Saxons of Kronstadt (Brașov) obtained permission from King Louis I to build a real castle, which became an important defensive stronghold during the Ottoman invasions. It also served as a customs post for merchants: 3% of goods passing in and out of Transylvania were retained. In addition to the lord of the castle elected by the king from among the Saxons, soldiers and mercenaries also resided in Bran castle. In 1419, King Sigismund of Luxembourg entrusted the castle to the princes of Transylvania, and it was one of them, John Hunyadi, who stopped the Turks in 1442. It was during those years that the legend arose that Bran Castle was the home of the ruthless Dracula: during his second reign (1456–1462), Vlad III attacked the Saxons of Brașov, who were demanding ever higher customs duties and supporting his rival to the throne. The attack was terrible: the Impaler burned the suburbs of the city and killed hundreds of Saxons. In the following centuries, the castle fell into ruin despite attempts at restoration.

The oldest part, which has remained fairly faithful to the medieval original, corresponds to the ground floor, which

• 193: Bran Castle (the word "bran" in Slavic translates as "gate"), guarded to the east by the Bucegi Mountains and to the west by the Piatra Craiului massif, dominates the Burzenland landscape from an inaccessible rocky hill. It is likely that Bram Stoker saw an illustration of the manor in the book "Transylvania: Its Products and Its People," written in the mid-19th century by Charles Boner. This explains why the description of the castle in his novel, where part of the story takes place, is so similar.

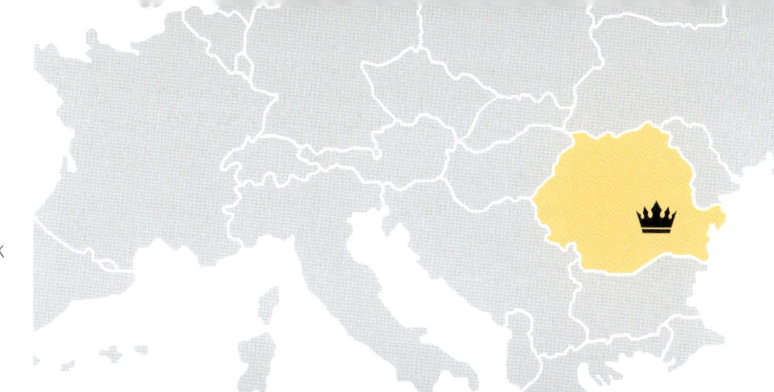

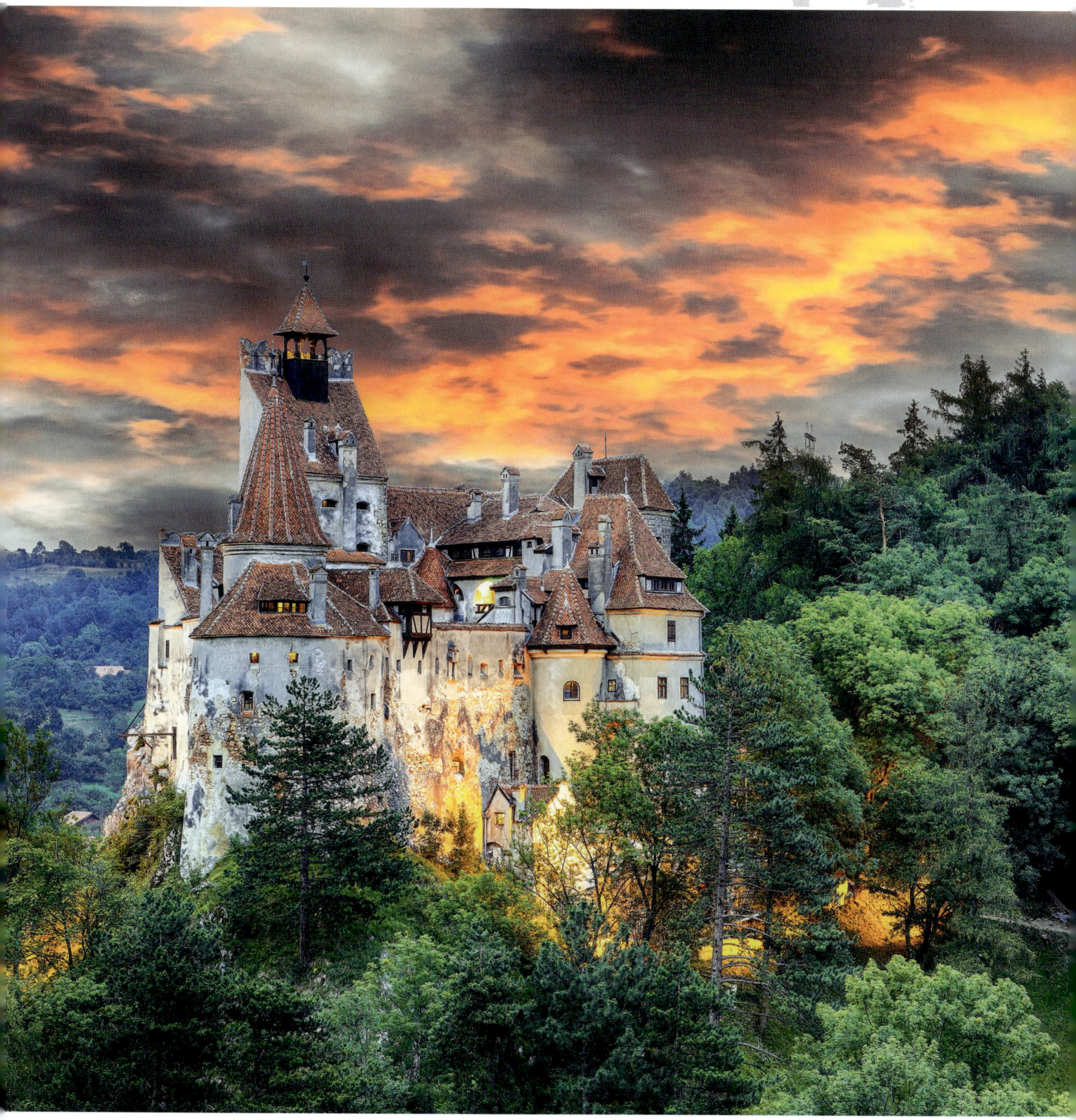

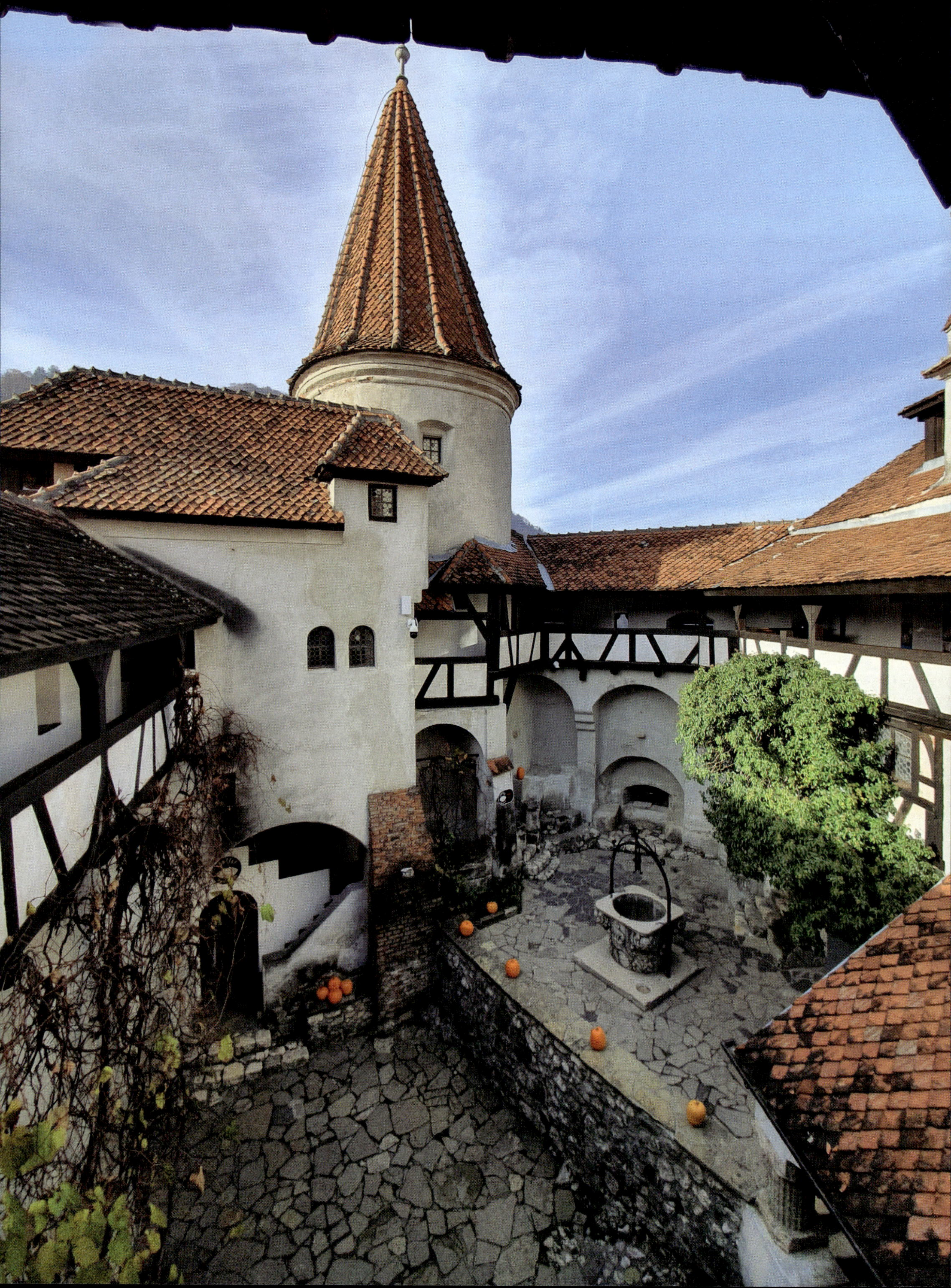

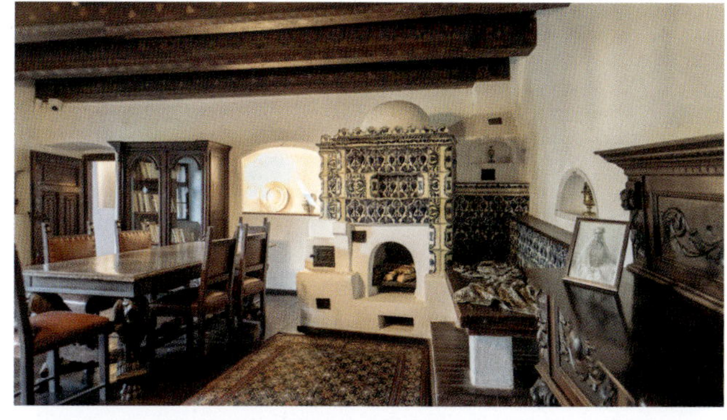

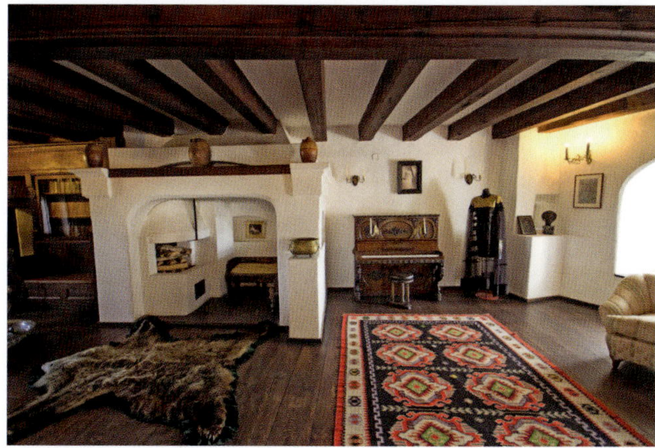

• 194: The castle has four floors with a series of corridors, rooms, and halls. The ground floor is the one that has best preserved its medieval appearance. The guard room, where the soldiers were stationed, leads to the courtyard, in the center of which there is a fake well made from a 19th-century capital.

• 195 top: The castle's dining room, which was restored and decorated by Czech architect Karel Líman between 1920 and 1932 at the behest of Queen Maria.

• 195 center: The cozy Music Room, much loved by Queen Maria of Romania, who, upon receiving the castle as a gift from the city of Brașov in 1920, made it her favorite residence.

was used for servants and guards, and the courtyard. In 1920, after Transylvania became part of Greater Romania, the city of Brașov donated the castle to Queen Maria, who transformed it into a residence for the royal family, restoring it and tastefully furnishing it with furniture collected from all over Europe, mixing eras and styles, works of art, carpets, and precious objects. Upon her death in 1938, the castle passed to her youngest daughter Ileana (1909–1991). During World War II, it was the princess herself who transformed the castle into a military hospital. After 1945, Bran was used to treat the wounded and maimed of war, but also the population of the region. Ileana herself cared for the patients as a nurse until 1948 when, along with the rest of the royal family, she was forced by the newly established Communist regime to leave Romania and take refuge first in Switzerland and then in the United States, where she took her vows in 1961. The castle was nationalized in 1948 and only after a long legal battle in 2009 was it returned to the descendants of the royal family, who have made it one of the most visited attractions in the country.

Legend and reality

The second of four brothers, the future "Impaler" was born into the noble family of Vlad II, who in 1428 had joined the Order of the Dragon ("drac" in Hungarian): for this reason he was called "Dracul," and his son "Vlad Draculea," son of Dracula. The terrifying nickname "Dracula" derives from a misunderstanding: since dragons did not exist in Romanian mythology and the term dracul meant "devil," Vlad III became "son of the devil" in Romanian. From Sighișoara, where he was born, Vlad became involved in a series of vicissitudes, forging alliances with the Ottomans, the Saxons, and the voivode of Transylvania, John Hunyadi. He managed to seize control of Wallachia, which had been lost a few years earlier, and showed himself for what he was: a bloodthirsty man. His first enemies were the Ottomans, against whom he launched a series of crusades. Other victims of his ferocity were his subjects who were reluctant to submit: it was particularly against the boyars and Saxons of Brașov that Vlad waged a campaign of terror, carrying out sadistic executions intended to deter any revolts; he preferred impalement to all other forms of torture, hence his nickname Tepeș. At the end of 1476 or early 1477, Vlad III died in battle against the Ottomans. His head was cut off and sent to Constantinople as a trophy. The location of his burial remains unknown. Printed engravings based on the accounts of those who managed to escape have revealed some of Vlad III's atrocities. One of the most widespread anecdotes tells of how the voivode ate his meals surrounded by his impaled victims, showing a macabre indifference. There are reports of children being killed, torture, prolonged agony, and people being burned alive.

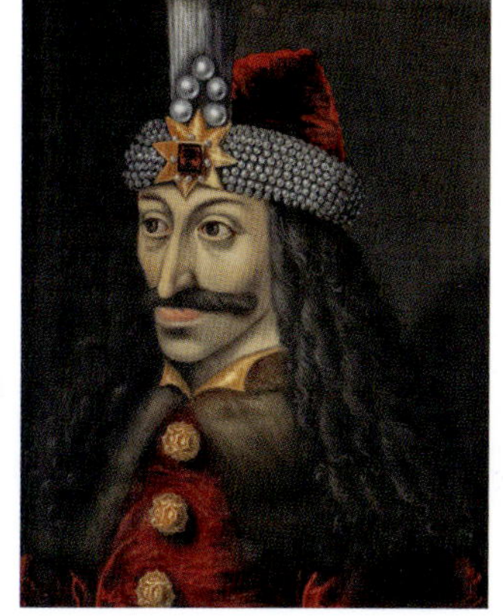

• 196–197: The imposing Topkapi complex overlooks the Golden Horn. In the center, the Tower of Justice, the tallest building in Topkapi, rises above the roofs and domes. It is located in the second courtyard or Council Square, between the entrance to the harem and the Kubbealti or Diwan, the stone-porticoed building where the sultan's council met.

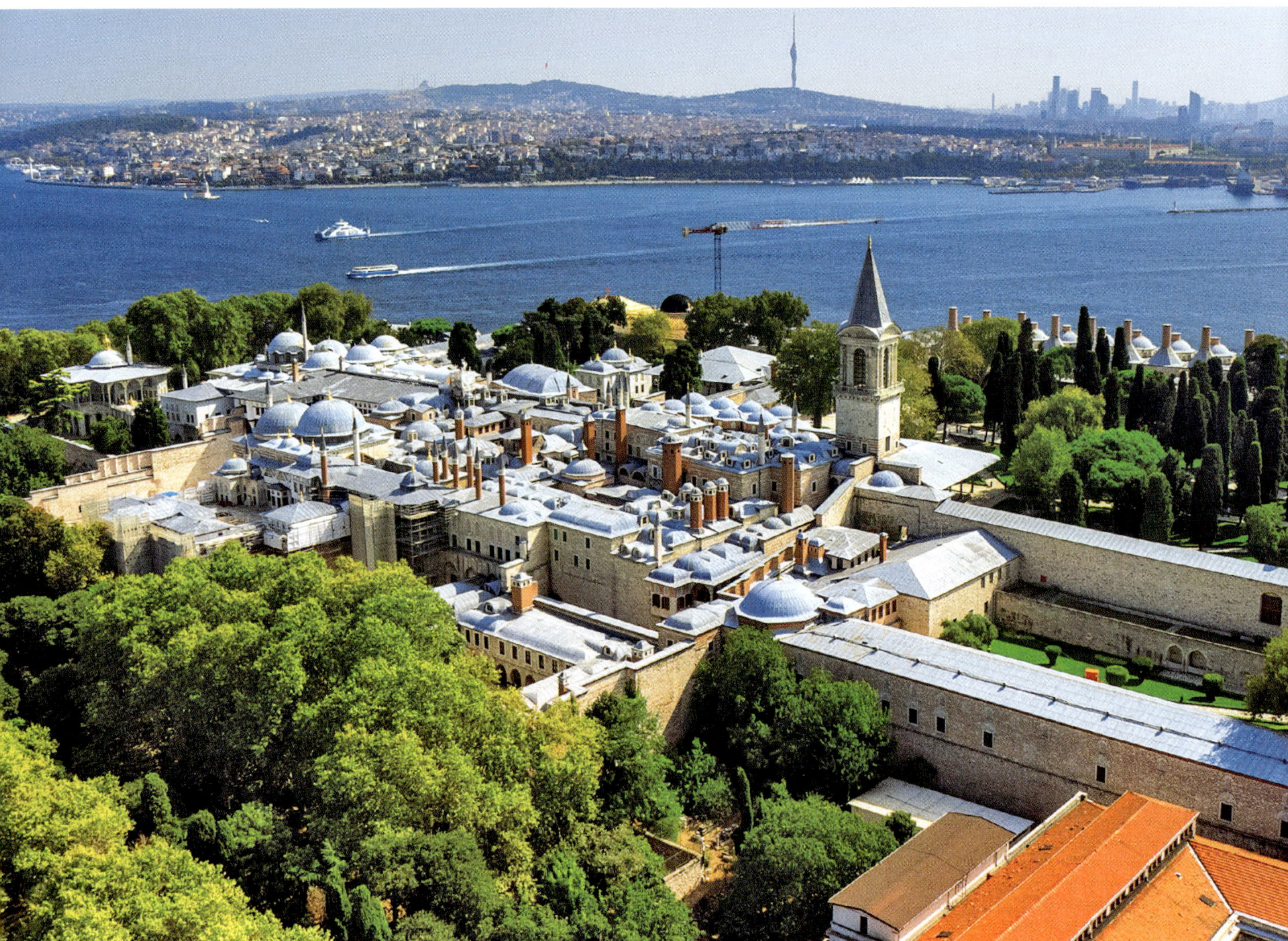

The Topkapi complex, surrounded by fortified walls with 28 watchtowers and consisting of a series of pavilions, courtyards, and gardens, was a veritable imperial citadel with thousands of inhabitants, but with a heart that was almost inaccessible beyond the last gate, the Gate of Happiness. The first nucleus of the palace, inhabited for four centuries by the Ottoman sultans, was built by Mehmed II the Conqueror, who began work a few years after the fall of Constantinople, the ancient capital of the Eastern Roman Empire, which took the name Istanbul in 1453. Over time, the various sultans who succeeded one another had the palace enlarged to accommodate the ever-increasing number of residents, including guards, dignitaries, concubines, eunuchs, servants, and kitchen staff. The result is a complex with buildings erected in different styles. Until the 16th century, architects adapted to the Turkish-Ottoman style, while the buildings added later were influenced by European styles. At least a dozen pavilions, dwellings, and other buildings disappeared in the 19th century. The part of the complex closest to the sea was demolished to make way for the Sirkeci railway sta-

TOPKAPI PALACE

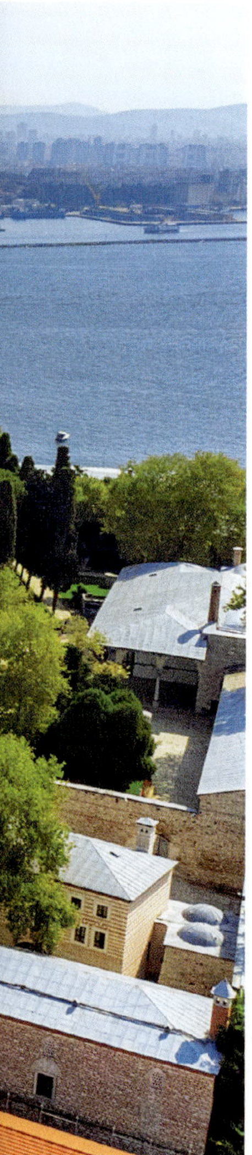

tion, the terminus of the Orient Express, which opened in 1890. The Ottoman sultans resided at Topkapi until 1856, when Abdülmecid I moved the imperial residence to the new Dolmabahçe Palace on the European shore of the Bosphorus. The visit to the complex—designed to become progressively more impenetrable as one enters its innermost and most private areas—begins at the monumental Imperial Gate (Bab-i Hümayun) located behind the Hagia Sophia. Only viziers, foreign ambassadors, and religious authorities were allowed to pass through it on horseback and then continue through the First Courtyard, or Arms Square, towards the Central Gate (Orta Kapi); all other visitors were forced to enter on foot. The selected few who had been given permission by the guards to cross the first courtyard on horseback

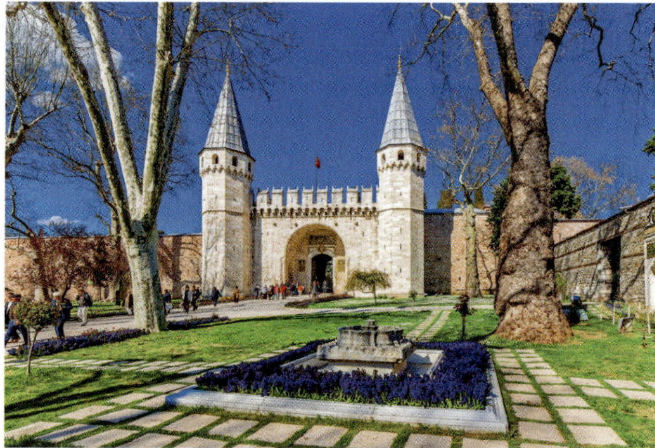

• 197 center: The Central Gate (Orta Kapi), flanked by two twin towers that served as prisons for those condemned to death, led to the second courtyard of the complex. Only the sultan could pass through it on horseback: everyone else had to dismount and continue on foot.

had to dismount in front of the enormous Central Gate (Orta Kapi), also known as the Gate of Greeting (Bab-üs Selam), and cross on foot: passing through this gate on horseback was an exclusive privilege of the sultan. Beyond the Orta Kapi was the second courtyard, also known as the Council Square, which was quieter than the first because only officials and important visitors were allowed to enter. This space was created by Mehmet II, but it took on its current appearance around the first two decades of the 16th century during the reign of Suleiman the Magnificent.

1453
During the siege of Constantinople by the Ottomans, led by Sultan Mehmet II, the last Roman emperor of the East, Constantine XI Palaiologos, died. Between May 18 and 29, the city fell.

1459
The young sultan ordered the construction of a new imperial residence on the promontory separating the Golden Horn from the Sea of Marmara. This marked the birth of the first nucleus of Topkapi, to which successive sultans would gradually add pavilions and gardens.

1520–1566
Suleiman I, known as "the Magnificent," inherited an empire stretching from the Balkans to the coasts of North Africa, Syria, and the Black Sea, which he further expanded by conquering Hungary and pushing as far as the gates of Vienna. Topkapi Palace was renovated.

1574
A fire destroyed the kitchens of Topkapi. Its reconstruction was entrusted by Selim II, son of Suleiman, to the chief imperial architect Sinan, who also worked on the expansion of the harem.

1665
On July 24, during the reign of Mehmet IV, a second fire broke out in Topkapi, devastating much of the harem, including the apartments of the Valide, the sultan's powerful mother. The damage caused by the fire was immediately repaired.

1719
Sultan Ahmed III had a library built in the third courtyard of Topkapi.

1856
On the initiative of Abdülmecid I, known as "the Reorganizer," the private residence of the sultans and the administrative center of the Ottoman Empire were moved from Topkapi to the new Dolmabahçe Palace on the European shore of the Bosphorus. The imperial treasury and mint remained in Topkapi.

1922
After defeat in World War I, the Ottoman Empire was abolished on November 1. The last sultan, Mehmet VI, born in Dolmabahçe Palace and circumcised in a ceremony at Topkapi, left Constantinople on November 19. He died in exile in San Remo.

1924
Topkapi Palace was converted into a museum that now attracts more than three million visitors a year.

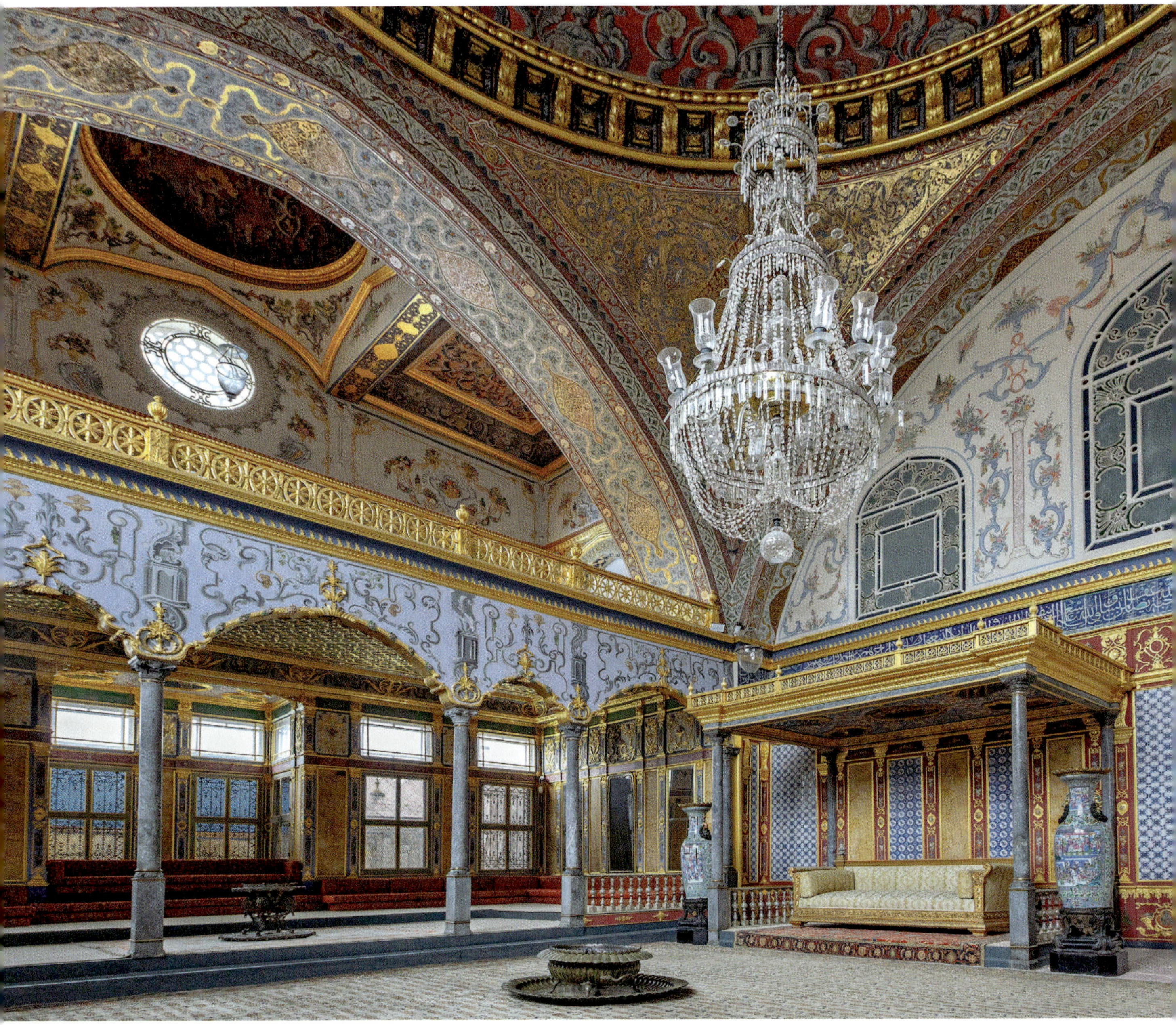

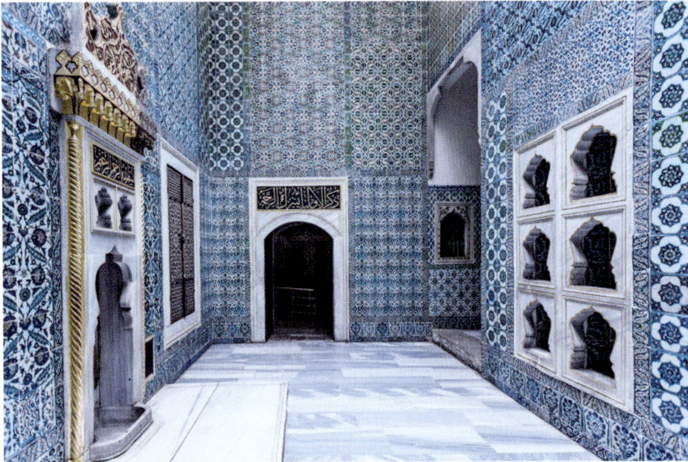

• 198-199: The Topkapi harem consisted of numerous rooms, many of which were decorated with tiles featuring plant or geometric motifs, with finely crafted wood paneling or mother-of-pearl and ivory inlays. The most important room was the Throne Room. The sultan sat on the sofa under the canopy, with his favorite concubine beside him, while the other concubines reclined on the spacious red sofa under the windows.

• 198 bottom: The rooms of the harem are decorated with glazed Iznik ceramic tiles. The main colors were cool tones, especially blue, obtained from cobalt imported from Persia, turquoise, and green obtained from copper oxide. These colors were later joined by bright red and purple, prepared with iron oxide and manganese oxide respectively. The designs were mainly floral, with tulips, the trademark of Iznik, appearing most frequently.

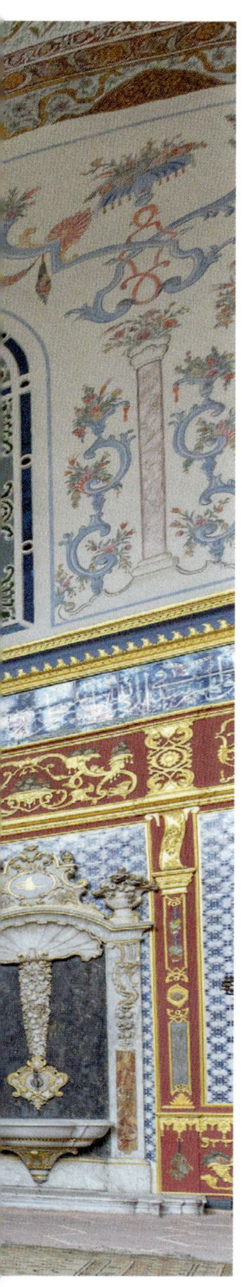

The second courtyard was overlooked by the Topkapi's service and administrative buildings: the former hospital, the enormous kitchens and bakery, the janissary quarters, the stables, the harem, and the Kubbealti or Diwan, the pavilion where the vizier's meetings were held. Here, well hidden behind a grille, the sultan attended the meetings of the council of ministers unseen. The entrance from the second courtyard to the harem was not far from the Kubbealti. It was called the Carriage Gate (Araba Kapisi) because the women who lived in the harem could only pass through it on condition that they remained enclosed in a carriage so as not to be seen. This section of the complex was created in the 16th century at the behest of Hürrem (Roxelana), wife of Suleiman the Magnificent. Comprising over 400 rooms on six levels connected by corridors and courtyards, it housed the apartments of the sultan and his mother, the bedrooms of the women and children, the quarters of the eunuchs and servants, the baths, and the service rooms. There were also two mosques and hammams. The sultan's wives, concubines, mother, favorites, sisters, daughters, and other female relatives could live in the harem only as long as their loved one remained in office: when the sultan died or was deposed, they all had to move quickly to the Eski Saray, the old palace, leaving the field open to the favorites of the next sultan. This section of the complex was also home to the black eunuchs responsible for guarding the doors and ensuring the safety of the women: there were about 200 of them, and they slept in quarters near the entrance to the harem. Including the maids and odalisques, the population of the harem numbered many hundreds of women. In short, it was a small village, at the top of which was the Valide Sultan, literally "sultana mother," the most important woman in the empire.

This part of the imperial complex also included the ten domed buildings and the chimneys of the imperial kitchens and pastry shops, which were immediately identifiable when looking at the palace from the sea. These were enormous spaces, having to cater for the needs of a multitude of people: it has been calculated that the Topkapi kitchens fed around 5,000 people every day; but when there were receptions at the palace, this number could rise to 10,000. As for the cooks, there were at least 800 of them, organized like an army.

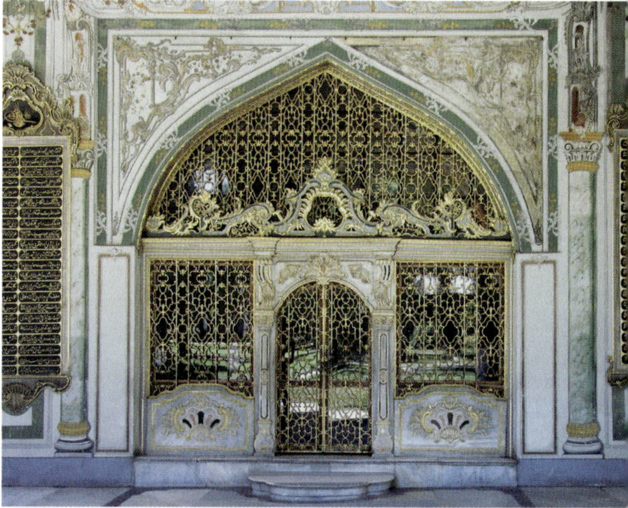

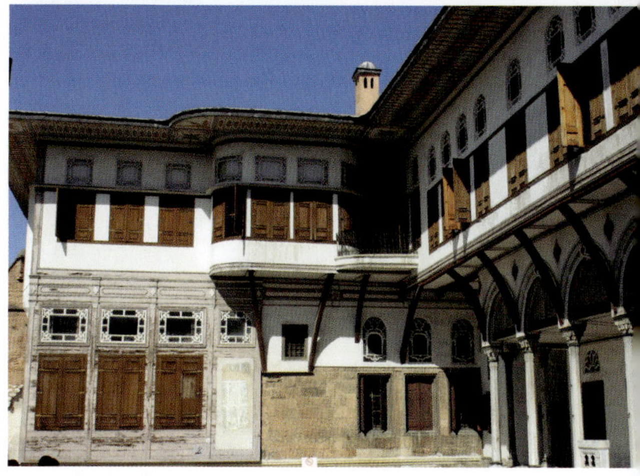

• 199 top - In the Kubbealti, the Diwan-i Hümayun, the Imperial Council (composed of the grand vizier, the most important viziers, the commander of the Janissaries, the admiral of the fleet, the heads of security, and high-ranking palace officials) discussed affairs of state.

• 199 bottom - The Courtyard of the Favorites was so called because it overlooked the apartments of the favorites, i.e. the concubines who had given the sultan a son and could aspire to become his wives. The fact that they were slaves meant that the sultan did not have to deal with their families.

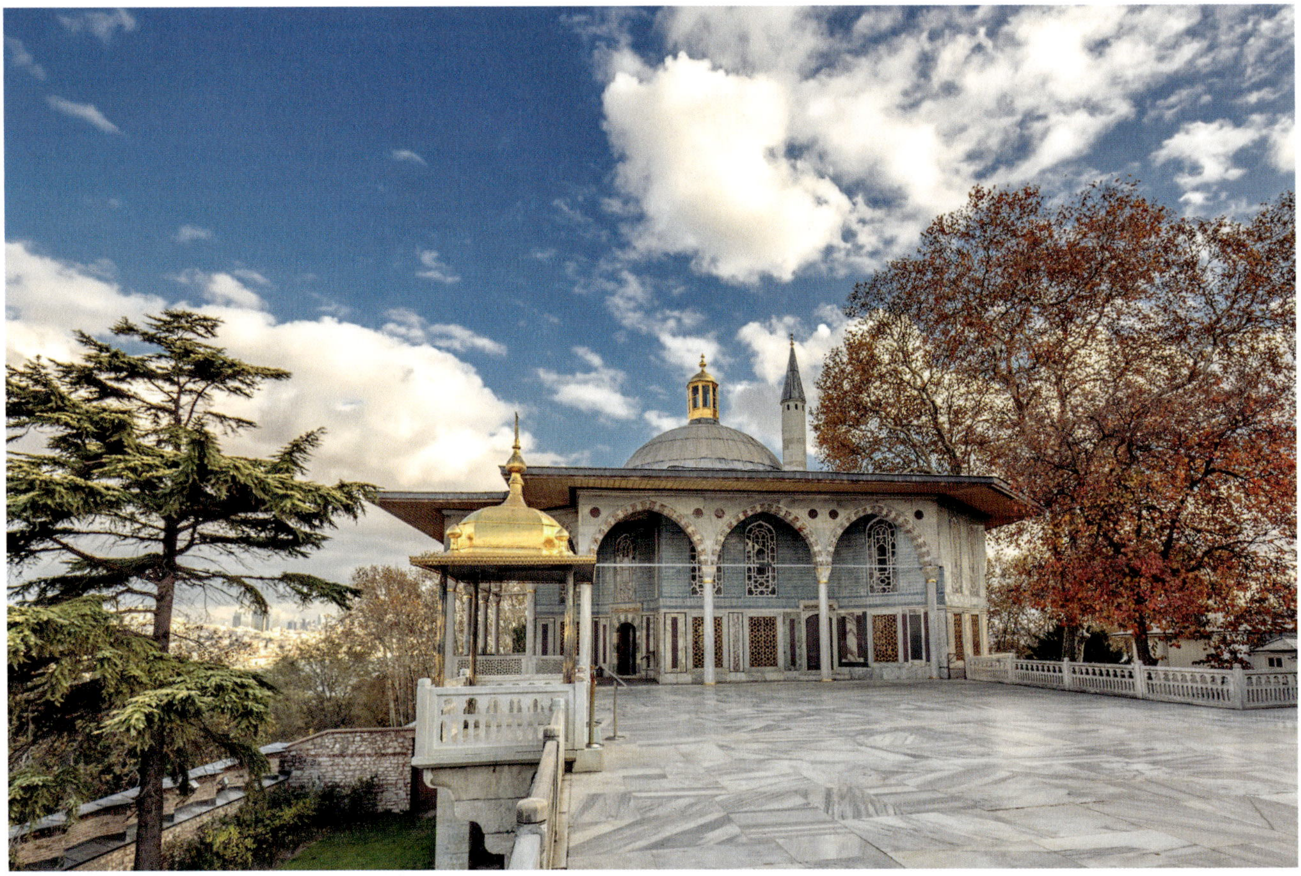

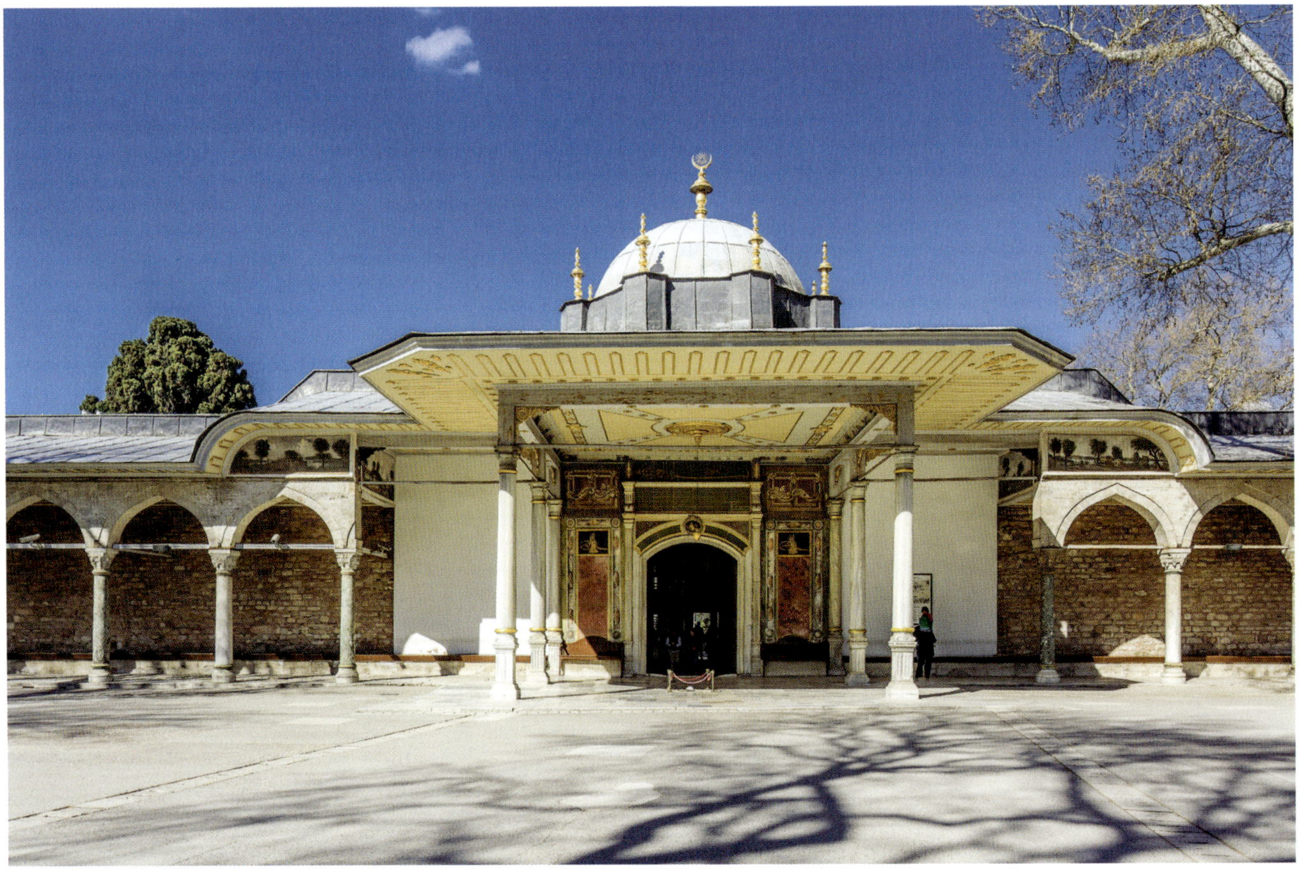

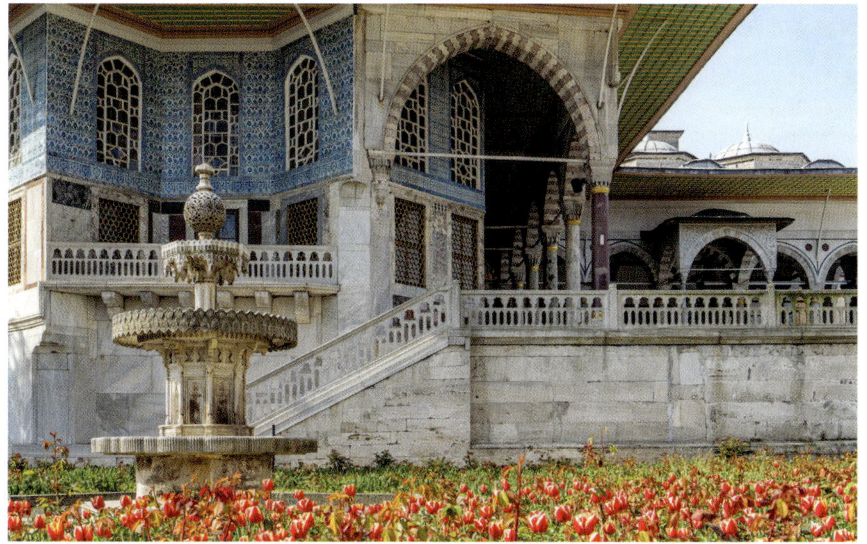

The third courtyard was the innermost area of the palace, reserved for the sultan and his pages and inaccessible to the rest of the world. The few privileged individuals authorized to enter did so through the Sublime Gate or Bab-i-Ali, which was later called the Gate of Happiness (Bab üs-Saade Kapisi). It was built during the reign of Mehmed II the Conqueror, and the most important ceremonies of the Ottoman Empire took place under its canopy, somewhat reminiscent of the ancient custom of the sultans' ancestors of performing their public duties on the thresholds of their tents. Coronations also took place in front of the Gate of Happiness, and it was here that the sultans, accompanied by the grand vizier and surrounded by high-ranking state officials, attended the most important religious ceremonies. When they finally died, their remains were displayed at this spot.

A narrow passageway, rather than a door, led from the third to the fourth courtyard, which, arranged on a series of terraces, was the sultans' private garden, an inviolable space embellished with gushing fountains and water basins and dotted with kiosks, pavilions, and canopies that provided shade on hot days or when it rained. Here are two of the most refined buildings in the entire Topkapi, built by Murat IV, known as the Warrior (1612–1640), to celebrate his military conquests. These are the Baghdad Kiosk (1639) and the Revan Kiosk (1635). The fourth courtyard was also known as the Tulip Garden, in honor of Sultan Ahmed III's favorite flower.

• 200 top: Among the attractions of the fourth courtyard, the one that generally impresses the most is the small Iftar pavilion, a sort of canopy with a gilded bronze roof supported by slender columns, offering magnificent views of the Golden Horn. During Ramadan, it was the sultans' favorite place to eat iftar, the date-based snack that breaks the fast at sunset.

• 200 bottom: The Sublime Gate or Gate of Happiness was surmounted by a domed roof supported by four columns. Passing through it, you can see a hole in the raised marble floor: it was used to support the royal banner when new sultans were crowned.

• 201 top: Revan's kiosk was erected by Murat IV to commemorate a victory in the Armenian city of Yerevan. The garden near the kiosk is embellished with a pretty fountain, an essential feature in a place like this, which was used for the sultans' rest and recreation.

The imperial treasures

Among the pavilions of the third courtyard is the one built by Mehmed II the Conqueror in 1460, which houses one of the most fascinating, incredible, and famous treasures in the world. The priceless objects on display were accumulated by the sultans during the approximately four centuries they ruled the Ottoman Empire from Topkapi. In addition to a fabulous collection of gold jewelry adorned with diamonds, rubies, emeralds, and other precious stones, there are weapons studded with precious stones and

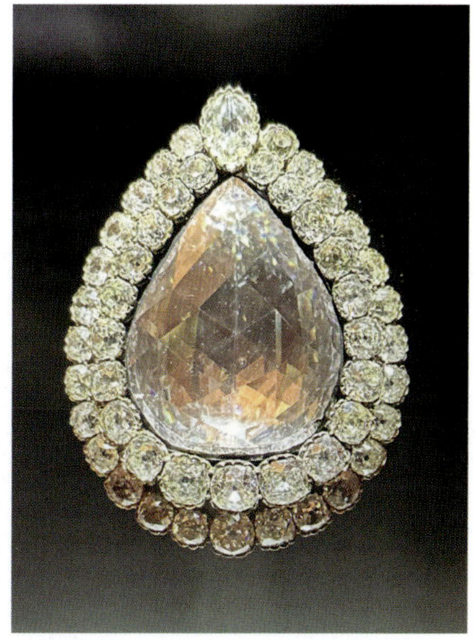

even furniture and furnishings adorned with gems, including solid gold candlesticks studded with diamonds and a throne covered in gold leaf. But the most famous pieces are undoubtedly the Spoonmaker's Diamond and the precious gold dagger studded with diamonds, with three huge Colombian emeralds mounted on one side of the hilt and a fourth emerald at the top of the handle that can be opened to reveal a small clock. The former is a pure, teardrop-shaped gem weighing 86 carats, or 0.6 oz, considered the fifth largest in the world (1.65 by 1.37 by 0.63 inches); adding to its value, if possible, are 49 diamonds set around the mount.

Hermitage Palace

1672
Peter, son of Tsar Alexei I Romanov and his second wife Natalya Kirillovna Naryshkina, was born in Moscow on May 30.

1696
With the death of his older half-brother Ivan V, Peter I was elected Tsar of Russia. Over the following two years, he traveled throughout Europe and, upon his return to his country, promoted a series of reforms aimed at Westernizing customs.

1703
Architects Domenico Trezzini and Jean-Baptiste Alexandre Le Blond were commissioned by the tsar to draw up plans for the construction of St. Petersburg.

1710
Domenico Trezzini began construction of the Summer Palace and Giovanni Maria Fontana laid the foundation stone of the Menshikov Palace on Vasilyevsky Island.

1712–1713
Peter I officially married Catherine Alekseevna in St. Isaac's Cathedral in St. Petersburg. Construction began on the first Winter Palace in St. Petersburg.

1713
The capital was moved from Moscow to St. Petersburg.

1754–1762
Commissioned by Elizabeth, daughter of Peter I, the current Winter Palace was built, designed by Francesco Bartolomeo Rastrelli: it's one of the five buildings that make up the Hermitage complex, on the site of Peter the Great's second palace. The palace remained the official residence of the Russian tsars until 1917.

1764–1775
Catherine II, who became empress in 1762, had the Small Hermitage built in 1764 to a design by architects Georg Friedrich Veldten and Jean-Baptiste Michel Vallin de La Mothe. Used as a small retreat, it is connected to the main building by a hanging garden.

1787
The Grand (or Old) Hermitage, designed by Georg Friedrich Veldten, was completed.

1783–1789
The Hermitage Theater, designed by Giacomo Quarenghi, was built. The interior was inspired by the Olympic Theater in Vicenza.

1839–1851
The German architect Leo von Klenze, commissioned by Nicholas I, designed the New Hermitage, built to be a museum.

1904–1917
In 1904, the last Tsar, Nicholas II, abandoned the Winter Palace with his royal family to escape popular uprisings. During World War I, the rooms on the second floor of the palace were used as a hospital for wounded soldiers.

1917
In October, the Bolsheviks stormed the Winter Palace, where the provisional government had established itself.

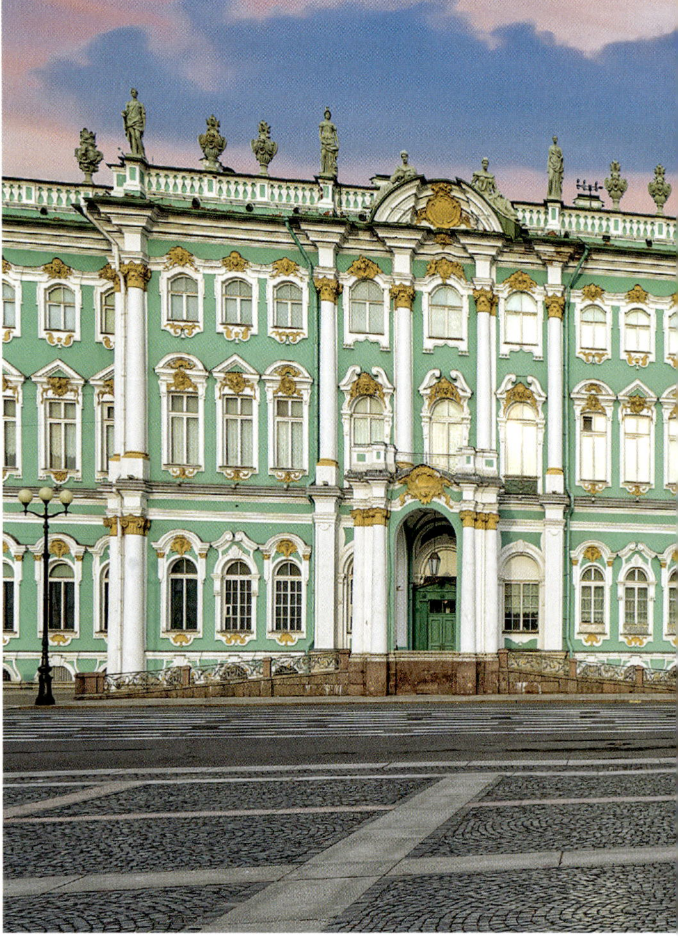

Four of the five palaces overlooking the Neva River in St. Petersburg were built between the 18th and 19th centuries. They make up the world-famous Hermitage complex, home to magnificent art collections gathered by the Russian tsars since the late 18th century. The most majestic is the Winter Palace, the official residence of the tsars until 1917.

At the time of Peter the Great, the "creator" of St. Petersburg, a first Winter Palace was built in 1710 to a design by Domenico Trezzini, a modest residence consisting of two floors and an attic topped by a slate roof in the Northern European style. Starting in 1721, the tsar commissioned Georg Johann Mattarnovy to build a second palace in its place, which, however, could not

• 202-203: The façade of the Winter Palace seen from Palace Square, the setting for various events in Russian history. In the center of the square stands the Alexander Column, dedicated to Alexander I to commemorate the victory over Napoleon Bonaparte in 1812.

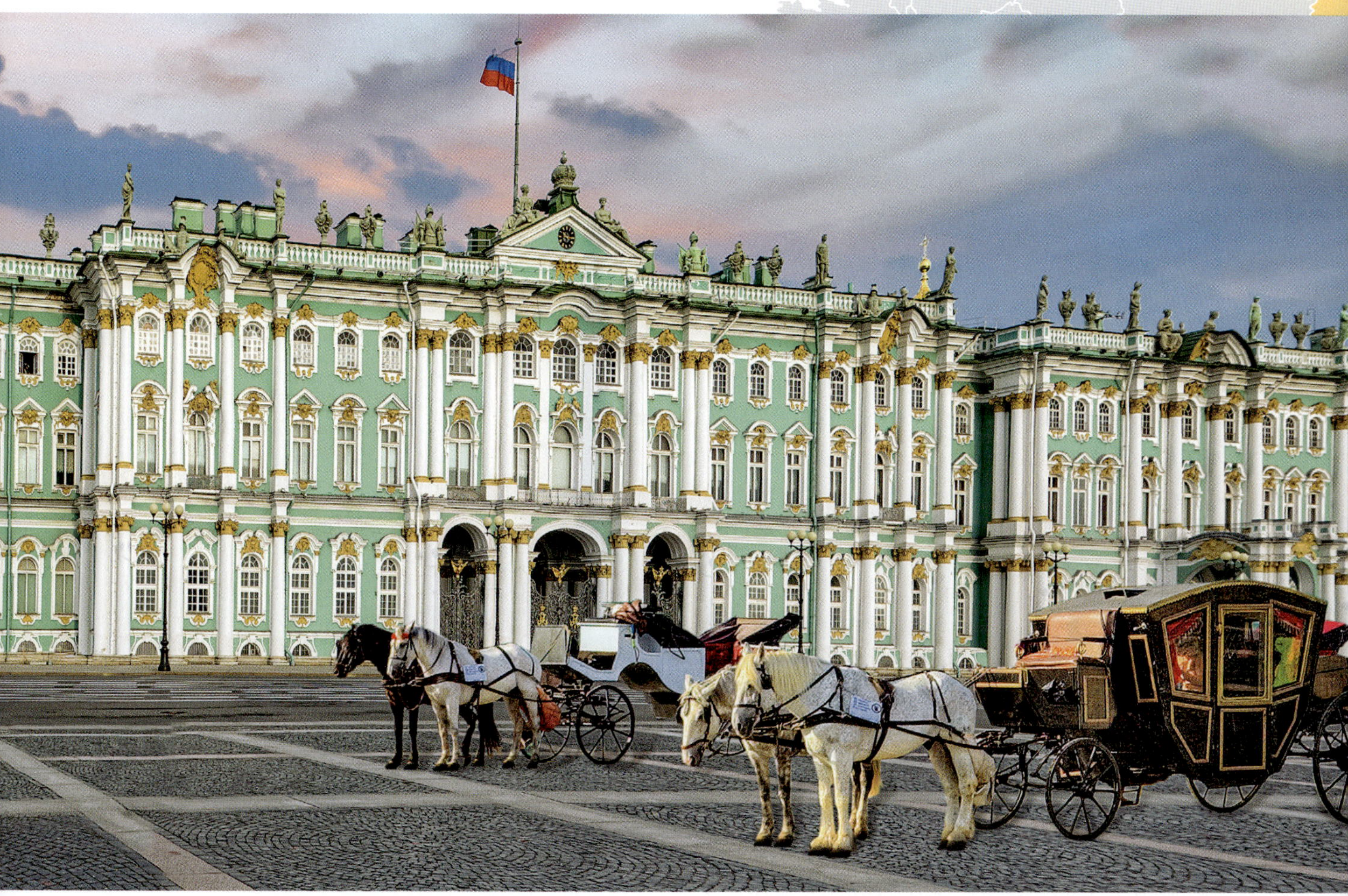

compete with the grandiose palaces of the European courts, nor even with those of Russian dignitaries. The palace was built on two levels above a rusticated ground floor; the façade was embellished with a central pediment supported by columns. The interior was more opulent, with oak furnishings and walls finished in red marble. It was in the study on one side of the hall on the first floor of that residence that Peter the Great died on January 28, 1725. The room did not survive subsequent renovations and the abandonment of the palace, but part of the ground floor below the study corresponds to the foundations of the Hermitage Theater, built about 20 years after the tsar's death on the site of his palace.

After the tsar's death, chaotic years followed in terms of succession. St. Petersburg was briefly abandoned in favor of Moscow, and the Winter Palace was no longer considered the main residence of the royal family. In 1741, a coup d'état proclaimed Elizabeth tsarina. It was Peter I's daughter who was responsible for the construction of the magnificent Baroque-style New Winter Palace. The project was entrusted to the Italian architect Francesco Bartolomeo Rastrelli in 1754, and work lasted eight years. Elizabeth, a lover of luxury and refinement with a passionate character and a penchant for entertainment, wanted the beauty of her new residence to eclipse that of the leading European palaces.

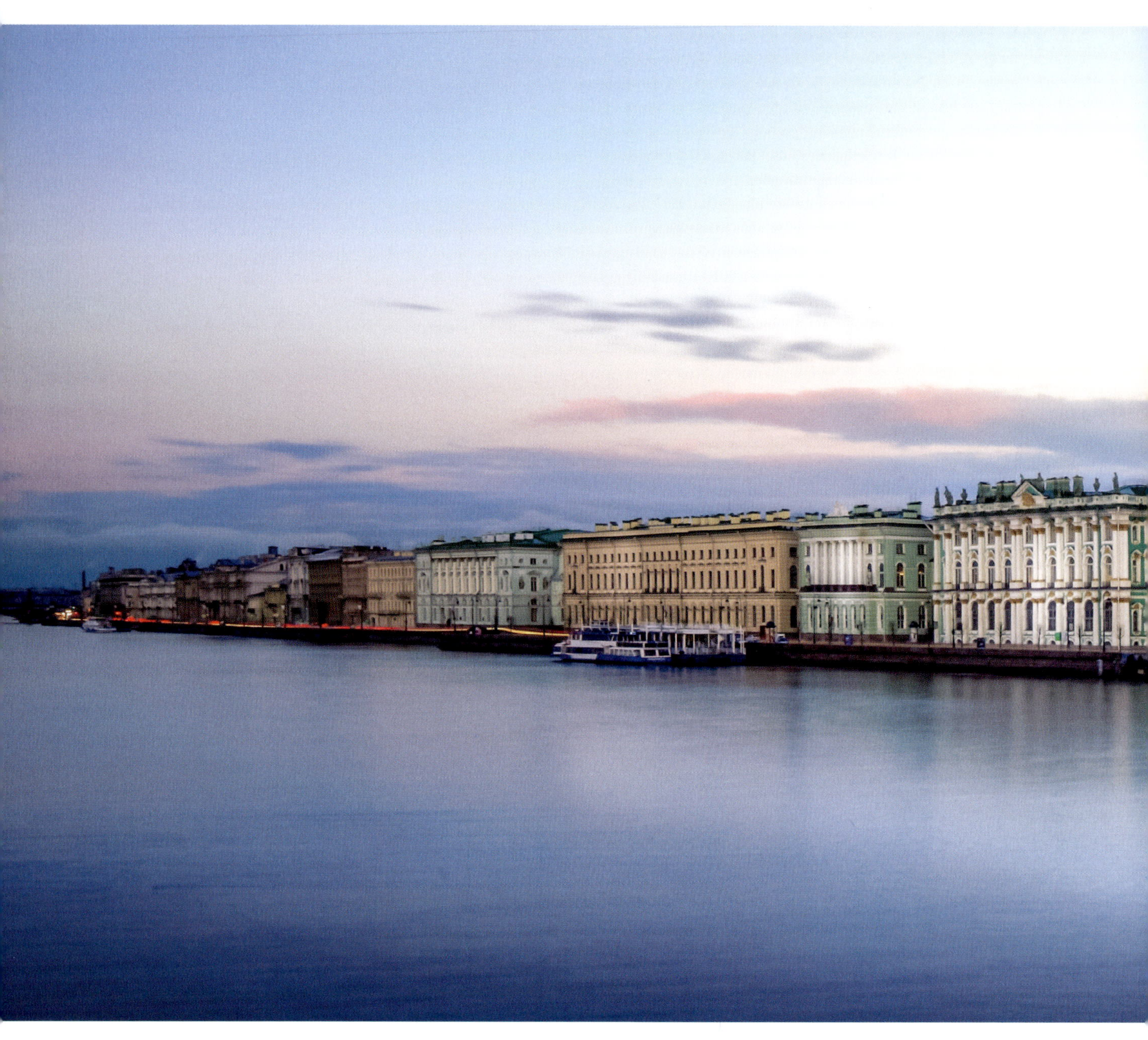

The construction required an enormous sum of money (the final cost of this project was 2,500,000 rubles), and a tax was even imposed on the city's taverns to raise the funds. The large number of workers involved, over 4,000 people, received a monthly salary of only one ruble. The protracted nature of the work inevitably led to a change of client: Catherine II, who became empress in 1762 after dethroning and probably assassinating her husband Peter III, chose the Neoclassical style for the interiors instead of Baroque, which was designed by architects Ivan Egorovich Starov and Giacomo Quarenghi, among others. During the reign of Catherine II, the construction of the so-called Neva Embankment was ordered: three other palaces appeared next to the Winter Palace, the Small and Large Hermitage and the Hermitage Theater overlooking the river. During her 34-year reign, the empress acquired the art collections that form the basis of today's Hermitage Museum. After Catherine II's death, the brief reign of her son Paul I (1754–1801) and the Napoleonic Wars, peace returned in 1815 and Alexander I demanded the return to Russia of many works that had been stolen during the French invasion. His brother Nicholas I oversaw the restoration of the Winter Palace after the fire of 1837 and

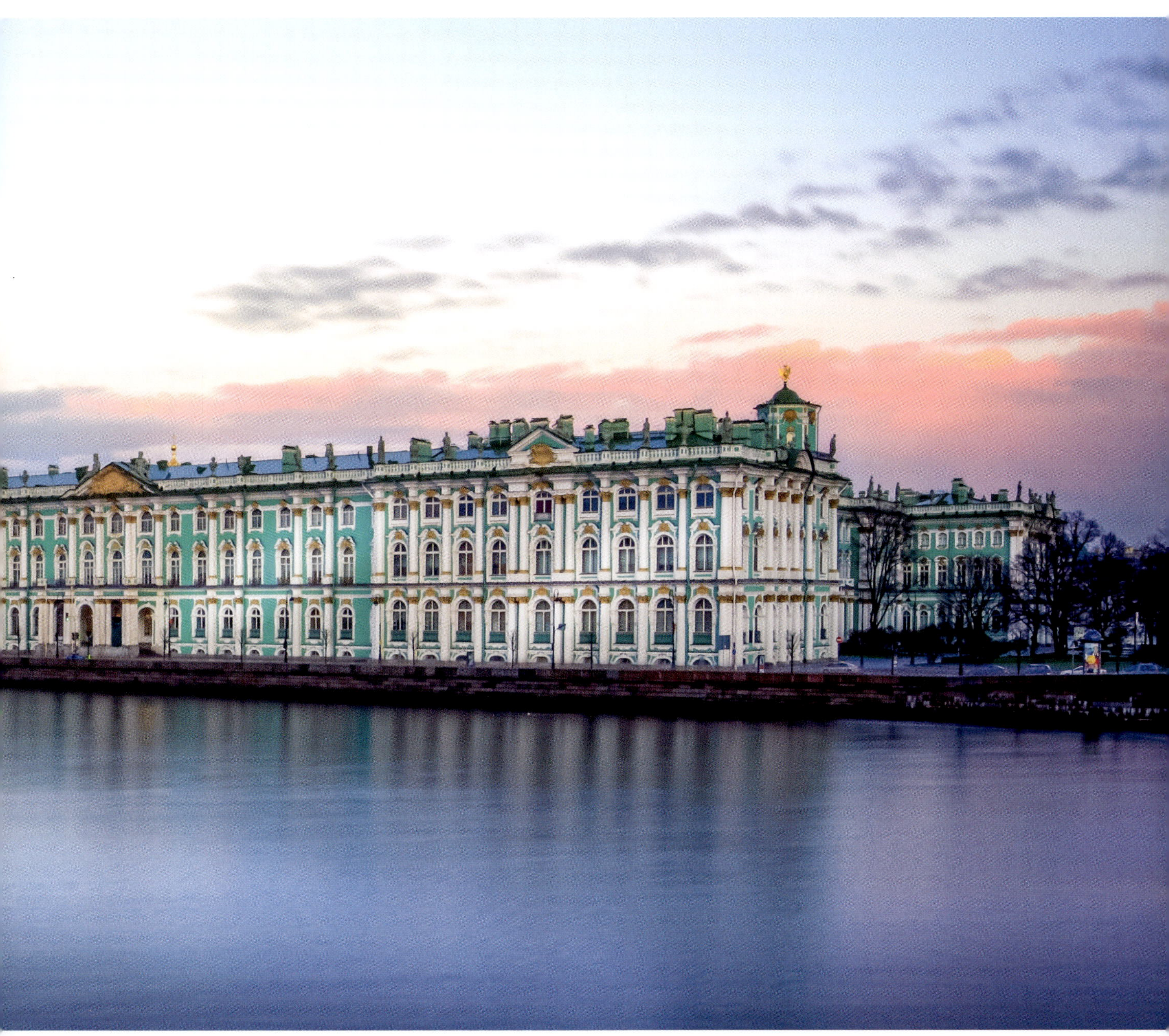

the construction of the New Hermitage, commissioned to house the ever-growing art collection. His wife, Alexandra Feodorovna, was the last empress to embellish the imperial apartments, such as the Malachite Salon. Alexander II (1818–1881) chose to reside in a remote corner of the palace furnished in the bourgeois style of the time. After his assassination, for security reasons, his son Alexander III (1845–1894) moved with the royal family to the Palace of Gatchina, where his successor Nicholas II, the last emperor of Russia, spent his childhood. The era of lavish ceremonies, balls, and banquets was coming to an end.

• 204-205: The Hermitage complex on the Palace Embankment. It was Catherine II who chose the name Hermitage, derived from the French word meaning "hermit's dwelling": the tsarina wanted an isolated place where she could spend time surrounded by the masterpieces of her collection, away from the social life of St. Petersburg. From left to right, the Hermitage Theater, the Winter Canal and the Hermitage Bridge, the Great (or Old) Hermitage, the Small Hermitage, and the Winter Palace. The New Hermitage, located behind the Great Hermitage, is not visible.

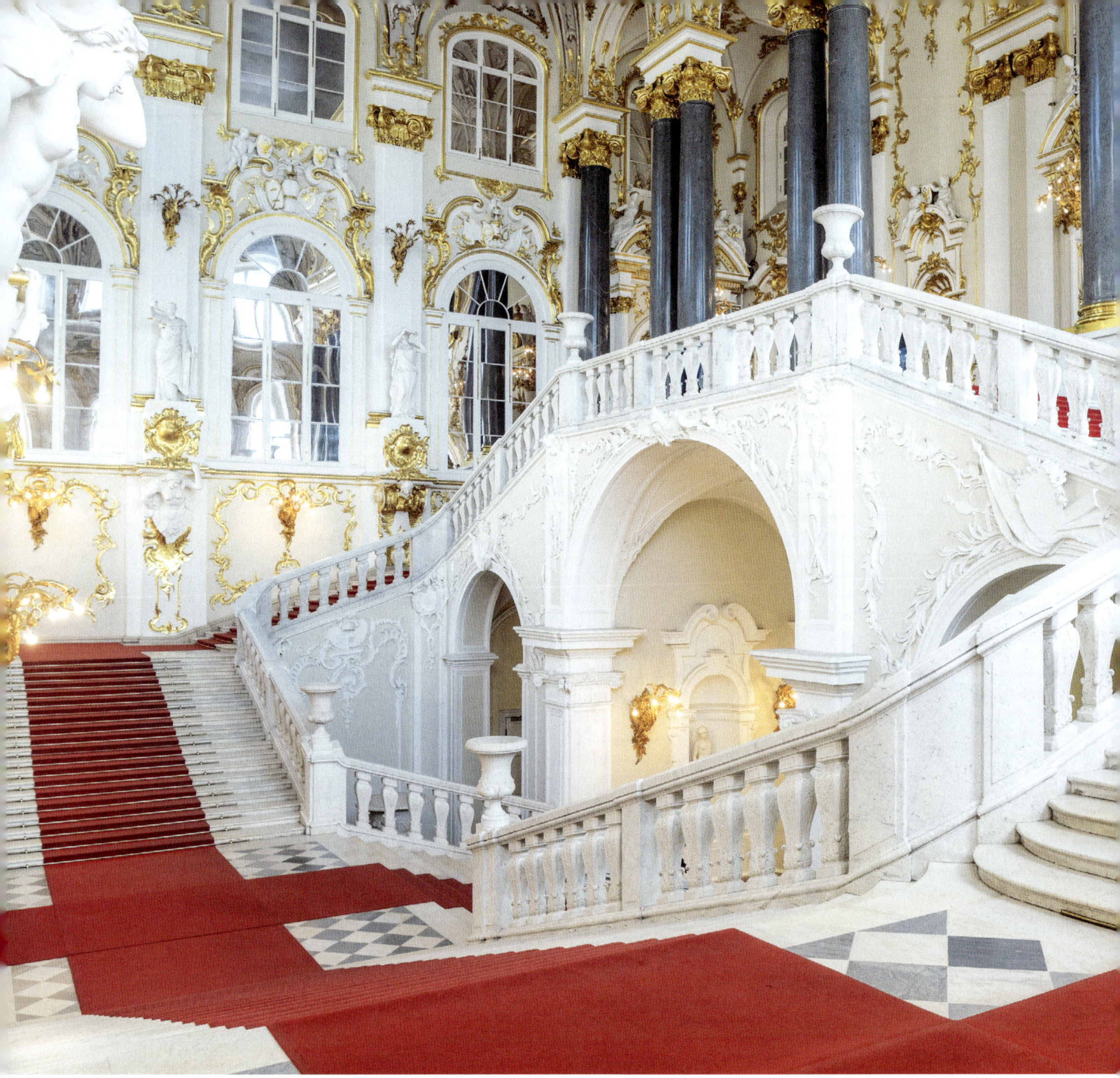

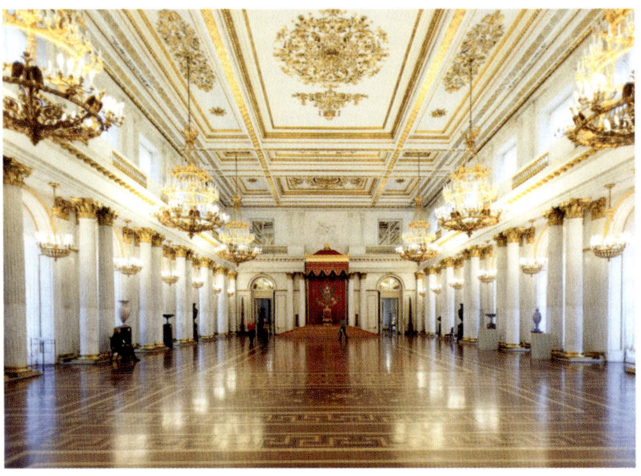

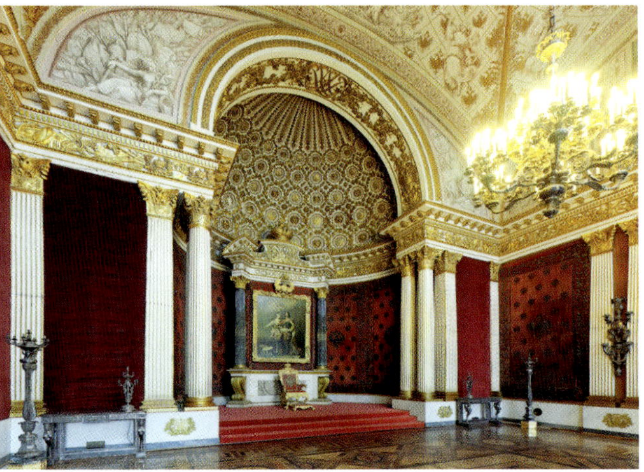

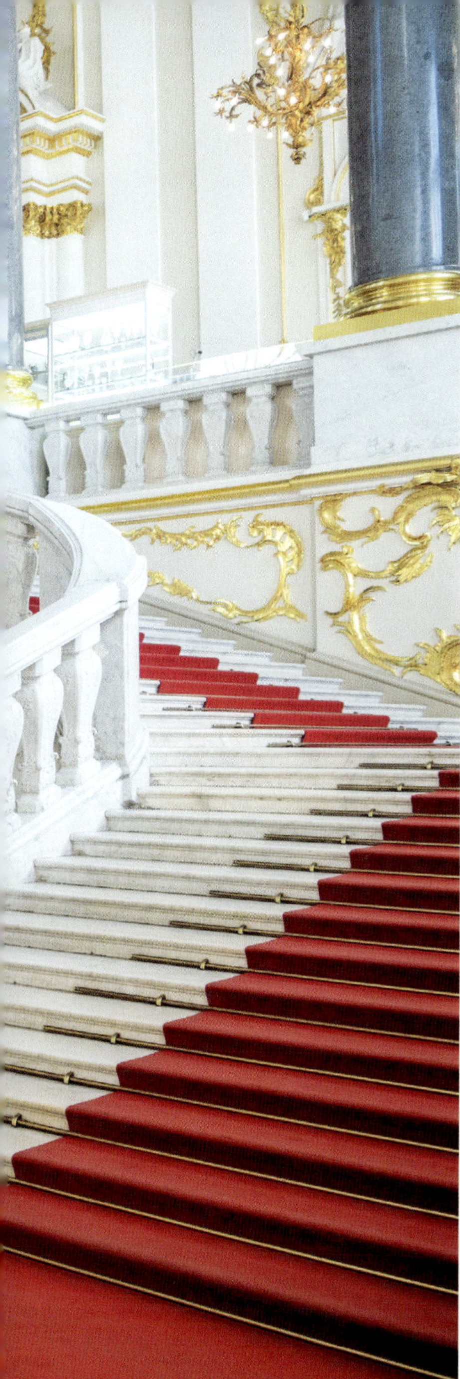

The marvels of malachite

The Malachite Salon was designed by the architect Aleksandr Pavlovič Brjullov after the great fire of 1837. The room, which is accessed from the landing of the Grand Staircase, separated the ceremonial rooms of the palace from the empress's private apartment. It was in this room that the brides of the Romanov imperial family were traditionally dressed by the tsarina before their weddings. The name of the room derives from the presence of objects, furniture, and coverings in malachite, a rare hard stone. From 1830 onwards, after the discovery of deposits in the Urals, this precious material was widely used by the tsars' artists to embellish their palaces. The complex technique of Russian mosaic was used: thin sheets of malachite were glued with a special mastic onto a base, such as a vase. This was then smoothed and polished to create the effect of a monolithic stone.

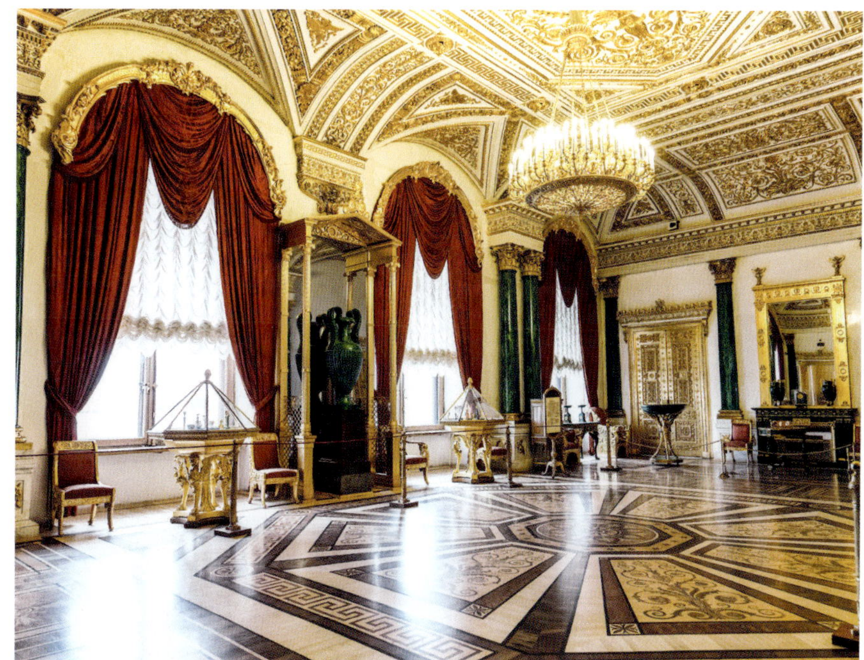

• 206-207: The Grand Staircase of the Winter Palace was designed by Francesco Bartolomeo Rastrelli and then rebuilt identically after a huge fire broke out between December 17 and 19, 1837, completely destroying the interior of the building. The architects Vasily Petrovich Stasov and Alexander Pavlovich Bryullov were commissioned to rebuild it. The staircase retained the characteristics of Rastrelli's style with its lavish golden stucco decorations and mirrors that create the illusion of a larger space.

• 206 bottom left: The Hall of St. George, or Grand Throne Room, is the center of the Winter Palace. After rejecting Rastrelli's design as outdated in its Baroque lines, the tsarina approved Giacomo Quarenghi's design from 1795. Unfortunately, the classicist architect's masterpiece, with its polychrome marble cladding, was destroyed in a fire. Nicholas I ordered Vasily Petrovich Stasov to rebuild the hall using white Carrara marble.

• 206 bottom right: Peter's Hall, also known as the Small Throne Room, was built in 1833 based on a design by Auguste de Montferrand and then rebuilt almost unchanged by Vasily Petrovich Stasov, who, along with Carlo Rossi, was one of the last representatives of Russian Classicism. The hall is dominated by the allegorical painting "Peter I with Minerva," by Jacopo Amigoni (1682-1752). The panels adorning the side walls exalt the military art of the tsar. The hall contains the throne of Empress Anna Ivanovna, made in London in 1731.

PETERHOF PALACE

1705
Tsar Peter I visited the coast of the Gulf of Finland for the first time and had a pavilion built where he stayed between military campaigns.

1714
Construction began on the Peterhof Palace: after the death of Andreas Schlüter, Johann Friedrich Braunstein took over the project. The Grand Palace was built, along with the Monplasir Palace that was erected in the garden.

1721
Water gushed from the park's fountains thanks to a system of communicating vessels designed by engineer Vasily Tuvolkov, which was more innovative than the Marly pump that supplied water to the fountains of the Palace of Versailles.

1723
The Peterhof Palace was inaugurated with a spectacular ceremony.

1721–1725
The Hermitage Pavilion was built by Johann Friedrich Braunstein to serve as a private dining room for the tsar and his guests.

1745–1755
Tsarina Elizabeth commissioned Francesco Bartolomeo Rastrelli to rebuild the Grand Palace in the Baroque style.

1941
In the fall, the palace was occupied by German troops. Before their arrival, over 8,000 objects and about 50 statues were brought to safety. However, all the waterfalls in the complex were damaged by artillery.

1990
The palace was added to the UNESCO World Heritage List.

During his trip to Europe between 1716 and 1717, Tsar Peter I of Russia was undoubtedly impressed by the Palace of Versailles, where he was a guest of the King of France. Upon his return, the Tsar brought with him to Russia twelve albums of engravings he had received as gifts, which would provide ample material and inspiration for his architects to design the Peterhof Palace on the shores of the Gulf of Finland, about 12.4 miles from St. Petersburg. Due to its location by the sea, the complex of the tsars' summer residence had something unique about it, with its lower park extending along a slope parallel to the coast and the Grand Cascade—originally designed by Peter I himself to glorify the victories of the Russian fleet—whose waters flow into the Baltic Sea through a picturesque canal. The sea was Peter I's obsession: the decision to build a castle in

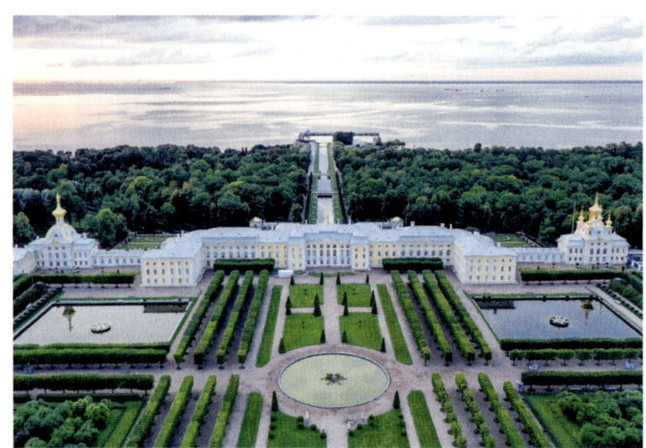

that location had political significance in the Tsar's mind. After securing Russia's outlet to the Gulf of Finland, wrested from the Swedes, and opening his country to the West thanks in part to his travels, there was no better place than Peterhof to build a palace outside the city that would rival those of the great European courts. In 1704, there was only a

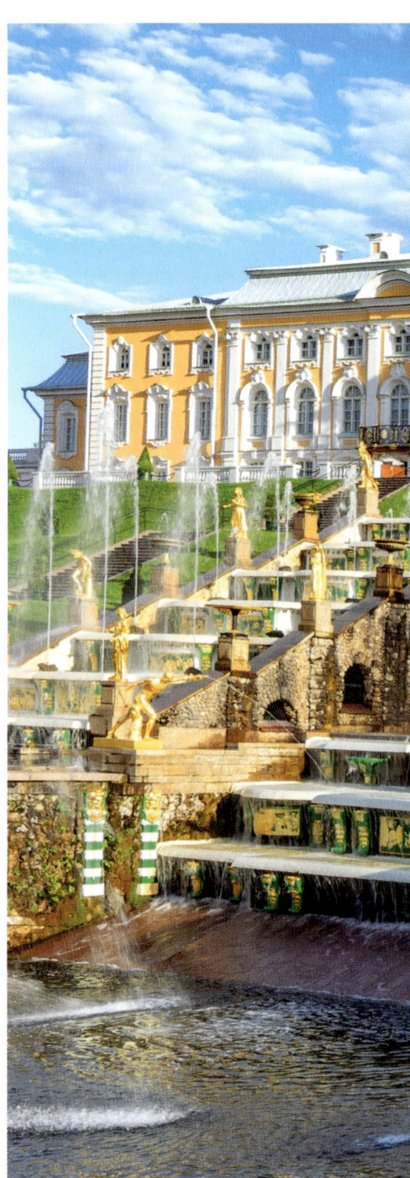

• 208 center - View of the Peterhof Palace, built by Peter I to rival Versailles. Architecturally, the palace is the result of all the reconstructions that have taken place over time, as shown by the distinct signs of different artistic tastes and styles. During World War II, the main building was burned and severely damaged, but it was later restored to its former glory.

• 208-209: The façade of the Grand Palace in Peterhof stretches for almost 984 feet and dominates the entire complex, connecting the Upper Garden to the Lower Garden. When it was built during the reign of Peter I, the palace was a modest building as wide as the Grand Cascade. It was enlarged after the tsar's death.

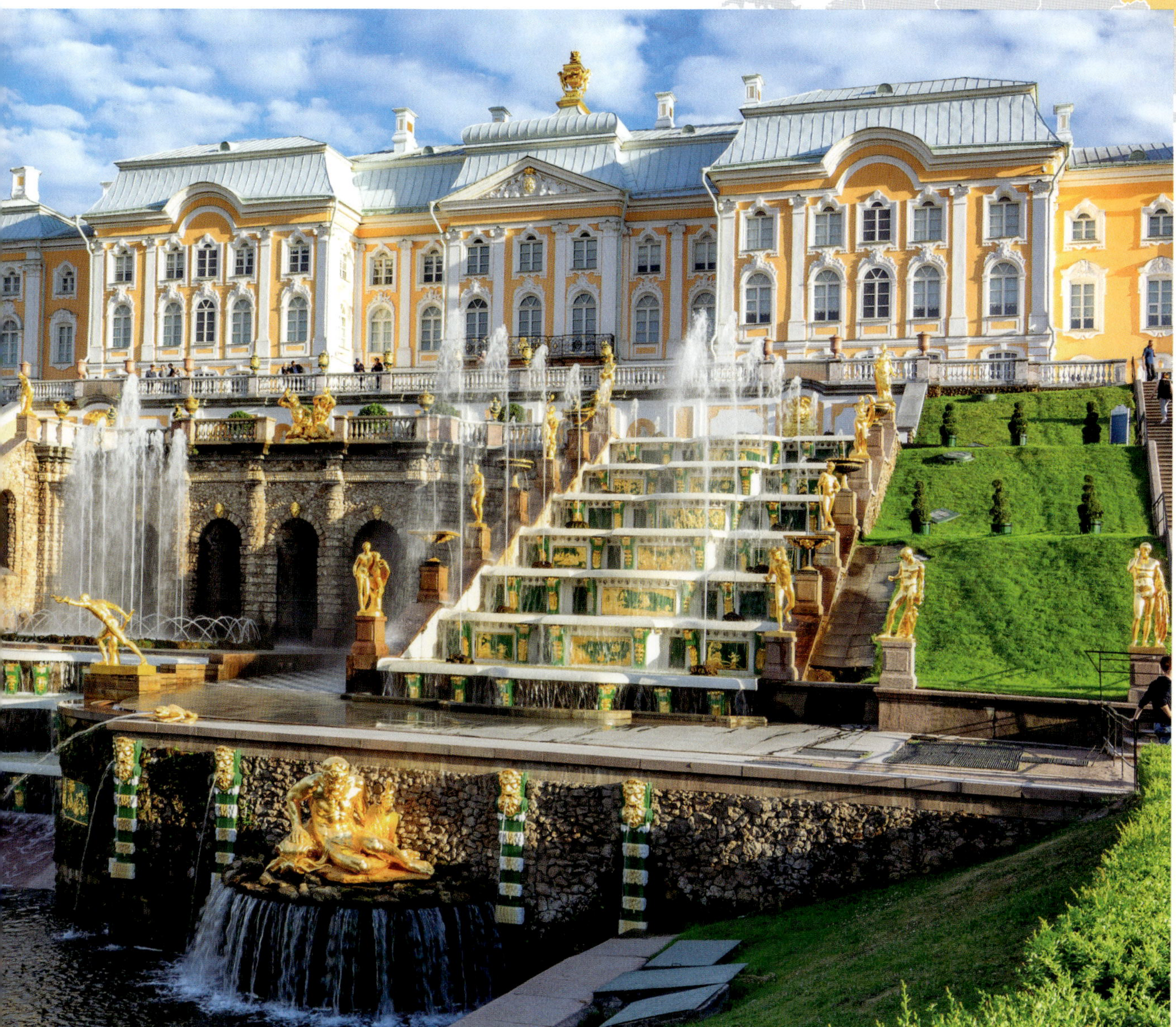

small country house on the site, where the tsar stayed on his travels to Kronstadt, the fortress built on a small island in the Gulf of Finland. Ten years later, thanks to the work of thousands of laborers, serfs, and soldiers, the first nucleus of the royal palace was built. There are autographed documents and sketches testifying to the fact that Peter himself spent time designing the interiors and sketching the façade of his future palace. The first comprehensive design for Peterhof was entrusted to the German architect Johann Friedrich Braunstein, an exponent of the Peterine Baroque style, who was active in Strelna—where Peter I initially wanted to build his Summer Palace—and in Carskoe Selo, on the estate where Catherine I's palace would later be built.

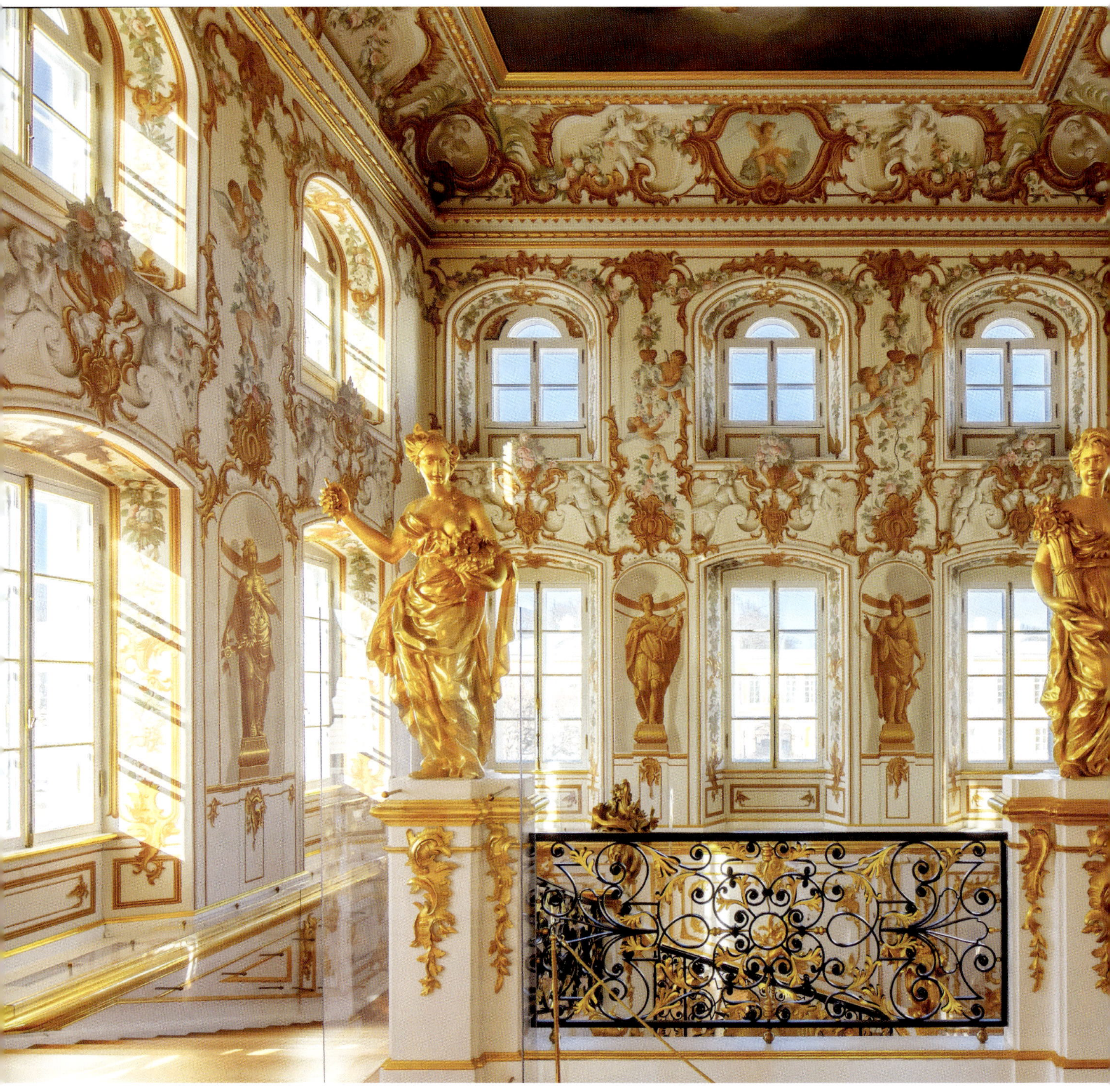

In Peterhof, he also worked on the Monplasir pavilion, where Peter the Great received his guests, who were unable to escape the heavy drinking; and on the Hermitage Pavilion, located in an isolated position on the shores of the Gulf of Finland. The Frenchman Jean-Baptiste Alexandre Le Blond, who had been in charge of the construction of the city of St. Petersburg since 1703, also followed the German's designs. Le Blond had been a pupil of André Le Nôtre, the creator of the park at Versailles. The architect laid out the upper garden, which was flatter than the lower one, in the formal French style, with geometric flower beds, sculptures, kiosks, and pergolas, as well as a large number of fountains and pools. Plants and shrubs, including mistletoe, elm, maple, and rose trees, were imported from other parts of Russia and abroad. The summer residence was completed two years before the

• 211 top - The magnificent Ballroom has hosted banquets, masked balls, and ceremonies for two centuries. During World War II, the palace was looted and destroyed by the Germans. Reconstruction began in the early days of liberation.

• 211 bottom - The Portrait Room is lined with 368 portraits of female faces. Legend has it that the Veronese painter Pietro Rotari was commissioned by Tsarina Elizabeth to find and paint the most beautiful girls in the kingdom, searching the entire country. In reality, there were only eight models, but the artist ingeniously depicted them in dozens of different poses and expressions, using his skill in combining colors.

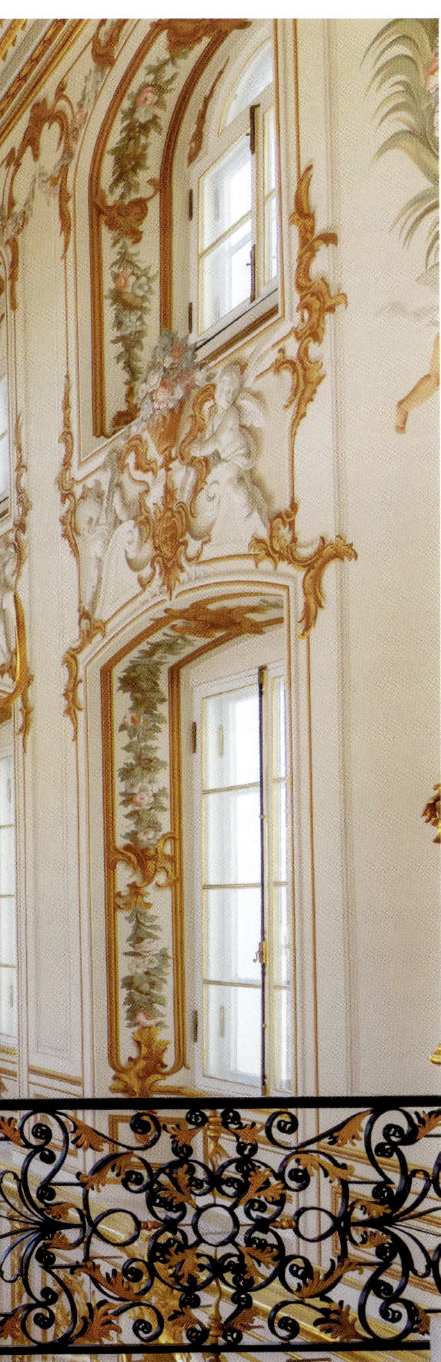

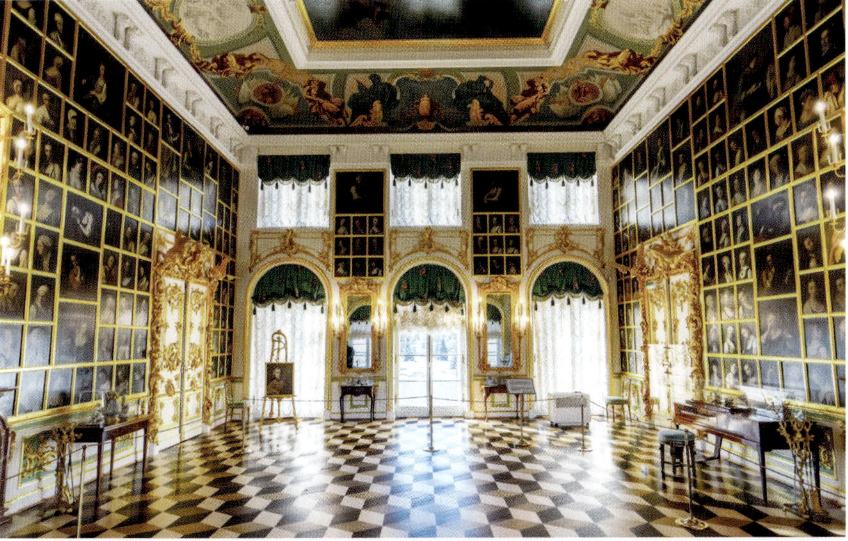

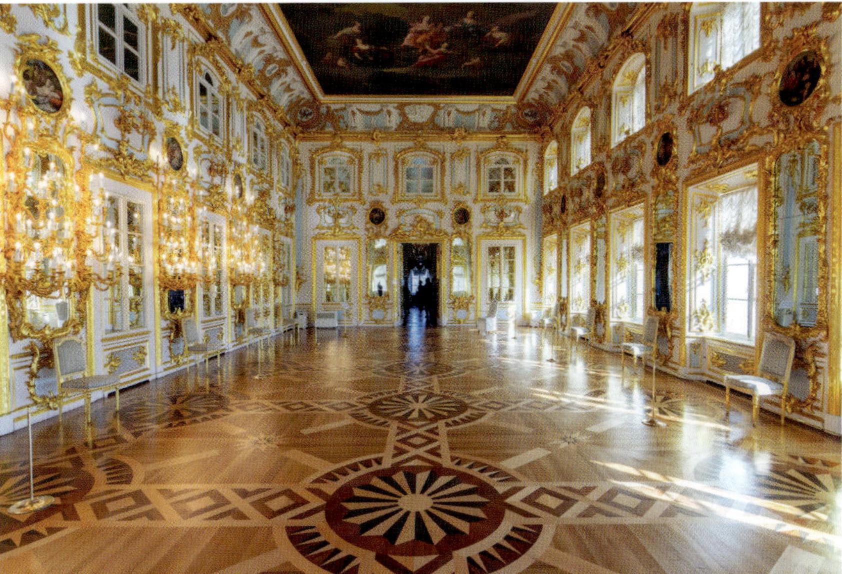

• 210–211: The central staircase, designed by Francesco Bartolomeo Rastrelli, is decorated with caryatids and gilded carvings. It leads to the Throne Room, which features a painting of Catherine II on horseback.

tsar's death. The palace looked rather modest compared to its magnificent surroundings. It was Tsarina Elizabeth, daughter of Peter I, who enhanced the palace's charm by hiring architect Francesco Bartolomeo Rastrelli, who between 1745 and 1755 added two wings to Peter I's Grand Palace and embellished the court church with five golden domes, where wedding ceremonies were held and prayers were said to celebrate military victories. The interiors were also renovated in Baroque style, with the exception of Peter the Great's study, which remained intact.

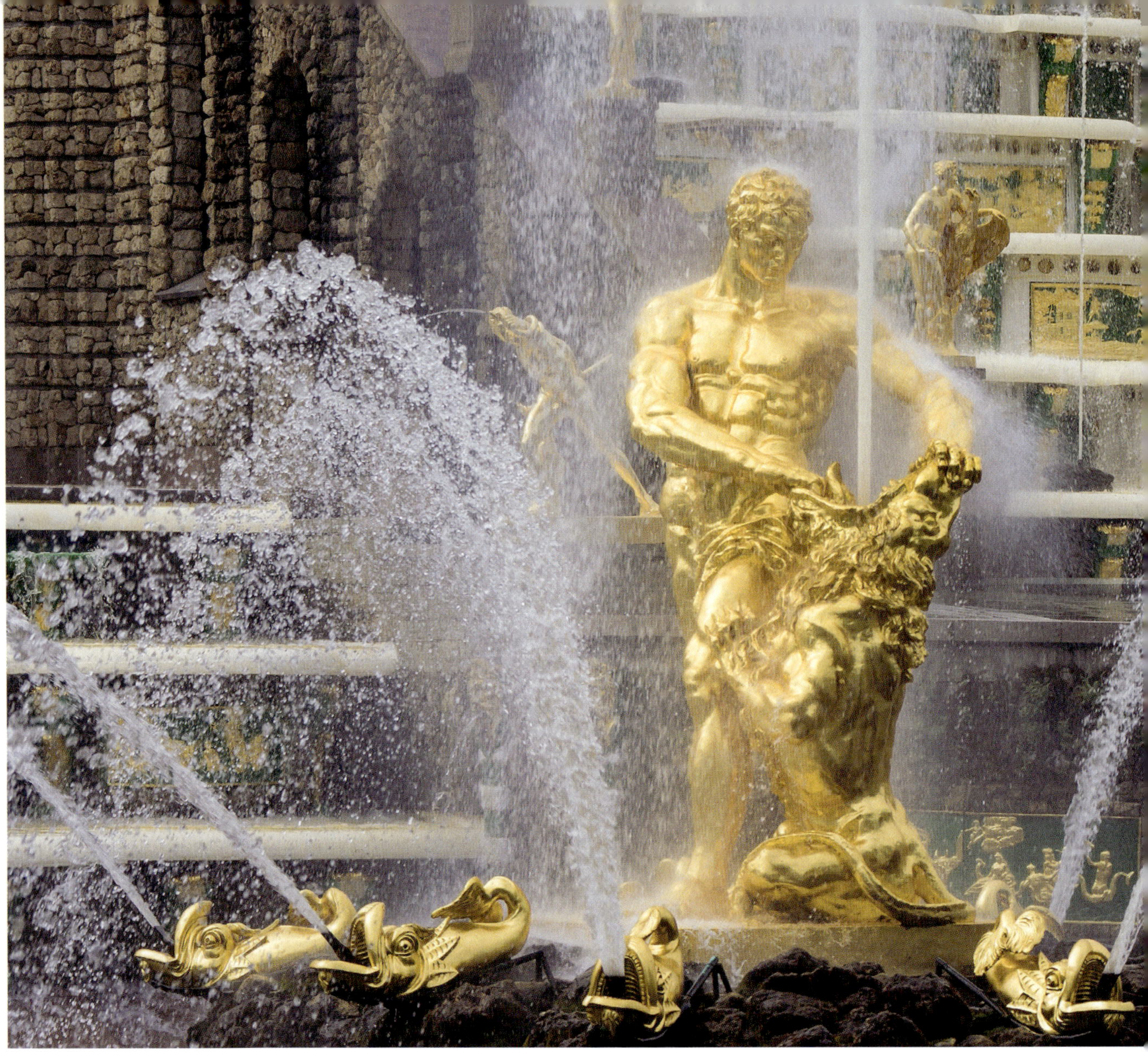

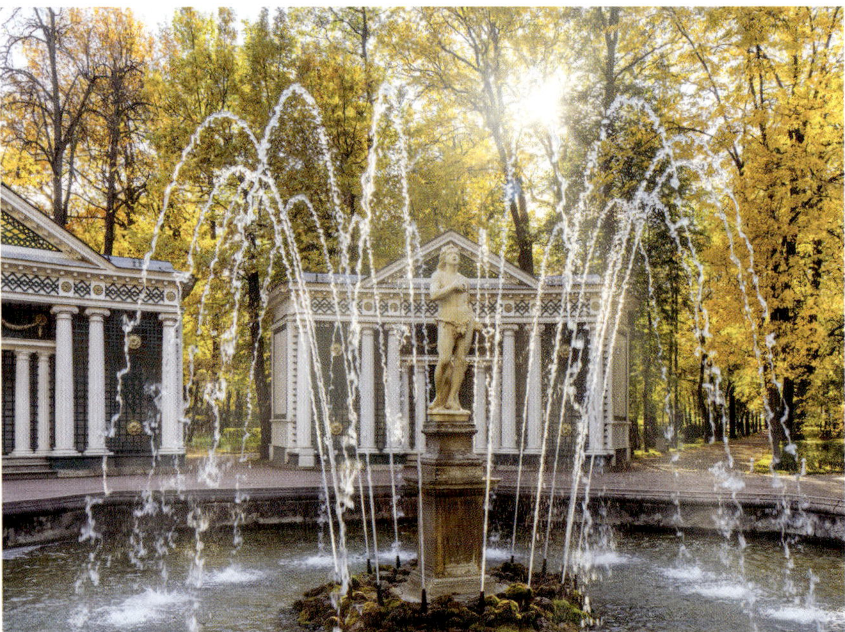

• 212–213: The Great Waterfall is dominated by a statue of Samson twisting the jaws of a lion, from which a jet of water shoots up to a height of 65 feet. The meaning is allegorical: Samson represents Russia and the lion represents Sweden, defeated in the Battle of Poltava in 1709. Unlike the gardens of Versailles, where the Marly machine used an ingenious system of pipes to pump water from the Seine to the palace, the fountains and pools at Peterhof were fed by water flowing from the nearby hills. The waterfall is decorated with 38 gilded bronze statues.

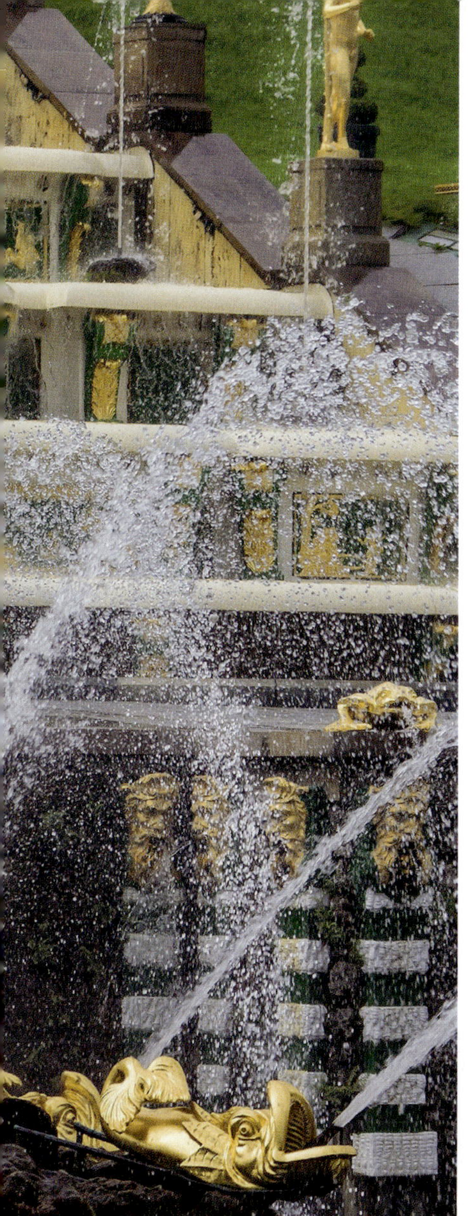

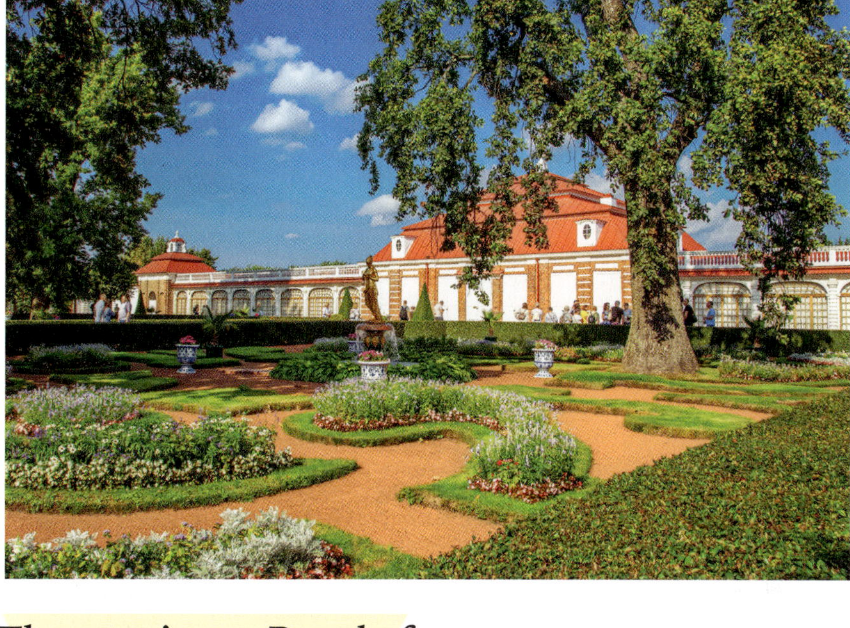

The meeting at Peterhof

It was in the Monplaisir pavilion that a dramatic confrontation took place between Tsar Peter I and his son Alexei, accused of betraying his father by publicly criticizing his reformist zeal. Russian artist Nikolai Nikolaevich (1831–1894) immortalized this moment on canvas, now preserved in the Tretyakov Gallery in Moscow. The details of the work perfectly convey the wealth that characterizes the room: the tablecloth is beautifully embroidered, the chairs are carved and covered with precious fabrics, and numerous paintings hang on the walls. History does not actually record this episode, but it is a fact that Alexei had to renounce the throne to save himself from charges of high treason. He was imprisoned in the Fortress of Saints Peter and Paul, where he died.

• 212 bottom: The two fountains dedicated to Adam and Eve were commissioned by Peter I from the Venetian sculptor Giovanni Bonazza, who in 1718 made two copies of the famous sculptures located in the Doge's Palace, as works by Antonio Rizzi, a master of the Renaissance period. The decoration of the Adam fountain was completed in 1722, while the Eve fountain was put into operation in 1726. In the 18th century, the fountains were surrounded by pergolas that served as shelters in case of bad weather.

• 213 top: The Monplaisir pavilion was Peter the Great's favorite place, perhaps because it overlooked the sea. From the small bedroom decorated with painted terra-cotta tiles, the tsar could see the fortifications of Kronstadt and its ships at anchor. From the palace, it was only a few steps to the dock where his boat awaited him.

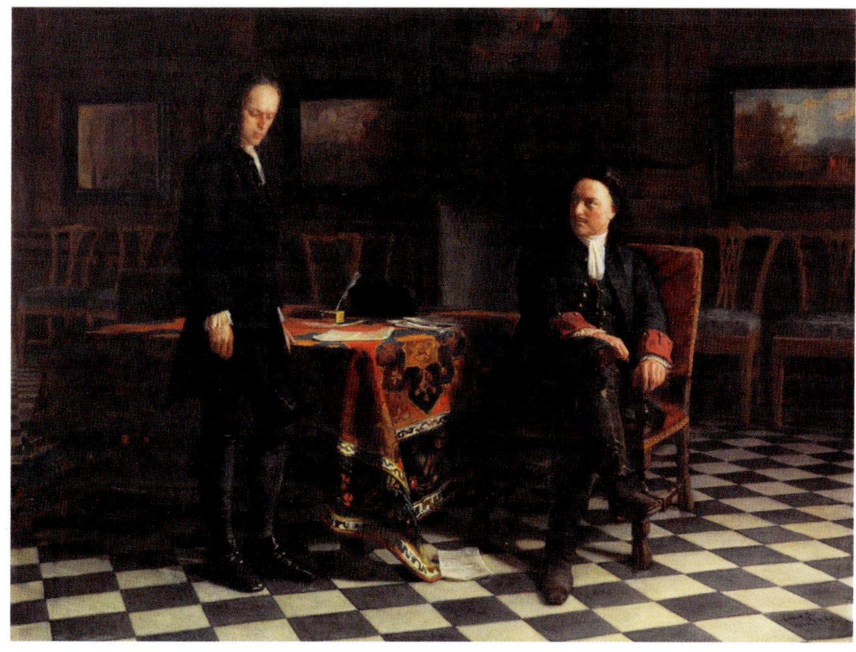

Tsarskoye Selo Palace

1707
Peter the Great secretly married Martha Elena Skowrońska, future empress under the name Catherine I. The marriage was officially celebrated in 1712 in St. Petersburg, in St. Isaac's Cathedral.

1710
With the Great Northern War, Peter the Great obtained the Sarskaya Myza estate from Sweden, about 15.5 miles from St. Petersburg, and gave it to his wife Catherine. The village was called "Tsarskoye Selo" ("Tsar's Village")..

1723
Based on a design by Johann Friedrich Braunstein, Catherine had a two-story cottage built in Tsarskoye Selo to replace the original wooden house.

1742–1743
On the throne since 1741, Empress Elizabeth, daughter of Peter and Catherine, decided to transform her mother's home in Tsarskoye Selo into a vast royal residence, which she named "Catherine Palace." She entrusted the project to Mikhail Zemtsov and his pupil. The palace was extended by 984 feet.

1752–1756
Francesco Bartolomeo Rastrelli, chief architect of the imperial court, was involved in the reconstruction of the palace. He was also responsible for the interiors and for designing the enormous surrounding park.

1770–1796
Catherine II, who became empress in 1762, had modifications made to the façade and interior of the palace. The Baroque architecture gave way to Neoclassical. The Scottish architect Charles Cameron was commissioned to modify the interiors.

1782–1796
Within the imperial estate of Tsarskoye Selo, Catherine II commissioned a new palace in the neoclassical style as a wedding gift for her grandson, the future Alexander I, emperor from 1801. The Italian architect Giacomo Quarenghi was responsible for the project.

1940–1944
During the German occupation, Catherine's and Alexander's palaces in Tsarskoye Selo were heavily damaged. The Germans dismantled the Amber Room from Catherine's Palace and transported it to Königsberg, where all traces of it were lost. The long restoration and reconstruction work began after the war.

After founding St. Petersburg in 1703 and beginning construction of the Winter Palace and Peterhof Palace on the Gulf of Finland, Tsar Peter the Great acquired the Tsarskoye Selo estate, about 15.5 miles from St. Petersburg, which had belonged to a Swedish nobleman, and gave it to his second wife, Catherine. Catherine, born in Latvia as Martha Elena Skowrońska to a family of peasants, had changed her name, as was customary, when she converted to Orthodox Christianity. She loved hunting and the outdoors, and the forest on the edge of the estate provided her with plenty of game for her leisure activities. The location was very pleasant, and the sovereign had a small brick residence built there by the architect Johann Friedrich Braun-

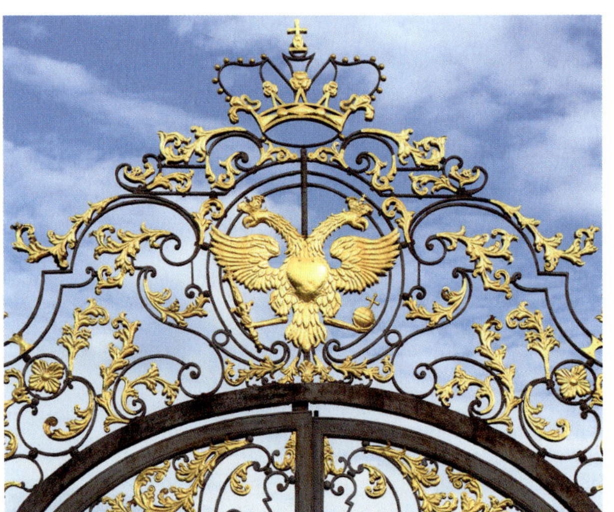

stein. After the couple died, the residence passed to their daughter Elizabeth. The new tsarina was not satisfied with her mother's modest home and had it transformed into a majestic palace in two separate phases. Between 1752 and 1756, the court architect Francesco Bartolomeo Rastrelli gave the palace its distinctive Elizabethan Baroque style, considered an expression of late European Baroque. The distinctive white columns and telamons appeared on the façade,

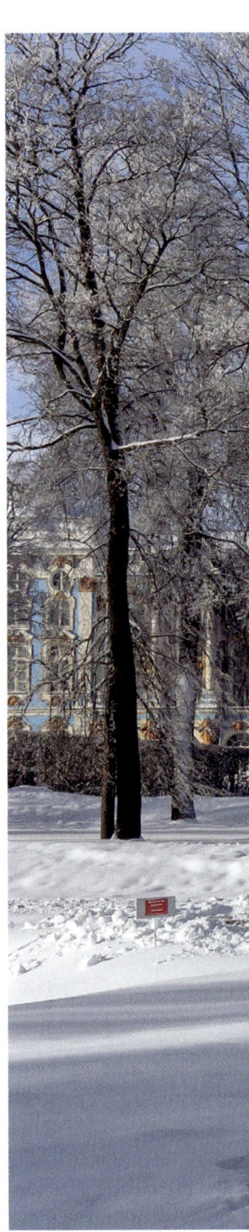

• 214 center: The gate of Tsarskoye Selo topped by the double-headed eagle of the Romanovs.

• 214–215: Catherine Palace and the surrounding park in winter. This magnificent residence is linked to three tsarinas: Catherine I, Elizabeth, and Catherine II. During Elizabeth's reign, it was decorated with gold, and even the roof appeared golden, as it was made of copper. The gold was later removed by Catherine II.

• 215 bottom: Aerial view of Catherine Palace, the most important building in the Tsarskoye Selo complex.

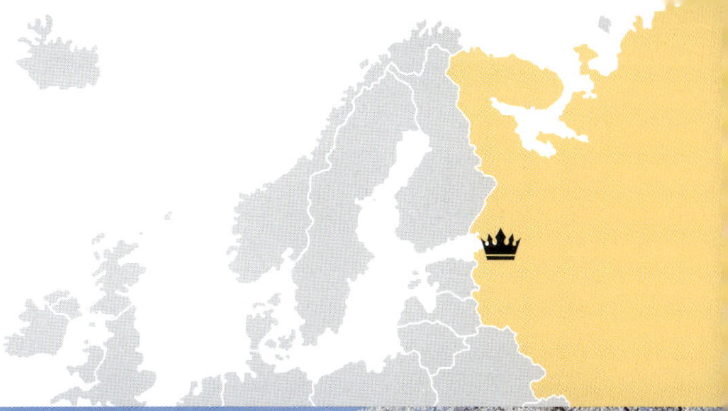

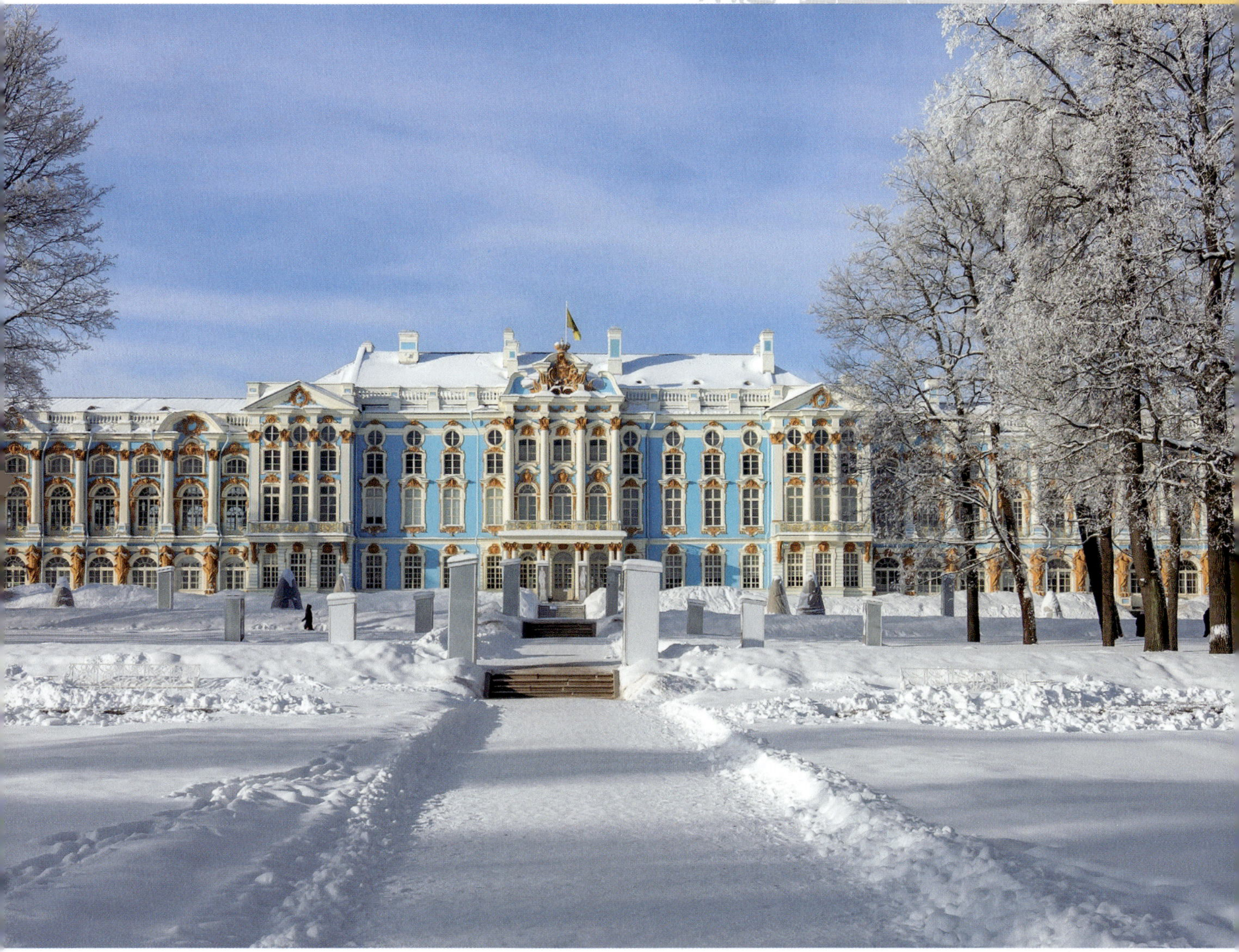

and gold was used lavishly, for example on the domes of the chapel and the sculptures. The architect also designed sumptuous interiors with a profusion of stucco, mirrors, and lighting effects.

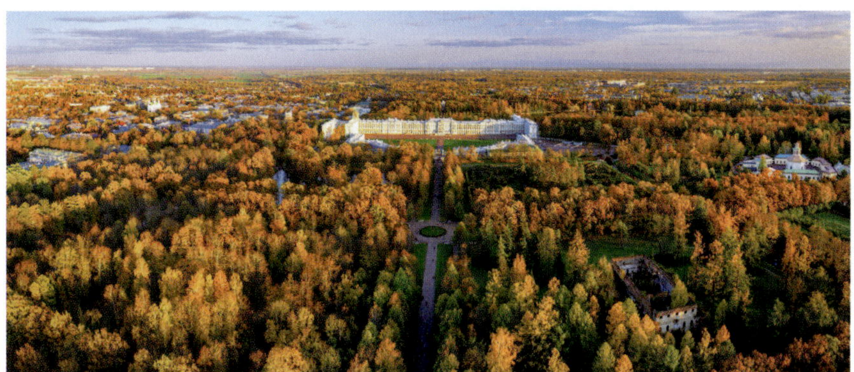

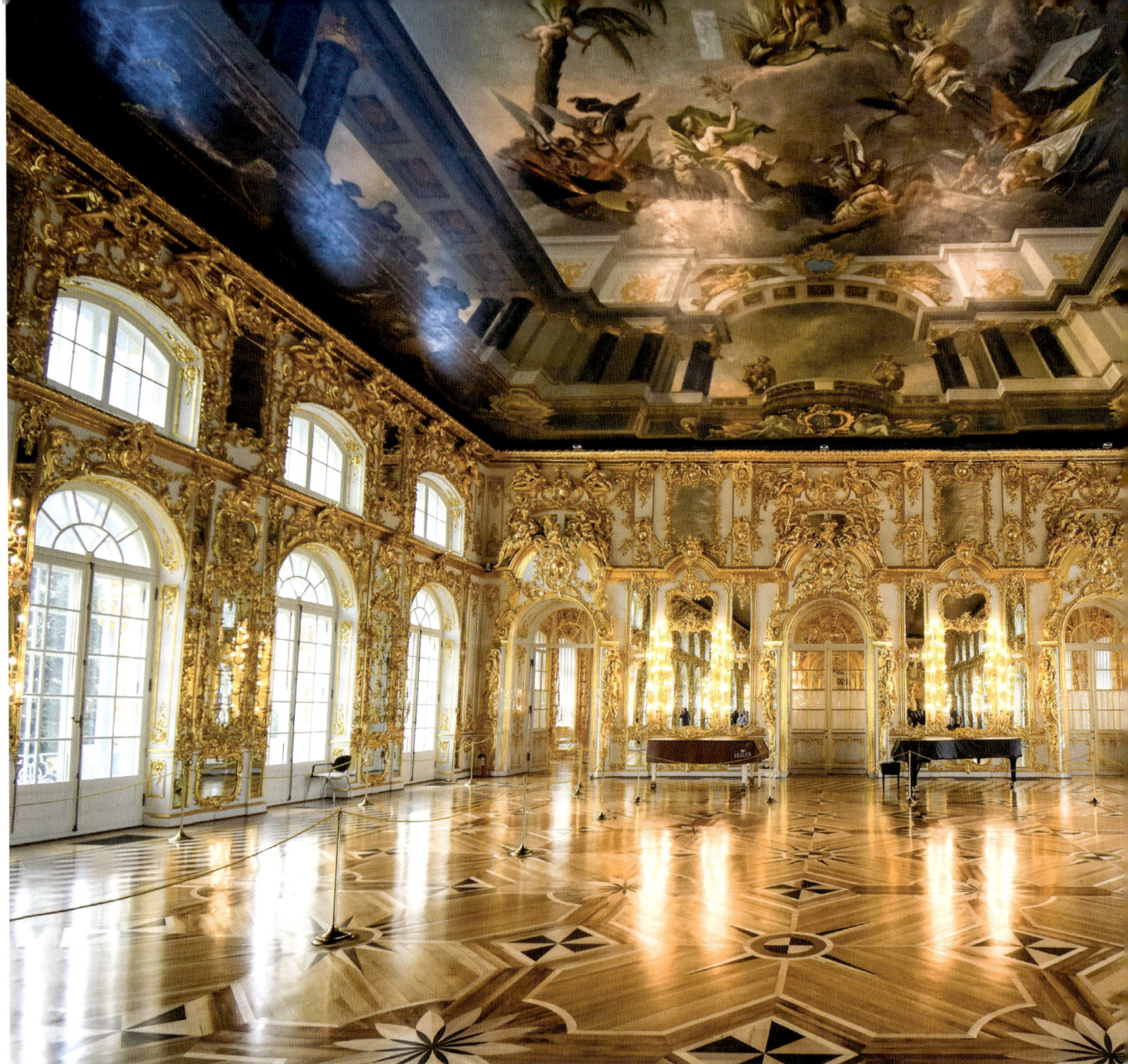

During Elizabeth's reign, the Amber Room—designed by architect and sculptor Andreas Schlüter—was relocated to Tsarskoye Selo. It had been donated by Frederick William I, King of Prussia, to Peter the Great in 1716. Further alterations to the palace were ordered by Catherine II, who ascended the throne in 1762. The empress considered Baroque architecture to be old-fashioned "whipped cream," and Rastrelli was relieved of his duties. The new mistress of the house preferred a more sober style in line with the new neoclassical taste that was beginning to prevail in the last decades of the 18th century. For her apartments in the northern part of the palace, Catherine II turned to a Scottish architect, Charles Cameron, who created more sober interiors of refined beauty, inspired by Roman and Greek antiquity. The same sobriety also characterized the State Study and some of the adjacent rooms furnished by Vasily Stasov for Alexander I, who commissioned the architect to celebrate Russia's victories against Napoleon in 1812. Finally, the new Grand Staircase was built in 1860 by Ippolit Antonovich Monighetti. After that, the Catherine Palace could finally be considered complete; but shortly thereafter, German forces intentionally destroyed the residence during World War II. Reconstruction began in the 1950s thanks to the work of Soviet archivists who had managed to document much of the interior before the war.

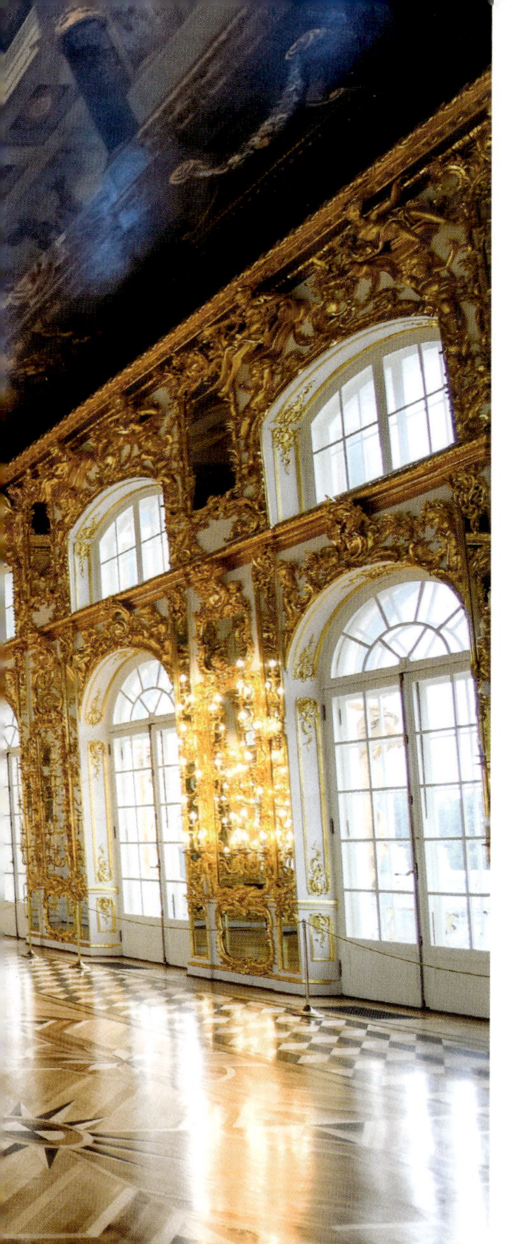

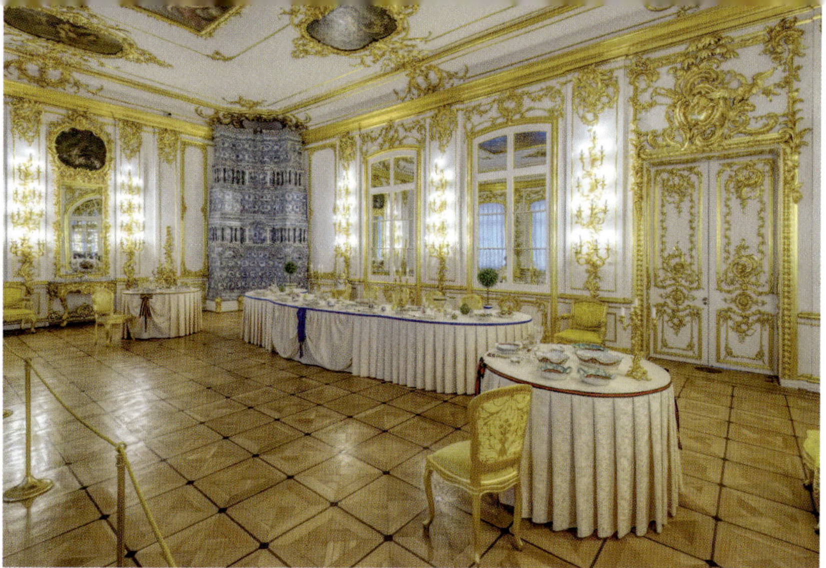

The Amber Room

In addition to being a masterpiece, the Amber Room has a truly curious history. Commissioned in 1701 by Frederick William I, King of Prussia, for his castle in Charlottenburg, it was given to Peter the Great by Frederick II after the Tsar, visiting Germany in 1714, was dazzled by it. The chamber was dismantled piece by piece, transported to St. Petersburg by sea, and from there pulled by sleigh to the Winter Palace, where, however, no one dared touch it for over 40 years for fear of damaging it. In February 1755, it was reassembled in Tsarskoye Selo on the orders of Elizabeth, thanks to craftsmen who had been brought in specially from Germany. Francesco Bartolomeo Rastrelli and one of his assistants adapted the panels to the dimensions of the room for which they were intended, adding others and no fewer than 24 mirrors. The Amber Room emerged unscathed from the 1917 Revolution, but not from the Nazi occupation. Before leaving the Catherine Palace, the Soviets tried to hide this masterpiece under layers of wallpaper, carpets, and other makeshift materials, but the Wehrmacht found it, dismantled it, and sent it to Königsberg Castle, from where it disappeared. Today's version is an exact copy, commissioned by the Soviet government in 1979 based on existing photographs and drawings.

• 216–217: Catherine Palace is famous for its Golden Gallery, a perspective created by a series of ten rooms arranged one after the other along a single axis, all decorated in late Baroque style with a profusion of gold and mirrors, starting with the Great Hall or Ballroom. Designed by Francesco Bartolomeo Rastrelli, it covers a rectangular area of almost 9687 square feet that was illuminated both by the light entering through the large windows and reflected on the mirrors, and by the glow of 700 candles.

• 217 top: Next to the Great Hall is the Knights' Hall, which was set up with a buffet where guests could refresh themselves on festive evenings and during balls. The tables display the porcelain services used by the imperial family. In one corner, a huge stove covered with blue and white Delft ceramics, each painted with different scenes that never repeat themselves, heated the room.

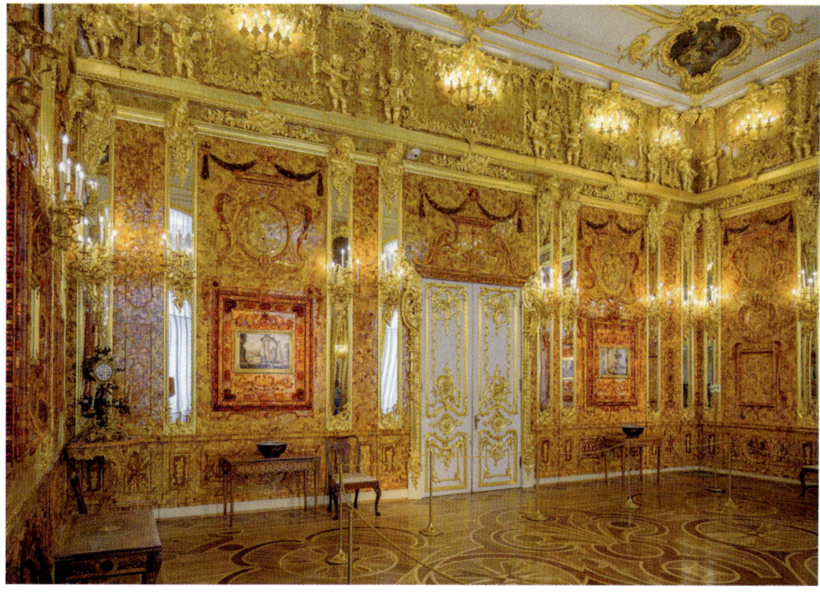

· 218-219: Built on top of a hill, Amber Fort was the seat of the ancient Rajput Kachhwaha clan until 1727, when the capital was moved to Jaipur. Just below Amber Fort, a garden seems to float on the waters of Lake Maota. This is Kesar Kyari Bagh, the saffron garden, because crocuses were once planted in its flowerbeds to produce the spice. It was created in the 17th century for the women of the harem, who could admire it from above and perhaps even reach it via an ingenious pulley system that served as a private elevator.

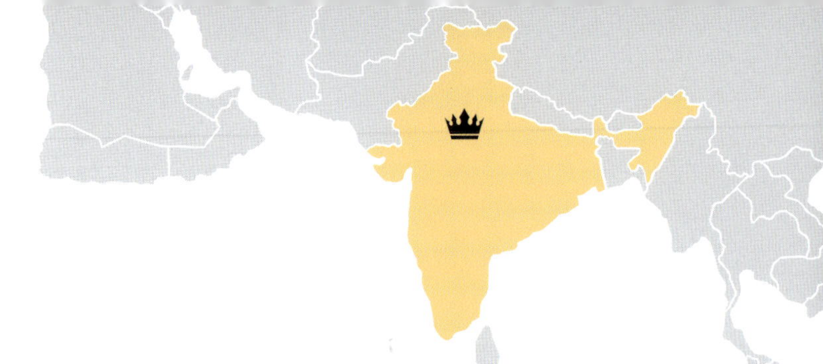

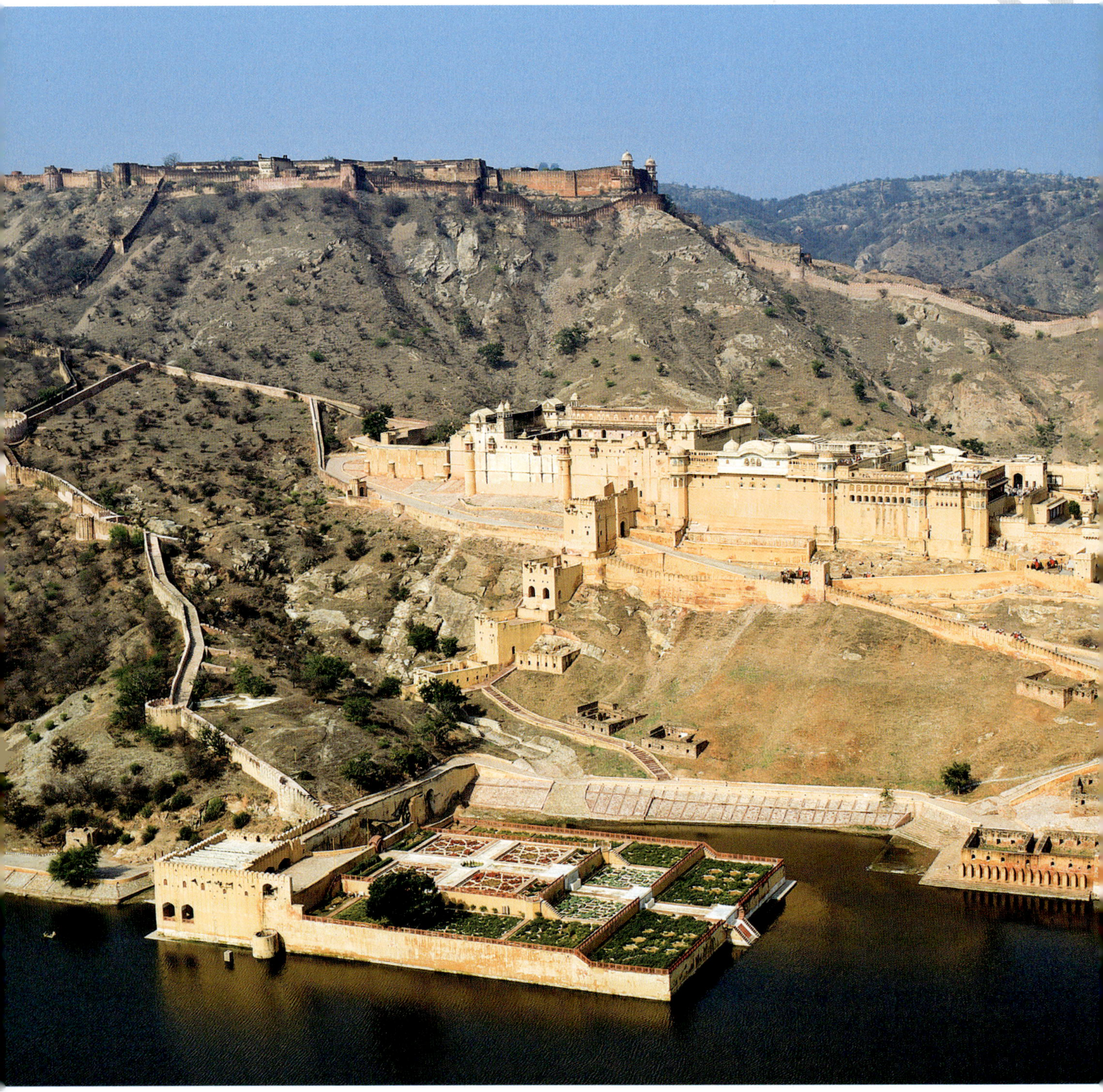

AMBER FORT

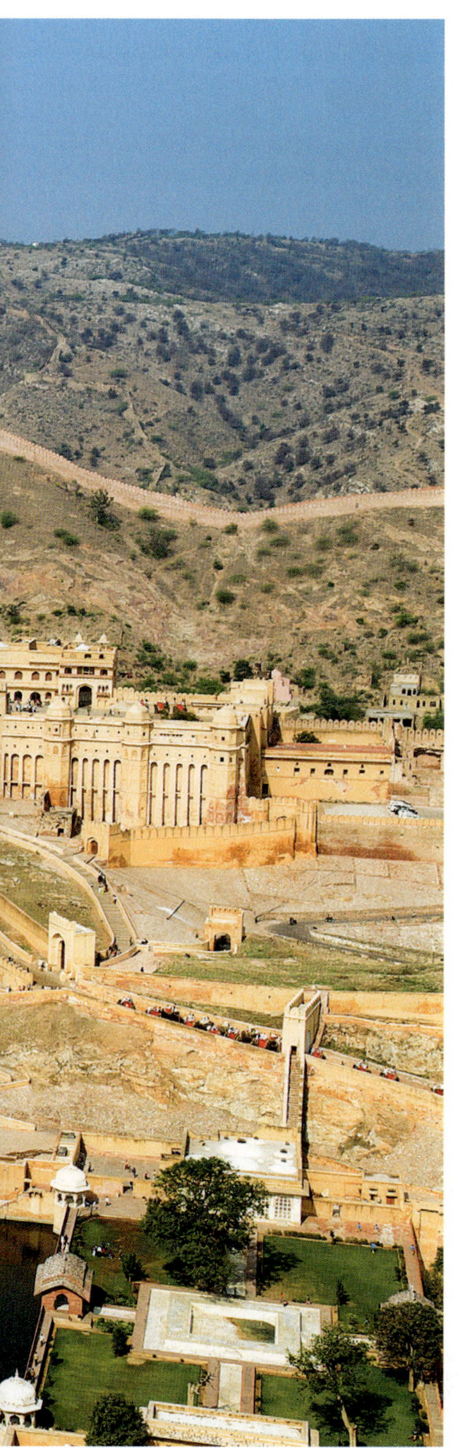

Situated 6.8 miles from Jaipur, capital of the Indian state of Rajasthan in western India, Amber Fort (or Amer) is considered the gateway to the magical land of the maharajas. This splendid palace-fortress guards the road to Delhi from the top of a hill at the base of which lies Lake Maota. Built in sandstone and marble, as was typical of Rajput and Mughal architecture between the 16th and 17th centuries, it was constructed by two maharajas belonging to the Rajput Kachwaha clan who were on good terms with the imperial family, Man Singh I and his successor Jai Singh I (1611-1667), rulers of the Kingdom of Amber. In his position as commander-in-chief of the Mughal imperial army, Man Singh I had accumulated immense wealth and wanted to spend it on the construction of a residence as opulent as the imperial ones that had so impressed him. Jai Singh I continued the work, completing and enlarging the fortress so that the Kingdom of Amber would also have its own magnificent royal palace. The Rajputs were a warrior caste and were well aware of the defensive requirements of architecture. For this reason, Amber Fort has mighty walls and is difficult to access due to its perched position. However, sheltered by the defensive structures, the luxury of the palaces, especially the private ones, is truly remarkable, starting from the narrow street—protected by the walls—that leads to the main gate, known as "Suraj Pol" ("Gate of the Sun") because it faces east. From there, you enter the Jalebi Chowk, the first courtyard, where the army gathered and victory parades were held upon returning from battle. Continuing along the path, you reach the second courtyard, which houses the Diwan-i-Aam or Hall of Public Audiences, characterized by a platform with 27 columns, each topped by an elephant-shaped capital. The magnificent Ganesh Gate leads to the third courtyard, where the maharaja's private apartments were located.

967
It is believed that a first fortress was built in Amber or Amer, a small town inhabited by the Meena clan, by Raja Alan Singh.

16th century
Around 1592, Raja Man Singh I of the Kachwaha dynasty expanded and modified the ancient fort, giving it its current appearance.

17th century
Jai Singh I added embellishments to Amber Fort, including the elaborate Ganesh Poll or Ganesh Gate, which leads to the third courtyard..

1727
The transfer of the capital from Amber to Jaipur marked the end of Amber's role as the main political center, but the fort continued to be used by the Kachwaha.

2013
Amber Fort, along with five other forts in Rajasthan, was added to the UNESCO World Heritage List..

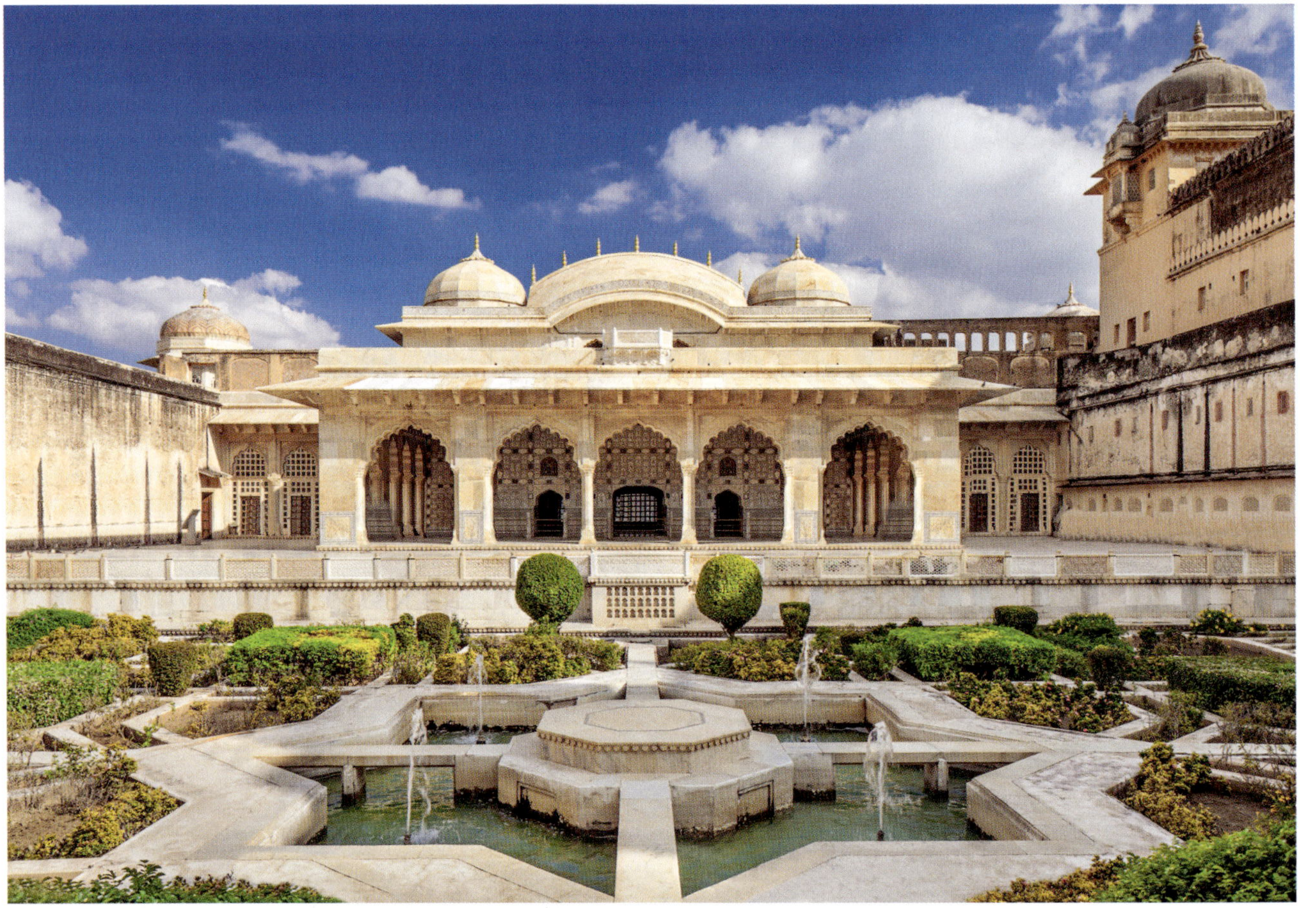

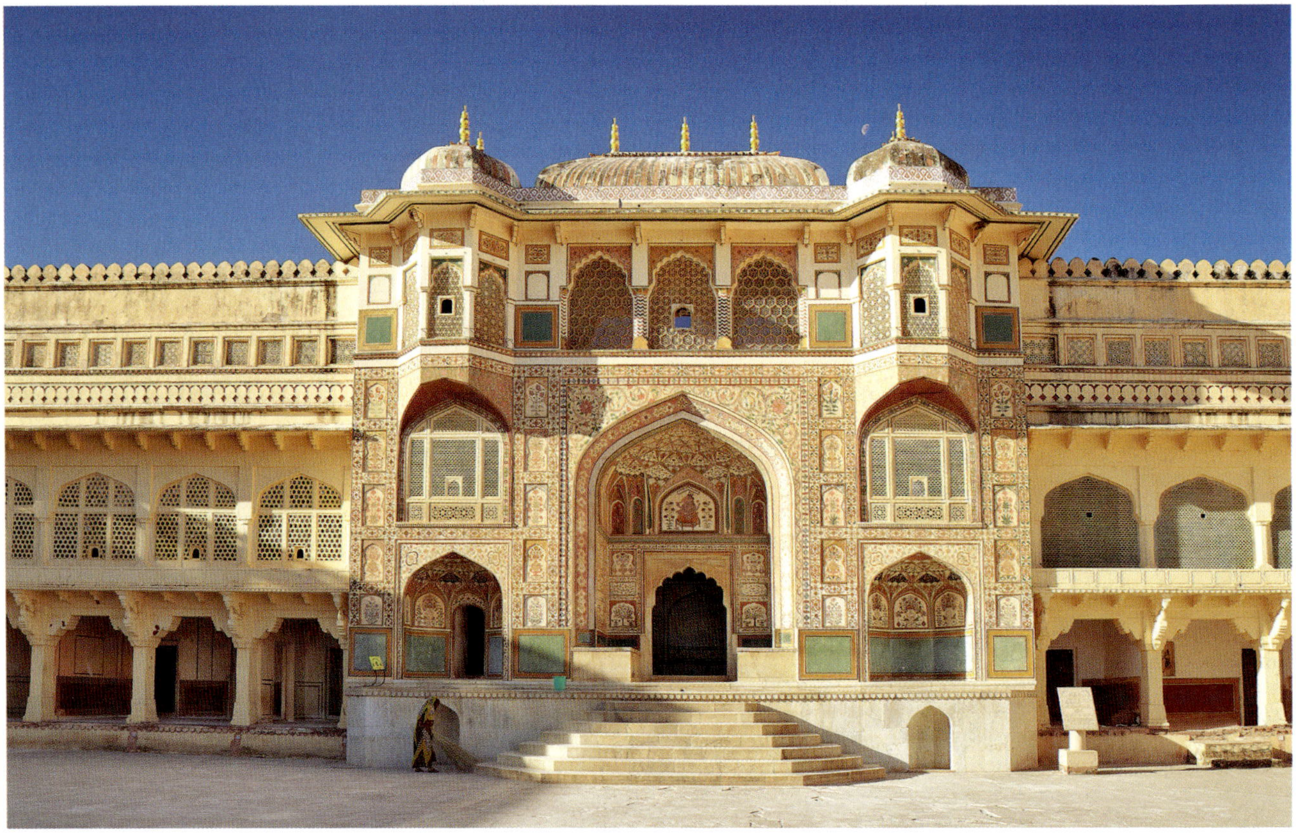

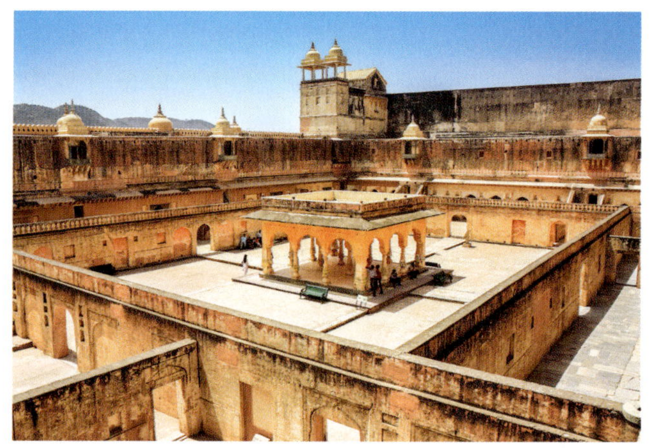

Two buildings face each other across a garden: the Shish Mahal or Palace of Mirrors, completely covered with mirrors and colored glass, intended as a place of rest for the maharaja, and the Sukh Mahal or Palace of Pleasure, where the maharaja found relief from the heat on hot days, thanks to a system of waterfalls that cooled the rooms. To the south of this courtyard is the palace of Man Singh I, which is the oldest part of the fort and the main palace of the complex. Finally, we come to the fourth courtyard, where the Zenana—the area of the residence where the women of the royal family lived, from the concubines and maids to the queen mother—was located. This courtyard also houses the Jas Mandir, a private audience chamber decorated with floral inlays in relief made of glass and alabaster.

· 220 top: The Shish Mahal, entirely covered with mirrors, is truly spectacular: the light of a single candle was enough to illuminate the walls with a thousand glimmers and transform the ceiling into an amazing starry vault. This wonderful effect was achieved at relatively low cost, considering that the mirrors and crystals cost less than the gems used profusely by the Mughal emperors and, in general, by the maharajas.

· 220 bottom: The Ganesh Gate is the entrance to the third courtyard of Amber Fort, which overlooked the private palaces. It owes its name to the Hindu god Ganesh, who is depicted just above the central opening. It has three floors, the third of which was reserved for women.

· 221 top: The Zenana, or harem, overlooked the fourth courtyard of Amber, the innermost courtyard of the fort. In the center of the courtyard stands the Baradari, an open pavilion created to provide shade and coolness on hot days, like a sort of parasol.

· 221 bottom: Located in the second courtyard, the Diwan-i-Am was the hall used for public audiences. Built on a platform, it has 27 columns in two rows, surmounted by an elephant-shaped capital.

The passage to Jaigarh Fort

Amber Fort is connected by an underground passage to Jaigarh Fort, located above it, on top of the promontory called "Cheel ka Teela" (Eagle's Hill) in the Aravalli Range. The passage was a useful escape route in times of war because it allowed members of the royal family and the court to move to the safer Jaigarh Fort, which had a more efficient defensive structure with thick red sandstone walls. In addition, from the 17th century onwards, Jaigarh Fort became one of the most efficient cannon foundries in the world thanks to the abundance of iron mines in the vicinity. Today, the Jaivana cannon is preserved in the museum: manufactured in 1720 at the beginning of the modern era, it was the largest wheeled cannon in the world.

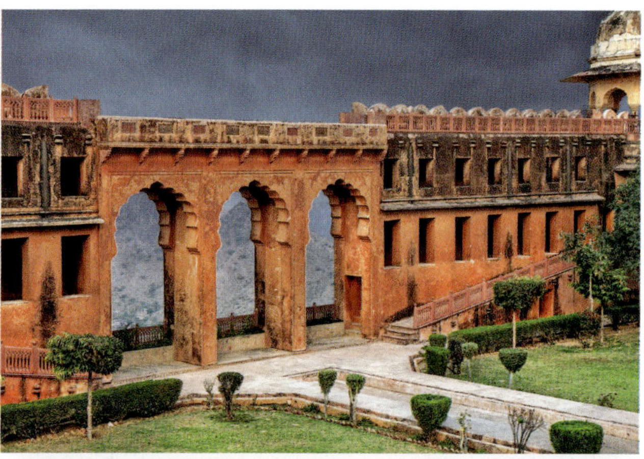

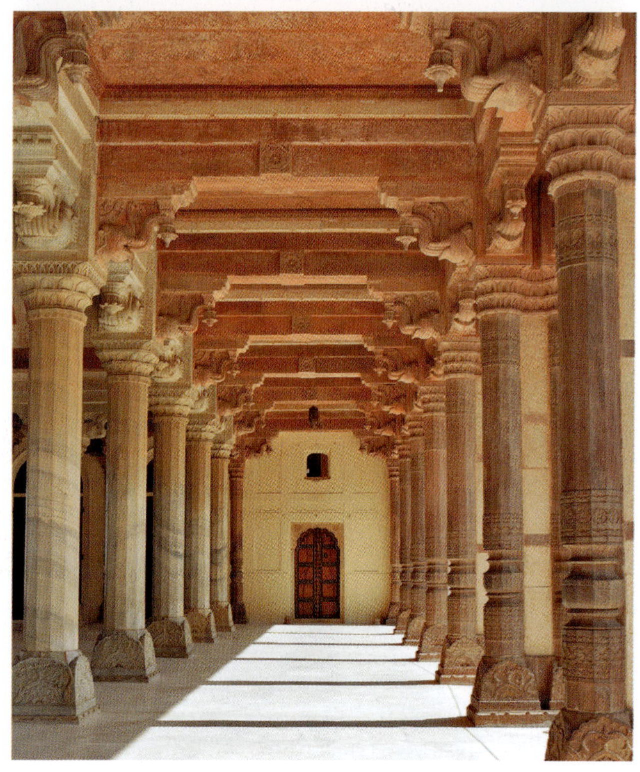

• 222-223: The colorful sloping roofs, golden spires, chedis, and Khmer-style towers of the Grand Palace stand out against the Bangkok skyline. A 6,233 foot-long circle of whitewashed crenellated walls surrounds the Grand Palace, which covers an area of 2,346,532 square feet. There are 12 gates in the outer walls and another 22 in the labyrinth of inner walls. The entrances along the outer walls are enormous because they had to allow the royal procession to enter on elephant-back. The most important gate is the Wiset Chaisri or Gate of Wonderful Victory, which leads to the Temple of the Emerald Buddha.

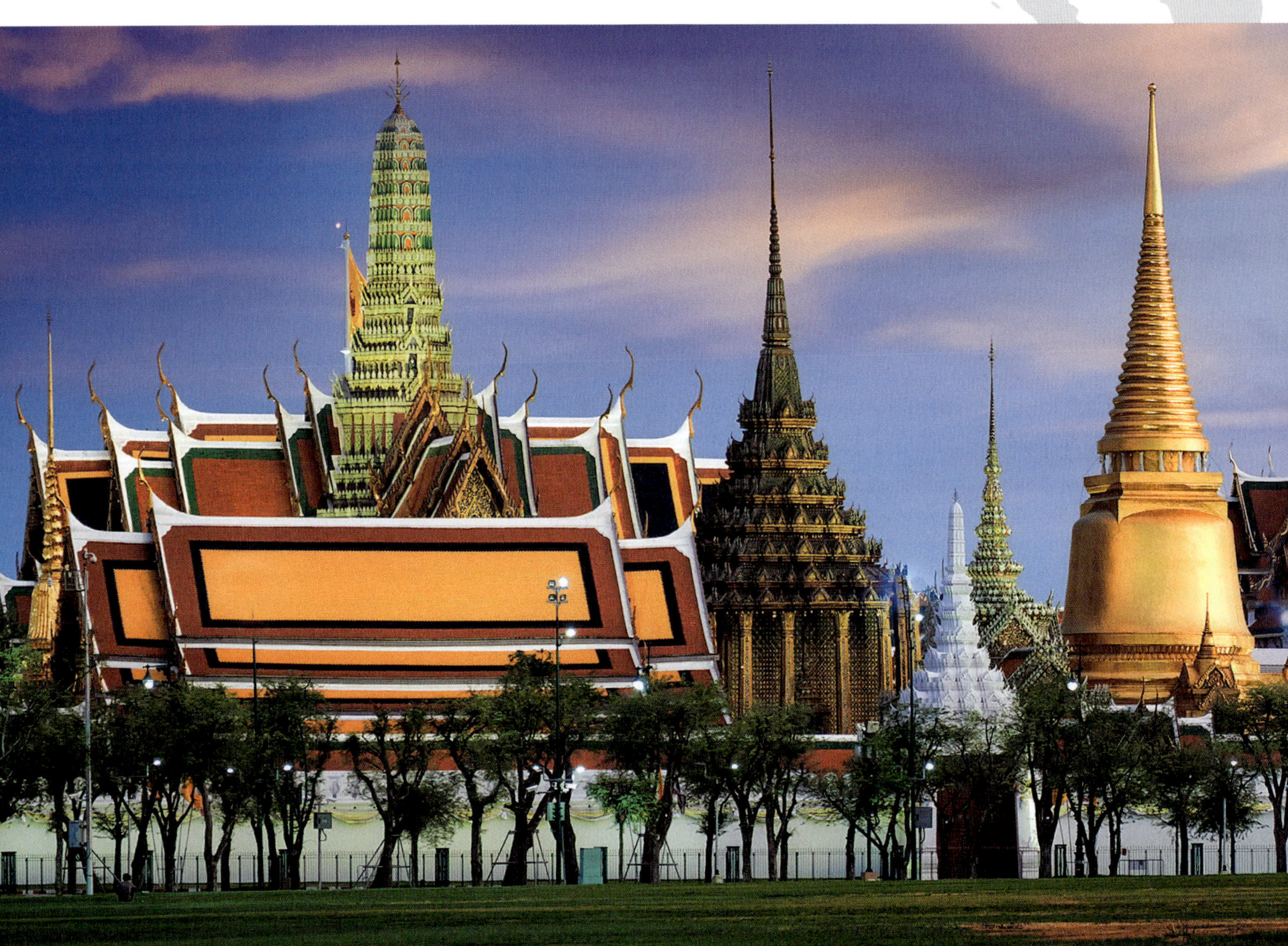

The Grand Palace in Bangkok was the residence of Thai monarchs, the seat of the court, and the administrative center of the kingdom for over two centuries. Even today, it is the most spiritually important place in Thailand because the Temple of the Emerald Buddha, the sacred heart of Thailand, is located within its grounds. In 1782, before construction work began on the palace complex, Rama I (the title Rama refers to the rulers of the Kingdom of Siam) chose to move the heart of his kingdom's capital from Thonburi to a village called "Bang Makok" or "Bang Kok," which was considered safer because it was protected by a river and a network of canals dug specifically for this purpose. The Grand Palace was built in the center of the island thus created. The new buildings were erected with bricks taken from the site of Ayutthaya, the ancient capital of Siam, destroyed by the Burmese about 15 years earlier, from which the Buddha statues were also recovered intact. Among the first parts to be completed was the Phra Ubosot (the shrine, the main temple) of the Wat Phra Kaew complex, built to house the most sacred image in the kingdom of Rattanakosin: the Emerald Buddha. Rama I's work was

Bangkok Royal Palace

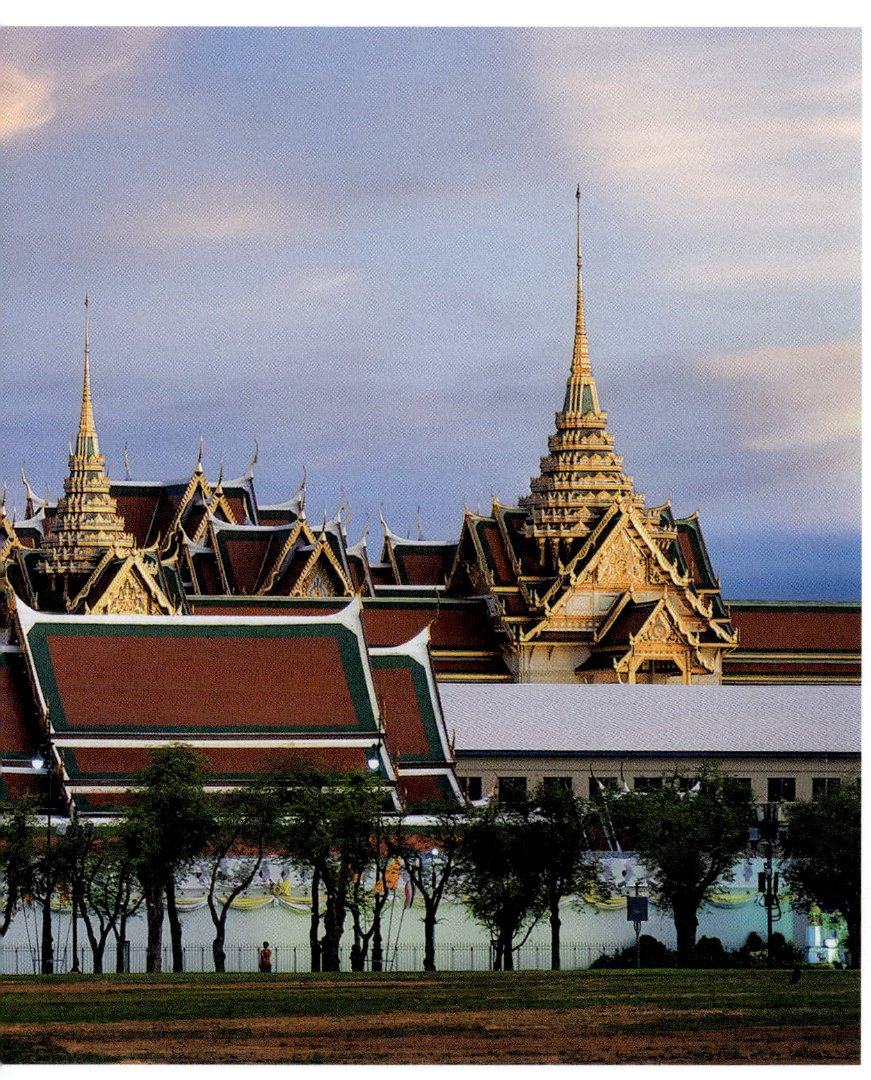

then continued by his successors of the Chakri dynasty, who over the course of two centuries added other palaces, pavilions, and temples to those already present within the complex (or demolished or restored the old buildings), resulting in a mixture of Siamese, Chinese, and even European artistic styles that make it quite a varied architectural complex. The unifying element, however, is the curved roofs covered with shiny colored tiles, with elegant pointed spires and sinuous golden decorative elements that shine in the sun, casting flashes of light. The complex consists not only of residential palaces, but also of royal offices and religious temples and monuments, making it look much more like a real city than a palace as it is understood in the West.

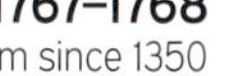

1767–1768
Ayutthaya, capital of the Kingdom of Siam since 1350 and one of the most prosperous cities in Asia, was invaded and destroyed by the Burmese. The capital was moved about 50 miles south to Thonburi, a town on the right bank of the Chao Phraya River, which is now a populous district of Bangkok.

1782
Rama I, founder of the Chakri dynasty, became ruler of Siam and moved the capital from Thonburi to the other bank of the Chao Phraya River. Here he created an artificial island called "Rattanakosin" and began construction of the Royal Palace complex.

1785
The Royal Palace of Rattanakosin was inaugurated by Rama I. The palace complex also included Wat Phra Kaew, where the sacred Emerald Buddha statue was transported.

1809–1824
During the reign of the second Chakri ruler, Rama II, the area of the Grand Palace was enlarged to the south, reaching its current size of 2,350,838 square feet.

1876–1882
Rama V entrusted two English architects with the construction of the Phra Thinang Chakri Maha Prasad, the new throne hall of the Grand Palace.

1893
The Grand Palace was in danger of being bombarded by two French warships that had managed to sail up the Chao Phraya River to Bangkok. To prevent this from happening, Rama V was forced to negotiate.

1897–1903
Upon his return from a trip to Europe, Rama V had a new royal district built with palaces similar to those he had seen in the Old Continent. The chosen site was a piece of land not far from the Grand Palace. Thus, Dusit was born.

1915
In the royal district of Dusit, the Ananta Samakhom throne hall was completed: it was an elegant palace in Carrara marble, commissioned by Rama V.

1939
On June 24, 1939, during the reign of Ananda Mahidol or Rama VIII, Siam changed its name and officially became "Thailand," land of free men.

2019
On May 5, the new king of Thailand, Maha Vajiralongkorn, also known as "Rama X," was crowned. He was born in the Dusit royal complex in 1952.

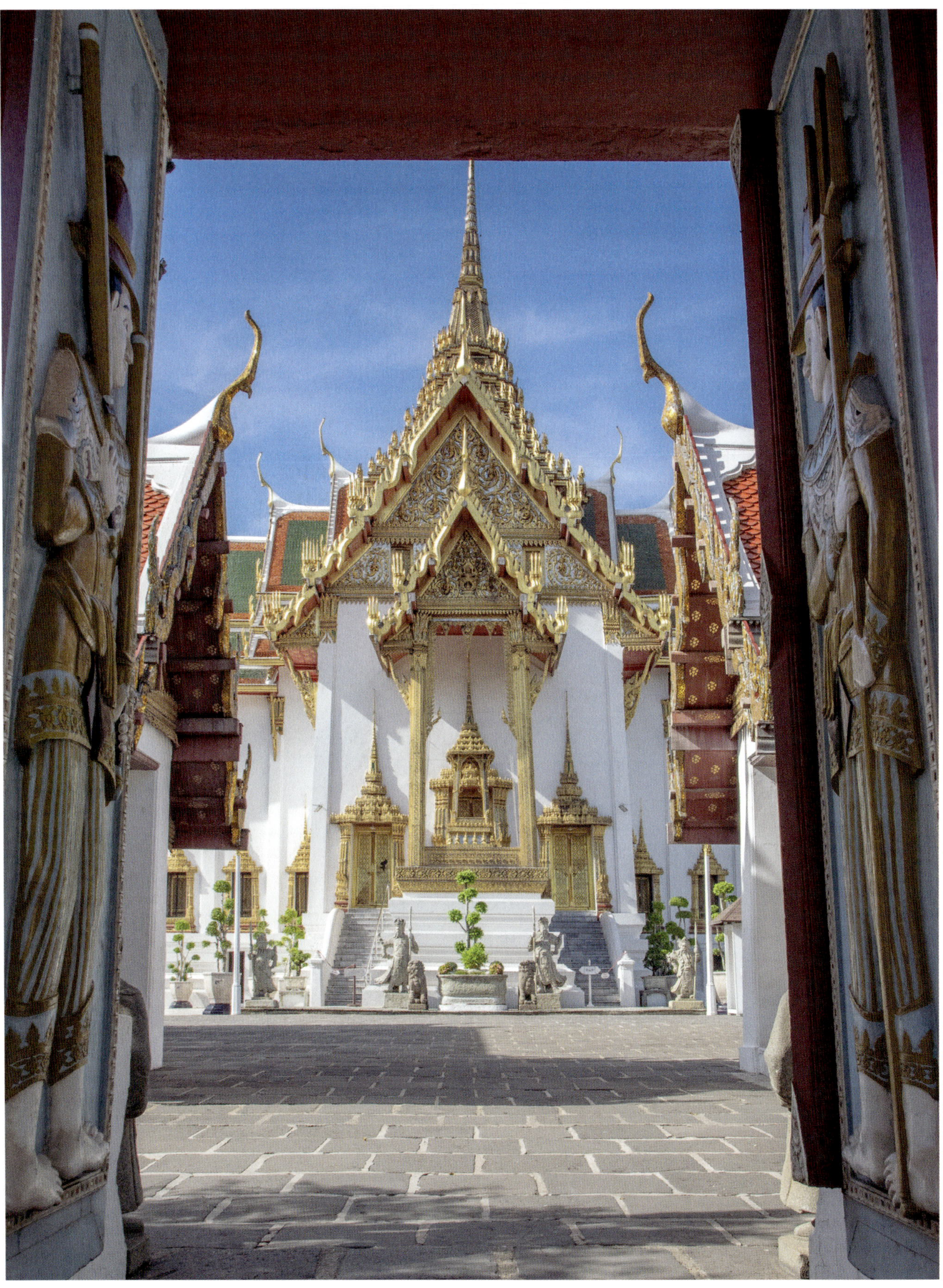

The residential and representative palaces where the Chakri kings lived and exercised their power are located in the central courtyard. Here, the king spent his days moving between his apartments and the throne rooms where he held court. Three groups of buildings can be identified: first, the ancient Phra Dusit Maha Prasad (in Thai style) and the Phra Maha Monthien (the true heart of the Grand Palace, because it was the residence of the kings and also housed some of the most important throne rooms in the complex). The private area was located in the innermost part, while the public area was in the outer part, near the entrance. From Rama II onwards, all Chakri monarchs were crowned here. The Chakri Maha Prasat, a Chakri palace dating back to 1882, reflects the modern and cosmopolitan taste of Chulangkorn or Rama V, who initially planned to cover it with European-style domes but then gave in to the Thai tradition of sloping roofs: a sign of Siamese resistance to Western imperialism, as well as the superiority of traditional architecture over modern architecture. The central spire of the palace houses the ashes of the Chakri kings and queens, while the side spires house those of the princes. Around the Sivalaya garden are buildings reserved for state guests, and in the center is the Emerald Buddha Temple. The current king of Thailand, Rama X, does not live in the Grand Palace, but in the Dusit Palace complex in another part of the city.

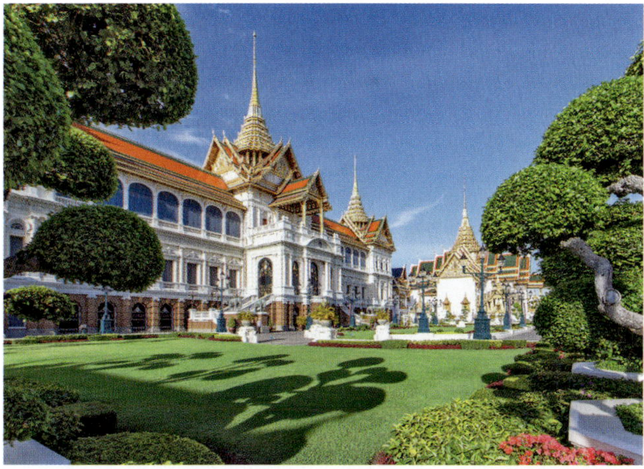

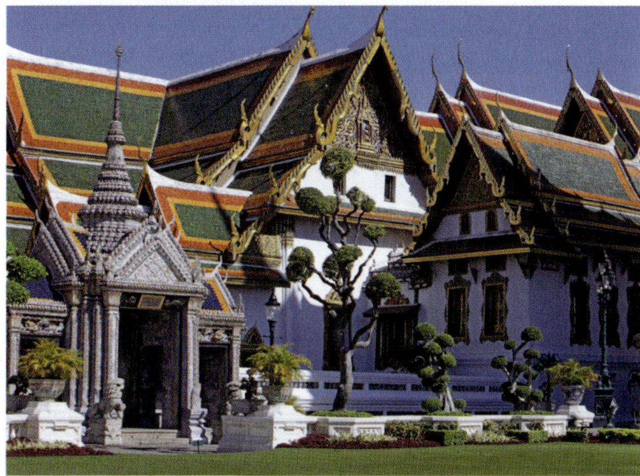

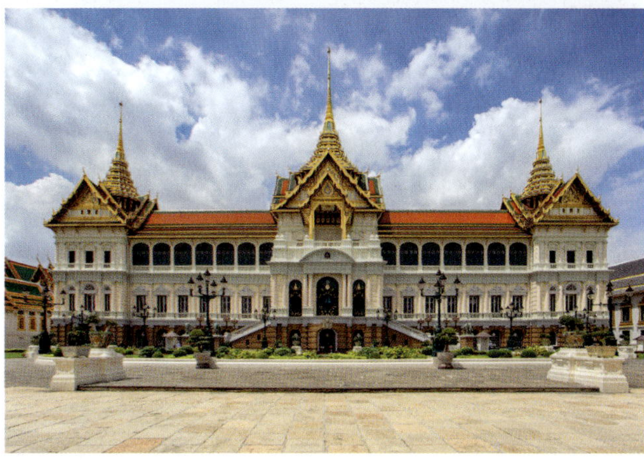

• 224: Phra Dusit Maha Prasad is one of the most elegant and spacious buildings in the Grand Palace: Maha, in Sanskrit, means "great" and Maha Prasad means "great hall." It was built for the coronation of Rama I and was later used for other ceremonies and audiences with a large number of people. Even today, this beautiful palace is used as a funeral chapel when a member of the royal family dies, before the body is taken for cremation.

• 225 top: In the central courtyard are the magnificent palaces that once formed the residences of the sovereigns and the throne rooms. The current royal family lives in the Amphorn Satharn villa in Dusit, but has kept its official residence here and returns to stay here for important ceremonies.

• 225 center: The group of buildings of Phra Maha Monthien, all connected to each other, is linked to the first kings of the Chakri dynasty, who lived here. Its construction began in 1785 under Rama I; subsequent rulers enlarged it by adding new throne rooms, pavilions, and even a portico, until Rama V moved the official seat of the kingdom to the adjacent Chakri Palace, built to celebrate the centenary of the Thai monarchy and the Grand Palace in 1882. The most intimate area of Phra Maha Monthien is the Chakraphat Phiman, the residential wing that includes the room where, according to tradition, all Thai kings spend their first nights after their coronation on the bed of their ancestors.

• 225 bottom: In the middle of the central area, between the Dusit Maha Prasad and Maha Monthien complexes, stands the imposing Chakri Maha Prasad or Chakri Palace. Chulalongkorn, or Rama V, entrusted the design to two English architects, John Clunich and Henry C. Rose, who were inspired by the Italian Renaissance.

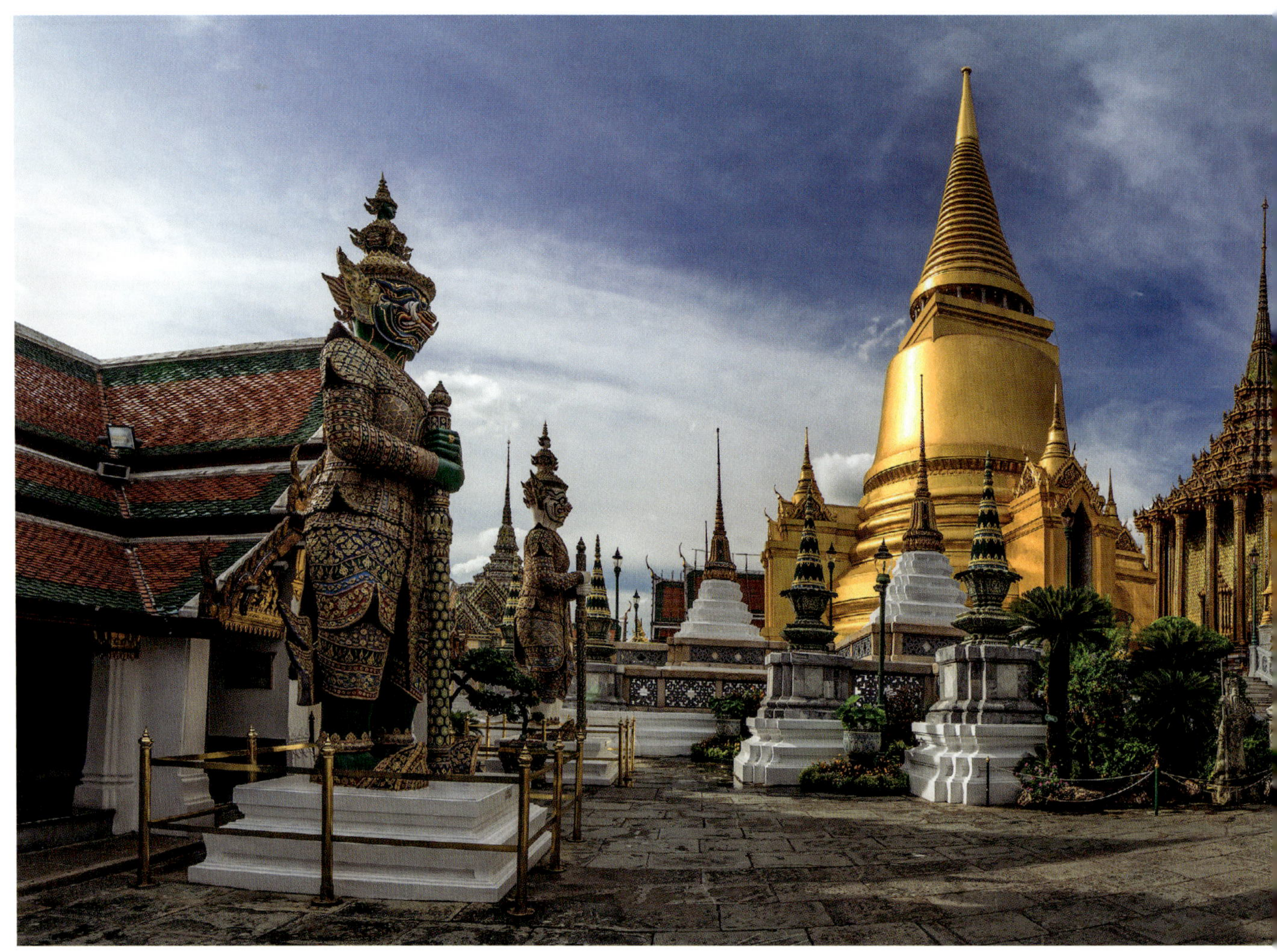

In the northeast corner of the outer courtyard of the Grand Palace is the Wat Phra Kaew complex, the temple of the Emerald Buddha, built between 1782 and 1795 by order of Rama I and then embellished, enriched, and restored by his successors. Since it is located inside the Grand Palace, albeit in an area separate from the residential area and enclosed by a high wall, no lodgings were built for the monks, who normally resided in Buddhist temples. For worship, it was sufficient to bring the monks from a nearby monastery. On March 22, 1784, the highly revered Emerald Buddha statue was transported in a solemn ceremony from Wat Arun, on the other side of the river, to its current location in a shrine inside the Phra Ubosot, or Buddha Chapel, surrounded by a low wall that further emphasizes its sacred nature. It is a rectangular building with a roof covered with shiny blue, yellow, and orange tiles. The entrance doors are decorated with mother-of-pearl inlays and the central door is used only by the king. Guarding the doors are 12 bronze lions placed at the base of the steps in front of them, in addition to the dozens of Garudas and Naga snakes with the same protective function which surround the building. The small green Buddha, a 26-inch-tall statuette carved, according to legend, not from an emerald but from a single block of jade, is said to be over 2,000 years old. In reality, it probably dates back to the 15th century: chronicles report that it was found in Chang Rai in 1434, hidden inside a larger plaster Buddha that was shattered during transport, revealing its precious contents. It was then transferred to Chiang Mai, in northern Thailand, in 1468.

• 226-227: The Wat Phra Kaew area is crowded with pavilions, tabernacles, statues, low walls, pinnacles, and trees. In the image, from left to right, you can see the large golden bell-shaped chedi commissioned by Mongkut or Rama IV in the mid-19th century, then the Mondop commissioned by King Rama I in 1785, then the Prasad Phra Thep Bidon with its tall Khmer-style prang and finally, on the right, you can glimpse the portico of the main chapel, the Phra Ubosot.

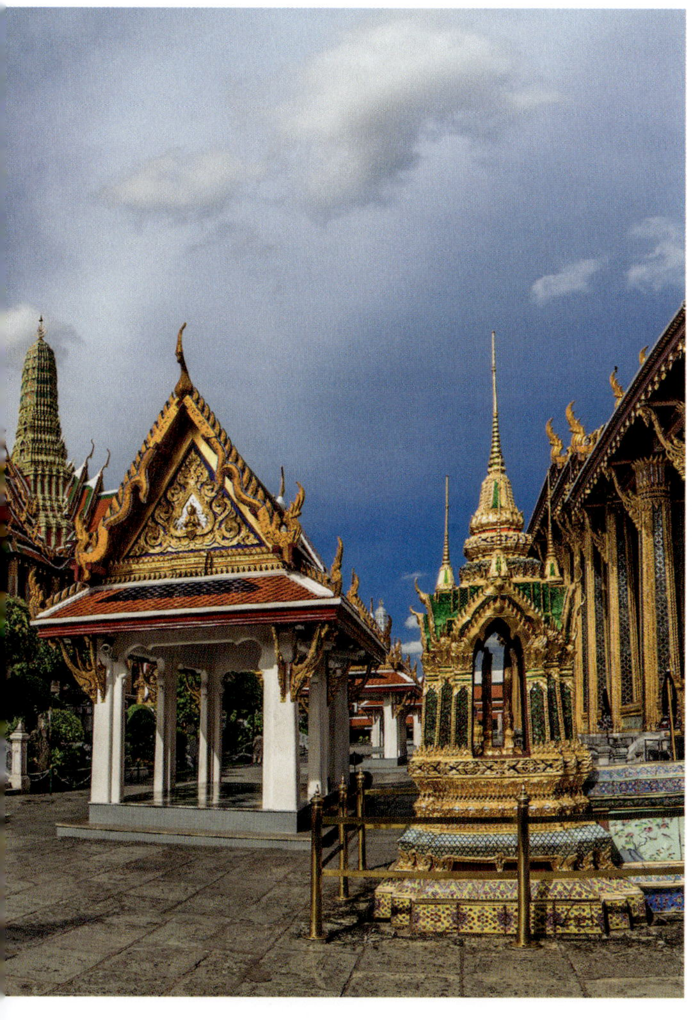

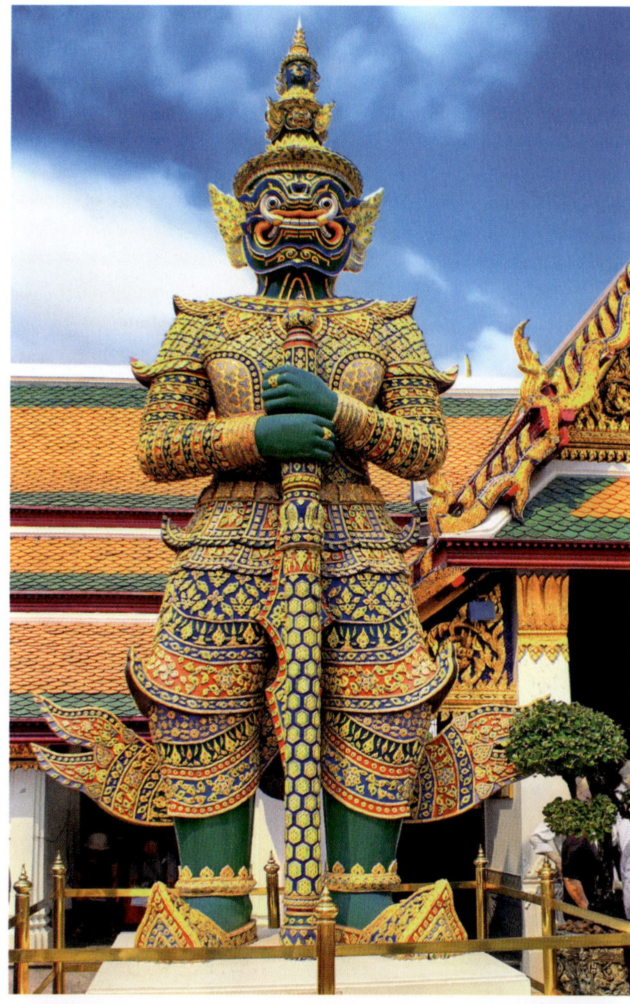

Buddha's clothes

At every change of season, usually in March, July, and November, since the time of Rama I, the King of Thailand himself (or, if unable to attend, a senior member of the royal family designated by him) goes to the royal chapel of the Grand Palace to change the clothes of the Emerald Buddha, of whom he is considered the guardian, and pray for the country and its people. In summer, he only puts on a pointed crown and various gold jewels with precious and semi-precious stones; in the rainy season, a monk's robe and a gold headdress studded with sapphires; in winter, a golden net shawl and a gold headdress studded with diamonds. At the end of the ceremony, the sovereign sprinkles holy water on those present.

• 227 top: The entrances to the temple area are guarded by colossal statues of 12 divine generals or Yaksha, supernatural beings who, in Hinduism and Buddhism, serve to ward off evil forces. These guardian spirits protect the Wat Phra Kaew, frightening men and demons with their imposing appearance and preventing evil spirits from approaching the chapel of the Emerald Buddha.

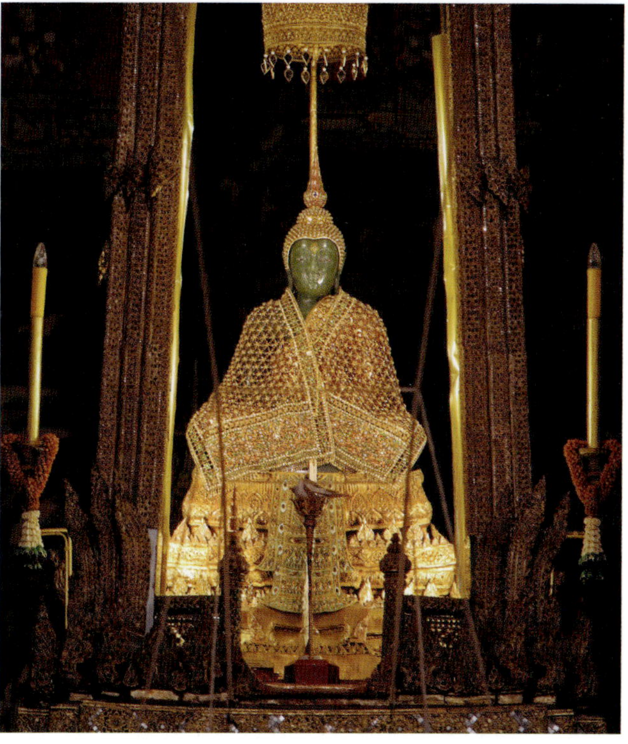

FORBIDDEN CITY

1206
Genghis Khan founds the Mongol Empire, which would extend over much of Central Asia. In 1234, the Mongols conquered northern China, replacing the Jin dynasty.

1279–1368
In 1215, the Mongols of Genghis Khan conquered Zhongdu (now Beijing), the "central capital" of the Jin dynasty. In 1264, Kublai Khan, founder of the Yuan dynasty in 1271, rebuilt the city, which took the name Dadu ("Great City"), also known as "Khanbaliq."

1368
Zhu Yuanzhang, a former Buddhist monk, led the uprising against the Mongols, conquered and destroyed Dadu in 1368, and proclaimed himself emperor under the name Hongwu, the first of the Ming dynasty. Nanjing was chosen as the capital of the empire.

1402
Yongle, having dethroned his nephew Jianwen, became the third emperor of the Ming dynasty and moved the capital from Nanjing to Beijing ("Northern Capital"). The new city was built on the ruins of Dadu.

1406–1421
The great construction site was opened in 1406, but it was not until 1421 that Yongle moved the throne to Beijing. Starting in 1416, thousands of workers were engaged in the construction of the Forbidden City, the immense imperial palace in the heart of the capital.

1420
While the Forbidden City was being completed, work began on the Temple of Heaven or Tian Tan.

1644
The last ruler of the Ming dynasty, Chongzhen, hanged himself on Jingshan Hill, or Coal Hill, before the Manchu army entered Beijing. The young Shunzi was proclaimed emperor of China: he was the first of the Qing dynasty.

1750
The fifth Qing emperor, Qianlong, who reigned from 1735 to 1796 like his predecessors, resided in the Hall of Mental Education within the Forbidden City (the Ming emperors resided in the Palace of Heavenly Purity).

1856
The Second Opium War broke out. The British army occupied the Forbidden City until the end of hostilities.

1861
Upon the death of Emperor Xianfeng in 1861, his favorite concubine Cixi, mother of the heir to the throne, became regent of the empire for 47 years. Several palaces in the Forbidden City are associated with her: the Palace of Concentrated Beauty, the Palace of Concentrated Excellence, and, next to it, the Palace of Universal Happiness.

1912–1924
Pu Yi, the last emperor, was deposed following the revolution led by Sun Yat-sen, which led to the proclamation of the Republic of China. Pu Yi was allowed to remain with his family in the inner part of the Forbidden City until 1924.

1987
The Forbidden City was declared a World Heritage Site by UNESCO.

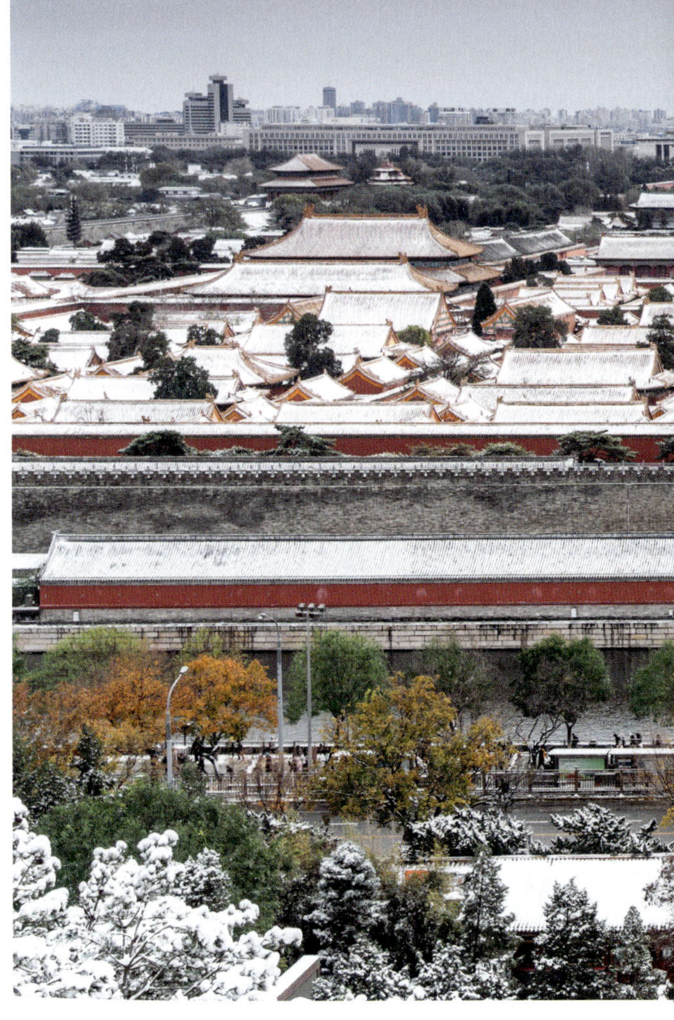

Over the course of five centuries, 24 emperors lived in the Forbidden City, the enormous palace in the center of Beijing, which was off-limits to subjects and therefore shrouded in an aura of sacredness and solemn respect. Its construction began in 1406 after Emperor Yongle of the Ming dynasty moved the capital from Nanjing to Beijing ("Northern Capital"), a city with ancient origins that met the need to defend and control the borders from invasions by the Mongols and the peoples of the steppe. Yongle's architects, in accordance with the laws of ancient Chinese geomancy,

• 228-229: View of the Forbidden City. In the foreground is the Gate of Divine Might, the northern entrance to the palace complex and, today, to the museum. The entrance gates used by the emperor, with the exception of the Glorious East Gate, were decorated with nine rows of nine metal studs. Nine is the magic number and recurs everywhere in the Forbidden City.

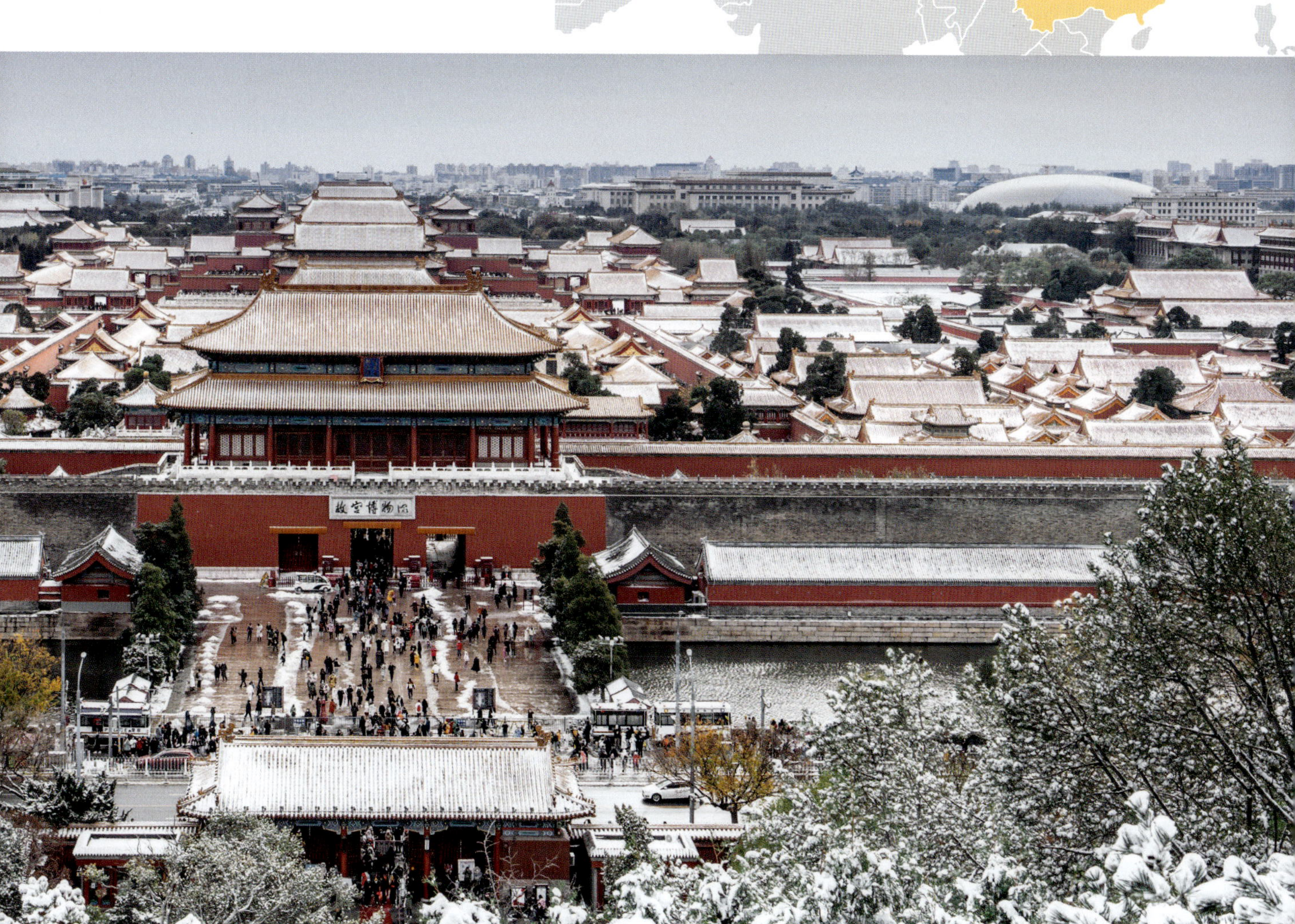

designed the immense palace of the Son of Heaven to recreate the harmony of the cosmos. Over the course of 15 years—the emperor did not move in until 1421—at least one million workers and about 250,000 craftsmen worked on the immense construction site. The necessary materials arrived by river: thousands of tons of precious nanmu wood from the southern provinces, millions of bricks made from Shandong clay, and tiles to cover 1,722,222 square feet of flooring. The craftsmen of Liulichang (a district of the Outer City) were experts in the production of a renowned colored lacquer ("Liuli" in Chinese): their kilns produced the yellow tiles, the color of the emperor, which covered the roofs of the Forbidden City. In a rectangular area (3153 x 2470 feet), 9,999 and a half rooms were built, counting the large halls, but also—according to the Chinese concept of "room," which differs from the Western one—the small rooms, even the corridors and connecting passages. The half room corresponds to a tiny room in the courtyard of the Imperial Library and, according to legend, is included to emphasize that the Son of Heaven possessed a palace only slightly smaller than the mythical palace of the Jade Emperor, the Lord of Heaven, which consisted of 10,000 rooms.

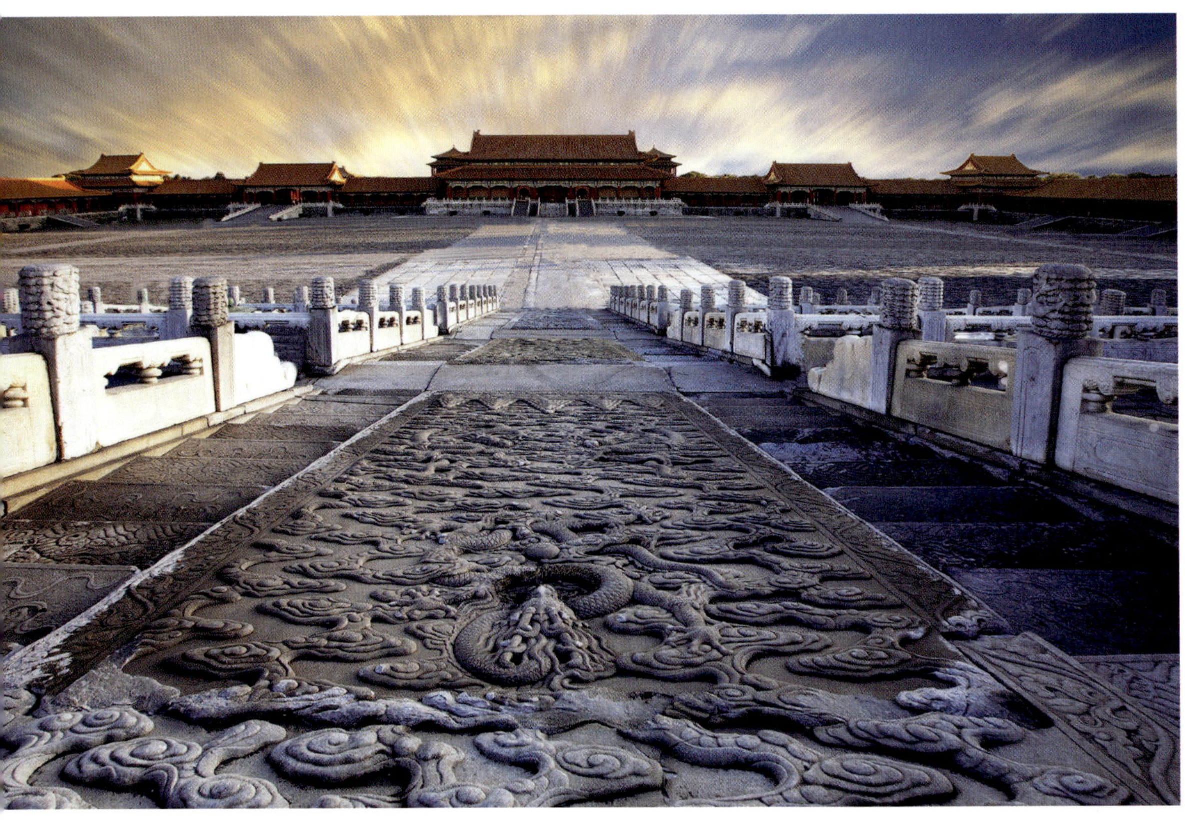

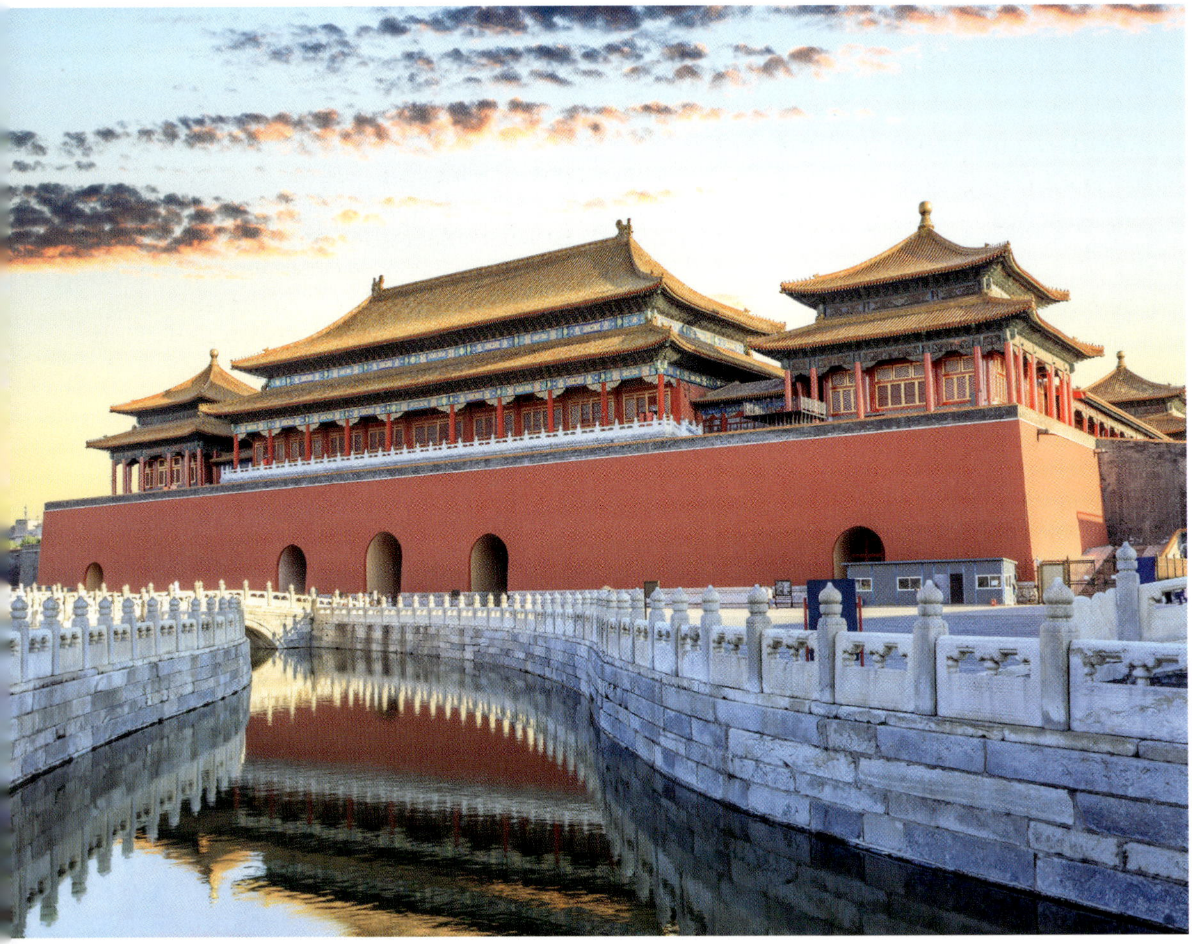

• 230 top: The spectacular courtyard between the Gate of Supreme Harmony and the Hall of Supreme Harmony, the heart of the Forbidden City: during collective audiences, it could hold 100,000 people. In the foreground is the access ramp to the Hall of Supreme Harmony, reserved for the emperor: it is a huge slab of marble finely carved with dragons, the imperial emblem, playing with pearls. Almost 56 feet long, 9 feet wide, and almost 2 feet thick, it weighs 275 tons.

• 230 bottom: In the courtyard between the Meridian Gate and the Gate of Supreme Harmony (656 feet long and 984 feet wide) flows the River of Golden Water, bordered by marble banks. It is crossed by five bridges representing the cardinal virtues of Confucianism: benevolence, righteousness, ritual, loyalty, and wisdom. The waterway was not only decorative, but also served as a useful water reserve in case of fires, which were a frequent occurrence in the Forbidden City.

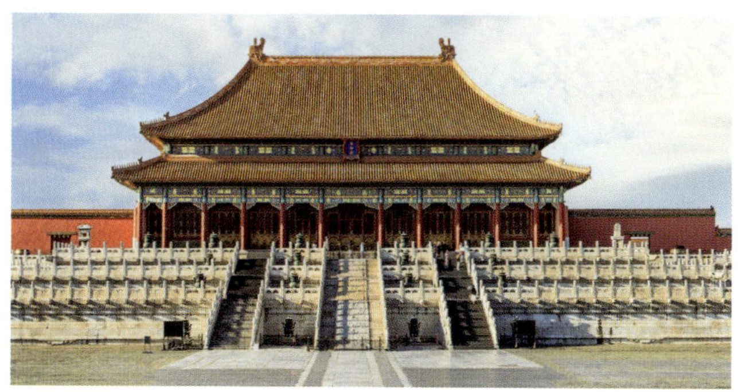

· 231 top right: On the raised corners of the roof covered with yellow tiles and supported by 24 columns, an odd number of fantastical figures stands guard: the dragon, the phoenix, the lion, the celestial horse, the sea horse, the leopard, the turtle, the unicorn, the fish, and the monkey, plus an immortal knight. They have the difficult task of defending the hall from fire, the worst enemy of the wooden structure, which has suffered several fires over the centuries. The last reconstruction took place in 1695 by the second emperor of the Qing dynasty.

The visit begins at the Porta Meridiana—131 feet high, including the masonry base—with its U-shaped architecture and three pavilions with elegant double-pitched roofs. From the tribune of the imposing central pavilion, emperors presided over official ceremonies, reviewed victorious armies returning from war campaigns, witnessed the punishment inflicted on high dignitaries guilty of offending the Son of Heaven (who were beaten to death with bamboo canes), and proclaimed official edicts. Once through the gate, you find yourself in the square opposite the Gate of Supreme Harmony. This space has nothing to do with the grandeur of the Meridian Gate, but is softened by the low architecture on the east and west sides, interrupted by side gates, and by the winding Golden Water River. Passing through the Gate of Supreme Harmony, you come to the iconic view of the courtyard—656 x 623 feet—in front of the Hall of Supreme Harmony which, together with the Hall of Middle Harmony and the Hall of Protected Harmony, corresponds to the so-called Front Palaces, used for official ceremonies. The first symbolizes the sacredness of the Empire and is located in an elevated position above the rest of the buildings of the Forbidden City, on three levels of marble terraces: a law established that no building could be taller. On the three-story terrace, 18 incense burners (each symbolizing a province of ancient China) emitted clouds of sandalwood and pine fragrance that seemed to float among the heavenly clouds above the pavilion where the throne of the Son of Heaven was located. Solemn audiences and the most significant events took place inside the Hall. To enter the Hall of Supreme Harmony, you must pass through a series of doors designed to gradually raise your expectations. After all, you are entering the largest wooden structure in China today: 114 feet high, 210 feet long, and 121 feet deep, covering an area of 25,586 square feet. Inside, the dragon, the imperial emblem par excellence, is the most represented animal, giving its name to the so-called Dragon Throne, a term also used in an abstract sense to rhetorically define the emperor himself and his kingdom. On either side of the space leading to the ideal center of the Forbidden City are pavilions that once housed libraries, offices, and warehouses.

The architects' ingenuity

The period during which the Forbidden City was built is relatively short when you consider that numerous buildings were constructed over a total area of 7,750,015 square feet and that the building materials came from several miles away from Beijing. For example, the logs used to make the columns of the three halls of the palace's inner court were brought from the forests of Sichuan, a province in southwestern China, crossed by a section of the Yangtze River. Cedar trees (whose wood is easy to work with, but also very strong and able to support heavy loads andis withstand temperature changes) were cut down during the rainy season and rolled down to the river, which was connected to the Grand Canal (which had to be partially rebuilt) through which they reached Beijing. The construction technique, used in China since the first millennium BC, was nothing short of ingenious and still amazes today: the columns, resting on a stone base, supported the roof connected to them through a wooden support. Not a single nail was used to hold the elements together, which were manufactured before construction of the Forbidden City began and only arrived at the construction site at the time of assembly.

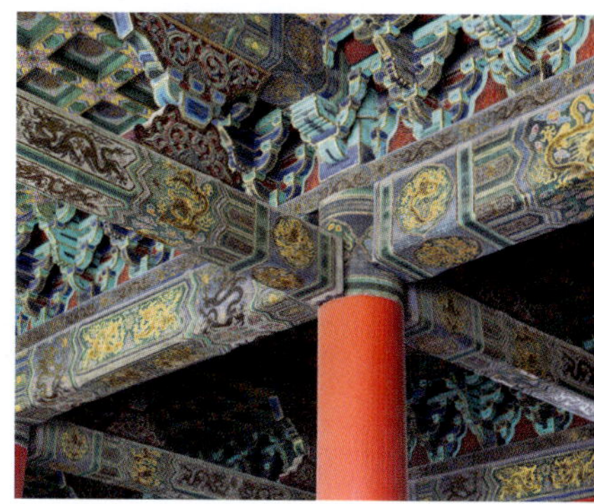

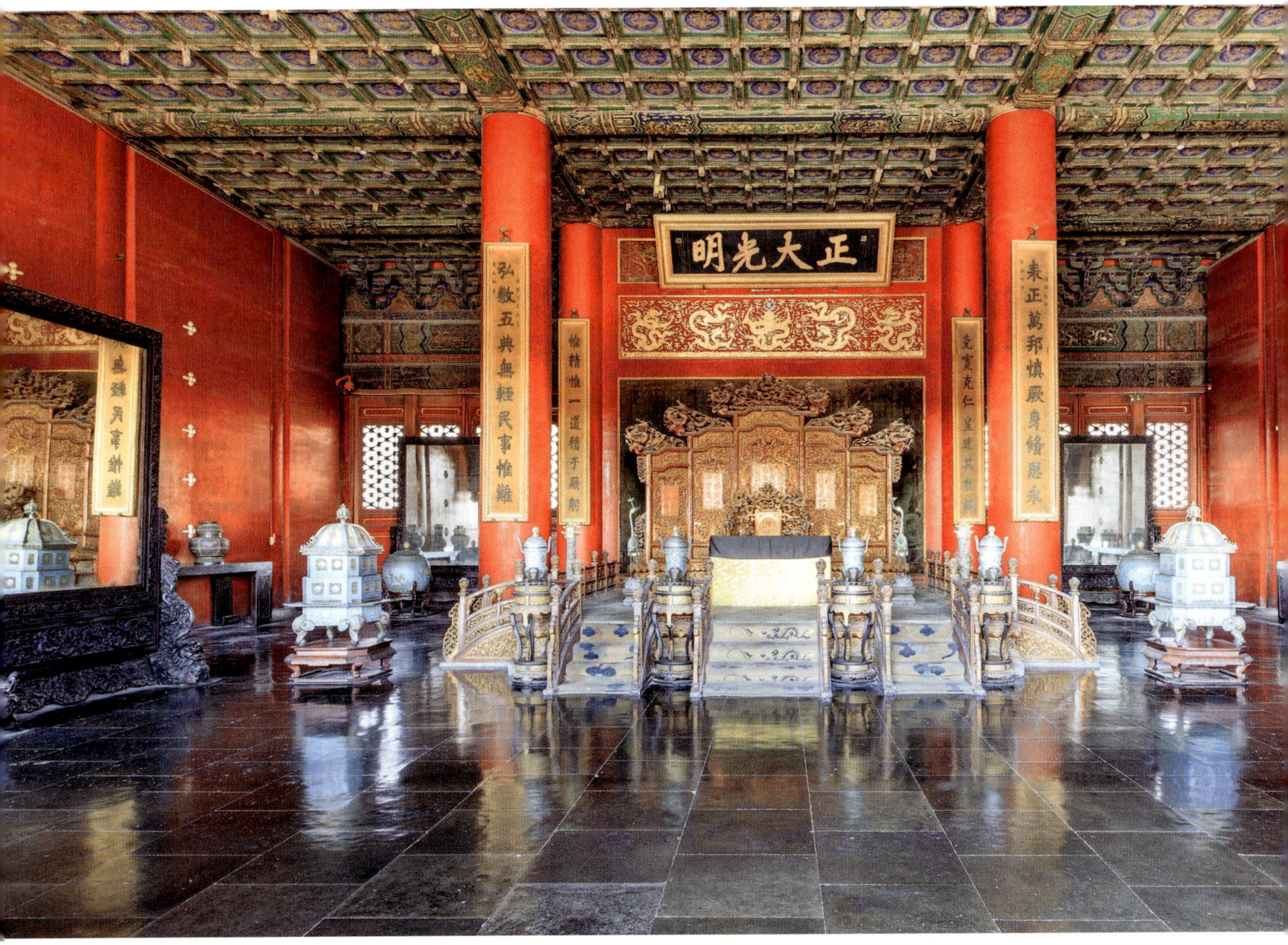

The emperors' banquets

Since ancient times, food has been considered a kind of medicine for the body and soul in Chinese culture, and great attention was paid to food and rituals related to banquets. Chinese emperors were well aware that the stories told by their guests would contribute to spreading the legendary image of the Sons of Heaven. Suffice it to say that banquets considered "modest" consisted of about 70 courses, while the most lavish ones consisted of 365 dishes, one for each day of the year, served over three consecutive days. To prevent the emperor from being poisoned—palace conspiracies were not uncommon—a silver chopstick was placed in each dish: if arsenic was present, the chopstick would change color. Around a hundred cooks worked in the kitchens of the Forbidden City, each specializing in the preparation of a single dish. To satisfy the palates of the diners and ensure the variety of the numerous courses, it was inevitable to resort to the use of unusual ingredients. Among the dishes served were stuffed bear paws, snails, various types of snake soup, seaweed swallows' nests, abalone seafood, dried shark fins, turtles, geckos, and the inevitable lacquered duck, whose recipe dates back to the Ming dynasty.

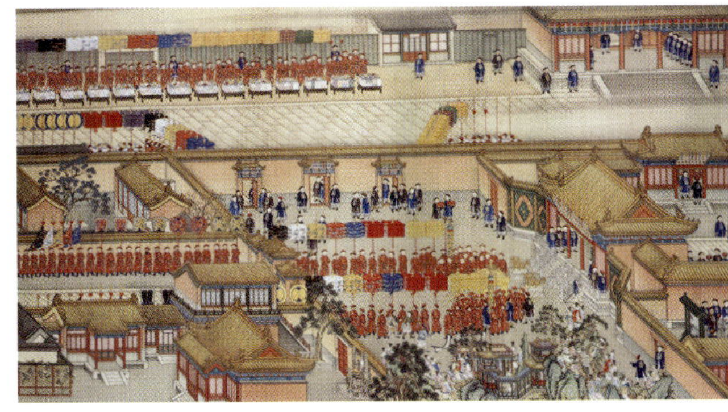

• 232 bottom: This 18th-century painting depicts the celebrations organized by Qianlong for his mother's birthday.

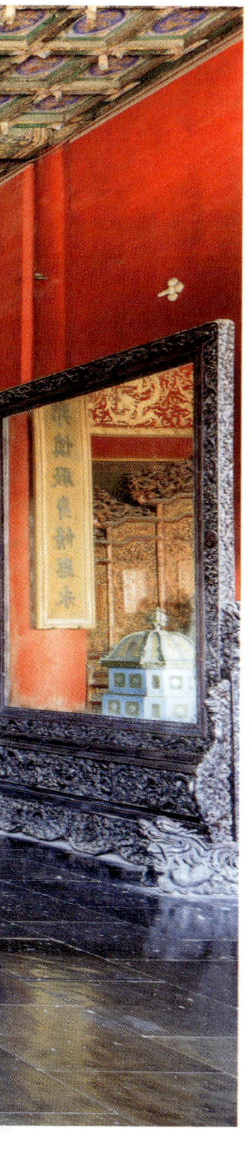

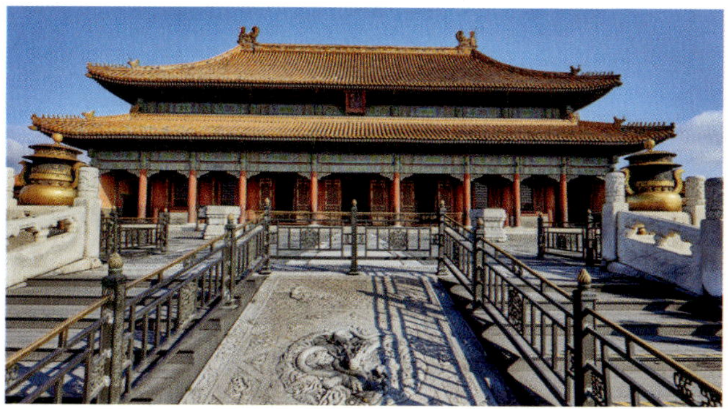

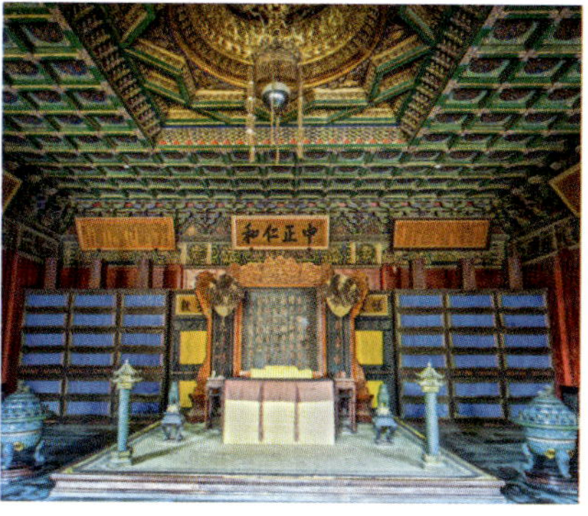

Living in the Forbidden City meant being segregated and subject to a complex set of rituals. Here the hierarchical system applied to everyone: even the emperor was not exempt, as he was still inferior to Heaven, of which he was the Son. Furthermore, despite being an absolute authority in all matters and revered as a deity, he was strictly bound by sacred etiquette and controlled by a special Court of Rites that dictated what he could and could not do. Leaving behind the Front Palaces, where the "public" life of the Son of Heaven took place, we enter the area of the Rear Palaces, a slightly smaller replica of the former. This was the emperor's residence, where he carried out his daily activities, always managed by others. Everything was controlled by the Empress Mother, who regulated the lives of some 6,000 people, including eunuchs, maids, servants, and concubines, who lived practically as prisoners in a sort of enclosure consisting of corridors, shady courtyards, narrow passageways, and yellow-roofed buildings on either side of the three main palaces: the Hall of Heavenly Purity, the Hall of Mutual Harmony, and the Hall of Earthly Tranquility. The Hall of Heavenly Purity was the residence of the Ming rulers and the first two Qing emperors (Yongzheng moved his private apartment to the Hall of Mental Education for security reasons, as did his successors). Here they lived, conducted daily state affairs, and granted audiences to ambassadors from other countries. Here the emperor's body received its final farewell before being transferred to the foot of Coal Hill for burial. The emperors of the Manchu dynasty preferred other halls for sleeping because this one was thought to be haunted, despite the presence of a large mirror to ward off evil spirits (which is still in place today).

• 232-233: The Hall of Heavenly Purity is the main hall of the Inner Sanctuary. Chronicles recount that in 1722, the great Emperor Kangxi started the custom of organizing banquets for the elderly inside and outside the hall. Former imperial officials over the age of 65 and mandarins were invited to the occasion, with up to 1,000 guests in attendance. His grandson Qianlong celebrated his 50th year of reign in 1785 by offering a banquet for 3,000 mandarins and 5,000 dignitaries. The imperial throne is located in the center of the hall. The wooden sign bears four ideograms meaning "Open, honest, and splendid as the sun."

• 233 left: The Hall of Heavenly Purity is located on a raised terrace, which also features enormous gilded bronze incense-burners, and the statues of a turtle and a phoenix made of the same material. These fantastic animals symbolized immortality and longevity. During the harsh winters, in addition to the large bronze braziers, the palaces were heated by a network of brick ducts through which air was heated by burning coal in pits located under the verandas.

• 233 right: The Hall of Mental Education was first built during the Ming dynasty and then renovated by the Qing emperor Kangxi, who transformed it into a workshop where clocks were designed and manufactured. From Yongzheng onwards, throughout the 18th century, the hall was the residence of the Son of Heaven. Immersed in his collections, Qianlong received mandarins there and dealt with affairs of state. The interior of the Hall is decorated with polychrome paintings, glazed tiles, and ancient thangkas (painted or embroidered Buddhist banners).

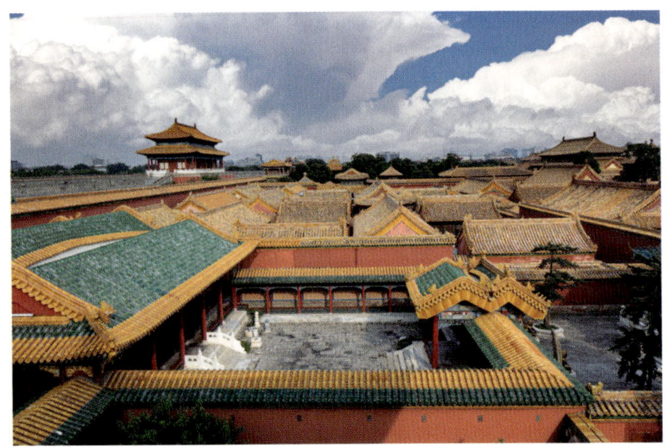

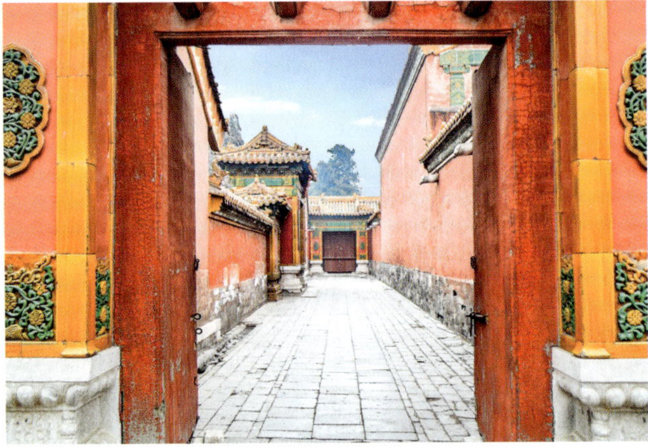

The design of the Forbidden City was intended to ensure perfect harmony between the opposites at the heart of Taoist philosophy: Yin, the negative principle, corresponds to the dark and cold north and to the feminine element, while Yang is the positive principle, corresponding to the brighter and warmer south and to the masculine element. It is no coincidence that the Hall of Supreme Harmony, used by the emperor, is located in the southern part of the palace complex, while (during the Ming dynasty) the Palace of Earthly Tranquility, used by the empress, is located in the northern courtyard. The architects also had to take into account the laws of feng shui, according to which there had to be water to the south of every building in the complex and a mountain on the opposite side of the palace to protect it from evil spirits and the cold coming from the north. There was neither water nor mountains in Beijing, so it was necessary to create them: the Golden Water River was dug to the south, and the so-called Coal Hill, now a public park called Jing Shan, was embellished with trees and pavilions to the north.

Even the pairs of lions placed in front of the halls and pavilions of the Forbidden City, like every other detail of the residence, were subject to the laws of feng shui. One is yang, the male, recognizable by his right front paw resting on a sphere apparently made of cloth, called an "embroidered ball"; the other is yin, the female, sculpted with a cub under her left paw to represent the cycle of life. Everything within the city was regulated by strict rules, especially the organization of public and private life, which would have been impossible without the presence of a host of officials—mandarins, eunuchs, servants, and concubines. The former were elected through an ancient three-level examination system open to all male subjects of the kingdom, regardless of age (except singers, actors, and dancers, who were considered impure). Those who passed were awarded the prestigious title of mandarin or literate official, and were appointed Jinshi, or doctor, in the Hall of Supreme Harmony. They were entrusted with the entire management of public affairs, becoming essential to the functioning of the empire. The daily tasks to be carried out in the emperor's residence were entrusted to a group of eunuchs, numbering around 10,000 during the Ming dynasty and reduced to 2,000 during the Qing, who were recruited from poor families or saved from death. Due to their supposed loyalty and the fact that they could not produce offspring, they gained more and more power at court, to the point of coming into conflict with the literate officials. Many eunuchs, such as Admiral Zheng He, were entrusted with important positions. Others were assigned to serve in the concubines' quarters, who were selected by the Empress Mother.

• 234 top: One of the many passages connecting the courts of the Sacred Inner City. Many were reserved for the emperor when he traveled on foot rather than in a palanquin. Those accompanying him had to walk alongside him at a fast pace as a sign of respect.

• 234 bottom: One of the gates of the Inner Holy. The green and yellow majolica floral decorations on the walls break up the severity of the Front Palaces and symbolize the different function of the northern area of the Forbidden City.

• 235: The rear courtyard of one of the palaces inside the Forbidden City in a striking winter view.

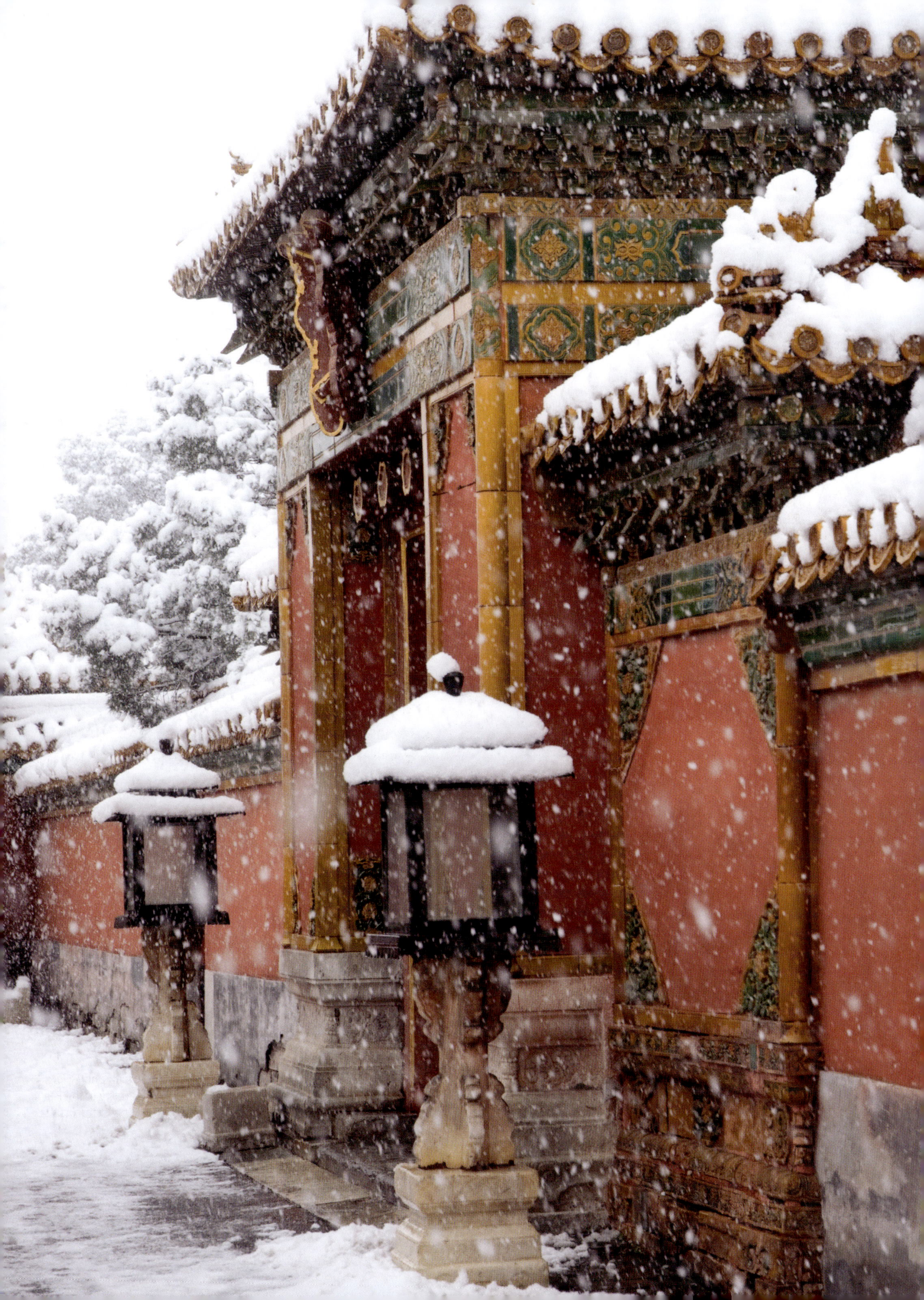

Himeji Castle

1333
In the early years of the Muromachi period, Akamatsu Norimura, head of the Akamatsu clan and governor of Harima Province, built a fort on Mount Himeyama to protect the city of Himeji.

1346
Norimura's son, Akamatsu Sadanori, had the fort demolished and erected a building known as "Himeyama Castle," which was completed in 1346.

1545
During the Sengoku period, Kuroda Shigetaka had the castle renovated, and it began to gain importance.

1580
Nobunaga took control of Harima and placed it under the control of Toyotomi Hideyoshi, who renovated the castle and built a small keep. Some remains of Hideyoshi's castle have remained intact because part of the walls were incorporated into the subsequent renovation.

1601
Ikeda Terumasa, an ally of Tokugawa Ieyasu in the Battle of Sekigahara (October 21, 1600), obtained the province of Harima and had the main keep of Himeji-jo built. It is thought that the outer walls were whitewashed during this renovation.

1617
Tadamasa Honda became lord of the castle and expanded it to include the inner walls of San-no-maru and Nishi-no-maru, as well as the outer walls to the west.

1941–1945
During the Pacific War, Himeji Castle was mildly damaged by bombing but withstood the fire. Documents show that the white outer walls of the castle were so visible that black nets were used to hide them from view during the war.

1993
Himeji Castle was listed as a UNESCO World Heritage Site.

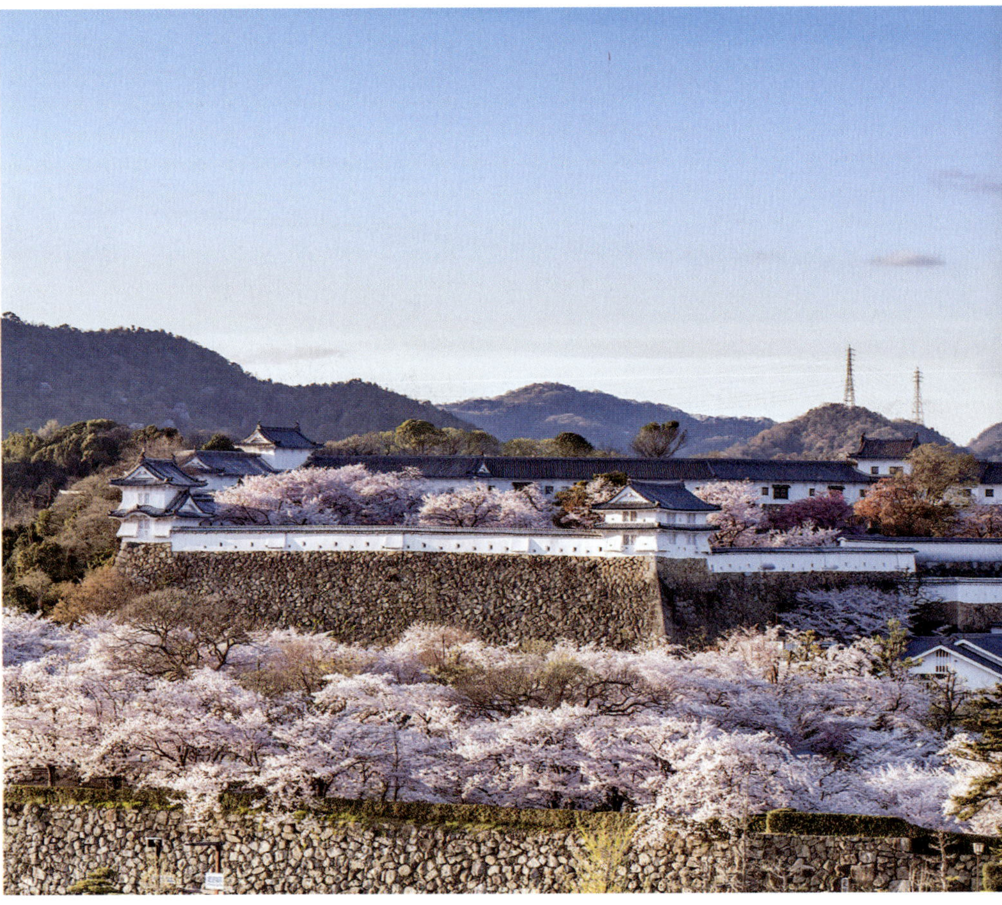

Shirasagi-jo, literally "White Heron Castle"—the suffix "jo" is simply the Japanese word for "castle," and the three towers flanking the central structure make it look like a bird ready to take flight—is located in Himeji, a city on the island of Honshū, capital of the historic province of Harima, about 93 miles west of Kyoto. The castle was built in several stages starting in 1333 when, at the beginning of Japan's long and turbulent feudal period, the samurai Akamatsu Norimura, governor of the province of Harima, had to protect it from attacks by neighboring warlords. Himeji-jo remained a modest fortification until 1580, when another samurai, Toyotomi Hideyoshi, had a three-story keep built there to use as a base for his military campaigns in southern Japan. After Toyotomi Hideyoshi's death, Himeji-jo was given as a fief in 1601 to Ikeda Terumasa as compensation for his valiant behavior in the Battle of Sekigahara, which had given control of Japan to another great statesman and warrior, Ieyasu Tokugawa, whose descendants would rule the empire until 1868. Ikeda Terumasa undertook the ambitious

• 236-237: View of the majestic Himeji Castle. The white outer walls are plastered with white lime, which not only gives them their characteristic color but also offers protection against fire. The castle is surrounded not only by defensive walls but also by a wide moat to protect it from enemy attacks. The complex includes over 80 buildings connected by a series of winding paths that resemble a labyrinth: they were designed specifically to deceive and confuse invaders because they appear to lead to the entrance but actually lead away from it. In the magnificent park, you can witness Hanami, the spectacular cherry-blossom season.

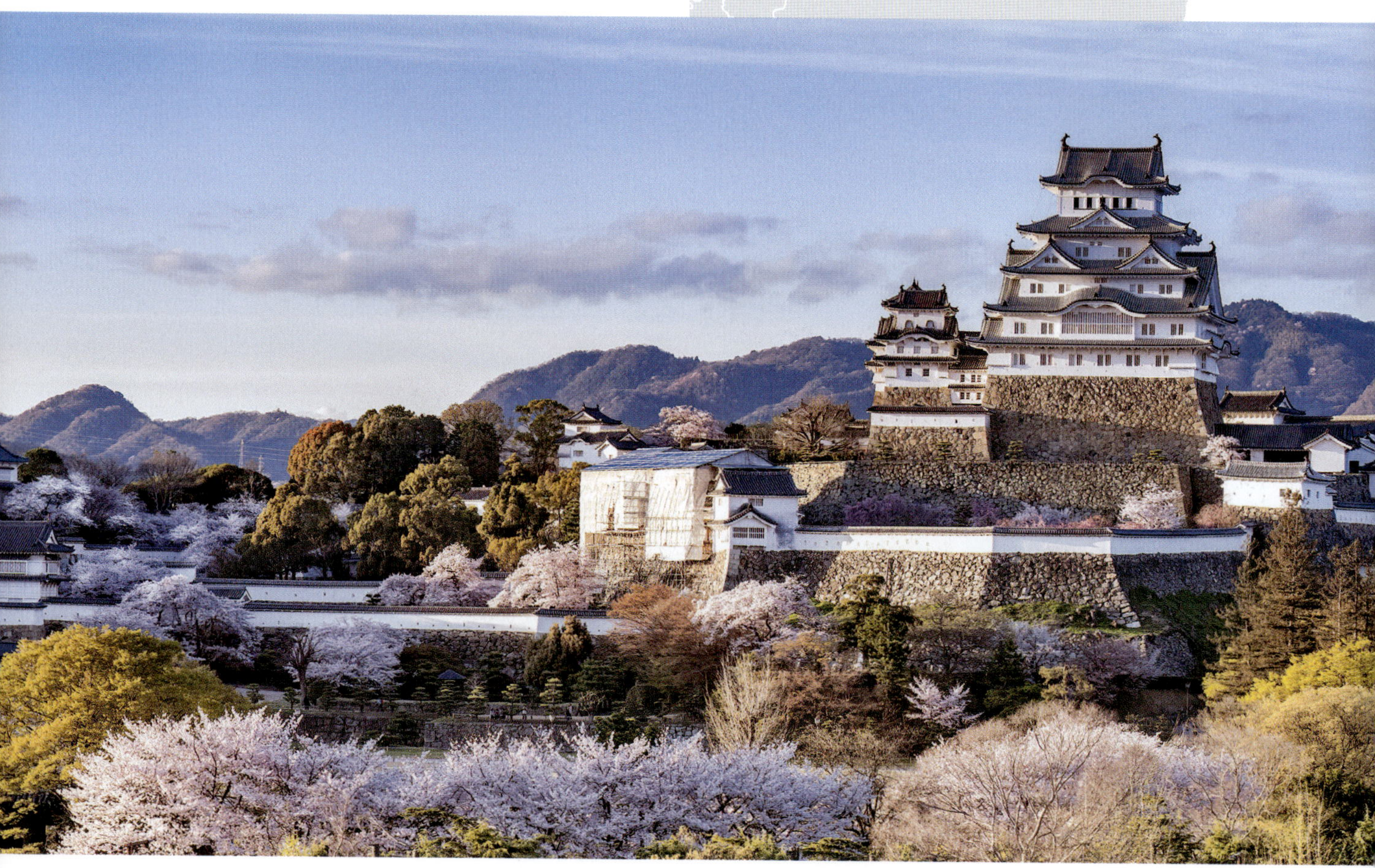

task of transforming Himeji into a siege-proof fortress: it took nine years and 5,000 workers, divided into competing teams, each responsible for building a different part and led by a hierarchical structure of skilled master carpenters. The stone and timber used were of the highest quality. The fortress covered an area of 568 acres, following a spiral plan, a true labyrinth. Kaempfer, a doctor with the Dutch East India Company, claimed that he had never seen anything like it in Europe. Himeji-jo acquired its final form under the daimyo Tadamasa Honda, who completed the work in 1618. This splendid example of military architecture is particularly noteworthy for its Tenshukaku, six stories high and 115 feet tall, practically a skyscraper for its time. In wartime, it served as a formidable observation point and was equipped with a large warehouse for weapons and rice. In peacetime, it was a symbol of the prestige of the lord who owned it. A complex network of moats and a labyrinth of high internal walls surrounded it, making it extremely difficult for anyone who attempted, by whatever means, to reach the central tower: in fact, the castle was never besieged. Japanese historians have calculated that it took between 25 and 50 million days of work to complete the "war machine" of Himeji-jo. Despite its large size, it does not clash with the surrounding landscape but, on the contrary, symbolizes the pinnacle of the Japanese concept of harmony between man and nature.

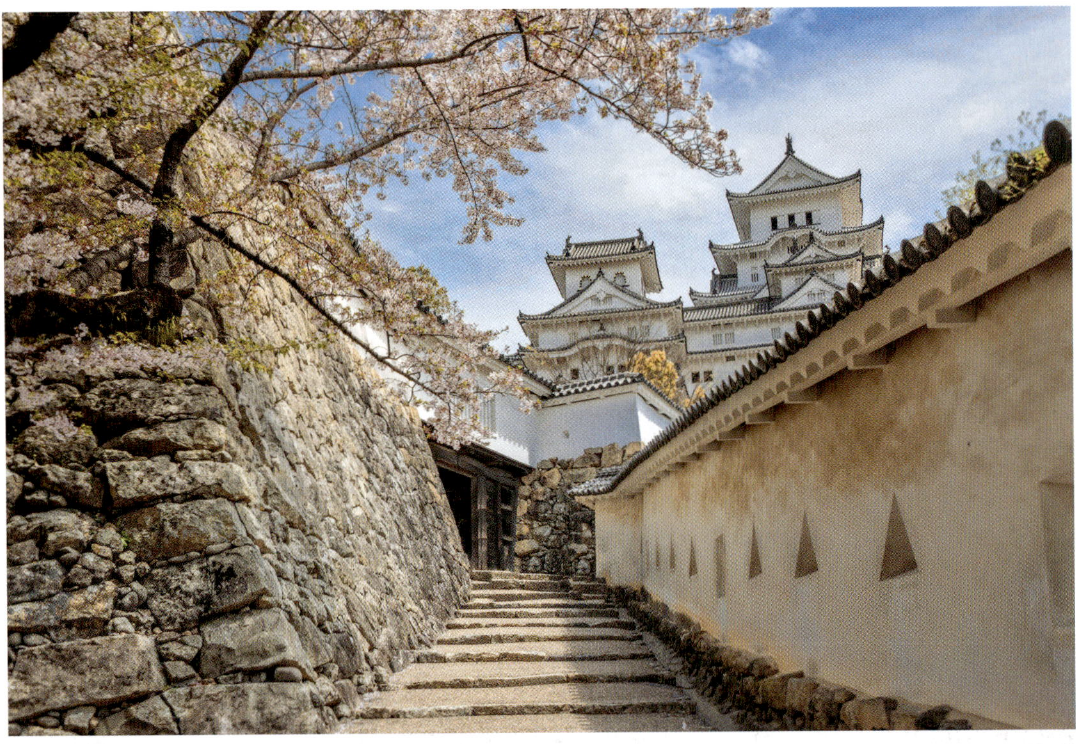

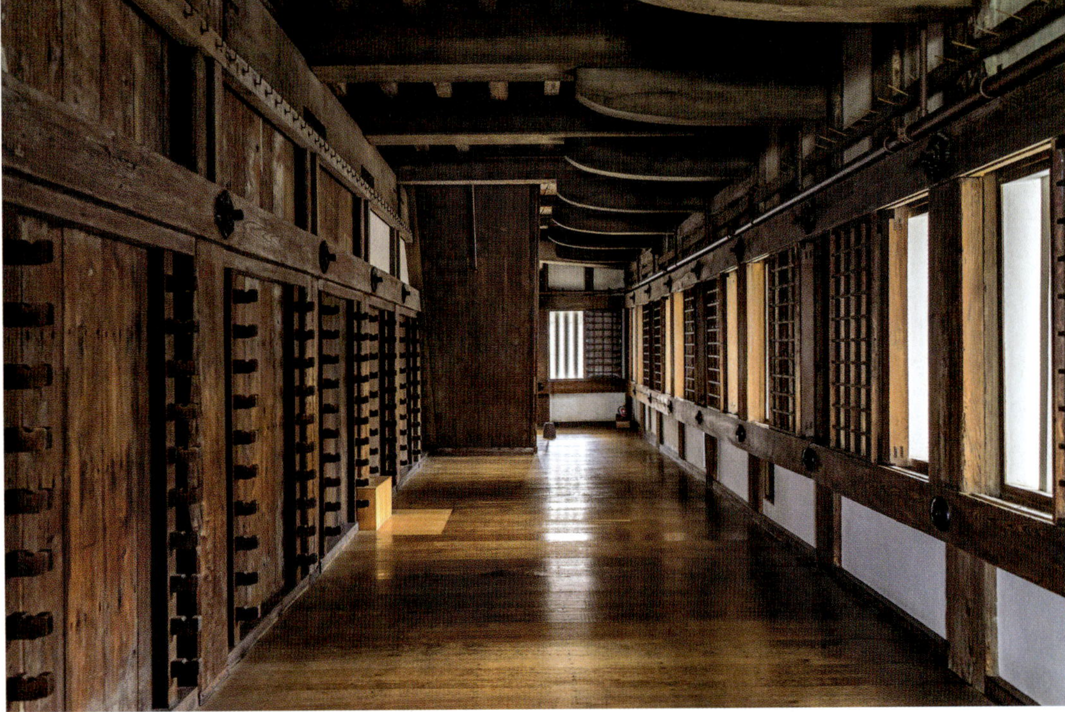

• 238 top: Along the perimeter of the walls, you can see the samas, holes dug into the walls that served as loopholes. There are four different types, often alternating along the same wall: square, rectangular, triangular, and round.

• 238 bottom: Interior view of the keep of Himeji Castle: weapon racks are still visible on the wall.

• 238–239: Himeji Castle has been the setting for many films, including two masterpieces by Akira Kurosawa, both set in feudal Japan: Kagemusha (1980), winner of the Palme d'Or at the Cannes Film Festival, and Ran (1985), winner of several awards including an Oscar for costume design and a David of Donatello. Some scenes from "007: You Only Live Twice" (1967) with Sean Connery were also filmed in this stunning Japanese fortress.

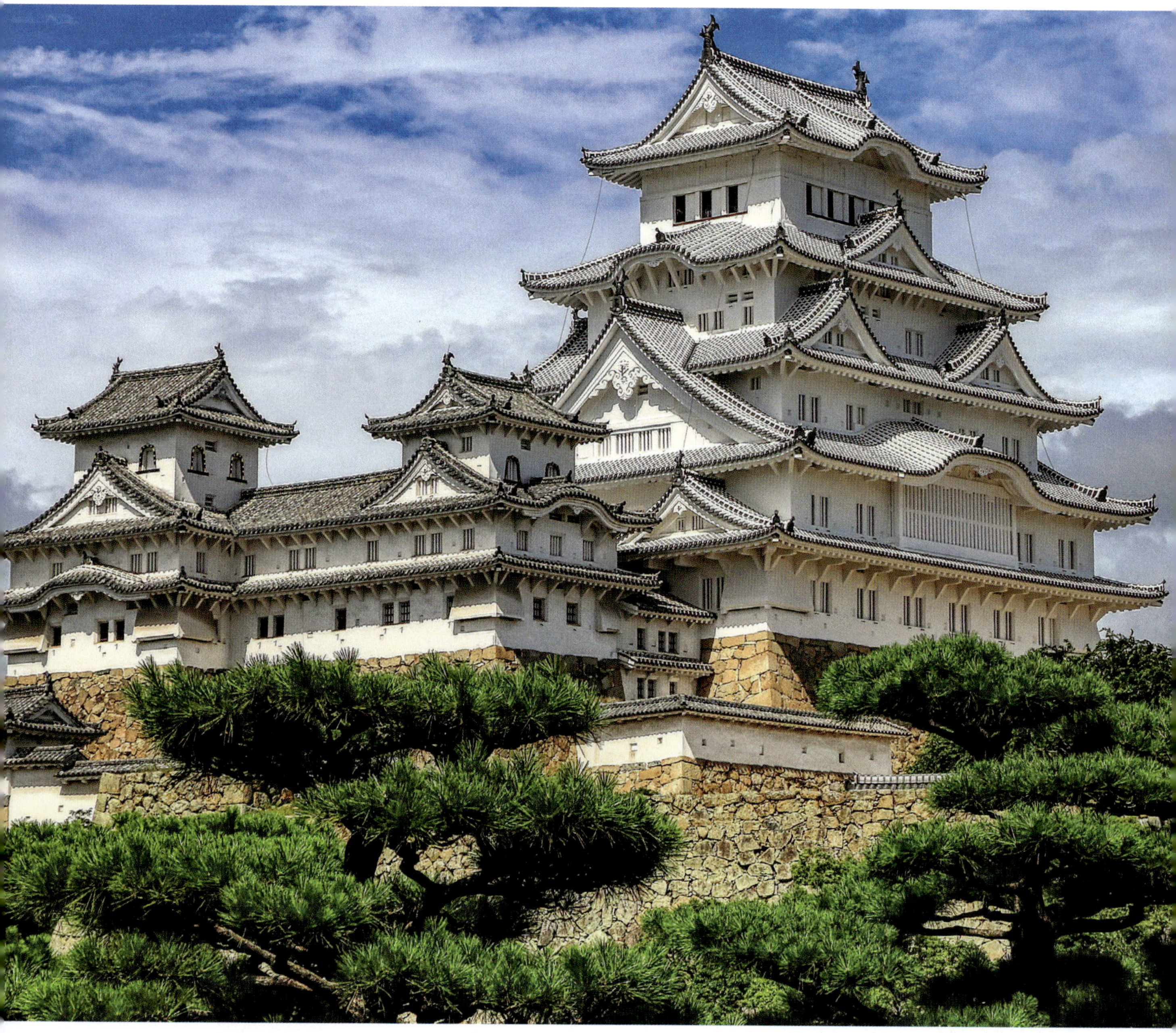

The castle guards

The strange creatures perched on the roofs of Himeji Castle, as on most Japanese castles, are called "Schachihoko." With the body of a fish and the head of a tiger, they act as guardian entities. According to legend, they have the extraordinary ability to quickly swallow large amounts of water, storing it in their bodies; in case of fire, they intervene by spitting it onto the flames and calling on the clouds to bring rain. The first to adorn his castle (Azuchi castle) with these mystical creatures was Nobunaga Oda, ruler of the province of Owari. Schachihoko are usually made of ceramic and covered with gold leaf, but in Nagoya Castle they were made of wood covered in pure gold (it is estimated that they used 474 pounds of it).

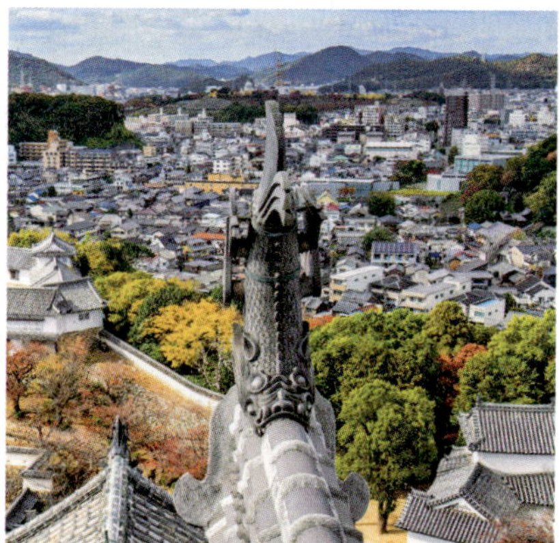

Author

Born in Milan in 1967 and married with two children, **Paola Hazon** studied history and philosophy and began working in publishing, starting with updating a prestigious encyclopedia. She went on to manage two publishing houses, working on periodicals and magazines focusing on history, including Storica National Geographic. In 2020, she founded Studio Hazon, which specializes in books about travel and nature, and she gave more space to her favorite activities: writing and storytelling.

Photo credits

All images are from Shutterstock except: p. 10 Eye Ubiquitous/Getty Images; pp. 10-11 by Andrea Pucci/Getty Images; p. 12 Larry Gatz/Alamy; p. 13 center Private collection; p. 13 bottom Private collection; p. 14 Urbanmyth/Alamy; p. 16 bottom Silver Screen Collection/Getty Images; pp. 18-19 Murat Taner/ Getty Images; p. 20 Peter Nicholls/Stringer/Getty Images; p. 21 top Allan Baxter/Getty Images; p. 22 Private collection; p. 23 left AFP/Stringer/Getty Images; p. 23 top right SHAUN CURRY/Stringer/Getty Images; p. 23 bottom right Rolls Press/Popperfoto/Getty Images; p. 24 MICHAEL DUNLEA/Alamy; pp. 24-25 ViewFromAbove/Alamy; p. 26 ViewFromAbove/Alamy; pp. 26-27 Charlie Harding/Getty Images; pp. 28-29 WPA Pool/Team/Getty Images; p. 29 top Private collection; p. 30 top Tim Graham/Getty Images; p. 30 center Dan Kitwood/Getty Images; p. 30 bottom Tim Graham/Getty Images; pp. 30-31 CHRISTOPHE ENA/Getty Images; p. 31 bottom imageBROKER.com/ Alamy; pp. 32-33 John Lamb/Getty Images; p. 36 top Pawel Libera/Getty Images; p. 47 top Private collection; p. 61 Private collection; p. 69 ONLY FRANCE/Alamy; pp. 70-71 ONLY FRANCE/Alamy; p. 71 top BERTRAND GUAY/ Getty Images; p. 73 DEA/S. VANNINI/Getty Images; pp. 74-75 JOEL SAGET/ Getty Images; p. 76 Private collection; pp. 76-77 Private collection; p. 81 bottom Private collection; p. 82 bottom D A Barnes/Alamy; pp. 84-85 Tuul and Bruno Morandi/Alamy; p. 87 top Private collection; p. 90 bottom DEA/C. SAPPA/Getty Images; p. 99 aerial-photos.com/Alamy; p. 104 center Private collection; p. 106 Private collection; p. 108 bottom Private collection; p. 112 Private collection; p. 115 Atlantide Phototravel/Getty Images; p. 118 Private collection; p. 119 DE AGOSTINI/Getty Images; p. 121 bottom Private collection; p. 124 top and bottom Private collection; p. 125 top Private collection; p. 128 ALEXANDER KLEIN/Getty Images; p. 135 top brandstaetter images/Getty Images; p. 138 center Culture Club/Getty Images; pp. 138-139 imageBROKER. com/Alamy; p. 141 bottom Private collection; p. 144 top imageBROKER.com/ Alamy; p. 144 bottom Image Professionals GmbH/Alamy; p. 148 Private collection; p. 148-149 Image Professionals GmbH/Alamy; p. 150 center Private collection; p. 150 bottom Diego Grandi/Alamy; p. 152 Private collection; pp. 154-155 ullstein bild/Getty Images; p. 156 center Private collection; p. 157 DEA/G.P.CAVALLERO/Getty Images; pp. 158-159 VASILIS VERVERIDIS/Alamy; pp. 160-161 JacobH/Getty Images; p. 160 bottom Private collection; pp. 162-163 Pavel Dudek/Alamy; p. 164 bottom ClarkandCompany/ Getty Images; p. 167 bottom Private collection; p. 171 center mk0x55/Getty Images; p. 171 bottom Private collection; p. 172 Witold Skrypczak/Alamy; p. 174 left Pavel Dudek/Alamy; p. 174 in destra Private collection; p. 175 top ewg3D/Getty Images; p. 175 bottom left Nathaniel Noir/Alamy; p. 175 bottom right brandstaetter images/Getty Images; p. 176 Zoonar GmbH/Alamy; p. 179 center Pavel Dudek/Alamy; p. 179 bottom Imagedoc/Alamy; p. 179 right Private collection; pp. 182-183 agsaz/Alamy; p. 183 top Private collection; p. 183 center MB_Photo/Alamy; p. 183 bottom AlexMastro/Alamy; pp. 184-185 Alois Radler Woess/Alamy; p. 185 Azoor Prague Photo/Alamy; p. 187 top Zoonar GmbH/Alamy; p. 188 Private collection; p. 189 Ian Trower/Alamy; p. 213 bottom Private collection; pp. 218-219 Anders Blomqvist/Getty Images; p. 220 bottom Jan Wlodarczyk/Alamy; p. 221 top benedek/Getty Images; p. 221 bottom ephotocorp/Alamy; p. 225 top and bottom Pakin Songmor/Getty Images; p. 226-227 chain45154/Getty Images; pp. 228-229 Ping Shu/Getty Images; p. 230 top ViewStock/Getty Images; p. 232 bottom DEA PICTURE LIBRARY/Getty Images; p. 234 bottom simon's photo/Getty Images; p. 235 Nancy Brown/Getty Images; p. 238 in alto imageBROKER.com/Alamy; p. 238 bottom Francesco Bonino/Alamy; p. 238-239 EOSGent/Alamy; p. 239 bottom Loop Images Ltd/Alamy

Editorial Project
D&D Consulting/Valeria Manferto De Fabianis

Graphic design
Paola Piacco

Layout
Maria Cucchi

Piazzale Luigi Cadorna, 6
20123 Milan, Italy
www.whitestar.it

Translation: Inga Pelosi Leighton / Editing: Phillip Gaskill

ISBN 978-88-544-2178-3
1 2 3 4 5 6 30 29 28 27 26

Printed in Romania

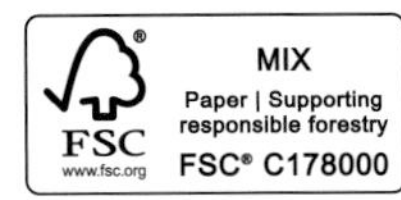